PROPHET OF LIBERTY
The life and times of Wendell Phillips

Engraved on steel expressly for
George L. Austin's **Life and Times**
of Wendell Phillips, Boston, 1884

PROPHET of LIBERTY

the life and times of

WENDELL PHILLIPS

by

Oscar Sherwin

BOOKMAN ASSOCIATES
New York

MANUFACTURED IN THE UNITED STATES OF AMERICA BY
UNITED PRINTING SERVICES, INC.
NEW HAVEN, CONN.

To the Colored Citizens of this Land
to whom Wendell Phillips was
always a Friend

ACKNOWLEDGMENTS

I wish to acknowledge my indebtedness to the following libraries for permission to examine the manuscripts and books in their possession: Public Library of the City of Boston, Library of Congress, Harvard College Library, Howard University (Moorland Foundation), Massachusetts Historical Society, New York Historical Society, New York Public Library (main division at 42nd Street and branch at 135th Street), and Yale University Library. Cornell University Library sent me photostats of manuscript letters in its possession. For many courtesies extended to me I am deeply grateful to Mr. Richard G. Hensley, Miss Elizabeth L. Adams, Miss Emily Hewins, and Miss Harriet Swift of the Public Library of the City of Boston, Professor Otto Kinkeldey of the Cornell University Library, Miss Carolyn E. Jakeman of the Harvard College Library, Mr. Allyn B. Forbes and Miss Shirley E. Wood of the Massachusetts Historical Society, Mr. Alexander J. Wall and Miss Susan Lyman of the New York Historical Society, Mr. F. Ivor D. Avellino and his assistants of the History Reading Room and Mr. Joseph Roberts of the Manuscript Room of the New York Public Library (42nd Street) and Mrs. Catherine Latimer of the New York Public Library (135th Street branch). The burden and nervous tempo of work were greatly lessened by their kindness. I am especially indebted to Miss Elizabeth L. Adams for patiently investigating many items which were not readily available and Mr. Richard G. Hensley, Mr. Zoltán Haraszti and Mr. Allyn B. Forbes for their prompt cooperation in forwarding photostatic and transcribed material.

I also wish to thank Professor Bower Aly of the University of Wisconsin, Mr. Lewis A. Dexter of Boston, and Professor W. Haynes Yeager of the George Washington University for information and material which they graciously mailed to me and Mr. Irving Rosenthal of the College of the City of New York for referring me to special files of clippings kept by the New York *Times*. I am indebted to the New York *Times* for permission to examine these clippings.

Above all I should like to express my debt to Professor Oscar Cargill of New York University for his helpful suggestions and encouragement. The author's enthusiasm for his subject found in him not just an enlarging soundboard, but an acute and directing intelligence.

CONTENTS

"*The cause of the slave had many advocates, many of them very able and very eloquent, but it had only one Wendell Phillips.*" FREDERICK DOUGLASS.

"*The worldly side of Phillips's life may be summed up in the words: 'He was born on Beacon Street and he died on Common Street.'*" Exercises at the dedication of the statue of Wendell Phillips.

"*Wendell Phillips's second centennial will be better observed than his first.*" WENDELL PHILLIPS STAFFORD.

"*Men of a thousand shifts and wiles, look here!*" JAMES RUSSELL LOWELL.

CHAPTER ONE

INTRODUCTION:

THE REVOLUTIONARY TRADITION

A sleepy man with a portly figure and brown wig reached the mansion of Governor Eustis in Roxbury at the wan hour of two o'clock on the morning of the twenty-fifth of August, 1824. The Governor was a fine old fellow with a bush of gray hair that stood out under a three-cornered beaver which he wore on state occasions. When his guest arrived at the door, he cried out with honest enthusiasm—"Oh, this is the happiest day of my life."[1]

A great cavalcade of heaving torches and a shower of rockets announced the arrival of La Fayette.

After a little more than two hours sleep, the Marquis was awakened at dawn by the booming of guns and the music of a band. He looked out of the window and there maneuvering on the lawn was his old Light Infantry, the Marquis's own, red and black plumes and all. Calling to his son and secretary and valet to come and see, he exclaimed, "My brave Light Infantry! It is exactly like that they were uniformed. What courage! What resignation! And how I loved them!"

The festivities of the day began. The crowds were so immense that they were two hours in covering the two miles from Roxbury to Boston. At the city limits they were met by Mayor Quincy in an open calash with the Common Council in carriages. The procession halted while bread and cheese, at the expense of the municipality, and free punch were served to the people.

Mayor Quincy in an address of welcome assured the Marquis that this vast and impressive demonstration was "not the movement of a turbulent populace excited by the fresh laurels of some recent conqueror. It is a grave, moral, intellectual impulse."[2]

There could be no doubt now that the Marquis had reached Boston.

The whole city was in commotion: drums beating, bugles echoing, horses prancing and troops marching in all directions. Bells in the steeples were pealing. On Boston Common a battery was firing a salute of one hundred and one guns, and the long procession (unlike other processions it started at the hour published),—the grand marshal, the bands, the cavalcades and trains of carriages, the open barouche drawn by four white horses—passed under triumphal arches and festoons of flags all the way to Boylston Street, the people cheering, the Marquis bowing graciously right and left. Some leapt up clapping their hands, others burst into tears. Along the route, the sidewalks, piazzas, windows, and roofs of houses were thronged with spectators. Banners, bonnets, and handkerchiefs waved from every hand. As the procession passed, LA FAYETTE! LA FAYETTE! sprang from the voice of the multitude; LA FAYETTE beat in every heart; LA FAYETTE glowed on every cheek; LA FAYETTE glistened in every eye; every tongue vibrated LA FAYETTE.

One of the arches thrown across Washington Street was incribed with the following lines written by the city's laureate, Charles Sprague:—

WELCOME LA FAYETTE!

Our fathers in glory shall sleep
That gathered with thee to the fight;
But the sons will eternally keep
The tablet of gratitude bright.
We bow not the neck, we bend not the knee,
But our hearts, La Fayette, we surrender to thee.[3]

The poet here hit upon the right word. It was a surrender complete and universal. The crowds were huzzaing with all their might.

On Boston Common three thousand school children were assembled, the misses in white frocks, the masters in white pantaloons and blue spencers. They also wore ribbons pinned on their jackets stamped with a miniature likeness of La Fayette. The Committee did not let the children wander about and did not wish them to sit down. They were so tired after four hours' waiting that they could scarcely stand. But when they saw the glorious old Frenchman—they could have stood until today.[4] They raised up their little hands and shouted with joy.

The procession moved up Park Street to State House. There in the Senate Chamber Governor Eustis began to read his address of welcome, but was so overcome by emotion that he broke down and gave his manuscript to one of his aides to read for him.[5]

At Harvard the next day the hero was harangued by Edward Everett: "Hail! Friend of our Fathers, welcome to our shores. Enjoy a triumph not bestowed on conquerors or kings: enjoy the assurance that here throughout America, there is not one heart that does not beat for joy and gratitude on hearing your name . . . . Lincoln and Greene, Knox and Hamilton are gone; the heroes of Saratoga and Yorktown have fallen before the only foe they could not meet. Above all, the first of heroes of men, the friend of our youth, the more than friend of his country rests in the bosom of the soil he redeemed. On the bank of the Potomac he lies in glory and in peace . . . . His voice cannot now break its silence to bid you welcome to his own roof. But the grateful children of America will bid you welcome in his name. Welcome! Thrice welcome to our shores! And whithersoever throughout the limits of the continent your course shall take you, the ear that hears you shall bless you, the eye that sees you shall bear witness to you, and every tongue exclaim, with heartfelt joy, Welcome! Welcome! La Fayette!"[6]

Bells were pealing for the Fourth of July all over the land, the boom of cannon and the sound of patriotic music. Amidst these anthems the stoutest leader of the North and the boldest statesman of the South closed their eyes in final sleep.

Thomas Jefferson expressed a strong desire to live until the Fiftieth Anniversary of the Declaration of Independence should dawn. His friends feared he would not endure so long. But life ebbed slowly from that strong frame. It was nearly one o'clock on that great day when he expired. John Adams died at Quincy a few hours later with the words, "Thomas Jefferson still survives" struggling from his lips. As the sun sank, a noise of shouting was heard in the village—the enthusiastic cheers called forth by Adams' toast—Independence Forever![7]

On a hot summer day when the windows of the schoolhouse were all open, the children heard the tolling of bells for Adams and Jefferson. They were informed why the bells were tolling and for the children it was a remarkable providence that the two patriots died on that day they had made sacred. Some heard their grandfathers sing that inspired battle hymn of the Revolution beginning with the lines:—

Why should vain mortals tremble at the sight of
Death and destruction on the field of battle?

They heard them tell of that bitter winter encampment in New York when the snow fell to five feet on a level, when they were short of provisions, without shoes, nearly naked, and huddled together in heaps under the straw for warmth.[8]

This is merely what it was to be a boy in those days.

The Revolutionary tradition was still fresh and vigorous. It was the native air of Wendell Phillips. It marked and dominated his life. It gave a moral depth to his nature and lodged the principle of devotion to great causes in the very beatings of his heart. All about were scenes immortalized by the Revolution. Almost every one of the city's houses had a legend. Every public building had held within its walls what was treasonable debate or bore bullet marks or bloodshed—evidence of royal displeasure.

Yonder from his door still loomed Bunker Hill. Here was the church tower whose lantern started Paul Revere upon his ride. There was Winter Hill whose cannon ball struck Old Brattle Street Church. Across the Common was the "Old South" dedicated to God by the Puritans and to liberty by Otis and Warren. Within five minutes' walk was Faneuil Hall and the very elm under whose branches Washington first drew his sword. What an environment! What an incentive!

CHAPTER TWO

A NEW ENGLAND BOYHOOD

Wendell Phillips's family was one of the best and most distinguished in New England. It dated in America back to 1630 when the Reverend George Phillips, one of a band of conscience exiles, sailed from Great Britain for the new world in the Arbella with Winthrop and Saltonstall and Johnson and settled at Watertown in the colony of Massachusetts Bay.[1] All of his descendants were eminent in colonial or early American affairs: ministers and deacons, judges and captains, legislators and governors. Two founded the famous Academies at Exeter and Andover and a chair of theology at Dartmouth College.[2] Wendell's father, John Phillips, a leader of the bar, an exemplary citizen, "disinterested, considerate, and candid," was the first Mayor of Boston.[3]

The Phillips mansion on Beacon Street—"the sunny street that holds the sifted few"[4]—was one of the show places of Boston and the center of the aristocratic quarter. A block away to the left was the Hancock House; next door on the right lived the Winthrops. In front stretched forty-three acres of Boston Common and around and about thronged the élite of the capital. Here on November 29, 1811, Wendell Phillips was born, the eighth in a family of nine.[5]

He was reared in the strict piety of a Puritan household.[6] His mother, Sally (Walley) Phillips, was profoundly religious. Her foremost purpose was to root him in faith and hope and love. She used to take him aside and pray with him and for him. Her earliest gift to him was a Bible. She taught him the

18

catechism as he sat on her lap, and when he could hardly toddle, she guided his steps to the family pew on Sunday mornings. "Wendell," she would say, "be good and do good; this is my whole desire for you. Add other things if you may— these are central."[7]

His love for her was a passion deepening and determining the current of his whole life.

John Phillips, prudent, cautious, conservative in the conduct of civil affairs,[8] was, nevertheless, in his home liberal and independent. He made this wise rule for his children: "Never ask another to do for you what you can do for yourself, and never ask another to do for you what you would not do for yourself if you could." Knowing also the uncertainty of fortune in America, and remembering, perhaps, the old saying: "He who does not teach his children a trade brings them up to steal," he encouraged them to master whatever tools of manual labor they could handle. Accordingly, as soon as he got on his feet, Wendell began to potter around with hammer and chisel and saw. Indeed his mother said: "A good carpenter was spoiled when Wendell became a lawyer."

Moreover he early developed another trait. Feeling the push of his clerical ancestry, he would place a Bible in a chair before him, and arranging other chairs in circles about the room, he would harangue these wooden auditors by the hour. "Wendell," said his father to him one day, "don't you get tired of this?"

"No, papa," replied the speaker, "I don't get tired, but it's rather hard on the chairs."[9]

He inherited his wit from his father. When a member of the convention for the revision of the Constitution of Massachusetts, John Phillips, in debating a certain proposed change, remarked— "I hope our case may not be like that of a man whose epitaph may be read in an Italian churchyard: 'I was right; I wanted to be better; I took medicine; and here I lie.'"[10]

Both parents were widely and variously interested in affairs beyond their doorstep. John Phillips was in public life. Hence questions and issues astir out there in the streets were brought into the household and talked over at the fireside and around the table. Persons were characterized, measures discussed, matters of historical moment dwelt upon in full family conclave. Thus the children gained an intellectual acquaintance with the outside world.

Wendell's nearest and dearest friend was John Lathrop Motley, the future historian of the Netherlands. Motley, not yet eleven years old, was writing a novel. It opened not with "one solitary horseman," but with two riding up to an inn in the Valley of the Housatonic. Neither of the boys had seen the Housatonic, but it sounded grand and romantic. Two chapters were finished.

Thomas Gold Appleton, son of one of the patriarchs of New England manufactures, also lived nearby and joined the boys. The three frolicked in the garret of Motley's house. Their favorite pastime was to strut about in any fancy costume they could find in the corner of the old attic and shout scraps of poetry and snatches of dialogue at each other.[11]

When they came downstairs, they would read to Motley's father from such authors as Channing and Irving, and he would criticize their way of reading. Mrs. Motley, a "regal beauty", lent the charm of her presence.[12]

In his eleventh year Wendell Phillips entered the famous Boston Public Latin School on School Street.[13] The institution has been one of the features of the city since Ezekiel Cheever from London established it in 1670. Cheever passed off the academic platform at the age of ninety-four, being buried from his schoolhouse where he had trained the most eminent citizens of an entire generation— "a skilful, painful, and faithful schoolmaster," Cotton Mather said of him in his funeral discourse. After his demise, no successor made his place good until Mr. B. A. Gould came in 1816. When young Phillips entered the school, Gould had been master six years.

Instruction was chiefly in Latin and Greek. They had a very bad Latin grammar made by Mr. Gould himself and to cultivate the verbal memory of the little boys, the first year was spent in committing the words of this grammar to memory.

The system of the School was rigid. In summer most of the boys wore long calico gowns quite like the gowns which ministers sometimes wear now, only without flowing sleeves.

The boys took turns at tag or some other game before the school bell rang. But at last, at eight o'clock in summer and at nine in winter, the bell began to ring. It rang for five minutes, and before the end of five minutes every boy was in his place. The masters stood in the meanwhile on the sidewalk in front of the school door. As the bell rang, they bowed to each other and repaired one by one to their rooms.

A strong quick boy was sent up into the belfry to ring the bell. He took hold of the tongue and struck it rapidly and sharply on the side of the bell. To do this for five minutes was an exhausting bit of labor, but for all that it was rather a privilege to be permitted to ring the bell. For in compensation for doing so, the boy was awarded certain credits on his conduct and recitation lists, and one who found himself going to the bad in his studies would ask to be assigned to the bell that he might work off these misdemeanors.

The favorite sport among the boys was kicking their pails to pieces at the end of the school term. They would subscribe for pails in which to keep the water which they wanted to drink on hot days, and when the term was done, not wishing to leave the pails to their successors, they kicked them about the sidewalk and street until they were ruined.

Ushers, whatever their age, were called old. It was old Dillaway, old Gardner, etc.[14]

Wendell was a vigorous and tall boy and ranked high among his school fellows on account of his beauty, elegant manners and social position. He was also a superior student, ranking fourth in a class of twenty-nine in scholastic standing.

Declamation was an important part in the curriculum. All boys were required to take part in several declamations held at regular times throughout the year. At the age of thirteen Phillips spoke in the Prize Declamation delivering an Extract from Patrick Henry's Speech. The program carries comments in pencil. After Phillips's name is written the word "Animated." The Faculty Records also mention a two dollar prize for third honors in the Prize Declamation. Perhaps the Latin School can be regarded as a factor in the development of Phillips the speaker.[14a]

Motley had gone to Northampton to fit for college at an institution directed in part by the historian Bancroft. Appleton remained as the chum of Phillips. Phillips struck up, besides, a friendship with an overgrown and awkward lad, Charles Sumner. "Gawky" Sumner, the fellows called him, and they disliked him, for he was a bookworm.

Phillips, on the other hand, was a lover of outdoor sports— a champion boxer and marksman, fencer, oarsman, and rider.[15] He was especially fond of horses and later became a personal friend of Rarey, the horse-tamer.

The school was close by Boston Common. The Common was still recognized as

1. A pasture for cows
2. A playground for children
3. A place for beating carpets
4. A training ground for the militia[16]

It had served these purposes for two hundred years and was not fenced till 1815.

The boys went to the Common for coasting. It was the winter sport par excellence. Prominent sleds were as well known among boys as race horses and yachts are today. Sleds were made with much care and skill. Black enamelled leather, bordered by gold or silver headed tacks, made a popular seat, and the irons were made of the best "silver steel," whatever that meant. They were kept burnished like glass, with constant care and fine emery and oil, and a streak of ashes or a bare spot was avoided as a yacht steers clear of rocks. Sleds bore such fanciful names as "Comet", "Cave Adsum", and "Dancing Feather".

There were the Jay Street Coast, Beacon Street Mall, and the "Big" or "Flagstaff" Hill. But the great coast was from the foot of Walnut Street leaving the great elm on the right as you went down. The cry of "Lullah" cleared the track.[17]

Dr. Jacob Bigelow's funny poems made him the boys' spokesman.

Mr. H******! Mr. H******! be a little kinder,
Can't you wink a little bit, or be a little blinder?

Can't you let us *sliding* fellows have a little fun?
Were you *born old*, or was't your way all childish
    sports to shun?
Did you ne'er know how *"sleek"* it is, to slide from
    top to bottom?
And can't we use our *ironers* and *plainers*, now
    we've got 'em? . . .
"Two dollars" make our *Pas* look *cross*—that's proper
    bad, you know;
Our *youth* will soon be *gone* alas! and sooner gone
    the snow.[18]

(Caleb Heyward was the police officer of the day.)

As the snow melted and the elms blossomed and the grass
came out, the Common opened itself to every sort of game.
Wendell and his chums played marbles in the holes in the walls,
flew kites everywhere, or sailed boats on the Frog Pond. (There
were no frogs, but some small horned pout left there, for which
the boys fished occasionally.) Some of the little fellows delighted to drive blunt arrows against the sides of the grazing
cows. There were poplars in front of Beacon Street and willows
here and there from which the boys made whistles when the
sap began to run.

Luncheon parties with ham, cheese, beer, crackers, and apples
would often sit under the trees. Later new iron seats were
placed on the Common. They prevented whittling.[19]

Bostonians made a practice of walking round the outside
of the Common every morning before breakfast. Daniel Webster
and Edward Everett were remembered as two of these. Rufus
Choate in his morning promenade was said to have studied his
German.[20]

The boys often interrupted their play to listen to the Town
Crier, for that office was still in use. The official drove down
West Cedar Street and after ringing a big dinner bell, stood
up in his wagon and proceeded to read from a paper: "Child
lost! four years old, wore a blue and white checked calico dress,"
etc. giving a minute description of the little girl. Then he started
up his horse with a "g'long!" and went on to the next corner,

where the performance was repeated.[21] Wendell and his friends followed him.

Stage coaches still clattered in from the country over the cobblestone streets. Signboards still swung from taverns and hotels inscribed with the names, "The Indian Queen", "The Bunch of Grapes", "The Lamb", etc.[22]

Boston looked like the quiet English provincial town it was.[23] It had not much over 40,000 inhabitants. Foreigners were comparatively unknown; servants were all American.[24] The Yankee from the country who came to Boston to sell his "notions"—apple sauce among them—filled up the time of waiting for customers by going into service. Just as he got licked into shape, he sold his apple sauce and wanted to leave—"All right, mister. I'll trouble you for them dollars! I've sold my sauce, and if the mouth of the man that bought it ain't soon like the puckers of your coat, I don't know."[25]

No Irish boys, no German boys, but plenty of Negroes. Boston Negroes colonized Negro Hill, a place of vague horror to the white boys. Boys white and black fought a great deal. And it was a settled axiom of the white boy, that if he kicked the Negro's shin, his nose would bleed, but he generally began with the nose.

Horse chestnut trees were the great favorites then in Boston.

Amidst such idyllic influences, Wendell Phillips was educated. As he grew older he expanded the range of his pleasures to include the thrill and fascination of great oratory. He lost no opportunity to hear the "masters of assemblies"—Harrison Gray Otis, Edward Everett, and Henry Clay. And he walked over the bridge to Charlestown and Bunker Hill to hear Webster, then the embodiment of eloquence and patriotism, Webster whose philippic against the slave trade of Plymouth in 1820 every schoolboy knew by heart—

"I hear the sound of the hammer: I see the smoke of the furnaces where manacles and fetters are still forged for human limbs. I see the visages of those who by stealth and at midnight, labor in this work of hell, foul and dark as may become the artificers of such instruments of misery and torture. . . . If the pulpit be silent whenever or wherever there may be a sinner bloody with this guilt within the hearing of its voice, the pulpit is false to its trust."[26]

CHAPTER THREE

HARVARD DAYS

Wendell Phillips entered Harvard in 1827, four years after his father's death.[1] His mother wept on his neck and told him never to forget his prayers and his Bible.

When Phillips matriculated, the Reverend Dr. John T. Kirkland was president. Two years later, in 1829, Josiah Quincy succeeded him.

Harvard was a conservative and donnish society. To the college faculty, politics only meant the success of Webster and the great Whig party. When Andrew Jackson visited the college, President Quincy was much distressed at having to confer the degree of LL.D on him; indeed all the faculty abhorred Jackson.

The student's life was hard. Morning prayers at six in summer, and in winter half an hour before sunrise in a bitterly cold chapel, the professors keeping watch over the congregation from a sort of raised sentry box and noting down the name of any one guilty of misdemeanor. Breakfast in the college Commons consisted solely of coffee, hot rolls and butter, except when members of a mess succeeded in pinning to the nether surface of a table, by a two-pronged fork, some slices of meat from the previous day's dinner.

The students lived in austere and bare rooms furnished with a pine bedstead, washstand, table and desk and cheap rocking chair, and two to four other chairs of the plainest fashion. Hardly any student owned a carpet. Some kept a cannon ball which on very cold days was heated to a red heat and placed as a calorific radiant on a metallic stand. At other seasons it was utilized by being rolled downstairs at such times as might most nearly bisect the proctor's sleep.

Students were invariably hostile to the faculty. If a student went unsummoned to the teacher's room, he almost always went by night. It was regarded as a high crime by the class for a student to enter the recitation room before the ringing of the bell or to remain to ask a question of the instructor. Recitations were mere hearings of lessons without comment or collateral instruction. There were no electives in those days.[2] Students were expected to wade through Homer as though the *Iliad* were a bog and it was their duty to get along at such a rate *per diem*. Then there was the horrid "scale of merit"—Quincy had each instructor's and monitor's report sent up to him weekly, and himself totted up every student's credits. He described the ideal college course as a "thorough drilling", and that is just what the Harvard course was.[3]

Occasionally Cambridge calm was disturbed by a gust of riots. Students broke windows, made bonfires, war danced and hooted under the windows of unpopular instructors. On autumn evenings members went out with large baskets and brought them back with apples, pears, grapes, and melons from Belmont. Sometimes they robbed hen roosts and market gardens.

Commencement was the occasion for disordered revelry. The entire Commons was completely covered with drinking stands, dancing booths, mountebank shows, and gambling tables. You never heard such a horrid din, tumult, and jargon of oath, shout, scream, fiddle, quarrelling, and drunkenness as on those two nights. The class of 1834 treated all comers to iced punch: crowds gathered to witness the ceremonies. And in 1836 the Reverend John Pierce entered this observation in his diary: "Be it noted that this is the first commencement I ever attended in Cambridge in which I saw not a single person drunk in the Hall or out of it. . . . There were the fewest present I ever remember."[4]

President Quincy, who had retired disgusted from public life, was a wilful, abrupt, and harsh man, but exceedingly good hearted. He improved the food and service, trusting that if the students were served like gentlemen, they would behave as such, and he broke an ancient tradition by addressing them as "Mr." But he did not go to the root of the trouble by providing athletics and other outlets for ebullient youthful spirits. Student riots continued. On one occasion the students burned the President in effigy in the college yard, and on another there was a terrific explosion in the chapel.[5]

Of the faculty Edward T. Channing was professor of rhetoric and oratory and George Ticknor professor of modern languages and belles lettres. Channing looked like Punch. Under his scornful countenance and merciless ridicule, the student sweated and squirmed. His custom was to take up a theme, hold it up, and call out X. X came to the chair by the professor's side and the professor read in a shrill voice—" 'The sable sons of Afric's burning coast.' You mean *Negroes*, I suppose." The student admitted that he did. The professor took his pen and drew a line over the sentence he had read and substituted the word "Negroes" above the line.[6]

Channing stood for simplicity: "I believe that showy writing is always cold and reaches but a very little way below the surface of men's minds." Channing may have been of great influence on Phillips, for he studied with Channing for four years, and one of the distinguishing marks of Phillips's speeches is simplicity.[6a]

Phillips stood well up toward the head of his class in his studies, and was later elected to Phi Beta Kappa. He learned easily and rapidly, was deeply interested in history and chemistry, and had a passion for mathematics. He was letting his Greek go, but never failed to read his Latin. He knew French well and some German—not much; he evaded the study of Spanish by beguiling his instructor, who was an old European revolutionist, to talk through the recitation hours about revolutionary themes and experiences. In fact there was one whole term in which he did not have a single real recitation.

One day Phillips went into Boston to attend the Whig meeting in Faneuil Hall. It was during the campaign of 1828 when Adams was running against Jackson. As he ascended the stairs, he heard the powerful metallic voice of Daniel Webster arguing in favor of the tariff. Not so musical, he thought, as Clay's was or Harrison Gray Otis's, but full of strength. As he entered the Hall and listened, he speedily detected that Webster's statement was "all argument." After this he heard Webster everywhere—in the courts and at political gatherings—always with admiration for his gifts. The great expounder, Phillips thought, was ponderous on ordinary occasions. It took a crisis to arouse him—then he was sublime.[7]

At college Phillips became intimate with the President's son, Edmund Quincy, who early in life devoted himself deliberately to the somewhat arduous profession of gentleman.[8] Phillips also continued his close friendship with Motley and Sumner.

Motley, though the youngest in the class, without any effort stood third or second in rank. He was so negligent after his first college year that he was "rusticated." In his room he had a small writing table with a shallow drawer filled with sketches, unfinished poems, soliloquies, a scene or two of a play, prose portraits of pet characters, etc. These he would read to Phillips, and every now and then he burned the whole and began to fill the drawer again.

Motley was a scapegrace, Sumner a hermit.

There were boats on the Charles, saddles, boxing gloves, and fencing foils. And social clubs[9] in which Phillips was everywhere among the first. He was president of the Porcellian and of the Gentleman's Club, and a member of the Hasty Pudding, organizations of young aristocrats. At the time the Porcellians were thought to be pro-Southern in their sympathies, and this club used to rally all the Southern students.[10] The Hasty Pudding was a literary society. Meetings were held on Saturday evenings. The members ate a hasty pudding and molasses and closed the exercises by singing a hymn. Phillips also belonged to a society called "The Owls," which only met at midnight, and the one who could make a face to look most like an owl was considered the best fellow. He was elected first lieutenant in a military organization called the Harvard Washington Corps and, representing the aristocrats, nearly won in the

balloting for class orator. He had so little interest in reform
that he succeeded in defeating the first proposition to establish
a temperance society at Harvard and his first speech was a
fervent defense of the status quo against the "untried theories"
and "mad schemes" of these "advocates of reform" who attempt to put the "wisdom of yesterday in competition with the
wisdom of the ages."[11]

He was the only student of the period for whom the family
carriage was habitually sent out to Cambridge on Saturday morning to bring him into Boston for Sunday.[12]

When Phillips was a student at Harvard, the Reverend Dr.
Lyman Beecher was the Jupiter of the Boston pulpit. Every
Sunday and often on weekday nights he thundered and lightened
in Hanover Street Church. He shook and kindled the town.
Thousands throbbed under his preaching.[13]

His special mission was to combat Unitarianism, which then
sat in all high places, and to rally and solidify the forces of
orthodoxy. Nothing was too bad or too bitter for him to say
against the offending sect. He rushed up and down the country like a field marshal, his coat tails flying, dropping the notes
of sermons from his hat, leaving his belongings in stages and
inns—the great gun of Calvinism—fulminating against baptism
of infants, against toleration, against innovation and democracy,
against separation of church and state. For seven years, his
mind had been "heating, heating, heating," as he put it, over the
awful peril to men's souls of this blasphemous doctrine, this
menacing heresy. He was confident that if Byron could have
talked with him, "it might have got him out of his troubles."[14]

One day someone said to him: "Well, Dr. Beecher, how long
do you think it will take you to destroy Unitarianism in Boston?"

"Humph!" was the gruff reply, "several years, I suppose,—
roots and all."[15]

He was a plain, ruddy, nervous old man. For exercise he sawed
all the wood for his own large family, and often finding that
exercise too mild, begged the privilege of sawing at the wood-
pile of his neighbor. He kept a load of sand in his cellar to which
he would run at odd intervals and shovel vigorously, throwing

it from one side of the cellar to the other to work off his nervous excitement.

When he mounted the pulpit or platform, the waiting audience had a new sensation. The first part of his sermon was dry, condensed, and clear as a series of mathematical axioms. The second part was a passionate and direct appeal. A sermon that did not induce anybody *to do anything*, he considered a sermon thrown away. He warned, he entreated, he pleaded, talking as if the audience were one individual whom he must, before he left the pulpit, persuade to take a certain step.

"Do you say, 'What shall I do?' One thing I will tell you, that if you do not do something more than you have, you will be lost. That you acknowledge, do you not?" Then changing the tone of his voice to the key of personal conversation, he would say— "Now there is one thing you can do; you can resolve before God from this moment that the salvation of your soul shall be your first object, and that, whatever it may mean to be a Christian, you will not rest till you are one. You can do that. Are you not conscious that you can? I put it to you—*will* you do it? You cannot refuse without periling your salvation."[16]

His style of appeal had a practical value. As he preached, he watched the faces of his hearers, and when he saw that one moved, he followed him. "A—B—," he would say, "has seemed to feel a good deal these several Sundays. I must go after him. Something seems to block his wheels." Often he would remark— "I've been feeling round to find where the block is. I put my fingers on this and that and it don't move; but sometimes the Lord helps me, and I touch the right thing and all goes right." He began to speak of his "Clinical Theology."[17]

When he first set up his evening meetings, not a bell tingled, but after a few weeks there was not a bell that didn't tingle. The number increased so fast it was overwhelming, so he kept a record. In this thing of revivals, all things came by showers. Each shower would increase, increase, increase, and when he saw it was about used up by conversion, he would preach so as to make a new attack on the mind and conscience and bring a new shower. The work never stopped for five years. No such religious movement had been known in Boston since the great awakening eighty years before.[18]

Wendell Phillips once heard Lyman Beecher preach on the theme, "You belong to God," and went home after that service, threw himself on the floor in his room with locked doors, and prayed: "O God, I belong to Thee; take what is Thine own. I ask this, that whenever a thing be wrong, it may have no power of temptation over me; whenever a thing be right, it may take no courage to do it."[19] In 1826 he passed through the experience of conversion.

This consecration of himself to God and His service made a deep impression on his classmates, awakening their reverence (the word is not too strong). They always remembered his appearance of devoutness during the morning and evening prayers in the chapel, which most attended to save their faces with the authorities. By those who knew him he was admired and loved as an open hearted, generous, and chivalrous fellow, a sincere and devoted friend. They praised his "brightness of mind" and spoke with pride and affection in their voices of "his perfect purity and whiteness of soul".[20]

His Bible was always open on the center table.

He was graduated at commencement in 1831 with a class which numbered sixty-five.[21] The psalm was pitched a little too high.

CHAPTER FOUR

A JUDGE, AN ACTRESS, A CORSAIR,

AND A CONSPIRATOR

The orthodox steps in the upward course of a wellborn and rich young Bostonian of a hundred years ago were: first, the Public Latin School; next Harvard College; and then the Harvard Law School. Two steps had already been taken; in the autumn of 1831,[1] Wendell Phillips took the third and seated himself to be instructed by Judge Story.

Story was a born teacher. The law which was harsh and crabbed became inviting under his instruction. He taught as a priest of the law seeking to consecrate other priests. His class exercises were not formal lectures but rather conferences to which both teacher and his little circle of pupils contributed. He lived with them upon terms of the most familiar intimacy and they dearly loved him. He exaggerated all their good traits and was blind and deaf to their faults. Wherever he went they flocked about him.[2]

When not writing Judge Story was talking. He was one of the most tremendous talkers long suffering Cambridge ever heard. On trips to Boston by daily omnibus (fare 25 cents) he entertained friends and strangers alike by an unquenchable stream of pleasantries, anecdotes, and observations. His extraordinary memory, copious learning, and long practical experience often caused him to wander widely from the starting topic. It was easy to draw the old Judge from the point under consideration

to a lengthy account of Chief Justice Marshall and his fellows—
and this was apt to be done every day. All his resources were
at his tongue's command—facts, arguments, theories, authorities,
history, illustrations. The bell announcing the expiration of
the hour would stop him in full tide, and if there was no lecture
immediately to follow, a spontaneous call of "go on" often went
up from the benches.[3]

This sort of thing may not have taught Phillips much sub-
stantive law, but it gave him something better—intimate contact
with a great legal personality.

The school was Story's pet and pride. He was continually
devising new and delightful plans for its improvement. He
fostered the custom of holding "moot courts". A case was given
out. The parts of junior and senior counsel were regularly assigned to two students on each side from among those who
chose to enjoy the privilege, and the case was publicly argued
before one of the professors, sitting as a judge, by whom the
decision was pronounced.[4] He doggedly refused any addition to
his original salary of one thousand dollars a year.

He was a low, heavy set man with very fair skin and blue
eyes, and very bald save for a little tuft of hair on the top of
his forehead which he often combed during the lecture with a
fine comb carried in his vest pocket.

Sweet and sunny Story! There is a saying: "Only a good man
can be a teacher; only a benevolent man; only a man willing to
teach."

The principal instruction, however, was given by Professor
Ashmun whose methods consisted largely of written lectures by
the Professor and recitations by the students. The latter were
arranged in two classes according to the extent of preparation,
it being still usual for many to enter the School after a year
or more of study in a law office.[5] Story's lectures were "on
the Law of Nature and Nations, and on Chancery, Commercial,
Civil, and Constitutional Law." Ashmun's were "on miscellaneous
branches of the Common Law."[6] Reviews and examinations in the
text books were had on four days in the week, lasting from one
to two hours for each class. The course of study was to be

completed in three years, but in 1832-1833 a two years' course was adopted with extra books suggested for those who desired the full three years.[7]

Lectures began at eleven o'clock and ended at one, Saturday being *dies non*. Usually the same professor occupied the chair for both hours, changing the subject at noon. Between the two lectures, there was an intermission of fifteen minutes. It was considered the proper thing to spend this interval in a visit to Lyon's beer cellar across the street and drink a glass of half and half. Result—a general somnolence during the succeeding hour.[8]

Fanny Kemble, the actress, came to town and the Harvard students went mad. They sold their books, clothes, and everything else for the price of a theatre seat. Charles Sumner was so enraptured with her that he spent every minute of his leisure time in hiking in sunshine or snow or storm to Boston and back again, and in pushing his way in with the dense crowd to see the divinity perform. "Come," young Sumner would say, buttonholing a friend on the street, "tell me something about Fanny Kemble. Tell me something she said."[9]

Judge Story in the course of his lectures would refer to Fanny Kemble's performances at the theater. Phillips asked him once, "Judge Story, you come of Puritan ancestors. How do you reconcile all this theater going with their teachings?"

"I don't try to reconcile it," answered the Judge. "I only thank God I am alive in the same era with such a woman."[10]

She was more than a flashing, independent character. She was somewhat of a genius.

In 1833 Wendell Phillips was graduated from Harvard Law School. Next year, with the blessings of Justice Story who foretold for him an unprecedented career, he was admitted to the bar.[11]

He went away on a short tour, travelling as far as Philadelphia. Here at a fashionable boarding house, he met a romantic figure— Arab features with raven black hair, high shoulders, and piercing eyes—Edward Trelawny, the English friend of Byron and Shelley. Trelawny, the Corsair, as he was called, was there in

attendance upon Fanny Kemble of whom he professed to be
an admirer. He moved among the mirrors, the teacups, and the
talk, spinning wild yarns and blazing out in fine rhetorical
damnation of all poppycock and snobbery. His narrations were
so interesting that, whether true or untrue, Phillips could not
but listen to them with as much pleasure as to the wonders of an
Arabian tale. But the Englishman shocked the young Puritan
by the open expression of his atrocious sentiments respecting
women—boasting of his success with them, and declaring that no
woman ought to live beyond the age of twenty.[12]

Among Trelawny's achievements in America was his holding
Fanny Kemble in his arms to give her a view of Niagara, his
swimming across the river between the rapids and the falls, and
his buying the freedom of a man slave.[13]

Facing homeward Phillips stopped for a few days at New
York. In some way he made the acquaintance of Aaron Burr—
a dry, bent, brownfaced little man, polite as Chesterfield himself, with a beautiful smile and exceedingly small ears. The
slayer of Hamilton so seldom interrupted, listened so eagerly,
so attentively, so modestly, made the young man who spoke to
him feel so important, so absorbing, so indispensable, that he
never forgot him. He showed Phillips the sights. Soon after his
return, Burr visited Boston. Phillips called on him at the Tremont Hotel and offered to act the part of cicerone. Among
other places, they went to the Athenaeum to see the pictures
and look at the library. As they walked down the hall, between
the alcoves, Phillips caught sight of a bust of Hamilton, one of
the ornaments of the library which he had forgotten was there.
He tried on some pretext to draw Burr in another direction, but he
too had seen the bust and marched straight up to it. He stood
facing it for a moment, then turned and said—"A remarkable
man—a very remarkable man." Upon this he wheeled on both
heels in military style and moved on again with great composure.[14]

To prepare himself thoroughly before engaging in practice,
young Phillips went to Lowell and entered the office of his

schoolmate Thomas Hopkinson.[15] He spent a few months there and then returned to Boston.[16]

And now at last Wendell Phillips with years of diligent preparation behind him, opened his office, hung up his sign, put up his library, and cried, "Ready!"[17]

He waited in a spic and span office for clients who did not come.

CHAPTER FIVE

THE MARTYR AGE

The afternoon of October 21, 1835, was charming, the air balmy with a touch of tonic in it. Wendell Phillips sat reading beside an open window in his office on Court Street. Suddenly his attention was attracted by shouting and the scurry of feet along the sidewalk. The young lawyer rose and leaned out over the window sill. He saw an excited crowd half a block away on Washington Street and wondered what was the matter. Leaving the window he put on his hat and went out.

Presently he found himself in the midst of a yelling and cursing mob that rapidly grew to several thousand. They were confronting the Anti-Slavery office at the head of Washington Street; four or five hundred angry, clamoring men were trying to push their way up the narrow stairs and into the hall which was up two flights.

Wendell Phillips stood and watched. He saw the Mayor Theodore Lyman come on the scene and heard him vainly beseech the people to disperse and preserve order. In a moment the Mayor disappeared into the building; soon afterwards some thirty women, pale but composed, came down the stairs and marched in procession along the street and so away, amid the hoots and insults of the rabble.

Then Phillips noticed a man bareheaded, with a rope coiled about his body, his clothing torn and bedraggled. The man's face was calm and pale, his bald head shining. "Kill him!" "Lynch him!" "Hang the Abolitionist!" shouted the mob.[1]

"Who is that?" asked Phillips.

"That?" answered a bystander, "Why, that's Garrison, the damned Abolitionist. They're going to hang him."

The young man saw Colonel Park, the Commander of the Boston regiment of which he himself was a member, and hurrying over to him said, "Colonel, why doesn't the Mayor call for the guns? This is outrageous."

"Why, you fool," retorted the Colonel, pointing to the crowd that surged and pressed before him, "don't you see that the regiment is in the mob?"[2]

Astonished, Phillips glanced quickly about to verify this fact and further noticed that the mob was kid-gloved, composed of "gentlemen of property and standing", his friends and associates on Beacon Hill. There was very little of the rough element in it. A justice of the peace standing nearby remarked— "I hope they tar and feather him. Though I would not assist, I can tell them five dollars are ready for the man that will do it."[3] Phillips turned away in disgust.

In the meanwhile Garrison had extricated himself from the rope and was seized by two or three powerful men, who led him along through the crowd, shouting—"He shan't be hurt! You shan't hurt him! Don't hurt him! He is an American." etc. This seemed to excite the sympathy of many in the crowd and they reiterated the cry—"He shan't be hurt, he shan't be hurt."[4]

Phillips followed the mob as it pushed along, but his view being suddenly cut off, and supposing that the authorities would keep Garrison in the City Hall until it should be safe for him to venture out to his home, he turned about and walked back to his office in deep thought.

Next day he learned that he had not seen the drama through, that Garrison had been taken to the Mayor's room, provided with clothing—a pair of trousers from one person, a coat from another; a third lent him a sock, a fourth furnished him with a cap—and driven to jail "as a disturber of the peace," but in reality to save his life. Rioters rushed madly upon the vehicle with the cry: "Cut the traces! Cut the reins!" flung themselves upon the horses, clung to the wheels, dashed open the doors, and tried to upset the carriage.[5] But the driver, with his whip lashing his horses and the heads of rioters alike, made an opening through the crowd and drove at tremendous speed for Leverett Street Jail where Garrison was safely locked in a cell, "accompanied," as he said, "by two delightful associates—a good conscience and a cheerful mind."[6]

Phillips also found out the occasion of the riot. The Abolitionists had given notice of a public meeting of the Boston Female Anti-Slavery Society to be held on October 14, to which women only were invited and which the English Abolitionist, George Thompson, was to address. Immediately there was a smoldering unrest in the city and the *Commercial Gazette* of Boston predicted trouble at the meeting. A few days before the attack, one independent military company, marching through Washington Street, bore a target to be shot at, on which was painted an image of Thompson and also the figure of a colored woman in close proximity.[7] To add to the tension, a false accusation was brought against Thompson by a Southern student at Andover, named Kauffman, who declared that Thompson had said in one of his addresses at Andover that slaves ought to be stimulated to cut their masters' throats.[8] The ladies, indeed, became so alarmed at the prospects of a riot that they petitioned the civil authorities for protection. No notice was taken of the petition. It became necessary to postpone the date of the meeting to October 21 and to change the place of meeting to a hall at 46 Washington Street, the headquarters of the anti-slavery office. The name of Thompson was dropped from the program, and the day before the announced meeting, he left Boston. The plotters of trouble believed he was still in town and threats were uttered freely by enemies of the cause. Only a few hours before the outrage, inflammatory handbills directed against Thompson were circulated throughout the city. They were printed at the office of the *Commercial Gazette*:

THOMPSON
The Abolitionist

That infamous foreign scoundrel Thompson will hold forth this afternoon, at the Liberator office, no. 46 Washington Street. The present is a fair opportunity for the friends of the Union to snake Thompson out! It will be a contest between the Abolitionists and the friends of the Union. A purse of $100. has been raised by a number of patriotic citizens to reward the individual who shall first lay violent hands on Thompson so that he may be brought to the tar kettle before dark! Friends of the Union, be vigilant!

Boston, Wednesday, 12 o'clock.[9]

The handbills did their work quickly, and by the time Garrison arrived at the hall, at twenty minutes before three in the afternoon, the crowd had already assembled in the street and was howling, "Thompson! Thompson!" The Mayor assured the rioters that Thompson was not in the hall. They knew, however, that Garrison was and so they clamored for his surrender. Garrison was urged to escape and reluctantly left the premises. The attempt, however, was unsuccessful. He was seen to go from the building into the narrow lane behind it. Pursued, he took refuge in a carpenter's shop only to be dragged out and mobbed. At this point Wendell Phillips arrived on the scene.

He who had gone gracefully through the drawing rooms of exclusive Boston homes suddenly came square up against a jolting reality. He had always been taught to believe in the forces of law and order. And now suddenly crashed into his sheltered existence this ugly business where friends of his were part of a disgraceful attempt of lynching. The Mayor had played an opera bouffe part dispersing the ladies instead of the rioters. Most surprising of all, the press extolled the mob and glorified in its shame and rioting.[10] He was rudely awakened from his pleasant dream to realize the fact that in this country of which he was a proud citizen an unpopular minority had no rights which the State was bound to respect, that a law was not worth the parchment it was written on when it stood in the way of popular prejudice—and that prejudice, abolition of Negro slavery.

2.

Five other men had written against slavery before Garrison had thought upon the subject at all. They had prepared the ground and sown good seed. Benezet, Woolman, and Lundy were saints who had yearned with remarkable sympathy for the black bondmen and were indefatigable in good works in their behalf. But they had not the stern and iron quality without which reforms cannot be launched upon the attention of mankind. What his predecessors lacked, Garrison possessed to a marvelous degree—the undivided interest, the supremacy of a single purpose, the stern stuff out of which the moral reformer is made and in which he is panoplied. They were all his, but there was another besides—immediatism.[11] That word became the unceasing trumpet blast of his weekly paper, *The Liberator*.[12]

He and his associates were like the early English Puritans who wanted "Reformation without Tarying for Anie." Burke once said: "Where there is abuse, there ought to be clamor, because it is better to have a slumber broken by the firebell than to perish amidst the flames in our bed."[13]

"Mr. Garrison," people said, "if you have immediate emancipation you will have chaos." Garrison seemed absolutely serene and answered: "That is no concern of mine. I know that slavery is wrong and freedom is right, but what you will deprecate, my dear sir, will be, not the results of freedom, but of slavery."[14]

His creed was simple, his language as imperious as the declamations of the ancient prophets. He contended that slavery was "a crime, a damning crime," and hence that all slaveholders were criminals and their supporters partakers of their guilt. He had more man to man respect for slave owners than for the safe and sane men of his time. He could not be bedfellows with anyone who preached half measures or who showed a lack of absolute principles. Abolition was a religious, a moral contest, a veritable Holy War.

When the fight was on, he was an Old Testament man and thought and wrote the sometimes clear and sometimes cloudy language of prophecy. His armory of Scriptural phraseology was always full of burnished weapons. To some his language seemed intemperate and vituperative. But what to critics sounded strident and abusive was to him the Trumpet of God. He believed in marrying masculine truth with masculine words.

"Every writer's style," he said, "is his own—it may be smooth or rough, plain or obscure, simple or grand, feeble or strong, but principles are immutable."

There was nothing pacific in his incessant demand for peace. "I will not waste my strength in foolishly endeavoring to beat down the great Battle with a feather. . . I am for digging under the foundations and springing a mine that shall not leave one stone upon another."[15]

Samuel May, descendant of the Sewalls and Quincys, of milder speech than Garrison, remarked at the close of an expostulation with him: "O my friend, do try to moderate your indignation and keep more cool; why, you are all on fire." Garrison stopped, laid his hand on May's shoulder with a kind but emphatic pressure, and said slowly, "Brother May, I have need to be *all on fire*, for I have mountains of ice about me to melt."[16]

Listen to him: "For myself, I hold no fellowship with slave owners. I will not make a truce with them even for a single hour. I blush for them as countrymen—I know they are not Christians; and the higher they raise their profession of patriotism or piety, the stronger is my detestation of their hypocrisy. They are dishonest and cruel—and God, and the angels, and devils, and the universe know that they are without excuse."

"Why so vehement?" he asked, "so unyielding? so severe? Because the times and the cause demand vehemence. . . . With reasonable men, I will reason, with humane men, I will plead, but to tyrants, I will give no quarter, nor waste arguments where they will certainly be lost."[17]

In an address in 1833 he said, "How, then, ought I to feel and speak and write, in view of a system which is red with innocent blood drawn from the bodies of millions of my countrymen by the scourge of brutal drivers;—which is full of all uncleanness and licentiousness;—which destroys the life of the soul; and which is too horrible for the mind to imagine or the pen to declare? How ought I to feel and speak? As a man! As a patriot! As a philanthropist! As a Christian! My soul should be, as it is, on fire. I should thunder, I should lighten, I should blow the trumpet of alarm long and loud. I should use just such language as is most descriptive of the crime. I should initiate the example of Christ, who, when he had to do with people of like manners, called them sharply by their proper names —such as an adulterous and perverse generation, a brood of vipers, hypocrites, children of the devil who could not escape the damnation of hell. . ."[18]

In contrast with these martial words, Garrison was an extreme non-resistant. He not only objected to all wars, but was a total disbeliever in force and coercive measures.

But the man into whose hands a copy of the *Liberator* came could no longer maintain a careless indifference on the subject of slavery. He might be alarmed or indignant but was forced to think and with many men there could be but one outcome. The paper made converts from the very start. It put Western and Eastern anti-slavery men into communication with each other.

Garrison had a genius for infuriating his antagonists. No banderillero ever more skillfully planted his darts in the flanks of an enraged bull. The "infamous Garrison," he was now called. The Southern press went into paroxysms of clamorous rage, denounced him as a murderer and a cutthroat, and every mail brought him from that quarter threats of assassination. Anonymous letters were studded with menaces and dire predictions: "You damned scoundrel," "Fiendish editor," "Hell is gaping for you, the devil is feasting in anticipation." One letter from Lowell (Mass.), signed "Revenge," promised death by poison or the dagger if the "infamous *Liberator*" should be published one month longer. "This information," commented Garrison, "afflicts us less than the postage—six cents."[19] When told by the Reverend John Breckenridge that he (Garrison) was "too debased and degraded in the community for me, occupying the station that I do, to hold a controversy with you," that was meat and drink to Garrison and his "mind was very tranquil."[20]

Nothing could daunt him. In South Carolina a reward of $1,500. was offered for the conviction of any white person circulating the *Liberator*, and the Georgia legislature provided

$500. for Garrison's arrest and conviction.[21] To this award Garrison replied: "A price set upon the head of a citizen of Massachusetts—for what? For daring to give his opinions of the moral aspect of slavery! Where is the liberty of the press and of speech? Where the spirit of our fathers? Where the immunities secured to us by our Bill of Rights? Are we the slaves of Southern taskmasters? Is it treason to maintain the principles of the Declaration of Independence? Must we say that slavery is a sacred and benevolent institution or be silent? Know this, ye Senatorial Patrons of Kidnappers! that we despise your threats as much as we deplore your infatuation; nay, more—know that a hundred men stand ready to fill our place as soon as it is made vacant by violence. The *Liberator* shall yet live—live to warn you of your danger and guilt—live to plead for the perishing slaves—live to hail the day of universal emancipation."[22]

The Southern planters, filled with rage, wrote protests to their Northern customers, and Northern merchants, yielding to their cupidity and fears, cried out against Garrison as a wicked and inexcusable conspirator. The press was their willing servant and so to a great extent was the pulpit; the Reverend Leonard Bacon once admitted publicly that "he rarely spoke of the devil in the pulpit and never of Mr. Garrison."[23]

To Northern lickspittle and Southern curses Garrison had but one reply: "I will be as harsh as truth and as uncompromising as justice. On this subject I do not wish to think or speak or write with moderation. No! No! Tell a man whose house is on fire to give a moderate alarm; tell him to moderately rescue his wife from the hands of the ravisher; tell the mother to gradually extricate her baby from the fire into which it has fallen—but urge me not to use moderation in a cause like the present. I am in earnest—I will not equivocate—I will not excuse—I will not retreat a single inch—and I will be heard."[24]

3.

A new reign of terror was dawning. Abolitionists were fanatics, disorganizers, amalgamationists, traitors, Jacobins, incendiaries, cutthroats, infidels, etc. Anybody, everybody, felt free to cuff and damn them. It became increasingly difficult for them to earn a livelihood in any line of trade; they were marked men.

They were stoned, clubbed, knocked down, and pelted with missiles, stripped of clothing, tarred and feathered, ridden upon rails or smeared with filth. Their houses were sacked, bonfires made in the streets of their furniture, garments, and bedding, their vehicles and harnesses cut and broken, and their domestic animals harried, dashed with hot water, cropped, crippled, and killed.

"These dangerous men," declared the Boston *Courier and Enquirer,* "must be met. They agitate a question that must not be tampered with. They are plotting the destruction of our government, and they must not be allowed to screen themselves from the enormity of their guilt."[25]

One Georgia judge addressed a suspect in this manner: "I have acquitted you simply for want of evidence, but I still believe you are an Abolitionist, a God damn Abolitionist, and you had better confess. You are," he continued, "a fool, a God damn fool. Have not your friends told you so? Do you not know it yourself?"[26] Leading Nullifier Hammond of South Carolina wrote the editor of the New York *Evening Star* that Abolitionism could be "silenced in but one way—*Terror—Death.*" A group formed to suppress Abolitionists, he believed, was "no more a mob than a rally of shepherds to chase a wolf out of their pastures."[27]

The editor of the *Emancipator,* Reverend Joshua Leavitt, made it a practice of sending his paper to every member of Congress. A small number (about twenty or thirty of the periodicals) were returned with indecent or insulting remarks. One read: "You damned infernal psalm singing negro stealing son of a bitch if you Ever show your damned hypocritical face in the dist. of Columbia I will make my negroes cowhide you to death."[28]

A casual report at the end of 1835 reads thus: "Brother Phelps has been mobbed in Worcester County. . . . Reverend Mr. Grosvenor has been mobbed in Worcester County. . . . Charles Stuart has been mobbed in the western part of the state of New

York. . . . Reverend George Storrs has been mobbed (according to law) in New Hampshire," etc.[29] Hezekiah Niles thought 1835 was the worst mob year. In one week he clipped one hundred items of mob violence, many of them over the slave question.[30]

A mob spurred on by Southern medical students and angered by rumors of the hobnobbing of colored and white people of both sexes, surged into Pennsylvania Hall, erected by the friends of freedom in Philadelphia at a cost of $40,000, pillaged what they thought of value, and then set the building on fire.[31]

The whole land was hot with pro-slavery wrath. Efforts were made to break up Abolition meetings everywhere.[32] The office of the anti-slavery *Philanthropist* was gutted, and desperate efforts were made to kill its editor, James G. Birney. At Marietta, Ohio, Samuel Hall, a student in college, when attempting to make an anti-slavery address, was assaulted with rotten eggs and other missiles and compelled to swim across Muskingum River to escape from the mob. Bigelow, a student in Western Reserve College, attempted to make an address in Aurora; a crowd gathered and fired a cannon and beat an anvil in front of the church until nearly all the glass in the windows was broken. Bigelow escaped unhurt, but his effigy was burned on a heap of stones nearby. At Canfield, an anti-slavery meeting was broken up, and for a long time afterwards the inhabitants showed the stain of a rotten egg on the pulpit Bible. At a schoolhouse meeting in a neighboring town, the lights were suddenly extinguished, and a pan of rotten eggs was poured upon the shoulders of the speaker.

Professor Hudson of Oberlin was sharp tongued and fearless. Nothing pleased him better than a scrimmage. He often conquered mobs by resolutely talking them down and making them ashamed of themselves. But on one occasion, looking through the window from the outside to see what awaited him in the room where he was to speak, he saw a pot of boiling tar on the stove which heated the room and a pillow case full of feathers conveniently near, while a half drunken crowd was in possession of the place. Hudson decided to run. However, he had been seen and was pursued. As his pursuers were better sprinters than Hudson and he was about to be captured, he dashed into the first house he came to and asked for protection. The proprietor was an Abolition sympathizer. He was an old man, but hearty and vigorous. He ordered his sons to take their guns and guard the other entrances while he took his stand in the front door with an axe in his hand. When the mob came up and demanded the Abolitionist, he gave warning that he would brain the first man that attempted to enter the house without his consent. So evidently in earnest was he, that the rowdies, after a little bluster, gave up the hunt and left in disgust.[33]

Even sleepy old Nantucket, in its sedentary repose by the sea, woke up long enough to mob a couple of Abolition lecturers.

There were plenty of Northern people to whom "amalgamation"—the word used to describe the union of races—was a veritable scarecrow. As soon as they were free, Negro men, it was said, would marry white wives. "Do you want your son or daughter to marry a Nigger?" was regarded as a knockout anti-Abolition argument. One young gentleman became devoted to the daughter of a Kentucky farmer and asked him for her hand. "But I am told," said the old gentleman, "that you are an Abolitionist." The young man agreed. "Then sir," roared the old man, "you can't have my daughter; go and marry a nigger."[34]

At Canaan, New Hampshire, where a manual training school for free Negroes was established, three hundred men appeared with a hundred yoke of oxen and pulled the school house into a neighboring swamp.

The Abolitionists were suspected of being "out of their heads." In one case the judge held that the question whether the witness was an Abolitionist was admissible as it related to the witness's sanity, and that would affect his credibility.

In 1837 not a single meeting house or hall of any size could be obtained for the annual meeting of the Massachusetts Anti-Slavery Society. It met in the loft of a hotel stable which enabled Garrison to declare, "Abolition today, as on every day, stands upon a stable foundation." On another occasion he said with his usual sting, there was no public hall which could not "be hired by jugglers, mountebanks, ballad singers, rope dancers, religious impostors, etc., etc."[35]

Northern merchants and manufacturers with anti-slavery tendencies were boycotted. A black list of New York Abolition merchants was made out by a committee, and the South was told to withdraw its patronage from these destroyers of the Union. Henry C. Bowen was on the list, and Beecher wrote for him a card which became famous: "My goods are for sale, but not my principles."[36]

In most financial and manufacturing circles, a pocket nerve was touched by the outcries of people who had cotton to sell and heavy orders to give. When the South called on the North to stay the Abolition frenzy to meet the wishes of their Southern friends, the first men of Boston called a meeting for August 21, 1835, in Faneuil Hall to discountenance the seditious principles of what even John Quincy Adams at that time wrote down as "a small, shallow, and enthusiastic party, preaching the abolition of slavery upon the principles of extreme democracy." The meeting was a Whig affair, and the principal speakers said the very things which were expected of them.

Great lawyers like Rufus Choate, statesmen like Van Buren and Buchanan, frontier leaders like Lewis Cass alternately pooh-poohed and scolded at the Abolitionists.

One Southside Adams conceived the idea that "Northern antagonism to slavery" might be "diverted into a mutual effort with the South to plan for the good of the African race." Among the Southern men thus addressed was Henry A. Wise of Virginia, who replied in a public journal: "What business have you to interest yourself about it [slavery]? Why take a thought about benefiting the race of my slave more than about benefiting the race of my ox, or my ass, or anything else that is mine?"[37] Yet after this snub Dr. Adams went on with his *Southside View* and remained "a veritable verigreen" to the day of his death.

Not alone did politicians of the South meditate schemes of vengeance—the clergy was filled with the same evil spirit. "Let your emissaries," said the Reverend Thomas S. Witherspoon of

Alabama, "dare to cross the Potomac, and I cannot promise you
that your fate will be less than Haman's. Then beware how you
goad an insulted but magnanimous people to deeds of despera-
tion."[38]

At the approaching meeting of the Presbytery, the Reverend
Robert W. Anderson of Virginia designed to offer the preamble:
"If there be any stray goat of a minister among you, tainted with
the blood-hound principles of Abolitionism, let him be ferreted
out, silenced, excommunicated, and left to the public to dispose of
in other respects."

If the Abolitionists," said Reverend William S. Plummer, D.D.
of Richmond, "will set the country in a blaze, it is but fair that
they should receive the first warning of the fire."

(As for the invective of the South, the Abolitionists were put
in mind of Major Jack Downing: "I met a man from Georgia
there, six feet, nine inches high, a real good fellow. Most all
these Southern folks are good fellows, if you don't say nothin'
about the tariff, nor freeing the niggers, but they talk pretty
big. I know how to manage them, the gineral tell'd me a secret
about that,—says he, 'Major, when they say they can hit a dollar,
tell 'em you can hit a four-pence ha'penny.' ")

Two causes célèbres illustrate the attitude of both North and
South.

Miss Prudence Crandall, a Quaker,[39] who was conducting a
Ladies' Academy at Canterbury, Connecticut, accepted Sarah
Harris, a colored girl, as a pupil. The white parents objected
and threatened to withdraw their children if Miss Harris were
allowed to remain, as they "would not have it said their daughters went to school with a nigger girl." "The school may sink,"
Miss Crandall said, "but I will not give up Sarah Harris." The
white children were withdrawn.

Not daunted, and to the consternation of Canterbury citizens,
she proceeded to convert the boarding school into an institution
for the training of Negro girls who should themselves become
teachers for the children of their race. She advertised in the
Liberator of March 2, 1833—

"Prudence Crandall—

"Principal of the Canterbury (Connecticut) Female
Boarding School, returns her most sincere thanks to those
who have patronized her School and would give information
that on the first Monday of April next, her school will be
opened for the reception of young Ladies and little Misses
of color. The branches taught are as follows: Reading,
Writing, Arithmetic, English, Grammar, etc."

The advertisement closed with a long list of references to
gentlemen of the highest character.

The notice threw the town into a furore of excitement. The
irritation too arose from the fact that members of the community
regarded themselves as the true friends of the Negro in their
capacity as members of the Friends of Colonization in Africa.
The Friends of Colonization actually opposed any education
for the Negroes beyond training them to be leaders of their race
in Africa. Letters from selectmen of the town to the Norwich,
Conn., *Republican* charged that Miss Crandall wanted to give
Negro misses fashionable airs and to train them to be brides
for white bachelors. A committee of Canterbury's leading citizens
remonstrated with her against the plan. But she replied, "I
have put my hand to the plow, and I will never, no never, look
back."

Twenty colored girls arrived at Miss Crandall's school largely
through the enthusiastic support of Garrison and his friends. The
irate Canterbury citizens invoked against her the Pauper and
Vagrancy Law, one of the early "blue laws" of the Connecticut
colony. This law required people not residents of the town to
pay a fine of $1.67 a week; if the fine was not paid or the person
gone in ten days, he was to be whipped on the naked body
not exceeding ten stripes. A warrant was issued against one
Negro pupil, Eliza Ann Hammond, from Providence. Reverend
Samuel J. May was eager that she should endure the punishment even to the stripes since the treatment would rouse the
country against Miss Crandall's persecutors. Another warrant
was issued for another pupil, but neither warrant was followed
by action, probably because May soon got a bond of ten thou-

sand dollars from gentlemen in his parish to cover the fines.

As Miss Crandall still held her ground, a new law was enacted by the Connecticut legislature on May 24, 1833, called the Black Law, prohibiting under severe penalties the instruction of any Negro from outside the state without the consent of the town authorities. When the new law was passed, bells were rung and cannon fired for half an hour. In the midst of all this Miss Crandall was unmoved. When the pupils walked out, horns were blown and pistols fired.

One of the exhibition exercises or gala days at Miss Crandall's school was a "Mental Feast" where four of the youngest scholars dressed in white sang the story of their trials in seven quatrains composed by the teacher.

> Sometimes when we have walked the streets
> Saluted we have been,
> By guns and drums and cow bells too
> And horns of polished tin.
>
> With warnings, threats, and words severe
> They visit us at times,
> And gladly would they send us off
> To Afric's burning climes. . . .

Difficulties came to a head when Miss Crandall was arrested and imprisoned. She spent one night in jail, but that one night's incarceration in a murderer's cell was bruited about the country.

Her case came to trial, but the jury disagreed. She was convicted on a second trial, but the verdict was quashed for lack of evidence in the higher court, the court tamely evading the constitutional question by declaring it "unnecessary for the court to come to any decision on the question as to the constitutionality of the law."

Despite legal attempts to stop her, Miss Crandall's school continued throughout the rest of 1833 and most of 1834. But popular resentment made life miserable for her. Her well was filled with manure; a minister was not allowed to preach in the Canterbury Church because he had visited the school; a physician summoned to attend a sick girl warned Miss Crandall

not to send for him again; a druggist refused to sell her medi-
cines; fires were started in the building, windows repeatedly
broken, and one temporary teacher was pelted with addled eggs.

Two events were more effective than law in bringing Miss
Crandall's school to a close. The first was her marriage to the
Reverend Calvin Philleo of Ithaca, New York, a Baptist preacher
who was far more prudent than Prudence. And the second,
occurring a few days later, was a final display of mob violence
that wrecked the school—the windows smashed by men carrying
iron bars and heavy clubs, and the front rooms rendered unin-
habitable. There was no assurance the attacks would not be
repeated; friends urged her to abandon the enterprise. Acting
on their advice, Prudence disbanded her school and sent the
twenty young girls to their homes. "When I gave that advice,"
said May, "I felt ashamed of Canterbury, ashamed of Connecticut, ashamed of my country, ashamed of my color."[40]

Amos Dresser, a young theological student, travelling South
for the purpose of selling "Cottage Bibles" and a few other
books, was arrested at Nashville, Tennessee, on the suspicion
of being an Abolition agent. He was brought before a Vigilance
Committee consisting of the principal citizens and seven leaders
of the Presbyterian Church. The trunk was lugged before the
Committee and emptied. In it they found three volumes written
by Abolitionists put in by Dresser for private reading and some
old newspapers of the same character used as stuffing to prevent his books from rubbing. His private journal was examined,
but as it was in pencil consisting only of memoranda and those
put in abbreviation, little could be made of it. The Mayor gave
up the attempt to read it aloud observing as he laid it down
that it was "evidently very hostile to slavery." The committee
acknowledged that Dresser had broken no law, but pleaded that
if the law did not sufficiently protect slavery against the assaults
of opinion, an association of gentlemen must make the law for
the occasion.

Dresser was therefore found guilty of three things—of being
a member of an anti-slavery society in another state, of having

books of an anti-slavery tendency in his possession, and of *being believed* to have circulated such in his travels. He was condemned to receive twenty lashes on his bare back in the market place.

To the market place he was marched amidst the shouts of the populace, and there by torchlight and just as the chimes were about to usher in Sunday, he was stripped and flogged. As the heavy cowhide whistled through the air, Dresser prayed. "God damn him—stop his praying," screamed someone in the mob. But Dresser did not stop it.[41]

He was given twenty-four hours to leave the city, but he thought it unsafe to remain a moment longer or to return to his lodging. Some kind people drew him into their house, bathed his wounds, gave him food, and furnished him with a disguise with which he left the place early in the morning.

The Augusta (Georgia) *Chronicle* remarked: "He [Amos Dresser] should have been hung up as high as Haman to rot upon the gibbet until the wind whistled through his bones. The cry of the whole South should be Death, Instant Death, to the Abolitionist, whenever he is caught."[42]

Such was the situation at the hour when the broadcloth mob fell under the eyes of Wendell Phillips in 1835—the South imperious, the North compliant, the Abolitionists few in numbers, uninfluential in position, despised as fanatics and hated as incendiaries, banned by the slave masters and mobbed at home.[43]

In the morning after his imprisonment Garrison inscribed with pencil upon the walls of his cell the following lines—

"William Lloyd Garrison was put into this cell on Wednesday afternoon, October 21, 1835, to save him from the violence of a 'respectable' and influential mob, who sought to destroy him for preaching the abominable and dangerous doctrine that 'all men are created equal' and that all oppression is odious in the sight of God. 'Hail Columbia!' Cheers for the Autocrat of Russia and the Sultan of Turkey!

"Reader, let this inscription remain till the last slave in this despotic land be loosed from his fetters."[44]

CHAPTER SIX

ANN GREENE

One day early in 1836 Wendell Phillips and Charles Sumner sat conversing in Phillips's office on Court Street when a mutual friend, Mr. Alford, burst in upon them. He informed them of his engagement to a Miss Grew of Greenfield, Massachusetts. He said too that he was going to Greenfield with his fiancé the next day and that a Miss Ann Terry Greene, a cousin of hers, was to accompany them. Would Phillips and Sumner take care of the young lady? After chaffing Alford the two friends agreed to go. Miss Greene was a clever and lovely girl, added Alford, but she was a rabid Abolitionist. And he warned Phillips and Sumner to look out or she would talk them both into that *ism* before they suspected what she was at.

The friends then disputed as to which one was the more likely to win Miss Greene's favor. Sumner maintained he had a better chance because he had read the *Liberator* longer than Phillips had. But the next morning it was storming furiously. When Sumner got up and looked out, he muttered, "I won't go on a stage ride on such a day for any woman!" And he ungallantly went back to bed.[1]

Phillips went. While his friend Alford devoted himself to Miss Grew, he listened to the Abolitionist Miss Greene. When the stage coach lumbered into Greenfield, he obtained permission to continue the acquaintance.[2]

Ann Terry Greene was the daughter of a wealthy shipping merchant of Boston. She had been left an orphan at an early age and was living with her uncle and aunt, Mr. and Mrs.

Henry G. Chapman, warm friends of Garrison and devoted to his cause. She was considered beautiful—of medium size with long light brown hair, very delicate features, and a waxen complexion. She was splendidly educated and a fine conversationalist. In moral fervor she resembled Wendell Phillips's mother.

Phillips came to see her, came again, and then kept coming. Within a year their engagement was announced.[3]

At Chapman's fireside he was introduced to Garrison. The two men, so unlike in family training and worldly prospects, were immediately attracted to each other. It was a strange alliance. Garrison was a plebeian, Phillips an aristocrat. The one was a selfmade man; the other the consummate product of New England culture.

Phillips and Ann Greene were married on October 12, 1837. Phillips married an invalid. Through some nervous defect, Ann, even as a child, was frequently confined to her room.

Beginning as lovers, Wendell and Ann remained lovers to the end. Because of her ill health, he became her nurse. She was passionately fond of reading, and when she was too sick to hold the book, Wendell would be her eyes. "My better three-quarters" was her favorite description of him.[4] Yet in spite of her sickness, she was always in good spirits, fond of fun and stories. "When I first met Wendell," she was accustomed to say, "I used to think, 'It can never come to pass; such a being as he is could never think of me.' I looked upon it as something as strange as a fairy tale.' "[5]

That meeting with Ann Terry Greene was a happy one. As a result of it, the lady secured an ideal husband and won to a great reform its most powerful advocate. Phillips obtained a wife who became his perennial inspiration. "Yes," he confessed in after years, "my wife made an out and out Abolitionist of me, and she always preceded me in the adoption of the various causes I have advocated. . . . A sick wife though she be, I owe the little I am and do almost wholly to her mature guardian spirit."[6]

Not long after meeting Garrison, Wendell Phillips openly announced his adoption of Abolition principles and took his place among the "fanatics." On June 14, 1837, he rode out to Lynn, ten miles away, for the first time to attend an Anti-Slavery Convention and made a maiden speech in which he paid a generous tribute to Garrison.[7]

When it became known in Boston that Phillips had become an Abolitionist, the town was horrified. Everybody said—"It is suicide—political, professional, and social suicide." So it was. Doors which before had opened to give him welcome were shut in his face. No more wealthy clients came to his law office.[8] His former friends called him "a friend of the niggers" and turned away from him in disgust. Some of his relatives declared he was insane and planned to have him confined in an asylum.[9]

The extraordinary thing, however, is not that they felt as they did, but that Phillips felt as he did. The fact that he so soon and so completely emancipated himself from the narrow prejudices of his environment is the best tribute to his character.

Here was a man endowed with every conceivable advantage for winning success—social standing and prestige, a profession he loved and for which he had every qualification, a taste for public affairs, and an almost unequalled aptitude for debate, every avenue of preferment and distinction open to him. And yet he deliberately abandoned them all.

He became a social pariah, but he never complained, never besought, never retreated an inch, nor filed down a principle, nor softened a phrase to regain his place and conciliate esteem.

A Boston gentleman once said to the Reverend Thomas Wentworth Higginson—"I am no Abolitionist, and yet, somehow, I never meet Wendell Phillips in the street, without wanting to pull off my hat to him. For I remember what he might have been, had he sacrificed, like the rest of us, his scruples to his ambition.[10]

CHAPTER SEVEN

"THOSE PICTURED LIPS"

On November 7, 1837, slavery murdered the Reverend Elijah Parish Lovejoy at Alton, Illinois.[1]

Lovejoy was a young Presbyterian minister, a graduate of Waterville College, Maine, and of the Princeton Theological Seminary, who had gone to St. Louis and started a religious paper called the *Observer*. His editorial career began peacefully enough, but a spirit like his could not be peaceful long. Fired by the expanding benevolence that inspired the church of the day, he enlisted his paper in "the Presbyterian war against slavery, intemperance, and popery."[2]

His first article on slavery was exceedingly moderate. But he soon grew bolder and proposed gradual emancipation and colonization. He was not an Abolitionist. But he saw enough, heard enough, felt enough in that slave-holding community to make him hate slavery. St. Louis, a river port for the lower South, would hear no discussion of the subject. A letter written to the editor by nine eminent citizens urged him "to pass over in silence everything connected with slavery." But Lovejoy said, "I have sworn eternal opposition to slavery, and by the blessing of God, I will never go back." He stood squarely on his constitutional rights which, he stated, gave him "a warrant for using, as Paul did, all freedom of speech." In addition, he pointed out that the citizens of St. Louis were establishing a dangerous precedent. "Today a public meeting declares that you shall not discuss slavery," he wrote. "Tomorrow another meeting decides it is against the peace of society that the principle of popery be

discussed. . . . The next day a decree is issued against speaking
against distilleries, dram shops, and drunkenness. And so on
to the end of the chapter. The truth is, my fellow citizens, if
you give ground a single inch, there is no stopping place."[3]

When falsely charged with transmitting Abolition newspapers
to Jefferson City, boxed and ready for distribution in Missouri,
he denied the charge yet claimed the right to send ten thousand
of them if he chose to as many of his fellow citizens.

At the request of the original proprietors of the *Observer*,
who were in debt, Lovejoy surrendered his editorship, but the
new owner called him back.

In the spring of 1836 a free mulatto resisting arrest stabbed
an officer and killed a prominent citizen. He was seized in
jail by a gang of lynchers, taken out of the city, chained to
a tree, and burned to death. Efforts were made to punish the
murderers. But the Judge, L. E. Lawless, promulgated the remarkable doctrine that a crime, punishable by death when committed by an individual, could be committed by a multitude
with impunity. He charged the jury as follows: If the violence
"was the act of congregated thousands, seized upon and impelled
by that mysterious metaphysical and almost electric frenzy which,
in all ages and nations, has hurried on infatuated multitudes
to deeds of death and destruction, then I say the case transcends
your jurisdiction—it is beyond the reach of human law." Of
course the jury did not bring in an indictment.[4]

Lovejoy protested against the outrage and instantly brought
down upon his head the wrath of the community. His office
was gutted and his press thrown into the Mississippi. He decided
to move his headquarters to Alton, Illinois, twenty-five miles up
the river.[5]

At the outset he encountered misfortune. The press arrived
from St. Louis on a Sabbath morning, and Lovejoy's Sabbatarian
convictions compelled him to leave it unpacked on the wharf.
Sometime during Sunday night it was dumped into the river. But
the good citizens of Alton called a public meeting, unanimously
denounced the act, and, carefully expressing disapproval of the
Abolitionists, pledged money for a new press. On his part,

Lovejoy expressed gratitude and announced that although he was an uncompromising enemy of slavery, he was not an Abolitionist, and that he had come to Alton to publish a religious, not an Abolition paper. The people of Alton understood that he pledged himself not to advocate or discuss Abolition. So a new press was bought for him, and by August, 1837, the *Observer* had secured two thousand subscribers.

But not for long could Lovejoy subdue the fire burning within him. Editorials appeared, each one more denunciatory than the rest. He soon began to advocate the formation of a state Abolition society, savagely attacked slavery, and branded the Vice-President of the United States a father of slaves. The flag itself, he said, was made of material raised by slaves.

Alton citizens were outraged. Their town was by far the wealthiest and most enterprising in Illinois. Its principal commerce was with the South, and it was ambitious to take the place of St. Louis as a distributing point and center of trade. The citizens feared that the activities of Lovejoy might endanger their prospects. On August 21, 1837, a mob entered the office of the *Observer*, destroyed the press, type, and material, and threw them into the river.

At first the mob attacked the editor as he was returning from the apothecary's with some medicine for his sick wife. A number of them, linked arm in arm, pushed by him and wheeled in the road before him, thus stopping him completely. They threw clods of dirt at him, yelling, "It is the damned Abolitionist; give him hell." Lovejoy spoke to them, asked them why they stopped him. By this time the cry all around him was, "Damn him, rail him, rail him, tar and feather him, tar and feather him." Then Lovejoy said to them quietly: "I have one request to make of you, and then you may do with me what you please." He then asked them to send one of their number to take the medicine to his wife, which he begged they would do without alarming her. This they promised, and sent one of their number to do it. Then he said to them: "You had better let me go. You have no right to detain me. I have never injured you." They began to curse and sneer, and Lovejoy added, "I am in your hands and you must do with me whatever God permits you to do." The men hesitated, consulted for a few moments, then told Lovejoy to go home.

Friends in the Ohio Anti-Slavery Society got him a new press. He offered to resign but was requested to stay. The third press arrived and was put in the warehouse. Late at night ten or twelve "respectable" ruffians, disguised with handkerchiefs over their faces, broke into the building, rolled out the press to the river bank, broke it all up, and cast it into the Mississippi. Lovejoy was mobbed again at his house, and dragged almost out while his wife became hysterical.

A fourth press was ordered from Ohio. The Mayor of Alton was appealed to for police protection but declared his inability to safeguard the editor. A group of Lovejoy's friends, about sixty young Abolitionists from towns nearby, therefore assembled with arms in their hands, determined that this press would not go the way of the others.

In the meanwhile a public meeting was held in Alton protesting against Lovejoy's agitation on slavery and asking him to leave. Lovejoy took his stand on the freedom of the press. But resolutions declaring the inalienable right of every citizen to freedom of speech, of freedom of the press, and urging protection of Lovejoy on the ground of principle solely, were voted down in the committee. Lovejoy made his own defense.

"It is not true, as has been charged to me, that I hold in contempt the feelings and sentiments of this community in reference to the question which is now agitating it. I respect and appreciate the feelings and opinions of my fellow citizens, and it is one of the most painful and unpleasant duties of my life that I am called upon to act in opposition to them. . . .

"I, Mr. Chairman, have not desired any *compromise*. I have asked for nothing but to be protected in my rights as a citizen— rights which God has given me, and which are guaranteed to me by the Constitution of my country. Have I, sir, been guilty of any infraction of the laws? Whose good name have I injured? When and where have I published anything injurious to the reputation of Alton?

"Have I not, on the other hand, labored in common with the rest of my fellow citizens, to promote the reputation and interests of the city? What, sir, I ask, has been my offense? Put your finger upon it—define it—and I stand ready to answer for it. If I have committed any crime, you can easily convict me. You have public sentiment in your favor. You have your juries, and you have your attorney [looking at the attorney general], and I have *no doubt* you can convict me. But if I have been guilty of no violation of law, why am I hunted up and down continually like a partridge upon the mountains? Why am I threatened with the tar barrel? Why am I waylaid every day, and from night to night, and my life in jeopardy every hour?

"You have, sir, as the lawyers say, a false issue; there is not two parties between whom there can be a *compromise*. I plant myself, sir, down on my unquestionable rights, and the question to be decided is, whether I shall be protected in the exercise and enjoyment of those rights—*that is the question, sir,*—whether my property shall be protected, whether I shall be suffered to go home to my family at night without being assailed and threatened with tar and feathers and assassination, whether my afflicted wife, whose life has been in jeopardy from continued alarm and excitement shall, night after night, be driven from a sick bed into the garret, to save her life from the brickbats and violence of the mobs; *that, sir, is the question.*"

(Here much affected and overcome by his feelings he burst into tears. The sympathy of the whole meeting was deeply excited. He continued:)

"Forgive me, sir, that I have thus betrayed my weakness. It was the allusion to my family that overcame my feelings, not sir, I assure you, from any fears on my part. I have no personal fears. Not that I feel able to contest the matter with the whole community; I know perfectly well I am not. I know, sir, you can tar and feather me, hang me up, or put me into the Mississippi, without the least difficulty. But what then? Where shall I go? I have been made to feel that if I am not safe at Alton, I shall not be safe anywhere. I recently visited St. Charles to bring home my family, and was torn from their frantic embrace by a mob. I have been beset night and day at Alton. And now, if I leave here and go elsewhere, violence may overtake me in my retreat, and I have no more claim upon the protection of any other community than I have upon this; and I have concluded, after consultation with my friends, and earnestly seeking counsel of God, to remain at Alton and here to insist on protection in the exercise of my rights. If the civil authorities refuse to protect me, I must look to God, and if I die, I have determined to make my grave in Alton."[6]

The press arrived at three o'clock in the morning on the seventh of November and intelligence of its arrival was made known by the blowing of horns. The Mayor, John Krum, went to the warehouse to aid in storing it. The press was placed under heavy guard.

Alton was in a fever pitch of excitement. Merchants closed their stores, and the whole city waited in dread for the night. The only talk on the street was of the Abolitionists, their stubborn attitude, their military preparations.

About nine in the evening, seeing no sign of an assault, most of the guard dispersed, entrusting the care of the press to Lovejoy and a dozen friends. Soon a gang of hoodlums, armed with muskets and waving torches, milled about in front of the building throwing stones and firing shots. The shots were returned, and one of the mob was killed. The mob retired but soon returned, many inflamed by drink, and renewed the assault. Bells of the city were rung, horns blown, and large numbers of citizens hurried to the scene, some counciling quiet, others urging vengeance. The Mayor came with a justice of the peace, and they were sent by the mob into the building to propose the surrender of the press on condition that its defenders would not be injured. To the demand of Gilman, the owner, who had property of great value in storage, that the Mayor should call upon the citizens to save his building, the latter replied that the mob was too strong, that he was powerless to protect the building. Admitting the lawful right of persons to defend their property, he retired and reported to the rioters that his terms were rejected whereupon they set up the cry, "Fire the building," "Burn them out," "Shoot every damned Abolitionist as he leaves."

The firing was furious. The building was surrounded and every means of escape cut off. Twice Lovejoy came out without being recognized and fired at the mob. Some of the rioters placed a ladder against a blind wall of the building which a man ascended and set fire to the roof. Those in the building could not get at him, and Lovejoy and two others stepped out of the door and fired at the man on the ladder but missed. The next moment a volley poured into them from rioters concealed behind a pile of lumber on the wharf. Lovejoy was hit in the breast. He had strength enough to run back and up the stairs crying out as he went, "I am shot, I am shot." When he reached the counting room, he fell back into the arms of a friend and died instantly.

His supporters offered to surrender, but the offer was refused. They scattered amid a fusilade of bullets, the building was fired, and the press for the fourth time flung into the Mississippi. . . .

It was a rainy, depressing day as the mourners walked through the mud and water to Lovejoy's grave. The burial service was simple, consisting merely of prayers by Lovejoy's constant friend, the Reverend Thomas Lippincott, no remarks being made lest the mob should disturb the rites of his friend. No inquest was made over the body, no flowers strewn over the coffin. Mob law not only reigned, but was insultingly triumphant.

The news spread like wildfire. "HORRID TRAGEDY! BLOOD CRIETH!" exclaimed the Cincinnati *Journal Extra*. "Voice of the Press! Horrid Outrage!—Lovejoy Murdered!!!" shouted the Lynn *Record*.[7] The *Liberator* printed an account of Lovejoy's murder between heavy black lined columns and ran an editorial with the heading—

A Martyr for Liberty
Slain by the hands of His Own Countrymen![8]

The martyrdom of Lovejoy became the battle cry of the Abolitionists. It lent credence to their claim that the fight for Negro
freedom involved a struggle for white freedom, that the two were
parts of the same whole.[9]

Boston flamed with indignation. A number of its eminent
citizens, headed by the Reverend Dr. Channing, applied for the
use of Faneuil Hall in which to denounce the outrage not as
Abolitionists, but as believers in free speech and a free press.
The Mayor and aldermen refused the hall on the ground that
the country might regard the meeting "as the public voice of the
city" and that the meeting would result in "a scene of confusion
which would be disreputable to the city and injurious to the
glory of that consecrated Hall."[10] "It is doubtless true," stormed
the *Liberator*, "that there are men in Boston calling themselves
respectable and honorable citizens who are rejoicing over the
Alton massacre and who would be highly displeased at any public
disapprobation of it! Monsters that they are! Will the Mayor
and Aldermen listen to the remonstrances of such? We will not
believe it."[11] The Lynn *Record* added: "The whole head is sick
and the whole heart faint. Who would have believed—who
could have believed that the very city which was first to rock
the cradle of liberty would be the first to abandon it?"[12]

The denial increased the agitation. Dr. Channing appealed
to Boston in an open letter which resulted in a crowded assembly protesting against the action of the Board. Another application signed by an enlarged number of influential names was
presented. Now the municipal authorities granted the request
and obliged: the hall was opened.

Faneuil Hall, "Cradle of Liberty," was built "at his own
cost" and presented to Boston in 1742 by Peter Faneuil, a
wealthy merchant of the city whose Huguenot ancestors had been
driven out of France by the tyranny of Louis XIV when at the
instigation of a mistress he revoked the Edict of Nantes. The
Huguenot hatred of despotism which Peter Faneuil built into the
hall was continued in the town hall which rose from its ashes
in 1763, for in the decade before the Revolution, the patriots made
its walls echo with denunciations of British tyranny.

At ten o'clock on the morning of December 8, five thousand people packed the hall to overflowing.[13] The throng was divided into three factions: free discussionists with a sprinkling of Abolitionists, mobocrats, and indifferent idle spectators, attracted by curiosity and swayed to and fro by each speaker in turn, but holding the balance of power.

Wendell Phillips came prepared to make a speech. His wife and her cousin Mrs. Chapman wished to go, and he accompanied them. He wore a long surtout, a brand new one, with a small cape, as was the fashion of the day.[14]

The proceedings opened quietly and decorously. The Honorable Jonathan Phillips, a wealthy Bostonian and kinsman of Wendell Phillips, took the chair.[15] Dr. Channing made a brief but impressive address speaking from a lectern set in front of the platform and well out towards the center of the hall, a position which he selected because he feared he might not be heard amid the rush and crush if he were farther back. (There are no seats in Faneuil Hall. At great gatherings the people stand. This, of course, increases the capacity of the hall and also in times of excitement the difficulty of hearing the speakers.)

Resolutions drawn by Dr. Channing were next offered and read by Benjamin F. Hallet. These were seconded by George S. Hillard, Esquire, in an incisive speech.

As Hillard concluded, there was a stir, then an outburst of applause, as a thickset man with sandy complexion and piercing eyes was seen to elbow his way down the great gilded eagle in the gallery over the main entrance with the evident purpose of making a speech not on the program. Everybody knew this official—James Tricothic Austin, Attorney General of Massachusetts, a parishioner of Dr. Channing, a popular politician and a masterly speaker. With a red face and bullying manner, he began an harangue clearly intended either to break up the meeting in a row or array it against the object of its callers.[16]

He maintained that there was a conflict of laws between Missouri and Illinois, compared the slaves to a menagerie "with lions, tigers, hyenas, an elephant, a jackass or two, and monkeys in plenty," and likened Lovejoy to one who should break the bars and let loose the caravan to prowl about the streets. The rioters of Alton, he said, were akin to the orderly mob "which threw the tea into Boston Harbor in 1776," and their victim had "died as the fool dieth." He closed by asserting that a clergyman with a gun in his hand, or one mingling in the debates of a popular assembly, was marvelously out of place. "He resorted to violence and he fell by violence. He excited the passions of men by conduct unwise, impolitic, rash, extravagant, and unchristian, and the consequence of his conduct was such as might have been anticipated."

A roar of triumph greeted the end of Austin's speech and the assemblage waited to vote down Channing's resolutions.

At this moment Wendell Phillips suddenly felt himself inspired, and tearing off his overcoat, started for the platform. His wife seized him by the arm and half terrified, said: "Wendell, what are you going to do?" He replied, "I am going to speak, if I can make myself heard."[17]

He pushed his way through the turbulent crowd and leaped upon the lectern. His youthful appearance, his calm dignity and the classic beauty of his face piqued the audience's curiosity. He commenced in quiet tones:—

"Mr. Chairman—We have met for the freest discussion of these resolutions, and the events which gave rise to them (cries of 'Question!' 'Hear him!' 'Go on!' 'No gagging!' etc.). I hope I shall be permitted to express my surprise at the sentiments of the last speaker—surprise not only at such sentiments from such a man, but at the applause they have received within these walls. A comparison has been drawn between the events of the Revolution and the tragedy at Alton. We have heard it asserted here, in Faneuil Hall, that Great Britain had a right to tax the Colonies, and we have heard the mob at Alton, the drunken murderers of Lovejoy, compared to those patriot fathers who threw the tea overboard! (Great applause.) Fellow-citizens, is this Faneuil Hall doctrine? ('No, no!') The mob at Alton were met to wrest from a citizen his just rights—met to resist the laws. We have been told that our fathers did the same; and the glorious mantle of Revolutionary precedent has been thrown over the mobs of our days. To make out their title in such defence, the gentleman says that the British Parliament had a right to tax these Colonies. It is manifest that, without this, his parallel falls to the ground; for Lovejoy had stationed himself within constitutional bulwarks. He was not only defending the freedom of the press, but he was under his own roof, in arms, with the sanction of the civil authority. The men who assailed him went against and over the laws. The mob, as the gentleman terms it—mob, forsooth!—certainly we sons of the teaspillers are a marvellously patient generation!—the 'orderly mob' which assembled in the 'Old South' to destroy the tea were met to resist, not the laws, but illegal exactions. Shame on the American who calls the tea-tax and stamp-act laws! Our fathers resisted not the king's prerogative, but the king's usurpation. To find any other account, you must read our Revolutionary history upside down."[18]

State archives, Phillips continued, were loaded with arguments of John Adams to prove taxes laid by the British Parliament unconstitutional—beyond its power. It was not till this was established that the men of New England rushed to arms. The arguments of the Council Chamber and the House of Representatives preceded and sanctioned the contest. "To draw the conduct of our ancestors into a precedent for mobs, for a right to resist laws we ourselves have enacted, is an insult to their memory."

The difference between the excitement of Revolutionary days and that of his own, added Phillips, was simply this: the men of that day went for the right, as secured by laws. They were the people rising to sustain the laws and the constitution of the province. The rioters of his own day went for their own wills, right or wrong.

"Sir, when I heard the gentleman lay down principles which place the murderers of Alton side by side with Otis and Hancock, with Quincy and Adams, I thought those pictured lips (pointing to the portraits in the hall) would have broken into voice to rebuke the recreant American—the slanderer of the dead!" (Tremendous applause.)

"The gentleman said he should sink into insignificance if he condescended to gainsay the principles of these resolutions. For the sentiments he has uttered, on soil consecrated by the prayers of Puritans and the blood of patriots, the earth should have yawned and swallowed him up!" (Applause and hisses with cries of "Take that back.")[19]

At this point the uproar became so great that for a time no one could be heard. At length the Honorable William Sturgis came to Phillips's side at the front of the platform. But he was met with the cries of, "Phillips or nobody," "Make him take back *recreant*." "He shan't go on till he takes it back." When it was understood that Sturgis meant to sustain, not to interrupt Phillips, he was listened to and said: "I did not come here to take any part in this discussion, nor do I intend to; but I do entreat you, fellow citizens, by everything you hold sacred—I conjure you by every association connected with this Hall, consecrated by our fathers to freedom of discussion—that you listen to every man who addresses you in a decorous manner."

Phillips resumed speaking. He proceeded to dissect the attorney general's argument.

"Sir, as I understand this affair, it was not an individual protecting his property; it was not one body of armed men assaulting another, and making the streets of a peaceful city run blood with their contentions. It did not bring back the scenes in some old Italian cities, where family met family, and faction met faction, and mutually trampled the laws under foot. No; the men in that house were regularly enrolled under the sanction of the mayor. . . . It was, therefore, you perceive, sir, the police of the city resisting rioters—civil government breasting itself to the shock of lawless men. . . . Some persons seem to imagine that anarchy existed at Alton from the commencement of these disputes. Not at all. . . . Anarchy did not settle down on that devoted city till Lovejoy breathed his last. Till then the law, represented in his person, sustained itself against its foes. When he fell, civil authority was trampled under foot. He had 'planted himself on his constitutional rights'—appealed to the laws—claimed the protection of the civil authority—taken refuge under 'the broad shield of the Constitution.' When through that he was pierced and fell, he fell but one sufferer in a common catastrophe.'

"If, sir, I had adopted what are called peace principles, I might lament the circumstances of this case. But all you who believe, as I do, in the right and duty of magistrates to execute the laws, join with me and brand as base hypocrisy the conduct of those who assemble year after year on the Fourth of July, to fight over the battles of the Revolution, and yet 'damn with faint praise,' or load with obloquy, the memory of this man who shed his blood in defence of life, liberty, property, and the freedom of the press! . . .

"*Imprudent* to defend the liberty of the press! Why? Because the defence was unsuccessful? Does success gild crime into patriotism, and want of it change heroic self-devotion to imprudence? Was Hampden imprudent when he drew the sword and threw away the scabbard? Yet he, judged by that single hour, was unsuccessful. After a short exile, the race he hated sat again upon the throne.

"Imagine yourself present when the first news of Bunker Hill battle reached a New England town. The tale would have run thus: 'The patriots are routed; the redcoats victorious; Warren lies dead upon the field.' With what scorn would that *Tory* have been received, who should have charged Warren with *imprudence!* who should have said that, bred as a physician, he was 'out of place' in the battle, and 'died as the *fool dieth!*' (Great applause.) How would the intimation have been received that Warren and his associates should have waited a better time? But, if success be indeed the only criterion of prudence, *Respice finem*—wait till the end.

"*Presumptuous* to assert the freedom of the press on American ground! Is the assertion of such freedom before the age? So much before the age as to leave one no right to make it because it displeases the community? Who invents this libel on his country? It is this very thing which entitles Lovejoy to greater praise, the disputed right which provoked the Revolution—taxation without representation—is far beneath that for which he died. (Here there was a strong and general expression of disapprobation.) One word, gentlemen. As much as *thought* is better than *money,* so much is the cause in which Lovejoy died nobler than a mere question of taxes. James Otis thundered in this hall when the king did but touch his *pocket.* Imagine, if you can, his indignant eloquence had England offered to put a gag upon his *lips.* (Great applause.)

"The question that stirred the Revolution touched our civil interests. *This* concerns us not only as citizens, but as immortal beings. Wrapped up in its fate, saved or lost with it, are not only the voice of the statesman, but the instructions of the pulpit and the progress of our faith.

"The clergy 'marvelously out of place' where free speech is battled for—liberty of speech on national sins? Does the gentleman remember that freedom to preach was first gained, dragging in its train freedom to print? I thank the clergy here present, as I reverence their predecessors, who did not forget their country in their immediate profession as to deem it duty to separate themselves from the struggle of '76—the Mayhews and Coopers—who remembered they were citizens before they were clergymen."[20]

And Phillips closed with these words:

"I am glad, sir, to see this crowded house. It is good for us to be here. When liberty is in danger, Faneuil Hall has the right, it is her duty, to strike the keynote for these United States. I am glad, for one reason, that remarks such as those to which I have alluded have been uttered here. The passage of these resolutions, in spite of this opposition, led by the Attorney-General of the Commonwealth, will show more clearly, more decisively, the deep indignation with which Boston regards this outrage."[21]

When the applause died away, the chairman put the resolutions and they were carried by an overwhelming vote. "Old Faneuil Hall," said the Boston *Times,* "has spoken in thunder

tones and her voice will go forth, as it has before, the watchword of freedom everywhere."[22]

The speech Wendell Phillips made, of course, was not exactly the speech he came prepared to make. The famous sentence, "I thought those pictured lips, etc." was clearly based
by an unconscious act of memory upon a passage written by
Whittier nearly two years before in an open letter of protest to
Governor Everett filling five columns of the *Liberator*. Phillips
undoubtedly read the letter to the governor and remembered
the passage in question.[23]

"The speech of the Attorney General Austin," said the Boston
Independent Messenger, "was so fraught with moral stupidity
and sulkiness, and all that is malicious, defamatory, mobocratic,
and murderous, as to justify the severe remark of a spectator
that he (Austin) exhibited in his own person the hideous spectacle of the ass and hyena combined in one animal [alluding to
Austin's comparison of the slave population to jackasses, hyenas,
monkeys, etc.]. The reply of the youthful, accomplished and
gifted Wendell Phillips electrified the mighty assembly. It
was sublime, irresistible, annihilating."[24]

That evening Mrs. Maria Chapman, "the born duchess" as
she was called, used all her arts of persuasion to induce Phillips
to relinquish his profession and cast his fortune to sink or swim
on the broad ocean of reform. Phillips argued that Webster and
Everett had the field, that years must elapse before he could
win equality with those veterans. But the arguments of the
"duchess" prevailed. She saw instantly what advantage could
accrue to the small band of Abolitionists from a close alliance
of the able young aristocrat with his suddenly revealed gift.[25]

CHAPTER EIGHT

WHIPMASTER AND SCOUTS

The Abolitionists were not all lambs and not all reasonable and Garrison was unsparing of his friends as well as his enemies. He was a natural autocrat who demanded from his followers implicit acceptance of all his views. "You exalt yourself too much," wrote Eliza Wright, one of his most loyal friends.[1] Whittier showed occasional flashes of impatience with Garrison, as when he dubbed Massachusetts "the Celestial Empire of the Uncle to the Sun and Cousin to the Moon," (that is, Garrison).[2] He had what his biographers call "an unyielding purpose to expose and refute the errors, fallacies, and misrepresentations of every proselyte to the cause, or every ally, however great his name or desirable his accession." Especially towards Channing he felt all the bitterness of the radical against the liberal, and characterized Channing's attack on slavery as "an inflated, inconsistent, and slanderous production . . . moral plagiarisms from the writings of the Abolitionists."[3] The Reverend Amos A. Phelps was for belaboring all "go-betweenites of the Channing kind." "Every such man who comes out should be reviewed without respect of his own person, and when he is naked, let his nakedness be made visible."[4] Differences with him he was prone to regard as gross departures from principle, as evidences of faithlessness to freedom. He was determined to thresh out each particle of chaff and leave only the pure grain.

A politician may conciliate, a dictator must have his way. Followers dubbed Garrison "the Pope." In the East, in New England, he kept his supremacy in spite of dissidents. Outside, his

73

control was not so sure. Disaffected clergymen spoke of his galling "yoke" and "brassy brow."[5] He fell upon men who did not see eye to eye with him with a literary tomahawk and scalping knife. He seasoned his replies to Birney with epithets such as "unfair," "improper," "libelous," "absurd," "folly closely allied to cool effrontery," "ridiculous," "disorganizing."[6] But Birney and Whittier and Wright and Gerrit Smith and other heretics, he apparently quite forgot, were actuated by motives similarly noble and were in their way as true to their convictions as he was to his. No, there was but one right way and in that way he stood with the feet of a pioneer. His way led directly, unerringly, to the land of freedom. All other ways twisted, doubled upon themselves, branched into the labyrinths of folly and self seeking. "Ho! all ye that desire the freedom of the slave, who would labor for liberty, follow me and I will show you the only true way."[7]

Once on the road to Philadelphia to attend a convention of the American Anti-Slavery Society, he got into conversation on the subject of slavery with a fellow passenger, who did not know him by sight. The stranger was favorably impressed by Garrison's exposition and said that if all Abolitionists were like him there would be less opposition to the cause. "But, sir, depend upon it, that hare-brained, reckless, fanatic Garrison will damage, if he does not shipwreck, my cause." "Allow me, sir, to introduce you to Mr. Garrison," said a fellow delegate.[8]

However, Garrison was the least Garrisonian of the Garrisonians. He had a substratum of common sense and practical wisdom.[9]

As a speaker he was usually monotonous, sometimes fatiguing, but always controlling. At public meetings where the order of addresses was arranged, he made an excellent president as he had a great felicity in introducing and interlocuting remarks. But at debate he did not answer so well, as he was rather too apt to do all the talking himself. The Bennington *Gazette* nicknamed him "Lloyd Garrulous" and said of him: "He is withal a great egotist and when talking of himself displays the pert eloquence of a blue jay."[10] Seated on the platform he wore that strange immobile smile of dominance and utter conviction that he was right.

He was inclined to procrastinate and was always unsystematic. Although he suffered from chronic illness he could endure long hours of drudgery and was rarely in low spirits. He cared little for native but always enjoyed sacred music. He was against smoking. Once he gave it soundly to his friend, N. P. Rogers, that he, an Abolitionist, on his way to an anti-slavery convention, should desecrate his anti-slavery mouth with a stupefying tobacco weed. As they proceeded, Rogers absentmindedly took out another cigar. "Is it any malady you have got, Brother Rogers," said Garrison to him, "that you smoke that thing, or is it habit and indulgence merely?" "It is nothing but habit," said Rogers gravely, "or I should say, it was nothing else," and he significantly cast the little roll over the railing. "A Revolution," exclaimed Garrison, "a Glorious Revolution without noise or smoke," and he swung his hat cheerfully about his head.[11]

Garrison was fond of the society of women, was perhaps a little sentimental and effusive in their presence and in correspondence with them. In a highminded and frank way he liked women.

His home life was gay and happy. He married Miss Benson, cozily called "Peace and Plenty" by her affectionate family, a very sane and wholesome woman but with some rebellious blood in her veins.[12] In times of financial stress he would put an arm around his anxious wife and walk up and down the room with her, saying, "My dear, the Lord will provide."[13]

Garrison was a man of middle size, completely bald and clean shaven, with large hazel eyes behind spectacles and a mild, benevolent expression. He walked erect and with a firm, brisk step. He appeared indeed more like a typical New England minister of the gospel than a relentless agitator. As the children's hands were exceptionally cold in winter, they often warmed them on their father's bald head.

Lowell wrote of him:

> There's Garrison, his features very
> Benign for an incendiary,

Beaming forth sunshine through his glasses
On the surrounding lads and lasses,
(No bee could blither be or brisker),—
A Pickwick somehow turned John Ziska.
His bump of firmness swelling up
Like a rye cupcake from its cup.[14]

But upon those he met he made a variety of impressions. One saw in "his beautiful countenance and clear eagle eye, that resolute spirit which makes the martyr." Miss Martineau said: "His speech is deliberate like a Quaker's but gentle as a woman's."[15] She was impressed with the saint-like impression and sweetness of his manner. (Garrison could bear what he met with from street to street and from town to town, but a kind look and a shake of the hand from a stranger unmanned him for the moment.) Another, on the other hand, styled him the "whipmaster general and supreme judge of all Abolitionists, as though he wore the triple crown and wielded an irresponsible sceptre."[16]

Emerson found Garrison "venerable in his place like the tart Luther." When Emerson suggested that Garrison had not considered the element of fate in the Negro question, Garrison neighed like a horse and could not understand the point.[17] His respect for Garrison grew with his knowledge of him and he wittily said of the Abolitionists: "They might be wrongheaded, but they were wrongheaded in the right direction."[18]

In the midst of so much that was dishonest, sordid, and time-serving, Garrison was doing his best with a single heart in every way for righteousness and for the good of mankind. He was an antidote to American complacency.

Grouped around Garrison were the "sappers and miners" of the anti-slavery army, the pioneers and scouts. Stephen S. Foster, Abby Kelley, Parker Pillsbury, Charles C. Burleigh, Theodore D. Weld were all persons of marked and picturesque character. They were resolute, sensational, irritating.

"I was a slave," Foster said, "I am a slave no longer. My lips have been sealed by man. They will never again be sealed till sealed in death. My body is freely yielded to the persecutors to torture at pleasure. But my spirit must and shall be free."[19]

Foster would go into the churches there to interrupt the services with his appeals and denunciations. Being a steadfast nonresistant, he bore with exasperating meekness assaults from minister, elder, or deacon to which as a result he was subjected. He was dragged twenty-four times from temples of worship and twice thrown from the second story of buildings careless of consequences. He was in jail often and had more power than any other anti-slavery lecturer to bring on a shower of rotten eggs and brickbats. Once in a Baptist meeting house someone gave him an evangelical kick in the side which left him for weeks an invalid. His method of stirring up an audience was by his favorite assertion that the Methodist Church was worse than any brothel in New York.

He was indicted for assault and battery, nearly put in irons, and once a mob of two thousand deliberately attempted to murder him. He was twice punished with fines for preaching the gospel. Yet he said: "My lot is easy compared with that of those for whom I labor. I can endure the prison, but save me from the plantation."[20]

A scraggy beard about an eager, intellectual face gave it a look of wildness. Wide, thin lips compressed and shut together in a thin line. Across his chin a wrinkle as if he held his face habitually in a scornful and truculent expression, and he looked as if he were always ready to jump at an enemy.

He was forcible and witty and ready in retort. On one occasion a slaveholder ventured on the platform to argue in behalf of the "peculiar institution." Foster contradicted some assertion by the man, who in return asked indignantly, "Do you think I would lie?" "Well," replied Foster, "I don't know as you would lie, but I do know that you will steal."[21]

A man with caoutchouc endurance,
A perfect gem for life insurance,
A kind of maddened John the Baptist,
To whom the harshest word comes aptest,
Who, struck by stone or brick ill starred,
Hurls back an epithet as hard,
Which deadlier than stone or brick,
Has a propensity to stick.[22]

Foster was logical to the point of unreason. Mary Grew, a Philadelphia Abolitionist, said of him in later years, smiling the while at some recollection: "Logic was the death of Stephen." His style of argument was as follows: Slavery is the sum of all villainies, such as theft, murder, and rapine; the Southern Church supports slavery; hence Southern clergymen are guilty of all villainies. Northern clergymen extend the right hand of fellowship to Southern clergymen: thus they condone and partake of their guilt. From such general premises he would proceed with unfaltering energy to the close of his personal conclusion. "Foster has proved," lamented another friend, "that X is a murderer and a thief—and yet he isn't."[23]

Foster was a sturdy, successful farmer of his New England fields. His property near Worcester was one of the best managed and most productive in the district. "I should hate farming in the West," he once said. "I should hate to put my spade into the ground where it did not hit against a rock."[24]

His hands were gnarled with toil and his gestures were ungainly. But his eyes were blue and kind, and his voice beautiful.

Foster's wife, Miss Abby Kelley, a Judith turned Quakeress, followed the same plan of causing "the truth to make a sensation by making it sensational."[25] Her eyes were small, contracted when she was speaking until they emitted sparks of fire.[26] Every woman thought she had a right to jeer at her. Men went to her meetings with brickbats and stones to pelt her. It was an unheard of thing to see a woman on the platform.

Brown, broad-shouldered Parker Pillsbury, blacksmith and chaise maker, had the temperament of a Hebrew prophet. When he spoke against the institution he abhorred, it was in the language of Jeremiah.

He was the ninth of thirteen children in a family of poor New Hampshire farmers. By great effort he succeeded in obtaining a theological education, and he was in attendance at Andover Seminary when he took up the cause of Abolition. He was warned by the faculty that if he persisted in addressing Abolition meetings, he need not expect to be provided with a parish. However, he unhesitatingly threw in his lot with the reformers and sacrificed his wordly future.

His ministry at Loudon was a stormy one. "You ask me in your note," he writes to a friend, "if I will not come into Massachusetts to assist you in the *struggle for freedom!* Why, my dear brother, I am here fighting for life. I am in a little den of pro-slavery as filthy as can be found this side of the caverns of the pit." His license to preach was revoked. During his first year of service as a field lecturer for the New Hampshire Anti-Slavery Society he received eighty-three cents a day; during the second year it was voted that he keep $400. for himself from the year's contributions by lecture audiences. He and the "lovely little wife" he left behind while he visited the towns lived in poverty.

He was a man of direct and vigorous speech, intense and earnest—"a tough oak stick of a man," said Emerson, "not to be silenced or insulted or intimidated by a mob, because he is more mob than they; he mobs the mob."[27]

A volley of stones came crashing through the windows of his lecture room. The women, he wrote, kept quiet, but the men babbled uneasily, and one cried out, "Let's adjourn, let's adjourn!" Pillsbury raised his voice above the din and asked, "Did your fathers adjourn at Bunker Hill when fired on by the enemies of freedom?" The confusion ended.

To emphasize the degradation attending the enslavement of Christians he asked his listeners assembled in church at Danvers, Massachusetts, to reverse the process and picture to themselves the spectacle in that sacred place of a dog called up for baptism with the solemn invocation, "Tiger, I baptize thee in the name of the Father and the Son and the Holy Ghost!" It is difficult to recapture in full the excitement this bit of business evoked.[28] Lowell termed him a giant

> Who tears up words like trees by the roots,
> A Theseus in stout cowhide boots. . .
> A terrible denouncer he
> Old Sinai burns unquenchably

Upon his lips; he might well be a
Hot blazing soul from fierce Judea,
Habakkuk, Ezra, or Hosea.[29]

"These Cotton slaveholders," declared this son of thunder in
Old Liberty Hall, "could turn all Heaven into Birmingham, make
weavers of the angels, and drown the music of the morning
stars with the eternal din of spindles."[30]

Later in life Pillsbury turned his sympathies to the laborer.
"With heavenly interference and aid, our hugest dragon, chattel slavery, is slain. Now," he observed, "we begin to see what
other monsters not less deadly beset us on every hand." The eight
hour day, the right to organize, restrictions on child labor, and
similar issues attracted his attention and formed the substance
of his articles and lectures.[31]

Another of the color guard of anti-slavery lecturers was
Charles C. Burleigh—a long, thin figure in high water pantaloons
that dangled above his ankles, with a downward curve of the
nose and flowing sandy beard. He was the laughing stock of
every audience until he began to speak. He was the ablest de-
bater among the Abolitionists—fluent, intense, logical, clear.
Samuel J. May characterized him as "a single minded, pure
hearted, conscientious, self-sacrificing man,"[32]—but so were all
the Abolitionists.

The Reverend Samuel May was the St. John of the Garrisonians. Kindly and brave with a rich fund of sympathy, he
thoroughly earned Bronson Alcott's epithet of "the Lord's chore
boy."[33] Then there were Francis Jackson, rich and philanthropic,
and Henry G. Chapman, who moved in the best society, dwelt in
a ceiled house and fared sumptuously every day, but who accepted the condemnation of his pastor, Dr. Channing, and of
his business and social intimates in order to become treasurer
of the Abolition cause. There were also the Reverend Moses
Thatcher and the Reverend Amos Phelps, Congregational ministers, and Ellis Gray Loring and Samuel E. Sewall, a brace of
conscientious lawyers. Loring's house was open to fugitives as
well, and perhaps he was the first lawyer to take a Negro boy

into an office and train him for the bar. He was moderate in views and urged moderate tactics in conducting agitation: by petitioning legislative bodies, by interrogating candidates publicly, and by using suffrage. He favored "gradualism" as opposed to Garrison's "immediatism."

Nor was Garrison the only editor in the humanitarian coterie. At his side stood David Lee Child. Professional scholarship was notably represented by Charles T. Follen, a liberty loving German who was professor of German Language and Literature at Harvard. Follen, looking German all over, was what Goethe used to call a "Schoene Seele"—beloved of all.[34] In 1834 he joined the New England Anti-Slavery Society and at its first convention held in Boston drafted the "Address to the People of the United States." This address was the immediate cause of the severance of Follen's connection with Harvard. When his tenure of professorship expired in 1835, it was not renewed, although his striking success as a teacher was widely and emphatically recognized. As teacher, lecturer, Unitarian minister, he never ceased to make the training of original and independent individuals his primary object.

Follen perished with many others by the burning of the steamer Lexington on January 13, 1840. Every Unitarian church in Boston refused the use of its edifice for holding services in his honor.

"Some men," said Follen, "are so afraid of doing wrong that they never do right."[35]

Theodore D. Weld was another great anti-slavery lecturer, "eloquent as an angel and powerful as thunder," who speedily made his name and fame continental. On his journeys he met with uproars, insults, and at last with rotten eggs and filth, a kind of treatment which only increased his fervor. He was "the most mobbed man in the United States."[36] Rowdy youths in the preliminary period of violence made an uproar which Weld overcame by raising his splendid voice above the din. Peaceable horses tied to posts were assaulted, snuff and sand thrown into women's eyes, eggs hurled into the meeting, and cannons fired. For such disorders Weld expressed a patient contempt. "I beg the audience will be composed," he told his nervous hearers as an egg broke upon his face. He wiped it away calmly and proceeded as deliberately as if he had paused to take a draught of water.[37]

Many times he was stoned even while he spoke from the pulpit. At Circleville, a large stone crashed through the church window, one so well aimed that it struck him on the head and for a moment stunned him. He paused for a few moments till his dizziness had ceased, and then went on and completed his lecture. Meanwhile some of the gentlemen had hung their cloaks up at the window so that his head could not be so easily used as a target. Once the disturbance lasted until it was too late to speak. Then lifting his mighty voice, he informed his hearers that he would speak the next night and the next. He would continue to plead for constitutional liberty until liberty or he was defunct.[38] Usually after the second night the violence died. Then Weld reaped his harvest.

In his closing lecture he asked converts to immediate Abolition to stand. "Friends, will all of you who believe, please rise to your feet?" Some enthusiasts sprang to their feet and turned to their neighbors with uplifted hands, who usually rose in a body in response to their lead.[39]

"Abolitionism is a two-fold revival," proclaimed Weld; "first of the law of love in relation to man, 'Love thy neighbor as thyself', and then of the principles of liberty as proclaimed by our forefathers. . . . The business of Abolitionists is with the heart of the nation rather than with its purse strings."[40]

As a student Weld's concern for the blacks became so poignant that every minute he could spare from his studies was devoted to them. "If I ate in the City, it was at their tables," he recalled. "If I slept in the City, it was in their homes. If I attended parties, it was *theirs—weddings—theirs, funerals—theirs, religious meetings—theirs, Sabbath Schools—Bible Classes—theirs.* During the eighteen months that I spent at Lane Seminary *I did not attend Dr. Beecher's Church once.*"[41]

Weld's thrilling triumphs were in Ohio and Pennsylvania. His greatness of heart and flaming zeal for Abolition exercised a powerful influence on the cause.[42] But he had one attribute inimical to the perpetuation of his fame. Friends called it modesty, but Weld himself believed it to be pride. "It is the great besetment of my soul," he declared, "the poisoned thorn that festers and corrodes. I am too proud to be ambitious, too proud to seek applause, too proud to tolerate it when lavished upon me —proud as Lucifer that I can and do scorn applause and spurn flattery."[43] Frederick Douglass testified that one of Weld's books, *Slavery As It Is,* was as influential in the earlier period of the anti-slavery movement as Harriet Beecher Stowe's *Uncle Tom's Cabin* was in a later day.[44]

Weld never would speak at anniversaries or conventions or even attend them. "The Stateliness and Pomp and Circumstance of an Anniversary I loathe in my inmost soul."[45] With Joshua Leavitt he started and kept alive an efficient anti-slavery lobby in Washington. But he was more than a lobbyist; he was an evangelist, the genius of Abolition revival. Samuel J. May said that Wendell Phillips as an orator was his only rival in the cause of liberty.[46]

Unhappily Weld's excessive labors and exposures caused the loss of his voice and did what slavery could not do—silenced him.

The tragedy at Alton brought in an important recruit, Wendell Phillips' aristocratic friend, Edmund Quincy. He was the litterateur of Abolition. But he also had his share of slander and abuse. He heard that he kept two mistresses, that he beat his wife, that he made her do the family work, that he made her cook for twelve "niggers" and afterwards wait upon them at table, that he brought two Negro wenches to the house and made her associate with them. He was called Prince of Bigots, His Anti-Slavery Highness, an aristocrat, a hyena, and a squash infidel.[47]

Even Charles Francis Adams, son of the ex-president, wrote at the time: "I wish I could be an entire Abolitionist, but it is impossible; my mind will not come down to the point."[48]

George Thompson, renowned orator of West India Emancipation and agent of the London Anti-Slavery Society, often came to the United States to spur on the cause of emancipation. To Garrison's ears Thompson's name was "as sweet as the tones of a flute," but it was not at all dear to the majority of Cis-Atlantic ears.[49] His visits were resented as intrusions on the part of a foreigner in affairs peculiarly our own. We were still too young, too raw to endure one who should tell us pointedly of our sins. We could barely tolerate Mrs. Trollope and Charles Dickens because they indicated our follies in certain and sometimes shrill tones. But Mrs. Trollope and Charles Dickens were "literary" and therefore harmless. George Thompson was by no means harmless. He was truly a terrible person, and he could not only wound, but rub salt in the raw. Even Garrison was not his superior in this respect.

As a result, he was maligned, hated, hunted. Newspapers from Maine to Georgia denounced him daily and called for his expulsion from this country. His meetings were broken up and he was often insulted in the streets. In New York he was threatened by a mob which refused to tolerate his "officious intermeddling," and he and his family were put out of the Atlantic Hotel in deference to the wish of an irate Southerner. At Augusta, Maine, his windows were broken and he was warned out of town. And once to escape the fury of a mob, he was conveyed in a small boat rowed by two of his friends from one of the Boston wharves to a small English brig and in that vessel carried safely to St. Johns.

Thompson was tall and graceful and had a sweet voice. His appeals were electrifying, "his action all that Demosthenes could desire," said Garrison effusively.[50]

The most remarkable addition to the number of Abolition lecturers was Frederick Douglass. Douglass was the son of an unknown father (white) and Harriet Bailey, a slave who had also some Indian blood. As a child he experienced neglect and cruelty, indulgence and hard work, but particularly the tyranny of a human being who was legally classed as real estate. Hearing his mistress read the Bible, he was consumed by a burning desire to learn to read. In response to his plea, his mistress taught him the alphabet and how to spell simple words. But the lessons ended the moment her husband learned of the boy's progress, shouting in Douglass' presence, "Learning would spoil the best

n———r in the world."[51] He made two attempts to escape—
the latter was successful and he married and settled in New
Bedford.

He had been christened Frederick Augustus Washington
Bailey, but his benefactor, Nathaniel Johnson, found the name
of Douglass in Sir Walter Scott's *The Lady of the Lake* a more
appropriate surname than his own for the escaped slave, and the
name by which he is known to history was chosen. Said Douglass:
". . . the free hills of old Scotland where the ancient Black
Douglass once met his foes . . . almost every hill, river, mountain, and lake of which has been made classic by the heroic
deeds of her noble sons. Scarcely a stream but has been poured
into song, or a hill that is not associated with some fierce and
bloody conflict between liberty and slavery."[52]

Learning that Garrison was to speak in Nantucket, Douglass
attended the meeting and was invited by a gentleman who had
heard him address a company of colored people, to support the
affirmations of the reformer by his testimony. Douglass told his
story with power and eloquence. The audience, previously calm,
was thrilled through and through. Garrison rose to speak, very
quiet, very serene. The contrast between the young Negro
man with his tawny leonine face and great bush of hair and
Garrison, spare of flesh, the light shining on his bald head, his
brown eyes enkindled, and his face expressing at once calm
benevolence and a deep surge of feeling, made the scene dra-
matic. When Garrison said: "Have we been listening to a
man or a thing?" the effect was like that of an electric shock.
And as he shouted with the full power of his voice (without the
loss of that dignity always attending the fixed poise of his
nature), "Shall such a man be sent back to slavery from the
soil of old Massachusetts?" almost the whole assembly sprang to
its feet and shook the walls and roof of the Athenaeum with the
cry, "No! No!"[53]

Undoubtedly, as John A. Collins pointed out, "The public have
itching ears to hear a colored man speak, particularly a slave.
Multitudes will flock to hear one of this class speak."[54] Douglass
could thrill his listeners with an account of how one day he

turned on his tormentor, a Negro-breaker, Covey, and soundly
thrashed him, at the same time getting his audience to burst
into laughter as he described the expression on Covey's face as
he went down in the filth of the cowpen. He could dramatically
portray his master Auld first being converted, the tears rolling
down his cheeks as he worshipped God, then the same Auld,
on the same day, dispersing a group of slaves who had assembled to worship the same God.[55] The colored people had a
parody on the "Heavenly Union," a hymn sung weekly in the
churches of the South.

> When Jesus from His throne on high,
> Beheld my soul in ruin lie,
> He looked on me with pitying eye
> And said to me as he passed by,
> With God you have no union.

Douglass composed his own version:

> Come, saints and sinners, hear me tell
> How pious priests whip Jack and Nell,
> And women buy, and children sell,
> And preach all sinners down to hell,
> And sing of heavenly union. . . . [56]

He defined slavery as "perpetual unpaid toil; no marriage,
no husband, no wife, no parent, no child; ignorance, brutality,
licentiousness, whips, scourges, chains, auctions, jails, and sep-
arations; an embodiment of all the woes the imagination can
conceive."[57]

Douglass at once was made agent of the Massachusetts Anti-
Slavery Society. He became the central figure in the famous
"One Hundred Conventions" of the New England Anti-Slavery
Society, was mobbed, mocked, and beaten, compelled to ride
in Jim Crow cars, and refused accommodations, but he carried
his program through to the bitter end. In the middle of his
speech he was often forced to leave the building followed by
a mob howling, "Get the nigger!" "Kill the damn nigger!"[58]

He wrote a striking book, *Narrative of the Life of Frederick Douglass*, which Wendell Phillips advised him to burn. It was a daring recital of facts and Phillips feared it might lead to his enslavement. Douglass published the book, however, and then to avoid possible consequences, visited Great Britain and Ireland. He remained in Great Britain two years visiting nearly all of the English liberals. He returned to the United States with money to buy his freedom and establish a newspaper for his race, *The North Star*. All agreed that Douglass was a man of extraordinary power and magnetism, the most eminent of his race in that period.

"Liberty is meaningless," he cried in Boston's Music Hall, "where the right to utter one's thoughts and opinions has ceased to exist. . . . There can be no right of speech where any man, however lifted up, or however old, is overawed by force and compelled to suppress his honest sentiments. . . . When a man is allowed to speak because he is rich and powerful, it aggravates the crime of denying the right to the poor and humble. . . .

"A man's right to speak does not depend upon where he was born or upon his color. The simple quality of manhood is the solid basis of the right—and there let it rest forever."[59]

The conversion of Channing to anti-slavery was slow, but a winter spent in the West Indies gave him the opportunity to see slavery face to face. His work, *Slavery*, attracted wide attention and might have been found on many a parlor table from which the *Liberator* was excluded with scorn. He was one of the few Americans who had a literary reputation in Europe. While not as extensive as that of Washington Irving, it was, in the opinion of Ticknor, "almost as much so, and deservedly higher." Emerson said Channing's sermons were sublime, and James Freeman Clarke that Channing spoke "with the tongues of men and of angels."[60] And so he did:

I know it will be said, 'You would make us poor.' Be poor, then, and thank God for your honest poverty. Better be poor than unjust. Better beg than steal. Better live in an almhouse, better die than trample on a fellow creature and reduce him to a brute for selfish gratification. What! Have we yet to learn that it profits us nothing to gain the whole world and lose our souls? . . . Has God's throne fallen before Mammon's? Must duty find no voice, no organ, because corruption is universally diffused? Is not this a fresh motive to solemn warning, that, everywhere, Northward and Southward, the rights of human beings are held so cheap, in comparison with worldly gain?[61]

Channing "so human and good, sweet as sunshine and fragrant as pine woods."

Women justified the saying of Luther: "I have oftentimes noted when women espouse a cause they are far more fervent in faith, they hold to it more stiff and fast than men do; as we see in the loving Magdalen, who was more hearty and bold than Peter himself."

There was no dearth of heroines. One was Lydia Maria Child, wife of the editor David Lee Child. She threw a bomb into the pro-slavery camps of the North and South with *An Appeal in Favor of that Class of Americans Called Africans*. The little book made many converts, but it aroused intense hostility. The sale of Mrs. Child's other books fell off badly and the Boston Athenaeum cancelled her free membership. But she kept on undaunted, attacking slavery in work after work and attending the tumultuous Abolition meetings. In old age she remembered collaring and pulling away a man who was shaking his fist in Wendell Phillips's face at a music hall mob— and her surprise when he tumbled down.[62] She edited the *National Anti-Slavery Standard*, the New York weekly newspaper, from 1841 to 1849.

She was a sweet impassioned soul and her letters reveal her faith, modesty, and unbounded charity.

In fact I think the want of faith produces a horror of infidelity. I could never bring my mind to read Harriet Martineau's book, and the reason was that I feared she might influence me in a way I did not want to be influenced. To put the soul on *such* a track is like sending a bird out into the long cold storm. Who can be sure that it will come back to the Ark with an olive branch in its mouth?[63]

Again to a friend:

I am strongly inclined to think that the reconstruction of society on a new basis is the only thing that can arrest the frightful increase of pauperism and crime. If it be true that you cannot change the outward structure of society till men are morally and intellectually improved, on the other hand, the masses *can not* be morally and intellectually raised until they are placed in a more comfortable physical condition. I know an excellent Quaker lady who went to England to preach to the poor. "When I gathered them into my meetings," said she, "I found that I could not gain their attention because they were hungry. At last I came to the place of meeting provided with a store of comfortable food. I fed them well, and after that, they listened to me, many of them with their hearts." This preaching about Christian brotherhood has slight effect, and he who from childhood has felt the hard grip of poverty, listens quite skeptically to accounts of the overflowing goodness of God and his equal love to the human race. Our religion and our institutions are so horribly discordant that one or the other must vanish.[64]

Lydia's means were never large. But her spirit was Spartan. When she had nothing for others, she worked to get it. She wrote Phillips once: "I have four hundred dollars to my credit at my publishers for my book on *Looking Towards Sunset*. Please get it and give it to the freedmen."[65] Phillips eulogized her as modest, womanly, simple, sincere, solid, real, loyal."[66] She certainly was the outgrowth of New England theology, tradition, habits—the finest fruit of all these.

Another woman champion of Abolition was Maria Weston Chapman:

There was Maria Chapman, too
With her swift eyes of clear steel blue. . .

> A noble woman, brave and apt,
> Cumaean sibyl not more rapt
> Who might, with those fair tresses shorn,
> The Maid of Orleans' casque have worn—
> Herself the Joan of our Ark.[67]

Then there were the sisters Sarah and Angelina Grimké. They were born in Charleston, South Carolina, of a slave-holding family noted for learning, refinement, and culture. Their parents were related to the Rhetts, the Barnwells, the Pickenses, and others of the Palmetto aristocracy. Sarah was born in 1792, Angelina thirteen years later.

Early in life they showed signs of dissatisfaction with their environment. Angelina was a typical crusader. Her sympathies from the first were with the slave. As a child she collected and concealed oil and other simple remedies so that she might steal out by night and alleviate the sufferings of slaves who had been cruelly whipped or abused. There was a statute in South Carolina against teaching slaves to read and write. The penalties were fine and imprisonment. The girls, however, had little fear of that law. Sarah took malicious satisfaction in teaching her little maid at night when the latter was supposed to be occupied in combing and brushing her long hair. The light was put out, the keyhole screened, and flat on their stomachs before the fire, with a spelling book under their eyes, they defied the laws of South Carolina.

In 1821 Sarah went North and met the Quakers. After many trying spiritual experiences she settled in Philadelphia and became a member of the Society of Friends. Sister Angelina followed. Both chafed under the discipline of the orthodox Philadelphia Friends. Angelina came to resent in them what seemed to her an equivocal attitude on slavery and Abolition. A life of modesty, economy, and charity seemed hollow when they longed for the opportunity to serve humanity.

In the religious meetings Negro women were consigned to a special seat. The Grimké sisters, having first protested against this discrimination, took their own places on the seat with the colored women.

Angelina was determined to express her growing sympathy with Abolition and she wrote to Garrison encouraging him in his work. The letter to her surprise was published in the *Liberator*. Eager to make a more positive contribution to the cause, she poured out her heart in *An Appeal to the Christian Women of the South*. The manuscript was handed to the officers of the anti-slavery society in the city, and as they read, tears filled their eyes. In this pamphlet Angelina urged Southern women to speak and act against slavery. "The women of the South can overthrow this horrible system of oppression and cruelty, licentiousness and wrong."[68]

The *Appeal* was immediately printed in large quantities for distribution in the Southern states. Copies sent to Charleston were seized by a mob and publicly burned. And when it was announced that Angelina intended to return to Charleston to spend the winter with her family, there was intense excitement. The Mayor of the city informed the mother that her daughter would not be permitted to land in Charleston, nor to communicate with anyone there, and that if she did elude the police and come ashore, she would be imprisoned and guarded until the departure of the next boat. On account of the distress caused for her friends, Angelina reluctantly gave up the trip.

The two sisters let their light shine among the Philadelphia Quakers. A series of parlor talks to women which had been organized by the sisters grew in interest until parlors became inadequate and the speakers were at last addressing large gatherings of women in the public meeting places of Philadelphia.

After pondering for months, the shy, gentle, blue-eyed Angelina took what seemed to her a momentous step. She decided to accept an invitation from the American Anti-Slavery Society to address small groups of women in New York and Boston. Sister Sarah also determined to risk the disapprobation of the Friends, and henceforth the sisters were on intimate terms with the Abolitionists.

In Massachusetts men began to steal into the women's meetings and listen from the back seats. In Lynn all barriers were broken down and the modest and diffident young Angelina found herself addressing an immense and enthusiastic audience of men and women.

The addresses made by the sisters were called lectures, but they were rather familiar talks, and occasionally a discussion, while many questions were asked and answered.

The sisters bore their difficulties cheerfully. For many weeks they held five or six meetings a week, in a different place each time, often poorly lodged and poorly fed, as they ate nothing which they did not know to be the product of free labor, taking cold frequently and speaking when ill enough to be in bed, but sustained through all by faith in the justice of their cause.

Angelina's eloquence was marvelous. Her voice was gentle, firm, impressive. Many traveled a long distance to hear her. Mechanics left their shops and laborers came in out of the fields and sat motionless throughout her meetings. Sarah's speaking was not so effective as Angelina's. She was never very fluent and cared little for the flowers of rhetoric. She could state a truth in clear and forcible terms, but her language was unvarnished, sometimes harsh, while her manner of speaking was often embarrassed. She understood and felt her deficiencies and preferred to serve the cause through her pen rather than through her voice.[69]

The halls were always packed. Sometimes the crowds around the place of meeting were so great that a second hall or church would have to be provided, and Sarah spoke in one while Angelina spoke in the other. At one place ladders were put up at all the windows and men crowded upon them and held their uncomfortable positions throughout the whole meeting. "But then their talk," said one, "oh, it is angel's food!"[70]

But the prejudice against the Grimké sisters found many expressions. Newspapers liberally bestowed ridicule and sarcasm upon the "deluded ladies."[71] Conservatives shut in their faces the doors of every church which they controlled—the vast majority. Finally a Protestant Bull or "Pastoral Letter" was issued by the General Association of Congregational Ministers of Massachusetts, a tirade against women preachers and women reformers.

The perplexed and agitating subjects which are now common amongst us . . . threaten the female character with widespread and permanent injury. . . . The power of woman is in her dependence, flowing from the consciousness of that weakness which God has given her for her protection. . . . But when she assumes the place and tone of man as a public reformer, our care and protection of her seem unnecessary, . . . her character becomes unnatural . . . the vine usurps the role of the elm.[72]

So great was the opposition to their speaking in public that the sisters felt compelled to defend woman's rights as well as Abolition, for in their minds the two causes were vitally connected. Sarah in her *Letters on the Equality of the Sexes and the Condition of Women* maintained that "the page of history teems with woman's wrongs" and that "it is wet with woman's tears." She entreated women to "arise in all the majesty of moral power . . . and plant themselves, side by side, on the platform of human rights, with man to whom they were designed to be companions and equals and helpers in every good word or work."[73]

What Wendell Phillips said of Angelina applies equally well to Sarah: "Were I to single out the moral and intellectual trait which most won me, it was her serene indifference to the judgment of those about her."

What applies to Sarah may be equally well said of the highminded, unselfish whipmaster and scouts of Abolition.

CHAPTER NINE

THE ARMORY OF GOD

How did this little band of Abolitionists, opposed to every element that was potent in America, to state and church, to trade and society, to law and learning, to politics and art, propose to fight their battle? They deliberately chose the Christian methods. They distinctly disavowed carnal weapons and adopted moral suasion. They believed in reason, not passion, in conscience, not force, in ideas, not bullets. Garrison was a non-resistant, as were many of his followers. Wendell Phillips was not. But he fully adopted the measures in vogue when he came into the movement.

The indictment of the Abolitionists had two contradictory counts. The slaveholders charged them with attempting to stir insurrection. Those who professed to abhor slavery, but who excused themselves from moving against it, accused them of impracticability. They answered the charge of sedition by pointing to their standards of faith and practice. They responded to the accusation of impracticability by proving they were acting under the inspiration of Jesus Christ and that they were therefore just as practical as the genius of His system would permit them to be. Did the Master preach immediate repentance? So did they preach immediate emancipation. Was it within the power of a sinner to let go of his sin? So was it within the power of a slaveholder to free his slaves.

Moreover, as a further reply to this assertion that they were impracticables, they called attention to the recent success of the English Abolitionists who on the same basis had assailed and abolished slavery in the British West Indies. Why was not what had been practicable there, after years of agitation, equally practicable here? Were Clarkson and Wilberforce, Buxton and Macaulay, Brougham and O'Connell hotheads? Then they too were content to be known as fanatics. And why should what was acknowledged to be statesmanship on one side of the Atlantic become fanaticism on this side?[1]

Nathan Appleton writing to a Southern friend declared that Garrison, Phillips, and the Abolitionists were "unfortunate fanatical monomaniacs—rather the objects of pity than of any other feeling."[2] When Theodore Parker found his clerical brethren refusing to exchange pulpits with him, he wrote: "To me it seems as if my life was a failure; here I am as much an outcast from society as though I were a convicted pirate."[3] Eastern colleges were strongholds of pro-slavery feeling. In 1848 Charles Sumner spoke to the students of Harvard College, and Longfellow remarked: "The shouts and hisses and the vulgar interruptions grated on my ears. I was glad to get away." When Emerson spoke on the fugitive slave law at the Cambridge City Hall, he was hissed and hooted by the young law students.[4]

The Abolitionists, however, recognized the fact that slavery and the free discussion of slavery could not exist within the same federation. They laid hold of the principle that free discussion is the breath of liberty, and that any institution which could not bear the light of inquiry, argument, and denunciation was a weak and dangerous institution.

The main reason for the spread of anti-slavery feeling was that the Abolitionists were taking hold of the "great wheel going uphill," that they were marching with modern civilization while the defenders of slavery were standing for the obsolete, the abnormal, and the impossible.

True, the Abolitionists made mistakes. But when the Reverend Samuel J. May was taken to task by Dr. Channing, he replied: "I am tired of these complaints. The cause of suffering humanity, the cause of our oppressed, crushed, colored countrymen, has called as loudly upon others as upon us Abolitionists. It was just as incumbent upon others as upon us to espouse it. We are not to blame that wiser and better men did not espouse it long ago. We Abolitionists are what we are—babes, sucklings, obscure men, silly women, publicans, sinners, and we shall manage this matter just as might be expected of such persons as we are. It is unbecoming in able men who stood by and would do nothing to complain of us because we do no better."[5]

If the reformers in the heat of conflict did not always deliberately weigh their words or carefully study the propriety of action, they found sanction in Burke's words: "Something must be pardoned to the spirit of liberty."[6] Their denunciations, at times, were too harsh, abusive, inflammatory. But was their treatment such to soothe their tempers into serenity?

They were by no means policy wise. They believed that they could drive people easier than they could lead them. They used no buttered phrases. They told the plainest truths in the plainest way. They called slaveholders robbers and man-stealers. They branded Northern politicians with Southern principles as "dough-faces." But they reserved their hardest and sharpest expletives for Northern clergymen who were either pro-slavery or non-committal. They blistered them with their lashings.

Most of the Abolitionists were of humble pursuits and circumstances. They were tanners, curriers, shoemakers, artisans, and tillers of the soil, yet possessed of a high degree of intelligence. In general they were people who paid their debts, attended divine service, and had the reputation of an orderly life. As the movement grew apace, however, it drew to itself freaks and cranks. At an anti-slavery convention Maria W. Chapman exclaimed: "The good Lord uses instruments for His purpose I would not touch with a fifty foot pole."[7] But she might have added that the good Lord also used men and women of extraordinary fine character. The very dangers they faced tied them together. Still more were they united to one another by the spiritual exaltation that comes when one gives one's life unselfishly to the cause of others.

They wanted neither office nor the loaves and fishes of office, but they wanted justice, righteousness, and truth, and these they felt in duty bound to promote with all their influence. And if those mighty spirits who kept the nation in a political uproar about frigates and gunboats, British influence and French influence, aristocrats and democrats, tariff and anti-tariff, State rights and Federal rights, Bank and no Bank, gold currency and paper currency, retrenchment, internal improvements, the public money and the public lands—if those mighty spirits, so the Abolitionists said, imagined that the religious and moral people of the United States were to be muzzled and trained on this question of slavery, they were miserably mistaken.

Their endurance of maltreatment rapidly became the very fibre of anti-slavery lore. They continued their crusade in the martyr tradition of the early Christians: they had soon learned that their effectiveness increased in direct proportion to the stamina they displayed in suffering for the cause.[8]

Their mission, their warfare, was a moral one. The appeal was ever to the spirit, the mind, the word, the example of Christ. They announced the moral law and proclaimed its constant and inevitable working. "Hear the message of the angels to the shepherds of Bethlehem—'Fear not: behold, we bring you good tidings of great joy which shall be unto All PEOPLE; for unto you is born this day in the city of David, a Savior, who is Christ the Lord."

Never in America has practical Christianity been so taught and so exemplified. James Freeman Clarke said: "I find here in the anti-slavery meeting a Church of Christ, a church in deed and truth."[9]

Moreover, many Abolitionist leaders turned in disgust and dismay from a money grubbing industrial society fast becoming dominant. Sons of socially prominent families of yore, a displaced class, of the old New England, of Federalism, farming and foreign commerce, reared in a faith of aggressive piety and moral endeavor, they disdained being shoved aside in a brawling struggle of crass monetary power. They faced a strange world, for social and economic leadership was being transferred from the farmer and preacher to the manufacturer and corporation attorney. Family tradition and education forbade idleness. Perhaps in the moral aura of Abolition many of the leaders found a chance of personal and social self-fulfillment.[9a]

"In morals as in mathematics," Theodore Parker stated, "a straight line is the shortest distance between two points."[10] The course of the Garrisonian Abolitionists was pursued without deflection, and for the very reason that they had no elections to carry, no conservatives to placate, no fear of results. Results! A reformer who concerns himself with results loses his vision and strength. That is the business of Jupiter, not his. His is to see and proclaim principles.

"The real progress of our cause," said Wendell Phillips, "is to be looked for from those who keep aloof—who have rid themselves not merely of old parties but of parties themselves—who feel that the real opposition to our enterprise lies deeper than the reach of the ballot box—that the objects at which we ought to aim are what no political party ever did, can, or meant to accomplish. . . . Those who cling to moral effort are the true champions in this fight. . . . We are working *with God,* and the times and the seasons are in his hands."[11]

The Abolitionist's confidence in the ultimate triumph of his principles never wavered. An adherent of the cause was discussing the slavery question with a minister. The minister was a staunch supporter of "the institution" which, according to his contention, firmly rested on biblical authority.

"How do you expect to destroy slavery as it exists in Kentucky, by talking and voting Abolition up here in Ohio?" asked the clergyman.

"We will crush it through Congress when we get control of the general government," replied the Abolitionist.

"But Congress and the general government have, under the constitution, absolutely no power over slavery in the States. It is a State institution," the clergyman countered.

The Abolitionist thought for a while. "Well," said he at last, "the good Lord has not taken me into His confidence, and I don't know what His plans for upsetting slavery are, but He will be able to manage it somehow."[12]

This spirit and purpose were indicated by the words of Garrison: "Our cause," said he, "is of God. It has been so from the beginning. Why did this nation tremble at the outset? Why were the slaveholders smitten as with the fear of death? Who were the Abolitionists? Confessedly, in a numerical sense, not to be counted. They had no influence, no station, no wealth. Ah, but they had the truth of God, and therefore God himself was on their side; and hence the guilty nation quaked with fear when that truth was uttered and applied. We have fought a good fight, and we yet shall conquer, God helping us. All the spirits of the just are with us; all the good of earth are with us; and we need not fear as to the result of the conflict."[13]

The victory was no less sure than the laws of seed time and harvest. "The sheaves shall yet be brought home with shouts of unmingled joy and the sunshine of unclouded peace."

> Listen to our solemn call
> Sounding from old Faneuil Hall,
> Consecrate yourselves, your all—
> To God and Liberty,
> On your spirit's bended knee
> Swear your country shall be free,
> Be free! be free! be free!
>
> Heed not what may be your fate,
> Count it gain when worldlings hate,
> Naught of hope, or heart, abate,
> Victory's before!
> Ask not that your toils be o'er,
> Till all slavery is no more!
> No more! no more! no more!
>
> Welcome then the crown of thorns,
> Which the faithful brow adorns,
> All complaint the brave soul scorns,
> Burdens are its choice,
> While within it hears a voice
> Ever echoing, rejoice,
> Rejoice! rejoice! rejoice!
>
> Soon to bless our longing eyes,
> Freedom's glorious sun shall rise,

Now it lights these glowing skies
Faintly from afar,
Faith and love her heralds are,
See you not his morning star?
Hurra! hurra! hurra![14]

As Edmund Quincy said, the warfare was to be no wild crusade, but a holy war, a sacred strife, waged not with arms forged
by human hands or tempered in earthly fire, "but with weapons
fresh from the armory of God . . . Prayer . . . Faith . . . and
the word of God." The Abolitionists never fell asleep on their
weapons.[15] The moral movement was always kept in vigorous
operation.

They worked out a thoroughgoing propaganda[16]—circulated
petitions by the thousands, showered them upon Congress and
state legislatures, appeared before legislative committees, sent
out traveling agents, busied themselves with the condition of
free colored people, slipped printed handkerchiefs bearing
anti-slavery cuts into bales designed for Southern markets
and mailed prints and pictures depicting the cruelties of slavery
and the delights of emancipation. Above all they held anti-
slavery meetings in all sorts of places, from stable lofts to
churches and public halls. From a total of sixty societies in the
nation in 1835, the number grew to more than a thousand in
1837, and by 1838 Birney calculated there existed more than
1300 with about 108,000 members.[17] No Abolitionist society had
a permanent fund or endowment. The largest source of income
was furnished by voluntary contributions.[18]

The American Anti-Slavery Society reported that during the
year 1837-38, 412,000 petitions reached the House and two-
thirds of that number the Senate. Henry B. Stanton calculated
that two million signatures in all had been gathered by the national society in 1838 and 1839. Since the total of Abolition
members was slightly above 100,000, it was clear signers included many who were not Abolitionists. In 1835 the American
Anti-Slavery Society embarked upon a pamphlet campaign intended to awaken the conscience of the nation to the evils of
slavery. A fund of $30,000 was appropriated to provide for

agents, periodicals, and free distribution of Abolition publications. It was planned to publish a different periodical each week
of the month. At the end of the fiscal year the Society had
printed and circulated more than a million pieces of anti-slavery
literature.[19]

The Massachusetts State Abolition treasury contained $2,036.74
in 1834, $10,883.45 in 1839, and in 1849, $6,188.02. With these
small sums the society made a prodigious amount of noise. Its
paid and unpaid lecturers made every possible sacrifice and
frequently went hungry. Their salaries were of the lowest[20]—
on one trip $12. per week each man with the exception of Abby
Kelley "who labors without price," remarked Phillips.[21] In all
camps, in all branches of the work, there was remarkable devotion and great unselfishness. They kept the community astir;
they made people think and talk.

Members held frequent meetings for discussions and lectures,
attended conventions far and near, read anti-slavery literature,
circulated papers and tracts and wrote for the *Liberator* and the
Herald of Freedom. They welcomed to their homes the Abolitionist orators that people might hear them tell in church or hall
or schoolhouse the story of those in bondage and the one duty
of the hour.

Town criers advertised the meetings. Once at Grafton, Massachusetts, since neither house, hall, church, nor market place
could be obtained in which he could speak to the people, but
determined to speak, Frederick Douglass went to the hotel and
borrowed a dinner bell. With this in hand, he passed through
the principal streets, ringing the bell and crying out—"Notice!
Frederick Douglass, recently a slave, will lecture on American
slavery on Grafton Common this evening at seven o'clock."[22]
The notice brought out a large audience. Lowell remembered
seeing some fine old radicals coming into the grand gatherings
in Boston, wearing the battered hats and torn coats which bore
witness to their encounters with the mob. He saw eloquent
Stephen Foster standing with a battered hat and beginning
his speech: "This hat was crushed for me by the Church in
Portland." Parker Pillsbury took the platform in a coat whose
complete rent down the back he turned round to show.[23]

One anti-slavery speaker went as a missionary into Bucks County, Virginia, where there were many German Democrats. He tried to convince the audience that a Democrat ought to ally himself to anti-slavery. "Why, what do you call a Democrat?" asked the orator. "Is he not one who believes in equal rights for all? Is he not one who believes in the freedom of all mankind?" An old German cried out, "That's not what I calls a Democrat. I call a Democrat a man what votes a Democratic ticket."[24]

Negroes were prominent as agents and speakers for the various Abolition societies. White Abolitionists took great pride in introducing Negro agents to doubting audiences to demonstrate what Negroes could do if given the opportunity. Many of these speakers were encouraged to carry the message of American Abolition to Europe. More than a score of the black Abolitionists went to England, Scotland, France, and Germany. Almost everywhere they were received with enthusiasm.[25]

The Abolitionists early learned the value of printed propaganda and had a special press of thirty or forty newspapers. Next to the *Liberator* came the *Genius of Universal Emancipation*. The *Emancipator*[26] and the *National Anti-Slavery Standard*, published in New York, were the organs of the Middle States. Then there was the *Abolitionist* under the editorship for a time of William Goodell; the *Philanthropist* in Cincinnati; and later the *National Era*, ably edited by Dr. Gamaliel Bailey in Washington.[27] No great daily took up the cause of Abolition previous to 1860, but the *New York Tribune* and many western dailies were anti-slavery in tone. The Abolitionist papers all had a limited circulation among the faithful, but were vigorously edited and widely quoted.

There were three centers of non-Garrisonian Abolitionists— New England, the Middle States, and Western. In New England the great moral force was Dr. Channing; in the Middle States, the Tappans and Gerrit Smith.

Arthur and Lewis Tappan, merchants of New York and crusaders against the pleasures of the godless, supported several struggling newspapers, issued tracts, and attempted to form a college for colored students. A friend of the Tappans pointed out that "if a man of business is also a philanthropist, he is in danger while he is laying up treasure in heaven of losing it on earth."[28] Of similar character to the Tappans was Gerrit Smith of Peterboro, New York, son of a New York slaveholder and owner of about 750,000 acres of land. Smith was a man of liberal ideas. He was against the tariff as an infringement of personal liberty, against the sale and manufacture of liquor, against national debt, against land monopoly, against secret societies[29] and above all—against slavery. He believed in woman suffrage, the "Free Religion" movement, and independent schools. He also held that all law was from the bosom of God and used the term "Bible Civil Government" on all occasions. Christians did not thank him for such a definition. The cry of "infidel," "Sabbath-breaker," and "preacher of politics" made him a little cynical. A man of considerable wealth Smith could afford the luxury of his convictions. His wealth also permitted him to carry some of these convictions into practice. He had "a sort of pecuniary plethora that requires constant bleeding to assure health and vigor."[30] In the course of years Smith gave to national and New York anti-slavery societies at least $50,000 in cash besides presenting 120,000 acres of land to deserving colored men.[31] His house was a caravansary for Abolitionists and a refuge for fugitives. He was one of the earliest of political Abolitionists in the country and helped in the formation of the Liberty Party in 1839.

The reason for the development of the three areas of Abolition is to be found in part in the difference of conditions. New England had no contact with slavery; the Middle States had about 3000 slaves in 1830 and were much more familiar than the New England States with the coming of fugitives and free Negroes. Slavery, therefore, to them was a more practical evil. In the West the relation was still closer and more pertinent, for almost the whole length of the Ohio River was a slaveholding frontier. Here the leaders of the non-Garrisonian Abolitionists were Salmon P. Chase, Gamaliel Bailey, and James G. Birney.

All three sections had a part in the great Abolition struggle.[32] New England raised up orators, poets, and satirists. The Middle States furnished a considerable part of the sinews of war, kept up the journals, founded schools, and aided colleges.

The Western Abolitionists organized the Underground Railroad and devised and set in motion the political Abolition party. The women in this section were more effective and better organized than the men. "Library associations," "reading societies," "sewing societies," and "Women's clubs" were but thin disguises for anti-slavery organizations. The members worked on quietly and effectively. The matron of a family would be provided with the best riding horse which the neighborhood could furnish. Mounted upon her steed, she would sally forth in the morning, meet her carefully selected friends in a town twenty miles away, gain information as to what had been accomplished, give information as to work in other parts of the district, distribute new tracts, seek out the best means of extending their labors, and return in the afternoon. In the course of time all disguise would be thrown aside, and a public speaker of national reputation would be invited to give a rousing Abolition speech.[33]

Garrison made no effort to build a following in the Middle and Western states owing to a series of conflicts which led to a split. The main grounds of difference between the Garrisonians and other Abolitionists were five: personal disagreements, the status of women, the interpretation of the Bible, non-resistance, and "politics."

Whatever the differences, Garrisonians and non-Garrisonians never permitted the agitation to lag. The former were better disciplined, welded together by the moral flame of their leader. They were seized with the consuming power of one idea—the awful sin of slavery—and they gave it their time, their thought, their strength, their means in full and glad surrender. To them the apathy of professing Christians and of people generally was "enough to make every statue leap from its pedestal, and to hasten the resurrection of the dead." And it was their inevitable purpose to take these Christians by a storm and "help to swell the triumphant shout bursting from millions of hearts on earth and answered from the battlements of heaven, which shall proclaim that the victory is won, that the slave is free!"

Hence the agitation of Garrisonian Abolitionists was constant, unyielding, intense. ("We can *agitate* for anything under the Constitution," wrote Phillips to Sumner, March 7, 1853. "You could not, constitutionally, vote a law in ye Senate—except under the war power as J. Q. A. proved—to touch South Carolina slavery, but you could agitate on that floor or on the free soil of Massachusetts as much as you choose to topple the old Palmetto sin down.")[34]

There was a perpetual round of annual meetings: annual meetings of the New York, the Massachusetts, the New England and the American Anti-Slavery Societies. Then there was the annual anti-slavery celebration of West India Emancipation on August 1 in the grove at Abington. In addition there were Anti-Slavery Bazaars to which English towns often contributed:— tidies and Afghan blankets and crocheted collars, fish scale baskets and bog-oak ornaments, Honiton lace pin cushions, etc. One gentleman from Dublin submitted Proudhon—*Revolutions de Paris*—("Unsold"). Anti-Slavery Fairs were also popular.[35] "Did you ever hear," wrote Phillips to an English friend, "of the man who sat devouring boiled eggs and seeing a little girl at the other end of the table help herself to salt, cried out, 'What do you want salt for?' 'I thought,' said she, 'if anybody should *ask* me to take any *eggs*, I would be all ready!' Well, if any of you think of sending to our fair this fall, do try and have them over early, soon enough for us to advertise before it opens that they have arrived. A polite way of asking for eggs?—isn't it?"[36] Anti-Slavery Soirees and Anti-Slavery Festivals were filled with resolutions and speeches. "Eloquence is dog-cheap at the Anti-Slavery chapel," said Emerson.[37]

The air of these gatherings resounded with the hymns of their faith:

The one by James Montgomery—

> The end will come, it will not wait,
> Bonds, yokes, and scourges have their date;
> Slavery itself must pass away,
> And be a tale of yesterday.[38]

The 15th by Garrison—

> The hour of freedom! come it must—
> 　O hasten it in mercy, Heaven!
> When all who grovel in the dust
> 　Shall stand erect, their fetters riven.[39]

Or the 7th by Mrs. Follen—

> "What mean ye, that ye bruise and bind
> 　My people," saith the Lord;
> "And starve your craving brother's mind,
> 　That asks to hear my word?"[40]

And Garrison's stanzas—

I.

> I am an Abolitionist!
> 　I glory in the name,
> Though now by Slavery's minions hissed
> 　And covered o'er with shame;
> It is a spell of light and power—
> 　The watchword of the free:—
> Who spurns it in the trial-hour,
> 　A craven soul is he! . . .

V.

> I am an Abolitionist!
> 　The tyrant's hate and dread—
> The friend of all who are oppressed—
> 　A price is on my head!
> My country is the wide, wide world—
> 　My countrymen mankind;
> Down to the dust be Slavery hurled;
> 　All servile chains unbind![41]

A MELANCHOLY TOUR

Wendell Phillips worked steadily for his new alliance. In a few months he was reported as one of the "interested and animated debaters among those who usually attend our meetings."[1] He closed the year 1838 by forming a city anti-slavery society in Boston and was chosen its first president.

In 1839 he was appointed General Agent of the Massachusetts Anti-Slavery Society. He threw himself into his work with the ardor of an enthusiast.[2] The duties were similar to those of a state missionary: to organize stations wherever there were schoolhouses. Meetings were to be held in churches, halls, and vestries, when they could be had, committees appointed, and lecturers assigned. To him it was a new, exciting, and strange undertaking. "I received your note informing me of the request of your society for a lecture from me a few days since," he writes in haste to Eliza J. Davis. "I have been so busy since as to leave no time to reply."[3]

The welcome offered by country villages was often doubtful and sometimes dangerous. Nevertheless he braved danger and hostility, going up and down the state among the hundred towns where no societies had been established and in which old prejudices were to be overcome and a new sentiment created. They asked: "What can we do?" He answered: "Bind yourselves together, agitate, discuss, read, petition, write your representatives and vote. By and by your ballots will settle every question and right every wrong." Societies sprang up in his circuit of the state—centers of information and proselytizing. Their influence

rippled out to other towns and these joined in county associations
to be represented in state conventions.

Once he spoke on the platform with an old Quaker. The people
waited to greet the old Quaker and asked him home for the
night, but they pelted Phillips with rotten eggs as he went
down the street in the dark. Afterwards Phillips said to the old
Quaker: "I said just what you did and yet you were invited home
to fried chicken and a bed, while I received raw eggs and
stones."

"I will tell thee the difference, Wendell. Thou said, 'If thou
art a holder of slaves, thou wilt go to hell!' I said, 'If thou dost
not hold a slave, thou wilt not go to hell!' "[4]

But Phillips would not butter parsnips with fine words.

There was a circle of wideawakes in Boston called "The
Friends"[5] meeting at irregular intervals usually in the pala-
tial apartments of Jonathan Phillips, that relative of the orator
who had presided over the meeting in Faneuil Hall, a wealthy
bachelor who lived at the Tremont House. Dr. Channing might
be found there, and the gentle philosopher Bronson Alcott, and
the heretic Theodore Parker. They were wont to discuss living
questions of all sorts. Once the theme was Progress. This was a
"Socratic meeting," Dr. Channing the Socrates. "Had the conversation been written out by Plato, it would equal any of his
beautiful dialogues."[6] A week later the discussion was upon
the personality of God. Phillips became a member of the society;
he used to refer to it as a rare school of dialectics.

In the meanwhile Mrs. Phillips's health weakened. The decline was so rapid that her puzzled physicians advised a European trip. Neither husband nor wife was willing to desert the
Abolition cause for a day, but the doctors, backed by the Phillips
family, who hoped Wendell might be "cured of his fanaticism,"
hastened the departure. The two delayed only long enough
to attend the annual meeting of the New England Anti-Slavery
Society held in Boston on May 30.

The Massachusetts body addressed to Phillips a letter indicating the esteem in which he and his wife were held:—"You
buckled on the Abolition armour when there were blows to take

as well as to give, and from that hour to the present we have ever found you in the front rank of the conflict, reckless of all consequences growing out of a faithful adherence to principle, and giving yourself as a freewill offering to the sacred cause of human liberty. . . . We shall regard your absence as a real loss to the board, to the society we represent, and to the great antislavery organization in the land—a loss which cannot be made up."[7]

With such a commendation Phillips and his wife sailed from New York in the packet *Wellington* on June 6, 1839.

"My dear Thompson, I am sorry to say No to your pressing request, but I cannot come to Glasgow," Phillips writes from London in July to his English friend. "My heart will be with you though on the first of August, and I need not say how much pleasure it would give me to meet on that day especially the men to whom my country owes so much and on the spot dear to every American Abolitionist."[8]

The appeals and exhortations which time to time came from England seemed to have fallen to the ground in vain. Far from it, Phillips assured Thompson.[9] They awakened, in some degree at least, a slumbering church to a great national sin—and they strengthened greatly hands which were almost ready to faint in the struggle with a giant evil. "We need them still. Spare us not a moment from your Christian rebukes. Give us line upon line and precept upon precept." The Abolition enterprise, explained Phillips, was eminently a religious one,—and dependent for success entirely on the religious sentiment of the people. It was on hearts that waited not for the results of West India Experiments—that looked to duty and not to consequences, —that disdained to make the fears of one class of men the measure of the rights of another,—that feared no evil in the doing of God's commands,—it was on such that the weight of their cause mainly depended. "I hardly exaggerate when I say that the sympathy and brotherly appeals of British Christians are the sheet anchor of our cause. . . . Your appeals sink deep. Distance lends them something of the awful weight of the verdict of posterity. May they never cease."

"England too is the fountain head of our literature. The slightest censure, every argument, every rebuke on the pages of your Reviews strikes on the ear of the remotest dweller in our country. Thank God that, in this, the sceptre has not yet departed from Judah—that it dwells still in the land of Vane and Milton, of Pym and Hampden, of Sharp, Cowper, and Wilberforce—

> the dead but sceptred sovereigns
> Who still rule our spirits from their urns.

May those upon whom rests their mantle be true to the realms they sway. You have influence where we are not even heard. The prejudice which treads underfoot the 'vulgar' Abolitionist dares not proscribe the literature of the world. In the name of the slave, I beseech you let that literature speak out in deep, stern, indignant tones, for the press, as Bulwer says,

> like the air
> Is seldom heard but when it speaks in thunder. . . .

"It is not the thoughtful, the soberminded, the conscientious for whom we fear. With them truth will finally prevail. It is not that we want eloquence or Christian zeal enough to sustain the conflict with such, and with your aid to come off conquerors. We know, as your Whately says of Galileo, that if Garrison could have been answered, he had never been mobbed—that May's Christian firmness, Smith's world wide philanthropy, Chapman's daring energy, and Weld's soul of fire can never be quelled and will finally kindle a public feeling before which opposition must melt away. But how hard to reach the callous heart of selfishness, the blinded conscience over which a corrupt church has thrown its shield, lest any ray of truth pierce its dark chamber? How shall we address that large class of men with whom dollars are always a mightier consideration than duties—prices current stronger arguments than proofs of holy writ.

"But India can speak in tones which will command a hearing. Our appeal has been entreaty—for the times in America are 'those parsy times' when

> Virtue itself of Vice must pardon beg
> Yea, curb and woo, for leave to do him good.

But from India a voice comes clothed with the omnipotence of self interest—and the wisdom which might have been slighted from the pulpit will be to such men oracular from the market place. Gladly will we make a pilgrimage and bow with more than Eastern devotions on the banks of the Ganges—if his holy waters shall be able to wear away the fetters of the slave."[10]

From London to Paris and Lyons. Then to Rome: Trajan's pillar and the Colosseum, the palace of the Caesars and the Pantheon, St. Peter's and the Vatican, Titus's Bath and the half-buried ruins of Nero's golden house where the frescoes were blooming and fresh after eighteen hundred years.[11]

Amidst all this came news of what interested Wendell and Ann Phillips more—that a World's Anti-Slavery Convention had been called to meet in London the following June, and that they had been appointed delegates with a number of other men and women. They immediately set out for London.

On June 12, 1840, at an early hour on a bright sunny morning, the anti-slavery delegates from different countries walked through the crooked streets of London to Freemason's Hall. At eleven o'clock, the spacious hall being filled, the Convention was called to order. The venerable Thomas Clarkson, who was to be President, on entering, was received by the large audience standing. Owing to Clarkson's feeble health, the chairman requested that there should be no other demonstrations.

There were about five hundred delegates on the floor, many of them Americans. There were several women: Ann Phillips, Maria W. Chapman, Lucretia Mott, Harriet Martineau (who, though an English-woman and a non-resident of America, was an honorary member of the Massachusetts Anti-Slavery Society), Elizabeth Cady Stanton, and others. Wendell Phillips was requested to present their credentials.

Upon doing so he was informed by the Executive Committee of the British and Foreign Society that they would refuse to admit women to membership.[12] He decided to appeal from their decision to the convention itself. Accordingly, as soon as Thomas Clarkson withdrew, Phillips made the following motion: "That a committee of five be appointed to prepare a correct list of the members of this Convention, with instructions to include in such list all persons bearing credentials from an anti-slavery body." This motion at once opened an angry debate on the admission of women delegates.[13]

English customs were outraged. Women sitting with men in a convention!—the idea was shocking. They might sit together at home, in church, at theatres, in ball rooms, at concerts, in public conveyances, anywhere, everywhere, except in a convention. "This insane innovation, this *woman-intruding delusion*" was severely rebuked.[14]

The Reverend J. Burnet, an Englishman, made a most touching appeal to American ladies to conform to English prejudices and custom so far as to withdraw their credentials, as it never did occur to the English and Foreign Anti-Slavery Society that they were inviting ladies.[15] But the "rhapsodists of the United States,"[16] as the women were called, determined to put up a fight.

The clergy with few exceptions were bitter in their opposition. Some of them kept dancing around with Bible in hand, shaking it in the face of the opposition, growing so vehement that at last George Bradburn, exasperated with their narrowness, sprang to the floor and stretching himself to his full height, remarked—"Prove to me, gentlemen, that your Bible sanctions the slavery of women—the complete subjugation of one half of the race to the other—and I should feel that the best work I could do for humanity would be to make a grand bonfire of every Bible in the Universe.[17]

Phillips was requested to withdraw his motion. But he rose again and said—

> "It is the custom there in America not to admit colored men into respectable society; and we have been told again and again that we are outraging the decencies of humanity when we permit colored men to sit by our side. When we have submitted to brickbats and the tar-tub and feathers in New England rather than yield to the custom prevalent there of not admitting colored brethren into our friendship, shall we yield to parallel custom or prejudice against women in Old England?

"We cannot yield this question if we would, for it is a matter of conscience. But we would not yield it on the ground of expediency. In doing so, we should feel that we were striking off the right arm of our enterprise. . . . We have argued it over and over again, and decided it time after time, in every society in the land, in favor of the women. We have not changed by crossing the water. We stand here the advocates of the same principle that we contend for in America. . . . Massachusetts cannot turn aside to succumb to any prejudices or customs, even in the land she looks upon with so much reverence as the land of Wilberforce, of Clarkson, and of O'Connell. It is a matter of conscience, and British virtue ought not to ask us to yield."[18]

When Phillips left to conduct the case, Ann addressed him as follows: "Wendell, don't shilly-shally."[19]

After a gallant struggle the ladies were overwhelmingly denied admission to the floor as delegates and shunted off into the galleries as spectators. A protest against the action, drawn up by Professor Adam of Harvard, signed by several American delegates and presented to the Convention, was laid on the table and ordered not to be printed among the proceedings. O'Connell called the exclusion of women, "a cowardly sacrifice of principle to a vulgar prejudice."[20] "We all felt discouraged," wrote Lucretia Mott in her diary.[21]

As she and Elizabeth Cady Stanton walked arm in arm down Great Queen Street that night reviewing the exciting scenes of the day, they agreed to hold a woman's rights convention on their return to America. Thus a missionary work for the emancipation of woman was then and there inaugurated.[22]

As the ladies were not allowed to speak in the Convention, they kept up a brisk fire morning, noon, and night in their hotel on the unfortunate gentlemen delegates who also lodged there. Mr. James G. Birney, with his luggage, promptly withdrew after the first encounter to some more congenial haven of rest. But the Reverend Nathaniel Colver from Boston, who always fortified himself with six eggs well beaten in a large bowl at breakfast to the horror of his host and circle of esthetic friends, stood his ground to the last, his physical proportions being his shield and buckler, and his Bible his weapon of defense.[23]

Garrison, delayed by storms on the ocean, did not reach London till the Convention was nearing its end. When he arrived he refused to enter the body, and as a silent protest against the rejection of his female coworkers, and to the great scandal of the delegates, took his seat in the gallery. "Haman never looked more blank on seeing Mordecai sitting in the king's gate with his hat on, than did this committee in conference on seeing us take the position we did." Garrison was besought to come down. They tried by every means in their power to seduce him down. Every time he was mentioned, the whole conference would applaud as if they thought they could clap him down. But they might as well have expected to remove the pillars upon which the gallery stood. "They could not argue away what they had done; they could not argue the seal off the bond."[24] Garrison sat upstairs calmly conversing with the poet's wife, Lady Byron.[25]

There were splendid entertainments. A Quaker banker, Samuel Gurney, sent out seven barouches to convey the delegates to his suburban seat. The Duchess of Sutherland, something very plenteous and beautiful and sunny in her aspect, came in all her splendor. She was a ripe, autumnal, exuberant person—"a personified Ceres always holding a cornucopia in her right hand."[26] Haydon made a picture of the Convention; Daniel O'Connell contributed some blistering eloquence.[27]

A monster public meeting was held in Exeter Hall as a grand finale to the Convention and went off with great éclat. Neither Garrison, nor Phillips, nor Thompson was invited to speak: two lesser lights represented America. When Daniel O'Connell made his appearance, the applause was deafening. He made a powerful speech, denouncing the American slaveholders and at the same time paying the highest compliments to the American Abolitionists. He spoke in thunder tones: "You seemed to hear the tones," said Wendell Phillips, "come echoing back to London from the Rocky Mountains."[28]

"Daniel O'Connell," said the London correspondent of Bennett's *New York Herald*, "is bellowing like a bull at all the anti-slavery meetings, and America is his standing theme of abuse. . . . It is good to be dyed black if you come up to London, for Negro love is filling all ranks, from Prince Albert and the Queen, down to her poorest subjects."[29]

Phillips went with Garrison soon afterwards to call on O'Connell. The Irishman had just begun to agitate for the repeal of the Union with England. He was to make a speech on the issue that very night in the House of Commons. They found him stretched on a sofa enjoying a novel by Charles Dickens.

They heard an amusing anecdote. O'Connell treated the House with scant respect. He remarked in a speech outside that it contained "five hundred scoundrels." Two years before he had charged the Tory Election Committee with gross bribery, for which he was censured by the Speaker. The admonition he received on his knees in the prescribed manner, and when he finished, he rose to his feet, and slowly dusting his trousers, exclaimed in an audible whisper—"What a damned dirty House!"[30]

O'Connell's familiar way of lecturing was to converse with an audience. His mind played before ten thousand and his voice flowed as clearly and as leisurely as in a circle round a fireside. His eloquence was simple and unadorned. He could speak to the people in their own idom with the smell of the turf smoke in every phrase. He used rough and truculent language on occasion, but he was always racy and to the point. "If I did not use the sledge-hammer, I could never crush our enemies," he said. Again: "When a fellow happens to be a scoundrel, I have a tolerably good tongue for describing him."[31] He was a flaming battery of scorn, invective, and vituperation to any member who assailed his cause, his religion, or his people.

In his hands the system of mass meetings by agitation reached a perfection never attained before and seldom since. Wendell Phillips learned many valuable lessons from him. . . .

The member for all Ireland swaggers into the House of Commons, his bulky form wrapped in an ample flowing cloak. A large round, ruddy face encircles laughing blue eyes. In his seat he takes off his cloak and puts on with a rakish cock his tall hat with its wide brim. . . .

Some advocates of slavery in Cincinnati addressed to the Repeal Association a document protesting among other things: "The very odor of the Negro is almost insufferable to the white." O'Connell replied: "The Negroes would certainly smell, at least, as sweet when free as they now do, being slaves."[32]

In London, Ann and Wendell Phillips struck up a friendship with a group of Abolitionists: Miss Elizabeth Pease, a young Quaker lady, and Richard D. Webb of Dublin, a rich Quaker printer, who put out an edition of non-resistant pamphlets just to raise a little bit of a row. They became best friends too with the orator George Thompson and went laughing through England and Scotland with this prince of raconteurs.

"Since last Xmas I have got into harness as Reporter for the Chancellor's Court," Phillips writes to Sumner from Lincoln's Inn Fields: "so you see I shall go down to posterity at least as one of the conduit pipes of the Law." In a subsequent letter we learn that Phillips had also been appointed a barrister for Shropshire.[33]

The world's anti-slavery convention adjourned on June 23 and was followed by an unceasing round of fetes and pleasures. The social pace was too fast for Ann's health, and in July, 1840, Wendell set out with her by way of Belgium and the Rhine for Kissingen in Bavaria. At Frankfort they saw the oldest printed Bible in the world and two pairs of Luther's shoes which Ann would not quit till Wendell mustered German enough to ask the man to let her feel them. So she was permitted to hold the great man's slippers in her own hands.

From Kissingen to Brückenau, another spa. Then a leisurely progress through Switzerland: Interlaken and up to Staubback Falls—"Have you seen them?" Phillips writes to Elizabeth Pease. "They come shooting over the precipice of black rock eight or nine hundred feet high—dissolved into mist ere halfway down—they compare them always to a lace veil thrown over the rock. . . . But truth to tell, to my vulgar mind it was impossible to get rid of the idea of a man standing up there and throwing over a shovel full of powdered sugar. They are beautiful, though."[34]

Northern and Southern Italy in the autumn. In Florence by November, to Leghorn for the sea breezes in winter. At the last spot they learned of the birth of a young son to Garrison away off in Boston whom the parents named after one of the wanderers, Wendell Phillips.

Naples and Rome in the spring, Paris in the early summer, and on to London once more after almost a year's absence.

"'Tis a melancholy tour, this through Europe," Phillips writes to Garrison, "and I do not understand how any one can return from it without being, in Coleridge's phrase, 'a sadder and a wiser man.' Every reflecting mind must be struck at home with the many social evils which prevail. . .

"Europe is the treasure house of rich memories, with every city a shrine. But all the fascinations of art and the luxuries of modern civilization are no balance to the misery which bad laws and bad religion alike entail on the bulk of the people. The Apollo himself cannot dazzle one blind to the rags and want which surround him. Nature is not wholly beautiful. For even when she marries a matchless sky to her Bay of Naples the impression is saddened by the presence of degraded and suffering humanity.

"In our own country the same contrasts exist, but they are not yet so sharply drawn as here. I hope the discussion of the question of property will not cease until the Church is convinced that from Christian lips *ownership means responsibilities for the right use* of what God has given; that the title of a needy brother is as sacred as the owner's own. . . .

"The moral stagnation here only makes us value more highly the stirring arena at home. None know what it is to live till they redeem life from monotony by sacrifice. There is more happiness in one such hour than in dwelling forever with the beautiful and grand. . .

"In one way I have learned to value my absence. I have found difficulty in answering others—however clear my own mind might be—when charged with taking steps which the sober judgment of old age would regret, without being hurried recklessly forward by the enthusiasm of the moment and the excitement of heated meetings. I am glad, therefore, to have had this space aside, this opportunity of holding up our cause calmly before my mind—of having

distance of place perform, as far as possible, the part of
distance of years—of being able to look back from other
scenes and studies upon the course we have taken the last
few years. Having done so, I rejoice now to say that every
hour of such thought convinces me, more and more, of the
overwhelming claims our cause has on the lifelong devotion
of each of us; and I hope to return to my place prepared
to urge its claims with more earnestness, and to stand fearlessly by it without a doubt of its success.

"When Paul's 'appeal to Caesar' brought him into this
Bay of Naples, he must have seen all its fair shores and
jutting headlands covered with bath and villa, imperial
palaces and temples of the gods. A prisoner of a despised
race, he stood, perhaps for the first time, in the presence
of the pomp and luxury of the Roman people. Even amid
their ruins, I could not but realize how strong the faith of
the Apostle to believe that the message he bore would triumph alike over their power and their religion. Struggling
against priests and people may we cherish a like faith."[35]

In London Phillips found his friend George Thompson busily
engaged in organizing a British-India agency for the cultivation
of cotton, the object being to compete with the South in the
markets of the world in the hope of superseding slave labor in
the production and sale of that staple. "They can procure," said
Thomas Clarkson, "not tens of thousands, but tens of millions
of free laborers to work; what is of the greatest consequence
in this case, the price of labor with these is only from a penny
to three half pence a day. What slavery can stand against these
prices?" Phillips lent his aid to the cause by publishing an open
letter to Thompson, but no lasting good resulted from the
British-India endeavor. Phillips must have had his misgivings
since the last sentence reads: "Take care that in driving our
cotton from your shores, you do not admit a single pound that
be equally blood-stained with our own."[36]

On July 4, 1841, after an absence of more than two years,
Wendell and Ann Phillips embarked from Liverpool for home,
crossing by steamer, a mode of travel then thought hazardous.

Unhappily the chief purpose of their trip was not achieved. Ann returned as she had departed—an invalid. Says Ann to Elizabeth Pease:

"It would be impossible to tell you how much we have felt your kindness to us: strangers, you took us into your heart of hearts, and have cherished us so tenderly. Since I have been ill, the world has worn quite another aspect to me, for many that I had thought friends have fallen off and many have misunderstood the nature of my state of health so much that there is no pleasure in communication with them. Judge then how touching and grateful your kindness has been to me: you have understood the little numerous ills that sickness brings, have kindly fallen into the sick one's ways, have made me happy. God bless you for it!"

And Phillips added: "Ann's lines, affectionate as they are, dear Elizabeth, tell you no more of her heart than a drop of water can image the ocean. She moans for you. I was forbidden to mention your name to keep away the tears. . . . I thought we were going home, but we leave full half of home behind us, where your kind heart is."[37]

They reached Boston on July 17 and were given a formal reception by the entire Abolition community in Chardon Street Chapel.[38] The voyage instead of benefiting Ann had exhausted her. "The little state room that you saw us in," she writes to Richard D. Webb, "was our sick home for thirteen days and bright and sunny was the day which welcomed us into the fair bay of Massachusetts." They had made no friends on board. Wendell had battled for freedom midst pro-slavery merchants and slaveholders. The captain, a Scotsman, was the only man who stood by him. "Your whiskey jug," continued Phillips to Webb, "served us a good turn on the voyage, or rather its contents did, and now we keep it in memory of you."[39]

For the remainder of the summer Ann and Wendell stayed in the "great wooden house" of Phillips's mother in Nahant, an isolated spot,—"a superb promontory of solid rock with grand beaches"[40]—a mile from any other habitation. But with fifteen

children and twenty grandchildren at intervals dropping in
upon the elder Mrs. Phillips, no one was ever alone. In the
evening Wendell and Ann played chess or backgammon, or
some brother or sister game to pass the night, and the family
disputed away on the great questions. "We are considered as
heretics and almost infidels," wrote Ann to Miss Elizabeth
Pease, "but we pursue the even tenor of our way undisturbed."
Sometimes Wendell went off abolitionizing for two or three days,
but Ann remained on the ground.

She suffered almost constantly from headaches, and despite
the beautiful beach, time lagged.

> "I do not feel right in this atmosphere and like Rip Van
> Winkle am ready to exclaim, 'I'm not myself. I'm somebody
> else—that's me yonder.' . . . Pray for poor feeble Ann—I
> cannot read about India, the pamphlets you have given us,
> the papers you send; my mind must remain unstored and I
> must become in that respect an even less worthy companion
> of you, but I hope through the help and favor of God my
> heart will grow. . . .
>
> "Do take care of your health; do not work too much or sit
> up late—there is no getting the truant back when once gone,
> but health I begin to think is most as hard to regain as lost
> virtue."[41]

In the autumn the couple moved into a tiny brick house of
English basement style on Essex Street, No. 26, which Ann
Phillips had inherited from her father. The house was in the
midst of the anti-slavery colony: the Garrisons, Chapmans,
Jacksons, Lorings were within five minutes walk.

"Ann all trouble and care which I relieve as much as I can,"
writes Phillips on Thanksgiving. "Enter house in evening with
two servants well recommended. Next cook tended by physician
and can't be about—takes to bed—the other girl ill-natured as
Cerberus, ignorant as possible, wants to be out half the time
and work for herself half the remainder—knows nothing and
is not willing to be taught—weather through one week, cook
gets better—uses one of her first week days to tell Ann she
should have preferred to have gone to another place she had

heard of—don't like young housekeepers. Ann tells her to go if she wishes whenever she chooses—at that draws in her horns and stays and seems now a good girl—the other like the zebra appears to be beyond taming. Well, I'll ramble on."[42]

Ann gives Elizabeth Pease some insight into life at No. 26 Essex Street:

> "There is your Wendell seated in the arm chair, lazy and easy as ever, perhaps a little fatter than when you saw him, still protesting how he was ruined by marrying. Your humble servant laughs considerably, continues in health in the same naughty way, strolls out a few steps occasionally, calling it a walk; the rest of the time from bed to sofa, from sofa to rocking chair; reads, generally, the *Standard* and *Liberator*, and that is pretty much all the literature her aching head will allow her to pursue; rarely writes a letter, sees no company, makes no calls, looks forward to spring and birds, when she will be a little freer. . . .
>
> "I am not well enough even to have friends to tea, so that all I strive to do is to keep the house neat and keep myself about. I have attended no meetings since I helped fill 'the Negro pew.' What anti-slavery news I get, I get second-hand. I should not get along at all, so great is my darkness, were it not for Wendell to tell me that the world is still going on. . . . We are very happy. . . . Dear Wendell speaks whenever he can leave me, and for his sake I sometimes wish I were myself again; but I dare say it is all right as it is."[43]

And again, to Webb: "I hope you and yours may never know the wearing suffering of protracted illness . . . but whatever is your lot, may your trust be in God. Farewell."[44]

CHAPTER ELEVEN

ULTRAISM AFLOAT—

"CLING BY THE ABOLITIONISTS"

The *Liberator* was reeling like a ship about to capsize. Abolitionists opposed to Garrison called it "foul-mouthed and abusive," "irreligious and Jacobin," and "a stumbling block in their path."[1] But Garrison replied in kind—"I am accused," said he "of using hard language. I admit the charge. I have not been able to find a soft word to describe villainy or to identify the perpetrator of it."[2]

An attempt was made to curb the wild horses of Garrison's eloquence by appointing a few gentlemen who should revise all articles written for the *Liberator* and try to persuade the editor to print nothing which should not have been approved by them. But the attempt failed. Garrison of all men could never have been kept in such traces.

Phillips rallied to Garrison's support. "I regard the success of the *Liberator*," he wrote in an open letter to the paper, "as identical with that of the Abolition cause itself. Though so bitterly opposed, it does more to disseminate, develop, and confirm our principles than any other publication whatever. The spirit which produced still animates it. . . . Pride of settled opinion, love of lifeless forms, undue attachment to sect are its foes. The spirit of the *Liberator* is the touchstone of true hearts. Success to it!"[3]

In an adjoining column was Garrison's article, "Watchman, What of the Night?" This abruptly declared: "Strong foes are without, insidious plotters are within the camp."[4]

122

The struggle between Garrison and his enemies and the controversy over the status of women in the anti-slavery societies had reached its climax during Phillips's absence in Europe. At the tenth anniversary of the American Anti-Slavery Society in 1840, the malcontents attempted to capture the national society, to reverse its action on the woman question, and to oust Garrison from a position of power.[5] As every Abolitionist present had a vote, Garrison chartered a steamer to take from Providence to New York an anti-slavery boatload to save his society from falling into the hands of the new organizers. He put the fare at a low rate and sent out a rallying cry through the *Liberator*. The call was promptly responded to. Over four hundred delegates were prepared to "preserve the integrity of the anti-slavery movement."

Never was there such a mass of "ultraism" afloat in one boat. Persons of all ages, complexions, and conditions, from veterans through ripened manhood down to rosy youth. They filled up berths, floors, in cabins or on deck.[6]

When they arrived at the convention, they made "clean work of everything with crashing unanimity," to use Garrison's words.[7] On a test vote Abby Kelley was nominated to the Business Committee by 557 votes for—451 against. Lucretia Mott, Lydia Maria Child, and Maria Chapman were put on the executive committee. Some of the opposition members were so exasperated by the result that they left the meeting. Garrison's enemies had made up their minds that Abolition and No Government, Non-Resistance, theological heterodoxy, and the political equality of the sexes could no more walk together than could Abolition and colonization. Garrison's theories, they maintained, weakened "the staff of accomplishment." Accordingly, Lewis Tappan soon after the resolution admitting women to membership was passed, invited those who voted against it to meet in the lecture room under the church for the purpose of organizing a new society. The great body of ministers present accepted the invitation as did many others, and the American and Foreign Anti-Slavery Society was speedily organized. "We have not left our brethren," said the Reverend Orange Scott: "They have left us."[8]

The new society recognized the "rightfulness of government," urged political action as a duty, and declared the admission of women to take part in its proceedings, an innovation that was "repugnant to the constitution of the society," "a firebrand in anti-slavery meetings and contrary to the usages of the civilized world."[9] It drew within the folds the more conservative and prudent members of the old society, those who "could not swallow Garrison." It became the weak wing of the anti-slavery movement. After a feeble existence of thirteen years, it expired.[10]

The schism, however, affected the original society considerably, the annual income dropping immediately from $47,000. to $7,000. and not rising above $12,000. until 1856. The number of local societies and of members was at once diminished and was never recovered.[11]

The Garrisonians as a result banded themselves more tightly together and reaffirmed their purpose to conduct a purely moral war against slavery. Once more they avowed their confidence in conscience and reason and discussion as the surest means with which to pull down the strongholds of oppression.

Throughout the controversy Phillips sided with Garrison. "Whence come divisions amongst us," he asked. "The man who joins an unpopular cause from impulse falls away as soon as his soul is fretted in feeling that half of life is spent merely kicking against the pricks. Some joined the Abolition crusade without ever counting the cost. "These reluct at the painful journey, the unwonted voyage, and their hearts are lead in their bosoms when they touch the hot sands of the Holy Land."

"Do you seek those who have really turned the world right side up? You must unearth them from beneath the ribaldry and foul scorn with which history has covered them. Catiline and Cromwell, Pym, Lilburne, Bunyan, and Vane, how long were they lost under epithets! If 'Truth be the daughter of time,' as the proverb says, she is surely the child of his very old age.

"The only man who can benefit a cause is he who comes to it self-impelled from sense of duty,—his eye fixed on God, careless of effects or of success, if he be only certain he has laid on its altar 'all that he had,' even all his living. *Fellow worker with God* is his title. . . . For such

> Fame is no plant that grows on mortal soil,
> Nor in the glist'ring foil
> Set off to th' world, nor in broad rumor lies:
> But lives and spreads aloft in those pure eyes,
> And perfect witness of all-judging Jove."[12]

Phillips was incensed at this hour by the action of Congress in denying the right of petition. Congress had been bombarded for years with petitions for emancipation in the District of Columbia. This aroused the anger of the pro-slavery members who in 1836 brought about the passage of the first "gag rule," the Pinckney resolution, which provided that all petitions relating to slavery should be laid on the table without being referred to the committee or printed.[13] In substance this resolution was readopted at the beginning of each of the succeeding sessions of Congress. An obsequious Senate made haste to concur. Nor was this all. Ex-president John Quincy Adams, a representative from Massachusetts, who had been active in presenting these petitions and contended that these "gag rules" were a direct violation of the Federal Constitution, was menaced with expulsion for his "impudence." Phillips eagerly championed Adams' gallant fight against an arbitrary Congress. At a meeting of the Massachusetts Anti-Slavery Society, four years before, after offering a resolution commending Adams, he had remarked in this, his first anti-slavery speech:

> "Who does not recollect the astonishment . . . with which we heard that the door of the Capitol was closed to the voice of the people? . . . .
> "The supineness of the North under the act of Southern aggression, and still more, the indifference with which Calhoun's bill was generally received, are the strongest arguments we can offer to our fellow citizens to induce them to look at this subject. Why, such a proposition on any other occasion would have set the county in a blaze! What is it that thus palsies our strength and blinds our foresight? We have become so familiar with slavery that we are no longer aware of its deadening influence on the body politic. Pinck-

ney's words have become true: 'The stream of general liberty cannot flow on unpolluted through the mire of partial bondage.' And this is the reason we render to those who ask us why we are contending against Southern slavery,—*that it may not result in Northern slavery;* because time has shown that it sends out its poisonous branches over all our fair land, and corrupts the very air we breathe. Our fate is bound up with that of the South, so that they cannot be corrupt and we sound; they cannot fall and we stand. Disunion is coming, *unless* we discuss this subject; for the spirit of freedom and the spirit of slavery are contending here for the mastery. They cannot live together: as well, like the robber of the classic fable, chain the living and the dead together, as bind up such discordant materials, and think it will last. *We* must prosper, and a sound public opinion root out slavery from the land, or there must grow up a mighty slaveholding State to overshadow and mildew our free institutions.

"I have said, Mr. President, that we owe gratitude to Mr. Adams for his defense of the right of petition. A little while ago it would have been absurd to talk of gratitude being due to any man for such a service. It would have been said, 'Why, he only did his duty, what every other man would have done; it was too simple and plain a case to need a thought.' But it is true that, now, even for this we ought to be grateful. And this fact is another, a melancholy proof of the stride which the influence of slavery has made within a few years. It throws such dimness over the minds of freemen that what would once have been thought the alphabet of civil right, they hail as a discovery."[14]

Phillips thus cut to the core of the problem—the preservation of civil liberties. In attacking anti-slavery and Abolitionist forces the South made the error of attacking the rights of the Northern white men as well. The liberties of speech, press, religion, assembly, and thought were, according to the *Richmond Enquirer* "curses to the North" because they were abused by the Abolitionists in "inciting to treason, polygamy, free love, vile superstition, and vile infidelities. . . . You must take away these liberties of the North," it warned, "or they will destroy private property, religion, marriage, nay government itself." James G. Birney, who perceived the wider implications of the controversy, wrote to Gerrit Smith: "It has now become absolutely necessary that Slavery should cease in order that freedom may be preserved to any portion of our land."[15]

The insistence upon the moral and legal right of a minority to speak and be heard with full protection from suppression or interference became in time to many citizens nearly as important as the abolition of the slave system. "The net effect was to gain for Abolition a body of supporters who thought less of the wrongs of the slave than of the rights of the white man, a fact that explains the contention of Lincoln and Seward that the Republican party was founded to protect white men, not black."[16] "It is no longer a question of slavery for the black man," cried one speaker, "but of liberty for the white man"— and Abolitionists drummed the point home from press and platform for more than twenty years. The movement became, as Phillips pointed out, inextricably bound up with the preservation of our heritage—civil liberties.[17]

2.

In the autumn of 1841, after Wendell Phillips's return from Europe, there came from Ireland a monster appeal signed by 70,000 Irishmen, with Daniel O'Connell and the great temperance leader, Father Mathew, at their head, condemning slavery and urging the Irish in America to identify themselves with the Abolitionists.

"The object of this address is to call your attention to the subject of SLAVERY IN AMERICA, that *foul blot* upon the noble institution and fair fame of your adopted country. But for this one stain, America would indeed be a land worthy your adoption; but she will never be the glorious country that her free Constitution designed her to be, *so long as her soil is polluted by the footprint of a single slave.* . . .

"SLAVERY IS A SIN AGAINST GOD AND MAN. *All who are not for it must be against it.* NONE CAN BE NEU-

TRAL. We entreat you to take the part of justice, religion, and liberty. . . .

"JOIN WITH THE ABOLITIONISTS EVERYWHERE. *They are the only consistent advocates of liberty.* Tell every man that you do not understand liberty for the white man, and *Slavery for the black man*: that you are for LIBERTY FOR ALL, of every color, creed, and country. . . .

"Irishmen and Irishwomen! *treat the colored people as your equals, as brethren.* By all your memories of Ireland, continue to love Liberty—hate Slavery—CLING BY THE ABOLITIONISTS—and in America, *you will do honor to the name of Ireland.*"

(Signed by): Daniel O'Connell, Theobald Mathew and ☞Seventy Thousand other inhabitants of Ireland."[18]

But at this crisis the Irish in America were almost without exception on the side of slavery. They belonged to the laboring class and were thus brought into competition with the Negroes. Moreover, finding as they did, the wealth, fashion, and political power of the country arrayed against the Abolitionists, and hungry themselves for the fleshpots of Egypt, they naturally went where they could fill their stomachs and their pockets. (Only a saint can prefer a lean right to a fat wrong.)

The Abolitionists, however, hailed the Irish petition with enthusiasm. Securing Faneuil Hall, they opened it on the evening of January 28, 1842, and filled it as it had not been filled since the Lovejoy meeting almost five years before. Wendell Phillips was the orator of the occasion. Fresh from the old world, with the rich Irish brogue of O'Connell still sounding in his ears, he mounted the rostrum and delivered an address which drove the Irish in the crowd wild.

"Ireland is the land of agitation and agitators. We may well learn a lesson from her in the battle for human rights. Her philosophy is no recluse; she doffs the cowl, and quits the cloister, to grasp in friendly effort the hands of the people. No pulses beat truer to liberty and humanity than those which in Dublin quicken at every good word from Abolition on this side of the ocean; there can be no warmer words of welcome than those which greet the American Abolitionists on their thresholds.

"I trust in that love of liberty which every Irishman brings to the country of his adoption, to make him true to her cause at the ballot box, till he throws no vote without asking if the hand to which he is about to trust political power will use it for the slave. When an American was introduced to O'Connell in the lobby of the House of Commons, he asked, without putting out his hand, 'Are you from the South:' 'Yes, sir.' 'A slave-holder, I presume?' 'Yes, sir.' 'Then,' said the great liberator, 'I have no hand for you!' and stalked away. Shall his countrymen trust that hand with political power which O'Connell deemed it pollution to touch? (Cheers.)

"Mr. Chairman, we stand in the presence of at least the name of Father Mathew; we remember the millions who pledge themselves to temperance from his lips. I hope his countrymen will join me in pledging here eternal hostility to slavery. Will you ever return to his master the slave who once sets foot on the soil of Massachusetts? ('No, no, no!') Will you ever raise to office or power the man who will not pledge his utmost effort against slavery? ('No, no, no!')

"Then may not we hope well for freedom? Thanks to those noble men who battle in her cause the world over, the 'ocean of their philanthropy knows no shore.' Humanity has no country; and I am proud, here in Faneuil Hall,—fit place to receive their message—to learn of O'Connell's fidelity to freedom, and of Father Mathew's love to the real interests of man. (Great applause.)"[19]

Resolutions denouncing Congress and demanding the abolition of slavery in the District of Columbia were adopted with a roar—a genuine Irish roar—and the meeting adjourned.

"Well," remarked Phillips as he left the Hall, "we will send our resolutions to Washington spite of the gag law. And we say, as Patrick Henry did in the House of Burgesses, when he spoke to George III across the ocean: 'If this be treason, make the most of it!'"[20]

When O'Connell read Phillips's speech he made a handsome return by pronouncing it the most classic short speech in the

English language, and he added: "I resign the crown. This
young American is without equal."[21]

But his immigrant countrymen, after bellowing their applause, went out and read what their newspapers had to say
on the other side of the question and accepted the counsel
of their pro-slavery Bishop Hughes of New York. The hierarchy
here through his lips impugned the genuineness of the Irish Appeal, and genuine or not declared it the duty of every naturalized
Irishman to resist and repudiate it with indignation as a foreign
interference. Thenceforward, as before, the race voted the
straight Democratic ticket—cheered for slavery and damned the
"niggers."[22] As the editor of the *Pilot*, who was against all current "isms", later declared: "As a general thing wherever you
find a free soiler, you find an anti-hanging man, woman's rights
man, an infidel frequently, bigoted Protestant always, a socialist, a red republican, a fanatical teetotaller, a believer in
Mesmerism, Rochester rappings, and in every devil but the
one who will catch him. You get in a rather dirty set, you perceive, when you join their ranks." The same point of view
was evident in the Catholic press in other parts of the country.
The Catholic population came to regard Abolitionists as enemies of religion, of public law and order, and of the Union
which they, as naturalized citizens, had sworn to support.
Members of the hierarchy by taking refuge in a conservative
church tradition contributed to the general impression that their
church was pro-slavery.[23]

Phillips posted an angry letter to Richard Allen in Dublin,
mentioning the manner in which certain newspapers received
the Irish address. "Those papers are the organs and influential
controllers of the Irish and Catholic population here. What
will you do? They deny its authenticity, say O'Connell signed
it without knowing or caring about the Abolitionists here."
And he put his finger on the underlying cause: the Repeal
Association feared it might lose the support of its members
in the South.

"Now what we want you and O'Connell to think it your
duty to do is to send us a startling, scorching, bitter, un-

sparing, pointed rebuke (and publish it in your own papers also as well and send it to us) telling the repealers here that you don't want the money or voices of slaveholders or their friends—that you repudiate all connection with a Repeal Society which holds its peace on Negro Slavery in order to cozen favor with those whose hands are bloody with its guilt—laugh, hoot, scorn, hiss, spit at the recreant Irishman who holds off from his sympathy the Abolitionist and clasps the slaveholder and slaveholding toady to his bosom—reject all aid from such with scorn. Tell them they pollute the cause they wish others to think they want to help. . . .

"I long to get a sight of the lightning flash, the bolt with which you will annihilate these mock pretenders to liberty. I spoke here once at a repeal meeting—never shall I do it again—O'Connell never could have breathed there unless his electricity had been able to purify the air—low, mean politics—demagogical, earthly, worldly—pah! the mouth tasted bad for days after. . . ."[24]

When O'Connell hesitated to back up his appeal, Phillips's temper flamed. "We are all red hot against O'Connell. He dares not face the demon when it touches *him*. He would be pro-slavery this side the pond,—'a mere peeler,' as we say. He won't shake hands with slaveholders, no—but he will shake *their gold*. Fool! how little he knows his real interest this side the water."[25] And Phillips raged on: "The fool of barroom demagogues" . . . "a mere brawler" . . . "How contemptible O'Connell behaves!"[26]

Eventually Dan's temporary backsliding was forgotten or effaced: certainly his heart was secure in the right place. And instead of a shipwreck, Phillips built a towering pillar to his American fame.

"Dear Lizzie," he once wrote to Elizabeth Pease, "but I want you to understand how the battle lies between the reformers 'without concealment and without compromise'—and those who are willing to uphold the gallows and not 'peep' about the Sabbath Question, conceal their creed on women, speak soft words about the church, in order to secure, as Shakespeare says, 'the most sweet voices of the people.' "[27]

CHAPTER TWELVE

KING OF THE LYCEUM

There was hardly a village schoolhouse in New England that had not its winter evening debates. In the larger towns and cities these were diversified by Lyceum lectures. The best speakers of the generation were in constant demand: Edward Everett, Rufus Choate, Horace Mann, Ralph Waldo Emerson, Henry Ward Beecher, and George William Curtis. For about forty years these lectures provided a vital and entertaining education for the people. Perhaps the appetite for them had been inherited from forefathers whose chief intellectual entertainment had been Sunday sermons two or three hours long.

The support of the lyceum came from what Holmes called "the average intellect." And he humorously described the typical audience: "Front seats: a few old folks—shiny-headed—slant up best ear towards the speaker—drop off to sleep after a while when the air begins to get a little narcotic with carbonic acid. Bright women's faces, young and middle aged, a little behind these, but towards the front,—(pick out the best and lecture mainly to that). Here and there a countenance sharp and scholar-like, and a dozen pretty female ones sprinkled about. An indefinite number of pairs of young people—happy but not always very attentive. Boys, in the background, more or less quick. Dull faces here, there,—in how many places! I don't say dull people but faces without a ray of sympathy or movement of expression. They are what kill the lecturer. These negative faces with their vacuous eyes and stony lineaments pump and suck the warm soul out of him."[1]

Certainly Wendell Phillips was more fortunate in his audiences. Invariably they were attentive, hostile or enthusiastic, never dull-eyed or indifferent. In time he became known as one of the Kings of the Lyceum system.[2]

His lecture on "The Lost Arts" belonged to that first phase of the Lyceum before it undertook to meddle with political duties and dangerous angry questions of ethics. It was first delivered in 1838 and perhaps repeated over two thousand times. Bronson Alcott wrote of Phillips: "More than any lecturer, unless it be Emerson, he has made the lecture a New England, if not an American, institution, is always heard with profit and pleasure by the unprejudiced auditor, any course in the cities and towns being thought incomplete without him."[3]

The town of Concord, twin scene with Lexington of the first battle of the Revolution, was dominated by half a dozen prominent and elderly squires. In the winter of 1842–43 the Lyceum out there invited Phillips to come and give his lecture on "Street Life in Europe"—an outcome of his travels.[4] He did so, confining himself in the main to sights abroad, but managing to give slavery a number of sharp thrusts as he went along. These passing references piqued curiosity, and he was invited to come again next winter and speak on slavery. He gladly accepted and the date was fixed. But a few days before he was to appear, a prominent citizen moved in the Lyceum that Phillips be asked to choose some other topic, adding that his sentiments on slavery expressed the year before were "vile, pernicious, and abominable." But a large majority in the Lyceum voted to hear Phillips on slavery and nothing else.[5]

So Phillips came and spoke for an hour and a half in a strain very galling to the squires, especially to two of them— Squire Keyes and Squire Hoar. He charged the sin of slavery upon the religion of the country with its twenty thousand pulpits, all dumb or advocating the iniquity. The church, he said, had accused the Garrisonians of infidelity, and there was some truth in it; they were infidels to a religion that sustained human bondage. As for the State, the curse of every honest man should be upon its Constitution. Could he say to Jefferson, Adams, and Hancock, after the experience of fifty years: "Look upon the fruit of your work!" they would bid him crush the parchment beneath his feet.

These utterances were worse than those of the year before, and so the next week the conservatives in the lyceum began

to debate Phillips's lecture and to denounce him. Word was
sent to Phillips by his friends, and he came into the meeting
while Squire Keyes was jeering at him for "leading captive
silly women." Squire Hoar then took the testimony against the
audacious "stripling" who had proclaimed such monstrous doctrines, complimented him on his eloquence, but warned the
young against such insidious and exciting oratory. About nine
o'clock, Phillips stepped forward from the rear of the hall and
asked permission to reply. He said:

"I do not care for criticisms upon my manner of assailing
slavery. In a struggle for life it is hardly fair for men who
are lolling at ease to remark that the limbs of the combatants are not arranged in classic postures. I agree with the
last speaker that this is a serious subject; had it been otherwise I should not devote my life to it. Stripling as I am,
I but echo the voice of the ages, of our venerable forefathers—of statesmen, poets, philosophers. The gentleman
has painted the dangers to life, liberty, and happiness that
would be the consequence of doing right. These dangers
now exist by law at the South. Liberty may be bought
at too dear a price; if I cannot have it except by sin, I reject
it. But I cannot so blaspheme God as to doubt my safety
in obeying Him. The sanctions of English law are with me;
but if I tread the dust of law beneath my feet and enter the
Holy of Holies, what do I find written there? 'Thou shalt
not deliver unto his master the servant which is escaped to
thee; he shall dwell with you, even among you.' I throw
myself then on the bosom of Infinite Wisdom. Even the
heathen will tell you, 'Let justice be done though the
heavens fall'; and the old reformer answered when warned
against the danger of going to Rome, 'It is *not* necessary
that I should live; it *is* necessary that I go to Rome.' But
now our pulpits are silent—whoever heard this subject presented until it was done by 'silly women' and 'striplings'?
The first speaker accused me of ambition; let me tell him
that ambition chooses a smoother path to fame. And to you,
my young friends, who have been cautioned against exciting
topics and advised to fold your hands in selfish ease, I
would say, Not so—throw yourselves upon the altar of some
noble cause! To rise in the morning only to eat and drink,

and gather gold—that is a life not worth living. Enthusiasm is the life of the soul."[6]

The audience applauded heartily. The meeting which was to vote Phillips down hastily adjourned and from that day on, he was the favorite speaker in Concord.

In the next year he gave a thrilling address there which Thoreau has commemorated, containing a prayer which concluded, says Thoreau, "not like the Thanksgiving proclamations, with 'God save the Commonwealth of Massachusetts!' but with 'God dash it into a thousand pieces, till there shall not remain a fragment on which a man who dare not tell his name can stand.' "[7] The reference here was to Frederick Douglass who in Boston was in momentary danger of arrest and rendition and whose liberty was conditioned upon the denial of his identity.

Shortly after the Concord episode Phillips was invited before a lyceum in some town in New Hampshire. Arriving at the place he went to the hall and was met outside by the President who said to him, "Mr. Phillips, what are you going to lecture about this evening?" Phillips replied, "Street Life in Europe." "You are not going to lecture on Abolition then?" Phillips answered, "No, sir, I was not asked to do so." "There seems to be some mistake, Mr. Phillips," resumed the President. "No mistake on my part," responded the lecturer. "I was asked to come and give a lecture here tonight and I have come." "Please walk into the hall," said the President of the lyceum. He then went on the platform and asked: "Is the Secretary of the Lyceum in the House?" Someone called out, "Yes" from the middle of the Hall. "I told you, Mr. Secretary, when you wrote to Mr. Phillips, to ask him to lecture tonight on Abolition. Did you do so or did you not?" "I did not," was the reply. "Why did you not do it when the committee told you to do so?" "Because," returned the other, "I do not mean to have Abolition rammed down my throat!" To which the President promptly responded, "I will give you to understand, Mr. Secretary, that we do not mean to have you rammed down our throats." A vote was taken and it was decided by a considerable majority that Phillips should lecture on Abolition and he spoke on that familiar topic for two hours.[8]

CHAPTER THIRTEEN

"A COVENANT WITH DEATH
AND AN AGREEMENT WITH HELL"—
"DUMB DOGS THAT DARE NOT BARK"

In October, 1842, a mulatto named George Latimer came to Boston from Norfolk, Virginia. He was soon arrested and thrown into jail on a charge of theft. Presently it was revealed that he was an escaped slave. Friends rallied to his side and demanded a trial by jury. "No," replied Judge Shaw, "he is a fugitive slave. The Constitution of the United States (Article IV, section 2) authorizes the owner of such an one to arrest him in any state to which he may have fled."[1]

The city was wild with excitement. Placards were distributed and handbills posted throughout the city denouncing the outrage, and summoning the citizens to an open meeting in Faneuil Hall "For the Rescue of Liberty."

"Bostonians! friends of the rights of man! descendants of the Pilgrim Fathers! sons of Revolultionary sires! followers of Him who came to open the prison doors and set the captive free! Shall Boston, shall MASSACHUSETTS, be made the hunting ground of HUMAN KIDNAPPERS? Shall our soil be polluted by the footprints of Slavery? Shall shelter and protection be denied to wronged and bleeding humanity?. . . .

"Shall Massachusetts stand erect no longer,
But stoop in chains upon her downward way,
Thicker to gather on her limbs, and stronger,
Day after Day' "[2]

136

A turbulent crowd attended the meeting. Samuel E. Sewall, chairman, in protesting against the arrest of Latimer was continually interrupted by cries of "We'd like to see you with darkies for a week"—"Get o' dat Nigger's heel"—"Whar-yah-hoo," etc. When Joshua Leavitt read the series of resolutions, the audience became so noisy that scarcely a word of the speaker could be caught by reporters, though they stood near the platform. In the midst of his remarks, the cry of "Fire! Fire!" sounded outside which was immediately responded to in the Hall. There was a temporary stop to the proceedings.

Joshua Leavitt spoke till he was hissed down. Edmund Quincy rose to move the adoption of the resolutions just read. His remarks, said the Boston *Daiy Bee,* were "all froth and no cider."[3]

Charles Lenox Remond, a young Negro active in the Abolition cause, now got up to speak. No sooner did he appear on the platform than he was greeted with groans, cries, shouts, hisses—"Down with the darkey," "Tip him into the pit!" "We won't hear the damned nigger!"

The mob refused to listen to young Remond, so Wendell Phillips rose. "Never did we hear such a volley of blackguardism and shameless abuse as came from the lips of this fanatic madman," remarked the Boston *Daily Bee.* "Our readers will scarcely believe it, yet we assure them that WENDELL PHILLIPS had the audacity, the shameless self degradation, to curse the Constitution of the United States in the *Cradle of American Liberty,* before an assemblage of American citizens. Our blood boiled in our veins."[4]

Wendell Phillips—"Fellow citizens, I will ask your attention but for a single moment. . . . No generous man will try to drown my voice, when I plead the cause of one not allowed to speak for himself. Many will cry 'Shame!' here when they are told of the imprisonment of an innocent man. But where shall that shame rest? On the head of a poor officer who, for a dollar, obeys his writ? On needy attorneys, who would sell the fee simple of their souls for an attendance fee of 35 cents a day? On ambitious lawyers panting to see their names blazoned in Southern papers as counsel for slave-catchers. No. They are but *your tools*. *You* are the guilty ones. The swarming thousands before me, the creators of public sentiment, bolt and bar that poor man's dungeon to-night. (Great uproar). I know I am addressing the white slaves of the North. (Hisses and shouts). Yes, you dare to hiss me, of course. But you dare not break the chain which binds you to the car of slavery. (Uproar). Shake your chains; you have not the courage to break them. This old hall cannot rock, as it used to, with the spirit of liberty. It is chained down by the iron links of the United States Constitution. (Great noise, hisses, and uproar). Many of you, I doubt not, regret to have this man given up—but you cannot help it. There stands the bloody clause in the Constitution—you cannot fret the seal off the bond. The fault is in allowing such a Constitution to live an hour. A distinguished fellow citizen is reported to have said in this hall, that the 'Abolitionists were insane enough to think that the duties of religion transcended those they owed to the Constitution.' Yes, silly men that we are! We presume to believe the Bible outweighs the statute book. (Continued uproar). When I look upon these crowded thousands, and see them trample on their consciences and the rights of their fellow men, at the bidding of a piece of parchment, I say, my CURSE be on the Constitution of these United States! (Hisses and shouts). Those who cannot bear free speech had better go home. Faneuil Hall is no place for slavish hearts. (Hisses). . . .

"Fellow citizens . . . I record here my testimony against this pollution of our native city. The man in the free States who helps hunt slaves, is no better than a bloodhound. The attorney who aids is baser still. But any judge who should grant a certificate would be the basest of all!

'And in the lowest deep, a lower deep
   Still threatening to devour him, opens wide.' "[5]

The hall was now in complete uproar. Rings were formed upon the floor and the popular dances of "Jim and Jo," "Take your time, Miss Lucy," and "Clare de Kitchen" were broken down. Every effort to silence the noise only inflamed the audience the more. There were several knockdowns and scuffles in the galleries. In the midst of the violent confusion, Joshua Leavitt rose and in a moderate voice requested those in favor of passage of the resolutions already read to say "Aye." Accordingly those upon the platform cried out "Aye" upon which they whirled their hats in the air in great triumph and left.

"Agitate! Agitate!" cried the *Liberator* of November 11, 1842. "LATIMER SHALL GO FREE!. . . . Be vigilant, firm, uncompromising, friends of freedom! friends of God!"[6]

Whittier sent a clarion call from Massachusetts to Virginia:

> What asks the Old Dominion? If now
>   her sons have proved
> False to their fathers' memory, false
>   to the faith they loved;
> If she can scoff at Freedom, and its
>   great charter spurn,
> Must we of Massachusetts from truth and duty
>   turn?
>
> We hunt your bondmen, flying from
>   Slavery's hateful hell;
> Our voices, at your bidding, take up
>   the bloodhound's yell;
> We gather, at your summons, above
>   our father's graves,
> From Freedom's holy altar-horns to
>   tear your wretched slaves! . . . . .
>
> Look to it well, Virginians! In calm-
>   ness we have borne,
> In answer to our faith and trust, your
>   insult and your scorn;
> You've spurned our kindest counsels;
>   you've hunted for our lives;
> And shaken round our hearths and homes
>   your manacles and gyves!
>
> But for us and for our children, the
>   vow which we have given

For freedom and humanity is regis-
    tered in heaven;
No slave hunt in our borders,—no
    pirate on our strand!
No fetters in the Bay State,—no
    slave upon our land![7]

Happily Latimer was saved, an offer being made and accepted to pay $400. for his release with free papers. Where-
upon the chattel became a man.

The precedent, however, was not likely to discourage other
slaveholders from the pursuit of fugitives. Consequently a
"convention of freemen" was held on November 19, and the
famous Latimer petition was drawn up and signed by 62,791
citizens of Massachusetts, praying the Legislature to forbid all
persons holding office under the laws of the State of Massachusetts from aiding in the arrest or detention of persons claimed
as fugitives from slavery; to forbid the use of jails or other
public property, for their detention; and to prepare amendments to the Federal Constitution that should forever separate
the people of the state from all connection with slavery.[8] This
was the basis of the Personal Liberty Act passed March 24, 1843.[9]

The case of Latimer opened Wendell Phillips's eyes to the
fact that in advocating the rights of the blacks, his real an-
tagonist was the Union. From this moment he began to denounce the Constitution. He went further. He personally seceded
from the Union and refused all voluntary action under it. He
closed his law office, for an attorney had to take an oath to
support the Constitution. He foreswore the ballot, for a voter
was an active participant in governmental affairs. Thus he
stood a man without a country, a political Ishmael. As the Revo-
tionary Fathers said: "If this be a Revolution, let it come,"
Phillips said: "If I must choose between the Union and Liberty,
then I choose Liberty first, Union afterward!"[10]

"The Union," he remarked with a calmness that enchanted
while it appalled—"the Union is called the very ark of the
American covenant, but has not idolatry of the Union been the
chief bulwark of slavery? Is not the Union as it exists the foe

of Liberty and can we honestly affirm that it is the sole sur-
viving hope of freedom in the world? Long ago great leaders
of our parties hushed their voices and whispered that even to
speak of slavery was to endanger the Union. Is not this enough?
Sons of Otis and of Adams, of Franklin and of Jay, are we
ready for Union upon the ruins of freedom? *Delenda Carthago!*
Delenda Carthago!"[11]

Phillips did not take this step in passion. He took it calmly,
soberly, as he did everything else, and with a perfect knowledge
of what it meant.

He studied the Constitution and discovered that in giving
"solemn guarantees" to slavery, it was "a covenant with death
and an agreement with hell." It erected the negation of God
into a system of government. For consider, here was the clause
which legalized the slave trade for a period of twenty years;
here was the clause which allowed the slave masters to count
three-fifths of their slaves to swell their representation in Congress, and here was the clause which pledged the military power
of the United States to put down servile rebellion and to enforce
the fugitive slave law—a trinity of evil, a compact of fatal compromise. ("We Americans," said Lowell, "are very fond of this
glue of compromise. Like so many quack cements, it is advertised
to make the mended parts of the vessel stronger than those
which have never been broken, but like them it will not stand
hot water.")[12] Then when Phillips lifted his eyes from the
parchment and looked back into the Convention which framed
it, he saw that these provisions expressed the exact purpose of
its authors—"the saturation of the parchment," as John Quincy
Adams put it, "with the infection of slavery, which no fumigation
could purify, no guarantee could extinguish."[13]

And when he glanced at the successive administrations since
that time, at decisions of the courts, at the practice of the country, at the existing situation, he was driven to the conclusion
that consistent Abolitionism was impossible under that document and that slavery was intrenched in the fundamental law
of the nation.

Yet Northern people exalted the Union above all that was
called God or that was worshipped. It was their ark and Shekinah

—not a symbol, but an actual embodiment of every political good. When it was assailed, they were all the more angry because they did not see how the assault could be successfully repelled.

Phillips was amazed at his own blindness in not sooner discovering all this. Well, he saw it now, and so he did, as his Puritan ancestors had done under the despotism of Charles I and Archbishop Laud—he came out.[14]

He was gratified to find that he was not alone. Other Abolitionists saw what he saw, felt as he felt, acted as he acted. There was a band of Come-Outers, among them his friends and co-laborers Garrison and Quincy.[15] The question was the topic of debate at every anti-slavery meeting, in every anti-slavery society.

Garrison the leader marshaled his forces. As early as 1832 he had announced disunion in the *Liberator*—"There is much declamation about the sacredness of the compact which was formed between the free and slave States on the adoption of the Constitution. A sacred compact, forsooth! We pronounce it the most bloody and heaven-daring arrangement ever made by men for the continuance and protection of a system of the most atrocious villainy ever exhibited upon the earth. . . . "[16]

In May of 1842 Garrison put the doctrine at the head of his editorial columns, where he kept it for the rest of the year—"A REPEAL OF THE UNION BETWEEN NORTHERN LIBERTY AND SOUTHERN SLAVERY IS ESSENTIAL TO THE ABOLITION OF THE ONE AND THE PRESERVATION OF THE OTHER."[17]

"Ef I'd my way," exclaimed Lowell's Hosea Bigelow,

> I hed ruther
> We should go to work an' part,—
> They take one way, we take t'other,—
> Guess it wouldn't break my heart.
> Men hed ough' to put asunder
> Them that God has noways jined,
> An' I shouldn't greatly wonder
> Ef there's thousands o' my mind.[18]

The Massachusetts Anti-Slavery Society adopted the "Come-Outer" resolutions in January, 1843. The question was wrapped up in Garrison's old favorite Hebraisms and he gave it its final shape—*"Resolved* That the compact which exists between the North and the South is a covenant with death and an agreement with hell—involving both parties in atrocious criminality and should be immediately annulled."[19]

At the New England Anti-Slavery Convention held in May, 1844, the vote on the "come-outer" resolution surprised everybody. At one time the Garrisonians thought it would not pass. But when the roll was called, it seemed as if there were no "nays" at all, they came dropping in at such distant intervals. The vote stood 250 to 24.

Among the twenty-four nays were those of Maria White and of her betrothed James Russell Lowell. The two young people—"The glorious girl with the spirit eyes"—Lowell's own words—and her lover, slight and small, with rosy cheeks and wavy hair parted in the middle—refused to become "hardened and narrowed." They could have sentiments about their country and love it with all its imperfections. As Lowell wrote—"I do not agree with the Abolitionist leaders in their disunion and non-voting theories. They treat ideas as ignorant persons do cherries. They think them unwholesome unless they are swallowed stones and all."[20]

Soon after Lowell and Quincy were requested to act as Corresponding and Associate Editors of the *Standard*, at a salary of $250. each. Why both? asked Lowell. "Our most active friends," Phillips replied smoothly, "wish to feel the hand of Quincy in the *Standard*. In our 'Punch' they wish to find the usual variety of ingredients.[21]

Lowell showed the detached interest of a literary person—lacked the deadly intensity and immediateness of purpose of a Garrison or Phillips.

At the convention the Hutchinsons, anti-slavery vocalists, sang Jesse Hutchinson's "Get Off The Track."

When Sumner charged Phillips with short-sightedness and inconsistency (1. all governments have something bad in them;

citizens should speak and vote to reform them; 2. why didn't
Phillips leave the country?) Phillips replied:

"Pray, how long thinking war sinful would you serve as
Generalissimo and act the part of Murat in order to make
Government cease warring? Doubtless I must use all my influence to reform Government. But I must exert that influence through right means—whether office taking be one, is
the question. Do you say that quitting it I lose all influence?
What, is there no paper in the world but that on which men
write ballots? If there be any, I'll get Channing to write a
book on it and demolish Constitutions—Brougham shall write
articles and Tom Paine shall pamphletise—I'll be an Edinburgh Review and abolish test acts—I'll be an O'Connell and
instead of swallowing an heretical 'Communion' in order
to get office, I'll batter outside the door till men brush
away the old cobwebs and let me enter with a clean face—
No influence but in the ballot! Nay verily in the name of
all women who never vote at all. . . . Where too are
        'the dead but sceptred sovereigns
        Who still rule our spirits from their urns?'
The dead Burke, the distant Cobden shall do something
toward affecting the Government of ours, albeit no voters. . .

"But to vote a man into office is morally the same as
filling it oneself. I will use all influence for the reform of
Government which conscience tells me is right, but I will
neither steal, rob, enslave, or murder to support the Constitution or qualify myself for office.

"Ought Luther to have denounced the Pope or supported
him in order to get his amendment? There is a 4 July, 1776,
to men as well as to nations. . . . It is necessary with old
Pompey to do right. Heaven knows it is very far from
necessary to hold office.

"Then as to your second point—that I should leave the
country to be consistent. . . What right you have to set
up a Government and *force* me to pay taxes and then tell
me that I must leave the country or be guilty of all the sins
you incorporate in your Government, I confess I cannot see.
The God who made the law is my God as well as yours—
how, when, and where he gave you and your friends the
exclusive right to dwell here and make governments which

should so compromise all others born here, whether they agreed to them or not, I can't see. To live where God sent you and protest against your neighbor's sins is certainly different from joining him in sinning, which the office holder of the country does."[22]

The declaration of disunion was generally accepted by Abolitionists in New England and the Middle States. But the Abolitionists in the West, offspring of the Union, and by federal action "dedicated to freedom," could not be brought to approve disunion sentiments.

Meantime those Abolitionists (the "New Ogs," as they were called) because they refused to give women equal rights, identified themselves with the Liberty Party. Professedly this party was actuated by the same motives as Garrison. In reality it was fatally hampered by the compromises of the Constitution. It could only propose such measures as the Constitution would sanction. It attacked slavery in the District of Columbia and in the Territories; for slavery in the States it claimed no direct responsibility. When the national government had exhausted its whole power, that which the Abolitionists hated and meant to destroy, the *slave system*, would remain intact. Under a Pro-Slavery Constitution, what chance had an Anti-Slavery Crusade?

Recognizing this difficulty, the Liberty Party claimed sometimes that the Constitution had been fatally misrepresented, that the text was blameless, that it was, in fact, an Abolition document. This was the view of William Goodell and Gerrit Smith and George B. Cheever—honest and able men. At other times, it asserted that the Constitution could be amended and made Anti-Slavery if it were not so. At all times the political Abolitionists derided and belittled moral suasion and cried for action. With revolution in the air they esteemed agitation that was educative and moral alone as inadequate. Thus Whittier and Sumner and Wilson and Hale and Chase were led to adopt political expedients.

Lecturers of the Old Organization, particularly Garrison, Abby Kelley, and Foster, were sent to the region where the Liberty Party was strongest. At Syracuse, Foster's violent abuse and Garrison's condemnation of the Church and clergy almost provoked a riot. Rotten eggs were thrown, benches were broken, and the opponents of Abolition took possession of the meeting. Garrison and his followers were threatened with tarring and feathering. Still Garrison declared the Liberty Party "ludicrous in its folly, pernicious as a measure of policy, and useless as a political contrivance."[23]

When partisans argued that Slavery was the creature of law and could only be abolished by statute, that therefore the great duty of every Abolitionist was to cast an anti-slavery vote—the ballot was the cure-all, the end-all of the whole matter, of what use was it to talk against slavery?—Phillips and the Garrisonians had an effective reply. Now in the first place, they said, it was not true that Slavery was the creature of law; on the contrary, the slave laws, in letter as well as spirit, were the creatures of slavery, born of a public sentiment which that vile system had first created; and the first thing to be done, therefore, was to form a public sentiment amid which slavery could not live. The mere act of changing the laws, after that, would be the easiest of all possible tasks; it would follow as a matter of course. One thing to be done, therefore, was to change public sentiment and for this, moral agitation, in other words, "the opposition of moral purity to moral corruption, the destruction of error by the potency of truth, the overthrow of prejudice by the power of love," was the chief instrumentality.[24]

Besides it would be dangerous, Phillips asserted, for the Garrisonians to align themselves with the Liberty Party, for they would expose themselves to strong temptations to lower their standard for the sake of political success. The purity of the movement would thus be sullied by ambition for office, its moral tone depressed. The best weapons for anti-slavery warfare were spiritual.

The leader of the Liberty Party was James Gillespie Birney. He was a Southerner by birth, a prominent lawyer and slaveowner who was talked of for the governorship of his State. But Birney decided that slavery was wrong and he washed his hands of it. He went to Kentucky and freed his slaves; he was warned to leave the state. He then went to Cincinnati and established a newspaper to advocate emancipation; a mob promptly invaded his office, destroyed the press, and dumped it into the river. This did not deter Birney. He continued to advocate emancipation, facing violence and a great deal of hatred and abuse. Twenty-three years before Lincoln's famous utterance that a house divided against itself cannot stand and before Seward's declaration of an irrepressible conflict between slavery and freedom, Birney said—"There will be no cessation of conflict until slavery shall be exterminated or liberty destroyed. Liberty and slavery cannot live in juxtaposition."[25]

He was convinced that the only way to fight for freedom was by organizing a political party—"a free Northern nucleus," as Elizur Wright put it, "a standard flung to the breeze—something around which to rally."[26] Accordingly he joined his followers in starting the Liberty Party and was twice nominated by it to the Presidency—in 1840 and again in 1844. The first time he received no more than 7,000 votes, but four years later he had a total of 62,300—just enough votes to take the election from Clay and throw the government directly into the hands of slavery—James K. Polk of Tennessee ("Who the devil is Polk?" echoed the common feeling).[27]

Possibly Clay's own vacillation in regard to the annexation of Texas accounted for his failure. From his wavering the man of compromise lost the votes of many that were opposed to annexation as well as those who were in favor of it. He had opposed annexation right along, and then in the summer of 1844, in the so-called Alabama Letters, he said he should "be glad to see Texas annexed *provided*, etc."[28]

The Democrats sang—

> O! poor Cooney Clay
> Alas! poor Cooney Clay
> He never can be President
> While Polk is in the way.

And the Liberty Party men—

> Clear the track for Emancipation!
> Cars cannot run on a Clay Foundation. . .[29]

The only hope of success for the Liberty Party men lay in the possibility that the Whigs or Democrats would unite with them in nominating a Liberty man, a contingency unlikely to happen. The party reached its greatest strength in 1846 when it received 74,000 votes. It had stood to its guns but fired them into vacancy for seven years. The result seemed to confirm Garrison's judgment.

Not one Abolitionist in ten voted for the Liberty Party. But there were many who hankered after an alliance with this world and served as a disintegrating influence. The Garrisonians intensified their agitation to keep their forces intact.[30]

No one was more active and vigilant than Wendell Phillips. His ability as an organizer and eloquent speaker anchored the doubtful and wavering, renewed and tightened the bonds with the faithful. In 1844 he was again chosen general agent of the Massachusetts Anti-Slavery Society and carried through a program of One Hundred Conventions in the Commonwealth adopted at the annual meeting. Notices appeared in the *Liberator*, printed placards were sent out to the towns, and the machinery of agitation was oiled to run smoothly and swiftly. "The more the opposers multiply obstacles," Phillips said, "the greater must be our patient, constant energy to overcome them."[31]

In 1845 he wrote and published an argument entitled, "The Constitution a Pro-Slavery Compact," based on the Madison papers. He proved that the Constitution, as it then stood, was the Gibraltar of human bondage.[32]

> "If, then, the Constitution be, what these Debates show that our fathers intended to make it, and what, too, their descendants, this nation, say they did make it and agree to uphold,—then we affirm that it is 'a covenant with death and an agreement with hell,' and ought to be immediately annulled. No Abolitionist can consistently take office under it, or swear to support it.
>
> "But if, on the contrary, our fathers failed in their purpose, and the Constitution is all pure and untouched by

slavery,—then Union itself is impossible without guilt. For it is undeniable that the fifty years passed under this (anti-slavery) Constitution show us the slaves trebling in numbers;—slaveholders monopolizing the offices and dictating the policy of the government;—prostituting the strength and influence of the nation to the support of slavery here and elsewhere—trampling on the rights of the free States, and making the courts of the country their tools. To continue this disastrous alliance longer is madness. The trial of fifty years with the best of men and the best of Constitutions, on this supposition, only proves that it is impossible for free and slave States to unite on any terms, without all becoming partners in the guilt, and responsible for the sin of slavery. We dare not prolong the experiment, and with double earnestness we repeat our demand upon every honest man to join in the outcry of the American Anti-Slavery Society,—

NO UNION WITH SLAVEHOLDERS!"[33]

"I am called the 'pamphlet man' now," Phillips writes to Webb. "An outer Barbarian like yourself can't know the magic there is in the name of 'Madison Papers' to an American ear. Therefore you'll think the whole thing stupid *as it is*, but we've sold one edition and I'm going to print 2000 more. As for my little poor thing—it was scissored and patched into existence in one day—and printed almost as quick to circulate at our annual meeting and keep Abby Kelley from teasing me awhile—she wanted something to sell after her lectures and I had to provide it."[34]

Phillips also published anonymously in the same year a pamphlet, "Can Abolitionists Vote or Take Office under the United States Constitution?" Here he marshalled the pros and cons in successive order under the title of objections and answers. The brochure was full of wit and pat applications. To the objection that his course was pharisaical, he replied—

"Because we refuse to aid a wrongdoer in his sin we by no means proclaim that we think our whole character better than his. It is neither pharisaical to have opinions nor presumptuous to guide our lives by them. He would be a strange preacher who should set out to reform his circle by joining in all their sins. This reminds me of the tipsy Duke of Norfolk, who, seeing a drunken friend in the gutter, hic-coughed: 'My dear fellow, I can't help you out, but I'll do better—I'll lie down by your side!"[35]

In noticing the objection that by the payment of taxes he recognized and supported the State practically while renouncing it in theory, he answered that he was responsible only so far as his ability and willingness went. Any evil which sprang from his acts incidentally, without his ability or will, he was not responsible for. Such responsibility reminded him of a principle in Turkish law called "homicide by an intermediate cause." And Phillips related a case mentioned by Dr. Clark in his travels. A young man in love poisoned himself because the girl's father refused his consent to the marriage. The Cadi sentenced the father to pay a fine of eighty dollars, saying: "If you had not had a daughter, this young man would not have loved; if he had not loved, he had never been disappointed; if he had not been disappointed, he would not have taken poison."[36]

Phillips thus referred to the assertion that the Constitution though pro-slavery, might be amended and that he could vote meanwhile in that hope—

"It is necessary to swear to support it *as it is*. Let me illustrate this argument by a dialogue.

"*Liberty Party.* 'Don't call the Constitution pro-slavery, my friend. We can amend and strike out the bad clauses.'

"*Non-Voter.* 'Oh, well, *when you have* done so, I won't any longer call it pro-slavery.'

"This objection to our position reminds me of Miss Martineau's story of the little boy who hurt himself, and sat crying on the sidewalk. 'Don't cry,' said a friend, 'it won't hurt you tomorrow.' 'Well, then,' whimpered the child, 'I won't cry tomorrow.' "[37]

To the common statement that his position was that of a hot head and a zealot, he responded—

"History, from the earliest Christians downward, is full of instances of men who refused all connection with government and all the influences which office could bestow rather than deny their principles or aid in wrong doing. Sir Thomas More need never have mounted the scaffold, had he only consented to take the oath of supremacy. He had only to tell a lie with solemnity, as we are asked to do, and he might not only have saved his life, but, as the trimmers of his day would have told him, doubled his influence. Pitt resigned his place as Prime Minister of England rather than break faith with the Catholics of Ireland. Should I not resign a ballot rather than break faith with the slave?"[38]

In the same connection he added—

"An act of conscience is always a grand act. Whether right or wrong it represents the best self of our nature. While an under-clerk in the War Office, Granville Sharp, that patriarch of the Anti-Slavery enterprise in England, sympathized with America in our struggle for independence. Orders reached his office to ship munitions of war to the revolted Colonies. If his hand had entered the account of such a cargo, it would have contracted, in his eyes, the stain of innocent blood. To avoid this pollution, he resigned his place and means of subsistence at a period of life when he could no longer hope to find lucrative employment. As the thoughtful clerk of the War Office takes down his hat from the peg where it had hung for twenty years, methinks I hear one of our critics cry out: 'Friend Sharp, you are absurdly scrupulous; you may innocently aid Government in doing wrong.' While the Liberty Party yelps at his heels: 'My dear sir, you are losing your influence.'"[39]

At the sixteenth annual meeting of the Massachusetts Anti-Slavery Society, Phillips explained his position fully. Did people ask why he did not trust parties, and plans, and churches and compromises, but wished to rase all out and begin anew? Phillips answered, everything that man could have done, united to the Constitution, had been done. He did not mistrust the Union and political parties because they had failed once but because, against slavery, they had always failed.

"Let me explain in an anecdote of Henry Clay on the stump. When some vote of his had offended his neighbors, an old friend took him by the hand, and said, 'Harry, I've voted for you always till now. I'm done forever.' 'Neighbor,' said Clay, 'do you own a rifle?' 'The best in Kentucky.' 'Suppose it should once miss fire, what would you do?' 'Pick the flint and try again!' 'That's it, my boy,' said Clay, clapping him on the shoulder, 'do so with your friend,—pick the flint and try him again.'

"That now was good sense. Our case is just the reverse. We've got a rifle that *always misses*—are we to stand picking the flint forever! (Cheers). Seventy years all wasted— the hopes of two generations cheated—how long shall we wait? how long to earn the reputation of patient men! moderate men! men of sound common sense! The fox turned back from the lion's cave when he saw the tracks all inward, and none returned. Wise beast! In the vast house of Slaveholding despotism, the long procession of hopes and promises, church plans, and cunning compromises, have been endlessly marching for seventy years. Who has ever seen one glad traveller of them returning from that bourne? Shall we not be as wise as the fable? . . .

"Mr. President, we hold ourselves a Grand Inquest for Freedom—Inspector Generals, may I say, of anti-slavery for Massachusetts. We mean to hold ourselves free from all contamination of slavery; we mean to give it no countenance or support; and we mean to see it abolished before we close our eyes in death, if we can. (Loud and continued cheering). Over all political scheming, over all anti-slavery apostasy, over all hypocrisy and pretence, will we hold ourselves vigilant. If we can help it, no man shall go about in an anti-slavery garment, without the anti-slavery heart in his bosom."[40]

The truth was, explained Phillips, that every man who goes into politics has his coat trimmed on both sides and turns it at his pleasure. The Liberty Party might work for her own ends. She might join what others she pleased to accomplish those ends. She might go for a homestead to the white man, land for everybody, etc. But she might not by putting on anti-slavery as a cloak, swallow up the enthusiasm of the honest Abolitionists of the North.

"I thought last night, as I listened to the eloquent appeals and remonstrances of William W. Brown, a fugitive, how powerless are the men of Boston—wealthy and powerful though they be—how utterly powerless they are to protect that man here in their own city! There is not, in all Massachusetts, the power which can save William W. Brown from his master's grasp, should he come and demand him here. (A voice, 'yes, there is!') Yes! there are in Massachusetts 800,000 beating hearts, which, if they would utter the word DISSOLUTION, would be omnipotent to shelter, to protect, to save him. But that word is to come, not by mustering parties, or choosing cunningly 'available candidates,' but by Massachusetts coming up, as of old, and breaking her chains in Faneuil Hall. 'Treason!' some will cry—'the powers that be are ordained by God.' 'The powers of God are the powers that shall be'—this I hold to be the true doctrine, and this ought to be the reading of the text. (Great applause).

"No, sir, we may not trifle or dally with this thing. What brought about the Reform Bill in England? What the Catholic Emancipation? Fear of the masses. What accomplished the independence of these States? A determined spirit of *revolution*—a purpose to put an end to the existing state of things. *Revolution* is the only thing, the only power, that ever worked out freedom for any people. The powers that have ruled long, and learned to love ruling, will never give up that prerogative till they find they must, till they see the certainty of overthrow and destruction if they do not! . . .

"To plant—to revolutionize—those are the twin stars that have ruled our pathway. What have we then to dread in the word Revolution—we, the children of rebels! We were born to be rebels—it runs in the blood."[41]

2.

The Abolitionists fulminated against the Churches as they fulminated against the State. They declared, for example, in the New England Anti-Slavery Convention of May, 1841, that "in regard to the existence of slavery . . . the clergy stand wickedly preeminent, and ought to be unsparingly exposed and reproved before the people." But other members wished to assert by resolution—"That the Church and clergy of the United States, as a whole, constitute a great BROTHERHOOD OF THIEVES, inasmuch as they countenance the highest kind of theft. i.e., man stealing."[42] And Abby Kelley presented to the tenth anniversary meeting of the Massachusetts Anti-Slavery Society a resolution—"That the sectarian organizations called Churches are combinations of thieves, robbers, adulterers, pirates, and murderers, and as such form the bulwark of American slavery."[43]

Wendell Phillips was equally severe. "The American church —what is it?" he asked. "A synagogue of Satan!" "a weathercock denoting with exactness the tone and level of the public sentiment and morality," a church of "dumb dogs that dare not bark," a church "rotten at the core."

"The American pulpit, what is it? What the pews make it. Your minister is not chosen to build up your moral and intellectual strength; if so, he would be a reformer. He is chosen to make Unitarians, or Orthodox, or Baptists, or Methodists, as the case may be. The voluntary system is beautiful, to a certain extent, but it can never be a reformatory system. It will always mark the precise point of respectability. Christianity, like the larva from the burning volcano, while it is warm, moves on resistless; but when it grows cold, it stops, it takes shapes, and forms itself into organized bodies, into churches—and ministers. An old Italian in 1542 said that no Christian could die in his bed. There is truth in it now. No Christian now can be *respectable*, in the entire community where he dwells."[44]

"We affirm" Phillips said again before the American Anti-Slavery Society, "that the fundamental principle which the American Anti-Slavery Society first announced to the world is the germ whence have sprung all the doctrines and measures which it has since proposed."[45] What was that principle? That slavery was a sin and that it was the duty of the slaveholder immediately to repent. And as Phillips went lower and lower down into the strata of the American mind and American institutions, he found the roots of the tree of slavery coiled around the altars of popular religion and deriving their support from the national Constitution. What had he done but proclaim that truth?

"No matter how broad may be the profession of the Church, if we find it tainted with slavery, we write upon its forehead, 'Ichabod'—the glory has departed! Of what avail are its protestations of innocence, when all over its surface, we see breaking out the leprous spots of its contamination? Blame us not, if, like the man in the classic fable, we come to you, year after year, with a lantern lighted by this truth. Blame us not for assailing the Church—for how can we avoid it without growing false to our cause? . . . ."[46]

There was a short method of determining the Church's relation to the cause of freedom, added Phillips.

"The American Church is not a pigmy, stealing out of sight in the shadow of a Colossus. She is not a shrivelled and shrunken body, whose voice it is difficult to hear. She is mighty; she stands at the fountain head of national education and influence, swaying the minds of the people at her will. When the Church speaks, no ear trumpet is necessary to enable us to hear her voice. The poet Wendell Holmes speaks of a time when all the world, at a given signal, was to see how much noise it could make by vociferating, 'Boo!' When the moment arrived, all except one blind man were so intent on hearing the noise, that they forgot to utter the word! Such will not be the case when the American Church becomes heartily enlisted in the work of Emancipation. The fact that men ask what she is doing for this cause is proof that she is doing nothing. When she utters her voice, it is not in a corner. When she awakes to her duty, she will shake the solid earth with her tread. . . . She should be, like Caesar's wife, above suspicion. If her hosts were marshaled on the side of Freedom, infidelity could not peep or mutter. Now, when we come forth from our obscurity and insignificance, and find the path of liberty with 'here and there a traveller,' blame us not if we conclude that the Church has taken some other road."[47]

Elsewhere Phillips remarked: "If I die before emancipation, write this for my epitaph. 'Here lies Wendell Phillips, infidel to a Church that defended human slavery—traitor to a government that was only an organized conspiracy against the rights of man.'"[48]

CHAPTER FOURTEEN

OF MARTYR BUILD—FATHER MATHEW

In 1822 at Charleston, Denmark Vesey, a free Negro, made an elaborate plot to rise, massacre the white population, seize the shipping in the harbor, and, if hard pressed, sail away to the West Indies. One of the Negroes gave evidence, Vesey was seized, duly tried, and with thirty-four other conspirators hanged.[1]

Suspicion was so strong against the Negro that South Carolina immediately passed a series of laws commonly called the "Negro seamen acts," which provided that the moment a vessel arrived in port with a Negro aboard, the Negro, even if he was a citizen of another state or country, should be seized. The sheriff was to board the vessel, take the Negro to jail, and detain him there until the vessel was actually ready to leave. The master of the ship was then to pay for the detention of the Negro and take him away or pay a fine of one thousand dollars and see the Negro sold as a slave. Within a short time after the enactment of this law, as many as forty-one vessels were deprived of one or more hands. From one British vessel almost the entire crew was taken. Northern states protested that their citizens were thus deprived of their "privileges and immunities," and the British government made similar remonstrances. The Attorney General Wirt declared the act unconstitutional and void. But it was not repealed, and though relaxed against England, continued to be enforced against the Northern States.

It was generally recognised that the act violated both the treaty with Great Britain and the power of Congress to regulate

157

trade. To all this South Carolina replied that as a sovereign state she had the right to interdict the entry of foreigners, that in fact she had been a sovereign state at the time of her entrance into the Union, and that she never had surrendered the right to exclude free Negroes. Finally she asserted that if dissolution of the Union must be the alternative, she was quite prepared to abide by the result.

In 1844 Massachusetts sent Squire Samuel Hoar, Phillips's opponent at Concord, as commissioner to Charleston to make a test case of a Negro citizen deprived of his rights. When he appeared on the scene, the South Carolina legislature voted that "this agent comes here not as a citizen of the United States, but as an emissary of a foreign government hostile to our domestic institutions and with the sole purpose of subverting our internal police."[2] The legislature passed a resolution demanding the exclusion of Hoar and he was notified that his life was in danger.

The Sheriff told him that the people regarded his visit as an insult from Massachusetts, that they were very much excited, and he advised him by all means to leave the city at once. To all this Hoar replied that he was too old to run and that he could not return to Massachusetts without an effort to perform the duty assigned him. Others came to see him. The danger was not only great but imminent. Excitement ran high; people were gathering in groups. All that was needed to bring on an attack was for somebody to say, "Now is your time." The Mayor, a bank president, a committee of seventy leading citizens added the weight of their appeal: he must remain no longer.

At noon one day, Hoar was called downstairs and found carriages before the door of the hotel, and in the hall and on the piazza and in the street a crowd of men. They were there, he was told, to escort him to the boat. Hoar's protests were of no avail. It was a question merely whether he should walk or be dragged to the carriage. He chose to walk, entered the carriage, was driven to the boat, and returned to Boston.[3]

All Massachusetts was deeply stirred by the treatment of its representative. She had been "dishonored" by South Carolina.

No longer, said Emerson, could the Boston merchant entertain the Southern planter as a respected guest at his dinner table.[4]

Phillips urged his state to demand that the President enforce Hoar's plain constitutional right to reside in South Carolina. In default of which he asked the Legislature to authorize the governor to proclaim the Union at an end.[5] Massachusetts blustered but did nothing.

But although she did nothing officially to resent an indignity, she did much through certain of her sons to aid and comfort the slavemasters. Slaves were constantly making their way to the North. One of these blacks secreted himself on board a Massachusetts vessel in 1846 bound from New Orleans for Boston. He was discovered, chained, brought on to the Puritan city, transferred there to another Massachusetts ship bound South, carried back to New Orleans—and remanded to slavery.

The Abolitionists protested and Faneuil Hall was secured. The venerable John Quincy Adams presided.[6] The philanthropist Dr. Samuel Gridley Howe recited the facts and John A. Andrew (afterwards war governor) presented the ringing resolutions. Charles Sumner, now enlisted for the war against slavery, made one of the speeches. Phillips followed. "Let us proclaim," he said, "that law or no law, Constitution or no Constitution, humanity shall be paramount in Massachusetts. I would send a voice from Faneuil Hall that should reach every hovel in South Carolina, and say to the slaves, 'Come here and find in Massachusetts an asylum.' "[7]

Daniel Webster was horrified at this. "You that prate of disunion, do you not know that disunion is Revolution?"

"Yes," retorted Phillips, "we do know it, and we are for a revolution—a revolution in the character of the American Constitution!"[8]

Amid these exciting happenings Phillips found time for other activities. One day he went with Garrison before a Committee of the Legislature to argue against capital punishment. His ideas on penology were definitely humane and modern. To Sumner, August 17, 1845: "Don't you agree with me that this old maxim underlies the whole philosophy of penalties and imprisonment—that man should never like land, cattle, cotton be made the mere means to an end, but always himself share largely in the *end*. A is never to be imprisoned merely in order that B and C may be secure: but the morally insane A is to be cured—so surrounded with moral influences as to develop his higher and bring under his animal propensities—this the State owes him—restraint is to continue till this is effected and to be used *mainly* that it may be effected."[9]

Another day Phillips bore witness to the superiority of phonography (then just come into use) over the old method of reporting. Still another day he responded to a resolution boycotting the products of slave labor:

> "The resolution under debate laid down the principle 'that it was wrong to purchase or use the product of *unpaid* labor'—I said—if this was the ground of the free labor argument, we must abstain from many things besides cotton— since there was much labor in the world which though, perhaps, a little better paid than that of the slaves, was still unpaid, uncompensated, in any just sense. Instance the shirtmakers of the cities—miners of England and factory operatives—their portion of the net profit of their several manufactures was far too small—unjustly so. Capital's skill took the lion's share. Such, too, I argued, were the laborers of Ireland—miserably underpaid—not paid in any just sense of the word. I call payment that which secures the necessaries of life—some time and means of mental improvement—and something against age and sickness—this every industrious human being deserves for a day's work."[10]

Finally Phillips labored tirelessly for the abolition of "Nigger schools" and "Jim Crow" cars.[11]

There was not a large city in the Free States but had its "nigger hell," "nigger lane," "nigger heaven" at the theaters, "nigger pews." The Knickerbocker City indulged an annual guffaw over the emancipation procession when epauletted black marshals with drawn swords and sable cits rode and strutted up Broadway to the music of a brass band on the fifth of July, travestying the celebration of white independence on the day before. In Philadelphia the directory printed the names of colored citizens with a cross prefixed to distinguish them. And in

Sabbatarian Boston custom permitted the Negro citizen to walk about the Common on "nigger election day" when the governor came in, but if seen on the ground at the time honored pageant of "artillery election day," he was booted off.[12]

Wendell Phillips set himself a huge task: to cure Boston of the epidemic of colorphobia.

He brought the question of discrimination before the School Committee of his native city in 1846. Colored children were not allowed to study with white children but were sent off into hovels and herded in exclusion to learn from inferior teachers. Phillips started a petition praying for the abolition of caste schools, but the Committee denied his request.[13] Phillips dissected their reasons and brought the matter up again and again. In fact, he made it the ghost of the School Committee, until a few years later they were driven to yield the point, and the free schools of Boston became free indeed.

At its annual meeting, the Massachusetts Anti-Slavery Society published Phillips's victory in this resolution: "*Resolved,* That this society rejoices in the abolition of the separate colored schools in the city of Boston as the triumph of law and justice over the pride of caste and wealth, and recognizes in it the marked advance of the Anti-Slavery sentiments of the State."[14]

At the same time Phillips appealed to the legislature of Massachusetts to compel the railroads as common carriers to admit Negroes to the cars their tickets demanded. In the end he was equally successful with this appeal. Meanwhile he urged his friends not to ride in buses placarded: "Colored people not allowed to ride in this omnibus." And he made it a habit to share with any black man in whose company he found himself whatever accommodations his friend was forced to accept.[15] Frederick Douglass mentions several instances. Once after delivering a lecture to the New Bedford Lyceum before a cultivated audience, when brought to the railroad station, Phillips, on hearing that Douglass was compelled to ride in a filthy "Jim Crow" box car, stepped to Douglass's side in the presence of his friends, and walked with him straight into the miserable dog-car, saying, "Douglass, if you cannot ride with me, I can ride with you."

On the Sound between New York and Newport colored passengers had to spend the night on the forward deck of the steamer with the horses, sheep, and swine. On such trips, when Douglass was a passenger, Phillips preferred to walk the deck with him to taking a stateroom. "I could not persuade him," said Douglass, "to leave me to bear the burden of insult and outrage alone."[16]

In the spring of 1847 Phillips, at his own expense, published a pamphlet in which he reviewed with great acuteness and a lavish display of legal learning, an able book by Lysander Spooner on "The Unconstitutionality of Slavery." The large edition was soon disposed of, and others followed.

"If the beautiful theories of some of our friends," said Phillips, "could oust from its place the ugly reality of a pro-slavery administration, we would sit quiet and let Spooner and Goodell convert the nation at their leisure. But alas, the ostrich does not get rid of her enemy by hiding her head in the sand. Slavery is not abolished, although we have persuaded ourselves that it has no right to exist. . . .

"If the Constitution be guiltless of any blame in this matter, then surely there must be some powerful element at work in the Union itself which renders it impossible for this to be an Anti-Slavery *nation,* even when blessed with an *Anti-Slavery* Constitution, and thus the experience of fifty years proves *Union* itself under any form, to be impossible without guilt. In such circumstances, no matter what the Constitution is, whether good or bad, it is the duty of every honest man to join in the war-cry of the American Anti-Slavery Society. 'No Union with Slaveholders.' "[17]

Phillips still continued to score the Church. At the Anti-Slavery Bazaar a few months before, he quoted approvingly the saying of Dr. Arnold that the Church exists "to put down all moral evils within or without her own body," and then proceeded: "Anti-Slavery Societies ought not to have any *raison d'être.* The Church should do our work. But she will have nothing to do with current sins. She has the sword of the Spirit, but glues it in the scabbard! She puts on the breastplate of righteousness, but never goes into battle! She has her feet shod with the Gospel of peace, but will not travel!"[18]

Such was not the case with Phillips's intimate friend, the pugnacious Reverend Theodore Parker. Buckling on his armor, Parker dashed into the thick of battle, smiting not dead Pharisees, but living sins and foes. Iconoclastic, vehement, radical, heretic, unswerving, he was of martyr build.

2.

An assembly of Unitarian ministers of Boston and the neighborhood. A dark-haired, dark-eyed young man of somewhat plebeian features, but with earnest eyes, is defending himself dexterously and keenly against the charges rained against him. He has written a book—a voluminous discourse on Religion—and the Unitarian Doctors aver that that book is "vehemently deistical" and "subversive of Christianity as a particular religion" and they would have him withdraw from their society. The young man replies that his book was meant to build up religion, not to pull it down. The quarrel waxes louder as the hands move round the clock. Faces flush and bitter words fly fast and fierce. But the young man holds his own and will not budge an inch. The storm of passionate reproach has no force in it to move him. But then one calmer and kinder than the rest speaks warmly of the young man's sincerity. Another follows in these more generous tones. And then another. The young man, unmoved by rebuke and denunciation, is conquered by the first touch of kindness, breaks into weeping, and hastens from the room.[19]

Seven or eight years further on. The infamous Fugitive Slave Bill has become the enacted law of the United States. Ellen Craft, a woman almost white, and her husband, William, have long lived peacefully in Boston, he a joiner, she a seamstress. They are of Parker's congregation. But bailiffs come from the South to catch them and bear them back to slavery, and they are hidden away in fear of capture. Ellen is in Parker's house and the door is chained all day. And Parker sits at his desk, writing his sermon for the Sunday services, and at his side is a loaded pistol.[20]

Again a public meeting with the spacious hall crowded from orchestra to gallery. The meeting is pro-slavery. An orator on the platform winds up some specious plea for the great abomination with the taunt: "I should like to know what Theodore Parker would say to that?" At once, through the crowd in the gallery, there pushes to the front a man of somewhat plebeian features and shouts—"Would you like to know? I'll tell you what Theodore Parker says to it." (Cries of "Throw him over," "Kill him"). But Parker plants himself firm and with a glance to the right and left exclaims, "Kill me? Throw me over? You shall do no such thing. Now I'll tell you what I say to this matter."[21]

It is the same man that stands on the platform of his church on the Sabbath day. Before him is the largest congregation in Boston. This vehement deist, this "subverter of a particular Christianity" rises to read from an ancient record that he loves, the old story of One who was condemned to death and wore a crown of thorns, and men mocked at Him, and spat at Him, and they bid Him carry His cross, and behold He could not, and they set the cross up on Calvary, and they crucified Him. He rises to read that record to his people, and the pathos of it overcomes him, and he breaks into weeping and he must sit down. He rises again to read it before his people and the tears blind his eyes, and the emotion chokes his voice again, and he cannot go on. . . .[22]

It was not the heroic age of Unitarianism. Members were about as complaisant a set of Christians as ever took ship for the kingdom. The clergy were petrified and asphyxiated. If they had any positive maxim, it was, to use the phrase of Emerson's—"By taste are ye saved"—by propriety. A Unitarian orthodoxy had been tacitly agreed upon and the main endeavor of the elders was to prevent any commotion, to keep things decently and in order.

When Theodore Parker, manlike, spoke, there could be but one result. The controlling men of the denomination said—"This young man must be silenced!" They closed their pulpits to him, tried to alienate his congregation, refused to occupy the same platform, trade at the same shop, remain in the same room with him. The Church dropped him. But the blood of

Parker's forefather was in him and he said—"I will go about and preach and lecture in the city and glen, by the roadside and fieldside, and wherever men and women may be found. I will go eastward and westward and northward and southward and make the land ring. . . . What I have seen to be false, I will proclaim a lie on the housetop, and fast as God reveals the truth, I will declare his word."[23]

Every pulpit and every newspaper in Boston vilified him, clerical friends would not speak to him in the street and refused to shake his hand. Several ministers lost their positions by inviting him into their pulpits. At this juncture a company of gentlemen met, passed a simple resolution and went home—"*Resolved,* That the Reverend Theodore Parker shall have a chance to be heard in Boston."[24]

It was a dreary, cold, and wet morning in February, 1845, when Theodore Parker first spoke in the hall hired by the gentlemen, the Melodeon. Snow lay on the streets and roofs, and the wind and rain plashed against the building. But there was no lack of eager listeners to the sermon—"The Indispensableness of True Religion for Man's Welfare in his Individual and Social Life."[25]

Brethren had said to Parker before—"You are right, you say the truth, but it won't do. Don't preach it. He that spits in the wind spits in his own face. You will ruin yourself and do nobody any good." And when the trial came, one after another on whom he had reckoned, fell back upon the Old Guard and was silent. "Alas!" he wrote, "for that man who consents to think one thing in the closet and preach another in his pulpit! God shall judge him in his mercy. But over his study and over his pulpit must be written, *Emptiness,* on his forehead and right hand, *Deceit, deceit!*"[26]

Parker remained the special object of the malediction of American Churches for twenty years. Priestly malice, said Wendell Phillips, scarred every inch of his garment, but "it was seamless; it could find no stain." He saw men stare at him in the street and point and say: "That is Theodore Parker" and look at him as if he were a murderer. During the great revival of '58, it was recommended that men and women, wherever they might be, in the shop or on the street, should pray for Parker daily when the clock struck one. "We know that we cannot argue him down," they said, "but O Lord, put a hook in his jaws so that he may not be able to speak!" "Hell never vomited forth a more wicked and blasphemous monster than Theodore Parker," said one of the noted evangelists, "and it is only the mercies of Jesus Christ which have kept him from eternal damnation already."[27]

And Theodore Parker himself, how did he conduct himself through all this? It did not surprise him, for he knew human nature. "I knew all this would come," he said. "It has come from my religion, and I would not forego that religion for all this world can give. . ."[28]

He spoke frankly of Jesus as a man, and a man liable to imperfections and mistakes, while he honored him as the greatest leader of humanity. He put religion on a purely natural basis. Christianity, he remarked, shines by its own light, is its own evidence, needs no miraculous support. He could shock people with, "If it could be proved that Jesus of Nazareth had never lived, still Christianity would stand firm and fear no evil."[29] Christianity he defined as "absolute pure morality, absolute pure religion." The ideal Christ "whom we form in our hearts" he held superior to the historic Christ "so blameless and so beautiful."

He spoke of the Bible and said men worshipped it as an unerring guide for all their ways, as the only message given by God to men in distant times. And in thus doing, he said, they were wrong, for they put a limit to God's love and the working of His Spirit in the world. He said to them: "The Bible is one thing, but religion is another. If there were no Bible, we should still hear God's voice within. His love is wider than men know, and He still lives and speaks to them as plainly as He spoke in days of old. Let each man, woman, and child keep open his soul and receive God's messages and we shall be inspired."

Those who defended the "peculiar institution" of the South on biblical grounds he held up to scorn. To a Southern correspondent who urged the curse of Ham in extenuation of slavery, he said, "Dear Sir, Christianity does not consist in believing stories in the Old Testament about Noah's curse and all that, but in loving your brother as yourself, and God with your whole heart."[30]

He was the Paul of Transcendentalism—wielding a mallet. Emerson, on the other hand, as Dr. Holmes said, was "an iconoclast without a hammer, who took down our idols from their pedestals so tenderly that it seemed like an act of worship." They stood for the same thing. Parker was Emerson's truth in the pulpit.[31]

The sum total of his system may be gathered up in this: "God is infinitely good: now, what follows?"[32]

Instead of preaching about the abstractions of dogma and the sins of Babylon, he preached about the sins of Boston: about merchants and politicians who debauched the conscience of the nation by cheering or countenancing the return of fugitive slaves, about smug church members who rented property to brothel keepers, about mill owners in Lowell who cut wages 10 per cent and paid extra dividends of 12 per cent. It was inevitable, he said, that nine tenths of all prisoners came from the "perishing" classes, the poor and ignorant. Society, not the individual, was at fault.

The Church is here in the world for nothing at all if not to hold up a higher standard of life and create a better society. So Parker attacked: intemperance, covetousness, ignorance, the wrongs of woman, war, political corruption, above all, Slavery. Against Slavery he struck as with a battleaxe. One phrase, underscored by Herndon, was by a twist of phrase immortalized by Lincoln: "The government of all, by all, and for all is a Democracy."[33]

Parker was not greatly concerned with the Constitution or tolerant of compromise. He was an honest man and a rugged man who must and would speak out the truth in him, a man whose every word was "fiercely furnaced in the blast of a life that had struggled in earnest."[34]

Adverse criticism did not worry him. "If a man called that a rowdy speech, it was because he had the soul of a rowdy," he retorted. "And if fifty men said so it was because there were fifty so ensouled.'[35]

He thought himself a second Luther commissioned to rebuke sin in high places. "Suppose," he wrote in his diary, "I could have given all the attention to theology that I have been forced to pay to politics and slavery, how much I might have done! I was meant for a philosopher, and the times call for a *stump orator*."[36]

The Melodeon was a great and gloomy building, uncomfortable and dirty. The congregation often saw the spangles of the opera dancers who had been there the night before. But to it the heretic Parker gathered such crowds of listeners that it was no longer large enough to hold them. The great Music Hall in Boston was then chosen for his use.

The earnest thousands who trooped up Sunday after Sunday to hear him preach were profoundly impressed. No trumped-up twenty minute speeches those such as some of our weak-backed congregations sit through with difficulty even, but solid sermons of an hour or two hours that sent people home with their ears tingling for a week. No place that for a lazy head, no school for exquisite graces, no rival of the dancing master— "You never made me your minister," he said, "to flatter or to please but to instruct and serve."[37] To listen to him regularly was indeed a liberal education not in theology or religion alone, but in politics, history, literature, science, art, everything that interests rational minds.

His figure was not imposing, nor his gestures fine, nor his action graceful. He moved little as he spoke; his hand only occasionally rose and fell on the manuscript before him as if to emphasize a passage to himself. The discourse was read in an unmusical, monotonous voice. The audience was held by the spell of earnest thought alone, uttered in simple language. He did not care to "file his line," and had no time to do it. He preferred Anglo-Saxon words.

"There he stands, looking more like a ploughman than priest,
  If not dreadfully awkward, not graceful at least,
  His gestures all downright and same, if you will,
  As of brown-fisted Hobnail in hoeing a drill;
  But his periods fall on you, stroke after stroke,
  Like the blows of a lumberer felling an oak."[38]

"Is that Theodore Parker?" once asked a plain man who heard him. "You told me he was a remarkable man, but I understood every word he said."[39]

Parker's audiences were singularly untractable. They did not assemble in the usual churchly fashion, from habit in a mood for reverence. They came in such clothes as they had, sat in such seats as were vacant, went out if tired. Some brought newspapers in their pockets which they read in the few minutes preceding the preacher's entrance. Some betrayed by their manner that they regarded the prayer as an impertinence, and others that they came for the sermon, not for the Scripture or hymn. The sittings were free; the expenses—never heavy, for Theodore Parker was ever "greedy of a small salary"—were met by voluntary contributions. No tie held his parishioners (at one time they numbered 7000) but that of intellectual and moral satisfaction.

In January, 1847, Parker took a house in Essex Place, directly in the rear of Phillips's residence, their gardens touching each other. It was a happy occurrence for both. They differed radically in their religious views. But they had much in common. With both, liberty was a passion.

The house was roomy, but books overflowed from top to bottom. The walls were lined with books. These gradually crept over the door, the windows, and the chimney pieces, thence into little adjoining rooms, and finally stepped boldly down the stairs one flight at a time, for three flights colonizing every room by the way and finally pausing reluctantly only at the kitchen door. The bathroom, the closets, the attic apartments were inundated with books.

Parker was a voracious reader. Often when some lecture engagement brought Phillips home late at night, from his own chamber window he saw the light burning in Parker's study. But those midnight carousals with books numbered the days of Theodore Parker.

3.

The great apostle of Temperance, Father Mathew, landed in New York on Monday, July 2, 1849. The city bade him welcome in the name of America. Mayor Woodhull's address was a triumph of bombast—"Frightful are the ravages of the plague and vast the preparations to stay its desolating course, but the destroying Angel of Intemperance has entombed more victims than any pestilence which has ever afflicted the human family."[40] In the evening the Common Council gave a public dinner at which healths were drunk in glasses of pure "Croton."

Father Mathew was no lean, sour visaged temperance reformer. He was a broad solid looking man with grey hair and mild intelligent eyes, a massive nose and countenance and full lips.

Having administered the pledge of total abstinence to some twenty thousand persons in New York and Brooklyn, he journeyed eastward and arrived in Boston on July 24. A barouche and four horses and a municipal committee awaited him at the city line. Temperance societies took charge of him. Throngs of men, women, and children—and not Irish alone—took of him medals and pledges in Faneuil Hall. In one street where there were sixteen grog shops his presence closed all but three.

The Abolitionists hailed him as a welcome ally. No sooner had he arrived than he received a letter of invitation to be present at a meeting to celebrate "the anniversary of the most thrilling event of the nineteenth century, the abolition of slavery in the West Indies." Garrison and Dr. Bowditch interviewed him. Turning to Garrison he said—"Mr. Garrison, your name is very familiar to me." "Yes," said Garrison smiling, "I am somewhat notorious, though not as yet very popular." He then added, "You have some very warm friends in Cork.' Garrison told him he was aware of the fact. And he went on to extend the invitation on behalf of the Massachusetts Anti-Slavery Society, handing him the letter containing the invitation in official form. Taking the letter with some agitation and embarrassment, Father Mathew said—"I have as much as I can do to save men from the slavery of intemperance, without attempting the overthrow of any other kind of slavery." Garrison reminded him that seven years before an Address was sent from Ireland signed by Daniel O'Connell, Theobald Mathew, and 70,000 others invoking the

Irishmen and Irishwomen of America to hate slavery and cling to the Abolitionists as the only true and consistent friends of liberty. "Oh," said Father Mathew, as if the act had long since passed from his memory into oblivion, "I do now recollect that I signed such an Address and I also recollect that at that time it subjected me to a good deal of odium." Finding nothing was to be gained by protracting the interview, Garrison and his friend left.[41]

Garrison published an account of the interview, together with a copy of his letter welcoming Father Mathew and of the Address of 1842, as a crushing indictment. "It is with great sorrow of heart," he said, "that I lay these facts before America, Ireland, and the world."[42]

Newspapers rushed to the defence of the apostle. The Boston Herald ran a headline—"Shameful Attempt of the Boston Abolitionists to Inveigle Father Mathew into their Ranks."[43] The Boston Daily Times declared Garrison "a lunatic, a harmless bore, whose only desire is 'to kick up a row.' "[44]

The Abolitionists kept up a barrage of attacks. They addressed five open letters to Father Mathew, made copious extracts of O'Connell's withering speeches on the blood guiltiness of America, and attacked the priest's neutral stand. Garrison called him a "false priest," holding him responsible "for leading his countrymen astray, and for adding to the anguish and despair of the slave." "We don't believe," remarked Elizur Wright in his Chronotype, "he cares the value of a copper cent for the cause of Freedom and Temperance, except so far as it will build up his own fame."[45]

Not a syllable on the question of slavery fell from Father Mathew's lips. He maintained throughout his visit a most discreet silence.

"It was the boast of O'Connell," wrote Wendell Phillips to his friend James Haughton of Dublin, "that he would never set foot on American soil, while it was polluted with slavery. Father Mathew not only visits us, but consents to go padlocked that he may be feted! . . . He has no right to sell his silence in slavery, that, with thirty pieces of silver, he may swell the treasury of Irish teetotalism. Silence from such a visitor is most significant support."[46]

The Abolition attack, however, never seriously hampered Father Mathew. Though Senator Davis branded him "a wolf in sheep's clothing to attack slavery,"[47] he was admitted to the floor of both Houses of Congress and was entertained by the President. The South welcomed him cordially; his heart was rather with the slaveholder than with the Abolitionist.

A slight misunderstanding with Georgia was neatly adjusted. Father Mathew was notified by Judge Lumpkin, President of the Georgia State Temperance Society, that the invitation extended by that body and accepted by Father Mathew was revoked—at least pending an explanation. The Judge had been supplied with a copy of the Irish Address of 1842 with Father Mathew's signature, and he wrote to ask if the document were genuine. The Apostle hesitated long, then sent the merest line in reply, saying nothing to the point, but referring the inquirer to a report of his interview with Garrison. This the Judge looked upon as shuffling, since it involved no recantation of the Address. And peace was not made till Father Mathew wrote again to this "honored and dear sir" with a profuse apology for not knowing he was a high and mighty judge and so addressing him before. He renewed his "solemn declaration (to Mr. Garrison) of being firmly resolved not to interfere in any the slightest degree with the institutions of this mighty Republic." More, he pleaded, should not be asked of him in "this emphatically free country." And thus placating Georgia, he earned the torchlight procession afterwards tendered him in Augusta.[48]

When he finally bade farewell to the citizens of the United States, the *Liberator* printed his speech and in the next column added an "*important omission in the foregoing—Address from the People of Ireland to their countrymen and countrywomen in America* signed by Daniel O'Connell, Father Mathew himself, and 70,000 other Irishmen."[49]

CHAPTER FIFTEEN

PLUNDER OF MEXICO—
THE FREE SOIL PARTY

1.

What should be the character of the new states into which the territories were to be mapped out? Should they be slave states or free states. How should the balance of power be kept?[1]

From the very start, this issue forced itself into Congressional discussion. It became angrier and angrier with the lapse of time and the development of sectional interests.

The states were admitted in pairs—one slave, the other free. Whenever two new Free State Senators came to Washington, two new Slave State Senators must come too and the South maintain the balance of power. The populous North was sure of controlling the House; the South clung desperately to the Senate.

When in 1819 Missouri applied for admission to the Union with a State constitution permitting slavery, there was a prolonged debate over the whole question throughout the country. In the following year, Congress passed a law providing for the admission of Missouri, but to restore the balance Maine was separated from Massachusetts and admitted to the Union as a free State. It was further enacted that slavery was to be forever prohibited from all territory of the United States north of the parallel 36° 30′, that is, north of the Southern boundary of Missouri. By this act the Mason and Dixon line was extended through the Louisiana purchase, westward to what were then the Spanish possessions.

In 1837 the thirteen slave states were balanced by a like number of free states. The South still had Florida which would in time become a slave state. Against this single territory was the immense region to the Northwest, equal in area to all the slave states combined, which, according to the Ordinance of 1787 and the Missouri Compromise, had been consecrated to freedom. The equilibrium would be destroyed, the very life of slavery threatened. Foreseeing this condition planters turned hungry eyes to the South and West, and started a movement for the seizure of more territory—"more pens to cram slaves in."

Bands of hardy farmers and lordly planters, droves of hunters, slave adventurers, outlaws poured into the flourishing Mexican province of Texas, started a Revolution, crushed the troops sent out against them "to restore order", and wrung from the defeated Mexican commander, Santa Anna, an official recognition of Texan independence. Having enrolled themselves "among the independent nations of the earth," they now turned with eager expectancy to the United States praying for admission to the Union. Their constitution guaranteed the existence of slavery. So the answer to the Texan overture was prompt and emphatic in the South: Mississippi, Alabama, and Tennessee by solemn resolution called upon Congress to admit the Lone Star State to the Union.

The North, however, vigorously protested. The annexation of Texas was pronounced unconstitutional and revolutionary.[2] Statesmen like John Quincy Adams, merchants like Abbot Lawrence, asserted that success of the plot would be equivalent to dissolution of the Union and urged forcible resistance. For years the country was agitated by the question. "Men who would have whispered Disunion with white lips a year ago," wrote Phillips to Elizabeth Pease, "now love to talk about it, and many leading men will talk as we were once laughed at for talking awhile ago."[3]

"I trust, indeed," exclaimed Channing, "that Providence will beat back and humble our cupidity and ambition. . . . I ask whether as a people we can stand forth in the sight of God, in the sight of nations and adopt this atrocious policy? Sooner perish! Sooner our name be blotted out from the record of nations!"[4] With a shout of defiance, Garrison called for secession of the Northern States if Texas came into the Union with her slaves.[5]

"As for Disunion," remarked Wendell Phillips, "it must and will come. Calhoun wants it at one end of the Union, Garrison wants it at the other. It is written in the counsels of God."[6] Besides, the Texas wrangle was a public education. Every speech was another nail driven in the coffin of the system he hated. For the one thing slavery could not abide was examination.

Senators Bate and Choate of Massachusetts were lukewarm. When the resolution against the annexation of Texas was pending in the Senate, Massachusetts Congressmen called upon them vehemently urging them "to feel, to think, and to act as Massachusetts men, who have been reared under the institution of the Pilgrim Fathers, should think, feel, and act."[7]

There was a widespread feeling in the North that the South would retreat before the storm of words. Phillips was not so sanguine. Calhoun had the power,—why should he not use it? Early in 1845 he wrote to Elizabeth Pease: "Well, Texas, you'll see, is coming in. We always said it would and were laughed at." And he added to Webb: "There's one pleasure in having Texas admitted. I have always told these 'Doughface Whigs' that they hadn't spunk enough to keep it out and they've cried out, 'Oh, you may trust a Whig Senate!' To which I've cried, 'Fudge!' —and now it proves so."[8]

His prophecy was fulfilled. On the last day of February, Calhoun, having failed to carry the Treaty of Annexation through the Senate by the requisite two-thirds majority, accomplished his purpose by resorting to a joint resolution of both houses which called for a mere majority. Texas, an empire in itself, was given the option of subduing its immense area into four states as soon as it should have sufficient population.

Money played as scandalous a part in annexation as did slavery. The independent Texas nation had had little cash. It had waged its war and managed its government only by issuing paper certificates, in reckless amounts. Millions of dollars of this scrip at face value had been bought by American speculators. Annexation to the Union would make the future of Texas safe, and every dollar of dubious script would be worth a hundred cents. Enormous fortunes were at stake and millions were floating around the capital for greedy Congressmen of easy consciences. Joshua Giddings asserted that a vote for annexation could bring $50,000.[9]

Annexation meant Disunion, the chiefs of the Whig party had declared. Now they backed down, ate their words, and went in for an era of "good feeling". But the agitation had roused the North.

A meeting to protest the admission of Texas as a slave state was held in Faneuil Hall on Tuesday evening, November 4. Rain and hail fell in torrents, thunder cracked and rolled, lightning blazed vividly—but 2,000 people were present. "I hail this moment, friends and fellow citizens," declared Wendell Phillips, "as one of kindred spirit. It says to Texas standing at our door with her constitutional provisions for slavery, 'only free women can pass this threshold. Only free men ought to dwell under this roof!' "[10]

Daniel Webster, three days later in the same hall, remarked— "I can only say for one that if it should fall to my lot to have a vote on such a question, and I vote for the admission into this Union of ANY State with a constitution which prohibits even the legislature from ever setting the bondsmen free, I shall never show my head again, depend upon it, in Faneuil Hall."[11]

The new settlement did not stay settled. Since Mexico had never recognized or accepted the independence of Texas, annexation to the United States was a spark applied to tinder. The spark was fanned to a flame by the slaveholder, President Polk.

On Saturday, May 9, 1846, Polk received the welcome news that a clash of arms had taken place on the eastern bank of the Rio Grande. On the following Monday he sent a message to Congress—"War exists, and notwithstanding all our efforts to avoid it, exists by the act of Mexico herself."[12]

But four months before, Polk had secretly ordered General Taylor to advance his forces to the disputed zone of the Rio Grande. The territory which General Taylor occupied was claimed by Mexico, and Texas herself had offered to arbitrate the question. Even a weak power like Mexico could not submit to being thus robbed.

Theodore Parker called the war a wicked one, "waged for the plunder of Mexico." He described the United States as "a great boy fighting a little one and the little one feeble and sick. What makes it worse is, the little boy is in the right, and the big boy is in the wrong and tells solemn lies to make his side seem right. . . . This is a war for slavery, a mean and infamous war, an aristocratic war, a war against the best interests of mankind. If God please, we will die a thousand times, but never draw blade in this wicked war." (Cries of "Throw him over"—he was speaking in the gallery.) "What would you do next?" (A shout—"Drag you out of the hall.") "What good would that do? It would not wipe off the infamy of this war, would not make it any less wicked."[13]

Lowell saw in the war a crime against God and man. Political sophistries found no mercy at his hands.

> Ez for war, I call it murder,—
> There you hev it plain an' flat;
> I don't want to go no furder
> Than my Testyment fer that;
> God hez sed so plump an' fairly,
> It's ez long ez it is broad,
> An' you've gut to git up airly
> Ef you want to take in God. . . .
>
> Aint it cute to see a Yankee
> Take sech everlastin' pains
> All to git the Devil's thankee
> Helpin' on 'em weld their chains?
> Wy, it's jest ez clear ez figgers,
> Clear ez one an' one make two,
> Chaps that make black slaves o' niggers
> Want to make white slaves o' you.[14]

Abolitionist leaders rejoiced that the annexation of Texas and the war with Mexico brought to their ranks recruits without number and that the State of Massachusetts officially protested both against annexation and war. The annual report of the Massachusetts Anti-Slavery Society for the year 1845 declared: "The triumphs of the American armies are the triumphs of cruelty, of injustice, of oppression" won by "a fanatical horde of banditti." Wendell Phillips was the author of a heated resolution, unanimously passed, denouncing Governor George N. Briggs "as perjured in his own principles, as a traitor by his own showing—as one before whose guilt the infamy of Arnold . . . becomes respectability and decency." Governor Briggs's "offence" was that he called on the commonwealth to rally to the war.[15]

America "conquered a peace" with Mexico. As a result she acquired the additional territory of New Mexico and California. She filched Mexico not to provide, as was said, "land for the landless" but as Benjamin Wade of Ohio said, "niggers for the niggerless."[16]

In the summer of 1846, when the war with Mexico was only a few months old, President Polk asked Congress to vote him two million dollars to be used in the acquisition of new territory. Judge David Wilmot of Pennsylvania, a quiet, stout, Dutch-built man, with light hair and florid complexion, offered an amendment. He awoke next day a famous man.

The words "Wilmot Proviso" were heard at every breakfast table, dinner table, and tea table throughout the country. "God raised up a David of old to slay the giant of Gath," said General James W. Nye of New York. "So hath David Wilmot with the sling of freedom and the smooth stone of truth, struck the giant Slavery between the eyes. He reels; let us push him over."[17]

Judge Wilmot was the real parent and undoubted prophet of the Proviso. Others cooperated—Hannibal Hamlin of Maine, Preston King of New York, and Jacob Brinkerhoff of Ohio. The essential language of the Proviso, however, was Jefferson's, the essence taken from the Ordinance of 1787: neither slavery nor involuntary servitude shall ever exist in any territory acquired from the Republic of Mexico.[18]

The House of Representatives passed the bill twice, but it failed twice in the Senate. The idea embodied in the Proviso, however, would not die. "It may be," roared Chase, "you will succeed in burying the ordinance of freedom, but the people will write upon its tomb, 'I will rise again.' "[19]

Wilmot defended his bill:

"Shall the South be permitted by aggression, by invasion
of the right, by subduing free territory, and planting slavery
upon it, to wrest these promises from Northern freemen,
and turn them to the accomplishment of their own sectional
purposes and schemes? This is the question. Men of the
North answer. Shall it be so? Shall we of the North submit
to it? If we do, we are coward slaves, and deserve to have
the manacles fastened upon our own limbs."[20]

Again Calhoun defended the slavocracy against the "foul
slanders" of its enemies. And the Cassandra of politics warned:

"Sir, the day that the balance between the two sections
of the country—the slave-holding and the non-slave-holding
states—is destroyed, is a day that will not be far removed
from political revolution, anarchy, civil war, and widespread disaster. . . . But if this policy should be carried
out, woe, woe, I say, to this Union!"[21]

The "furioso" utterance of Calhoun frightened the mercantile
and political classes of the North. But the renewed agitation
rendered further service to liberty—it made more Abolitionists.
There was irony in Wendell Phillips's remark in Mrs. Chapman's
Abolition annual, the well printed and well edited *Liberty Bell*—
"It may yet come to pass that professors of Harvard College will
give it out to future generations, as a subject for themes, 'Which
did the most, Garrison or Calhoun, for the downfall of American
slavery?' "[22]

In protest against the arrogance and cupidity of the South
the Abolitionists broadcast petitions calling on the Legislature
of Massachusetts to propose a dissolution of the Union. On
March 17, 1848, Wendell Phillips made an earnest and vigorous
speech on the Disunion Petitions before the Legislative Judiciary Committee.

"Mr. Chairman—we ask for Disunion, and we are ready
to meet all the obloquy which such a proposition begets.
Disunion is not a rare word in our national history. Dis-

appointed ambition has often, for a moment, longed for separate confederacies, in which there would be more Presidential chairs than one. Parties, in the hour of defeat, have talked of revolution, when revolution was their only chance of success. And sometimes, even a State thwarted in its favorite purpose has threatened to shoot madly from its sphere. But the Abolitionists are the only men who have ever calmly, soberly, and from mature conviction, proclaimed at the outset, their purpose to seek the dissolution of the American Union; and this from no bitterness of personal or party disappointment, but solely at the bidding of principle, and from a sense of duty.

"These petitions are called revolutionary. We accept the description. They are intended to be. We hope they are in another sense also, Revolutionary—that is, akin to the measures and principles of our 1776. Wise lawyers doubt, it is said, whether a State can constitutionally secede from the Union. No matter how that question is settled. We do not propose this as a constitutional measure. If such a course be not allowable under the Constitution, there is such a thing as going over it. The right of the people to alter their form of government has never been denied here. It is upon that right we stand, the sacred right of Revolution. If, as the South has so constantly contended, Secession is a constitutional right, well—we will commend the poisoned chalice to her lips. . . . But if the better law of New England rejects that doctrine—well, also. There is a right beneath, and more ancient than the parchment,—the right of each generation to govern itself."[23]

Phillips spoke for two hours. After he finished at six o'clock, Garrison arose, but it was night and most of the people left the Hall. "Why does it (Disunion) create so much excitement now?" asked Phillips before the fourteenth annual meeting of the American Anti-Slavery Society. "The very men who launched the Constitution, and watched it with a feeling made up of two-thirds of doubt, and one of hope, and nothing of expectation, as a boy launches his shingle boat on the pond, hardly thought it would swim. . . ."[24]

Phillips again returned to the theme of Disunion at the next meeting of the Society.

> "We make no secret of our determination to tread the law and the Constitution under our feet. Shall I tell you why? Society in this country is a pyramid resting upon its base, while that of the Old World tottles upon its apex. Public opinion here is mightier than laws and constitutions; and where the statute favors oppression, we take an appeal against it directly to the conscience and moral sense of the nation. The American people do not dare to be logical—they shrink from carrying out their own theories. When those theories come in conflict with some favored interest in Church or State, they turn a short corner, and bow submissively to the Devil of Compromise! Not so, however, with the Abolitionists. Laws and Constitutions are nothing to them, when they are found conflicting with the higher, the eternal law of God. . . .
>
> "Daniel Webster says you are a law-abiding community, but thank God, you are not. Massachusetts, at least, is not. She is not quite so low as her statute book, for we defy despotism by disobeying the law.
>
> "Men talk of Southern chivalry! It is mere froth and syllabub! We oppose to it the old Puritan idea of Duty. It is by this alone that any thing can be done. . . ."[25]

"O noble lawlessness!" Phillips exclaimed later, "Christian trampling on majorities! Holy rebellion! But I want organized rebellion. I want a legal rebellion. I want a recognized rebellion. I have no regard for what is called constitution law. The day has gone by when the Constitution was anything more than a roll of parchment, and we are continually paying less regard to it."[26]

"Wendell Phillips never forgets his taste or his breeding," remarked the *Liberator;* "he is always the gentleman, however vehement or fierce his denunciations."[27]

Out of the furor aroused over Texas annexation and Mexican strife, Wilmot Proviso and Disunion activity, rose the Free Soil Party. In the election of 1848 it split the old parties in nearly every Northern State.

On May 22, the Democratic National Convention nominated
Lewis Cass of Michigan upon a platform framed to suit the
South, and from all over the Free States there broke out at once
cries of rage and disappointment. "Had a bombshell fallen into
our quiet city yesterday, it could not have created more consternation," said the Whig Chicago *Journal.*[28]

But when on the 10th of June, the Whig National Convention
nominated Zachary Taylor without any platform and howled
down the Wilmot Proviso, Western Reserve Whigs rose as one
man to repudiate him. "As we anticipated," said the *True Democrat*, "the Whigs have nominated Zachary Taylor for President.
And this is the cup offered by slaveholders for us to drink. We
loathe the sight. We will neither touch, taste, nor handle the
unclean thing."[29]

Liberty Party men, Conscience Whigs, Free Soil Democrats,
New York Barnburners (those who supported the Wilmot Proviso) banded themselves together into a Free Soil Party. They
nominated the adroit Martin Van Buren and Charles Francis
Adams as candidates for president and vice-president respectively and adopted a ringing platform—"We declare that Congress
has no more power to make a slave than to make a king. . . . We
inscribe on our banner: 'FREE SOIL, FREE SPEECH, FREE
LABOR, AND FREE MEN,' and under it will fight on, and
fight ever, until a triumphant victory shall reward our ex-
ertions."[30] Joshua Leavitt, an enthusiastic Garrisonian Abolitionist, gained the floor to make Van Buren's nomination unanimous, his utterance choked by feeling: "The Liberty Party is
not dead," he shouted, 'but translated."[31]

The choice of Van Buren was unfortunate. Thousands who
had vowed never to support Taylor preferred to eat their words
rather than vote for hated "little Van." Old line Democrats
("Hunkers") called him the traitor, the hypocrite, the Judas
Iscariot of the nineteenth century. But the Liberty Party had
secured its principles, and given others the men.

The campaign was colorful and tuneful. Free Soilers sang
themselves hoarse up to election day.

> The North is ripe for the Proviso,
>   Hurrah! Hurrah! Hurrah!
> She'll back the names from Buffalo,
>   Hurrah! Hurrah! Hurrah!
>
> Whigs, Democrats, we'll all unite
> And Liberty boys—for our cause is right
>   Hurrah! Etc.[32]

Greeley brought the *Tribune* around to a sour espousal of Taylor. "The country does not deserve a visitation of that pot-bellied, mutton-headed cucumber Cass." But Bryant and the *Evening Post* warmly espoused Van Buren: "Shall the Great Republic," he asked, "no longer be known as the home of the free and the asylum of the oppressed, but as the home of the slave and the oppressor of the poor?"[33]

Van Buren received 291,263 votes—four times the number given to Birney in 1844. In New York where he received 120,510 votes, he held the balance of power. Taylor was elected by the vote of New York which, except for the split in the Democratic ranks, would have gone to Cass.

The Free Soil vote was so large that the *Liberator* remarked: "The Slave Power is beginning to falter—fresh adherents are daily rallying around the standard of Liberty, and the cry of 'No Union With Slaveholders' is causing the knees of the oppressor to tremble."[34]

But the Free Soil Party found as little favor in the eyes of the Abolitionists as the perishing Liberty Party which it had swallowed.[35] Garrisonians felt that any attempt to restrict slavery by law was precisely equivalent to damning up the Mississippi with bulrushes.

"*Free Soil* party, indeed!" exclaimed Henry Wright. "Do they go for Free Soil in Virginia?—in any existing slave states now covering one million of square miles? No! They are pledged to sustain and perpetuate it there; they only go for free soil in newly acquired—PLUNDERED—territory. . . ."[36]

Wendell Phillips poked fun at those Abolitionists who hankered after the ballot and office. "A man fancies that, at whatever cost, he must go up and be a citizen, even if he sacrifice to idols, to gain permission to touch a ballot. As Andrew Fair-service said, if you put a pudding on one side of hell, and an Englishman on the other, he will spring for it. So with an American, if you put him on one side of the crater and a ballot on the other, he will risk all to get it."[37]

Later, before the New England Anti-Slavery Society, Phillips defended the stand of the Abolitionists against the Free Soilers.

"The only real dispute between us and those who allow the Constitution to be pro-slavery, is one regarding personal honor and integrity. Shall a man, for any purpose, promise to do what he does not intend to do? I know it is rare, in our days, to see men refuse office and power from any such scruples. But history, from the earliest Christians downwards, is full of instances of men who refused all connection with government, and all influence which office could bestow, rather than deny their principles, or aid in doing wrong. Yet I never heard them called either idiots or over-scrupulous. Sir Thomas More need never have mounted the scaffold, had he only consented to take the oath of supremacy. He had only to tell a lie with solemnity, as we are asked to do, and he might not only have saved his life, but as the trimmers of his day would have told him, doubled his influence. . . .

"Indeed we are only doing what all honest men have done in all ages of the world. Look at the course of the British Catholics, submitting to exclusion, for more than a century, from professions and offices, from the House of Commons and the House of Lords, rather than qualify themselves by an oath abjuring the Pope. They might have purchased power and office by the price of one falsehood. One lie would have placed the Duke of Norfolk, any time during the century, in the seat of his father! Do we honor him less that he refused power on such considerations?

"Look at the course of O'Connell. Remember his love of office, of power, of political influence—with a nation in his right hand, shut out, as a Catholic, from the House of Commons. Did he take the oath of abjuration that he might gain his rightful place? No. He stayed outside the door of that House till after two elections; in 1828, the oath being

abolished, he pushed door and oath before him and strode
to his rightful place and influence like an honest man.
(Great cheering.). . . .

"Yet when in a nation like ours, we strive to be worthy
followers of these I have named, men call us 'impracticable'
and 'morbidly scrupulous,' and priests taunt us with folly
for 'throwing away our influence.'. . .

"If Free Soilers go to Congress, holding themselves free
from every supposed compromise relating to slavery, let
them tell the nation so. (Cheers.) If they go holding themselves at liberty to disregard, in their official capacity, the
laws of the land, let them tell the nation so. (Cheers.) If,
as we are told, Free Soil Senators adopt it, as a rule of their
official conduct, to appoint no man to office who is willing
to obey the laws of the land, we shall criticise, and *criticise,*
and *criticise,* till they avow the fact in the face of the Senate
itself, instead of leaving their friends to claim it for them
in our meetings. (Cheers.)

"The frankest man of the party, one standing in the very
front of the van, when asked how he justified his oath, answered— 'Oh, I've sworn so often, I never think anything
about it!'

"Our quarrel with politicians and parties will never cease
till their anti-slavery be like Cicero's noble description of
law—not one thing at Christiana and another thing at Washington—not one thing at Faneuil Hall and another thing at
Pittsburgh—not one thing in an anti-slavery meeting to gain
confidence, and another thing in November to gain votes
—but everywhere, at all times, and in all capacities—radical,
defiant, aggressive, trampling on all slave laws, and either
openly defying the legality of slavery itself, or repudiating
the government as a covenant with death and an agreement
with hell. (Cheers.)

"The conviction that *SLAVERY IS A SIN* is the Gibraltar
of our cause. We cannot make crises but we can prepare for
them. Perhaps slavery is finally to be starved out, rather
than reasoned down or prayed down. Selfish and material
interests, the laws of labor and trade, may be the direct and
immediate causes of its abolition. Disunion—war, civil or
foreign—may break the chain. It should be our object to
create such a public opinion as will soonest set these

agencies in motion, and most effectually use the opportunities that occur."[38]

After 1848 the tide set against the Free Soil Party. "Barnburners," Free Conscience Whigs, insurgents rejoined the old parties and the movement collapsed.

The results were mainly educational. "Free Soil" shaped the principles, forged the arguments, and trained the leaders who in 1856 formed the Republican Party.

Some in the Abolition ranks growing fainthearted questioned the meagre fruits of moral agitation. Phillips replied—

"Some Abolitionists are discouraged at what they call our ill success. 'What have you done?' they ask. Done? Set the nation on fire. Driven the frightened slave holders to Mexico to get land and help in their despair; and they will yet find that this attempt to save their system is like a man's catching up a red hot iron to defend himself with. Done? Broken two or three of the greatest sects in pieces—this John Quincy Adams says is the only thing which will ever uproot slavery. Done? Scattered to the four winds the most gigantic effort of the age—the Evangelical Alliance, because it would betray the slave. Confounded both political parties —and fixed the eye of Europe upon our infamy, so that most Americans are forced to be hypocrites and pretend to be Abolitionists or get no rest on the other side of the ocean. Is not this enough success for a few men and women in a dozen years? If this is called failure, I should like to have someone describe what success would look like! If Providence will only grant us such another dozen years of failure, you and I will find occasion to join the slave in his shout of jubilee."[39]

2

When one thousand dollars funded in ebony took to its heels and ran away, the slavemasters felt in their pockets a vacuum which like nature they abhorred.

Towards the end of May, 1849, several of the "chattels personal" suddenly appeared in Boston en route for Canada. Two of these were William and Ellen Craft, husband and wife. Ellen, almost white, impersonated a planter seeking medical treatment in the North while her husband acted the role of her "Negro boy." She carried her right arm in a sling so that she would not be expected to write, bandaged her smooth face, and put on a pair of green goggles. Thus disguised she succeeded in buying tickets for herself and "servant" without discovery. In the train she was terrified to see a gentleman who had known her from childhood. He even sat down by her and spoke to her, but saw in her only an invalid going North for her health. The most dangerous spot was Baltimore where every white man with a slave was required to make a written statement proving his right of property before he could be allowed to go to Philadelphia. But Ellen could not write for she had bound up her arm in a sling. After some conversation, Ellen told the officer that she knew no one in Baltimore and had no proofs her "boy" William was her slave, but that he was necessary to her on account of her illness and she must take him on. As the train was about to start, the officer relented and Baltimore was safely passed. In a few hours they not only escaped but were entertained as heroes. They took refuge in Boston.[40]

Wendell Phillips greeted them in Faneuil Hall on May 31, 1849, amid thunders of applause.

"We say that they may make their little motions and pass their little laws in Washington, but that *Faneuil Hall Repeals Them* in the name of the humanity of Massachusetts. (Great applause.)

"Give us the Bible for a text book, and Faneuil Hall for a pulpit, and we will yet control the moral sentiment of this nation, though we give you the odds of thirty thousand pro-slavery ministers. (Cheers.)

"Fellow citizens, when such a man as Frederick Douglass tells you his history, the result of American prejudice—speaks the honest indignation of his race against his wrongs—when he tells you of your own conduct towards him—keep your hands by your sides. Hush those echoing plaudits of yours; keep silent. What right have you to applaud? What have you done to aid the slave to his liberty? What have you done to open this Hall for his welcome? . . . You who swear so often personally or by deputy, to support the laws from which he fled, why do you bless his flight? Can he find shelter in any pulpit in Boston? How many? One, two, or three, alone. Do one of two things—confess that your hearts blush for the deeds your hands are not ashamed to do; or go, coin your plaudits into statutes, and then we will all cry, 'God save the slave sheltering Commonwealth of Massachusetts.' "(Applause.)[41]

Zachary Taylor recommended Friday, August 3, as a day of fasting on account of the cholera, and on that day the Abolitionists met at Worcester, Massachusetts, to celebrate the anniversary of West India Emancipation.

Fourteen cars carried the throng from Boston. They came from a distance of a hundred miles and in almost every direction. The grove where the meeting was held was not sufficiently level or shady. The heat was terrific and every seat broke down before noon. It was not comfortable either to stand or sit on the ground. Yet for six or seven hours the audience stood packed together listening eagerly to speeches by Burleigh, Parker, Emerson, Adin Ballou, and Wendell Phillips. A proposal was made to adjourn to the spacious town hall. "How many people will the hall hold?" it was asked. "2500," was the response. "Then not more than half of those who are assembled here can get into it," was the rejoinder. And they voted to remain in the grove even without seats and with discomfort. Hymns and songs were sung during the proceedings.

Phillips made a fiery speech—

"The world is our jury and we indict the cowering slaveholder before it.

"Law forms are only parchment. Hearts, Thoughts, Dollars, Truth rule the world. Give the American people, give the North, the wish, and any unprincipled Democrat or Whig (perhaps the adjective is superfluous) will find the *way*. . .

"The West India experiment,—was it successful? Ask the American clergy and people throughout. Oh, yes! And why?

Because the exports did not fail! . . . There is as much sugar in the Liverpool market from those islands as before they were freed!

"As if there were nothing but sugar in God's world! As if man was made to work and for nothing but work! As if the American people were to test a great moral event by hogsheads of sugar and puncheons of rum! I do not care whether the slave worked or not. I do not care whether the slave made one ounce of sugar or one pint of rum. It would not grieve me much to learn that he lay lazily under the graceful palm of his native land. I do not care much to know what he did. There is nothing worse than slavery. If he did not cut his master's throat, the experiment was successful. There is nothing but anarchy that is worse than slavery. . .

"Suppose that a man had met Sam Adams after the Revolution, and asked him how it had succeeded. Sam says to him, Look round on these thirteen free and independent colonies. But, says our friend, how are the stores on Long Wharf? Do they let for as much now as they used to in '65? Are you as rich as you were? Is your house in Beacon Street, Mr. Hancock, worth what it was? This depreciated currency that I hear so much about, how is it as to that? Where is the industry of Massachusetts? At a discount. Where are your wharves? Grass grown. Where are your people? Broken up in all their habits of industry, would be the answer. Where is your capital? Wasted. Where are your farms? Untilled. Where is Charlestown? Burnt. Where are your young men of twenty? 'Their bones lie mingled with the soil of every state from New England to Georgia.' Where is the garnered capital of the thirteen industrious colonies? Scattered, most of it, to the winds.

"Ah, has the Revolution, then, been a failure? Was Sam Adams mistaken? Was John Hancock a fool? . . . So ought the American newspapers to tell you now, when they ask us to prove the success of the West India experiment, by their exports; when the cane is as fruitful, and that the docks are as full as they were before.

"It is a sad commentary on the spirit of the age that the experiment of emancipation in the West Indies is judged of, always, by figures, by dollars and cents, not by the moral consequences. Shame on such reasoners!"

At the close of his speech, Phillips remarked: "You shall have the most eloquent lips, if you want them. Go home and call for him, and the mighty Daniel himself shall become a speaker for immediate emancipation; only set up a steeple where he can see the weathercocks setting North instead of South."[42]

The Oregon Bill organizing Oregon as a territory was before the Senate. Webster shook his mane like a lion and spoke as he had pledged himself to speak:—"I shall oppose all slavery extension and all increase of slave representation in all places, at all times, under all circumstances, even against all inducements, against all supposed limitation of great interests, against all combinations, against all compromise."[43]

CHAPTER SIXTEEN

"FIVE BLEEDING WOUNDS"

The whole country from San Francisco to Maine and New York was echoing the cry of "Gold, gold, gold." Along the docks, in shops and hotels, at wayside taverns, in stage coaches and canal boat cabins, it was the one absorbing topic of conversation—everyone had "the gold or yellow fever."

As fast as sails or steam could bear tidings to different points of the compass, adventurers hastened from China, from the Sandwich Islands, from Australia, and from the whole Pacific coast from Vancouver's Island to Valparaiso. "Ho for California" was a rallying cry of the press in the Atlantic cities.[1]

The census of 1850 gave California 92,597 inhabitants. Within ten years the number grew to 379,994.[2] The motley gold diggers needed a settled system of government so they asked President Polk to provide it. He failed to grant it. Congress could not do so because of the deadlock over slavery. Finally, seeing no immediate relief, the people of California took matters into their own hands. A convention was duly elected and met at Monterey in 1849. Provided with a copy of the constitution of Iowa by one of the delegates, the members at once entered upon grave and decorous deliberations, offering to the people at the close a "free state" constitution. In a burst of enthusiasm the proposed constitution was ratified by a huge majority of more than 12 to 1. With her document in hand, California knocked at the door of the Union.[3]

General Taylor, the incoming President, took the oath under a gloomy sky while a raw wind blew from the East and the intermittent snow flakes were falling. . . . There was just time

191

left before the Christmas holidays for Congress to receive the President's message dated twenty days earlier. The message was brief and frank, but modest in what it recommended. It favored most heartily the admission of California as a State at once with its anti-slavery constitution. As the people of New Mexico were taking steps likewise to frame a constitution after their own choice, he advised Congress to await their action. The vital principle of the Wilmot Proviso was not to be abandoned.[4]

Southerners flew into a rage at the prospect of losing the richest fruits of the Mexican War. "My Southern blood and feelings are up," wrote Alexander H. Stephens, "and I feel as if I am prepared to fight at all hazards and to the last extremity."[5] "God preserve the Union is my daily prayer," wrote General Scott.[6]

Henry Clay, now seventy-four, with one foot in the grave and cured of his ambition to become President, came to the capital[7] intending to remain "a calm and quiet looker-on." But all the ill blood and angry menace stirred the old cloud-compelling spirit within him to allay the storm. He had not lost his power to charm and he was a good manager. For the executive he felt amiable contempt.

Late in January he took the lead in the Senate and offered his "comprehensive scheme" of adjustment for healing the country's "five gaping wounds." For every wound Clay had a plaster: (1) Speedy admission of California as a free state; (2) Organization of the territories of New Mexico and Utah without mention of slavery, leaving them to decide that question for themselves; (3) Prohibition of the slave trade in the District of Columbia; (4) Enactment of a more stringent fugitive slave law; (5) Payment to Texas of ten million dollars cash from Uncle Sam's strong box for her pretense of a claim to New Mexico.

Except for the trivial exclusion of the hammer and auction block from under the eyes of Congress, all its concessions were favorable to the South.

Taylor threatened to destroy the plan. The mettle of the old warrior was rising; he stood firm as adamant against all threateners of disunion. There was danger of a breach between him and Clay. The latter, who had taken the fullest advantage of Taylor's modest demeanor when the session started, showed plain chagrin that the executive would not yield to him. In a disrespectful speech he objected to the President's policy that it stopped short of what the national situation required. Five "bleeding wounds" he countered off rhetorically on the fingers of his left hand. "Does the President heal them?" asked the orator. "No such thing. It is only to heal one of the five, and to leave the other four to bleed more profusely than ever by the sole admission of California." To which Senator Benton replied sarcastically, if Clay had had more fingers, he would have counted more wounds.[8] When Clay passed Taylor on the avenue without speaking to him, the President believed he had been deliberately cut. Henceforth Old Zach growled at Clay openly.[9]

He disliked the whole compromise of iniquities, wished the admission of California granted upon its own merits, and the integrity of the Union maintained at every hazard. "I would rather," he said impetuously to Webster, "have California wait than bring in all the territories on her back."[10] Fellow slave-holders from the Gulf States tried to drive the President from this attitude. A committee was appointed to call upon him. The delegates found him stubborn, and their interview was a stormy one. Would he pledge himself to sign no bill with the Wilmot Proviso in it? The old warrior replied that he would sign any bill that Congress presented him. The committee next threatened to break up the Union: "Southern officers," added one of them, "will refuse to obey your orders if you send troops to coerce Texas." "Then," responded Zachary Taylor in high excitement, "I will command the army in person, and any man who is taken in treason against the Union, I will hang as I did the deserters and spies at Monterrey." The committe withdrew crestfallen.

Senator Hannibal Hamlin of Maine approached the door of the President's room as they came out. Hamlin found the President pacing the floor and raging like a lion. He walked across the room three or four times before he even noticed Hamlin. Then he spoke to him, but still continued pacing the room. "Mr. Hamlin," he said, "what are you doing in the Senate with the

Omnibus Bill?" (Clay's compromise measures) "Mr. President, I believe the bill wrong in principle and am doing what I can to defeat it." The President's rejoinder was prompt and decided. "Stand firm, don't yield! It means disunion, and I am pained to learn that we have disunion men to deal with. Disunion is treason"—then with a blunt expletive, "If they attempt to carry on their schemes while I am President, they shall be dealt with as by law they deserve and executed."

General Scott used to say that when he spoke of General Taylor as "an upright man," his wife quickly added, "Yes, and a downright one." Among army officers there was a saying— "General Taylor never surrenders."[11] Though Polk and Marcy swore at him, the soldiers swore by him. They trusted him implicitly. A hero in homespun, "he looked more like an old farmer going to market with eggs to sell than anything I can think of," commented one captain.[12]

On February 5 and 6 the Great Pacificator defended his compromise by making a passionate plea for "a union of hearts" between the North and South through mutual concession. The infirmities of old age began to tell upon him. Walking up to the Capitol he asked a friend who accompanied him, "Will you lend me your arm, my friend? I find myself quite weak and exhausted this morning." He ascended the long flight of steps with difficulty, frequently stopping in order to catch his breath. His friend remarked, "Mr. Clay, had you not better defer your speech? You are certainly too ill to exert yourself today." "My dear friend," answered Clay, "I consider our country in danger, and if I can be the means in any measure of averting that danger, my health or my life is of little consequence."[13]

When he arrived at the Senate Chamber he beheld an inspiring spectacle. For several days his intention to address the Senate on February 5 was known, and from far and near, from Baltimore, Philadelphia, New York, Boston, thousands came to hear him. Women richly dressed waved their fans and smiled from the semi-circle which surrounded the grave deliberators—a "vast assemblage of beauty, grace, elegance, and intelligence," as the speaker himself said on the second day. Calhoun's place was vacant by reason of his sickness; Webster too was absent, arguing before the Supreme Court, but most of the other Senators were in their places.

The orator rose gracefully and majestically—a tall stooping man in black with a halting step, iron grey hair and sunken cheeks. An outburst of applause greeted him. It spread to the dense crowd outside the chambers until they lifted up such a shout that the officers of the Senate had to go out to clear the entrance. Then Clay began. His voice was faltering at first, but as he spoke, his vitality returned to him and he seemed to fling away all the ailments of old age by force of his undauntable will. Hour after hour he urged the advantages of his "comprehensive compromise." Southern opponents did not this time interrupt him.[14]

"I have witnessed many periods of great anxiety, of peril and of danger, even, to the country," he said, "but I have never before arisen to address any assembly so oppressed, so appalled, so anxious. . .

"Mr. President, it is passion, passion—party, party, and intemperance—that is all I dread in the adjustment of the great questions which unhappily at this time divide our distracted country. Sir, at this moment we have in the legislative bodies of the Capitol and in the States twenty odd furnaces in full blast, emitting heat, and passion, and intemperance, and diffusing them throughout the whole extent of this bright land. Two months ago all was calm in comparison to the present moment. All now is uproar, confusion, and menace to the existence of the Union, and to the happiness and safety of this people. Sir, I implore Senators, I entreat them, by all that they expect hereafter, and by all that is dear to them here below, to repress the ardor of these passions, to look to their country, to its interests, to listen to the voice of reason . . .

"What do you want? What do you want who reside in the free States? You want that there shall be no slavery introduced into the territories acquired from Mexico. Well, have not you got it in California already, if admitted as a State? Have not you got it in New Mexico, in all human probability also? What more do you want? You have got what is worth a thousand Wilmot Provisos. You have got Nature itself on your side. You have the fact itself on your side.

You have the truth staring you in the face that no slavery
is existing there. Well, if you are men; if you can rise from
the mud and slough of party struggles and elevate yourselves to the heights of patriots, what will you do? You will
look at the fact as it exists. You will say this fact was unknown to my people. You will say they acted on one set of
facts, we have got another set of facts here influencing us
and we will act as patriots, as responsible men, as lovers of
unity, and above all of this Union. . . ."[15]

Clay ended his supreme effort. Men crowded about him to
take his hand and women to kiss his face. Never had he appeared
so grand. He had been the darling of his friends. Now he was
almost their God.

Clay's self-esteem was so great, that he could tolerate no
commendation of others, eulogized but the dead and would
never himself speak in laudatory terms of a contemporary.
John Quincy Adams found him only "half-educated." More generous is the petulance of Calhoun—"I don't like Clay. He is a
bad man, an impostor, a creature of wicked schemes. I won't
speak to him, but by God, I love him."[16]

A month later Calhoun, hawkeyed and gaunt looking, in a
long black coat, with a thick mass of white hair falling to his
shoulders, tottered into the Senate Chamber and was helped
to his seat, his hands clenching the arms of his chair. He brought
with him a carefully written manuscript upon the question
dealt with in Clay's resolutions.[17] Senator Mason of Virginia
was selected to read it. Calhoun listened to the delivery as
though all were new to him, moving not a muscle of his face—
"like some disembodied spirit reviewing the deeds of the flesh."
Occasionally he turned half round, and his spectral eyes searched
face after face as if to read the effect of his words. It was like
a great funeral ceremony with the corpse sitting by. Webster
and Clay sat like statues.[18]

The speech was inhumanly dry, precise. The argument ran
coherently from proposition to proposition. He was unwilling
to accept either President Taylor's plan or that of Clay. The
South demanded a full measure of justice: equal rights in the

acquired territories, return of fugitive slaves, restoration of the political equilibrium by a constitutional amendment providing for two Presidents of the United States, one representing the Slave States and the other the Free States, each with a veto upon the acts of Congress.

"It is time, Senators, that there should be an open and manly avowal as to what is intended to be done. . . . The cry of 'Union, Union—the glorious Union'—can no more prevent disunion than the cry of 'Health, health, glorious health' on the part of the physician can save a patient lying dangerously ill. (Can then the Union be saved?) Yes, easily. . . . The North has only to will it to accomplish it. . . . As things now stand, the Southern States cannot remain within the Union. . . ."[19]

The reading was concluded. Webster stepped to Calhoun's side, then Henry Clay. The Triumvirate stood together behind the Vice President's desk. Then a group of Calhoun's fervent young admirers closed in on him, and gentle hands led the old man slowly out of the Senate Chamber. The next day he remarked: "If any Senator chooses to comment upon what I have said, I trust I shall have health to defend my position."[20]

It was not to be. On March 31, four weeks after the address, a message flashed over the country: "John C. Calhoun is dead."

To his friends it was told that his last words were: "The South, the poor South, God knows what will become of her."[21]

The eyes of the nation were on Daniel Webster. Upon him and the conservative Eastern support depended the outcome of Clay's measure. Would he challenge the arrogant South? Or would he seek refuge in the ark of compromise?

In anticipation of the oratorical event, people had been traveling to Washington from all over the country for several days. Chairs, sofas, temporary seats made of public documents piled one upon another, were crowded into every available corner of the Senate Chamber. When the Senators arrived they found that for hours their seats had been occupied by women while members of the House and distinguished men of the nation filled the aisles. Foreign ministers were present, alertly attentive. The galleries were packed, the corridor and every approach to the Senate room densely crowded by the throngs struggling to get within sound of Webster's voice. Senator Foote sarcastically moved that the ladies be permitted to remain in the Senatorial chairs they had taken. They did remain, and formed a brilliant array.[22]

Promptly at 12 o'clock, on March 7, an amiable and dignified gentleman, blue eyed with slightly silvered hair took the chair and rapping sharply with his ivory mallet before him called the Senate to order. The Vice President said that Senator Isaac P. Walker of Wisconsin, not having finished his speech the day before, was entitled to the floor. That gentleman rose and said— "Mr. President, this vast audience has not come together to hear me, and there is but one man in my opinion who can assemble such an audience. They expect to hear him, and I feel it to be my duty, therefore, as it is my pleasure, to give the floor to the Senator from Massachusetts."[23]

Webster, deep bronzed and copped hued, rose and stood for a moment in silence. He wore his customary blue dress coat with shiny brass buttons, a buff vest and a beautifully starched neckcloth. He spoke for three hours and eleven minutes.[24]

"I wish to speak today," he said "not as a Massachusetts man, not as a Northern man, but as an American . . . I speak for the preservation of the Union. Hear me for my cause."

He puffed aside the Wilmot Proviso; geography and climate, he declared, "had settled beyond all terms of human enactment" that slavery could not exist in New Mexico or California. To cover them with a Wilmot Proviso would be needlessly to "reaffirm an ordinance of nature" and "to reenact the will of God." "I should put in no Wilmot Proviso for the purpose of a taunt or a reproach . . ."[25]

He denounced the Abolition movement as a "rub-a-dub agitation, whose only result was a little noise . . . I think their operations for the last twenty years have produced nothing good or valuable . . ." He frankly admitted that the North was unfaithful to its constitutional vows regarding the return of fugitive slaves and declared himself ready to support an effective fugitive slave law.[26]

The entire speech was a fervent appeal for the perpetuation of the constitution and above all of the Union. But New England, which had hoped for a defence, was smitten in the face. So intent was the orator in espousing the grievances of the South that he quite forgot some of the Northern wrongs to counterbalance them.[27]

While he was speaking a tall gaunt figure with a long black cloak gathered around him entered with slow and dragging steps from the lobby behind the Vice President's desk. The apparition, unobserved by Webster, sank trembling into a chair hardly able to stir. Webster swept on—

"Secession! Peaceable Secession! Sir, your eyes and mine are never destined to see that miracle. The dismemberment of this vast country without convulsion! The breaking of the fountains of the great deep without ruffling the surface! . . . There can be no such thing as a peaceable secession. No, sir! No, sir! I see as plainly as I see the sun in heaven what that disruption must produce; I see that it must produce war, and such a war as I will not describe, *in its twofold character.*

"Peaceable   secession!—peaceable   secession! . . . What would be the result? . . . What is to remain American? . . . What am I to be? An American no longer? . . . Where is the flag of the Republic to remain? Northern states under one government, and Southern states under another government! A Southern Confederacy! I am sorry, sir, that it has ever been thought of, talked of, or dreamed of, in the wildest flights of human imagination. I would rather hear of natural blasts and mildews, war, pestilence, and famine, than to hear gentlemen talk of secession . . . No, sir! No, sir! There will be no secession! Gentlemen are not serious when they talk of Secession! . . .

And now, Mr. President, instead of speaking of the possibility of secession, instead of dwelling in these caverns of darkness, let us come out into the light of day; let us enjoy the fresh air of liberty and union; let us cherish those hopes which belong to us; let us raise our conceptions to the magni-

tude and the importance of the duties that devolve upon
us; let our comprehension be as broad as the country for
which we act, our aspirations as high as its certain
destiny. . . ."[28]

Monied men, owners of bank, railroad, and manufacturing
stocks applauded Webster's speech. It melted away the stern
resolution of the Nashville Convention before it gathered. Union
papers of the South rejoiced. "The People were always for
Compromise and Adjustment," exclaimed the Alexandria *Gazette.*

> All hail for the Union!
> (Let no one gainsay)
> Of States in communion
> Oh, last it alway,

sang the *Southron* in an ecstasy of rejoicing.[29]

Washington society was delighted, but one of Webster's colleagues cynically remarked: "Wait till you hear from Boston."

On March 15 the *Liberator* printed half of Webster's speech
and said: "The remainder of this indescribably base and wicked
speech must be postponed till our next number." In a desire to
discredit his opponent, Garrison declared that Webster kept
a harem of colored women, some of them "big black wenches
as ugly and vulgar as Webster himself." And Garrison alleged
that because of remorse Webster's face became "sallow and
shrunken, and his eyes languid and glazed." Repeatedly Garrison styled him "the great slave hunter and brazen advocate
of slave catching."[30]

Emerson damned Webster in an epigram—

> "Why did all manly gifts in Webster fail?
> He wrote on Nature's grandest brow, *For Sale.*"[31]

"Mr. Webster," he added, "perhaps, is only following the laws
of his blood and constitution . . . He is a man who lives by his
memory: a man of the past, not a man of faith and hope. *All the
drops of his blood have eyes that look downward.*"[32]

"I believe no one political act in America since the treachery of Benedict Arnold has excited so much moral indignation," declared Theodore Parker.[33] And Phillips doubted whether the vainest man who ever lived dreamed "in the hour of his fondest self conceit, that he had done the human race as much good as Daniel Webster has brought it harm and despair."[34] At another meeting, when someone in the audience called for three cheers for Webster, Phillips exclaimed—"Yes, three cheers for Sir Pertinax M'Sycophant, who all his life long has been bowing down to the Slave Power to secure the Presidency . . . and destined to be outwitted at last." (Cheers)[35]

"For thirty years—for thirty years," declared Baron Humboldt, "you have made no progress about slavery. You have gone backward, very far backward. . . . I think especially of your law of 1850. That I always call the *Webster* law. I always before liked Mr. Webster. He was a great man. I knew him and always till then liked him. But, ever after that, I hated him. He was the man who made it. If he wanted to prevent it, he could have done it. That is the reason why I call it the Webster law. And ever after that, I hated him."[36]

Massachusetts Abolitionists groaned at the mention of Webster's name, and the poet Whittier pilloried him in the famous lines—

So fallen! so lost! the light withdrawn
Which once he wore!
The glory from his gray hairs gone
Forevermore!

Revile him not, the Tempter hath
A snare for all;
And pitying tears, not scorn and wrath
Befit his fall!

Let not the land once proud of him
Insult him now,
Nor brand with deeper shame his dim,
Dishonored brow.

Of all we loved and honored, naught
Save power remains;
A fallen angel's pride of thought,
Still strong in chains.

All else is gone; from those great eyes
The soul has fled:
When faith is lost, when honor dies,
The man is dead!

Then, pay the reverence of old days
To his dead fame;
Walk backward, with averted gaze,
And hide the shame![37]

On Monday, March 25, a meeting was held in Faneuil Hall of "citizens of Boston and vicinity who have read with surprise, alarm, and deep regret the speech of Honorable Daniel Webster in the United States Senate on the subject of slavery." Samuel E. Sewall presided, Theodore Parker introduced a series of resolutions, and Phillips followed with a scorching attack on Webster's speech.

"Daniel Webster is false, no matter how impregnable his logic be or seem. (Hear, hear.)

"We call upon him to come up in his age, and fulfil the promise of his youth; and if he is wanting, if he has betrayed us, let him be like Arnold or like Gregory—let the axe sever forever the tender cords that bound him to the heart of hearts of Massachusetts. (Loud cheers.) If he has so little knowledge of the moral sense of New England as to think that he can stand up in the face of this community, after he has pledged himself to be a slave hunter, let him at least learn to respect the intelligence of New England, which knows at least when it is betrayed." (Applause.)

As for the contention that it was impossible for slavery to exist in the territory of New Mexico:

"Mr. Webster . . . tells us to trust to what? To trust to chance, fairly interpreted, to the providence of God. But

whoever trusts to chance, under the Constitution of the
United States, trusts to loaded dice and packed cards.
(Cheers). He trusts to a Webster surrendering the forces
of liberty, while Calhoun, like the guards, 'never yields,—
he dies.' ('Hear, hear.') That is the chance. No—we will
'take a bond of fate,' before we will trust that. (Cheers.)

But we need not talk in this strain. On our side is every
attribute of the Almighty. It will take greater apostates than
even this one to doom that fair land long to slavery. God
never scooped the Valley of the Mississippi as the cradle
of bondage, nor piled the Rocky mountains as ramparts
for tyrants. That valley is to be trodden by free feet; those
fastnesses held by free hands. Such indeed the 'will of God,'
which mocks all the wickedness of man to gainsay it." (Long
continued applause.)[38]

In the same week Phillips published a *Review of Webster's
Speech on Slavery*.

"This is statesmanship!" declared Phillips. "Yes, of the
kind Coleridge describes: 'There are men who never exert
themselves to cure an evil, but seek merely to hold it at
arm's length, careful only that things may last out their
day.' "

"Who can blame us," he asked, "for detesting that Moloch
Constitution to which the fair fame of our statesman is
sacrificed?"

And he denounced Webster's speech as a "cold, tame, passion-
less, politic commodity."

"His total surrender of what he so vain-gloriously called
'his thunder' and 'the Whig ground,' is flat apostasy, nothing
else. . . . In the streets they link his name with Arnold
and such humble traitors; but his crime is greater. Nothing,
as has been well said by Charles Sumner, resembles it but
the deliberate and calculating apostasy of Strafford. It is not,
as in Arnold, the surrender of a fort, or the desertion of a
single man. Here the proper, and by some younglings, the
expected leader of the North, not only leaves the camp, but

sets himself, like Strafford, to corrupt with his glazing soph-
istry the conscience and hoodwink the eyes of his countrymen, yields up the safety of one race, and uses the influence, too generously given him, to mould the other into
supple and unconscious tools of a Despotism which he is all
the while affecting to abhor. If Slavery sets her foot on the
strand of the Pacific, let her thank our Strafford. Mirabeau
was bought with gold, but Death took him before he could
earn it, Strafford with a peerage, but Puritanism winnowed
him and his plots on its inexorable threshing floor, the scaffold. There is a spirit awake at the North as inexorable as
Puritanism or Death; and now, as formerly, God gives to
Liberty nothing but victories. . . .

"We come to Mr. Webster's admission of there being just
grounds of Southern complaint against the North. The only
point in this part of the speech that interests us is the inutter-
able baseness of the slave hunt pledge. . . . Thanks to Mr.
Webster for his plain, unvarnished villainy. Villain, gentle
reader, is none too harsh a name for a man who professes
his readiness to return fugitive slaves. Our glorious old tongue
was made for use, not to be laid up in dictionaries. It is
rich indeed in the capacity for rebuking sin, but alas! the
Saxon race far out-does it in its capacity for sinning.

" 'What is to remain American?' . . . . 'What am I, Daniel
Webster, to be?' . . . 'How is each of the thirty states to
defend itself?'. . . . 'Where is the flag of the republic to
remain? Where is the eagle still to tower?' asks Daniel Webster. What fustian is all this! 'Liberty first and Union afterwards,' said Patrick Henry. 'Where freedom dwells, there is
my country,' was Franklin's motto ('Ubi Libertas, ibi patria)
'If this breach in the Constitution cannot be healed, Let Discord Reign For Ever,' said England's Demosthenes, Lord
Chatham. Besides these, how poor and tame seem the idle
questions of our Demosthenes! . . .

"And this, then, is the end of the political career of Daniel
Webster! Thirty years ago, he spoke brave words at the
Rock about that 'work of hell,' the slave trade, and eulogized
the 'religious character of our origin,' hoping that he might
leave to those who should come after him, 'some proof of
his attachment to the cause of good government, and of
civil and religious liberty; some proof of a sincere and ardent

desire to promote everything which could enlarge the understandings and improve the hearts of men';—and this is the result! Verily,

His promises were, as he then was, mighty;
But his performance, as he is now, nothing."[39]

It is not necessary to charge that Daniel Webster in his Seventh of March speech was bidding for the Presidency. Let it stand that a united country was his end and aim. He bargained away moral conviction for the sake of national harmony. He could see "an ordinance of nature" and "the will of God" written on the mountains and plateaus of New Mexico, but he failed to see an ordinance of nature and the will of God implanted in the hearts of men who refused to assist in reducing to bondage their fellows. Seward summed up the question in a dozen words: "The moral sense, the conscience of the age, has outgrown Mr. Webster."[40]

When Christian rights, the rights of justice and humanity, have been trampled upon, as Seward said, there is a higher law than the Constitution, a higher law than the Union.[41]

The fourth great speech on Clay's compromise measure was delivered by the young Senator from New York, William Henry Seward. He upheld President Taylor's course and pleaded for the admission of California under her free state constitution. To this young man listened all of the triumvirate, hardly taking their eyes from him while he spoke of things strange to them. He seemed really younger than he was—a slightly built and agile figure clad in black, with reddish hair turning brown, penetrating eyes, pointed New England features in which shrewdness and benevolence were blended. He had no reputation in Washington—he was known at the capital only as a new man who represented radical Northern opinion. So when he rose to speak, no fashionable ladies smiled on him or waved their fans. The galleries were almost deserted and but few Senators were in their places. There was "no one to approve and none to admire," sneered the Washington *Union*. He read his speech from a manuscript.

Trying indeed it was for Seward on this, his first national occasion, to face the withering scorn and distrust of the Gods of the Senate. When he first arose, he spoke with hesitation as though his heart failed him, and he seemed commonplace by comparison. Some of the passages he delivered with almost painful deliberation and monotony, and his speech seemed very dull, heavy, prosy. But the substance was striking and when he came to speak of human rights, his tones were less husky and his plain features lighted up, until the warmth of his eloquence stirred the whole chamber. He condemned all political compromises which involved matters of conscience; he confidently presaged the power of the American people to maintain their national integrity under whatever menace of danger.[42]

"It is insisted that the admission of California shall be attended by a compromise of questions which have arisen out of slavery. I AM OPPOSED TO ANY SUCH COMPROMISE, IN ANY AND ALL THE FORMS IN WHICH IT HAS BEEN PROPOSED, because while admitting the purity and the patriotism of all from whom it is my misfortune to differ, I think all legislative compromises radically wrong and essentially vicious . . .

"But there is yet another aspect in which this principle must be examined. It regards the domain only as a possession to be enjoyed . . . by the citizens of the old States. It is true, indeed, that the national domain is ours; it is true, it was acquired by the valor and with the wealth of the whole nation, but we hold, nevertheless, no arbitrary power over it. . . . We hold no arbitrary authority over anything, whether acquired lawfully, or seized by usurpation. The Constitution regulates our stewardship; the Constitution devotes the domain to Union, to justice, to defence, to welfare, and to liberty.

"But there is *a higher law than the Constitution* which regulates our authority over the domain, and devotes it to the same noble purposes. The territory is a part—no unconsiderable part—of the common heritage of mankind, bestowed upon them by the creator of the Universe. We are his stewards, and must so discharge our trust as to secure, in the highest attainable degree, their happiness . . ."[43]

Calhoun sat riveted, with glassy eyeballs fixed intently upon the speaker, muttering what sounded like a malediction. Webster interrupted Seward several times to ask whether he understood correctly and would then sink back in his place with a sneer of contempt.

The immediate impression on the listeners was not great. But that night the *Tribune* correspondent telegraphed that Seward's speech would "wake up the nation." Within a few days anti-slavery Democrats, Free Soilers, and Abolitionists praised it enthusiastically. Before the end of the month, 100,000 copies were sent out from Washington. The speech, condensed into an aphorism, shaped conviction.[44]

The most angry words that Calhoun ever spoke in the Senate were against Seward on account of this speech. Senator Foote had said that he knew the opinions of most of his colleagues and was on good terms with everybody.

Calhoun replied: "I am not—I will not be on good terms with those who wish to cut my throat. The honorable Senator from New York justifies the North in treachery. I am not the man to hold social intercourse with such as these."

Foote (in his seat): "I think he (Mr. Seward) will have to be given up."

Calhoun: "I recognize them as Senators—say good-morning, and shake hands with them—but that is the extent of my intercourse with such as those, who, I think, are endangering the Union."[45]

Seward's opponents interpreted his speech as incendiary and revolutionary. Clay said—"It has eradicated the respect of almost all men for him."[46]

The House wrangled along in a blind alley common to popular assemblies where no master mind directs. The spell of Old Man Eloquent was missing. In the Senate the violence of party feeling exploded in a bitter feud between Senator Foote of Mississippi and the burly Senator Benton of Missouri.

Foote, who had blown hot and cold, was a garrulous little man with a large bald head who wore green spectacles and had made his debut in the Senate two years before in a speech

which contained a page of bad Latin and misquoted Byron.
But his influence grew as he proved himself irrepressible. Beginning the term a violent secessionist his blood cooled down
under Clay's influence.

Benton had aroused the bitter hostility of his colleagues.
Southerners looked at him as a renegade for, though a slaveholder from a slaveholding state, he was staunchly opposed to
their object, and the Senator from Mississippi was selected to
taunt him. In a rasping speech, Foote exclaimed—"The Senator
need not think of frightening anybody by a blustering and dog-
matic demeanor. . . . The honorable Senator now says, 'I am
the friend of California . . . I announce—I, sir—I announce
that I will from this day henceforward insist—I, the Caesar, the
Napoleon of the Senate—I announce that I have now come into
the war with sword and buckler.'" Foote continued in this
goading manner. Benton retorted that he believed personalities
were forbidden by the laws of the Senate. "And now, sir," he
said, "I will tell you what I know. I know that the attack made
upon my motives today and heretofore in this chamber are
false and cowardly." Foote's rejoinder was no less cutting than
his former remarks. Greatly irritated, Benton exclaimed—"I pronounce it cowardly to give insults where they cannot be chas-
tised. Can I take a cudgel to him here?" Calls to order by the
Vice President and several Senators terminated the incident of the
day. But for some time afterwards ill blood between the two
gentlemen was brewing. Finally on the 17 of April the pent-up
enmity burst forth.

Benton made the charge that the whole excitement under
which the country labored was due to the Southern members
of Congress and that "there has been a cry of wolf when there
was no wolf, that the country has been alarmed without reason
and against reason." Foote defended the members accused,
said their action was "worthy of the highest laudation" and
that they would be held in "veneration when their calumniators,
no matter who they may be, will be objects of general loathing
and contempt." When the word "calumniators" was uttered,
Benton rose from his seat, pushed his chair violently from him,
and without a remark or gesture, but with a wrathful face,

quickly strode towards the seat of Foote which was about twenty feet distant from his own. Benton had no weapon of any kind in his hands or about his person. Foote, seeing at once the movement of Benton, left his place on the floor and ran towards the secretary's table, all the while looking over his shoulder. At the same time he drew a five-chambered revolver, fully loaded, and cocked it. Then he took a position in front of the secretary's table. Meanwhile Senator Dodge followed Benton, overtook him and grasped him by the arm. "Don't stop me, Dodge," exclaimed Benton. To which Dodge replied, "Don't compromise yourself or the Senate." Benton was on the point of going back to his seat when he happened to see the pistol in Foote's hands at which he became greatly excited and again started towards Foote. Struggling with those Senators who were hanging on to him and dramatically throwing open his coat, he exclaimed, "I am not armed; I have no pistols; I disdain to carry arms. Let him fire. Stand out of the way and let the assassin fire." In the meantime other members rushed in and disarmed Foote, and Benton was led back to his seat.[47] The Sergeant at Arms at last restored order. But when Clay suggested that both parties should give a bond to keep the peace, Benton arose and said, "I'll rot in jail, sir, before I will do it! No, sir! I'll rot in jail first. I'll rot, sir!" and poured a fresh torrent of bitter words upon "Hangman Foote" (so named because of the declaration that if John P. Hale came to Mississippi, he would be hung to "one of the tallest trees of the forest," and that he (Foote) would himself assist in the operation.[48]

But "Old Bullion" Benton of the hooked nose and pompous manner was a man of tremendous passions and an unrivalled hater. He had a keen mind but was unreasoning and preeminently unforgiving. He hated Calhoun with real vengeance, styling him "John Catiline Calhoun" and branding him as a "cowardly cur that sneaked to his kennel when the Master of the Hermitage blew his bugle horn." He seemed to relent a little when the great Carolinian's strength was ebbing away, and on one occasion he declared: "When God lays his hand on a man, I take mine off."[49] But in refusing to eulogize the dead Calhoun, he said, "My people cannot distinguish between a man and his principles. . . . They cannot eulogize the one and denounce the other."[50]

Benton loved the Union and hated both Nullifiers and Abolitionists. "The world's last hope for free government on this earth" might be destroyed by needless quarrels.[51] He heartily approved of Northern mobs that "silenced the gabbling tongues of female dupes and dispersed the assemblages, whether fanatical, visionary, or incendiary."[52] Yet for Clay's Omnibus Bill or "five old bills tacked together" he had a downright contempt. He compared them to old Dr. Jacob Townsend's sarsaparilla.[53]

CHAPTER SEVENTEEN

BOWERY TOUGHS

1.

The sickly air of compromise was filling the land. To the American public at large it was welcome because it seemed to bring external peace. Any action breaking the drugged calm was sure to be unfavorably received.

No wonder then that the annual meeting of the American Anti-Slavery Society in New York should be the signal for mob violence and a satanic outburst of the press.

James Gordon Bennett in the New York *Herald* of May 7 ran the headlines. "The Annual Congress of Fanatics—The Disunionists, Socialists, Fourierists, Communists, and other Abolitionists. May the seventh has come, and with it a host of fanatics, worse than the locusts of Egypt."[1]

The language of the New York *Globe* was even bolder. It listed the speakers:

"Wendell Phillips, of Boston, white man merely from blood.

"Frederick Douglass: If this Douglass shall proclaim his treason here, and any man shall arrest his diabolical career . . . thousands will exclaim, 'Did he not strike the villain dead?'"

"What are the designs of these men?" continued the *Globe*. "To have immediate emancipation or disunion—to incite the Negroes of the Southern States to rise upon their masters, to butcher them in cold blood, to violate and use their wives and sisters and daughters as the innocent victims

211

of Negro brutality; to scatter fire, rapine, and murder all through the South."[2]

The meeting was held on May 7 in the Tabernacle, a Congregational place of worship situated on the Northwest corner of Broadway and Anthony (now Worth) Street, the auditorium of which was a large square hall with its floor sloping down to the platform. Tiers of seats from behind the platform were carried around the sides to join the gallery. Isaiah Rynders, a bully-rook and tough and meeting smasher of wide experience, who had been a boatman on the Hudson and a gambler in the Southwest, a Tammany district boss and idol of a rowdy political organization called the "Empire Club," took possession of the hall. He posted himself at one side of the organ loft and behind the platform where he could command the battlefield with his eye. His gang of Bowery Boys were about him, ready to surge down on the platform when the time should come.

Garrison dressed himself with scrupulous care. In order to avoid the least appearance of singularity, he even changed the turn-down collar, which he was in the habit of wearing, for a stand-up collar such as was customary at the time. He opened the meeting with a reading from the Scripture and began his address without interruptions. But he had not gone far before Rynders heckled him. The din increased. The Hutchinsons who were wont to sing at Anti-Slavery meetings were in the gallery and attempted to raise a song to soothe the audience with music. But it was of no avail. Rynders drowned their fine voices with noise and shouting.

Douglass followed Garrison, and then came the Reverend Samuel Ward, editor of the *Impartial Citizen*. From the back of the platform came forward a large man, so black that, as Wendell Phillips said, when he shut his eyes you could not see him. "Well," said Rynders, "this is the original nigger." Ward made so eloquent a speech that the mob applauded him, and the meeting for the day ended with a triumph for the cause.[3]

In the evening, speeches were again interrupted by noises, and on the following day Rynders and his guerillas, having learned that intellectual weapons cut their fingers, confined themselves to physical disturbances. The hall was a bedlam of jumping rowdy devils, yelling, hooting, bellowing, snuffing, coughing, sneezing. The appearance of Charles Burleigh with the flowing sandy beard was the signal for roars of laughter mingled with cries of "O, look at his head!" "Go pay yer barber's bill!" "Hell, what a hairy arss." In spite of the tumult Burleigh went on, but no one could hear him. Rynders put his arm round Burleigh's neck and affectionately stroked his beard. A call was made for the Chief of Police. Rynders replied, "Oh, don't call him! you'll frighten us all to death!" (Cheers) Burleigh finally gave up the contest.

Phillips, the next speaker, also was greeted with a storm of hisses, cheers, clapping of hands, etc. This continued for five or ten minutes. He began by abusing the disturbers.

"Shall we submit to the control of the rabble? In Boston, where I come from, such scenes are not permitted." (Cheers, hisses, and great confusion. Voice in the crowd—'Say, Garrison, this is an imposition you have made upon us. You have given us a whitewashed nigger instead of a real black one; put him out; put the red-head down; we won't listen to him.')

Phillips continued: "Let Webster go on in his traitorous course at Washington." (Voice in the crowd—Three cheers for Washington; he set all his Negroes free and died an Abolitionist." Cheers and hissing.)

Phillips: "The Southern men here, who are leading on this riot, are not to blame; but I despise the Northern men who call themselves the friends of freedom, and say this is liberty, yet prevent the free expression of opinion. You call the Constitution sacred. Well, then, the Constitution guarantees the right of free speech. You profess to love the Constitution. I place it under my feet, where it ought to be." (Suiting the action to the word and stamping violently upon the stand.)

This was the signal for a tornado. Cries and curses: "Put him out," "Three cheers for the Constitution." (Great cheering.) "Three more." Followed by three cheers for Henry Clay, three cheers for New York, three groans for all fanatics. "Oh, you damned impostor, you are disgracing our city, stay home." Phillips withdrew.[4]

At last the rabble put forward its representative (an ex-policeman of the eighth ward who had lately been broken for being found drunk in a house of prostitution) to propose a resolution against the abolition of slavery and urging "these humanity mongers" not to use scurrility, blasphemy, and vituperation. Rynders put the resolution and his creatures carried it by acclamation.

Finally under protest Garrison was obliged to declare the meeting closed. The proprietors of the New York Society Library where the last two sessions were held, fearing a riot and consequent damage to the building, shut it against the Abolitionists.

"Thus," remarked the New York *Tribune* the next morning, "closed Anti-Slavery free discussion in New York for 1850."[5]

The Graham Institute in Brooklyn was secured for Wendell Phillips by a friend. A committee of the Institute, however, withdrew the invitation on account of the intense excitement. When Henry Ward Beecher heard of their action, he immediately invited Phillips to Plymouth Church. He went to the trustees man by man and most of them gladly gave their written permission. One or two were inclined to withhold it. Beecher, however, made it a personal matter. "You and I will break if you don't give me this permission," and they signed.[6]

Henry Ward Beecher was the spiritual fountainhead of Brooklyn. There was nothing clerical in his face, figure, dress, or bearing. He looked more like a street evangel: a long mane sweeping his coat collar, over-red cheeks, hard eyes, and low square-toed shoes.

Plymouth Church had no stained glass windows, no ecclesiastical ornaments, no architectural beauty. It was absolutely unadorned. The galleries were deep, the preacher not hidden behind the pulpit rampart, and the pews were swept in a circle about the platform. There was no broad central aisle to stare like an empty lane in the speaker's face. The white walls were plain.

A hush fell as Beecher rose for the hymn. Instead of resting a pale forehead on a pallid hand, and closing his eyes as if in silent prayer while the people sang, Beecher held the book in his red fist and sang with all his might.

Love was Henry Ward's remedy for slavery—love and Christian piety. But as Frederick Douglass, who was unimpressed with Beecher's high sounding rhetoric, said: "With a good cowhide, I could take all that out of Mr. Beecher in five minutes."[7]

The Mayor and a strong squad of detectives were on hand when Phillips arrived at Plymouth Church. A highly fashionable audience attended. Beecher opened the meeting with a few remarks:

> "When I heard the place of meeting had been, from prudential motives, closed against him, I felt it in my blood and in my bones, that this right should be vindicated. If he had been denied free speech in New York, I wished him to come to Brooklyn, where the right should be restored to him. I claim for him the same right to speak his sentiments that I claim for myself. . . . If he were 10,000 times blacker than he is (I mean in his *belief*, and not in his *skin*), I would still stand up for his right to speak his own sentiments, and I cannot but think the church a proper place to vindicate this important principle."[8]

Phillips rose serene, self poised, and began his speech. He made a statement that was very bitter and a cry arose over the whole congregation. He stood still with a cold, bitter smile on his face and waited till they subsided. Then he repeated the statement with more emphasis. Again an uproar went through the church. He waited and repeated it more intensely and beat them down with that one sentence until they were still and let him go on.[9]

> "The Abolitionists are charged with using hard language; the question is, is the language true? . . . It is easier to sit on the heights of criticism, and look down with a scrutinizing eye upon the work done by others, which we ought to have done ourselves, and to say, 'but for these rude guns,

I would be a soldier.' (Laughter) Men engaged in such
rough work as the Abolitionists', with the majority against
them, cannot always be very choice in their language;
if they were, they would probably not obtain the public ear.
The scholar may sit in his study, and take care that his
language is not exaggerated; but the rude mass of men are
not to be caught by balanced periods—they are caught by
men whose words are half battles. From Luther down,
the charge against every reformer has been that his tongue
is too rough. Be it so. Rough instruments are used for rough
work. . . ."[10]

To lift up one's voice against a system reeking with blood
and cruelty was called blasphemy and infidelity. But it was the
Abolitionists, insisted Phillips, who were the true friends of
the Bible, because they denied that its pages were stained with
any sanction of slavery. We send our Christian missionaries
to the banks of the Ganges on the principle that it is our duty
to care for our brother man, no matter how distant his position
on the globe may be from our own. Should we not, asked Phillips, care for our brother on the other side of the Potomac?

"I do not attack the sects, but I say this—that with 40,000
Christian pulpits, 70,000 slaves have grown into 3,000,000
and that statutes so bloody have been enacted under their
teaching, that those of Draco are light in comparison. Instead of the Jeffersons, the Henrys, and the men of the first
era of the republic lamenting slavery as an evil, we have
Calhoun declaring it a blessing, and McDuffie saying it is
the corner stone of the political edifice. Mr. Webster, as far
as we can judge from his last speech—(applause, hissing,
and cheering alternately for five minutes,)—I was going to
say, that although Mr. Webster has described what were the
views of the Romans and Greeks about slavery, it would
puzzle ten Philadelphia lawyers to tell what are his own.
(Laughter and hissing)"[11]

The almighty dollar was at the bottom of slavery. It was
not only a question of morality, but of property—an investment
of one hundred million dollars. An American's logic was as clear

as the sun at noonday upon every subject in the world except one. If it related to the white man, it was lucid and bright, but the moment it touched a black man, it veered about like the needle of a compass when it comes near a mass of iron.

Daniel Webster, when speaking of Kossuth, expressed anxiety for his escape from the bloody tyranny of his pursuers; but put Douglass in the place of Kossuth escaping from a far bloodier despotism. Would he respond? Not a bit of it.

"You love the American banner. But every sixth man under its stripes and stars is a slave . . . Patrick Henry confessed that slavery was a sin. That is all that we Abolitionists want the churches to proclaim. Let them confess themselves sinners, rather than file down their religion to their degraded practice or pervert the Bible to sustain it. Slavery is a sin, and no Constitution, no religious principle is binding that endeavors to sustain it. This is the great question of the age, that, like Aaron's rod, swallows up tariff, internal improvement, Democracy and Whiggery alike. . . .

"God has given us a conscience superior to all law, and whenever a slave touches our free soil, let him be free beyond the reach of his tyrant. Remember that though you may unsettle respect for old institutions, and for law and Constitution, by refusing to obey them, you will only establish the truth, that the Bible is heavier than the statute book. Remember the words of the Indian poet—

'Alone thou wast born,
Alone thou shalt die,
Alone thou shalt go up to judgment!'"

(Applause and some hissing.)[12]

At the close of Phillips's lecture, Beecher thanked the audience—not for being gentlemanly—but for proving that Brooklyn deserves its name—the City of Churches—and that they had shown what churches can do, in freely conceding the right of liberty of speech which was denied in New York.[13]

In Boston two weeks later, at a meeting of the New England Anti-Slavery Society, an attempt was made to reenact the scenes in New York—with but partial success.[14]

When Wendell Phillips, in Faneuil Hall, quoted old Fuller on Shakespeare, three cheers were given for Shakespeare, three groans for Phillips, three cheers for Christianity. (Blowing of horns, crowing in the style of barnyard fowls, groans and hisses.) When Phillips alluded to the Union and Webster, he was interrupted by three cheers given for the Union, Daniel Webster, Henry Clay, three for Cass, three for the President.

Voice—"You're a fanatic."

Wendell Phillips—"Thank God, I am a fanatic."

"Yes I am a fanatic. In a day when Liberty is gagged that stocks may sell at par, when pulpits preach peace instead of purity, and statesmen laugh at any higher authority than the parchment of human laws, thank God, I am a fanatic, as such men judge fanaticism!" (Applause)[15]

Phillips delivered two other speeches before the New England Society, refuting the charge of abuse and denunciation at the same time uttering a blistering criticism of Daniel Webster.

"There is a maudlin charity which shuts its eyes upon the sins of society, and seems to think that vice is to be taken out of the body politic as Eve was out of Adam, by putting him to sleep. We cannot thus wheedle the community. The devil is wiser than we think. The slaveholder is not appeased by delicate language. If he perceives in the individual an earnest purpose and a pledged determination against his system, he hates him just as much for that purpose wrapped up in a honied phrase, as if it were expressed in rough old Saxon. The only thing that such a writer gains is the Irish loss of being unintelligible, dull, or doubted by the community."[16]

Dr. Channing wrote with a calmness, with a carefully chosen phraseology which no man could expect to go beyond. Was he liked? Did the slaveholder when he perceived Channing to be in earnest welcome him as an agreeable critic? Not at all. Dr. Channing had his portion of abuse on the floor of Congress and in the Southern press, side by side with John Quincy Adams.

He was doing a masterly work for the disciplined and thoughtful, for the secluded and peaceful.

"There was something more to be done in taking this torch of truth, and carrying it forward so as to arrest the attention of the masses. This can only be done by the plainest speech, by words so spontaneous that they alone prove the speaker sincere and in earnest, and secure him a hearing.
    For men in earnest have no time to waste
    In patching fig leaves for the naked truth.
"If then, you dislike our terms, show us that they are not true."

And Phillips took a parting shot at Webster:

"If Mr. Webster knows nothing of any higher law than the Constitution, if when he fixes those great, dark, eloquent eyes of his on the blue vault of heaven he sees nothing higher than that Parchment of 1787, then he is the creature of the parchment of 1787, and not of the Lord God Almighty . . ."[17]

But though the godlike Daniel was, according to Phillips, no creature of the Lord God Almighty, he was certainly an attractive and rousing subject for a speaker's abuse. At Cochituate Hall Phillips remarked:

"The time has been when if you asked a Whig if he would return fugitive slaves, he would have answered, 'Is thine servant a dog to do this thing?' Now in 1850 you answer —'Not a dog, only a Webster.' (Applause and hisses) Why, do you hiss your Constitution? Do you hiss me for not supporting the Constitution, or Daniel Webster for supporting it. ('Both') I am ready to join in opposition to him. Let every man stand up before the New England public and profess his readiness to return the fugitive slave, and lay his hand on the bondman and help the slave pursuer carry him back to bondage, and see how, like vegetation before the early frost, his prospects will wither! No! No man will undertake it. We have placed that stock at a sad discount. And that is the first triumph against the Constitution.

"Our duty is this—to make it impossible in any future contingency that the anti-slavery sentiment of Massachusetts shall be so represented on the floor of the United States Senate, that we cannot trust it. Boston stands by itself. Its great wealth and manufactures make men pigmies, and they crouch at the feet of the Lawrences and Appletons, and we give them up. But out in the country, there stand men who are not Abolitionists, but who do not intend to be slavehunters."[18]

2.

Had a visitor arrived in New York City late in June or early in July, he would have noticed that the lobbies of the Astor, St. Nicholas, Fifth Avenue, St. Denis, Clarendon, and the Metropolitan hotels were thronged with Southern merchants and planters. And he would have observed newspaper advertisements by many firms, emphasizing that they specialized in merchandise exclusively for the "Southern" trade. Many firms mentioned they had branches in the South.

As J. De Bow said, New York was "almost as dependent upon Southern slavery as Charleston itself. In reply to a query by the London *Times* asking what would New York be without slavery, De Bow said, "The ships would rot at her docks; grass would grow in Wall Street and Broadway, and the glory of New York, like that of Babylon and Rome, would be numbered with the things of the past."[19] No inconsiderable part of Southern cotton, tobacco, and other products was exported from New York City.

Down to the outbreak of the Civil War, New York dominated every single phase of the cotton trade from plantation to market. The total business provided for New Yorkers by the five cotton states amounted to much more than two hundred million dollars.

To their credit no groups in the North were more active in opposing the "Nebraska infamy" than the "solid men" of Boston, Philadelphia, and New York. ("The City of New York is awake at last," declared the *Post* joyfully.)[20] But the panic of 1857 aroused a considerable resentment in the South against New York dominance of the cotton market. The only way to meet the growing hostility to New York City among Southerners was to demonstrate to them that New York merchants were the strongest defenders of Southern institutions. By 1859 the New York merchants were spoken of as "leading Northern defenders of slavery." The Southern trade was so vital to New York business men since the panic and the subsequent decline in Western business that they could not take chances of being mistaken for enemies of the South.

"The City of New York," declared the *Post*, "belongs almost as much to the South as to the North." The *Tribune* put it bitterly: "The city is rotten from center to circumference."[21]

CHAPTER EIGHTEEN

"HUSH, DON'T AGITATE."

The hot July sun saw Congress still in angry session vaporing over the new legacy of territories. Both Houses adjourned over the Fourth on which day the President attended a patriotic celebration at Washington Monument and listened to an oration of Senator Foote's. The heat was of unusual intensity. The President was a long time exposed to the sun and to quench his raging thirst drank large quantities of ice water. Returning to the White House he ate freely of wild cherries and wild fruits and took copious draughts of iced milk. An hour after dinner he was seized with cramps, which took the form of violent cholera morbus. The usual remedies were applied, but his illness increased. Typhoid fever set in. On the night of July 9 the President died. His last words were: "I am about to die. I expect the summons very soon. I have endeavored to discharge all of my official duties faithfully. I regret nothing, but am sorry that I am about to leave my friends."[1]

All spoke of his stern integrity, his unyielding firmness, his frankness, his moderation, and his modesty.[2]

Taylor's death was fortunate for the Compromise because he was bitterly opposed to the measure and would have used his executive influence to destroy it. With his passing, the opposing Whig faction came into power. Vice President Fillmore reorganized the Cabinet under Clay's advice, and Webster became Secretary of State. At length one by one the Compromise measures were passed by Congress and approved by President Fillmore.

When the affair was practically concluded, Webster wrote: "I confess I feel relieved. Since the seventh of March, there has not been an hour in which I have not felt a crushing weight of anxiety and responsibility. . . . It is over. My part is acted and I am satisfied."[3]

On September 12, 1850, the Fugitive Slave Act was carried through the House by 109 to 76. Thirty-one Northern members voted for it. Thirty-three others were either absent or paired, or dodged the vote. Thaddeus Stevens duly remarked: "I suggest that the Speaker should send a page to notify the members on our side of the House that the Fugitive Slave Bill has been disposed of, and that they may now come back into the Hall."[4]

The slaughter of shambles was completed, and Congress emerged into the light of day. On September 18, Fillmore set his hand to the Fugitive Slave Bill and signed his death warrant as a statesman.

The measure intended to quench only inflamed the fire. The whole country to Whittier was "about to become a hunting ground of the slave catchers," for it made slave hunting a duty. The harsh and infamous provisions outraged the North: a Negro might be identified through a mere affadavit of the slaveholder agent; the slave could not testify himself; there was no trial by jury; the commissioner's fee was doubled if the slaveholder prevailed; the bystanders could be summoned to aid in preventing an escape, and in case any person assisted the escape, such a person was to be fined a thousand dollars or imprisoned for six months.

But the tide of anti-slavery feeling rose to a point where law or no law, decision or no decision, the return of fugitives was openly resisted.[5] Phillips and the others refused to cry peace when there was no peace. Peace was slavery and sleep was death. The act opened a new era in the Abolition movement, an era in which non-resistance had no place. The period of pure moral agitation was at an end.

New England leaders recommended Northern nullification and secession. Massachusetts passed an act which inflicted a penalty of five years imprisonment upon any man who aided in

the enforcement of the Fugitive Slave Law. The Supreme Court
of Wisconsin went so far as to declare the same law unconstitutional and five years later the legislature claimed the right
of immediate secession in case the State was overruled by the
Federal Supreme Court or in case any attempt was made to
enforce the obnoxious act. Nearly every other Northern State
passed Personal Liberty Laws which were designed to nullify
it. Buchanan called these Personal Liberty Laws "the most
palpable violations of constitutional duty which have yet been
committed."[6]

Richard Henry Dana of Boston said that men who called
him a traitor a few years before now stopped him on the street
to talk treason.

At a meeting of Boston refugees, held October 5, 1850, an
appeal was issued to the clergy of Massachusetts imploring
them to "lift up their voices like a trumpet against the Fugitive
Slave Bill recently adopted by Congress."[7] When the law
took effect, bands of runaways came to Ontario, Canada, "by
fifties every day like frogs in Egypt."[8] After the panic subsided,
they remained in neighborhoods where conditions were favorable to their society. Theodore Parker stated publicly that there
were in Boston from four hundred to six hundred fugitives.

A Vigilance Committee through whose hands most of the
fugitives passed was organized in Boston in October, 1850.
Timothy Gilbert, a piano manufacturer, was president; Wendell
Phillips was on the Executive Committee. The purpose of the
Committee was to resist, defy, baffle and nullify the Fugitive
Slave Law by every possible means. A public appeal was made
for money and clothing. One of the earliest expenditures recorded was "for posting 300 bills describing the personal appearance of slavehunters." Shortly afterwards another entry
appeared for "printing 2,000 handbills warning Fugitives and
the People against the Slave Hunters."[9] People used to write
to Phillips from the South just before the slaves were about
to start by sea. Phillips got the letters and so would be on the
lookout when vessels got into Boston harbor. He would know
the name of the vessel, and who was on board, and be all ready
to help them. On one occasion he sent this note to his friend

McKim: "A physician has just waited on me and says a merchant living in North Carolina, a patient of his, has fallen in love with a slave girl—valued at $2,000—he can't afford to redeem her, wants to run her off to Canada and marry her. Is there any person in Philadelphia whom he can . . . communicate with . . . You see, I know nothing of the man or case. The Doctor is a republican, but his correspondent may be honest or wishing to get someone into a scrape. Can you name anyone in Philadelphia who would aid if he proved honest in his effort? Answer immediately."[10]

About 300 fugitives were given aid during the Vigilance Committee's active operation of ten years. The house of Lewis Hayden, a member of the committee, was the object of much spying, and one time he was so fully convinced that a raid was contemplated that he placed two kegs of gunpowder in the cellar, and himself sat by ready to touch them off rather than sur- render himself and his charges to the kidnappers.[11]

When William and Ellen Craft were hunted in Boston, they took refuge among friends. Ellen stayed with Theodore Parker who wrote his sermons during her stay with his sword in a drawer under his inkstand and a pistol in his desk. Their pursuers, stopping at the United States Hotel, dared not go into the streets for fear of the mob. Handbills were placed everywhere and cries of "Slavehunters, there go the slavehunters" were heard on all sides. At last the Southerners were compelled to leave the city. But William and Ellen Craft no longer felt safe, and went to England.

Before they set sail, Parker married them. In an open letter to President Fillmore he gave an account of the marriage ceremony, stating his own determination to break the law if it was necessary to protect his brethren who had been slaves. "William Craft and Ellen were parishioners of mine. They have been at my house. I married them a fortnight ago this day; after the ceremony I put a Bible and then a sword into William's hands and told him the use of each."[12]

Asa Mahan, President of Oberlin College, said he "liked the Fugitive Slave Law. (Sensation) He liked it because it could not be executed, and again because it was political death to the party that originated and executed it."[13]

Wendell Phillips urged fugitive slaves to arm themselves and kill their pursuers in order to secure a jury trial for homicide and he openly advocated insurrection. "You will say this is bloody doctrine—anarchial doctrine; it will prejudice people against the cause . . . I know it will," he said in his quiet voice.[14]

At a meeting held in Faneuil Hall on November 6, Sumner declared:

> "In the dreary annals of the past there are many acts of shame—there are ordinances of monarchs, and laws, which have become a byword and a hissing to the nations. But what act of shame, what ordinance of monarch, what law can compare in atrocity with this enactment of an American Congress. (Shouts of 'None'.). . . .
>
> "Other Presidents may be forgotten; but the name signed to the Fugitive Slave Bill can never be forgotten; ('Never'.) There are depths of infamy as there are heights of fame. (Applause.). . . . Better for him had he never been born! (Renewed applause.) Better far for his memory and for the good name of his children, had he never been President! (Repeated cheers.)"[15]

The result was seen in November when the Whig party was snowed under by Massachusetts ballots. The next year Charles Sumner was elected to replace Webster in the Senate.

"Repeal the law! Repeal the law!" became the anti-slavery war cry throughout the North. "Let the fanatics howl on," exclaimed the conservative Unionist Alexandria *Gazette*.[16]

Speakers went all over the land to denounce the wicked Abolitionists. Foremost among them was Daniel Webster. He bitterly assailed the higher law doctrine: "Gentlemen, this North Mountain is high, the Blue Ridge higher still, the Allegheny higher than either, and yet this higher law ranges farther than an eagle's flight above the highest peaks of the Allegheny. . . . The hearing of common man never listens to its high behests and therefore one should think it is not a safe law to be acted on in matters of the highest practical moment. It is a code, however, of the fanatical and factious Abolitionists of the North."[17]

Once stung by abuse, Webster burst out—"Northern Abolitionists and free soilers and Southern disunionists are the most reckless men, I think, I ever met with in public life."[18] And he described the Abolitionists as made up of "silly women and sillier men."[19] In a calm moment, he declared, "I shall say nothing which may foster the unkind passions separating the North from the South."[20] Southern Whigs were almost incredulous that the king of men should stand up to the rack so boldly. "I have hopes of him now," wrote Alexander H. Stephens from the capital pleasantly.[21]

In April of 1851 Faneuil Hall was denied to Wendell Phillips and the Abolitionists. In the same month, however, the Board of Aldermen with consistency refused the use of it to the friends of Webster who wished to unite in a public reception to him. But everyone understood the action to be a reflection on Webster's course for the past year. This awoke a storm of indignation. Afterwards the Common Council offered Webster the use of Faneuil Hall, but he declined it in a grandiloquent manner.[22]

Wendell Phillips remarked—"The Whigs one day invited Daniel Webster to address them in Faneuil Hall, but the great Daniel was pettish that day and declined. It was well, for Faneuil Hall is a good refuge for a fugitive slave to flee to, but a poor place of refuge for recreant statesmen."[23]

The Whig National Convention met at Baltimore on June 16, 1852. Despite the glittering eloquence on behalf of Webster, the roars of approval, the bouquet of roses, the prize went to "Old Fuss and Feathers," General Winfield S. Scott. Not a delegate from the South was for Webster and the North turned its back upon him. When the telegraphic dispatch was put into his hand, Webster opened it and read—"Scott, 159, Fillmore 112, Webster 21." His only comment was—"How will this look in history?"[24]

He had longed passionately for the Presidency. He had wanted it not only because of the glory of the office, but because of the vindication which it would give him. The rebuke of his party at the National Convention was a great shock to him. He feigned a cheerfulness to people but was disconsolate and could not drive from his mind the thought that his life was a failure. Heartbroken, the godlike Daniel died before the day of election.

When the bells for Webster's funeral at Marshfield had barely ceased to toll, Theodore Parker in a paroxysm of rage made a sensational attack upon him as a man and politician— "keeper of slavery's dogs," "Ally of the worst of men," "assassin of liberty," and "tool of slaveholders." "No living man had done so much to debauch the conscience of the nation."[25]

Wendell Phillips wrote a two column obituary which was printed in the *Liberty Bell*. Again, unjustly, he accused Webster of bargaining for the Presidency. But invective against a "miscreant" statesman was blunted and softened by the fact of his death and by Phillips's profound sympathy for slavery's oppressed poor.

"Daniel Webster is dead. If the Fugitive Slave Law could have died with him, he would indeed have slept in blessings. But the evil that men do lives after them: when it does not, we will speak nothing but praise of the dead."[26]

What is greatness in statesmanship? asked Phillips. It is, in one form, by instructive sympathy or preeminent ability, to understand and guide one's own times; in another form, it is to outrun one's own age, and mould the future. Had Webster either of these? Did he understand or guide his own age? His friends boasted for him as proof of "practical statesmanship" that he so often sacrificed his convictions to popular opinion. Strange, added Phillips, for he always contrived to make the sacrifice just when the people were coming round to his own opinion. In simple intellect few Americans ever equalled him. But that massive brain contented itself with saying common things uncommonly well. It never went sounding on and on to pilot the people into a broader and deeper life.

"We argue greatness from a man's aims. This man aimed to be President, and died, as his most intimate friends say, broken hearted because he failed. Had he followed his in-

stincts, and led the way of American ideas, he had been tenfold more than President.

"Ideas rule a thinking people like ours, and it is only
by incarnating some great popular ideas that any intellect,
or even any will, can govern America. Baptised into the
spirit of the age, a great man may become the people's idol,
his self-forgetful consecration shall give him tenfold manhood and even tenfold might, and from his position he shall
gain an influence ten times greater than manhood and mind
could together bestow. After all, the only leadership possible
with us is best expressed in the war cry of LaRoche Jacque-
lin, the Vendean chief—

> Si j'avance, suivez mois;
> Si je recule, tuez mois!
> Si je tombe, vengez mois.

If I advance, Follow Me. If I Retreat, be true to your idea,
and sacrifice even Me.[27]

"He is mourned in ceiled houses and the marts of trade.
But the dwellers in slave huts and fugitives along the high-
ways thank God they have one enemy the less . . . Pericles
consoled his death bed with the thought that he never caused
a Greek to wear mourning. Not poppy, nor mandragora,
nor all the drowsy syrups of the world could have medicined
our Pericles to that sweet sleep—had he remembered the
many homes one ruthless act of his selfish ambition had
made desolate, and the hundreds of children it had made
orphans."[28]

CHAPTER NINETEEN

STEALERS OF MEN

On October 29, 1850, George Thompson, the English orator, landed at Boston on a second visit to America. The Massachusetts Anti-Slavery Society arranged a reception for him in Faneuil Hall on November 15. But the press sounded the alarm to the mob and what happened was a repetition of the Rynders outbreak in New York. Wendell Phillips's appearance was the signal for an outburst of confusion. In rapid succession cheers were given for Daniel Webster, the Union, the Constitution, Abby Folsom, the Hen Convention. "It was hell let loose and no mistake." The Mayor and police were present, but they looked on with indifference. The meeting was finally adjourned.

"Not short of ten thousand of the funniest, noisiest, leather-lunged kick-up-a-dust, disposed spirits of Boston responded last evening," declared the *Daily Mail*. "Wendell Phillips sawed away dreadfully, but it was no use, the yelling was terrific. Phillips hung on, but the persistence of the groundlings was too much."[1]

Shouted down in Boston the Abolitionists with their guest went to Worcester. There they gave Thompson "a royal welcome."[2]

In January of the new year there was a soirée in Cochituate Hall, Boston, to celebrate the twentieth anniversary of Garrison's paper, the *Liberator*. The time selected was the close of the annual meeting of the Massachusetts Anti-Slavery Society. Thompson had been very ill in the country and was looking ghastly, fit for a sick bed, but he spoke gloriously and his presence was an inspiration to the rest. Add to that Garrison in tears and the company scarred with many a struggle. "Such hours come rarely in life," remarked Wendell Phillips.[3]

Thompson concluded his speech by placing in the hands of his friend a testimonial in the shape of a gold watch. Totally surprised, and very much embarrassed, Garrison rose in acknowledgment and said: "Mr. President, if this were a rotten egg (holding up the watch) or a brickbat, I should know how to receive it. (Laughter and cheers.) . . . But the presentation of this valuable gift is as unexpected by me as would be the falling of the stars from the heavens, and I feel indescribably small before you in accepting it." Phillips's speech was largely in a sportive vein, but he showed a serious appreciation of the role of the *Liberator*.

"John Foster used to say that the best test of a book's value was the mood of mind in which one rose from it. To this trial I am always willing the most eager foe should subject the *Liberator*. I appeal to each one here, whether he ever leaves its columns without feeling his coldness rebuked, his selfishness shamed, his hand strengthened for every good purpose; without feeling lifted for awhile, from his ordinary life, and made to hold communion with higher thoughts and loftier aims; and without being moved—the coldest of us—for a moment, at least, with an ardent wish that we, too, may be privileged to be co-workers with God in the noble purposes for our brothers' welfare which have been unfolded and pressed on our attention."

And Phillips followed with a generous tribute to Garrison. If of the Abolitionist it might be said that he had broken the shackles of party, thrown down the walls of sect, trampled on the prejudices of his land and time, risen to something like the freedom of a Christian man, how much was owing to the influence of such a leader. By him he had been redeemed into full manhood, taught to consecrate life to something worth living for. "Let us thank God," added Phillips, "that He has inspired anyone to awaken us from being these dull and rotting weeds—revealed to us the joy of self-devotion—taught us how we intensify this life by laying it a willing offering on the altar of some great cause!"[4]

2.

A sudden shout was heard in the law offices of Richard Henry Dana, Jr. on Court Street, and all rushed to the windows. The shout became a yell of triumph as two big, powerful Negroes dashed down the Court House steps dragging along an arrested fugitive named Shadrach between them, his clothes half torn from his back, through the Court Square and off towards Cambridge, "like a black squall," Dana said. A crowd drove along with them, cheering as they went. All was done with incredible swiftness, and there was no time for pursuit and arrest. Telegrams were sent by the police to stop all trains at the State line. But Shadrach, now in charge of the Underground Railroad, was removed by agents from the train at a stop before the State line was reached and driven in a sleigh over the border. Then he was put on a train for Canada and safety.

The excitement was intense. The facts were telegraphed to Washington with the inquiry, "What is to be done?" The President answered by a proclamation which declared the laws must be obeyed.[5]

Garrison's editorial in the next *Liberator*: "The Arrest—The Rescue—The Flight" reads like a psalm of triumphal thanksgiving, a chapter of the Hebrew prophets: "Thank God Shadrach is free! and not only free but safe under the banner of England. . . . A hundred free white citizens of the North may be thrown into prison, or tarred and feathered, or compelled to flee for their lives from the South on suspicion of being morally averse to slavery—but who cares?"[6]

Theodore Parker wrote in his Journal: "This Shadrach is delivered out of his burning fiery furnace without the smell of fire in his garments. . . . I think it the most noble deed done in Boston since the destruction of the tea in 1773"[7]

The aftermath of the Shadrach affair was the famous "Rescue Cases." A number of men credited with having a hand in the kidnapping of Shadrach were arrested and tried separately. Funds were collected by the Vigilance Committee to aid and defend them, and Richard Henry Dana, Jr. appeared as counsel. In all cases the jury disagreed. Sometimes they stood six to six; sometimes one single obstinate juryman prevented conviction.

A few years later Dana was driving through the White Mountains and had mounted the top of the stage coach when the driver greeted him: "How do you do, Mr. Dana?" Dana with his usual brusqueness replied, "I don't know you; how do you happen to know me?" The driver: "I heard you argue for the defendants in the Shadrach cases when I was on the jury." Dana: "I was very much surprised by the disagreement of the juries as the cases seemed to me to be entirely made out by the government. I should like to ask you, if it is proper, what it was caused the jury to disagree." The driver: "I was the one who disagreed." Dana, still unsatisfied: "Would you mind telling me why you disagreed?" The driver: "I was one of the men who helped him to escape."[8]

The next fugitive slave case did not end so happily as that of Shadrach. On April 3 the city police arrested Thomas Sims, an escaped slave, on a false charge of committed theft, and hustled him to the Court House. Fearing an attempt at rescue, a strong police force (thence styled the "Sims Brigade") was put on duty, and the Court House was surrounded with heavy chains. The Judges of the Supreme Court were compelled to creep under the chains on their way to the bench, and "so loyal," said the Massachusetts *Annual Report*, "were those magistrates to the dominant power that they submitted without a murmur."[9]

Boston bitterly opposed the outrage. Bells were tolled in the country towns. Meeting after meeting was held at which Phillips, Parker, Garrison, and Quincy spoke, and there was a monster demonstration on the Common where the orator addressed acres of excited people.

"We are met in the open air," said Phillips, "because Faneuil Hall is refused to us. . . . In our effort at this crisis to arouse Massachusetts to the outrage about to be perpetrated against her laws, in this effort, the State and City officials have betrayed us and joined the enemy. About to be perpetrated, did I say?—already consummated.

"What shall we do? Sir, I think this meeting is rather to plan action than discuss opinions. To plan what? To devise all possible means of preventing the return of a fugitive slave from the soil of the State—of preventing the full execu-

tion of this iniquitous law. If Yankee ingenuity cannot drive
a four-wheeled wagon load of slaves through any law
which drunken legislators can make, let us hide our
heads. . . .

"It will be a damning disgrace to Massachusetts if a man,
standing on free soil, and entitled to the presumption that
he is a freeman, is dragged from her limits back to bondage,
without a jury trial, without anything worthy of the name
of a trial or of evidence against him. It will be a damning
disgrace if such a man can be dragged back without the
rails of every rail track being torn up, without every village
on the route rising en masse to block the wheels of government."[10]

Placards were posted at all corners by the Vigilance Committee:

PROCLAMATION!!
to all
THE GOOD PEOPLE OF MASSACHUSETTS.
Be it known that there are now
Three Slave-Hunters or Kidnappers
in Boston
Looking for their prey.
One of them is called Davis
He is an unusually ill looking fellow
about five feet eight inches high, wide-shouldered.
He has a big mouth, black hair, and a good deal of
dirty, bushy hair on the lower part of the face. He
has a Roman nose; one of his eyes has been knocked out.
He looks like a Pirate, and knows how to be a Stealer of Men.
The next is called
Edward Barrett . . .
He wears his shirt collar turned down, and has a
black string—not of hemp—around his neck
The third Ruffian is named
Robert M. Bacon, alias
John D. Bacon . . .
He has a red, intemperate-looking face and a retreating
forehead. His hair is dark and a little grey. He wears a

black coat, mixed pants, and a purplish vest. He looks
sleepy and yet malicious.
Given at Boston, this 4th day of April, in
the year of our Lord 1851, and of the
Independence of the United States the fifty-fourth.
God Save the Commonwealth of Massachusetts.[11]

On Sunday a request was sent to the clergymen of Boston and
vicinity, and in several instances it was feelingly complied with.

"The undersigned, a freeman, in peril, desires the prayers
of this congregation that God may deliver him from his
oppressor, and restore him to freedom.

his

Thomas   X   Sims.

mark

S. E. SEWALL

Witnesses

E. W. JACKSON

Boston, April 5, 1851."[12]

"Give me a knife," the poor slave begged of his counsel, "and
when the Commissioner declares me a slave, I will stab myself
to the heart before his eyes."[13]

All attempts to free Sims failed. "COME BY THOUSANDS,"
urged the Vigilance Committee of the people of Massachusetts
the day before the rendition of Sims, "Come to witness the last
sad scene of the State's disgrace."

At five o'clock in the morning of Saturday, April 12, Sims
was taken from his cell, placed in a hollow square of 300 policemen armed with guns and sabres, marched to the head of Long
Wharf, and placed on board the brig Acorn. The slave guard
was drilled for an hour and a half before the final move to the
vessel. All along Court Street they were greeted with cries of
contempt. "Where is Liberty?" cried one spectator. "She is dead!"
shouted another. "Shame! Shame!" cried others. "Is this Boston?"
"Is this Massachusetts?" "Is that Charlestown and Bunker Hill?"
Just as Sims reached the deck of the vessel, a man standing on
the Wharf cried out, "Sims! preach liberty to the slaves!"

The scene was solemn. All the sails lay unfurled and ready for sea. Immediately the rattling of the jib halyards commenced and the white sail arose that was to carry the poor fugitive back to bondage. The assembly prayed and sang hymns, then friends of Sims moved up the Wharf and street singing "Old Hundred." Pausing on the spot where Crispus Attucks fell, members of the Vigilance Committee resolved to meet at once at the anti-slavery office. They adopted a resolution asking the people of Massachusetts to toll their bells as news reached them of the rendition of Sims.[14]

Several notices of "The Knell of Liberty" appeared in the next *Liberator*: "The bells of the Orthodox, Methodist, and Universalist Churches of Waltham were tolled on Saturday when the news of the man stealing was received. The bell on the Unitarian Church being clogged with cotton would not sound."[15]

The *Commonwealth* of Saturday, April 12, announced "The Victim has been sacrificed!"[16] "Massachusetts, God forgive her! She is kneeling with the rest," said the Massachusetts *Spy*.[17] "This Boston," declared the Ohio *Star*, "yes, that same old Boston, world renowned as the cradle of Liberty, has been turned into a military despotism! Austria with her Haynaus has found her rival!"[18]

Theodore Parker wrote: "If a monument were built to commemorate the events which were connected with the Salvation of the Union, the inscription might be—

Union Saved by Daniel Webster's Speech at
Washington .... March 7, 1850.
Union Saved by Daniel Webster's Speech at
Boston .... April 30, 1850.
Union Saved by the passage of the Fugitive
Slave Bill .... Sept. 18, 1850.
Union Saved by the arrival of Kidnapper
Hughes at Boston .... Oct. 19, 1850.
Union Saved by the Union Meeting at Faneuil Hall .... Nov. 26, 1850.
Union Saved by the kidnapping Thomas
Sims at Boston .... April 3, 1851.

Union Saved by the rendition of Thomas
  Sims at Savannah .... April 19, 1851.

Oh, what a glorious morning is this!"[19]

Twelve days after the return of Sims, Massachusetts declared itself in a practical protest, and the Anti-Slavery leader Charles Sumner was elected to the United States Senate. A salute of one hundred guns was fired on Boston Common, and all over New England bells were rung, guns fired, and houses illuminated. A procession formed in State Street and marched to Sumner's house, thence to the house of Richard Henry Dana, Senior, in Chestnut Street, thinking that the younger Dana, Sim's counsel, lived there. The old poet came to the door and told them that his son lived not there but in Cambridge. As they turned away, the crowd gave three hearty cheers for "the old gentleman, Mr. Dana's father."

The Boston *Daily Advertiser* next day issued a call to all business men of Boston to boycott Dana.[20]

As New York City was still dominated by the Rynders mob, the American Anti-Slavery Society was denied a hall there in which to hold its annual May meeting, and found shelter in Syracuse. The health of Ann Phillips was so precarious that Wendell was kept at home. He was able, however, to attend the annual New England Anti-Slavery Convention held at Boylston Hall, May 27. In his speech dealing with the attempt to rescue Sims he bitterly accused the people in the towns surrounding Boston of being lax in their duty to the runaway slave. When one person in the audience protested that the country towns had waited for a summons from Boston, Phillips angrily replied: "Waited for an invitation! When Hampden went to London Tower, under the order of Charles the First, two thousand armed men came up to London to know why their representative was in the Tower. They did not wait for an invitation!" It was not true, he added, that the Vigilance Committee of Boston discouraged a resort to force. They had made the best resistance they had the power to make. They called upon the Commonwealth to aid them and the Commonwealth was deaf to the call.

"My friend says it is expensive to come to Boston. It costs 25 cents to come from Lynn—one dollar to come from Plymouth—$1.25 to come from Worcester. Now, I will venture to say that all these men, so warmly interested for Sims as to arm themselves in his behalf, have had their daguerreotypes taken, more than once, those of their wives and children, and they will all come up to Boston next Fourth of July to see the fireworks; but they could not spend a dollar to come to Boston and prevent the rendition of Sims."[21]

On August 1 Phillips slipped down to Worcester to take part in the celebration of West India Emancipation. His speech was the feature of the day—a harsh attack on Webster and a fervent defence of anti-slavery. "This is the First of August," he began, "a day in which, as Lamartine said, 'Wilberforce went up to the throne of God with 800,000 broken fetters in his hand.'" The question was not, he went on, was the whistle a good one, but whether Americans could buy it cheap or dear. But the prosperity that was bought at the cost of justice, liberty, and honor came too dear, though it paved every street with gold, and built a marble palace in every village. As for Webster's speeches, they resembled the balloons sent up in Paris and London: distended and gassy they sailed well over the Capitals but fell flat and empty in the country when some higher law spire or Town Hall cupola touched them. And Phillips's anger flamed when he spoke of Webster's attempt to curb anti-slavery agitation.

"Mr. Webster, with an insolence which the history of this country cannot parallel, standing upon the steps of a hotel, tells his fellow citizen that 'this agitation must stop!' Not while God creates tongues! (Tremendous cheerings.) . . .
"'Stop that noise!'—so endeth the first lesson. And then the preacher goes down to Virginia, and considers Southern agitation. Does he say that must stop? No. Southern disunionists are 'learned and eloquent,'—indeed—'animated and full of spirit,'—truly!—'high-minded and chivalrous,'—no 'rub-

a-dub men' those!. . . . But, then, recollect, they were
born South and own slaves!—conclusive evidence of their
right to complain without cause, disturb the Union and
break it up, if they please, and still be the 'respected' of Mr.
Webster; while as far North as unhappy Faneuil Hall, no
man may peep or mutter. . . . 'Stop that agitation! You
are neither learned nor eloquent, high-minded nor chivalrous, and I'll speak as I please of you. And judging others
by myself, it's your vocation to be spaniels and doughfaces.'
    "Ay, the bone that is thrown at us is good enough, unless
we vindicate our right to speak, by speaking so loudly that
even the deafest ear can hear. Let us teach these politicians
that we know well enough what they mean when they would
hold up to us the value of the Union in protecting iron and
cotton, and the decks of fishing vessels; remind them that
we share the love of property with the brute creation; with
the bee that fashions its tiny warehouse, and the beaver that
builds dams across the streams; but that we possess also a
higher attribute, the gift of thought and speech, and mean
to value them accordingly, as the distinguishing characteristic of our superiority and allying us to God."[22]

This, added Phillips, is the true spirit of the Constitution.
Webster had said he spoke in the spirit of Samuel Adams. But
Samuel Adams, on going home one day, found a colored woman
sitting at his fireside. On asking his wife who she was, he was
told that she was a slave that a friend had presented her. "No
woman," said the old patriot, "crosses my threshhold who does
not bring her liberty with her." Spoken in the spirit of Sam
Adams? asked Phillips. Why, Webster was "not worthy to unloose the latchet of his shoe! (Applause.) Compare Samuel
Adams, the incorruptible Cato of 1776, to the Whirligig McSyc-
ophant of 1851!—as well liken an English bulldog to a lady's
fan!"
Phillips then launched into an examination of the Constitution. The Revolutionary patriots did not worship the Constitution as an end; they looked upon it as a means. They no more
mistook it for liberty than we mistake the railroad which brings
us to the city for the city we seek. They trusted that their

children, if it did not serve that end, would, in the spirit of its
founders, beat it down and do better. Judge Harrington of Vermont, one of the earliest Judges under the Constitution, asked
the first slaveholder that went to him for his property, for his
bill of sale. The slave hunter asked how it should be signed.
"Signed," said Harrington, "if signed at all, by the Almighty.
If you claim a man as your property, He alone is competent to
give a bill of sale." That, insisted Phillips, was the true spirit
of the Revolution.

"Whatever they meant, this remains true—the true traitor
of the Constitution is he who upholds the Fugitive Slave
Law. The worst foe to the Union is he who proves such a law
necessary for its preservation. As well put gunpowder under
the Capitol as wickedness into the statute book. The man
who would do his whole duty either to his country, his
religion, or his ancestry, is bound to devote himself, heart
and soul, to get rid of this great blight that rests upon our
national escutcheon. We owe it to the purity of our common
religion to prove that Christianity does not sanction bondage.
We owe it to our fathers, and their great guide, our institutions, to prove them fathers of men capable and ready for
the great work God lays upon us—doing justice and making
atonement to the colored race in our midst."[23]

CHAPTER TWENTY

TWIN REFORMS: WOMAN SUFFRAGE

AND TEETOTALISM

At an anti-slavery meeting held in Boston in 1850 an invitation
was given from the speaker's desk to all those who felt interested in a plan for a National Woman's Rights Convention to
meet in the ante-room. Nine solitary women responded and
went into the dank and dingy room to consult together. A call
was issued by prominent men and women, including Ann and
Wendell Phillips. The convention met in Brinley Hall, Worcester, on October 23 and 24, 1850. The attendance was large and
a national organization was started with the appointment of
a central committee of which Phillips was made treasurer.

Over in England the *Westminster Review* noticed the convention in an elaborate article by Mrs. John Stuart Mill and
endorsed it. But in America the newspapers pelted it with
abuse. It was "the Hen Convention" and its members "ismizers
of the rankest stamp." One Universalist clergyman announced
a proposed meeting from his pulpit in these words: "This evening, at the Town Hall, a hen will attempt to crow!"[1] This was
thought to be a huge joke. Lydia Maria Child had her own tart
retort, "Some of the communications of women in the newspapers are very amusing," she wrote to a friend. "They seem to
flutter together like a set of hens, terribly frightened lest you
and I and other 'strong-minded hawks' should pounce down
upon 'em and carry them off from their chickies."[2]

The most ridiculed and mercilessly persecuted of all the
suffragists was Susan B. Anthony. The newspapers were filled

with caricatures showing her in man's attire, with hip boots and a slouch hat from under which flashed a pair of fierce eyes from a countenance at once evil and formidable. The first sight of Susan B. Anthony on the platform gave one a flash of amazement. Patience and gentleness shone from her mild blue eyes, and in her plain black dress, relieved only by a white frill at the neck, and with her smoothly brushed hair parted over her forehead and coiled neatly at the nape of her neck, she looked what indeed she was, a Hicksite Quaker of a sturdy New England stock.

Lucy Stone, "a little independent piece," who picked berries and chestnuts for money to buy books with and while in college did housework at three cents an hour, was called by the press the she-hyena of the Suffrage movement. She went through Massachusetts from town to town, engaging her own halls, nailing up her posters and conducting her meetings. The average man and woman regarded her as a freak. Once she was hit on the head by a large prayer book hurled across the hall.[3]

Early in her career as a public speaker she met Henry Blackwell, who finally persuaded her to marry him. His pledge to accept the idea of complete equality was sincere and was expressed in the famous Protest which he wrote and they both signed. After acknowledging their mutual affection, they repudiated the laws of marriage that gave the husband "injurious and unnatural superiority, investing him with legal powers which no honorable man would exercise and which no man should possess." The Boston *Post* jubilantly hailed the marriage in derisive verse—

"A name like Curtius' shall be his,
On Fame's loud trumpet blown,
Who with a wedding kiss shuts up
The mouth of Lucy Stone!"

But no such thing happened. "Mrs. Stone" continued to lecture. She even permitted her baby's cradle to be sold for the taxes she refused to pay because by having no vote she was not represented in the government.[4]

The *Southern Literary Messenger* found amusement, even in wartime, in printing these verses from an English magazine:

1.

"Take a pretty girl,
The prettier the better,
Give her naught to read
But novel and love-letter.
Let her go to plays,
Circuses and dances,
Fill her heart with love,
Murder, and romances.

2.

Furnish her with beaux
Too numerous to mention,
Send her to attend
Each 'Woman's Rights' Convention,
Humor her to death
Whene'er she has the vapors,
Verses let her write
For magazines and papers.

3.

Tell her of her charms
On every occasion,
Make her 'talents' rare
The theme of conversation;
Let 'affairs of state'
And politics be taught her—
And she'll wear 'short skirts and pants'
Or at least she 'orter.' "[5]

Phillips's advice on woman suffrage policy was always eagerly sought. When Caroline H. Dall suggested the establishment of a Journal, he reminded her that Woman Rights funds were too small even to contemplate such a thing.[6] In October, 1851, the Second National Woman's Rights Convention met in Worcester. Phillips made an elaborate speech, examining all angles of the question.

Every step of progress, remarked Phillips, has been from scaffold to scaffold and from stake to stake. The ideas of justice and humanity have been fighting their way like a thunderstorm against the organized selfishness of human nature. And woman suffrage was a protest against the wrong of ages. In every great reform, the majority have always said to the claimant, no matter what he claimed, "You are not fit for such a privilege." Luther asked of the Pope liberty for the masses to read the Bible. The reply was that it would not be safe to trust the common people with the word of God. "Let them try!" said the great reformer.

"Woman stands now at the same door. She says, 'You tell me I have no intellect; give me a chance. You tell me I shall only embarrass politics; let me try.' The only reply is the same stale argument that said to the Jews of Europe, 'You are fit only to make money; you are not fit for the ranks of the army or the halls of Parliament.' How cogent the eloquent appeal of Macaulay: 'What right have we to take this question for granted? Throw open the doors of this House of Commons, throw open the ranks of the imperial army, before you deny eloquence to the countrymen of Isaiah or valor to the descendants of the Maccabees.' It is the same now with us. Throw open the doors of Congress, throw open those court-houses, throw wide open the doors of your colleges, and give to the sisters of the Motts and the Somervilles the same opportunities for culture that men have, and let the result prove what their capacity and intellect really are. When, I say, woman has enjoyed, for as many centuries as we have, the aid of books, the discipline of life, and the stimulus of fame, it will be time to begin the discussion of these questions,—'What is the intellect of woman?' 'Is it equal to that of man?' Till then, all such discussion is mere beating of the air."[7]

Phillips and the other suffrage reformers made no attempt to settle what should be the profession, education, or employment of woman. What they asked was simply this—what all other classes have asked before: leave it to woman to choose for herself her profession, her education, and her sphere. "We deny the right of any individual to prescribe to any other individual his amount of education or his rights." The sphere of each man, of each woman, of each individual is that sphere which he can, with the greatest exercise of his powers, perfectly fill.[8]

Another aspect of the question—true for his day—appealed to Phillips: the value of the contemplated change in a physiological point of view. Dainty notions had made woman such a hot house plant that one-half the sex were invalids. "Better that our women," added Phillips, "like the German and Italian girls, should labor on the highway and share in the toil of harvest than pine and sicken in the indoor and sedentary routine to which our superstition condemns them."

"One word more. . . . Do you ask me the reason of the low wages paid for female labor? It is this. There are about as many women as men obliged to rely for bread on their own toil. Man seeks employment anywhere and of any kind. No one forbids him. If he cannot make a living by one trade, he takes another; and the moment any trade becomes so crowded as to make wages fall, men leave it . . . Not so with women. The whole mass of women must find employment in two or three occupations. The consequence is, there are more women in each of these than can be employed; they kill each other by competition. Suppose there is as much sewing required in a city as one thousand hands can do. If the tailors could find only five hundred women to sew, they would be obliged to pay them whatever they asked. But let the case be, as it usually is, that there are five thousand women waiting for that work, unable to turn to any other occupation, and doomed to starve if they fail to get a share of that; we see at once that their labor, being a drug in the market, must be poorly paid for. She cannot say, as man would, 'Give me so much, or I will seek another trade.' She must accept whatever is offered, and often underbid her sister that she may secure a share. Any article sells cheap when there is too much of it in the market. Woman's labor is cheap because there is too much of it in the market."[9]

It was not the capitalist's fault, Phillips conceded. It was
as much the fault of society itself. It was the fault, to put it
bluntly, of that timid conservatism which set its face like flint
against everything new, of a servile press which knew so well
how much fools and cowards were governed by a sneer. It
was, too, the fault of silly women, ever holding up their idea of
what was "lady-like" as a Gorgon head to frighten their sisters
from earning bread. It was the fault, again, of that pulpit which
declared it indecorous in woman to labor, except in certain occupations and thus crowded the whole mass of working women
into two or three employments, making them rivet each other's
chains.

"But open to her now other occupations. . . . and the
consequence will be, that, like every other independent laborer, like their male brethren, they may make their own
terms, and will be fairly paid for their labor. It is competition in too narrow lists that starves women in our cities;
and those lists are drawn narrow by superstition and prejudice.

"The question is intimately connected with the great
social problem—the vice of cities . . . Facts will jostle
theories aside. Open to man a fair field for his industry,
and secure to him its gains, and nine hundred and ninety-
nine men out of every thousand will disdain to steal. Open to
woman a fair field for her industry, let her do anything her
hands find to do, and enjoy her gains, and nine hundred
and ninety-nine women out of every thousand will disdain
to debase themselves for dress or ease . . .

"Understand us. We blink no fair issue. We have counted
the cost; we know the yoke and the burden we assume. We
know the sneers, the lying frauds of misstatement and mis-
representation, that await us. We have counted all; and it
is but the dust in the balance and the small dust in the
measure, compared with the inestimable blessing of doing
justice to one half of the human species. . . ."[10]

Once during his speech, Phillips was interrupted by hisses.
He said—"There are two kinds of creatures that hiss—serpents

and geese," and he hoped there were none of these in the Convention. There was no further hissing.[11]

When Phillips met Theodore Parker after returning from the Convention, the clergyman said to him—

"Wendell, why do you make a fool of yourself?"

"Theodore," Phillips replied, "This is the greatest question of the ages; you ought to understand it."

Before the year had passed, Parker espoused the cause and preached four sermons upon it.[12]

Phillips could not stop so long as there were evils to be discovered and wrongs to be righted or thoughts to be spoken. One of these evils was intemperance. It was not a new evil nor the first time he had met and attacked it. Prohibition he regarded as the best remedy for general drinking. And he pleaded frequently for the enactment and the enforcement of laws to stop the sale of liquor at every tenth door in Boston and in the taverns of every village. Yet he was broad enough to state the other side: that the saloon was the workingman's clubroom and that his twelve hours of labor left him but twelve more for eating, sleeping, and such pleasures as boozing. Phillips trusted largely to moral suasion and offered as a reward for temperance individual happiness. Contrasted with the sour figure of the modern Prohibitionist, Phillips, like his fellow reformers, was a happy and generous person, eager to allow every liberty to mankind and never happy himself so long as injustice and unkindness remained on earth.

The question of temperance was a difficult one in those days, for liquor flowed freely. Two bottles of champagne per guest at a little Whig affair of Daniel Webster's were mere chasers to the real liquid refreshments served on that occasion. Long before champagne corks began to fly, gentlemen took aboard a full cargo of brandy and whiskey, cocktails, claret, Rhenish wines, sherry, madeira, and port.

In hardly any state was drunkenness the cause for divorce. Fuddled lawyers pleaded before fuddled judges in the highest courts; fuddled physicians came to the childbeds of women; whiskey, rum, and gin could be bought by children in grog shops and saloons. Even ministers of the Gospel drank. In moderation they claimed. At all events it was not uncommon for them to accept part of their salaries in kegs of liquor.

A few individuals, deeply concerned over this situation, met together in Boston in the autumn of 1825 to consider the question: "What shall be done to banish intemperance from the United States?" The result of the conference was a determination to form an American Temperance Society, whose cardinal principle should be abstinence from strong drink. In February, 1826, at a convention of interested men a constitution was adopted.

Twelve years later the Massachusetts Temperance Union was formed. It induced the General Court to enact the "Fifteen Gallon Law," the first prohibitory law of the state, and it was the first to emblazon on its banner the motto—*"Total abstinence from all intoxicating drinks."*[13] The principal impediments to total abstinence, declared a report of the society, were fashion, public festivities, weddings, and cider.

Agents all over the state endeavored to train up children as teetotalers by organizing them into Cold Water Armies. The children had frequent picnics, wore badges, carried banners in all processions, and sang songs. The pledge was set to music and sung with great glee at all the meetings:

> This youthful band
> Do with our hand
> The pledge now sign
> To drink no Wine,
> Nor Brandy red
> To turn the head,
> Nor Whiskey hot
> That makes the sot,
> Nor fiery Rum
> To turn our home
>   Into a hell,
> Where none can dwell,
> Whence peace would fly,
> Where hope would die,
> And love expire
> 'Mid such a fire:—

So here we pledge perpetual hate
To all that can intoxicate.[14]

Even a paper in the interest of this movement for the young
was published, called the *Cold Water Army*.

A monster demonstration was held on Boston Common by the
Washingtonian Temperance Societies on May 30, 1844. The
city was in gala attire. Banks were closed and most business
houses arranged for a half holiday. About fifteen thousand persons including many children joined in the procession. The
song, "The Teetotalers are Coming," was sung; "The Drunkard's
Dream" and other pieces were recited; twenty-three brass bands
of music played; and addresses by various persons were made
during the day. There were interesting floats. The South Boston
Washingtonian Society presented a moss-covered well with two
men drawing buckets of cool water from its depth. After the
exercises on the Common picnic suppers were served in several
parts of the city.[15]

Other Temperance Societies were organized. The secret Independent Order of Rechabites was not only a total abstinence organization but a benefit institution also, providing for all their
members in case of sickness and death. It took the name from
the ancient Rechabites mentioned in the Scriptures who refused to drink wine. It was not popular, however, because of
its foreign origin. Then there were "The Sons of Temperance,"
"The Daughters of Temperance," "The Temple of Honor," "The
Cadets of Temperance," "The Crusaders of Temperance," "The
Temperance Watchmen," "The Carson League," "The Independent Order of Good Templars" (the first temperance society
to open its doors to women), "The Young Home Guards" (any
young person enrolled was entitled to a beautiful diploma on
payment of fifteen cents for same. Any boy or girl procuring
the names of fifteen volunteers received a diploma gratis), "The
Juvenile Templars," "The Good Samaritan Brotherhood", etc.

"The Washingtonians" was made up entirely of reformed old
soaks, and their confessions were told in every lurid detail, more
thrilling to listen to than the most earnest arguments in favor
of a godly, righteous, and sober life. Like the revivals of evan-

gelical sects they put up a pretty good show. Nearly all of them had gone through delirium tremens or claimed the experience anyhow, and their battles with snakes and demons, their hideous agonies of body and mind were graphically described. If in their cups they had nearly or quite murdered a loved one, preferably a child, so much the better. John B. Gough's zeal for temperance was like that of Garrison for Abolition. After seven years of vagrancy and intemperance, he had signed the Washingtonian pledge and devoted himself unfalteringly to the cause. As he said: "While I can talk against the drink, I'll talk. When I can only whisper, I'll do that. And when I cannot whisper any longer, faith, I'll make motions—they say I am good at that."[16]

Even lesser lights among the temperance lecturers had a good sense of the theatre. One favorite carried along his little boy whom he carefully planted in an obscure corner of the church or hall. At the moment of his speech when the audience was exactly at the proper pitch of emotion, the speaker demanded: "As for the rum seller, the rum seller, my friends, what name black enough shall we find to call him?" He paused and gesticulated wildly, searching for a sufficiently scurrilous word. Which was the little boy's cue to shrill out at the top of his lungs—"Devil, devil!" (Hysterical screams from the women and loud amens from the men.)[17]

Another successful platform light was accompanied by a pathetic little girl who in blue ribboned ringlets and frilled pantalets stood beside his chair and sang a temperance song—the classic "Father, dear father, come home with me now," or the tear compelling, "Father's a drunkard and mother is dead."

> Mother, oh! why did you leave me alone?
> With no one to love me, no friends and no home.
> Dark is the night and the storm rages wild,
> God pity Bessie, the Drunkard's lone child."[18]

Companies of strolling players found the temperance theme popular bedewing it with such tender lyrics as "The Rumseller's Lament," "Dry that Flowing Tear," and "The Drunkard Wife's Lament." A few theatrical managers saw in it the possibility of increased profits. "The Drunkard or the Fallen Saved" ran for one hundred and forty consecutive performances before enthusiastic audiences in the Boston Museum. "One Cup More, or the Doom of a Drunkard" was also a success.

Timothy Shay Arthur's "Ten Nights in a Bar Room" and stories by Lucius M. Sargent (whose temperance tales were collected in a large edition of six volumes to supply the demand in the United States and Great Britain) were old standbys. Poetry, fiction, periodicals, pamphlets, broadsides streamed from the press of the American Temperance Union.[19]

The *Liberator* was often enlisted in the cause. One issue published the following which sums up the attitude of the early Temperance Reformer.

THE TREE OF DISSIPATION

The
sin   of
drunkenness
expels   reason,
drowns memory, dis-
tempers the body, defaces
beauty,   diminishes   strength,
corrupts the blood, inflames the
liver, weakens the brain, turns men
into walking hospitals, causes internal, external, and incurable wounds, is a witch to the
senses, a devil to the soul, a thief to the pocket,
the beggar's companion, a wife's woe, and the
children's   sorrow—makes   men   become   a
beast and a self murderer, who drinks
to others' good health and robs
himself of his own! Nor is this
all; it exposes to the
Divine

DISPLEASURE HERE!
AND HEREAFTER TO
ETERNAL MISERY!!

The
root of all is
D R U N K E N N E S S ! ! ![20]

CHAPTER TWENTY-ONE

GUEST OF THE NATION

"*Kossuth.* Tell him of American Slavery! Save Him! Save him!" cried Henry C. Wright in a letter to the *Liberator.* "His doom is sealed if he comes here. 'HERE LIES KOSSUTH—THE AMERICAN SLAVEHOLDER'—must be his epitaph, if he touches our shore. Friends of freedom in Europe and America— to the rescue!"[1]

But heedless of Abolitionist protests President Fillmore was directed to offer one of the ships of the Mediterranean squadron to convey Kossuth and his associates to the United States. The execution of the Fugitive Slave Law was now over-shadowed by the interest taken in the visit of the Hungarian patriot.

Kossuth waited a day at Staten Island in order to give the New York City fathers time to prepare a grand reception. One hundred thousand people were waiting on the Battery. Castle Garden was full to overflowing. When Kossuth landed and could be seen, a tumultuous roar broke forth. It seemed as if the shout would raise the vast roof of the reception hall.[2]

A torchlight procession in honor of Kossuth was held on the evening of his arrival and the city of New York gave him a banquet at Irving house. An imposing reception by the bar of New York and an afternoon entertainment by ladies at the Metropolitan Opera House were a fitting close to the honors showered on the Hungarian leader. It was a curious spectacle to see descendants of sober blooded Englishmen and phlegmatic Dutchmen roused to such a pitch of enthusiasm over a man whose only title to fame was that he had fought bravely and acted wisely in an unsuccessful revolution. But we were then an excitable people.[3]

A cordial reception was given Kossuth in Washington. He was presented to the President, dined at the White House, and was received by Congress. The occasion prompted Sumner to make his maiden speech. Kossuth deserved our welcome, he exclaimed. "He is grandly historic, a living Wallace—a living Tell—I had almost said a living Washington. . . ."[4]

The "Guest of the Nation" was a dignified and impressive gentleman with an Asiatic countenance—a thin, thoughtful face, full beard, and dark eyes. He held in his hand a broad brimmed soft hat, already the symbol of European revolutionists.

The keynote of hospitality thus struck in New York rang out clear and lusty in the other cities which Kossuth visited and where he gave full scope to his rare powers of picturesque eloquence. When he passed, it seemed as if every home for miles back from the railroad was deserted and that all the inhabitants had gathered along the tracks to see and hear the great Magyar. In Cincinnati alone he raised from thirty to fifty thousand dollars for the Hungarian cause.[5]

Not a word fell from Kossuth's lips regarding slavery. He would have Americans feel for the robbed, peeled, hunted Magyar while he had no word of sympathy for the Fugitive Slave. This was a bitter mortification to Phillips who was among his most ardent admirers and deeply sympathized with his poor country. But as he watched his triumphal course and saw him deliberately sacrifice the Negro to aid the Hungarian, his indignation grew hot. In vain he called on him to be "faithful and fearless."

Kossuth used to create wild enthusiasm by "Your own late glorious struggle with Mexico." But when he reached that climax in his Pittsburgh speech a dead silence fell upon the vast cheering audience.[6]

In a speech delivered at the Anti-Slavery Bazaar on December 27, 1851, Phillips condemned Kossuth's course. The speech was a criticism rather than a diatribe on a person whose chief desire, like his own, was for freedom, but whose partial advocacy of it was repellent to one who never did anything by halves.

"Senator Foote spoke truly when he said, from his seat in the Senate chamber, 'There is a great struggle going on through the world. It is between despotism and liberty. . . . No man can fail to be on one side or the other. He that is not with us is against us.' To which John P. Hale replied with such readiness, 'Exactly.' . . . . Now, wherever there is the war of ideas, every tongue takes a side. There is no neutrality. Even silence is not neutrality; but he who speaks a word of sympathy to his brother-man is on the side of humanity and progress. (Loud cheers.). . . ."[7]

Take Kossuth's speeches, added Phillips. Did they differ from those of the most pro-slavery American? Did he qualify his eulogy? Had he a word of sympathy for the oppressed? Our country was "great, glorious, and free, the land of protection for the persecuted sons of freedom among the great brotherhood of nations." This was his language.

"What! free as the land where the Bible is refused to every sixth person! Free as the land where it is a crime to teach every sixth person to read! Free as the land where, by statute, every sixth woman may be whipped at the public whippingpost! Free as the land where the murderer of the black man, if the deed is perpetrated only in presence of blacks, is secure from legal punishment! Free as the land where the fugitive dares not proclaim his name in the cities of New England, and skulks in hiding places until he can conceal himself on board a vessel, and make his way to the kind shelter of Liverpool and London!. . . ."[8]

Kossuth was a patriotic and devoted Hungarian—grant him that, said Phillips. He loved Hungary so much that his charity stopped at the banks of the Danube. He was a lover of his motherland, but, still, it was a local patriotism. Even Webster loved the whites. It is something to love one's race, and so much is patriotism. But people claimed for Kossuth that he represented the cause of liberty the world over.

"Men say, 'Why criticise Kossuth, when you have every reason to believe that, in his heart, he sympathizes with you?' Just for that reason we criticise him; because he endorses the great American lie, that to save or benefit one class, a man may righteously sacrifice the rights of another. Because, while the American world knows him to be a hater of slavery, they see him silent on that question, hear him eulogize a nation of slaveholders, to carry his point. What greater wrong can he do the slave than thus to strengthen his foes in their own good opinion of themselves? He whom tyrants hated on the other side the ocean, is the favored guest of tyrants on this side. He eats salt with the Haynaus of Washington. . . .

Dulce et decorum est pro patria mori. Every heart responds to the classic patriot, and feels that it *is* indeed good and honorable to *die* for one's country; but every true man feels likewise, with old Fletcher of Saltoun, that while he 'would die to serve his country, he would not do a base act to save her.' "[9]

The protests of Phillips and Garrison were drowned in salvos of applause as Kossuth wended his way through New England.

On April 25, he arrived in Boston and was received at State House by Governor Boutwell amid cheers of the great multitude gathered to do him honor. The road was choked up with footmen, horsemen, and carriages. The streets were crammed with people. Windows were full of ladies who waved their welcome.

"Though Kossuth's welcome roars through our streets," wrote Phillips to Sumner, "I may as well sit down and answer you, more especially as your Free Soil friends have sent me no ticket of admission to the State House, not thinking it delicate perhaps to suppose me willing to look at him!"[10]

It was announced that Kossuth would speak in Faneuil Hall on April 29, Thursday evening, and that no one would be admitted to the hall who could not exhibit a Hungarian bond to the doorkeepers. When the doors opened at six o'clock the street before the hall was so packed that several ladies fainted. Kossuth was received with nine thundering cheers.[11]

When the brave Magyar left Boston on May 18, his car was adorned with flowers and flags. It bore the words "Cradle of Liberty" on each side and had a gilded eagle at each end with the name Kossuth beneath.

By the middle of June the excitement had wholly died down and the name of Kossuth was rarely heard in New York or Boston. Even Phillips and the Abolitionists neglected him.

Congress came to audit the hotel bill of the Hungarian patriot and his suite. The bill amounted to nearly $40,000 and was considered by the Senate as enormous in magnitude. The dignity of the Senate compelled them not to pry into the items. The House had no such scruples, and before passing it, examined narrowly every itemized statement.

The debate was lively and entertaining.

Mr. Jones of Tennessee (in the course of his speech on contingent expenses of the Senate)—"Now, sir, here is a bill paid to the Messrs. Brown, hotel keepers of this city, for Louis Kossuth and his suite, of $4,566.32. For that I never intend knowingly to vote, directly or indirectly."

Several voices—"Read the items."

Mr. Jones—"The items are as follows: 'To board for Governor Kossuth and suite having ten parlors and twenty-two chambers, thirteen and a half days—twenty-three persons: $3,588.00; sundries: champagne, sherry, madeira, cigars, lemonade, bar-bill, washing, . . . Then, sir, they stopped at the National Hotel about four days, and their bill was $74. being $3.08 per day for each person, when they were paying their own expenses, and something over $14. per day for each person when this government was paying their expenses.

"These are the facts, and some of the reasons why this appropriation is asked for by the Secretary of the Senate."

Mr. Freeman, "Has the money been paid?"

Mr. Jones. "It has been paid out of the $150,000 appropriated in the civil and diplomatic appropriation bill of last year.

Mr. Freeman. "Then how are you to get it back?"

(Here the hammer fell.)[12]

CHAPTER TWENTY-TWO

A BEST SELLER

With Parker, Phillips assisted early in 1852 in the formation of a moral reform society for the protection of poor girls. The object of the organization was twofold: to instruct waifs in the means of earning an honest livelihood and then to remove them into a more wholesome environment.

The Anniversary of the Massachusetts Anti-Slavery Society occurred in January. On the 28 of that month, Phillips addressed the Society in one of the ablest of his speeches—that on Public Opinion.

"No matter where you meet a dozen earnest men pledged to a new idea,—wherever you have met them, you have met the beginning of a revolution. Revolutions are not made; they come. A revolution is as natural a growth as an oak. It comes out of the past. Its foundations are laid far back . . ."[1]

Phillips launched into a discussion of the fourth estate. Napoleon said, "I fear three newspapers more than a thousand bayonets." So too, Phillips felt, the government was wrecked the moment the newspapers decreed it. The penny papers of Massachusetts did more to dictate the decision of Chief Justice Shaw than the legislature that sat in the state House. The penny papers of New York did more to govern this country than the White House at Washington.[2] Webster said we live under a government of laws. He was never more mistaken, even when he thought the anti-slavery agitation could be stopped. We live under a government of men and morning newspapers. Bennett

and Horace Greeley were more really Presidents of the United
States than Millard Fillmore.

From the lordship of the press Phillips shifted to the lordship
of institutions.

> "The difficulty of the present day and with us is, we are
> bullied by institutions. A man gets up in the pulpit, or sits on
> the bench, and we allow ourselves to be bullied by the
> judge or clergyman, when, if he stood side by side with us,
> on the brick pavement, as a simple individual, his ideas
> would not have disturbed our clear thoughts an hour. Now
> the duty of each antislavery man is simply this,—stand on
> the pedestal of your own individual independence, sum-
> mon these institutions about you, and judge them."[3]

No law could abide one moment when public opinion demanded its abrogation. We live in an age of democratic equality
—the moment a party stands against the age, in the end it goes
by the board. "The man who launches a sound argument, who
sets on two feet a startling fact and bids it travel from Maine
to Georgia, is just as certain that in the end he will change
the government, as if, to destroy the capitol, he had placed gunpowder under the Senate Chamber."

Natural philosophers tell us, remarked Phillips, that if you
will only multiply the simplest force into enough time, it will
equal the greatest. So it is with the intellectual progress of
the masses. It can scarcely be seen, but it is a constant movement; it is the shadow on the dial—never still, though never
seen to move; it is the tide, it is the ocean gaining on the proudest bulwarks on the shore, those bulwarks which art or strength
can build. It may be defied for the span of a brief moment but
in the end Nature triumphs. Phillips went on:

> "There is nothing stronger than human prejudice. A crazy
> sentimentalism like that of Peter the Hermit hurled half of
> Europe upon Asia, and changed the destinies of kingdoms.
> We may be crazy. Would to God he would make us all crazy
> enough to forget for one moment the cold deductions of in-
> tellect, and let these hearts of ours beat, beat, under the

promptings of a common humanity! They have put wickedness into the statute-book, and its destruction is just as certain as if they had put gunpowder under the Capitol. That
is my faith. That it is which turns my eye from the ten
thousand newspapers, from the forty thousand pulpits,
from the millions of Whigs, from the millions of Democrats, from the might of sect, from the marble government,
from the iron army, from the navy riding at anchor, from
all that we are accustomed to deem great and potent,—
turns it back to the simplest child or woman, to the first
murmured protest that is heard against bad laws. I recognize it in the great future, the first rumblings of that volcano destined to overthrow these mighty preparations, and
bury in the hot lava of its full excitement all this laughing
prosperity which now rests so secure on its side."[4]

The sessions of the Massachusetts Anti-Slavery Society lasted
two days. In the evening of the third day, the Abolitionists
met at Faneuil Hall and Phillips spoke upon the recent surrender of Sims. He introduced resolutions condemning the great
obstacle that for twenty years had stood in the way of freedom
—the commercial interests.

"Do you ask why the Abolitionists denounce the traders
of Boston? It is because the merchants chose to send back
Thomas Sims,—pledged their individual aid to Marshal
Tukey, in case there should be any resistance; it is because
the merchants did it to make money. Thank God, they have
not made any! (Great cheering.) Like the Negro who
went to hear Whitefield, and rolled in the dust in the enthusiasm of his religious excitement, until they told him it
was *not* Whitefield, when he picked himself up, crying
out, 'Then I dirty myself for nothing.' So they dirtied
themselves for nothing! (Tremendous cheering.) If only
slave-hunting can save them, may bankruptcy sit on the
ledger of every one of those fifteen hundred scoundrels
who offered Marshal Tukey their aid! (Tumultuous applause.) . . ."[5]

Webster had, on various occasions, intimated that the cotton mills of Lowell, the schooners of Cape Cod, the coasters of Marblehead, the coal and iron mines of Pennsylvania, and the business of Wall Street were the great interests which the United States government was framed to protect. He intimated that property was the great element, the test by which the success of a government was to be appreciated.

"Perhaps it is so; perhaps it is so; and if the making of money, if ten per cent a year, if the placing of one dollar on the top of another, be the highest effort of human skill; if the answer to the old Puritan catechism, 'What is the chief end of man?' is to be changed, as according to modern statecraft it ought to be, why, be it so. Nicholas of Russia made a catechism for the Poles, in which they are taught that Christ is next below God, and the Emperor of all the Russias is next below Christ. So, judging by the tenor of his recent speeches, Daniel has got a new catechism, 'What is the chief end of Man?' The old one of the Westminster divines, of Selden and Hugh Peters, of Cotton and the Mathers, used to answer, 'To glorify God and enjoy him forever'; that is treason, now. The 'chief end of man'?—why, it is to save the Union!"[6]

The meeting was stormy. The hall was crowded with foes of the Abolitionists. Speaker after speaker was shouted down. Phillips himself had to fight for a hearing. Every name he ventured to censure was cheered. But his brilliance and wit turned the laugh upon his interrupters. When after a bitter attack on Webster, a voice called for "Three cheers for Daniel Webster," the cheers were given so faintly that a shout of derision went up from the audience. At the conclusion of Phillips's speech, an invitation was extended to any one in the hall to come forward, take the platform and defend Daniel Webster from imputations cast upon him. The invitation brought up one Abraham Gunnings Drake. "He was a perfect Roaring K. Rouser," said the *Daily Herald*. He struck a fierce attitude and walked the platform like a stag at bay. Finally a volcano of eloquence burst forth:

"When the Declaration of Independence was signed, wasn't there slavery? Yaas! Didn't Peter Faneuil advertise slaves in the city? Yes, sirree! What then? Was it wrong? I go for my Kedentry, right or wrong. Wrong commenced in the Garden of Eden—what o' that? I am a red-hot loco foco of the pro-slavery stamp. ('Good') I go for the Fugitive Slave Law, and so does the great Daniel . . . I am determined to rescue the immortal Daniel from the rank and file of the red hot, infuriated, and, insane, crazy, demented, imbecile Abolitionists. Why, because England only freed her black slaves in consequence for jealousy of the United States. Therefore I go for Daniel Webster, head and foot, in all over, although I wouldn't vote for him."[7]

The orator stalked off the stage amid bursts of laughter.

2

A cool headed London printer took a book home at night to read with the view of deciding whether it would be a paying publication. He was so affected first by laughter and then by tears that he ended by distrusting his own literary judgment, thinking his emotion was due to physical weakness. So he tried the story on his wife, a strong minded woman, and got her approval before he deemed it wise to print the book.

The book was Mrs. Harriet Beecher Stowe's *Uncle Tom's Cabin* and its publication in America on March 20, 1852, proved an event for two continents. Lowell described the impression made by the book as a "whirl of excitement."[8] Three thousand copies were sold the first day, ten thousand in a week, 300,000 in a year. Eighteen different publishing houses in England were issuing the book at one time and a million and a half copies were sold in Great Britain. The power presses, running night and day, were barely able to keep pace with the demand. It was translated in at least twenty-three languages including Illyrian (two distinct versions) Roman or modern Greek, Wallachian (two distinct versions), Welsh (three distinct versions), Armenian, Bohemian (one version).[9]

Rufus Choate read the book, wept over it in spite of himself, and slamming it down exclaimed angrily, "There! That will add two million or more to the ruff scuff Abolitionists."[10]

Prince Albert and the Queen, Charles Dickens and Macaulay praised it. The Reverend Charles Kingsley in the midst of his illness wrote—"Your book will do more to take away the reproach from your great and growing nation, than many platform agitations and speechifyings."[11] Lord Palmerston, who had not read a novel for thirty years, read *Uncle Tom's Cabin* three times and admired the book "not only for the story, but for the statesmanship of it."[12] Heinrich Heine, poet and cynic, was so moved by the book that he returned to the reading of the Bible—"Astonishing that after I have whirled about all my life over all the dance floors of philosophy and yielded myself to all the orgies of the intellect and paid my addresses to all possible systems without satisfaction, like Messalina after a licentious night, I now find myself on the same standpoint where poor Uncle Tom stands—on that of the Bible."[13] In a long review in a Paris journal George Sand concluded that Mrs. Stowe was "in the true spirit of the word, consecrated."[14]

Uncle Tom's Cabin was presented on the stage. When the Chatham Street and Bowery Boys, who belonged to the mobs that hooted and insulted the Abolitionists and broke up their conventions, when they saw "Abolition dramatized," as the play was cleverly called, they went wild at the escape of Eliza across the river, applauded the allusion to human rights, were disgusted with the professional slave auction and the business like action of Negro buyers in the slave market scene, and wept sincerely at the death of Uncle Tom. When it was the fashion of metropolitan theatres to change programs nightly, *Uncle Tom's Cabin* ran for one hundred nights, and it was played to crowded houses in two theatres each in London and Paris.

Mrs. Stowe's tour through England was a pageant. Crowds reverently watched for her at the railway stations, hymns were composed in her honor. She was showered with gifts which ranged from enormous inkstands because she was an author, to gold bracelets which by an inverted symbolism represented the breaking of shackles. She received a penny offering amounting to thousands of pounds for the anti-slavery cause and accepted a monster petition in twenty-six folio volumes solidly bound in morocco signed by 562,448 women of England urging the abolition of slavery.

In Scotland she met everywhere with a warm welcome. The plain, common people greeted her. The butcher came out of his stall and the baker from his shop, the miller dusty with flour and the blooming young mother with a baby in her arms, all smiling and bowing.

A reception was given her by the Duke and Duchess of Sutherland at Stafford House. When reports of this Stafford House meeting reached America, Calhoun remarked that it would make Abolition fashionable. A despised movement was indeed made fashionable for a while by a little Yankee woman "just as thin and dry as a pinch of snuff."[15]

The lasting results were not immediately evident. "It deepens the horror of servitude," wrote George Tichnor, "but it does not affect a single vote."[16] The impression made upon bearded men was not so powerful as its appeal to women and the future fighters of the Civil War—boys.

The South responded more in contempt than in wrath. "*Uncle Tom's Cabin*" was "a plot against the peace of society," exclaimed a preacher and professor at Annapolis, Reverend E. J. Stearns. A Southern woman reviewing Mrs. Stowe's "*Key to Uncle Tom's Cabin*," which appeared a year later than the novel, observed that Mrs. Stowe's books had "sunk so low" it was charity to make note of them.[17]

Letters and letters poured in upon the author. Friends applauded, slaveholders heaped angry reproaches upon her. On one occasion Professor Stowe opened an envelope which contained a Negro's ear, pinned to a bit of cardboard, and a few words scrawled which hinted that this was one of the effects of her defense of the "Damn niggers."[18]

"Uncle Tom," as Phillips justly remarked, would never have been written had not Garrison developed the facts, and never would have succeeded in America had he not created readers and purchasers.[19] The book is not a novel; it is a record of facts. The story is as distinctly intended to inform Northern ignorance and to remove Northern prejudice as it is to justify the conduct of Abolitionists. It lets in the daylight on the essential nature of slavery.

Slavery in no form, Mrs. Stowe contended, was justifiable. There were ten chances of a slave's finding an abusive, tyrannical master to one of his finding a considerate and kind one, and even when he chanced to be sold to a kind master, either the loss of the master's fortune, as in the case of Mr. Shelby, or his death, as in that of St. Clare, usually rendered the slave's condition even more wretched than it could have been, had he never enjoyed kindly treatment.

To stirring stories of fugitives who had escaped from European despotism, Mrs. Stowe remarked: "When despairing Hungarian fugitives make their way to America against all the search warrants of their lawful governments, press and political cabinet ring with applause and welcome. When despairing African fugitives do the same thing, it is—what is it?"[20]

Encouraged by the popularity of Mrs. Stowe's novel, the Abolitionists decided to observe the anniversary of Thomas Sims' surrender. Accordingly, on April 12, 1852, a great meeting was held in Boston at which Phillips spoke. He openly asserted the inalienable right of the slave to protect himself and to use every means that he had to resist arrest.

"I say in private, to every one that comes to me, 'But one course is left for you. There is no safety for you here, there is no law for you here. The hearts of the judges are stone, the hearts of the people are stone . . . Do not linger here.

"Still, circumstances may prevent flight . . . He may be seized before he succeeds in escaping. I say to him, then, There is a course left, if you have the courage to face it. . . . It has now reached that pass when even the chance of a Boston gibbet may be no protection from a Georgia plantation; but if I were in your place, I would try! (Tremendous cheering.) The sympathies of the people will gather round you, if put on trial for such an act. There may be something in an appeal to a Massachusetts jury impanelled to try a man's INALIENABLE RIGHT TO Liberty, the pursuit of happiness, and to protect himself.

"Mark me! I do not advise any one to take the life of his fellow,—to brave the vengeance of the law, and run the . . . unequal risk of the hard technical heart of a Massachusetts jury. I can only tell the sufferer the possibilities that lie before him,—tell him what I would do in his case,—tell him that what I would do myself I would countenance another in doing, and aid him to the extent of my power."[21]

The anti-slavery cause was a wonder to many, continued Phillips. They wondered it did not succeed faster. William Cobbett, with his *Political Register,* circulating seventy thousand copies per week, appealed to the working men of Great Britain, and in a few years he carried his measures over the head of Parliament. Cobden talked the farmers of England, in less than ten years, out of a tyranny that had endured for generations. The difference was, apologized Phillips, the Abolitionists had no such selfish motives to appeal to. They appealed to white men who could not see any present self interest in the slave question. It was impossible to stir them, for they must first ascend to a level of disinterestedness which the masses seldom reach. "I do not know when that point will be gained," confessed Phillips.

But the slave question haltered and lingered because it could not get the selfishness of men on its side—and that was the lever by which the greatest political questions have been carried. There was another motive: fear. Cobbett and his fellows gathered the people of Great Britain in public meetings of 200,000 men—and though the Duke of Wellington ordered his Scotch greys to rough grind their swords, as at Waterloo, he feared to have them drawn in the face of 200,000 Englishmen. That gathering was for their own rights.

"I do not believe that, if we should live to the longest period Providence ever allots to the life of a human being, we shall see the total abolition of slavery, unless it comes in some critical conjuncture of national affairs, when the

slave, taking advantage of a crisis in the fate of his masters,
shall dictate his own terms. . . ."[22]

How did French slavery and the French slave trade go down.
When Napoleon came back from Elba, when his fate hung
trembling in the balance, and he wished to gather around him
the sympathies of the liberals of Europe, he no sooner set
foot in the Tuileries than he signed the edict abolishing the
slave trade. How did the slave system go down? When in 1848
the Provisional Government found itself in the Hotel de Ville,
obliged to do something to draw to itself the sympathy and liberal
feeling of the French nation, they signed an edict—the first
of the nascent Republic—abolishing the death penalty and
slavery.

And in one of the finest passages the great orator ever
spoke, Phillips went on:

"The hour will come—God hasten it!—when the American people shall go stand on the deck of their Union, 'built
i' th' eclipse, and rigged with curses dark.' If I live to see
that hour, I shall say to every slave, Strike now for Freedom! (Long continued and deafening cheers.) The balance
hangs trembling; it is uncertain which scale shall kick the
beam. Strain every nerve, wrestle with every power God
and nature have put into your hands, for your place among
the races of this Western world; and that hour will free the
slave. The Abolitionist who shall stand in such an hour
as that, and keep silence, will be recreant to the cause of
three million of his fellow-men in bonds. I believe that
probably is the only way in which we shall ever, any of us,
see the downfall of American slavery. I do not shrink from
the toast with which Dr. Johnson flavored his Oxford
Port,—'Success to the first insurrection of the blacks in
Jamaica!' I do not shrink from the sentiment of Southey
in a letter to Duppa,—'There are scenes of tremendous horror which I could smile at by Mercy's side. An insurrection
which should make the Negroes masters of the West Indies
is one.' I believe both these sentiments are dictated by
the highest humanity. I know what anarchy is. I know
what civil war is. I can imagine the scenes of blood through

which a rebellious slave-population must march to their rights. They are dreadful. And yet, I do not know that, to an enlightened mind, a scene of civil war is any more sickening than the thought of a hundred and fifty years of slavery. Take the broken hearts, the bereaved mothers, the infant wrung from the hands of its parents, the husband and wife torn asunder, every right trodden under foot, the blighted hopes, the imbruted souls, the darkened and degraded millions, sunk below the level of intellectual life, melted in sensuality, herded with beasts, who have walked over the burning marl of Southern slavery to their graves, and where is the battlefield, however ghastly, that is not white—compared with the blackness of that darkness which has brooded over the Carolinas for two hundred years? (Great sensation.) Do you love mercy? Weigh out the fifty thousand hearts that have beaten their last pulse amid agonies of thought and suffering fancy faints to think of, and the fifty thousand mothers who, with sickening senses, watch the footsteps that are not wont to tarry long in their coming, and soon find themselves left to tread the pathway of life alone,—add all the horrors of cities sacked and lands laid waste,—that is war,—weigh it now against some young, trembling girl sent to the auction block, some man like that taken from our court-house and carried back into Georgia; multiply this individual agony into three-millions; multiply that into centuries; and that into all the relations of father and child, husband and wife; heap on all the deep moral degradation both of the oppressor and the oppressed, —and tell me if Waterloo or Thermopylae can claim one tear from the eye even of the tenderest spirit of mercy, compared with this daily system of hell amid the most civilized and Christian people on the face of the earth!"[23]

"You are very sensitive over *Uncle Tom's Cabin*", Phillips chided his audience. But if hearts answered instead of nerves, every Abolitionist would rise up, ready to sacrifice everything rather than a man should go back to slavery. The city of John Hancock had proved that her soil was not holy enough to protect the fugitive; Bunker Hill was not too sacred for fettered feet; the churches, planted in tears, in prayers, and in blood,

had no altar horns for the fugitive; the courts, too, had shut
its doors on the fugitive.

"I would say all this to the men about me, and add,—There
is one gleam of hope. It is just possible that the floor of the
State's prison may have a magic charm in it. That may
save the fugitive, if he can once entitle himself to a place
there. When, therefore, the occasion shall demand, let us
try it! (Great cheering.) It is a sad thought, that the possibility of a gibbet, the chance of imprisonment for life,
is the only chance which can make it prudent for a fugitive
to remain in Massachusetts.

"You will say this is a bloody doctrine,—anarchical doctrine; it will prejudice people against the cause. I know it
will. Heaven pardon the judges, the merchants, and the
clergy, who make it necessary for hunted men to turn,
when they are at bay, and fly at the necks of their pursuers!
It is not our fault! I shrink from no question, however desperate, that has in it the kernel of possible safety for a
human being hunted by twenty millions of slavecatchers in
this Christian republic of ours. (Cheers.) I am willing to
confess my faith. It is this: that the Christianity of this
country is worth nothing, except it is or can be made capable
of dealing with the question of slavery. I am willing to
confess another article of my faith: that the Constitution
and government of this country is worth nothing, except
it is or can be made capable of grappling with the great
question of slavery. . . . The greatest praise government
can win is, that its citizens know their rights, and dare to
maintain them. The best use of good laws is to teach men
to trample bad laws under their feet.

"On these principles, I am willing to stand before the
community in which I was born and brought up,—where I
expect to live and die,—where, if I shall ever win any reputation, I expect to earn and keep it. As a sane man, a Christian
man, and a lover of my country, I am willing to be judged
by posterity, if it shall ever remember either this meeting
or the counsels which were given in its course. I am willing
to stand upon this advice to the fugitive slave—baffled in
every effort to escape, or bound here by sufficient ties,
exiled from the protection of the law, shut out from the

churches—TO PROTECT HIMSELF, and make one last
appeal to the humane instincts of his fellow-men."24

☞ "Daniel Webster, the endorser of the Fugitive Slave Law,
died at Marshfield, Massachusetts, October 24, 1852, in the
very height of the Law's triumphant operation.

☞ "The following may not improperly, find a place here.
Where will the demands of slavery be stayed?"25

CHAPTER TWENTY-THREE

HORACE MANN AND PHILLIPS—

"INFIDELS" OR "FEMALE PESTS"

The rising tide of Anti-Slavery sentiment was attributed by those hostile to the Abolitionists to anybody and everybody save Garrison, Phillips, and their followers. They were bigots and fanatics, their weapons the whoop and tomahawk of savage abuse and denunciation; their blind, childish, reckless, hot-headed zeal injured the cause they professed to serve; Sumner and Mrs. Stowe, and Henry Ward Beecher were the vital in-fluences that moved the swelling flood in New England—so they asserted.

At a meeting of the New England Anti-Slavery Society on January 27, 1853, in a speech called "The Philosophy of the Abolition Movement," Phillips took up these charges which had just been ably presented in the columns of the *London Leader* under the signature of "Ion." He dispelled the old bugaboos of indiscriminate abuse and misrule dogging the steps of the Abolitionists and paid a stirring tribute to the work and leadership of Garrison. He claimed nothing for himself, but did feel the slight to the veterans who surrounded him.

Abolitionists, he said, must plead guilty, if there be guilt, in not knowing how to separate the sin from the sinner. They were fighting a momentous battle against desperate odds—one against a thousand. Every weapon that ability or ignorance, wit, wealth, prejudice, or fashion could command was pointed against them. The guns were shotted to the lips. The arrows were poisoned. Fighting against such a determined array, Abolitionists could not afford to confine themselves to any one weapon. The cause was not theirs so that they might rightfully postpone or put in peril the victory by moderating their demands, stifling their convictions, or filing down their rebukes to gratify any sickly taste of their own or spare the delicate feelings of their neighbor. "Our clients are three millions of Christian slaves, standing dumb supplicants at the threshhold of the Christian world. They have no voice but ours to utter their complaints or to demand justice. God has given us no weapon but the truth, faithfully uttered and addressed, with the old prophet's directness to the conscience of the individual sinner."

Against the Abolitionists were arrayed the elements which controlled public opinion and molded the masses. Anti-Slavery could but pick off here and there a man from the triumphant majority. They had facts for men who reasoned, but he who could not be reasoned out of his prejudices must be laughed out of them, contended Phillips. He who could not be argued out of his selfishness must be shamed out of it by the mirror of his hateful self held up relentlessly before his eyes.

"We live in a land where every man makes broad his phylactery, inscribing thereon, 'All men are created equal,' —'God hath made of one blood all nations of men.' It seems to us that in such a land there must be, on this question of slavery, sluggards to be awakened, as well as doubters to be convinced. Many more, we verily believe, of the first than of the last. There are far more dead hearts to be quickened, than confused intellects to be cleared up,—more dumb dogs to be made to speak, than doubting consciences to be enlightened. (Loud cheers) We have use, then, sometimes, for something beside argument."[1]

What was the denunciation with which Abolitionists were charged? asked Phillips. And the answer came vehemently from his lips—it was endeavoring in faltering human speech to declare the enormity of the sin of making merchandise of men, of separating the husband and wife, taking the infant from its mother, and selling the daughter to prostitution. What was this harsh criticism of motive with which Abolitionists were charged? It was simply holding the intelligent and deliberate actor responsible for the consequences of his acts. Was there anything inherently wrong in such denunciation or such criticism, countered Phillips. This Abolitionists made plain: they never judged a man but out of his own mouth. They seldom, if ever, held him to account, except for acts of which he and his friends were proud.

"Prove to me now that harsh rebuke, indignant denunciation, scathing sarcasm, and pitiless ridicule are unjustifiable, else we dare not throw away any weapon which ever broke up the crust of an ignorant prejudice, roused a slumbering conscience, shamed a proud sinner, or changed the conduct of a human being. Our aim is to alter public opinion. Did we live in a market, our talk should be of dollars and cents, and we would seek to prove only that slavery was an unprofitable investment. Were the nation one great, pure church, we would sit down and reason of 'righteousness, temperance, and judgment.' Had slavery fortified itself in a college, we would load our cannons with cold facts, and wing our arrows with arguments. But we happen to live in the world,—the world made up of thought and impulse, or self conceit and self interest, of weak men and wicked. To conquer, we must reach all. Our object is not to make every man a Christian or a philosopher, but to induce everyone to aid in the abolition of slavery. We expect to accomplish our object long before the nation is made over into saints or elevated into philosophers. To change public opinion, we must use the very tools by which it was formed. That is, all such as an honest man may touch. . . .' [2]

Abolitionists did not play politics, insisted Phillips. Anti-Slavery was no half gesture with them. "It was a terrible earnest with life or death on the issue!" It was no lawsuit where it mattered not to the good feeling of opposite counsel which way the verdict went and where advocates could shake hands after the decision as pleasantly as before. When Phillips thought of such a man as Henry Clay, his mighty influence and irresistible fascination cast always into the scale against the slave, his conscience acknowledging the justice of the Abolition cause and his convictions sacrificed remorselessly to his ambition, he could not find it in his heart to do him honor. "Haynau on the Danube is no more hateful to us than Haynau on the Potomac. Why give mobs to one, and monuments to the other?"

The Abolitionists never claimed to be courteous. They sought only to be honest men and speak the same of the dead as of the living.

"History is to be written. How shall a feeble minority without weight or influence in the country, with no jury of millions to appeal to,—denounced, vilified, and contemned, —how shall we make way against the overwhelming weight of some colossal reputation, if we do not turn from the idolatrous present, and appeal to the human race? saying to your idols of today, 'Here we are defeated; but we will write our judgment with the iron pen of a century to come, and it shall never be forgotten, if we can help it, that you were false in your generation to the claims of the slave!' (Loud cheers.) . . .

"Before that jury we summon you. We are weak here, —out-talked, out-voted. You load our names with infamy and shout us down. But our words bide their time. We warn the living that we have terrible memories, and that their sins are never to be forgotten. We will gibbet the name of every apostate so black and high that his children's children shall blush to hear it. Yet we bear no malice. In our necessity we seize this weapon in the slave's behalf, and teach caution to the living by meting out relentless justice to the dead."[3]

The concluding part of Phillips's speech was in warm praise of Garrison:

"We are perfectly willing—I am, for one—to be the dead lumber that shall make a path for these men into the light and love of the people. We hope for nothing better. Use us freely, in any way, for the slave. When the temple is finished, the tools will not complain that they are thrown aside, let who will lead up the nation to 'put on the top-stone with shoutings.' But while so much remains to be done, while our little camp is beleaguered all about, do nothing to weaken his influence, whose sagacity, more than any other single man's, has led us up hither, and whose name is identified with that movement which the North still heeds, and the South still fears the most."[4]

In the course of his speech Phillips attacked the educator, Horace Mann, then a Free Soil Congressman from Massachusetts, for his non-committal position on slavery. Horace Mann answered and a long controversy filling columns and columns of the *Liberator* was started. Mann was a little testy at the pertinacity of Phillips in distinguishing between Free Soilers and Abolitionists. He charged Phillips with seventy-five misstatements. And he was unjust and harsh. He took offence at Phillips's rebuke of him five years before in regard to colored schools, saying: "When the mental and manual labor of three or four men was daily thrown upon me, Mr. Phillips came stealthily up behind me and struck dastardly blows. He uttered and printed the most palpable untruths respecting me, alienating friends and diffusing ill will towards me through a wide circle. In the criminal courts, and in reference to those who are convicted over and over again, they speak of 'third' or 'fourth comers.' To me Mr. Phillips is at least a 'fifth comer.'" But Mann, then head of the school system of Massachusetts, was an officer of the commonwealth and Phillips had a right to criticise his public acts.[5]

It was the tendency of Horace Mann, however, to impute wrong motives; his charity for men was too small, his estimate of their goodness ungenerous. In controversy he would take advantage of petty quirks and quibbles, give himself to cheap devices and petty defences and toy with the truth.[6]

One correspondent in Maine remarked:

"Horace, you're a fool! We told you to say nothing. Phillips is right, and he knows it, and we know it, and had you taken counsel of prudence, rather than of passion, you would have seen it too, but you've got us into a pretty fix! We can't contend—it won't do to back out—and all we can do is, to cry 'Ultraism! Ultraism! Ultraism!' "[7]

In May, 1853, Phillips fired a scornful parting shot:

"I have repeatedly asked Mr. Mann his opinion of the Fugitive Slave Clause. *He has never given me an answer.* . . . If I debate, it shall be with a man, one who holds his opinions with his whole heart and soul and mind and strength, and has none to conceal. Life with me is too busy and earnest to waste its hours with a fencer whose only aim is to chop logic."[8]

In the midst of the controversy, Phillips found time to address a Committee of the Constitutional Convention of Massachusetts, then in session, in behalf of a petition signed by the women of the state asking for equal political rights with men. The Convention heard the orator, and then threw the petition into the waste basket.

The month of May, 1853, found Phillips in New York City where the American Anti-Slavery Society had returned for its anniversary (a peaceful one, this time) after its exile of two years. Phillips resumed his speech at the point where Captain Rynders had stopped it—a fiery attack on the Union. In the course of his remarks he referred to the offer of the Rev. Dr. Orville Dewey, the eminent Unitarian clergyman, to return his mother into slavery if that were necessary to preserve the Union. A hurricane of cheers and hisses broke forth. Phillips paused blandly, and when the storm had subsided, said quietly: "For once I have the whole audience with me; some of you are applauding me and the rest are hissing Dr. Dewey!" This sally was followed by applause and laughter. Phillips went on:

"It is because Americans dare not call things by their right names—it is because we refuse to tear off these folds of acceptable and agreeable self deception, it is because we spread a mist of beauty around the Union, praise it, and worship the idol we have made, that slavery is so strong as it is. Now, the mission of the anti-slavery cause is to tear off from this subject the disguises of honeyed words and agreeable self-adulation which the nation itself and its leaders have wrapped around it. It is an endeavor to awaken Americans to their own true position."[9]

Friends at a little distance and in Boston, said Phillips, told him that the Union must be preserved. It was organic, autochthonic; it was part of the soil; it was part of the blood; it was not to be spoken of; it was not to be debated—much less was it to be abjured. Now, what was this Union? asked Phillips. What had it done for Americans? Undoubtedly there were benefits connected with the Union. But the greatest privilege was that of free speech. That was the best government in the world where a man could think noble thoughts, and act them, without suffering martyrdom. Was that the Union? The clergyman, with here and there an exception (here Phillips pointed to Henry Ward Beecher, and the audience applauded), who spoke freely, spoke himself out of his pulpit. The press—what was it? Pro-slavery. Why? Because to be otherwise was to be poor. Free speech for the priest, for the lawyer, for the statesman, for the merchant, and for the editor, repeated Phillips, was to be bought in these states at the price of martyrdom. Slavery was planted in South Carolina, but it gagged the free lips of the Berkshire and Vermont pulpits, and that was the "glorious Union."

"A 'glorious Union'—autochthonous, part of the blood. We cannot print an English book without expurgating it. Such is your literature. Your American Bible Society dare not offer a Bible in this very country to a man who has a drop of black blood in his veins. Your Sunday School and Tract Society dare not publish a tract with anti-slavery in it for fear of its Southern supporters. It is a 'glorious Union!' Thomas Jefferson, they used to say, was an infidel. He took the New Testament, and cut out those portions that displeased him, and called the rest his Testament. They told it in all the 'Federal' pulpits of New England, and men's blood grew cold at the blasphemy. But we blot out half the Bible to suit a hundred thousand men South of Mason and Dixon's line, and he is an 'infidel' who objects. ('Hear, hear.') What a 'glorious Union!' Men walk about and dare not tell their names—dare to travel only by midnight; to give a fellow being a crust of bread or a drop of water (witness Thomas Garrett) shall make you a poor man, a bankrupt. Verily it is a 'glorious Union.' . . .

"They sell a little image of us in the markets of Mexico, with a bowie knife in one side of the girdle and a Colt's revolver in the other, a huge loaf of bread in the left hand, and a slave whip in the right. That is America!"[10]

What was our whole history since 1820? asked Phillips. An attempt to bulwark the slave system. We had one great State paper—the Declaration of Independence—and in two-thirds of the country it was voted fustian. As for Uncle Tom's Cabin, in every conservative paper, in every respectable pulpit, it was voted a libel. "That is your Union. (A hiss.) I do not misrepresent. There is many a man that weeps over Uncle Tom who votes the Whig or the Democratic ticket. There is many a man that weeps over Uncle Tom and swears by the New York Herald." (Laughter and applause.)

The governing mind of this country, rightly argued Phillips, was not in the pulpit. Nor was it in the editor's chair. It was in the counting house. The energy, the ability of this young, growing enterprising twenty million nation were all concentrated there. The counting house was the great, the strongest, the most respectable representative of the real brains of America.

"When men say to me, we have not given to the world a literature, it is true to a certain sense; but we have subdued an empire; if we know not how to play the flute, we can say with Pericles, we know how to make a wilderness into an empire. That is the peculiar merit of the American people. Now, these merchant princes of ours, all over the country, are they anti-slavery? Do they report progress on Uncle Tom? Do they stand by the side of the anti-slavery question? Merchant princes—princes! pedlers, who sell their principles before they sell their goods (Applause), and worse than that, who do not stop to sell their principles, but are willing to throw them in to make a bargain for their goods!" (Great applause.)

"You think I am a fanatic, today. You think I am talking wildly, and insanely . . .

"No. The noblest sentence in our literature, I had almost said, was that of Patrick Henry: 'It is a duty which we owe to the purity of our religion to show that it does not sanction slavery.' It is our duty to show that the Christianity which the Puritans left us, which Winthrop, and Edwards, and Hopkins, and Channing have bequeathed to us, is a Christianity which does not veil its thrust before a hundred thousand aristocrats, or two thousand millions of dollars, but which can originate and sustain an anti-slavery cause, even though men go to their graves stamped as 'infidels,' and although a nation dies in the struggle—can originate and sustain a cause which thinks Right of more importance than any necessity, however great. . . ."[11]

Phillips denied that when he talked of the Union as a curse, he was talking fanaticism. He insisted he was talking nothing but political economy, nothing in the world but the coldest and lowest and most common principles of the counting house. Could slavery have existed in this country had Americans permitted the keen competition of the nineteenth century to come pouring its life-giving energy and warmth directly upon the South? But it was because the Union had placed itself as a shield over this old relic of Barbarism that it lived, contrary to the expectations of men. "It is a mere question of dollars and cents, after all, and slavery, entrenched in self interest, entrenched in dollars and cents, must be met with the same weapons of warfare with which she fights."[12]

In September Phillips attended two riotous conventions in New York. The World's Temperance Convention excluded women as delegates, and when Phillips protested, he was greeted by a storm of hisses. He was pronounced out of order and tried to speak amid innumerable calls to order, motions, interruptions, decisions, cries of "Go on, Phillips!" "Put 'em out!" etc. Finally he was excluded from the hall.

The proceedings of the Woman's Rights Convention were interrupted by rowdies. Roars of laughter and songs were interspersed with shouts of "Let's hear the women," "Wha-t's that?" "Shame!" "Oh, hush." Hisses. "Does your mother know you're out?" Scuffle in the gallery, rapping of canes, clapping of hands, sneezes, shrieks, and groans. When Wendell Phillips arose and begged that Mrs. Matilda Anika, an advocate of Woman's Rights, be heard in German, voices broke in: "We don't want to hear you." "We have heard enough of you already!" "Go it, boots."

Phillips begged the assembly to give the stranger a hearing. Just as he was about to continue, someone inquired in a hollow, sepulchral tone, "What's her name?"

Phillips, standing up—"Her name is Matilda Anika."

Voice—"What's her name?"

Phillips—"Matilda Anika."

Another voice—"What's that?" (Laughter. Hisses. General uproar.)

The German woman again essayed to speak. Mrs. Ernestine L. Rose said she would interpret the speech if they would only listen. (Hisses. Squealing. Groans. Yelling.)

Phillips—"Go on with your hisses. Geese have hissed before now. (Laughter and hisses.) You are proving, at least, that some men are unworthy of political liberty. You prove that men of the City of New York often do not know what the meaning of teetotalism and free discussion is. (Hisses.) When you will answer our argument, we shall cease to be agitators—but not till then.

Bowery Boy—"Speak in Dutch." (Laughter.)

Phillips—"If you hate this movement, the very best thing you can do for us is to come down here and disgrace your city, as you are now disgracing it." (Renewed cries of "Put him out!" "Go home, old fellow," "Give him a cigar," "O dear!" etc.)

Phillips—"Your Revolutionary fathers fought for freedom—"
Voice—"Niggers excepted." (Laughter.)
An old white-haired lady on the lower floor jumps up, greatly
excited, and clenches her fist at somebody.
Mrs. Rose—"I invoke the intervention of the police. Is the
Chief of Police present? Where are the police? Will they come
up here?"
The German woman makes another attempt to be heard but is
greeted with a succession of jeers, jests, and roars of laughter.
Phillips—"Elective franchise . . . ("Take off your coat") "un-
fathomable infamy . . . tyranny . . . atrocious absolution . . ."
("Sit down. We came to hear women, not you.")
Phillips—"I will add, on sitting down, ("Yes, sit down") that
if any man in the audience will come forward and reason with
us, it . . ."
At this juncture the police arrest one or two noisy fellows
in the gallery, an operation which produces new confusion.
Voices near the door—"Fire, fire, fire." (Consternation and
symptoms of panic. Order finally restored.)
Phillips, unable to get a hearing, at length takes his seat.
Lucy Stone comes forward—("Take your time, Miss Lucy!"
"Whar do you come from?" "Louder!" People yelling and hooting in the gallery.)
And so on in the same strain until the end of the meeting.
Lucretia Mott—"It is moved and seconded that the meeting
do now adjourn *sine die*. All who are in favor will say 'aye' "
The "ayes" have it numerically, but the "noes" are the loudest
and the noisiest.
Denouement: a rush for the doors. People requested to beware of pickpockets. The fresh air reached. The crowd dispersing. The doors shut. The gates closed. A man turning off
the gas.[13] Quiet.
The New York *Daily Times*: "The Female Pests."[14]
The New York *Herald*: "We saw in broad daylight in a public
hall in the city of New York, a gathering of unsexed women. . . .
Is the world to be depopulated? Are there to be no more children? Or are we to adopt the French mode which is too well
known to need explanation?"[15]

Phillips returned to Boston. Two weeks later he gave a fine definition of the functions of the reformer and politician.

"The reformer is careless of numbers, disregards popularity, and deals only with ideas, conscience, and common sense. He feels, with Copernicus, that as God waited long for an interpreter, so he can wait for his followers. He neither expects nor is over-anxious for immediate success. The politician dwells in an everlasting NOW. His motto is 'Success—his aim, votes. His object is not absolute right, but, like Solon's laws, as much right as the people will sanction. His office is, not to instruct public opinion, but to represent it. Thus, in England, Cobden, the reformer, created sentiment, and Peel, the politician, stereotyped it into statutes."[16]

CHAPTER TWENTY-FOUR

PHILOSOPHER OF AGITATION

Wendell Phillips was the first and greatest American agitator. He chose the part from a deliberate and profound conviction. In a free country all real progress, he believed, must be brought about by agitation. He accepted Sir Robert Peel's definition of the word—"the marshaling of the conscience of a nation to mould its laws."

Not only was agitation the sole means by which reforms could be carried through, it was the only means by which governments could be kept free. A people that is satisfied with the institutions it has gained, that worships the past and refuses to go forward, has already ceased to be free. In Phillips's own words—"If the Alps, piled in cold and still sublimity, be the emblem of despotism, the ever restless ocean is ours, only pure because never still."[1]

Brought face to face with the problem, Phillips was led to adopt a characteristic method of agitation. He made a platform outside of the state, outside of the church, with no political and no ecclesiastical creed to guard, a platform devoted to the freest, broadest, most critical discussion of questions and issues. And he summoned parties, sects, trades, social usages for judgment before it. Others for a special purpose dipped into agitation as a bather wades into the surf and then returned to their wonted vocations. Phillips had no other calling.

He expected that the role he filled would survive him and find an endless succession of occupants, because he claimed for this function of outside observation and criticism an essential and permanent place in American life. He based this claim on a thoroughgoing and planned philosophy. This philosophy embraced five cardinal principles.

(1) He believed absolutely in the supreme power of ideas. They were rulers by their own nature, victors in their own right. Charge these with the dynamite of righteousness and conscience and they would blow any and every form of opposition to atoms. "The man who launches a sound argument," he reiterated, "who sets on two feet a startling fact and bids it travel across the continent, is just as certain that in the end he will change the government, as if to destroy the Capitol he had placed gunpowder under the Senate Chamber."[2] Hence he discountenanced force in a republic. Why resort to bayonets when ideas are stronger? He had no patience with anarchy and anarchists. "Agitation," he said, "is an old word with a new meaning."

"It is above-board—no oath-bound secret societies like those of old times in Ireland and of the Continent today. Its means are reason and arguments; no appeal to arms. Wait patiently for the slow growth of public opinion. The Frenchman is angry with his government; he throws up barricades. A week's fury drags the nation ahead a hand-breadth, reaction lets it settle half-way back again. As Lord Chesterfield said a hundred years ago: 'You Frenchmen erect barricades, but never any barriers.' An Englishman is dissatisfied with public affairs; he brings his charges, offers his proofs, waits for prejudice to relax, for public opinion to inform itself. Then every step taken is taken forever; an abuse once removed never reappears in history."[3]

Ideas were Phillips's stock in trade, his armory, his jewels— what you will. To know them, to present them, to discuss them, to make them prevail—that was his life work.

(2) Next to ideas Phillips believed in the people—in the average common sense and capacity of the millions. He held with John Bright that the first five hundred men who pass in the Strand would make as good a Parliament as that which sits at St. Stephens. The party leaders of the time had a qualified faith in the people. Phillips's was unqualified. "The people always mean right," he said, "and in the end they will have

the right."⁴ He saw that it is never for the interests of the masses that injustice should be done. Hence while it is not safe to trust any class by itself, it is safe to trust the people. Not any one race, not either sex, but all races, both sexes, all sorts and conditions of men, good and bad, learned and ignorant, rich and poor. He would give the suffrage to all. He would put the ballot even in the hands of the most ignorant and then turn him to the State and say—"Here is one of your rulers. Now see to it that he is educated or he may give you trouble." He believed in universal suffrage because it took bonds of the rich and powerful to do their duty by the weak and poor.

Though he cherished this profound faith in the people, he never flattered the mob, nor hung upon its neck, nor pandered to its passion.

(3) The next point in Phillips's philosophy of agitation was the moral timidity of men under free institutions.

"It is a singular fact that, the freer a nation becomes, the more utterly democratic the form of its institutions, this outside agitation, this pressure of public opinion to direct political action, becomes more and more necessary. The general judgment is, that the freest possible government produces the freest possible men and women, the most individual, the least servile to the judgment of others. But a moment's reflection will show any man that this is an unreasonable expectation, and that, on the contrary, entire equality and freedom in political forms almost inevitably tend to make the individual subside into the mass and lose his identity in the general whole. Suppose we stood in England tonight. There is the nobility and here is the Church. There is the trading class and here is the literary. A broad gulf separates the four, and provided a member of either can conciliate his own section, he can afford in a very large measure to despise the judgment of the other three. He has to some extent a refuge and a breakwater against the tyranny of what we call public opinion. But in a country like ours, of absolute democratic equality, public opinion is not only omnipotent, it is omnipresent. There is no refuge from its tyranny; there is no hiding from its reach; and the result is that, if you take the old Greek lantern and go about to seek among a hundred you will find not one single American who really has not, or who does not fancy at least that he has, some thing to gain or lose in his ambition, his social life, or his business from the good opinion and the votes of those around him. And the consequence is that, instead of being a mass of individuals, each one fearlessly blurting out his own convictions, as a nation, compared with other nations, we are a mass of cowards. More than all other people we are afraid of each other."[5]

The great agencies through which public opinion here found expression were the pulpit, parties, and the press.[*] These Phillips thought inadequate to deal with what the French call "burning questions" like slavery, woman suffrage, temperance, and labor, with issues ahead of public opinion, chiefly because in the nature of the case, they voiced and were bound by the average sentiment.

"The pulpit, for instance, has a sphere of its own. It is too busy getting men to heaven to concern itself with worldly duties and obligations. And when it tries to direct the parish in political and social ways, it is baffled by the fact that among its supporters are men of all parties and of all social grades, ready to take offence at any word which relates to their earthly pursuits or interests, and spoken in a tone of criticism and rebuke. As the minister's settlement and salary depend upon the unity and good-will of the people he preaches to, he cannot fairly be expected, save in exceptional and special cases, to antagonize his flock. If all clergymen were like Paul, or Luther, or Wesley, they might give, not take orders. But as the average clergyman is an average man he will be bound by average conditions."[6]

This defeat in the Church Phillips also found in parties and the press: If his audience were a caucus and he their orator,

---

[*] The advent and phenomenal progress of the radio and television as a vital force in public opinion modify Phillips's list, but not his conception. For the same elements at work in the press, of necessity, have manifested themselves on the air.

explained Phillips, they could not get beyond the necessary and timid limitations of party. They not only would not demand, but they would not allow him to utter one word of what they really thought and what he thought. They would demand of him—and his value as a caucus speaker would depend entirely on the adroitness and vigilance with which he met the demand—that he should not utter one single word which would compromise the vote of next week. That was politics. So with the press. Seemingly independent, seldom really so, the press could afford only to mount the cresting wave, not go beyond it. "The editor might well shoot his reader with a bullet as with a new idea." He must hit the exact line of the opinion of the day.

"I am not finding fault with him; I am only describing him. Some three years ago I took to one of the freest of the Boston journals a letter, and by appropriate consideration induced its editor to print it. As we glanced along its contents and came to the concluding statement, he said: 'Couldn't you omit that?' I said, 'No; I wrote it for that; it is the gist of the statement.' 'Well,' said he, 'it is true; there is not a boy in the streets who does not know that it is true; but I wish you could omit that.' I insisted, and the next morning fairly and justly, he printed the whole. Side by side he put an article of his own in which he said: 'We copy in the next column an article from Mr. Phillips, and we only regret the absurd and unfounded statement with which he concludes it. . . .' He had kept his promise by printing the article; he saved his reputation by printing the comment. And that, again, is the inevitable, the essential limitation of the press in a republican community. Our institutions floating unanchored on a shifting surface of popular opinion, cannot afford to hold back or to draw forward a hated question, and compel a reluctant public to look at it and to consider it. Hence, as you see at once, the moment a large issue, twenty years ahead of its age, presents itself to the consideration of an empire or of a republic, just in proportion to the freedom of its institutions is the necessity of a platform outside of the press, of politics, and of the Church, whereon stand men with no candidate to elect, with no plan to carry, with no reputation to stake, with no object but the truth, no purpose but to tear the question open and let the light through it."[7]

Phillips's tribute to Charles F. Hovy, a Boston merchant, well represents the cardinal principle in his own life and practise. "To be independent of the world, it has been well said, is little. To differ, when reason bids, from our immediate world, is the test of independence."[8]

Behind Webster and Everett and Clay was always a great or organized party or an intrenched conservatism of opinion. They spoke accepted views—moved with the masses of men and were sure of applause. Phillips stood alone. He was not a Whig nor a Democrat nor a graceful panegyrist of an undisputed situation. Both parties denounced him. Public opinion condemned him. With no party behind him and denouncing the established order and acknowledged tradition, his speech was necessarily a popular appeal for a strange and unwelcome cause.

"I know that human nature is like a pendulum, and never goes in the centre, but is always oscillating from side to side; but I know this also, that it is by the fanaticism of the ages that this lower world has been dragged out of its bed of sloth into some decent progress. (Applause.) You do not trace the children of reform, of progress, of ideas, back to the thrones, to ceiled houses, to colleges, to respectable boards . . .

"What we call an anti-slavery man is one who is awake to the necessity of the hour . . . who is willing to go behind words, who is willing to call things by their right names, who dares to trust God so much that he does not believe His Church will fall if he describes a church of slaveholders as a synagogue of Satan . . . Throw out of the catalogue the Union and the Church! Give us ideas, not symbols. Do not let your religion consist in sitting in the pew your grandfather sat in, and singing from your mother's hymn book—in the emotional, the association of tender memories, that make up one portion of religion; but recognize the fact that the religious element, in times like ours, has a keen battle to fight to vindicate itself."[9]

"There is nothing higher than the individual conscience," Phillips declared elsewhere. "That is the corner stone of the reformer . . . We must each learn to feel in determining a moral question as if there was no one else in the Universe but God and ourselves."[10]

(4) Another principle in Phillips's theory stressed the need for constant stir and vigilance in a Republic. If the work of the Revolution was to be saved, and independent America to become free America, the first and paramount necessity was to arouse the country. Agitation was and is the duty of the hour.

"Each man here, in fact, holds his property and his life dependent on the constant presence of an agitation like this of anti-slavery. Eternal vigilance is the price of liberty; power is ever stealing from the many to the few. The manna of popular liberty must be gathered each day or it is rotten. The living sap of today outgrows the dead rind of yesterday. The hand intrusted with power becomes, either from human depravity or *esprit de corps,* the necessary enemy of the people. Only by continual oversight can the democrat in office be prevented from hardening into a despot; only by an unintermitted agitation can a people be kept sufficiently awake to principle not to let liberty be smothered in material prosperity . . ."[11]

Some men, said Phillips, suppose that in order to have the people govern themselves, it is only necessary, as Fisher Ames said, that the "Rights of Man be printed, and that every citizen have a copy." Even so the Epicureans, two thousand years ago imagined God as a being who arranged this marvelous machinery, set it going, and then sank to sleep. Republics exist only on the tenure of being constantly agitated. Thus the anti-slavery agitation was an important, nay essential, part of the machinery of state—it was no disease or medicine. Never could we afford to do without prophets like Garrison to stir up the monotony of wealth, to reawake the people to the great ideas that are constantly fading out of their minds, to trouble the waters that there might be health in their flow.

"A republic is nothing but a constant overflow of lava. The principles of Jefferson are not up to the principles of today. It was well said of Webster, that he knows well the Hancocks and Adamses of 1776, but he does not know the Hancocks and Adamses of today. The republic which sinks to sleep, trusting to constitutions and machinery, to politicians and statesmen, for the safety of its liberties, never will have any. The people are to be waked to a new effort, just as the Church has to be regenerated, in each age. We must live like our Puritan fathers, who always went to Church, and sat down to dinner, when the Indians were in their neighborhood, with their musket lock on the one side and a drawn sword on the other."[12]

"Friends, I know the weariness of the cause in which you are engaged," remarked Phillips to those who attended the anniversary of British West India Emancipation at Abington.

"There is no Canaan in reform; there is no rest ahead; it is all wilderness. As long as the devil lasts you are in for it. The agitation you began is just as necessary today as it was thirty years ago. A thousand years ago, the Dutch built their ramparts,—a wall of mud—against the ocean. Do they trust them? Nay, day by day, the peasant steals an hour from toil for his children's bread, to go to the ocean and fill up the breach, repair the willow which the insects have eaten, and save the land which his father gave him, while the ocean roars over his head, endeavoring to clutch what man has snatched from its grasp. So it is with this little island of anti-slavery feeling, which we have clutched from a reluctant public. The waves of hatred, of time-serving politics, or partisan ambition, of servility and compromise, are raving around it. The rampart of public opinion which you have built is daily eaten away. Each day, some servile hunter for office caves in, and falls into the bottomless pit. Every day, one part of the rampart falls."[13]

At another time Phillips injected a dose of red blood into the veins of the faint-hearted: "If there is anybody here who does not like quarreling, I advise him to go and join the con-

servatives, for he will find reformers always in a tempest."
When the time comes, said Phillips, that the advocates of any
reform cease to criticize each other, its efficiency is gone. An
aggressive Christianity—the Christianity that attacks everything
and everybody until it secures something no longer capable of
being found fault with—that is the element of all reform.
Never fear, he added, that anybody with a reputation worth
preserving will be hurt or that any institution that ought to
live will die.

"I affirm it as a truth self-evident, as well as established
by all history, that no constitution or government ever came
to an end by efforts from within, that did not deserve to
come to an end. If our Constitution goes to pieces by discussion inside, it will only be because it deserved to go to
pieces, not for any other reason."[14]

Plant an oak in a flower pot; the flower pot will go to pieces
the moment the oak begins to grow. But as long as you see
the flower pot whole, you may be certain the oak is dwarfed.
Later Phillips defended his position:

"Unfortunately the power of writing is tenfold greater
than the power of thinking, and the result is we are covered with a swash of mere words, except when now and
then by some unaccountable mistake, a thought crops out.
Struggling up amid these waste acres of weeds comes now
and then a head which thinks as well as talks, and put
institutions to the question. This is the Agitator. He is
not always right. He may be often wrong. He may say
the very worst thing that can be said, but he says something that sets everybody thinking—he says something
that stirs the whole atmosphere. We are crystallizing constantly down into unwise rest intellectually, and he comes
and disturbs the process and sets all the elements and
atoms into a general movement and they crystallize round
a new centre.

"Sometimes up in Washington, when great papers don't
say much, they put their ears close down and see what the
little independent ones say. It is a very wise method. . . .

These little goading Agitators can anticipate, they can explain a little ahead how you will put your coats on the day after. It is a great thing."[15]

(5) Phillips's final axiom as an agitator was "the truth, the whole truth, and nothing but the truth." No concealing half of one's convictions to make the other half more acceptable; no denial of one truth to gain a hearing for another; no compromise, or as Daniel O'Connell phrased it, "Nothing is politically right which is morally wrong." Under this rule he used a plainness of speech which shocked his hearers. He was one outspoken man in a host of shifters and euphemizers. He said slavery is slavery, not "a form of economic subordination." The idols of a purely conventional virtue he delighted to shatter because no public enemy seemed to him more deadly than the American who made moral cowardice respectable. Should the partiality of friendship, should the learning, renown or public service of the offender, save him from the pillory of public scorn? Shall a gentleman whose compliance weakened the moral fibre of New England and fastened the slave's chain more hopelessly, go unwhipped of a single word of personal rebuke? "No," replied Wendell Phillips

"Call us fanatics, revile us for our personality, say that we attack reputations—what of that? We did not come into the world to keep ourselves clean. It is not our first and only duty to see that you love us. Popularity is not the great end of creation. We came into the world to give truth a little jog onward; we came into the world to help our neighbor to his rights; we came into the world to take one link of the fetter off the limb of the slave. In order to do it, it is necessary to cut the line that binds yon vassal to the pulpit, and let you know that when you look up, you do not see an independent intellect, but you see the reflection of wealth. A hard thing to say; it makes man odious to say it; but necessary to be said, necessary for you to learn, necessary for you to act upon."[16]

In vindicating Daniel O'Connell's plainness of speech, Phillips applied his remarks to his own position:

"O'Connell has been charged with coarse, violent, and intemperate language. The criticism is of little importance. Stupor and palsy never understand life. White-livered indifference is always disgusted and annoyed by earnest conviction. . . . Premising that it would be folly to find fault with a man struggling for life because his attitudes were ungraceful, remembering the Scythian king's answer to Alexander, criticising his strange weapon: 'If you knew how precious freedom was, you would defend it even with axes,' we must see that O'Connell's own explanation is evidently sincere and true. He found the Irish heart so cowed and Englishmen so arrogant, that he saw it needed an independence verging on insolence, a defiance that touched the extremest limits, to breathe self-respect into his own race, teach the aggressor manners, and sober him into respectful attention."[17]

It was the same with the Abolitionists, added Phillips. It needed with them an attitude of independence that was almost insolent; it needed that they should exhaust even the Saxon vocabulary of scorn, fitly to utter the loathing, the righteous and haughty contempt that honest men had for slave-stealers. Only in that way could they wake the North to teach the South that at length she had met her match, if not her master.

"On a broad canvas meant for the public square the tiny lines of a Dutch interior would be invisible. In no other circumstances was the French maxim, 'You can never make a revolution with rose-water,' more profoundly true. The world has hardly yet learned how deep a philosophy lies in Hamlet's
        'Nay, an thou'lt mouth,
        I'll rant as well as thou.' "[18]

CHAPTER TWENTY-FIVE

ANIMATED CONVERSATION

How does he look? The man who stands out for the slave amid the hisses of multitudes, the exciter of mobs, the agitator, the radical reformer, the fanatical philanthropist. What sort of man is this that is impelled by such a spirit? He is passing up the aisle through a crowded audience to the lecturer's platform in an old Baptist Church in one of the towns of Massachusetts. We see him for the first time.

We are surprised at his appearance. Can this be the fiery reformer? The ruddy complexion, the classic face, the light hair and eyes, the uncommon distinction in look and bearing. We conceived him to be a ferocious ranter and a blustering man of words. We find him instead, a quiet, dignified, and polished gentleman, in temper and manner as calm and soft as a summer's evening. No one would take him for the world's ideal of an agitator.

As he rises to speak he slowly buttons his black frock coat and advances to his position on the platform with the easy deliberation of a gentleman stepping across a drawing room. He has no manuscript or notes in his hand and he needs no support of a desk or table. His pose is easy and natural.

He starts to speak. He has not a strong voice; indeed it might be called somewhat soft. Its tones express—"I do not wish to be harsh; I wish to be kind to all; I wish to be careful, logical, true, and calm, but I must carry out what I see to be my duty and no man shall stay me from my course"—that is the language of his tones.

Mark the grace throughout of all his motions, the pointed pungent finger, the total absence of bombast, splurge or affec-

294

tation,—nothing but reasonable, honest, solid Anglo-Saxon—uttered with calmness, candor, conscientious good will, yet with firmness and independence.

The effect is absolutely disarming. The common conception of an orator is of a man violently swinging his arms and sing-songing rhetorical and flowery phrases. Phillips uses few gestures, and these, most modest. There is no stark theatric in his sincere manner. He does not shout, never seems to be excited, never hurried, never sing songs, speaks to his audience as if he were simply repeating in a little louder tone what he had just been saying to some familiar friend at his elbow.

The compelling power lies in the force of his ideas, in his simple, earnest, direct language. It is this astonishing contrast between the matter of his speech and his manner that bewilders while it rivets our attention. No other speaker puts such intense feeling into so small a compass of voice. He is the orator of the colloquial. He is vigorous, keen, rich and apt in illustration, sarcastic, splendid and terrible in invective, aggressive, bold, armed with moral weight and momentum. His words are nervous, swift, vital, stinging. Still he speaks quietly, naturally. It is simple colloquy—a gentleman conversing. But he holds us by his quietness; it never seems to occur to him to doubt his power to hold us. The colloquialism is never relaxed, but it is familiarity without loss of keeping. When he says "isn't or "wasn't," "can't" or "don't," or even like an Englishman drops his "g's" and says "bein" and "doin," it does not seem inelegant. From his refined lips they seem almost to gain authority and propriety. He might almost have been ungrammatical and it would not have impaired the fine air of the man.[1]

At times we are tempted to wish he would wake up and show his mettle: thunder, stamp, and fume—but we listen and hang breathless on every word. Then the first thing we notice is that people are taking up their hats—he is done. There is no sense that the time has passed. He has bound us with a spell. And we believed what he said while he spoke.

He puts on his Homburg hat—a common, low-crowned, careless wool hat like a schoolboy's or farmer's—and we go out with the thinking audience.[2]

A sense and feeling of his magnetic power remain. Only from him do we have that touch which is from generation to generation the laying on of the hands of life.

Wendell Phillips never wrote out his speeches. He disliked writing and thought it "a mild form of slavery—a man chained to an inkpot." His custom was to jot down a number of points and study them well, then write out and memorize an introduction to make terms, as it were, with his audience and leave the rest to the inspiration of the moment. His mind worked simultaneously in two divisions: one was supervising and directing the immediate utterance; the other was arranging the argument far ahead.

"The chief thing I aim at," he said, "is to master my subject. Then I earnestly try to get the audience to think as I do."[3]

At the outset he sometimes prepared his speeches with care, but afterwards he relied generally upon his vast store of facts and illustrations and his tried habit of thinking on his legs. Of course, his lectures were all carefully prepared—though never written out. So also were some of his elaborate speeches, but he was never so thrilling, never so commanding as when most extemporaneous.

He denied having trained himself for a public speaker. He drew habitually from but a few books, Tocqueville's *Democracy in America* being among the chief of these. But he read newspapers enormously and magazines a good deal and he had the memory of an orator, never letting pass an effective anecdote or a telling fact. These he turned to infinite account, never sparing ammunition and never fearing to repeat himself.

Stumping New England, it was said, made him an orator, and that, in some respects, is the right name for it. It was refined and elegant as could be, but still stump oratory. It became so inevitably from the nature of the case. And in one sense this is to his credit, for it would seem to prove that he cared more for the cause than for his own reputation. He never attained to the finished architectural productions of Webster or Burke. In delivery and interest he undoubtedly excelled both, but he lacked the patience and logical depth necessary to create a sustained elaborate argument such as that of the

Nabob of Arcot's debts. Nothing was more fatiguing, however, to untrained minds than a consistent and elaborate argument and the mixed character of Phillips's speeches, like a great bonfire made of all inflammable materials, was remarkably well suited to the audiences he addressed. Like Yancey, the fire eater, he was simple and direct, because he saw and purposed clearly. He was appealing from politicians to the people and he spoke a language which the people understood. If there was one element he lacked it was the pathetic. Full of compassion as he was and tenderhearted, he did not move his audience to tears. Perhaps his prevailing moods, defensive and aggressive, did not much favor pathos. ("Why cannot I make an audience cry as you do?" he once asked Anna Dickinson. "Because, Mr. Phillips, you never cry yourself" was the truthful reply.[4])

A friend told him that it had been noticed at Brown University that in competitive declamation any student was certain to win the prize who chose for recitation a passage from one of his speeches. "The professors say," added his friend, "that there seems to be something about your speeches which gives advantage to the reciter. They do not know what it is; do you?"

He answered—"It is because mine are speaking sentences. They were composed to be spoken."[5]

"Be yourself," he once said in golden advice to Frederick Douglass as the colored orator was starting for a speaking tour in England. "Be yourself, and you will succeed."[6]

> There with one hand behind his back
> Stands PHILLIPS buttoned in a sack,
> Our Attic orator, our Chatham,
> Old fogies, when he lightens at 'em,
> Shrivel like leaves; to him 'tis granted
> Always to say the word that's wanted, . . .
> His eloquence no frothy show,
> The gutter's street-polluted flow,
> No Mississippi's yellow flood
> Whose shoalness can't be seen for mud;—
> So simply clear, serenely deep,
> So silent—strong its graceful sweep,

None measures its unrippling force
Who has not striven to stem its course.[7]

Phillips was not moody or variable, or did not seem so. Yet he always approached the hour of speaking with a certain reluctance and never could quite sympathize with the desire to listen either to him or to anyone else. As he walked towards the lecture room, he would say to a friend, "Why do people go to lectures? There is a respectable man and woman; they must have a good home: why do they leave it for the sake of hearing somebody talk?" This was not an affectation but the fatigue of playing too long on one string. Just before coming on the platform at a convention, he would remark with perfect sincerity. "I have absolutely nothing to say" and then he would go on to make, especially if he were hissed or interrupted, one of his very best speeches. Nothing spurred him like opposition and it was not an unknown thing for one of his young admirers to take a seat in the hall in order to stimulate him by a counterfeit hiss if the meeting seemed tame.[8]

He never lost his head. Addressing as he did audiences bitterly hostile to him through the great part of his career, his serene self possession won him a hearing. The most prolonged applause could not disturb a muscle in his face and a storm of hisses had as little effect on him. And he had superb physical courage. He faced an infuriated mob in New York. He stood on the platform, rousing his listeners to a rage. Once some of the leaders rushed forward, cut a curtain rope and cried out, "We're going to hang you." "Oh, wait a minute," said Phillips quietly, "till I tell you this story."[9]

How well he could tell a story! Here is a passage from one of his earlier speeches:

"That most eloquent of all Southerners, as I think Mr. Seargent S. Prentiss, of Mississippi, was addressing a crowd of four thousand people in his State, defending the tariff, and in the course of an eloquent period which rose to a beautiful climax, he painted the thrift, the energy, the comfort, the wealth, the civilization of the North, in glowing colors—when there rose on the vision of the assembly, in the open air, a horseman of magnificent proportions; and just at the moment of hushed attention, when the voice of Prentiss had ceased and the applause was about to break forth, the horseman exclaimed, 'D- - - the North!' The curse was so much in unison with the habitual feeling of a Mississippi audience that it quenched their enthusiasm, and nothing but respect for the speaker kept them from cheering the horseman. Prentiss turned upon his lame foot, and said:

"'Major Moody, will you rein in that horse a moment?' He assented. The orator went on:

"'Major, the horse on which you ride came from Upper Missouri; the saddle that surmounts him came from Trenton, New Jersey; the hat on your head came from Danbury, Conn.; the boots you wear came from Lynn, Mass.; the linen on your shirt is Irish, and Boston made it up; your broadcloth coat is of Lowell manufacture, and was cut in New York; and if today you surrender what you owe the "d-North" you would sit stark naked.' "[10]

Most orators coax, excite, or argue with the audience. Phillips simply stood before it and took it up quietly in his hands, turned it around as if it were a plaything, and made it behave as he wanted it to.

His resources as a speaker were amazing. In power of invective he was unsurpassed. Here is one passage in the classic style of Rufus Choate, delivered quietly, naturally, as if he were conversing with a few chosen friends at his own dinner table. His calmness enchanted while it appalled—

"Yet this is the model which Massachusetts offers to the pantheon of the great jurists of the world!

"Suppose we stood in that lofty temple of jurisprudence,— on either side of us the statues of the great lawyers of every age and clime,—and let us see what part New England —Puritan, educated, free New England—would bear in the pageant. Rome points to a colossal figure, and says, 'That is Papinian, who, when the Emperor Caracalla murdered his own brother, and ordered the lawyer to defend the deed, went cheerfully to death, rather than sully his lips with the atrocious plea; and that is Ulpian, who, aiding his prince to put the army below the law, was massacred at the foot of a weak, but virtuous throne.'

"And France stretches forth her grateful hands, crying, 'That is D'Aguesseau, worthy, when he went to face an enraged king, of the farewell his wife addressed him— 'Go! forget that you have a wife and children to ruin, and remember only that you have France to save.'

"England says, 'That is Coke, who flung the laurels of eighty years in the face of the first Stuart, in defence of the people. This is Selden, on every book of whose library you saw written the motto of which he lived worthy, "Before everything, Liberty!" That is Mansfield, silver-tongued, who proclaimed,

"Slaves cannot breathe in England; if their lungs
Receive our air, that moment they are free."

This is Romilly, who spent life trying to make law synonymous with justice, and succeeded in making life and property safer in every city of the empire. And that is Erskine, whose eloquence, spite of Lord Eldon and George III, made it safe to speak and to print.'

"Then New England shouts, 'This is Choate, who made it safe to murder; and of whose health thieves asked before they began to steal.' "[11]

Phillips once said to a friend—"I never yet had towards any man whom I criticised, the slightest unkind feeling. I criticised them always from a moral standpoint and as sinners against a race or a principle."[12]

In private life Phillips was the most delightful of men. He did not seem to have been bred to good manners, but born to them, so natural and unconstrained was everything he did or said. He was never self-conscious, never self-forgetful; where consideration was needed he was sure to be at hand. He never talked too long or too brilliantly but seemed on the watch to give everyone present a fair chance. He was possessed of a singular charm, the gift that moved Emerson to say—"I would give a thousand shekels for that man's secret."[13]

His imitations of other orators were highly amusing, especially what he called Webster's Rochester speech: "The public

debt; it must be paid; and it shall be paid;—how much is it?"
He would go through the performance and then resume his
seat at the table laughing like a child.[14] When Emerson and
Phillips dined together, they would look at one another with
a kind of awe as if they were more wonderful to each other
than to ordinary mortals. It was after such an occasion that
Emerson said—"This man is such a perfect artist that he ought
to be walking all the galleries of Europe and yet he is fighting
these hard questions."[15]

At another time Emerson remarked—"Strange as it may seem,
it is true, the world owes the finest orator of the age to the
movement that enlisted Wendell Phillips in the service of the
poor, despised slave." In his journal he added: "Everett and
Webster ought to go to school to him."[16]

Theodore Parker when speaking of Edward Everett said—
"He (Everett) has an eloquence—it is surpassed only by one
voice"—pointing at the same time to Wendell Phillips. Parker
spoke the truth.

Everett's was the grand manner. It was over-ornate and too
perfect. He never left anything to the inspiration of the moment. Everything with this man was carefully worked out,
studied, perfected. The result was artificial. Some of his orations would have been better if they had not been so good.
Even at his simplest, he is still very far from Wendell Phillips's
ideal of oratory—"animated conversation." Everett's standard
was quite different. He was seldom animated and seldom wholly
conversational. He never wished to give the impression of an
unpremeditated speech. When he came upon the platform to
deliver his "Washington" for the fiftieth or the hundredth time,
he had his manuscript with him and placed it carefully upon
a desk or table. He never by any chance referred to it. But
there it was in plain view of the audience as though to say to
them: "This is no casual, unprepared address to which I ask
your attention. It is something that has been carefully studied,
and worked over at great length."

Andrew D. White happened to sit beside him at a public
dinner in Boston where he was to be the chief speaker. When
the table was being cleared, White noticed that Everett mo-

tioned to the waiter not to remove a bouquet of flowers that stood before his plate which contained two American flags. Later in the evening, in the course of his speech, and at just the right point, Everett caught up the flags as if without premeditation and waved them. "Everything with Everett as with Choate," added White, "seemed to be cut and dried so that even the interruptions seemed prepared beforehand."[17]

There was nothing polemical about Edward Everett. He had no passion, and passion was an element in almost all of Phillips's speeches.

The period was rich in great orators. The Southerners excelled in outburst power; the Northerners were less volcanic. Choate with his lank, ungainly form, wild and fantastic hair, and witch eyes was more electric than Phillips, but bombastic and flowery, and delighted in long sentences. One sentence in his Eulogy on Webster, probably the longest ever spoken by human lips—"Consider the work he did in that life of forty years," etc. included twelve hundred words and took ten minutes to finish.[18] Webster had greater splendor and majesty but was ponderous. Calhoun's was a subtle brain; he was rather a metaphysician than an orator; Clay's charm was in his manner, his utterance; he wielded audiences and molded Senates, but he did not ever in his life greatly influence those who never met and did not personally hear him. Prentiss was more picturesque,[19] Sumner more pretentiously the scholar, Beecher abounded more in bravuras of oratory. But in the sum of oratorical powers Wendell Phillips surpassed them all. He was more interesting and instructive than any of his contemporaries in their palmiest days.

True, his judgment was not always sound nor his estimate of men always just, nor his policy always proved by the event. He would have scorned such praise. But no better friend of freedom and of man ever breathed upon this continent and none offered to the future generations of his countrymen a more priceless example of inflexible devotion to conscience and to public duty. He belonged to the heroic type. He had that quality which Emerson thought the highest of all qualities— of being "something that cannot be skipped or undermined."

And he revolutionized oratory in America. He made the old "spread eagle" and bombast ridiculous. Such rantings put one in mind of savages who beat tom-toms and yelled and screeched to appal their enemies. Viscount Bryce called him "one of the first orators of the century, . . . remarkable for the transparent simplicity of his style," his direct and natural method.[20] His style indeed, set a fashion. It taught the bar, the pulpit, the platform, the value of conversationalism in oratory. With his advent roar and rant went out of date. The era of trained naturalism opened. Thus he made every audience his debtor.

CHAPTER TWENTY-SIX

"WE ARE ONE, YOU KNOW"

No. 26 Essex Street—"dear, delightful dusty spot." A flight of stairs with old fashioned mould candle banisters and at the bottom a well-worn cheap carpet. The walls covered with dark greenish paper that had been there for more than a quarter of a century. A high old time hat rack with wooden pegs painted white long ago. A dining room and a kitchen on the ground floor; a double parlor at the top of the stairs—small but suitable for a literary workshop, painted a yellowish white with an old but neat reddish carpet on the floor; front and back bedrooms on the third floor with attic accommodations for servants. The furniture old fashioned and made chiefly of mahogany. Everything cozy and comfortable.

It was a saying of Phillips that there was more sun and fun in no. 26 Essex Street than anywhere else in Boston.[1] Ann Phillips's bedroom looking out on Harrison Avenue was always bright with flowers of which the invalid was passionately fond—nasturtiums and smilax in mid-winter, later brilliant tulips, and then the blossoms of the spring—May flowers and anemones until the garden rose and sweet briars appeared. Ann had good color, a strong voice, and a hearty laugh, so that it was difficult to think her ill. Her conversation never flagged. She was eager to hear and discuss the news of the day, especially the progress of the Anti-Slavery cause. "Gay as the gayest bird is Ann Terry Greene," declared one of her schoolmates.[2]

She was fond of music but, debarred from going to concerts, she found pleasure in listening instead to the hand organs which were frequently played beneath her window. When Phillips was ready to go out, his wife habitually said: "Wendell, don't forget the organ money."[3]

Phillips personally did the marketing every morning and he might be seen walking home with his hands full of parcels "for Ann." He would go over a bushel of potatoes to get a peck of one size to bake for her breakfast. In purchasing peas, he would handle every pod to see that they were soft and tender "as Ann wanted them."[4]

Meals were served in Ann's apartment on a tiny table. "We eat in French," said Phillips referring to their habit of talking in French at their meals. He was a good eater and a good sleeper—the secret no doubt, of his excellent health and spirits. He often quoted the saying of William Cobbett: "The seat of civilization is the stomach" to which he would tack on: "add an easy conscience and a pillow steeped in poppy juice."[5]

As colonial women banned tea in pre-revolutionary days, so Ann Phillips would use neither cane sugar on her table nor employ cotton fabrics in her household as long as these were the products of slave labor. This was what she called an *argumentum ad hominem*—logic that would penetrate through the pockets into the heads of the labor stealers.

Phillips was constantly out in the thick and throng of the world. He saw everybody and had all sorts of adventures and would tell Ann of them. He was her eyes and ears.

Both were passionately fond of children. Deprived of any of their own, they adopted the children of their friends who were always running about the house. Phillips opened his mail and even conducted his reading while carrying on a conversation with his little friends.

At this period they met Eliza Garnaut, a woman of Welsh birth. She had married a Frenchman and came with him to Boston. He soon died leaving her with an only child, a girl. Without means, she managed to support herself and daughter, Phillips helping her at times with cash. When she fell a victim to the cholera, he adopted her daughter as his own, and Phoebe Garnaut became Phoebe Phillips.

In the summer, they spent two or three months in the country devoting the time to treatments for Ann Phillips, all of which proved futile. One was a preparation of sarsaparilla which in-jured, not helped her; another was mesmerism. It was difficult to secure a good operator and her husband was the best she had, "so the poor, devoted Wendell," Ann writes to her English friend, Miss Pease, "is caught one hour of his busy day and seated down to hold my thumbs. I grow sicker every year, Wen-dell lovelier. I more desponding, he always cheery, and telling me I shall live not only to be 'fat and forty,' but fat and scolding at eighty."[6]

But in another letter she added despondingly: "I am tired not of life, but of a sick one." And once when ill with fever and low she called her house "the hospital."[7]

This melancholy note of Ann's illness runs through all of Phillips's correspondence: "Shall I begin my letter by telling you of Ann? She has been worse than usual all this summer—more weak and more ill." "Ann was so seriously ill I could not bring myself to leave her." (He had got up ready to leave by train for an anti-slavery meeting). "When one pain ceases, another begins—and sometimes they are not even kind enough to wait thus for each other but very impolitely come two at once." Still more cheeringly: "Ann seems very slowly gaining—a trifle, a very trifle every day." Finally: "We hope on hope ever."[8]

When Phillips was asked once what he really meant by his customary reply to inquirers that his wife was "about as usual," he meant, he said, that she was able to enjoy looking out of the window upon Essex Street where she saw the bustle and stir of life. Sometimes she came downstairs to the floor below her bedroom and looked around the house, but she never stayed an hour outside of her own chamber and never took a meal out of it.[9]

She had a naive, girlish way of speaking. "We are one, you know," she said simply and sweetly, speaking of herself and her husband.

"Ann is as usual:" Phillips writes to Elizabeth Pease, "little sleep, very weak; interested keenly in all good things, and sometimes I tell her, so much my motive and prompter to every-thing good that I fear, should I lose her, there'd be nothing left of me worth your loving."

His devotion to her was idyllic. Once when she was dangerously ill, he waited on her as both wife and child. Was she secluded? He shut himself in. Was she lonely? He became her companion. Was she in pain? He nursed her with sympathy. Did she want this, would she have that? It was laid at her feet.

She was a fitful sleeper. Phillips occupied the room just back of hers, and she frequently aroused him a dozen times in the course of the night. When the family physician called in the early morning, he often counted fifteen burned matches about, mute witnesses to the number of her calls and his answers. And this continued for more than forty-six years without a murmur on his part.

Of course there were times when Ann's illness made her fretful and exacting. Wendell never lost his temper or his patience on such occasions, was never hurried or flurried but remained soft-voiced, uncomplaining and attentive. Jokingly to Anne Weston: "We see in the *Liberator* that I am to be in Weymouth *October 12.* Ann and I consider it the height of audacity in you to presume to suppose that I can spend the evening of that, the anniversary of our wedding day—away from her. . . . Don't plead ignorance."[10]

Affairs in the house moved like clock work. He rose at seven in the morning, breakfast was ready at half past seven, dinner was served at two o'clock, and a plain supper at half past six. At ten in the evening all was whist. When, as was often the case, a lecture engagement or a public meeting kept him out beyond that hour, he let himself in quietly and went to bed.

He liked to tinker about the house—when a door was to be eased, a fireplace to be overhauled, a window to be tightened, he went about, hammer or saw in hand, supremely satisfied. He was always amiable. No one ever heard him scold. The servants idolized him.

He was not a great talker at home. Indeed Ann Phillips used to say: "Silence would reign at 26 Essex Street unless I broke it."[11] When he came in, however, with a budget of news to open, he made the whole place merry. But his life had no events; his speeches were its only incidents.

He was a constant reader. When not with his wife or tinkering about the house, he was busy with his books or devouring the newspapers. In preparing his speeches he went down to his "den," locked the door, and denied himself to everyone, sometimes for days, only emerging to eat and sleep. His favorite position when so engaged was to be on the sofa. As he disliked the pen, a letter from him was a supreme token of his regard. Such was the fiery agitator at home.

One eccentricity Lydia Maria Child poked fun at and he playfully replied:

"Oh! My! . . . What insanity hath seized thee? Didst thou fancy I was about to become . . . an author? or that I too could be crazy and waste such material on my editorials—which I always write in pencil and on wrinkled scraps?. . . .

"Do you remember how acutely Mrs. Gaskell notes that each person has some article wherein he *must* be saving and stingy? wrapping paper—twine—a candle, pencils, etc. Well, my father's strong point was pens. Paper he was lavish of—in ink comfortably free—but to the extravagance of pens he never could cheerfully rise. Dr. Kirkland's last note, written in our house, swore he'd never write another there until he could have at least one moderately decent pen.

"My individuality starves in paper. It took me a year or more to undergo the wastefulness of envelopes and assume a virtue in this respect, but often detect in myself a twinge of reluctance at the prodigality of the age—keeping a little shrine in my heart for those old saints, Stoddard of Northampton and one of my great uncles, who copied a hundred sermons into their tiny pocket books and of course left their descendants such poor eyes that only by microscopic help can they profit by their forbears' piety. Now you whelm and tempt me—this poor sparer of drops—in an Atlantic. Suppose you should live to see me wasteful as a Congressman in his first session . . . Lucky I'm never likely to be in any public office. . . .

"Goodbye, I'll try to be good and learn ease in spending my treasure."[12]

In his personal habits Phillips was as conservative as he was radical in his thought and speech. He frequented one tailoring establishment for half a century. He had his hair trimmed by one barber for nearly two generations. He loved Washington Street, in Boston, as Dr. Johnson did Fleet Street in London, and strolled along its pavements with serene enjoyment, indifferent to newer thoroughfares. His dress was simple but neat; he never wore a loud cravat or ultra coat.

His patrician air never quite left him. Once when he spoke contemptuously of those who dined with a certain Boston Club which had censured him, as "men of no family," his real mental habit appeared. An English visitor pointed out to George Ticknor two men walking down Park Street and added the cheerful remark—"These are the only men I have seen in your country who look like gentlemen." The two were Edmund Quincy and Wendell Phillips.[13]

CHAPTER TWENTY-SEVEN

ON FREEDOM'S SOUTHERN LINE

Our nation's capital was full of eager life on the day when Franklin Pierce became President. The weather was variable: snow fell in large flakes during the morning and a raw north-easterly wind made the spectators shiver, but towards noon the storm ceased, there were signs of clearing weather, and the sun peeped out. The roll of drums and the sound of music were heard since daylight as the wakeful military and fire engine companies moved about in various directions. The crowds in-creased by thousands with the arrival of each morning train while pedestrians and horsemen streamed in from the country roads. Throngs paced the broad sidewalks—hundreds of them to escape the extortionate hotel keepers, having slept over night in the rotunda and warm passages of the Capitol where Con-gress was finishing its session.

About noon President Fillmore called for the President elect, and in an open barouche escorted by the usual military and civic escort, they made their way down Pennsylvania Avenue. The throngs waved their handkerchiefs and cheered. The in-coming magistrate rose erect in the carriage and lifted his hat again and again in response to the cheers. Hail to the chief!

The procession quickened its pace, for it began snowing again, but the Capitol was not reached until one o'clock. After the usual formal reception in the Senate Chamber, the tardy ceremonies of inauguration were begun at the east front. Here Chief Jus-tice Taney administered the oath of office and Pierce broke a nation-old precedent by affirming rather than swearing. He did not kiss the Book after the Southern fashion but laid his hand upon it, and held his right hand aloft, having previously bared his head to the falling snow. Then the new ruler over twenty-five million inhabitants took off his overcoat, stepped to the front of the temporary platform, and amid cheers of the vast concourse of spectators, delivered his inaugural address.

He broke another precedent: he did not read his address but spoke from memory, without the sign of a manuscript or note, in a remarkably clear and distinct voice. His young and handsome face heightened the force of his oration, which was well prepared and more than once interrupted by hearty applause. The keynote was self-confidence and breathed the spirit of frankness and cordiality, filled with the good intentions of inexperience.[1]

"I hold that the laws of 1850, commonly called the 'Compromise Measures', are strictly constitutional and to be unhesitatingly carried into effect . . . I fervently hope that the question (of slavery) is at rest, and that no sectional or ambitious or fanatical excitement may again threaten the durability of our institutions or obscure the light of our prosperity. . . .[2]

"That this repose," remarked the President in his first annual message congratulating the country upon its sense of calm and security, "is to suffer no shock during my official term, if I have power to avert it, those who placed me here may be assured."[3]

Less than a month later, without warning or suggestion, Stephen Arnold Douglas as chairman of the committee on territories reported the first draft of the Kansas Nebraska Bill. "Slavery takes the field," was the instant comment of the North.[4]

The measure held a phrase which Benton called "a stump speech injected into the belly of the Nebraska Bill."[5] This was that it was the true intent and meaning of the act not to legislate slavery into any territory or state, or to exclude it therefrom, but to leave the people thereof perfectly free to form and regulate their institutions in their own way subject only to the Constitution. In addition, Nebraska was to be divided into two territories, the Southern to be called Kansas and the Northern, Nebraska; and the Missouri Compromise of 1820, which had dedicated that territory to freedom, was declared "inoperative and void."[6] Douglas professed the most profound indifference as to the outcome. "I do not care whether slavery is voted up or voted down"; his main anxiety was, he contended, to vindicate the doctrine of popular or "squatter sovereignty."[7]

Douglas acted under a multiplicity of motives. Missouri factional quarrels, Indian titles, railroads, land grants, personal ambition were all bound up with the bill. It was the twofold desire of Douglas and the group of railway capitalists for whom he was spokesman to build up the Northwest and to make Chicago the eastern terminus of a proposed transcontinental railroad:—Chicago to Oregon, not the lower Mississippi to San Francisco. Put into the language of the promoters of the Pacific railroad, one territory meant aid to the central route; two territories meant an equal chance for both the Northern and Central routes. But it was a financial impossibility to build and operate a railroad across a thousand miles of waste and unproductive land without freight or any kind of traffic, without stations, without protection from Indian attacks and depredations. Obviously, civil government must be organized, Indian titles extinguished, the country thrown open and the industrious white population permitted to occupy it, if a railway was to be built, and maintained across it. And, as representative of the Chicago interests, Douglas must act quickly or the Southern route would be adopted. In order to insure passage of the bill by attracting to its support Southern votes in Congress, he added the clause which repealed the Missouri Compromise.

The bill had strong roots also in the political conditions in Missouri during 1853-1854 when Thomas H. Benton was running against David R. Atchison. Atchison had repeatedly given pledges to his slaveholding constituents who were eager to bring about the repeal of the old restriction and to enter Nebraska with their slaves. By championing repeal, Atchison would help his friends and place the South under obligation to himself and thus materially increase his chances in the presidential nomination.

But as Douglas is said to have confessed subsequently: "His party in the election of Pierce had consumed all its powder, and therefore without a deep reaching agitation, it could have no more ammunition for its artillery."[8]

A storm of protest broke through the North. The feeling was spontaneous, fierce, sincere. Pike described Douglas as chief of the doughfaces. Benton spoke of him as "a poor white man who had married a woman with niggers." Chase wrote a violent attack which was widely read.[9] The Bill was "a proposition to turn the Missouri Compromise into a juggle and a cheat," said one Northern journal.[10] "Could anything but a desire to buy the South at the next presidential shambles dictate such an outrage?" Even friends of the measure took alarm. The object of Douglas was "to get the inside track in the South"; he had betrayed "an indiscreet and hasty ambition."[11]

Whigs and Democrats, Silver Grays and Woolly Heads, Softs and Hards were "boiling over." Petitions poured in on Congress. The North, in Lincoln's phrase, was determined to give her pioneers "a clean bed with no snakes in it."[12] Even lovers of concord and harmony like Edward Everett denounced Douglas as an ambitious politician who dared to "sell the birthright of the free States for a mess of pottage."[13] He presented a memorial to Congress signed by more than three thousand clergymen of various religious denominations in New England protesting against the Bill. The memorial was made the occasion for a savage onslaught by Douglas—"It is presented by a denomination of men calling themselves preachers of the gospel, who have come forward with an atrocious falsehood and an atrocious calumny against the Senate, desecrated the pulpit, and prostituted the sacred desk to the miserable and corrupting influence of party politics.[14]

"The Fugitive Slave Law did much to unglue the eyes of men," said Emerson, "and now the Nebraska Bill leaves us staring."[15] "If the Nebraska Bill should be passed," wrote a Southerner in Boston, "the Fugitive Slave Law is a dead letter throughout New England. As easily," he continued, "could a law prohibiting the eating of codfish and pumpkin pies be enforced as that law be executed."[16]

Newspapers were accustomed to refer to the vulgarity and vehemence of Douglas's abuse, his "Senatorial billingsgate,"[17] his style of attack "more becoming a pothouse than the Senate."

> The Dropsied Dwarf of Illinois
> By brother sneaks called, 'Little Giant,'
> He who has made so great a noise
> By being to the Slave Power pliant.[18]

Douglas had underestimated the force of Northern indignation and partly despised it whatever its intensity. He had underestimated it because he felt himself no moral repugnance to slavery. His attitude was completely, exclusively materialistic. When it paid, it was good, and when it did not pay, it was bad.[19]

"My friends, we deserve all we have suffered," said Theodore Parker. "We are the scorn and contempt of the South. They are our masters and treat us as slaves. It is ourselves who make the yoke. A Western man travels through Kentucky and hears only this rumor: 'The Yankees are cowards; they dare not resist us. We will drive them just where we like. We will force the Nebraska Bill down their throats, and then force Saint Domingo and Cuba after it.' That is public opinion in Kentucky. My brothers, it is well deserved."[20]

The Charleston *Courier* replied—"We cherish slavery as the apple of our eye, and are resolved to maintain it, peaceably if we can, forcibly if we must."[21] Southern sentiment was overwhelmingly in favor of the measure. "The South flies to the bill," wrote Francis Lieber from South Carolina, "as moths to the candle."[22]

"It is, at once, the worst and the best Bill on which Congress ever acted," declared Sumner. "The worst bill inasmuch as it is a present victory of slavery. The best bill, for it annuls all past compromises with slavery, and makes all future compromises impossible. Thus it puts Freedom and Slavery face to face, and bids them grapple. Who can doubt the result?"[23]

Through the hectic hours of March 3, the debate dragged on, enlivened now and then by angry words, by wit and laughter, and sometimes by flashes of eloquence. Twilight fell and the candles were lighted. At eleven o'clock, Douglas, wearied and disgusted, moved to adjourn. The Senators objected. Douglas offered to waive his right to close if the Senate came to a vote at once. But no! Sumner wanted to speak. Houston wanted to speak. At last, near midnight, Douglas took the floor.

His appearance was striking—a dwarfish figure with an enormous head. Late as was the hour, the galleries, aisles, and corridors were crowded. All listened with bated breath.

"You cannot fix bounds to the onward march of this great and growing country. You cannot fetter the limbs of the young giant. He will burst all your chains. He will expand, and grow, and increase and extend civilization, Christianity, and liberal principles. Then, sir, if you cannot check the growth of the country in that direction, is it not the part of wisdom to look the danger in the face, and provide for an event which you cannot avoid? I tell you, sir, you must provide for continuous lines of settlement from the Mississippi Valley to the Pacific Ocean. And in making this provision you must decide upon what principles the territories shall be organized; in other words, whether the people shall be allowed to regulate their domestic institutions in their own way, according to the provisions of this bill, or whether the opposite doctrine of Congressional interference is to prevail. Postpone it if you will, but whenever you do act, this question must be decided."

Never in the United States in the arena of debate was a bad cause more splendidly advocated. Douglas was adroit, audacious, vehement—showed the most perfect courtesy to his antagonists. Frequently Seward interrupted with suavity and politeness and always Douglas yielded with equal graciousness. Once Seward could not restrain his admiration for the Senator—"I have never had so much respect for him as I have tonight". Douglas answered—"I see what course I have to pursue in order to com-

mand the Senator's respect. I know now how to get it." (Laughter) The little giant made it appear that he was the self-
sacrificing patriot and that his critics were actuated by an unworthy ambition. He spoke till daybreak and the crowd remained to hear his last words. Then at twelve minutes after
five o'clock on the morning of March 4, a vote was taken and
the Kansas Nebraska Bill was passed by a majority of almost
three to one. Running messengers shouted the news throughout
the slumbering capital.[24]

As the Senators sought their boarding houses or hotels on that
sombre March morning, they heard the boom of cannon from
the navy yard proclaiming the triumph of what Douglas called
popular sovereignty. In utter despondency Chase and Sumner,
devoted friends, walked down the granite steps of the Capitol together and as they heard the thunders of victory, Chase exclaimed
—"They celebrate a present victory, but the echoes they awake
will never rest until slavery itself shall die."[25]

"Pierce and Douglas," said Greeley, "have made more Abolitionists in three months than Garrison and Phillips could have
made in half a century.[26] Crowds of people who had hitherto
denounced the Abolitionists flocked to hear them. One journal
asked in derision: "Who names Douglas for the next President
now?" Not a response came from the North.

Douglas for a time was regarded with execration. He himself said that he could ride from Boston to Chicago by the light
of his blazing effigy in the night and in sight of his hanging
effigy by day. When after the adjournment of Congress, he
returned to Illinois and attempted to speak in Chicago, flags
were hung at half mast, bells were tolled, and at one of his
meetings, the hooting, jeering crowds refused to hear him.
For more than two hours, from eight o'clock in the evening,
Douglas struggled for a hearing, edging in a word whenever
he could, expostulating, defying, shaming, entreating, as the
moods of the mob appeared to vary. His angry cry that he
would stay until he was heard was answered by a chorus of
"We won't go home till morning, till morning, till daylight doth
appear." Finally he was forced to give way before the belligerent crowd, and, uttering a few words, strode off the platform.[27]

To radical Forty-eighters like Karl Heinzen, Douglas was a "Douglas Iscariot" and his popular sovereignty doctrine but another name for treason to the Republic and the whole human race. The Senator's likeness was displayed in the Chicago Market House under the caption "the Benedict Arnold of 1854."[28]

The Kansas Nebraska Bill sealed the doom of the Whig party, caused the formation of the Republican party on the principle of no extension of slavery, roused Lincoln and gave the bent to his great political ambition, and made the Fugitive Slave Law a dead letter at the North.

David Wilmot remarked: "I am determined to arouse the people to the importance of the slavery issue and get up an organization through which they can get control of the government. And if I become satisfied that these efforts will fail, and that the people will not assert their rights, then I'll be damned if I don't join the party that I think will send the country to hell the quickest."[29]

2

"Come on, then, gentlemen of the slave states," remarked Eli Thayer, "since there is no escaping your challenge, I accept it in behalf of freedom. We will engage in competition for the virgin soil of Kansas and God give the victory to the side that is stronger in numbers as it is in right."[30]

In February, three months before the Kansas Nebraska Bill became law, Thayer organized the New England Emigrant Aid Company with an authorized capital of five million dollars. The whole object of the Society was to save Kansas to freedom by actually doing it. As Thayer said: "Our work is not to make women and children cry in anti-slavery conventions by sentimental appeals, but to go out and put and end to slavery."[31]

In July the first band of twenty-four strong left Boston speedily followed by another of seventy which founded the town of Lawrence. Great crowds gathered at the railroad station to witness their departure and cheering throngs lined the tracks for several blocks. Whittier gave the colonists a marching song—

We cross the prairies as of old
Our fathers crossed the sea,
To make the West as they the East
The homestead of the free!

We go to rear a wall of men
On Freedom's southern line
And plant beside the cotton-tree
The rugged Northern pine!

Upbearing, like the Ark of old,
The Bible in our van,
We go to test the truth of God
Against the fraud of man.[32]

Thayer not only assisted the emigrants to reach their destination, but helped them develop their farms. For this purpose he installed saw-mills and flour mills, furnished machinery and implements, built churches, school houses, and hotels. Also, he proposed to earn dividends for the stockholders of his company. As he expressed it: "When a man can do a magnanimous act, when he can do a decidedly good thing, and at the same time make money by it, all his faculties are in harmony."[33]

One day Senator Atchison of Missouri was standing with some others on the wharf in Kansas City when a river boat approached with an engine on its deck. Atchison turned to those on his right and asked, "What is that on the deck of the steamboat?" His companion answered: "Senator, that is a steam engine and a steam boiler." Turning to the others, he repeated the question. They repeated the answer. Atchison replied: "You are a pack of damned fools. This is a Yankee city going to Kansas, and by G - - in six months, it will cast a hundred Abolition votes."[34]

North and South now vied with each other in encouraging emigration to Kansas. Colonel Buford of Alabama sold a large number of slaves and devoted the proceeds to meeting the expense of conducting a troop of three hundred men into the territory. They went armed with "the sword of the spirit" and all provided with Bibles supplied by the leading churches. They arrived in Kansas duly furnished with more worldly weapons and drilled for action. About the same time a deacon in one of the churches in New Haven, Connecticut, enlisted a company of seventy bound for Kansas. The meeting was held in the church to raise money to defray their expenses. The leader of the company declared that they also needed rifles for self defense. Forthwith Professor Silliman of the University subscribed one Sharp's rifle and others followed with like pledges. Finally Henry Ward Beecher, who was the speaker of the occasion, rose and promised that if twenty-five rifles were pledged on the spot, Plymouth Church in Brooklyn would be responsible for the remaining twenty-five that were needed. Sharp's rifles, he had said, were a greater moral agency than the Bible. And so the weapons were nicknamed "Beecher's Bibles."[35]

A subscription, which included among others the names of Phillips, Samuel Hoar, and A. A. Lawrence, raised $2670. for such "Bibles."[36]

On election day for members of the territorial legislature of Kansas, five thousand Missourians, armed with guns, bowie knives and revolvers, streamed over the border, seized power in the precincts, stuffed the ballot boxes, and chose pro-slavery delegates with but one exception. The outraged Free State men repudiated the "bogus" legislature and immediately began the importation of rifles. Two distinct and bitterly hostile governments came into existence in the Territory, and the bloody Kansas war began. Robbery, pillage, arson, and murder were the order of the day.

"I am more than ever of the opinion," Theodore Parker wrote, "that we must settle this question in the old Anglo-Saxon way— by the sword."[37]

With his fellow Abolitionists Phillips exerted himself to expose and defeat the Kansas Nebraska Bill. When it passed he redoubled his efforts to hasten Northern immigration to Kansas in order to secure it for freedom. In February he visited New York and spoke for two hours and a quarter in the Broadway Tabernacle on "Squatter Sovereignty" before a breathless and cheering audience. At the annual meeting of the American

Anti-Slavery Society he condemned the Slave Power and the Union which had made the Kansas Nebraska Bill possible.

"I said there were two Massachusetts. There is one that sends Everett to the Senate. There is one that follows in long procession the dust of Webster to his grave; that meets year after year to celebrate his obsequies, or his birth; that is always crying 'Peace,' 'Peace,' 'Let us go and make money,' that is busy at Lowell and Lawrence in making a tariff that shall fill the United States treasury to enable them, with the surplus funds, to buy all the real virtue there is at Washington, and to vote for this Nebraska Bill, that stands bent over her forge and looms, diligently forging her own chains. But, thank God, there is another Massachusetts; it is the Massachusetts which crowds, Sunday after Sunday, the spacious four thousand people holding walls of Theodore Parker's church (Great applause)—whom no broad sign of infidel blasphemy, written by a recreant over its portals, can scare away. There is another Massachusetts that sends Charles Sumner to fill her Webster's place, (applause), and hopes if he is not perfect, he is at least an improvement. (Laughter.) There is another Massachusetts which feels, as we do here, that it owes a deep debt to liberty and justice. . . . This is the other Massachusetts, and we mean to make her so restive, so disorganizing, that if the South will not go out of the Union, she will kick Massachusetts out. We will not stay together; we will not assist in this great conspiracy against justice. . . ."[38]

It was no great matter for liberty if Nebraska triumphed. All political triumphs are deceptive. "In the true sense of the word, liberty is never beaten; she is always victorious." If the South added Nebraska to her territory, in the end she only would fall with a greater crash.

Phillips pointed out the position in which he stood. It was this: the Union of which he had spoken was permanent. The government was in constant session; it never went away; it never intermitted. Wellington, when he fought the battle of Waterloo, stationed a solid square of infantry in the center of his post, six or eight deep. They stood with fixed bayonets—

and no matter what cavalry, no matter how many cannon, no matter what force was catapulted against them, they never changed their places. If a cannon ball went through them, they closed up; if the French cavalry made an onset, and one rank was broken, on their dead bodies another stood fixed, and it was by this central anchor that he gained the day.

"Now the government, which is the Slave Power, is just like this—a constant thousand men and twenty millions of dollars capital in constant session, with nothing else to do but to bribe Everetts, to buy up Websters, and to seduce Mitchels; with nothing else to do but to create public opinion; and if it cannot be created today, can wait till tomorrow. There it sits perpetually—no spring, no winter, no night, no day—sleepless and vigilant. If Nebraska is defeated today by the hot fury of the North, the government can wait until it cools. She can say with the old English baron, 'I bide my time.' If Mr. Sumner and Mr. Hale, if Mr. Greeley and Mr. Benton, if Sam Houston and the North, defeat the South today, you cannot keep the North at a white heat forever . . . She will cool tomorrow. The merchant goes home to his counting room, the lawyer to his client, the doctor to his patient, the clergyman to his parish, and the flying militia of reform is dissolved. . . ."[39]

Men must eat and drink, attend to business, and support their families. But in the meantime, the government, the Slave Power, unrelenting, always rich, stood ready to buy up and bully, to circumvent and to undermine—that was the reason, insisted Phillips, why she carried all questions. She was ever there—and the moment the weak hour came, she seized it for her purpose.

"A man can at times be wound up to the pitch of heroism and fling down martyrdom under his feet, and face the stake; but a million of men are not martyrs. Martin Luther was at a burning heat all his life; and the white ashes have never yet covered the burning enthusiasm of the pioneer of the Anti-Slavery cause, Mr. Garrison. But saints do not march in regiments, and martyrs do not travel in battalions; they come alone, once in an age. You cannot create an anti-slavery sentiment so durable, so unrelenting, so vigilant that the government cannot outwit and undermine it; consequently the only way in which you can save the slave is so to arrange political circumstances that there shall be no such government in existence."[40]

What had the Union done for us? Absolutely nothing, answered Phillips in deluded fashion. "It has not manufactured cotton at Lowell . . . It has not dug coal from Pennsylvania; it has not raised wheat in Illinois; it has not settled the West, it has not ploughed the ocean with New York commerce."[41] But soon Phillips came to solid ground—

"No, thank God, New York does not make money because South Carolina whips Negroes. She can do it without. I proclaim my belief that a Yankee can make money, even if the Southerner does not scourge his slave, that the sons of the men that fought at Bunker Hill can maintain peace in the streets of Boston, although there are no women writhing under the lash on the plantations of Louisiana. No union to which Adams and Hancock and Jay put their hands was ever meant to have for its cement the blood of the slave. (Applause)"[42]

On May 30 the Kansas Nebraska Bill was signed by President Pierce. "The deed is done," remarked the *Liberator*. "The Slave Power is again victorious. . . . A thousand times accursed be the Union which has made this possible."[43]

CHAPTER TWENTY-EIGHT

SONS OF OTIS AND HANCOCK

Shortly after six o'clock on the evening of the 24 of May, 1854, a Negro named Anthony Burns was arrested by a deputy United States marshal and his aides near the corner of Brattle and Court Streets, Boston, upon the charge of breaking into and robbing a jewelry store. The prisoner was lifted up bodily, rushed to the court house, and hurried up several flights of stairs to the jury room of the United States Court.

A few minutes later the door opened and the marshal entered the room accompanied by two men. Stepping towards the prisoner, Colonel Suttle, one of them, taking off his hat with mock politeness, made a low bow and said—"How do you do, *Mr.* Burns?" adding, "Why did you run away from me?"

Burns answered—"I fell asleep on board of the vessel where I worked, and before I woke up she set sail and carried me off."

"Haven't I always treated you well, Tony?"

Burns replied, "You have always given me twelve and a half cents once a year."[1]

Under a strong guard Burns was locked up for the night.

The next morning, a little before nine o'clock, as Richard Henry Dana was going past the court house, a gentleman told him that there was a fugitive slave in custody in the United States jury room. Dana went up immediately and saw the Negro sitting in the usual place set aside for prisoners, surrounded by a large corps of officers. United States Commissioner Edward G. Loring, who was also a Massachusetts Judge of Probate, was hearing the case. Dana offered his services, but Burns declined them. "It's of no use," he said; "they will swear to me and get me back, and if they do, I shall fare worse if I resist."[2]

Meanwhile Theodore Parker and others, who had accidentally heard of the arrest, entered the court room and Parker had a conference with Burns. He told the frightened fugitive that he was a minister, that by a meeting of citizens he had been appointed special pastor of fugitive slaves, and he asked whether Burns did not want counsel. The Negro again replied—"I shall have to go back. My master knows me. His agents know me. If I must go back, I want to go back as easily as I can."

"But, surely," said Parker, "It can do you no harm to make a defense."

"Well," replied Burns, "you may do as you have a mind to about it."

"He seemed," Parker afterwards said, "to be stupefied with fear."[3]

News of the arrest spread quickly through the city. Inflammatory handbills were circulated urging the people to "Watch the Slave Pen!!"

"THE KIDNAPPERS ARE HERE!
MEN OF BOSTON! SONS OF OTIS AND HANCOCK,
AND THE 'BRACE OF ADAMSES!'
See to it that Massachusetts Laws are not outraged with
your consent.
See to it that no Free Citizen of Massachusetts
is dragged into Slavery,
WITHOUT TRIAL BY JURY! '76!"[4]

MURDERERS, THIEVES, AND BLACKLEGS
Employed by
MARSHALL FREEMAN!!!

Marshall Freeman has been able to stoop low enough to assault even the United States Marines by employing Murderers, Prize Fighters, Thieves, Three-Card-monte men, and Gambling House Keepers to aid him in the rendition of Burns. . . .
Will you submit quietly to such insults?"[5]

On Friday morning the following card appeared in all the papers—"A MAN KIDNAPPED—a Public Meeting will be held at Faneuil Hall this (Friday) evening, May 26, at 7 o'clock to secure justice for a man claimed by a Virginia kidnapper."[6]

By Friday evening the city was in a ferment. Not since revolutionary days was there such excitement. Agitators were running to and fro, setting all the city in an uproar. The pent up feeling was ready to burst forth with fury. The crowd that gathered in Faneuil Hall was roused to such a pitch of excitement that when Wendell Phillips rose to speak they waited the word to do violent deeds.

"Mr. Chairman and Fellow Citizens—You have called me to this platform—for what? Do you wish to know what I want? I want that man set free in the streets of Boston (Great cheering.) . . .

"When law ceases, the sovereignty of the people begins. I am against squatter sovereignty in Nebraska, and I am against kidnapper sovereignty in the streets of Boston. (Great applause.) I went to see that poor man this morning, and stood with him face to face. He was arrested . . . with the customary lie that he was taken up for breaking into a store, and that if he would submit quietly, and be examined for half an hour, there would be no difficulty. And with that lie, he was got into the Court House and there, between four walls, with a dozen special officers about him, the pretence was dropped, and his master appeared. Mark me! his master appeared. (Cries of 'No!' 'No!' 'He has no master!') See to it, fellow citizens, that in the streets of Boston, you ratify the verdict of Faneuil Hall tonight, that Anthony Burns has no master but God! (Sensation, followed by enthusiastic cheers.)

"The question tomorrow is fellow citizens whether Virginia conquers Massachusetts. ('No!' 'Never!') If that man leaves the city of Boston, Massachusetts is a conquered State. There is not a state in the Union—not one, even the basest —that would submit to have that fugitive leave it . . . Tomorrow the question is, which way will you stick? Will you adhere to the precedent of Thomas Sims? ('No!' 'No!') Will you adhere to the case of Sims and see this man carried down State Street between two hundred men? ('No!' 'No!') . . . Nebraska, I call knocking a man down, and this spitting in his face after he is down. . . .

"Fellow citizens, I will not detain you any longer. (Cries of 'Go on! Go on!') But there is no use of Faneuil Halls. Faneuil Hall is not here. I do not know these pictures. I do not know these walls. Faneuil Hall is up in the purlieus of that Court House, where, tomorrow, the children of Otis and Hancock are to prove that they are not bastards. (Applause.)

"My resolution is, for one, that I will try so to behave in this case that we shall wipe off the stain of Thomas Sims, so that no kidnapper shall again dare to show his face in the city of Boston (Cries of 'Good' and cheers.) Make your resolution as I do. See that man for yourselves, and never lose sight of him, so long as his feet rest in Massachusetts soil. Who says aye to that? (Clamorous shouts of 'Aye, aye' and enthusiastic applause.)"[7]

Parker now came forward and delivered a wild, disjointed speech:

"Fellow-subjects of Virginia—(Loud cries of 'No!' 'No!' and 'you must take that back!') Fellow-citizens of Boston, then—('Yes!' 'yes!')—I come to condole with you at this second disgrace which is heaped on the city . . . There was a Boston once. Now there is a North suburb to the city of Alexandria—that is what Boston is. (Laughter.) And you and I, fellow subjects of the State of Virginia—(Cries of 'No!' 'no!')—I will take it back when you show me the fact is not so—Men and brothers (brothers, at any rate), I am an old man; I have heard hurrahs and cheers for liberty many times; I have not seen a great many *deeds* done for liberty. I ask you, are we to have *deeds* as well as words? ('Yes!' 'yes!' and loud cheers.). . . ."[8]

And so on in the same manner: "Now, I am going to propose that when you adjourn, it be to meet at *Court Square, tomorrow morning at nine o'clock.* As many are in favor of that motion will raise their hands." A large number of hands were raised, but many voices cried out, "No, let's go tonight," "Let's pay a visit to the slavecatchers at the Revere House," "Let us go now." One man rushed frantically from the platform crying,

"Come on," but none seemed disposed to follow him. Parker continued: "Do you propose to go to the Revere House tonight, then show your hands. (Some hands were held up.) It is not a vote. We shall meet at *Court Square, at nine o'clock tomorrow morning.*"⁹

The scene was tumultuous. The audience was shouting and cheering. Above the roar of voices could be heard cries of "To the Court House," "To the Revere House for the slave catchers." Parker tried in vain to still the storm but could not get a hearing. The persons on the platform were bewildered and hesitant how to control the excitement. At last Wendell Phillips rose and said—

> "Fellow citizens—Let us remember where we are, and what we are going to do. You have said, tonight, that you are going to vindicate the fair fame of Boston. You do not do it by going to groan before the Court House. ('Give them a coat of tar and feathers.') You do not do it, fellow citizens, by attempting the impossible feat of insulting a kidnapper. (Great cheering.) If there is any man here who has got an arm ready in the cause of justice; if there is any man here who is ready to sacrifice anything for the liberty of an oppressed man, he is to do it tomorrow. (Great applause.) No, fellow citizens, I pledge you that if I thought it would be done tonight, I would go first to the Court House, or the Revere House. . . . It is for Marshall Tukey to skulk down State Street between sunlight and moonlight, but when the sons of Fanueil Hall take that man out of the hands of the kidnapper, they shall do it in the face of the sun. . . ."¹⁰

They would baulk their efforts by showing themselves a tumultuous and aimless mob before the pillars of the Revere House, urged Phillips. They would only put the enemies of liberty more upon their guard, only give the garrison notice, only rob themselves of the sympathy of the city. No, it was not thus that liberty was to be served; it was not thus that the laws of Massachusetts were to be vindicated. Those who were to do the real work, who were ready to sacrifice something in behalf of Burns, were not to be carried away by a momentary impulse, a fatal indiscretion which would wreck the ship before it could be piloted into a safe and secure harbor.

"Let us go home tonight, fellow citizens. The zeal that will not keep till tomorrow never will free a slave. If there is any man here who is afraid that his enthusiasm is so transient, like the crackling of thorns under a pot, that it will all be spent by tomorrow morning, let him put on his hat and go home—this is no place for him. (Cheers.) But if there is any man here, who, as Scott says—

'Like red-hot steel is the old man's ire,'

Let him wait and be ready to do his duty to God and his brother tomorrow. (Renewed cheers.)"[11]

Phillips was carrying the audience with him when a man at the lower end of the hall cried out—"Mr. Chairman, I am just informed that a mob of Negroes is in Court Square, attempting to rescue Burns. I move we adjourn to the Court Square."

The hall became quickly empty and the crowd rushed to the scene of action.[12] There they found a small party under Thomas Wentworth Higginson attempting to break down one of the doors of the Court House with a long plank used as a battering ram. The Faneuil Hall men lent a hand. Brickbats were thrown at the windows and glass rattled in every direction. The leaders shouted: "Rescue him! Bring him out! Where is he?" etc. Shots were fired by the rioters. The whole square was thronged with people. At last a breach was made in the door and the men entered. But they encountered within a strong guard of fifty officers armed with cutlasses. In the melée one of the marshal's posse, a truckman by the name of Batchelder, was shot in the stomach. Higginson received a sabre cut across his chin and his followers were roughly handled and driven back into the street. The crowd thought themselves repulsed and started to retreat also; Higginson stood on the steps calling out to them— "You cowards! Would you desert us now?" A few responded feebly.[13]

There was a moment's pause in the midst of which emerged calmly from the crowd the venerable form of Amos Bronson Alcott, philosopher, poet, writer, dreamer. Pausing ere he

ascended the steps, he turned to one of the ejected rescuers
and asked, "Why are we not within?"

"Because," came the answer, "these people will not stand
by us."

Without saying a word, Alcott placidly continued his ascent,
his familiar cane tapping the stone with a clear and leisurely
sound. He paused again at the top. A revolver shot sounded
from within, the bullet speeding past him. Alcott turned, and
finding himself unsupported, retreated, but without hastening
his step.[14]

By this time the police were getting among the crowd and
carrying off a number to the station house. The spirit of the
rioters was gone and the attack came to an end.

Two companies of artillery were ordered out by the Mayor
to preserve the peace. The marshal also called out two companies of United States troops. He reported this action to the
President and received the reply: "Your conduct is approved.
The law must be executed."[15]

The attack on the Court House was ill-advised and premature—and against the wishes of the Vigilance Committee.[16] In
the morning and afternoon of the twenty-sixth, members of the
Committee including Parker, Phillips, Higginson, Stowell, and
Dr. Howe had discussed the proposal of making a sudden attack
and of using the Faneuil Hall crowd to this end. The plan,
however, was voted down three to one. The meeting was
adjourned about five o'clock and those making addresses that
evening were cautioned not to permit the audience to break up
for any unprepared assault on the courthouse. During the
Faneuil Hall meeting, however, Higginson changed his mind
and obtained the promise of a few men in the anteroom to aid
him in the rescue of Burns. Accordingly he started for the Court
House, leaving a messenger to inform his friends on the platform and ask them to bring the meeting to the scene of action.
The message was never delivered or was misunderstood. Hence
when cries were heard round the doors, they were supposed
to be mere efforts to break up the meeting. But in Colonel Higginson's own words: "It was one of the very best plots that ever
failed."[17]

"Incur any expense," the President had wired—and in compliance Marshal Freeman had sworn in a guard of 124--the sweepings of the slums. A precious crew, this Marshal's guard: jailer Andrews recognized among them forty-five of his regular customers. While they served, said Dana, Boston was reformed. "The people have not felt it necessary to lock their doors at night." "Marshall Freeman," stormed Theodore Parker, "raked the bowels of Boston. He dispossessed the stews . . . gathered the spoils of brothels, prodigals not penitent who upon harlots wasted their substance in riotous living, pimps, gamblers, fighters, drunkards, public brawlers, convicts . . . whom the subtlety of counsel or the charity of the gallows had left unchanged."[18]

Rumors flew wild round the city: there would be another attack upon the Court House; the Virginians would be hounded out of town; Wendell Phillips would be shot; Garrison would be mobbed; Parker would be arrested. Law abiding citizens carried pistols and respectable women stood on street corners and hissed the guardsmen and the soldiers as they passed by.

From Phillips's house Anne Weston presents a graphic picture: Wendell came and told Ann the house was to be mobbed that night. The city was in excitement—everybody at shop doors and down Washington Street, groups of people talking on the sidewalks—at night great rumors and panic among friends. "There was great passing and repassing and groups of men came and looked at the door and people swore before the House. Wendell was out and Ann was at 9 lying on the bed when word was sent up that Theodore Parker must see her *immediately*. Only a dim light was burning in Ann's room and Phoebe ran down with that to light him up. It was extinguished in the hurry and so Theodore entered her room in almost entire darkness. She was on the bed. Theodore expressed some surprise at not finding her able to sit up and then told her she must go at once to his house as hers might be sacked in 10 minutes. Wendell was away. Ann was somewhat frightened, but in a few minutes rallied and refused to leave. She would wait Wendell's return . . . Wendell returned and of course refused all such stuff."[19] Tom Phillips ran to the Mayor. But the Mayor told him he knew the house was in danger and the police were watching it.

On the day of the "trial" Boston was never so crowded. Every train disgorged its delegation from some country town; there were 900 excited partisans in from Worcester alone. Twelve men had been arrested for the murder of Batchelder. Colonel Suttle was being entertained by the Harvard professors, but the churches of the city sent up prayers for the unfortunate fugitive.

On Monday, the 29 of May, the examination of Burns began. The Court House had the air of a beleaguered fortress. Soldiers with fixed bayonets lined the walls and blocked the stairs. Only one door of the court house was open and before that were stationed three cordons of police and two of soldiers. Also a special force of Southern young men, students of Harvard College, formed the bodyguard of Colonel Suttle. None but functionaries could enter with a special permit from the marshal. The counsel for the fugitive made a strong defense. Burns was undeniably the slave of Colonel Suttle, although the proofs were clumsy, and on technical grounds, he might have been set free. But the United States officer was determined to win, and on June 2 Commissioner Loring adjudged the Negro to the owner.

Attempts to purchase Burns failed. Colonel Suttle had his mind set on defeating "the damned Abolitionists" and was "bound to take the nigger back if all hell stood in my way."[20]

It was a lovely, cloudless day in June when Burns was sent out of Boston. A large body of city police, twenty-two companies of Massachusetts soldiers, and a battery of artillery guarded the streets through which Burns and his guards must pass. The streets were cleared by a company of cavalry. The soldiers all had their guns loaded and capped and the officers carried revolvers. Each man around the hollow square was armed with a short Roman sword and one revolver hanging on his belt.

No martial music here, only the dull tramp of feet and the clatter of horses' hoofs. The men gripped their muskets and stared stolidly down, closing their ears to the jeers and taunts of the crowd.

Windows along the line of march were draped in mourning and lines of crepe were stretched across the streets. From the window opposite Old State House was suspended a black coffin on which were the words, "The Funeral of Liberty." Farther on the American flag, the Union down, was draped in mourning. The solemn procession was witnessed by fifty thousand people who hissed, groaned, and cried, "Kidnappers! Kidnappers! Shame! Shame!"[21]

Old Thomas Garrett, liberator of a thousand slaves, was there, carpet bag in hand. There too was good Dr. Howe, tears streaming down his cheeks "for sorrow, shame, and indignation." Higginson was there with his Worcester guard, his chin swathed in bandages. Two boys were there with famous names, Charles Lowell and Henry Lee Higginson. "Charley," said Henry, "it will come to us to set this right." (Easy enough. Just ten years more and Lowell would be dead at Cedar Creek and Henry left for dead on the field of Aldie Gap.)

The vast throngs crowded the sidewalks, filled the doors and windows of the shops, the balconies and even the roofs. "There was lots of folks," said Burns "to see a colored man walk down the street."

A shower of cayenne pepper, cow-itch, etc., thrown from the Commonwealth building, greeted the procession as it passed through State Street. Near the Custom House, the crowd surged forward. Instantly some lancers rode their horses furiously at the surging crowd and struck with the flat of their sabres. Then a detachment of infantry charged upon the dense mass at a run with fixed bayonets. Some were pitched headlong down cellars, some were forced into doorways and up flights of stairs, and others were thrown down and trampled upon.

The soldiers struck up the tune, "Carry me back to Old Virginny" which they sang on past the Custom House to the back of Long Wharf. There the fugitive was put on a United States revenue cutter, sailing towards Virginia.[22]

"Triumph of the Slave Power—THE KIDNAPPING LAW ENFORCED AT THE POINT OF THE BAYONET—Massachusetts in Disgraceful Vassalage," shouted the *Liberator*.

Loring, "the Kidnapper's commissioner," was hung in effigy all over the State. In North Bridgewater the inscription upon the image was

Commissioner Loring
The Memory of the Wicked Shall Rot.[23]

On Sunday Theodore Parker preached in the Music Hall in his finest Old Testament mood. He flung open his Bible with the gesture of a man who draws a sword and in tones that rang like the cry of battle, he thundered out his text: "Exodus XX:15— 'Thou shalt not steal.'" The face of the preacher was aflame.[24]

And stern Ezra Gannett who kept the law and who asked, "What is one man set against the safety of the Union?" Gannett heard the news and flung himself sobbing into a chair saying, "God forgive this guilty nation."[25]

"The government has fallen into the hands of the Slave owner completely," wrote Wendell Phillips in dismay to Elizabeth Pease. "So far as national politics are concerned, we are beaten —there's no hope. We shall have Cuba in a year or two, Mexico in five, and I should not wonder if efforts were made to revive the slave trade . . . Events hurry forward with amazing rapidity: we live fast here. The future seems to unfold a vast slave empire united with Brazil and darkening the whole West. I hope I may be a false prophet, but the sky was never so dark. Our Union, all confess, must sever finally on this question. It is now with nine-tenths only a question of time."[26]

The rendition of Burns cost the government about one hundred thousand dollars. "We rejoice at the recapture of Burns," said the fiery Richmond *Enquirer,* "but a few more such victories and the South is undone."[27]

Burns was the last fugitive ever seized on the soil of Massachusetts.

"I'm but a poor counsellor," Phillips writes to Higginson who, after being arrested, inquired about his line of defence:

"Don't rest wholly on me, though I appreciate justly and thank you for the confidence you give me. But I have no doubt, *not the shadow of one* that in your case I should plead *not guilty*.

"The only difficulty comes afterward—what shall be the line of defence? First, by this plea, secure a jury—then how much and what shall you confess? Of course doctrines,— principles—advice we gave we shall neither of us deny. In your case the jist of the matter is not your principle (e.g. that you *would* resist) but a *fact*, did you resist? I should, I think, make the government prove this—avowing all the while that you *approved* what was done—justifying it, but saying to the government, 'Grant all this, still what is it all to *me*, T.W.H.? Shew ye that I *did* break that door.'— (Still on this point I should like to know more before deciding. My idea is they cannot identify you at all.)

"Again there are various law questions—you had as much right as Freeman to that door—neither of you had any right to shut it. The United States hire only two rooms—have only a *right of way* through the entry. At the time of the attack the Supreme Court was in *session*, and you, as a citizen, had a right to pass. Even then if you confess the *act*, claim on this and other grounds that you had not, at the moment specified, violated any law.

"Then, by all means, by a plea of *not guilty*, gain a jury in order to argue before them the *higher* law—you do all your honor and conscience can claim if you avow all you before professed—but if with this banner nailed yet to the mast, you face a jury with success you not only help the agitation by a trial but by beating the government, a great point."

Finally Phillips came to the main point: "The opportunity of preaching to that jury is one of the things you fought for, perhaps the most important object."[28]

On the Fourth of July, the Abolitionists held their annual celebration at Framingham. Garrison led the proceedings. After Scripture readings and some remarks, he proceeded to manifest "the estimation in which he held the pro-slavery laws and deeds of the nation." First he burnt a copy of the Fugitive Slave Law. Borrowing the formula from Deuteronomy, he said—"And let all the people say, Amen." The audience applauded. Then he burnt the decision of Commissioner Loring remanding Burns to slavery, then the charge as to the treasonable nature of the attack on the Court House in an effort to rescue Burns. Finally holding up the United States Constitution, he branded it as "a covenant with death and an agreement with Hell."—and burnt it to ashes on the spot, exclaiming—"So perish all compromises with tyranny! and let all the people say Amen!"[29]

Phillips spoke at the gathering. "What we want in reality," he said, "is a spot, however small—whether it be the State of Massachusetts or half of it—which we can truly say is a free state; of which we can say, that a fugitive slave is safe there; that no matter how many laws are made to the contrary, Constitution or no Constitution, law or no law, the moment a slave sets his foot on that soil, he never goes back. (Loud cheers.)"[30]

In the autumn Phillips went off on a lecturing tour, travelling through central New York as far as Detroit and returning by way of Philadelphia. In this circuit of three weeks, he spoke everywhere to enthusiastic audiences. His theme was always the same: a call to abhor slavery as they abhorred "sheep-stealing, piracy, and murder."

When he got home from the trip, Phillips was arrested. Benjamin R. Curtis of the Supreme Court and Benjamin F. Hallett, the United States District Attorney (in turn a radical Antimason, a Jacksonian Democrat, a Hunker, and a Doughface steering by Southern charts) indicted Phillips and Theodore Parker for "obstructing the process of the United States," meaning the Fugitive Slave Law. Phillips gave bail with six securities. Sumner wrote to him—

"Well, Wendell . . . your treasonable efforts . . . have at last, . . . overtaxed the mercy of a long-suffering government; Franklin Pierce has struck back. You are indicted! What a small mouse for so big a mountain to bring forth— and after such prolonged travail, too. All right. Everything helps us!"[31]

Parker was ready to give the government agents "their belly-ful."[32] But the case never came to trial. Through technical defects the indictments were quashed. And on December 21 Phillips lectured in Tremont Temple, Boston, before a huge crowd on "The Nature and Extent of the Anti-Slavery Feeling."

CHAPTER TWENTY-NINE

"SIR, I AM A FANATIC"

Anti-slavery Massachusetts had now two objects at heart. One was the removal from the Probate Judgeship of Edward G. Loring, who as United States Commissioner had returned Anthony Burns to Virginia. The other was the making of such acts impossible within her borders in the future. Petitions praying for legislative intervention choked the mails. "I have lost all pride in Massachusetts," said Wendell Phillips, "till she redeems herself from that second day of June. Let us roll up a petition, a hundred thousand strong, for the removal of Judge Loring."[1]

Who should present the petitions? The popular choice turned instinctively to Phillips. On February 20, 1855, he went before a designated committee of the Legislature and pleaded for the removal of Judge Loring.[2] Crowds besieged the doors outside and hundreds were turned away. Phillips contended that it was not necessary in order to remove Loring by a Legislative Address that he should have violated any law. He might be removed, said Phillips, for any cause which the Legislature might deem a fitting cause. Again, Loring had violated the Personal Liberty Statute of 1843 which inflicted a fine of $1,000. and imprisonment for a year on any officer of the State who should aid in enforcing the Fugitive Slave Law of 1793. Besides, added Phillips, Loring had acted in an improper manner in the arrest of Burns and had prejudiced the case. "This Legislature has the power to redeem the ermine of Massachusetts from disgrace and make it honorable."[3]

Phillips's speech had an immediate effect. The House voted to remove the "disgraced" official by a vote of 207 to 111; the Senate concurred in the request. Governor Gardner, however,

337

vetoed the act. But again the Legislature asked the removal of
Judge Loring and again the Governor refused to comply with
the request. For the third time the Legislature presented its
demands. Finally Judge Loring was removed, though now by
Governor Banks.[4]

Paeans of praise alternated with clamors of condemnation.
Liberator: "The deed is done. The knowledge of it elicits the
warmest congratulations of the friends of freedom universally."
Boston *Post*: "Why should Judge Loring be removed? Is it be-
cause of the howl of a squad of fanatics and traitors?" Portland
Journal and Inquirer: "We do most heartily rejoice," etc.[5]

Massachusetts not only manifested its resentment by removing Judge Loring, but passed an "Act to protect the rights
and liberties of the people of the Commonwealth."[6] The Latimer
case had resulted in a mild Personal Liberty Bill. Now the law
was made to match the Compromise of 1850. Phillips led in
presenting and supporting the bill. Habeas Corpus was secured
to the fugitive, and the burden of proof was thrown upon the
claimant. For a state officer to issue a warrant under the law
was tantamount to a resignation; for an attorney to assist the
claimant was to forfeit his right to practise in the State courts;
for a judge to do either was to make himself liable to impeachment. Counsel was to be provided by the governor. Police,
sheriffs, jailors, militia were to keep their hands off.

The governor again defied public sentiment by vetoing the
Bill. But the Legislature overrode the governor's veto on May
21, the vote in the Senate standing 32 for and 3 against; in the
House 229 to 76. Thus did the Bay State nullify the Fugitive
Slave Law.

When Governor Gardner came up for reelection, Phillips
remarked:

"At the time I was commencing my speech against Judge
Loring, Mr. Dana said to me, 'I cannot trust your doctrine
that the people, the popular sentiment, the popular conscience may invade the judicial bench.' I said to him, 'We
can trust the people.' 'Nonsense,' said he. 'You know it's
humbug. You can't trust the people'. I believe if Massachu-

setts elects Gardner three times over, I shall be half converted to Richard Dana's opinion. Why, we have tried him
twice. He has insulted us. He has cheated us. The chair
of State, like the boy's plummet, has touched bottom; for
God's sake, let it begin to ascend!" (Applause.)[7]

Phillips, a third time within a month, addressed a legislative committee, but on this occasion he made a plea for the
abolition of capital punishment.

"Who are the men that are hung?" he asked. "Are they
the rich, the educated, the men that are cared for by society? No, that is not the class that supplies the harvest
for the gallows. The harvest for the gallows is reaped from
the poor, the ignorant, the friendless—the men who, in the
touching language of Charles Lamb, 'are never brought up,
but *dragged* up.' Society cast them off. She never extended
over them a single gentle care; but the first time this crop
of human passion, the growth of which she never checked,
manifests itself,—the first time that ill-regulated being puts
forth his hand to do an act of violence, society puts forth
her hand to his throat, and strangles him! Has society done
her duty? . . ."[8]

There are two objects of punishment, said Phillips. First, to
restrain the offender from repeating his offence, and, second,
to deter other people from imitating it. Now, if the object be
simply to prevent the individual from repeating the offence,
why not shut him up in prison? The state could keep him there;
the people could deny to the governor the power to pardon
such persons. Here Phillips was following closely the doctrines
of Beccaria.[9] "Nobody can say that a million of men and women,
with one poor hapless man in chains, are so afraid of him that
they are obliged to take his life in order to prevent the offence."
Phillips made another point. If this idea of hanging men
were correct, then why not make executions as public as possible?
Why not hang men at the centre of the Common? If example is
the object, the sight of punishment would seem to be essential
to its full effect.

"Why, Homer tells us, two thousand years ago, that a thing seen has double the weight of a thing heard. Everybody knows that a child will recollect what he sees ten times as well as what he hears. You know that in old times (not to make a laugh of it), in Connecticut, they used to take the children to the line of the town, and there give them a whipping, in order that they might remember the bounds of their township by that spot. Now, there are fourteen states in the Union that have made executions private, and in England they are private. Only a few men—some twenty or thirty or fifty—are allowed to witness them. . . . The reason given for hiding the gallows was that its influence was demoralizing; it was found to be the universal testimony that executions were great promoters of crime."[10]

Here was another singular thing about capital punishment, added Phillips. An ordinance commanded us to execute our fellow men, and yet in all civilized society, the man who executed that law, the hangman, was not esteemed fit for decent society. "To call a man a hangman is the greatest insult you can cast upon him."

Dr. Beecher, interrupting: "I suppose that is because he has touched sin and been polluted."

Phillips: "But the mob does not pelt the clergyman who takes the man's hand only the moment before he is executed!" This remark excited great merriment, the audience loudly applauding. "No, Mr. Chairman, it is a very remarkable circumstance that in all time the man who did his duty in obeying this statute has been infamous."

Phillips endorsed Lord Brougham's remark that if government had no other way of protecting society against the repetition of offences except by punishing the offender severely, then government was a failure. (Lord Brougham was no morbid philanthropist or sentimentalist, but a cool, hard-headed lawyer).[11] Take possession of your offender, urged Phillips, and subject him to moral restraint. Make our jails moral hospitals, make the men over again if we can and in that way protect society from that man henceforth. "As Bulwer has well said: 'Society has erected the gallows at the end of the lane, instead of guide-posts and direction-boards at the beginning.'"

Men used to say: "We cannot get rid of the gallows. Why, murder is so rife in the land that if you don't have the very worst punishment man can devise, no man's life will be safe." If this were so, said Phillips, why didn't they impale the criminal as in Algiers, or crucify him as the Romans did. If they wanted the terror of example, if they wanted the blood to freeze in the hearts of men, why did they not make the punishment as severe and cruel as possible? But that was not the spirit of the age. For if they did so, the humanity of the nineteenth century would rebuke them.

"If you can come down one step, if you can give up the rack and the wheel, impaling, tearing to death with wild horses, why cannot you come down two, and adopt imprisonment? Why cannot you come down three, and instead of putting the man in jail, make your prisons, as Brougham recommends, moral hospitals, and educate him? Why cannot you come down four, and put him under the influence of some community of individuals who will labor to waken again the moral feelings and sympathies of his nature?

"Who knows how many steps you can come down? . . . Society has been forced, by the instinct of humanity, against its logic, to put away cruel penalties. Men have been crying out continually against this instinct of mercy which sought to make the dungeon less terrible . . . Now we ask you to abolish the gallows. We ask you to take one more step in the same direction. Take it, because the civilized world is taking it in many quarters! Take it, because the circumstances of the time prove you may take it safely! Take it, because it is well to try experiments for humanity, and this is a favorable community to try them in."[12]

The various Anti-Slavery Societies held their annual meetings in New York and Boston in May of 1855. The New York *Daily News* called the gathering of the American Anti-Slavery Society "a kraal of howling maniacs," a "Bedlamite Congress."[13] But the New York *Christian Inquirer* truly remarked: "It is only within three years that a hall could be procured anywhere in the city for the meeting of the society. Now, the only diffi-

culty is to find one large enough to hold the crowds who flock
to hear the most ultra utterances of Anti-Slavery."[14]

At the anniversary of the New England Anti-Slavery Society
held in the Melodeon, Phillips declared:

"We do not tear down merely because we ourselves are
trodden down. I tear the parchment of the Union asunder
because it stands between me and my duty to the Carolina
slave. (Cheers.)

"*Punch* says that a cat, even if she be most kindly, never
approaches you in a straight line—she comes up sideways—
turning round your stupidities, rubbing against your anti-
pathies; and when she reaches you, perhaps she begins to
scratch. (Laughter.) So it is with truth. It comes up sideways; it turns round old habits, makes its way through narrow views, bigoted attachments to things we have never
examined, faith in words, not things,—*catch words,* that have
kept our infant minds in leading strings, though we be eighty
years old; when it gets near us, we repel it . . .

"In one scale you put two thousand millions of dollars,
the aristocracy of the three-fifths slave basis, the wealth
of State Street, the servility of the *Daily Advertiser*—a press
bought and paid for—a pulpit bought, and not worth paying
for—(great cheering)—literature emasculated—all this in
one scale, and in the other, the Sermon on the Mount. Give
it time—yes! give it centuries, and it will make all that
wealth and prejudice kick the beam! . . ."

Phillips had this to say of the Governor's refusal to remove
Loring:

"Our course is a perfect copy of Sisyphus. We always
toil up, up, up the hill, until we touch the soiled sandals of
some Governor Gardner, and then the rock rolls down
again."[15]

Dartmouth College invited Phillips to speak before its Literary Societies. He chose as his theme, "The Duties of Thoughtful
Men to the Republic." He came forward in front of the desk
without a single note which was considered venturesome be-

fore a learned body. But when he finished he was given "three times three," and in the evening was honored with a serenade at his lodgings.[16]

In October he spoke at the celebration of the twentieth anniversary of the Garrison mob, which took place in the very hall (Stacy Hall) out of which Mayor Lyman had driven the members of Boston's Female Anti-Slavery Society who had assembled there to discuss the "peculiar institution." Phillips recited the story of the mob, then said—

"Let us open for a moment the doors of the hall which stood here, and listen to the Mayor receiving his lesson in civil duty from the noble women of this Society.

"Mr. Lyman.—'Go home, ladies, go home.' (The mob was howling outside.)

"President.—'What renders it necessary we should go home?'

"Mr. Lyman.—'I am the Mayor of the city, and I cannot now explain, but will call upon you this evening.'

"President.—'If the ladies will be seated, we will take the sense of the meeting.'

"Mr. Lyman.—'Don't stop, ladies, go home.'

"President.—'Will the ladies listen to a letter addressed to the Society, by Francis Jackson, Esq.?'

"Mr. Lyman.—'Ladies, do you wish to see a scene of bloodshed and confusion? If you do not, go home.'

"One of the Ladies.—'Mr. Lyman, your personal friends are the instigators of this mob; have you ever used your personal influence with them?'

"Mr. Lyman.—'I know no personal friends; I am merely an official. Indeed, ladies, you must retire. It is dangerous to remain.'

"Lady.—'If this is the last bulwark of freedom, we may as well die here as anywhere.'"

"There is nothing braver than that," said Phillips, "in the history of the Long Parliament or of the Roman senate."

"I dreamed, in my folly, that I heard the same tone in my youth from the cuckoo lips of Edward Everett;—these women taught me my mistake. They taught me that down in those hearts which loved a principle for itself, asked no men's leave to think or speak, true to their convictions, no matter at what hazard, flowed the real blood of '76 . . . My eyes were sealed, so that, although I knew the Adamses and Otises of 1776, and the Mary Dyers and Ann Hutchinsons of older times, I could not recognize the Adamses and Otises, the Dyers and Hutchinsons whom I met in the streets of '35. These women opened my eyes, and I thank them and you (turning to Mrs. Southwick and Miss Henrietta Sargent, who sat upon the platform) for that anointing. May our next twenty years prove us all apt scholars of such brave instruction!"[17]

The autumn of 1855 Phillips devoted to lecturing. The Lyceum system was at its noon and people throughout the free States flocked to hear the great speakers of the country. It was a kind of church without a creed and with a constant rotation of clergymen, a kind of party without a platform and with orators of every opinion. Questions of any and every sort were discussed —and all sides were given a hearing.

Phillips closed the year with a speech at a dinner of the Pilgrim Society at Plymouth. He told a story—

"One day a man went into a store, and began telling about a fire. 'There had never been such a fire,' he said, 'in the county of Essex. A man going by Deacon Pettingill's barn saw an owl on the ridge pole. He fired at the owl, and the wadding somehow or other, getting into the shingles, set the hay on fire, and it was all destroyed,—ten tons of hay, six head of cattle, the finest horse in the country,' etc. The Deacon was nearly crazed by it. The men in the store began exclaiming and commenting upon it. 'What a loss!' says one. 'Why, the Deacon will well nigh break down under it,' says another. And so they went on, speculating one after another, and the conversation drifted on in all sorts of conjectures. At last, a quiet man, who sat spitting in the fire, looked up, and asked, 'Did he hit the owl?' (Tumultuous applause.) That man was made for the sturdy reformer, of one idea, whom Mr. Seward described.

"No matter what the name of the thing be; no matter what the sounding phrase is, what tub be thrown to the whale, always ask the politician and the divine, 'Did he hit that owl?' Is liberty safe? Is man sacred? They say, sir, I am a fanatic, and so I am. But, Sir, none of us have yet risen high enough. Afar off, I see Carver and Bradford, and I mean to get up to them." (Loud cheers)[18]

CHAPTER THIRTY

BARBARISM AT THE CAPITOL—

THE MOTHER OF ISMS

One day Daniel Webster reminded his young successor Charles Sumner of the importance of looking on the other side —a shield that was gold on one side might at least be silver on the other. Sumner replied—"There is no other side."[1]

Sumner's mother was Miss Relief Jacob (or Jacobs), a name in which one can distinguish at once the mixture of Hebrew and Puritan. He belonged, in fact, to a Christianized Jewish family.[2] It is easy to recognize the Hebrew element in Sumner's character; the inflexibility of purpose, the absolute self devotion and even prophetic forecast. Sumner was an old Hebrew prophet in the guise of an American statesman.

All his speeches in Congress, all his lectures on the platform had a single theme: Liberty is national, Slavery is sectional; Liberty must be established, Slavery must be destroyed. Limitations like the banks to a river increase the strength of the current for the mill-wheel. Sumner's concentration made his enemies call him a narrow man and a fanatic. But Paul was narrow when he said—"This one thing I do." Luther was narrow when he nailed his theses to the door of the church in Wittenberg.

Sumner never aspired to the Presidency. That lingering malady which victimized Clay, Webster, Calhoun, Seward, Chase, Sherman, and Blaine, never attacked Sumner. He who probably read more than any other five Senators together objected to being in the Senate because it interfered with his reading. He treated his mind as a reservoir and into it he steadily pumped learning of every kind.

In May of 1856 he made the most remarkable effort of his career—his speech on "The Crime Against Kansas."

Two days before delivering the speech, he wrote to Theodore Parker that he would "pronounce the most thorough philippic ever uttered in a legislative body."[3] It was prepared with great care but the smell of the lamp spoiled its eloquence. One of the most striking passages was so close an imitation of Demosthenes' great orations that Sumner was charged with plagiarism. The speech was crowded with quotations in Latin, French, and Italian, quotations from poets, ancient and modern, Virgil, Ovid, Milton, Lowell. Precedents were sought in the history of the ancient Egyptians, from the Druids, from Northern mythology. Some illustrations were drawn from the battlefields of Marathon, Crécy, Agincourt, the massacre of St. Bartholomew, the Spanish Inquisition, the cannibals of the Fiji Islands, and the diabolical atrocities of the Thugs and Assassins. Occasionally we catch a glimpse of a hero—of Miltiades, William Tell, Milton—but the prominent characters we see stalking across the stage were those of the worst monsters and fiends of history and fable—Mephistopheles, Catiline, Verres, and Danton, with Satan at the head of the procession.

Nothing was attributed to the heat of debate, for every word in the speech was carefully selected, weighed, and measured in Sumner's study. The Scripture was ransacked for words, not of peace, but of wrath, and then the whole was saturated with vitriol. For example, he described the pro-slavery men of Kansas as "murderous robbers from Missouri, hirelings picked from the drunken spew and vomit of an uneasy civilization, having the form of men," and "leashed together by secret signs and lodges" in order to "renew the incredible atrocities of the Assassins and the Thugs—showing the blind submission of the Assassins to the Old Man of the Mountain in robbing Christians on the road to Jerusalem, and the heartlessness of the Thugs, who, avowing that murder is their religion, waylay travelers on the great road from Agra to Delhi—with the more deadly bowie knife for the dagger of the Assassin, and the more deadly revolver for the noose of the Thug."[4]

The bitterness of Sumner's vituperation offset its reasoning. It lacked what Carlyle calls "the virtue to produce belief." The most irritating parts of the speech were those in reference to Senator Butler of South Carolina and to Senator Douglas, all the more irritating as Senator Butler was not present in the Senate at the time the speech was delivered. Comparing Butler and Douglas with Don Quixote and Sancho Panza, Sumner said:—

"The Senator from South Carolina has read many books of chivalry, and believes himself a chivalrous knight with sentiments of honor and courage. Of course he has chosen a mistress to whom he has made his vows, and who, though ugly to others, is always lovely to him—though polluted in the sight of the world, is chaste in his sight—I mean the harlot, Slavery. For her, his tongue is always profuse in words. Let her be impeached in character, or any proposition made to shut her out from the extension of her wantonness, and . . . the frenzy of Don Quixote in behalf of his wench, Dulcinea del Toboso, is all surpassed. . . . If the slave States cannot enjoy what, in mockery of the great fathers of the Republic, he misnames equality under the Constitution—in other words, the full power in the national Territories to compel fellow men to unpaid toil, to separate husband and wife, and to sell little children at the auction block then, sir, the chivalric senator will conduct the State of South Carolina out of the Union! Heroic Knight! Exalted senator! A second Moses come for a second exodus!"[5]

The speech infuriated the pro-slavery members of the South. Denunciation of slavery had been heard before from Chase, Seward, and others, but never before had there been heard in the Senate a speech so full of gall and wormwood as that of Sumner. It occupied two days, May 19th and 20th. When it was concluded, the gathering storm burst forth. Douglas and Sumner each lost his temper and resorted to offensive personalities befitting a barroom brawl, unbecoming in Senatorial debate. "Is it his object to provoke some of us to kick him as we would a dog in the street, that he may get sympathy upon the just chastisement?" asked Douglas.[6] He charged that Sumner's speech was made up of old pieces like a Yankee bed-quilt and sneered at the classical quotations by saying—"We have had another dish of the classics served up—classic allusions, each one only distinguished for its lasciviousness and obscenity—each one drawn from those portions of the classics which all decent professors in respectable colleges caused to be suppressed as unfit for decent young men to read. Sir, I cannot repeat the words. I should be condemned as unworthy of entering decent society, if I repeated those obscene vulgar terms which have been used at least a hundred times in that speech. It seems that his studies of the classics have all been in those haunts where ladies cannot go, and where gentlemen never read Latin." Sumner's remarks, Douglas said, were not made in the heat of debate. On the contrary, Douglas charged—"It happens to be well known it has been the subject of conversation for weeks, that the Senator from Massachusetts had his speech written, printed, committed to memory, practised every night before the glass with a Negro boy to hold the candle and watch the gestures, and annoying the boarders in the adjoining rooms until they were forced to quit the house! (Laughter.) It was rumored that he read part of it to friends, and they repeated in all the saloons and places of amusement in the city what he was going to say. The libels, the gross insults which we have heard today have been conned over, written with cool, deliberate malignity upon men who differ from him—for that is their offence . . ."[7]

To Douglas's personalities Sumner retorted as follows: "Sir, this is the Senate of the United States, an important body under the Constitution, with great powers. Its members are justly supposed from age, to be above the gusts of vulgarity. They are supposed to have something of wisdom and something of that candor which is the handmaid of wisdom. Let the Senator bear these things in mind, and let him remember hereafter that the bowie knife and bludgeon are not proper emblems of senatorial debate. Let him remember that the swagger of Bob Acres and the ferocity of the Malay cannot add dignity to this body. The Senator has gone on to infuse into his speech the venom sweltering for months,—ay for years; and he has alleged facts that are entirely without foundation in order to heap upon me some personal obloquy. I will not go into the details which have flowed out so naturally from his tongue. I only brand them to his face as false. I say also to that Senator, and I wish him to bear it in mind, that no person with the upright form of man can be allowed—(Hesitation.)

Douglas—"Say it."

Sumner—"I will say it—no person with the upright form of man can be allowed, without violation of all decency, to switch out from his tongue the perpetual stench of offensive personality. Sir, that is not a proper weapon of debate, at least, on this floor. The noisome, squat, and nameless animal, to which I now refer, is not a proper model for an American Senator. Will the Senator from Illinois take notice?"

Douglas—"I will—and therefore will not imitate you, sir."

Sumner—"I did not hear the Senator."

Douglas—"I said if that be the case, I would certainly never imitate you in that capacity, recognizing the force of the illustration."

Sumner—"Mr. President, again the Senator has switched his tongue, and again he fills the Senate with its offensive odor."[8]

On Thursday, May 22, two days after the delivery of his speech, the Senate adjourned early, but Sumner remained writing letters. While he was thus engaged, with his legs stretched out under his desk, which was firmly screwed to the floor, Preston S. Brooks, a son of Senator Butler's cousin and a representative from South Carolina, came up and said—"Mr. Sumner." Sumner looked up and saw a tall, dark-faced stranger, who without giving his name, said: "I have read your speech over twice carefully. It is a libel on South Carolina and Mr. Butler who is a relative of mine"—then without completing his sentence, struck Sumner a blow on the head with a heavy gutta percha cane. The Senator, half stunned and blinded by the unexpected attack, struggled to rise and free himself from his desk. The blows still continued, but the desk held him till in the agony of his struggles he wrenched it from its fastenings and staggered towards his assailant. A reporter of the New York *Times* rushed to Sumner's assistance, but Representative

Lawrence Keitt, who had accompanied Brooks in order to render him necessary assistance, thrust himself forward saying—"Let them alone, God damn you," and threatened those who attempted to interfere. Brooks grabbed Sumner by the collar and continued to rain blow after blow upon his head as hard and fast as he could until Sumner sank prostrate and bleeding at his feet and the cane was broken to pieces. A number of persons gathered around crying—"Don't interfere! Go it, Brooks! Give the damned Abolitionist hell!"[9]

Shortly afterwards Sumner still stunned, his head and face covered with blood, was rescued from his assailant and taken from the Senate chamber.

In the course of proceedings in the Senate, Senator Wilson of Massachusetts asserted: "Mr. Sumner was stricken down on this floor by a brutal, murderous, and cowardly assault." Senator Butler impulsively cried out. "You are a liar." Shortly afterwards Brooks sent Wilson a challenge. Wilson declined the challenge saying: "I have always regarded dueling as the lingering relic of a barbarous civilization, which the law of the country has branded as a crime."

Senator Slidell of Louisiana stated that he and others who were in the anteroom of the Senate heard of the beating of Sumner, but that "we heard this remark without any particular emotion. For my own part I confess I felt none." Senator Toombs of Georgia stated: "As for rendering Mr. Sumner any assistance, I did not do it. As to what was said, some gentleman present condemned it in Mr. Brooks. I stated to him or to some of my friends, probably, that I approved it. That is my opinion."[10]

An effort was made in the House to expel Brooks. He was censured, but the necessary two-thirds vote for expulsion could not be secured. Brooks resigned on July 14, 1856, but before doing so made an elaborate explanation in the House. "I went to work very deliberately, as I am charged—and this is admitted—and speculated somewhat as to whether I should employ a horsewhip or a cowhide, but knowing that the Senator was my superior in strength, it occurred to me that he might wrest it from my hand, and then—for I never attempt anything I do not perform—I might have been compelled to do that which

I would have regretted the balance of my natural life." Later
Brooks referred to one gentleman from Massachusetts who had
denounced the assault: "In my country the cock that crows
and won't fight is despised by the hens and even by the pullets,
who know a thing or two instinctively." (Great laughter.)[11]

Brooks was at once triumphantly reelected by his South Carolina constituents with only six votes against him, and on August
1 he again took his seat in the House.

In the House the most vigorous speech made in denunciation
of the assault was that of Anson W. Burlingame of Massachusetts. "On the 22nd day of May when the Senate and the House
had clothed themselves in mourning for a brother fallen in the
battle of life in the distant state of Missouri, the Senator from
Massachusetts sat in the silence of the Senate Chamber engaged in the employments appertaining to his office, when a
member from the House who had taken an oath to sustain the
Constitution, stole into the Senate, that place which had hitherto
been held sacred against violence, and smote him as Cain
smote his brother."

Keitt (in his seat). "That is false."

Burlingame. "I will not bandy epithets with the gentleman.
I am responsible for my own language. Doubtless he is responsible for his."

Keitt. "I am."

Burlingame. "I shall stand by mine. One blow was enough,
but it did not satiate the wrath of that spirit which had pursued
him through two days . . . Sir, the act was brief, and my comments on it shall be brief also. I denounce it in the name of the
Constitution it violated. I denounce it in the name of the sovereignty of Massachusetts which was stricken down by the
blow. I denounce it in the name of humanity. I denounce it
in the name of civilization which it outraged. I denounce it
in the name of that fair play which bullies and prize fighters
respect. What! strike a man when he is pinioned—when he
cannot respond to a blow! Call you that chivalry?"[12]

On account of these words Brooks sent a challenge to Burlingame. Upon several occasions before this, challenges had
been given by the South to the North, which had been de-

Daguerreotype by Hawes,
artist of Boston, n.d.

Photograph presented by Miss O. H.
Varrell of Egypt, Mass. 1856 (?)

clined by the recipients, and thereby the challengers without incurring any danger had achieved some notoriety among their constituents. But much to the surprise of Brooks, Burlingame promptly accepted, selected a second, and as he had a right to name the terms under the code of duelling, fixed them as follows: "Weapons, rifles; distance, 20 paces; place, District of Columbia; time of meeting, the next morning."

The place of meeting was afterwards changed by Burlingame's second to Canada, but Brooks declined to accept the terms on the pretense that it would be dangerous for him to travel through the North in order to reach Canada, and so the duel did not come off.[13]

The whole South applauded the attack on Sumner, gloated over it, extolled it as the highest exhibition of chivalry. Everywhere, in the public press, in legislative halls, in public meetings Brooks was hailed as a hero. Canes were voted to Brooks inscribed—"Hit him again—Use knockdown arguments." One cane was presented by students of the University of Virginia, suitably inscribed, and bearing upon it "a device of the human head badly cracked and broked."[14]

"Sumner and his friends," wrote the hotblooded Governor Wise of Virginia, "lie like people with brains already soft . . . Such skulking poltroonery would hurt a man anywhere that the institution of slavery exalts masters to a pride of genteel manhood. At first I regretted the caning; now I am glad of it."[15]

Still more insulting was the comment of the Richmond *Enquirer*—"We consider the act good in conception, better in execution, and best of all in consequence. The vulgar Abolitionists in the Senate are getting above themselves. . . . They have grown saucy, and dare to be impudent to gentlemen! Now, they are a low, mean, scurvy set, with some little book learning, but as utterly devoid of the spirit of honor as a pack of curs. . . . The truth is, they have been suffered to run too long without collars. They must be lashed into submission. Sumner, in particular, ought to have nine-and-thirty early every morning. He is a great strapping fellow, and could stand the cowhide beautifully. Brooks frightened him, and at the first blow of the cane, he bellowed like a bull calf. There is this blackguard

Wilson, an ignorant Natick cobbler, swaggering in excess of muscle, and absolutely dying for a beating. Will not somebody take him in hand? Hale is another huge, redfaced, sweating scoundrel, whom some gentleman should kick and cuff until he abates something of his impudent talk. These men are perpetually abusing the people and representatives of the South, for tyrants, robbers, ruffians, adulterers, and what not. Shall we stand it? . . ."[16]

Brooks, however, before his death, which occurred in the following January, confessed to a friend that he was sick of being regarded as the representative of bullies and disgusted at receiving testimonials of their esteem.

Sumner, though silenced, was eloquent in a new and more effective way. Half a million copies of The Crime Against Kansas were printed and circulated.

The assault shocked and angered the entire North. The titles of articles and editorials are suggestive—"Blood in the Senate"—"Brutal and Cowardly Assault upon Charles Sumner" —"Another Outrage Upon Massachusetts"—"A Border Ruffian in the Senate"—"The Last Argument of Slavery"—"Barbarism at the Capitol"—"Shame! Shame!"[17]

The shock of the assault was felt even across the Atlantic and moved the London Morning Star to denounce it as "without parallel in the annals of civilized communities." "That outrage," said Sir George Cornewall Lewis, "is no proof of brutal manners or low morality in America; it is the first blow in a civil war."[18]

The legislature of Massachusetts adopted a series of resolutions in which the assault was denounced as one "which no provocation could justify, brutal and cowardly in itself, a gross breach of parliamentary privilege, a ruthless attack upon the liberty of speech, an outrage of the decencies of civilized life, and an indignity to the Commonwealth of Massachusetts."[19]

"Sumner Indignation Meetings" were held at Tremont Temple and at Faneuil Hall. "Where are we?" asked Wendell Phillips. "Just where we were twenty years ago, battling for the liberty of speech on the Senate floor. Once we had no men there to speak. Now, the men are brave enough, but speak at the risk of assassination. I thank God, tonight, that I never sullied my lips with that absurd phrase 'the chivalry of the South.'"[20]

Three days later, at a meeting of the New England Anti-
Slavery Convention, Phillips continued his attack.

"Our purpose, our policy, ought to be, from this time
forth, to deny the existence of constitutional government
in this country. (Loud applause.) It is a magnificent conspiracy against justice. It is the plot of assassins—it is not a
government. It is a cheat. . . .

"There are but two words to be uttered at our meeting
today—one is 'Kansas,' the other, 'Sumner.' . . . .

"If Massachusetts chooses to walk on her downward way,
we can be honest men at least; we can live and die rebellious slaves, at least. We can at least perpetuate a protest.
If Massachusetts stands the events of this week, there
is nothing she will not stand. You may take Bunker Hill
down stone by stone—you may throw even the *Daily Advertiser* into the dock—you may sell slaves in State Street,
if Massachusetts can submit to what is done today. . . .

"In years gone by, we never had men at Washington
brave and true enough to speak the truth; now we have got
the men there, but they speak at their risk. That is the
Union! South Carolina says to us practically, 'Send me
Everett—a moon that reflects myself. (Cheers.) Send me
Webster, that crawls at the dictate of some Southern caucus.'
(Cheers and hisses.)

"We have dropped down to the level of a ruffian civilization. I would have had all Massachusetts aghast at this outrage. Aged, venerable men, conservative by wealth and
position, say: 'We must send men to Congress who can fight;
no matter for their principles, if they can fight.' What a
satire on the freest government in the world!"[21]

On November 3, Sumner returned to Boston. Crowds in the
streets greeted him and the authorities welcomed him in the
name of the Bay State. But the windows of every house in the
élite quarter of Beacon Street through which he passed, except
those of Prescott and Samuel Appleton, had their blinds closed
to show their indifference or contempt.[22]
Sumner's injuries were serious. Despite them he made two
attempts to resume his place in the Senate. Phillips exhorted
him:

"I have talked with men of all parties (on your case there is but one party worth naming), and without a dissentient voice they deplore your anxiety to return this session to Washington. . . . I know you can make speeches worth dying for, but let me tell you just now, to the nation's heart your empty chair can make a more fervent appeal than even you. . . . I conjure you as you love freedom save yourself. We need you more in the future than now—you are not the best judge. Don't dream of resignation—that must not ever come into your thoughts."[23]

Sumner found himself unable to remain. Yet when his term expired, he was, as Phillips predicted, almost unanimously elected. For years his desk was vacant. Massachusetts insisted that his empty seat should proclaim to the world her abhorrence of barbarism that betakes itself to clubs and murder.

Much of his time for three and a half years Sumner spent in Europe. In June, 1860, he again addressed the Senate. The subject under discussion was still the admission of Kansas as a free state and as he remarked in the opening sentences, he resumed the discussion precisely where he had left off more than four years before—"the Barbarism of Slavery."

2

A spontaneous movement was going on all over the North. Early in 1854 a Mr. Bovay of Ripon, Wisconsin, a Whig, Mr. Bowen, a Democrat, and Mr. Baker a Whig, called a meeting which was held in the Congregationalist Church and largely attended by men of all parties at which it was resolved to "throw old party organizations to the winds and organize a new party on the sole issue of the non-extension of slavery."[24]

It was necessary to find an appropriate party name. A rose may smell as sweet by any other name, but not so with a political party. The Democrats would not fight under the old Whig name, nor would the Whigs and Free Soilers fight under the Democratic name, nor would either Whigs or Democrats fight under the Abolition banner. Mr. Bovay thus suggested that the new party be christened the Republican Party.[25]

At Philadelphia on June 17, 1856, the first national convention met, the fusion consummated, the name officially coined,— and the Republican Party commenced its career. Amid riotous enthusiasm a platform was adopted. It welcomed all without regard to past differences who were opposed to repeal of the Missouri Compromise—all who favored the admission of Kansas as a free State—all who stood firmly and solidly on the young party's chief plank—*"That the Constitution confers upon Congress sovereign power over the Territories of the United States for their government, and that in the exercise of their power, it is both the right and the imperative duty of Congress to prohibit in the Territories those twin relics of barbarism—Polygamy and Slavery."*[26] John C. Fremont, the explorer, was nominated for the Presidency. The enthusiasm of the Republican convention soon communicated itself to the country. Wide awake clubs, torchlight processions, frenzied meetings, rousing songs made up a lively campaign.

> The people are roused! They've slumbered too long,
> While Freedom grew weak, and tyranny strong,
> But now they are coming from hill and glen,
> They come to the rescue—the Free Soil men! . . .
>
> A yoke for our necks, a drag and a chain,
> If despots can lull us to slumber again.
> Sound trumpets aloud from mountain to glen!
> And gather the forces of Free Soil men![27]

The Democrats chose James Buchanan. The chief use of language in their platform was to conceal their thoughts. The remnants of the Whigs condemned "geographical parties" and nominated Millard Fillmore, a man "eminent for his calm and pacific temperament."

Phillips welcomed the advent of the Republican Party. He regarded its canvass as a public education. But he claimed that it afforded alleviation, nothing more. The Republican party clamored for the non-extension of slavery. He sought its death. The Republican party said: "Localize it. Slavery must let go of Kansas." He retorted: "Slavery must set every bondsman free." The Republican Party said: "Bind the Devil." He advised: "Cast him out."

"Republicanism! What is it?" he asked before the New York Anti-Slavery Society. "I will tell you. Its cardinal principle is this: Resist the last enormity of slavery, and endorse all that went before. When Texas is the last enormity, resist it, and say nothing about the past; Texas once in, and the Fugitive Slave Law on the table, resist that, and say 'Amen' to Texas. When Kansas comes to the door, resist that, and say nothing about the past; now she is in, why, resist Cuba, and kiss Kansas. That is Republicanism . . ."[28]

At the annual July Fourth celebration in Framingham, Phillips criticised the timidity of political parties and the economic bulwark of the Slave Power.

'I do not know anything against Colonel Fremont, except that the Boston Post says he once ate dog's meat; and I do not wonder every Democratic puppy objects to that. (Laughter and applause.)

"The only fault with the Republican party is, that it is one of defence. The Liberty party was on the defensive, the Free Soil party was on the defensive, the Republican party is on the defensive, and each one of them has been driven back, back, back, until now the Republican has nothing to defend. The glory of the anti-slavery movement is, that it never stops to be attacked. The only possible anti-slavery movement in this country is an aggressive one. We are very small in numbers; we have got no wealth; we have got no public opinion behind us; the only thing that we can do is, like the eagle, simply to fly at our enemy, and pick out his eyes. (Applause.)"[29]

The North let the South gain half the battle by allowing her to begin the attack. There is no gallantry in defense—no enthusiasm in it. In all great contests, it is the minority that attacks if it carries the day. The great defect of Phillips's day was that the North was always crying out mercy: "We don't mean that"; "Beg your pardon, we only want to defend the territory over there beyond." Every political party in the coun-

try commenced its platform and its speeches with a lavish
eulogy of the Union. It got down on its knees first and said—
"I beg pardon for being suspected of *Abolitionism*."

But what was the merit of Abolitionism, asked Phillips. "It
is that we have earned the right to be called traitors and infidels.
We must hold that right." (If one wanted to learn who had
benefited his age, one need merely examine history and see
whom the rascals in office opposed.) The party that had as the
sharpest edge of its axe, this motto: "We go for the abolition
of slavery first, whether the Union survives it or not"—that
party would penetrate.

> "The government is not office; the government is the
> Slave Power—nothing else. The present President, so called—
> what is his name? (Great laughter. A voice—'Pierce') Yes,
> Pierce is not President of the United States; it is the Slave
> Power behind him. The Slave Power is the government.
> The merchants of Boston are the Slave Power, who want the
> profits of the government; the manufacturers of New Eng-
> land are the Slave Power, who want the profits of cotton. It
> is the wealth of the country. A man said to me in Boston
> streets, 'If you were to thrash Charles Sumner twenty
> times, you could not thrash him into a gentleman!' You
> will find hundreds of such men walking the pavement of
> Boston, owning the wealth of a hundred thousand dollars.
> That is the Slave Power, just as much as the 'nephew of
> my uncle,' who held the cane over Sumner's head, and let
> it down with so much force; that is the government. Now,
> put Fremont into the Presidential chair, and if he endeavored
> to be an anti-slavery President, it would break the Union.
> If he continued to be President, he must be a pro-slavery
> President, for the very elements of strength are on that
> side."[30]

The country lay beaten to the dust. If its spirit did not revive
soon, said Phillips gloomily, it would never revive, except by
some great convulsion like the Revolution. "Men will say—
'This is rant; God reigns; Ideas will govern; the Right will triumph.' No doubt of it. But gentlemen, you know many efforts
for liberty have failed." And Phillips cited Wycliffe, Huss, and

half a dozen others who set up the banner of reform as Luther
did, but went down to the grave defeated. If Luther had not
succeeded, we would never have heard so much about them.

Reform movements may fail, and be trodden out of sight
for a century. It may be so with this anti-slavery reform.
It is by no means certain that this very effort will free the
slaves. Money and interest, the love of the Yankee for the
dollar, the hatred of the Negro because he is black, the
peculiar condition of the country, may smother out ideas
that, like Cromwell, had triumphed for a time. A century
of despotism may follow it; and then some other Garrison
will rise up, like a phoenix, from the ashes of the first, and
perhaps God will bless him with the absolute redemption
of the slave. That the time will come, I know it; but we
cannot count too much upon the certainty of our success
because ideas will triumph. . . .
"I want one single earnest step from the North that shall
convince the South that she loves the freedom of the slave
more than she loves the Union; and the moment I get that,
I am as certain of the liberty of the slave as I saw it. I want
a million of men in Massachusetts—a million of souls. We
sometimes say there are a million of souls in Massachusetts.
Bless me! that is giving a soul to everybody! (Laughter.) I
want a million of souls in Massachusetts, penetrated with an
idea, willing to die for it, willing, better than that, to *live*
for it, and by it, and up to it."[31]

Phillips continued his attack on candidates and parties at
the Anniversary of West India Emancipation held on August 1
in the grove of Abington. Unlike the fourth of July which was
wet and gloomy, this day was bright and beautiful. The grove
with its pines extending to the edge of the golden sheet of
water added its own note of peace and beauty. When Phillips
rose to speak, a solemn stillness settled upon the assembly,
and the scattered audience pressed close around him, anxious
to catch every word, gesture, expression. His first words startled
them like the crack of a rifle shot. "I will call the House of
Representatives a 'Chamber of Assassins' while Preston S. Brooks

sits in it, and the Senate likewise. I want to stamp fifteen States not only as slaveholding, but as barbarous. . . ."

When a man entered the House of Representatives, said Phillips, or when he entered the political canvass, the first thing he did was to say: "I go for the Union. I am no Garrisonian. I am no Disunionist." "Don't suspect me," said a New York Republican journal, "don't suspect me of being a Black Republican. I am only a White one." What Phillips and the Abolitionists criticized in the Republican movement was this: they wanted a platform, no matter who was the candidate, that would drag the whole anti-slavery cause, moral as well as political, right into the center of the cauldron of political discussion.

> "The men of our generation are hucksters; they speak today, and take it back tomorrow, whisper at home what they would be afraid to have heard at Washington, and say at Washington what they would be afraid to have heard at home, and are politically dead when the two places meet and compare notes. (Cheers.) We are a huckstering, half-hearted, paltering, small-patterned, half-in-earnest race; none of the broad, intelligent, earnest, practical, devoted, in one sense, reckless enthusiasm of the revolutionary day, except in those whom the anti-slavery struggle has stirred into life. Now we are bound to keep that spirit alive; to let no political emergency, no compromise swallow it up. Mr. Seward says the day of compromise has passed. I want a party on that basis."[32]

"If Jessie is an Abolitionist, put her up for President," continued Phillips. But he did not want her husband put up while he allowed himself bound by a Constitution that made slavery in the Carolinas safe from the interference of the United States government. He had got beyond Constitutions and Unions.

> "I want no man for President of these States, I will acknowledge no man as an anti-slavery candidate for any office, who has not got his hand half clenched, and means to close it on the jugular vein of the slave system the moment he reaches it, and has a double-edged dagger in the other hand, in case there is any missing in the strangulation.

(Loud cheers.) I want a politics that inscribes on its banner
'Freedom—Justice!' and then, if they can find any room
below them for 'The Constitution of the United States,' put
it in; but Freedom first, Justice first."[33]

James Buchanan was elected but by a narrow margin. The
Democratic Party was no longer master of 27 of the 31 States;
all the free States but five went against it; its candidates no
longer had a majority of the popular vote. For the first time in
the history of the country an avowed anti-slavery candidate
had obtained an electoral vote.[34]

The final vote stood:

	Popular Vote	Electoral Vote
Buchanan	1,838,169	174
Fremont	1,341,264	114
Fillmore	874,534	8

3

On November 25 and 26 the Seventh National Woman's
Rights Convention met in the Broadway Tabernacle, New York.
In spite of a violent storm, a large number assembled. Phillips
was the principal speaker of the evening.[35]

"Tell me the position of woman, and you answer the question of the nation's progress. Step by step as woman ascends,
civilization ripens. The time was when a Greek dared not
let his wife go out of doors, and in the old comic play of
Athens, one of the characters says, 'Where is your wife?'
'She has gone out.' 'Death and furies! What does she do
out?' . . . But in spite of the anchored conservatism of
others, women get out of doors . . . Now the pendulum
swings one way, and now another, but woman has gained
right after right until with us, to the astonishment of the
Greek, could he see it—she stands almost side by side with
man in her civil rights. The Saxon race has led the van. I
trample under foot contemptuously, the Jewish—yes, the
Jewish—ridicule which laughs at such a Convention as this;

for we are the Saxon blood, and the first line of record that is left to the Saxon race is that line of Tacitus, "On all grave questions they consult their women."[36]

Phillips examined three phases in the development of Europe. The first was the dominion of force, the second the dominion of money, the third was beginning—the dominion of brains. When the last came, women would step out on the platform side by side with man. The old Hindu dreamed that he saw the human race led out to its varied fortune. First he saw a man bitted and curbed—and the reins went back to an iron hand. Then he saw a man led on and on, under various changes, until, at last, he saw the man led by threads that came from the brain and went back to an invisible hand. The first was despotism, the reign of force, the upper classes keeping down the under. The last was the type of the nineteenth and following centuries— the dominion of brains.

"Ideas reign. I know some men do not appreciate this fact, they are overawed by an iron arm, by the marble capitol, by the walls of granite—palpable power, felt, seen. I have seen the palace of the Caesars, built of masses that seemed as if giants alone could have laid them together, to last for eternity, as if nothing that did not part the solid globe could move them. But the tiny roots of the weeds of Italian summers had inserted themselves between them, and the palace of the Caesars lies a shapeless ruin. So it is with your government. It may be iron, it may be marble, but the pulses of right and wrong push it aside; only give them time. I hail the government of ideas.

"There is another thing I claim. You laugh at Woman's Rights Conventions; you ridicule socialism (I do not accept that): you dislike the anti-slavery movement. The only discussion of the grave social questions of the age, the questions of right and wrong that lie at the basis of society— the only voices that have stirred them and kept those questions alive have been those of these three reforms. Smothered with material prosperity, the vast masses of our countrymen were living the lives of mere getters of money; but the ideas of this half of the nineteenth century have been bruited by despised reformers, kept alive by the three radical movements, and whoever in the next generation shall seek for the sources of mental and intellectual change will find it here; and in a progressive people like ours that claim is a most vital and significant one . . ."[37]

We did not educate woman, contended Phillips, in the sense that we used education. She had no motive. We furnished a woman with books—we gave her no motive to open them. We opened to her the door of science—why should she enter? Public opinion drove her back, placed a stigma upon her of bluestocking, and the consequnce was, the very motive for education was taken away. A privileged class, an aristocracy, a set of slave-holders did just as much harm to itself as it did to the victimized class. "When a man undertakes to place woman behind him, to assume the reigns of government and to govern for her, he is an aristocrat and all aristocracies are not only unjust, but they are harmful to the progress of society."

"I would have it constantly kept before the public, that we do not seek to prop up woman; we only ask for her space to let her grow. Governments are not made; they grow. They are not buildings like this, with dome and pillars; they are oaks, with roots and branches, and they grow, by God's blessing, in the soil, He gives to them. Now man has been allowed to grow, and when Pharaoh tied him down with bars of iron, when Europe tied him down with privilege and superstition, he burst the bonds, and grew strong. We ask the same for woman."[38]

Phillips spoke at the festival in commemoration of the twenty-fifth anniversary of the formation of the Massachusetts Anti-Slavery Society. Four hundred guests attended at Faneuil Hall and took their seats at the tables which had been spread by the caterer, Joshua B. Smith.

"This commonwealth," said Phillips, "is called the mother of isms. It is true. She is the brain of the Union and furnishes it with its ideas.

"My boast is, that when in the volumes of our statesmen—of Clay, Webster, and every other,—you can find no
great social question touched,—when their speeches are
dead, because transient,—when their cowardice is apparent
from the very fact that they dared not analyze the social
wrongs that lay around them—the very service that has
earned us the epithets of 'traitor' and 'infidel,' is, that in an
age swallowed up by materialism, smothered in old institutions, this enterprise, beginning with a single purpose,
has enlarged the intellect of the continent to grapple with
all social questions—Woman—Punishment—Peace—and every
other idea. These have all been kept alive in the cauldron
of our agitation, and earned us properly, deservedly, the
title of 'infidel' and 'traitor.' 'Infidel' to a church that could
be at peace in the presence of sin! 'Traitor' to a State that
was a magnificent conspiracy against justice."[39]

With such convictions Phillips signed the call for a Disunion Convention to be held in Worcester, Massachusetts, in
January, 1857. The convention met on the fifteenth with a large
attendance. The Boston *Evening Ledger* captioned an editorial
"The Lunatics Let Loose." The Worcester *Bay State* published
"The Black List" containing the names of the principal signers
to the Convention. Garrison spoke at length, advocating his
familiar maxim—"No Union with Slaveholders," Phillips made
two speeches.

"We have a right to abolish and change governments,"
he said at the evening session, "certainly we have. 'Treason!'
It ought to be. Treason runs in the blood that flowed out
on Bunker Hill. I hope we shall never submit to inoculation
to avoid the disease. The dog runs naturally to water; so
the Yankees run naturally to treason—treason to any institution that seeks to gag his lips . . .
"What I want to do in regard to this question of Disunion is, to direct public attention to the possibilities of Disunion, to familiarize the public ear to the word Disunion—
at any rate to disarm it of its hitherto terrors. I want to
familiarize the idea to the people of Massachusetts and when
that is done, leave events to stereotype it into practice."[40]

Later an attempt was made to hold a monster Northern Convention at Cleveland "to consider the practicability, probability, and expediency of a separation of the Free and Slave States." Nearly seven thousand persons summoned the Convention by affixing their names to the call. But the convention was postponed because of the panic of 1857. Wendell Phillips served on the Committee of arrangements.[41]

At the twenty-fourth anniversary of the American Anti-Slavery Society, Phillips allayed the fears of his audience on the question of Disunion—

"I believe that if the dissolution of the Union were the dissolution of the government, it would not be frightful. Why? Because the blood and bones of the genuine Yankee are constitutionally orderly, and he does not need a government. (Laughter.) Put a Yankee baby six months old on his feet, and he will begin to say 'Mr. Chairman,' and call the next cradle to order. (Great applause.) A genuine Yankee on the prairies carries a school house, a meeting house, a town house, and a ballot box all in him, and they crop out the moment they are needed. (Laughter.)

"The South . . . plays her game adroitly," Phillips went on to say; "she hides herself behind judicial ermine; she attacks the Saxon blood through the bench and through the law abiding element. She says—'Have I not got a Constitution?. . . Is not this the opinion of the Supreme Court? Is not this law? Bow!' "[42]

The Disunion Convention had hardly adjourned when the Supreme Court of the United States announced a decision that startled the whole country from one end to the other.

CHAPTER THIRTY-ONE

NINE OLD MEN

On March 6, 1857, Chief Justice Taney, seated in a secluded semi-circular room in the basement of the Capitol began the reading of an opinion.[1] Stooped, flatchested, Taney was bent with years, his face deeply furrowed, his hair, which he frequently brushed away, hanging carelessly over a high forehead. His arms and fingers were long, bony, and hairy, his voice hollow and consumptive. And yet when he began to speak the audience never thought of his personal appearance—so terse, so pointed, so luminous, so logical and convincing were his words. He used no gestures. There was not a redundant syllable, not a phrase repeated. He gave to his decision an air of intellect, dignity, and authority. William Pinckney once said of him: "I can answer his arguments, I am not afraid of his logic, but that infernal apostolic manner of his there is no replying to."[2]

The room was queer and small, broken by pillars and arched walls and shaped overhead like the quarter section of a pumpkin shell. A feeble light trickled in through the windows of ground glass in the rear, and as the Justices sat with their backs to the light, the counsel who addressed them at times could scarcely see their faces. The effect was gloomy and depressing. After gazing around a moment, one newspaper correspondent exclaimed: 'I don't wonder at that decision in the *Dred Scott Case*. Why! what a potato hole of a place this is! The old men ought to be got above ground where they can breathe fresh air and see real daylight once in a while."[3]

One Dred Scott (first called Sam),[4] a slave belonging to a young army surgeon named John Emerson, was taken from his home state of Missouri, first into the free State of Illinois and then to Fort Snelling in the territory of Wisconsin. Emerson stayed two years, then was transferred back to St. Louis, and Dred without protest went with him. In 1842 Emerson left the army because of ill health. Two years later he died and the Negro became the property of his wife. In the fall of 1846, eight years after his return to Missouri, Dred Scott brought suit for his liberty against Mrs. Emerson in the State Court of St. Louis. The ground of the suit was that by living in Illinois he had been made free under the Constitution of that State, and his sojourn in the territory of Wisconsin also made him free because the Missouri Compromise of 1820 prohibited slavery in the domain acquired from France north of 36° and 30′ except the State of Missouri. In this trial court, Dred Scott won, but Mrs. Emerson appealed to the State Supreme Court which reversed the judgment on the ground that having returned to Missouri voluntarily the Negro resumed his status as slave under the laws of that State.

But in the meanwhile Mrs. Emerson had removed to Springfield, Massachusetts, and in 1850 had married Dr. Calvin C. Chaffee, a Know-Nothing and an Abolitionist member of Congress. Under Missouri law Mrs. Chaffee, because of her remarriage, could not act in any capacity with respect to Emerson's estate which had been left in trust to a daughter. Full control over Dred now rested on the other executor, Mrs. Chaffee's brother, John F. A. Sanford of New York.[5] Scott now transferred his suit from the State to the Federal Courts under the power given them to try suits between citizens of different states. The case of Scott as a citizen of Missouri against Sanford as a citizen of New York was brought before the United States Circuit Court. But the latter Court also decided against Scott, upholding the decision of the Missouri Court on the ground that it was the custom for Federal Courts to follow the decision of State Courts in such cases of personal freedom.

When the case on appeal came up before the Federal Supreme Court, the only point to be decided was the right of the

Circuit Court to follow the Missouri Court, and the way seemed clearly marked out by precedent. By a unanimous opinion of the Court in the case of *Strader v. Graham*, 1851, it had been held that when a slave returns to a slave state his status is determinable by the Courts of that State. Scott was a slave because the Supreme Court of Missouri had decided that he was a slave. The judgment of the lower Court should therefore be affirmed.

The duty thus laid on the United States Supreme Court was an unimportant one: Was Scott a free man or a slave? Indeed when the Judges met in consultation, the majority held to the plain path of precedent and agreed among themselves to ignore the thorny question of the Missouri Compromise that was agitating the country. To Judge Nelson, a rigid States rights man, was assigned the duty of writing the opinion of the Court.

Within a few days, however, Taney found that the two dissenting Judges, McLean and Curtis, intended to write lengthy opinions in the nature of stump speeches on the troublesome point, maintaining the constitutionality of the Missouri Compromise and the power of Congress to abolish slavery in the territories. The other Judges now felt compelled to discuss that point as well themselves. Justice Wayne had the patriotic idea that by settling forever the constitutional question of the Missouri Compromise and by stripping Congress of the power of ever again meddling with slavery, the whole disturbance would be ended and the States would all live happily together. Wayne's earnest appeal was successful, the assignment to Justice Nelson was withdrawn, and Chief Justice Taney was asked to write an opinion upon all the questions involved.

Justice Grier of Pennsylvania, however, did not want to pass upon the Missouri Compromise. President-elect Buchanan was informed, and a few days before inauguration wrote to his lifelong friend Justice Grier urging him to fall in line.

Friction between the judges by this time had become so acute that Taney had to exercise the role of disciplinarian. On one occasion the judges in their excitement rose from the conference table arguing and gesticulating. "Brothers" snapped Taney, "this is the

Supreme Court of the United States. Take your seats." The Judges sat down like rebuked schoolboys.[6]

McLean and Curtis determined to make political capital out of the Dred Scott controversy. McLean was a perennial candidate for the presidency. He had been a candidate in the Anti-Masonic Convention of 1831, was nominated by the legislature of Ohio five years later, was mentioned in the Whig Convention of 1848, received 196 votes in the Republican Convention of 1856, and although seventy-five years of age, still hankered after the nomination in 1860. He took the unusual ground that a judge was under no obligation to refrain from political discussion and stoutly defended the propriety of his candidacy for the presidency. He wrote frequent letters on political questions to personal friends and to the press for publication.

Quite otherwise was the case of Judge Curtis. Curtis was an old line Whig who as a lawyer had been identified with the slave interest. In 1836 in the case of the slave Med, he had maintained that an owner might bring a slave to Massachusetts and hold her there in slavery until returning to a slave state. Surely it was a far cry from this contention to the one that Curtis took in the Dred Scott case. In 1850 he defended the fugitive slave law in a speech in Faneuil Hall. Immediately after his appointment to the Supreme Court he procured the arrest of Wendell Phillips and Theodore Parker for obstructing the execution of that law. His course was unpopular in Massachusetts. The Northern press denounced him savagely. "He is not a Massachusetts judge," said the New York *Tribune*, "he is a slave catching Judge, appointed to office as a reward for his professional support given to the Fugitive Slave Bill."[7]

At first Curtis thought of concurring with the majority and not touching the Missouri Compromise. In 1854 before the Dred Scott case came before the Supreme Court, Curtis had written to George Ticknor complaining of the salaries paid to the Court. "They are so poor," he wrote, "that not one judge on the bench can live on what the government pays him." Soon after the decision rendered in the Dred Scott case, Curtis resigned from the bench, at the same time writing ex-president Fillmore that he had done so on account of the inadequacy of salary. Obviously,

if he were to return to Boston to practice law, it was necessary
to rehabilitate his reputation in Massachusetts. Within a week
after his resignation he received seven retainers in important
cases. His receipts from fees during the succeeding years
amounted to $650,000 which was much better financially than
being a justice of the Supreme Court.[8]

The moment the Court departed from the plain path of precedent, there was no possibility of unanimity. When Taney
read his decision "upon all questions involved," one judge
only—Wayne—concurred with him; five others concurred separately in partial and irregular fashion, and two, McLean and
Curtis, dissented point blank.

Taney decided First: That Dred Scott was not and could
not be, because he was of slave descent, a citizen of the United
States and therefore could not sue in the United States Courts.

Second: That the Missouri Compromise Act of 1820 was unconstitutional and void for the reason that one of the constitutional functions of Congress was the protection of property, that
slaves had been recognised as property by the Constitution,
that they might be taken wherever other property was taken,
and that, therefore, Congress was bound to protect, not to prohibit slavery in the Territories.

"It is difficult at this day," said Taney, "to realize the state
of public opinion in relation to that unfortunate race which
prevailed in a civilized and intelligent portion of the world
at the time of the Declaration of Independence and when the
Constitution of the United States was framed and adopted. . . .
They had more than a century before been regarded as beings
of an inferior order . . . and so far inferior, that they had no
rights which the white man was bound to respect."[9]

The phrase "that they had no rights which the white man
was bound to respect," was wrenched from its context, seized
upon, and promulgated throughout the North until in the mind
of the masses the name of Taney was the incarnation of injustice
and judicial infamy.[10]

"Well," commented Phillips as he finished reading the dictum
of Chief Justice Taney, "the Supreme Court sustains my claims
for a dozen years. It is infamous. But it is the law of the United

States. How now about the pro-slavery character of the Union? Am I not right in seeking to withdraw?"[11] In an angry mood he exclaimed: "I want a collision. I don't care how it comes. I want the Federal Government divided; I want State sovereignty assumed. Success to the strongest arm. Might makes right today."[12]

The New York *Independent* headed a special article: "The Decision of the Supreme Court is the Moral Assassination of a Race and Cannot Be Obeyed."[13] "A high judicial lie has been palmed off upon you," shouted Frederick Douglass to an Abolitionist audience in New York.[14]

To the Chicago *Tribune* came "visions of coffle gangs on their way through Illinois . . . Chicago might become a slave market and men, women, and children may be sold off the block in our streets." "Freedom and white men are no longer safe," declared the Illinois *Daily State Journal*.[15]

Seward was outspoken in the Senate: "The people of the United States never can and never will accept principles so unconstitutional, so abhorrent. Never! Never! Let the Court recede. Whether it recede or not, we shall reorganize the Court and thus reform its political sentiment and practices and bring them in harmony with the Constitution and the laws of Nature."[16]

Though the decision opened a Pandora's box and let loose all the perplexing questions supposed to be shut in, it had a far reaching and invaluable effect: it revived the Republican Party. The party was nearly bankrupt for lack of an issue. The Kansas issue was worn out: people were tired of hearing of "Bloody Kansas." Just at the right moment the Dred Scott case provided a new issue.

Besides the decision destroyed Douglas. Lincoln took occasion at Freeport to ask Douglas if he did not support the Dred Scott decision; also if he still adhered to the doctrine of popular sovereignty as a means of settling the slavery problem in the Territories. Douglas answered affirmatively to both queries. Whereupon Lincoln showed that if the Dred Scott decision were held, Congress must protect slavery in all the territories, and if the popular sovereignty idea prevailed, squatters of any territory might by popular vote prohibit slavery in any territory. "Judge

Douglas," Lincoln replied, "says that a thing may be lawfully driven away from a place where it has a lawful right to be."[17] Douglas recognised the predicament but replied that in spite of the Court's decision, settlers of a new territory might by "unfriendly" local legislation make slavery impossible. When the newspapers of the country published this reply, Southern men everywhere denounced "the demagogue who promised one thing in Congress and another in Illinois."[18]

There were several curious angles to the Dred Scott case. A week after the decision was rendered, constituents began to complain of Representative Chaffee. Did his wife have any interest in the ownership of Dred Scott and his family? "No!" answered Chaffee—which was obviously a lie. Two months later Chaffee and his wife sold the Scott family to Taylor Blow of St. Louis "for the purpose solely of emancipation." Ten days afterwards they were free.[19]

This same Taylor Blow had signed Dred Scott's appeal bond. He was the son of Peter Blow, from whom Scott had been bought by Dr. Emerson, and had been the Negro's childhood playmate. Blow was opposed to slavery and later became a prominent Republican in St. Louis. One fact that must be accounted for in every discussion of the case is the constant appearance of some member of the Blow family at every stage of its progress, except the actual inception.[20] Another anti-slavery adherent, a lawyer named Hugh A. Garland, appeared for the fictitious defendant Sanford.

Six months before the case was entered on the docket of the United States Supreme Court, a pamphlet entitled: "The case of Dred Scott in the Supreme Court of the United States, December Term, 1854," was printed at St. Louis and circulated. It contained a preface dated July 4, 1854, and was signed by the mark of Dred Scott, appealing to all who might read it for sympathy and help. Whoever wrote the preface was an adroit politician and master propagandist. It appears certain that the outlay for printing and distribution was made by the same person that bore the expense of the whole litigation. But who that person was, is not positively known.[21]

Finally: the Kansas Nebraska Bill had repealed the Missouri Compromise Act by declaring it "inoperative and void." The power of Congress to legislate over the subject of slavery had also been denied by the Bill. The slave oligarchy thus had little to gain by risking a ruling in the Court on a point which Congress had already effectively decided for itself. But not so with the anti-slavery party. An adverse judicial decision would not make their position any worse than it was under the Kansas Nebraska Bill, and a favorable decision might give the cause a moral impetus.

Perhaps the Dred Scott case was merely a test case begun and prosecuted by an ardent supporter of anti-slavery and Dred Scott a mere pawn in the hand of his subtle brain.

Taney, "the votary and pillar of the slave power," was opposed to slavery. In early life he had incurred the odium of the South by defending a Methodist minister indicted for inciting a slave insurrection through having preached a sermon condemning slavery.[22] Taney freed the slaves he had inherited except two who were too old to take care of themselves and these he supported until his death. The position he took in the Dred Scott case was the result of a mistaken sense of duty and not of any partiality for slavery. He had been brought up in the tradition that slavery was national and at his advanced age it was doubtless difficult for him to change his opinions.

When a bill for placing a marble bust of Taney in the Supreme Court Room (where already the busts of Jay, Ellsworth, and Marshall had been installed) came up for debate in the Senate, Sumner replied—"The name of Taney is to be hooted down the page of history . . . The Senator says that he for twenty-five years administered Justice. He administered justice, at least, wickedly, and degraded the Judiciary of the country and degraded the age." The debate was closed by Sumner: "Taney shall not be represented as a saint by any vote of Congress, if I can help it."

The bill was lost at this session of Congress, but later, a month before Sumner's death, a bill for the bust of Taney was passed without debate. Senator Trumbull of Illinois said—"Suppose he did make a wrong decision. No man is infallible. He was a great and learned and able man." Taney was indeed a great magistrate and a man of singular purity of life and character.[23]

The forces of slavery and anti-slavery were now sharply drawn. The folly of the Dred Scott decision opened the eyes of Northern leaders. For the first time they saw what the Abolitionists had seen for twenty years—the impossibility of mixing oil and water, fire and snow, life and death. Abraham Lincoln, in a speech at Springfield, Illinois, exclaimed: " 'A house divided against itself cannot stand,' " and the United States he likened to the divided house. In the same strain spoke Seward at Rochester, New York: "Shall I tell you what this collision means? They who think it is accidental, unnecessary, the work of interested and fanatical agitators, and therefore ephemeral, mistake the case altogether. It is an *irrepressible conflict* between opposing and enduring forces, and it means that the United States must and will, sooner or later, become either entirely a slaveholding nation or entirely a free-labor nation."[24]

On May 26, 1857, at a meeting of the New England Anti-Slavery Society, Phillips spoke on "the necessity of the hour which is revolutionary." Again he demanded the firm resolve and absolute purpose of the forces of anti-slavery.

"In 1789 the vessel of State was launched. At that same moment, the devil hovered over Charleston and dropped a few cotton seeds into the soil. Presto! sixty years, and the seeds of cotton have annihilated Wythe, and Lee, and Rutledge, and Jay, the Constitution, the Revolution, and everything else, and we are nothing but a cotton bag today. . . .

"Why has the South always conquered us? Because she writes one single word on her catalogue of requests, that is—'Slavery!' It is the first, it is the second, it is the third; turn the leaf and it is—'Slavery!' All through the book it is—'Slavery!' The North writes—'Kansas'—'Tariff'—'Internal Improvements'—'Railroads'—'Edward Everett'—and many other insignificant quantities, to the end. (Laughter and applause.) What is the consequence? The party that has but one object, knows what it wants, and is willing to sacrifice everything for it, conquers;—of course it must!"[25]

As Phillips explained, this was the history of moral struggles in all times. It was this willingness to sacrifice everything that turned impotency into power, a dwarf into a giant. "Beware of the man driven to the last ditch—beware despair," says the proverb, for the man who was willing to risk his own life was master of every other. Were Massachusetts willing to risk everything in order to break the fetters of the slave, then her million men and her handkerchief patch of territory would start up into omnipotence and move the mass prejudice of the nation.

"Suppose, when Warren, Putnam, and Prescott were on Bunker Hill, and 'Old Put' gave that order, 'Don't waste your powder, boys, wait till you see the whites of their eyes,'— suppose, instead of that, somebody had come to him and said, 'The British have fired Charlestown, and the shingles on the Congregational Church are all in a flame,' and he had said to his men, 'Stop. Let's put out the fire on that Church'—should we ever have conquered?"[26]

The strength and obduracy of Wellington's Old Guard at Waterloo which stood like a granite wall, hurling back every impetuous charge—that was the kind of resolution Phillips wanted for the purpose of the North. In the struggle between two mighty and determined parties, that party that had no looking back, that meant to write its history in the ditch, that meant to leave nothing alive unless it conquered—that party conquered.

"I want this purpose announced on the part of anti-slavery men. If I could have the twelve hundred thousand men that voted for Fremont, if I coud have those few hundred pulpits that redeem the Sodom and Gomorrah of the thirty thousand Bethunes and Nehemiah Adamses, (Applause)— if I could have them say, 'We are not technically Garrisonians, but we have laid life and reputation on the altar of justice. We have made up this purpose: Let the Union go; let the Church go; let Commerce go; let grass grow on the wharves; let another generation be wasted, as our fathers wasted one in the struggle for ideas, we care not. God willing, we will write out as the history of this generation, that at the sacrifice of every present interest, they melted

every fetter beneath the flag of the empire!' (Applause.)
—if I could have them say this, I should be sure of the
victory."[27]

But as long as the North did not announce this, as long as
the North faltered, just so long did the South tempt, day after
day, one class after another, buying up politicians and eating
out the virtue and strength of Northern opinion. If a man began
to form a virtuous resolution, it melted away in the temptation
of time serving politics and a qualifying religion. "The gallantry
and bravery of an absolute purpose is what converts multitudes
of men. He that rides forward and takes the lead, forms the
purpose of the millions that lag behind."

Abolitionists, said Phillips, never found fault with any man's
method. They never said to any man, "Toe the mark!" But when
others went off to side issues, they were wasting time.

"Today we stand with the triumph of the Slave Power
written on the forehead of the government itself; and that is
the reason why men ought to recognize the necessity of the
hour, which is revolutionary. It is useless to disguise it;
it is useless to doubt, to cajole men with equivocal words,
with half measures. . . . What is the use of your talk? There
is the law. The Supreme Court, the final interpreter of the
Constitution, has made it all, and the North says what the
Supreme Court has decided to be law, it bows to. 'What
are you going to do, Mr. Wilson? What are you going to do,
Mr. Cheever, Mr. Beecher? Do you mean to submit?' 'No!'
every voice answers. 'Do you mean to rebel?' 'No!' (Laughter.) Well, where is the middle course? There is no course
but to say to the popular mind—for it is on the basis of the
people, at last, that the heavy machinery of the anti-slavery
movement rests—it is to say to that people, and say it today,
'You must be ready for revolution. You must be ready to
look the law in the face and say, "We will not submit to it!" '
And when you have produced that readiness in the public
mind, then you are ready for the first attempt to carry that
decision of the Supreme Court into effect. But you must
begin to preach today. You must preach from sentiment to
conviction, and from conviction into character, and from
character into prejudice, and from prejudice into instinct."[28]

CHAPTER THIRTY-TWO

THE IMPENDING CRISIS

A North Carolinian named Hinton Rowan Helper published in 1857 a striking volume called—*"The Impending Crisis in the South and How to Meet It."* Dedicated to non-slaveholding whites, the theme was that slavery was a blight upon the Southern people and a political peril.

Much of the book was rabid, shallow, and in some respects downright silly, but with the monotony of rhodomontade was included a fine array of statistical proof that slavery was throttling the progress of Southern society. Page after page of comparisons between the North and the South were given. In every instance the North far outstripped the South. If the middle and lower classes of the South were to prosper, Helper argued, if the South were ever to develop a varied commerce and industry, slavery must go.

The Impending Crisis raised the question. If slavery was so good a thing, *for whose good was it?* Helper emphasized with relentless force facts in the United States census that the direct benefits of slavery accrued to only a part of the whites in the South, that the splendor, luxury, and culture of the South which had been so praised was the possession of a small minority who ruled for their own particular benefit six million whites and nearly four million blacks.

"The liberation of millions of 'poor white trash' from the second degree of slavery and of millions of miserable kidnapped Negroes from the first degree, cannot be accomplished too soon. That it was not accomplished many years ago is our misfortune. . . . It is madness to delay. If today we could emanci-

378

pate all the slaves in the Union, we would do it and the country and everybody in it would be vastly better off tomorrow. Now is the time for action; let us work."[1]

Helper urged the non-slaveholding whites to organize to combat slavery, that they refuse to cooperate with the slaveholders in politics, religion, business, and social life generally, that they give no recognition to pro-slavery men except as ruffians, outlaws, and criminals, that they hire no more slaves but give the greatest possible encouragement to free white labor, and that slaveholders be taxed out of existence.

"The slaveholders have hoodwinked you, trifled with you, and used you as mere tools for the consummation of their wicked designs. A speedy and perfect abolishment of the whole institution is the true policy of the South. Will you aid us? Will you assist us? Will you be freemen, or will you be slaves?"[2]

As for compensated emancipation. "Preposterous idea!" Helper exclaimed. "Shall we pat the bloodhounds for the sake of doing them a favor? Shall we free the curse of slavery to make them rich at our expense? Pay these whelps for the privilege of converting them into decent, honest, upright men?"[3]

Colonization? "A humane farce." Slaves were increasing in the country at the rate of nearly 100,000 per annum. Within the last ten years the American Colonization Society had sent to Liberia less than five thousand Negroes. "Fiddlesticks for such colonization," added Helper.[4]

To the "knights of bludgeons, chevaliers of bowie knives and pistols, and lords of the lash," he addressed a hotheaded and boastful challenge: "Frown, Sirs, fret, foam, prepare your weapons, threaten, strike, shoot, stab, bring on civil war, dissolve the Union, nay annihilate the solar system if you will,—do all this, more, less, better, worse, anything—do what you will, Sirs, you can neither foil nor intimidate us; our purpose is as firmly fixed as the eternal pillars of Heaven; we have determined to abolish slavery, and so help us God, abolish it we will! Take this to bed with you tonight, Sirs, and think about it, dream over it, and let us know how you feel tomorrow morning."[5]

The publication of *The Impending Crisis* was greeted with denunciation. Southern postmasters refused to deliver it. Great bonfires were made of such copies as could be found in the South. The ownership of a copy in a Southern State was sufficient to invite violence. Because John Sherman was reported to have contributed to a fund for its circulation, he was defeated for the speakership of the House of Representatives. But thirteen thousand copies were sold in 1857, and in the campaign of 1860 more than a hundred thousand were distributed. "Virginia will in vain banish Helper," declared Wendell Phillips. "She will in vain fight against the multiplication table—for Helper's book is nothing but the multiplication table printed two hundred times over."[6]

But a modern sociologist takes a dismal view: if the common white had no worth while interest at stake in slavery, if his real interest ran the other way about, he did, nevertheless, have that, to him, "dear treasure" of his superiority as a white man which had been conferred on him by slavery. He saw in the offensive of the Yankee as great a danger to himself as the august planter. Moreover this struggle against the Yankee provided a perfect focus for his romantic and hedonistic instincts, for his love of self-assertion and battle. "You can understand . . . how farmer and white trash were welded into an extraordinary and positive unity of passion and purpose with the planter—how it was that . . . Hinton Helper . . . and others could get no response."

His participation in the legend went even further yet. For continually from every stump, platform, and editorial sanctum, the planter captains gave him on the one hand the Yankee—as cowardly, avaricious, boorish, half Pantaloon and half Shylock—and on the other the Southerner—as polished, brave, generous, magnificent, wholly the stately aristocrat, fit to cower a dozen Yankees.[7]

The customary First of August Emancipation Address of Phillips in 1857 was a skillful appeal for funds to send out agents "to plant the seeds of radical, disinterested, fearless anti-slavery in the virgin soil of the West." It was in this long speech that he

turned aside to answer the Unitarian clergymen who were
"always picking at him because he was orthodox." He did this
by comparing the freedom displayed at a recent orthodox Yale
commencement with the restraint at libertarian Harvard, which
he attributed to its bond of union with the commercial interests
of Boston. Yale too had honored Charles Sumner with a degree
before Harvard had remembered her son.

"You go to Harvard," Phillips said, "and the young men
have no power. They are all young, it is true, but they all
speak on the Everett model; they are all as correct and as
cold. They are like the man who went up to Worcester with
an awful cold in his head. His friends asked him where he
got it. He replied, 'I called on Governor Everett, and stayed
too long.'" (Laughter and applause.)[8]

At the Yale Commencement to which Phillips alluded, he had
been invited to deliver the Phi Beta Kappa oration. He accepted
on one condition—that he be permitted to take for his theme,
"The Scholar, in a Republic, Necessarily an Agitator." His own
defence was of his chosen vocation—the agitator's,

"Whose purpose is to throw the gravest questions upon the
conscience and intellect of the masses, because they are the
ultimate governors in a republic, and therefore should be
educated by agitation up to the idea of national and universal freedom. If the people do not rule it is because they
are willing to have politicians rule instead. It is their in-
dolence which has allowed the Government to drift toward
despotism. This is the present danger in a country which is
not homogeneous. One-half is seventeen hundred years behind the times, where the faggot and tortures rule. Argument only is found in an entirely Republican country, and
its only safety is in agitation and distrust of politics."[9]

Some aggrieved Southerners protested against his topic, but
Phillips's eloquence took the town by storm, and the following
week he was invited to deliver a similar oration at Brown University. "He is undoubtedly the most brilliant man thrown up

to celebrity by the Abolition passion," reporters wrote to New York and Boston journals.[10]

Occasionally the spice of variety enlivened Phillips's somewhat monotonous career. In February of 1858, he paid a visit to the town of Cortland, New York, where he lectured on "Street Life in Europe," Saturday evening; on "Woman's Rights" Sunday morning; "Toussaint L'Ouverture" in the afternoon; and in the evening on "American Slavery." Trust a country town to exhaust a privilege and a celebrity!

2.

Bad blood was breaking out in the House of Representatives. A violent altercation took place between Lawrence M. Keitt of South Carolina and Galusha A. Grow of Pennsylvania. Grow was standing near the Democratic side talking to a Democrat when Keitt ordered him away, calling him "nothing but a Black Republican puppy." "No matter what I am," returned Grow, "no nigger driver can crack his whip over me."

Keitt grabbed him by the throat, but Grow knocked him down. In a moment the House was in an uproar, Republicans and Democrats mixing in a free-for-all. The Sergeant-at-arms, bearing the mace of the House, was at once in the midst of the combatants and after some minutes, with the "utmost energetic efforts on the part of the Speaker" succeeded partially in restoring order.[11]

At the next session Keitt apologized to the House, after previously submitting the language of his apology to Grow to see if the Pennsylvanian had any objection to the form. Keitt frankly admitted that the fault was his, but he saved his "honor" by alleging that he was not aware of being struck by anybody, which obviated the necessity for a duel.

The ruction became internationally famous. Over in London *Punch* published an epic beginning—

"Sing, O Goddess, the wrath, the ontamable
dander of Keitt
Keitt of South Carolina, the clear grit, the tall, the
ondaunted—

Him that hath wopped his own niggers till Northerners
all unto Keitt
Seem but as niggers to wop, and as hills of the smallest
potatoes.[12]

Some time afterwards Representative Roger A. Pryor of Virginia challenged Representative John F. Potter of Wisconsin to a duel. Potter as the challenged party immediately accepted and named bowie knives as weapons. Pryor protested that bowie knives were not recognized by the code and were "barbarous and inhuman." But Potter was serious. He was not used to dueling weapons and would be sure to be killed if he used any: with bowie knives he and Pryor were on even terms. Pryor wrote a note accepting Potter's terms, but the second was arrested and the deadly encounter averted.[13]

3.

The year of 1859 opened calmly. Disorders continued in Kansas, but the country had grown accustomed to that. The South, complacent over the Dred Scott decision and intrenched behind three lines of fortification—the White House, Congress, and the Supreme Court—was resting on its arms. At the North the Republicans were preparing for the campaign of 1860.

The great anniversaries were held as usual—the meetings crowded, the speakers trenchant, the discussions touching every phase of current affairs. On May 10 the American Anti-Slavery Society held its gathering in the Assembly Rooms, New York City. "The Abolitionists Down in the Mouth," the New York *Herald* commented. "They are down upon everybody and everything except their own little set of crazy demagogues and fanatics."[14] "The Abolitionists Again," ran a caption in the New York *Times*. "People go to hear them just as they would go to a bull baiting, or rat killing match, if these were respectable."[15] "All Played Out," remarked the New York *Express*.[16] But the *Liberator* truthfully declared: "Of all the anniversaries held by the Society since its organization, none has given more cheering signs of progress than this."

While in the city Phillips spoke before the New York Anti-Slavery Society:—

"We believe that the American Church is rotten to the core. (Applause and hisses.) Why these hisses? Who educates the American people . . . a slave-hunting, woman-whipping, soul-selling people, not knowing yet the difference between a sheep and a man—who educates them? The American Church, whose moral sense groans out of 40,000 pulpits. I hold the Church responsible for the character of the nation . . .

"It is a very easy thing for a dozen fastidious men, now sitting in these seats, to say that I am a vulgar utterer of Billingsgate, and they could have made a great deal prettier speech. No doubt they could. Scholarship folds its arms and says, 'These agitators are vulgar fellows;' and it turns its phrases, and balances its periods, and says, with Shakespeare, that war would have been a mighty gallant thing if it had not been for this villainous saltpetre. (Laughter and applause.)"[17]

On May 12 Phillips attended a turbulent session of the National Women's Rights Convention also held in New York City. One after the other the orators of the occasion were hooted off the platform until Phillips was called. For two hours he held the hitherto mocking audience in the hollow of his hand. In closing he said—

"I will not attempt to detain you longer ("Go on"—"go on") I have neither the disposition nor the strength to trespass any longer upon your attention. The subject is so large that it might well fill days, instead of hours. . . . If this experiment of self-government is to succeed, it is to succeed by some saving element introduced into the politics of the present day. You know this: your Websters, your Clays, your Calhouns, your Douglases, however intellectually able they may have been, have never dared or cared to touch that moral element of our national life. Either the shallow and heartless trade of politics had eaten out their own moral being, or they feared to enter the unknown land of lofty right and wrong."[18]

None of these great names, continued Phillips, linked its fame with one great moral question of the day. They dealt with money questions, with tariffs, with parties, with State law. If by chance they touched the slave question, it was only like Jewish hucksters trading in the relics of Saints. The reformers, the fanatics, as the Abolitionists are called, were the only ones who launched social and moral questions.

I risk nothing when I say that the anti-slavery discussion of the last twenty years has been the salt of this nation; it has actually kept it alive and wholesome. Without it, our politics would have sunk beyond even contempt. So with this question. It stirs the deepest sympathy; . . . it enwraps within itself the greatest moral issues. Judge it, then, candidly, carefully, as Americans, and let us show ourselves worthy of the high place to which God has called us in human affairs. (Applause.)"[19]

At this meeting a resolution was adopted to memorialize the legislatures in the Union. But owing to the general unrest and forebodings of the people on the eve of Civil War, the resolution commanded little attention.[20]

Two weeks later, Phillips addressed the New England section of the Women's Rights Reform. Whenever a new reform is started, he remarked, men seem to think that the world is going to take at once a great stride. But the world never takes strides. The moral world is exactly like the natural. "The sun comes up minute by minute, ray by ray, till twilight deepens into dawn, and dawn spreads into noon. So it is with this question. Those who look at our little island of time do not see it; but a hundred years later, everybody will recognize it."[21]

In the summer of 1859 the State permitted the statue of Webster to be placed in the State House yard with ostentatious ceremonies—Edward Everett eulogizing the recreant statesman. A few weeks later on October 4, Phillips opened the "Fraternity" lecture course—the most popular Lyceum platform in Boston. The result was his lecture on "Idols." Referring to Webster's statue, he said, again harshly, uncompromisingly:[22]

"No man criticises when private friendship moulds the loved form in

> Stone that breathes and struggles,
> Or brass that seems to speak.

Let Mr. Webster's friends crowd their own halls and grounds with his bust and statues. That is no concern of ours. But when they ask the State to join in doing him honor, then we claim the right to express an opinion.

"We cannot but remember that the character of the commonwealth is shown by the character of those it crowns. A brave old Englishman tells us the Greeks had officers who did pluck down statues if they exceeded due symmetry and proportion. 'We need such now,' he adds, 'to order monuments according to men's merits.' Indeed we do! . . . When I think of the long term and wide reach of his influence, and look at the subjects of his speeches,—the mere shells of history, drum-and-trumpet declamation, dry law, or selfish bickerings about trade,—when I think of his bartering the hopes of four millions of bondmen for the chances of his private ambition, I recall the criticism of Lord Eldon,—'No man ever did his race so much good as Eldon prevented.' Again, when I remember the close of his life spent in ridiculing the Anti-Slavery movement as useless abstraction, moonshine, 'mere rub-a-dub agitation,' because it did not minister to trade and gain, methinks I seem to see written all over his statue Tocqueville's conclusion from his survey of French and American democracy,—'The man who seeks freedom for anything but freedom's self, is made to be a slave!' "

The echo of these sentences had hardly died away when others were heard—sharper, fiercer, more ominous and deadly —John Brown's rifles among the hills of Virginia.

CHAPTER THIRTY-THREE

ST. JOHN THE JUST[1]

On February 18, 1858, Gerrit Smith of Peterboro, New York, wrote in his diary: "Our old and noble friend Captain John Brown of Kansas arrives this evening."[2] Thomas Wentworth Higginson, pastor of the Free Church at Worcester, George L. Stearns, a successful lead pipe manufacturer of Boston, and Frank B. Sanborn, fresh from college, young and enthusiastic, all were invited. Higginson could not go; neither could Stearns; to Sanborn the invitation was particularly attractive because of the presence at Gerrit Smith's of his classmate Edwin Morton, then a tutor in Smith's family. Sanborn was met by Smith's sleigh and drove up over the hills to his house.

Brown arrived on Washington's birthday. That evening after dinner the friends sat before the fire in Morton's room upstairs and listened to an astounding revelation. Its audacity filled them with apprehension, but every obstacle had been foreseen by Brown and to every objection he had an answer. He was positive and terribly in earnest. Gerrit Smith, already convinced, walked nervously in and out of the room while the argument proceeded. When the time came to read the Provisional Constitution, he sat down with the others and heard it out. Smith, a bland and impressive elderly man, filling the chair with large complacency, and Sanborn, the young schoolmaster with romantic notions, in disturbed silence heard the voice reading each word with slow emphasis—"Whereas, slavery throughout its entire existence in the United States, is none other than a most barbarous, unprovoked, and unjustifiable war of one portion of its citizens upon another portion. . . ." The conference broke up past midnight.[3]

Next day the discussion went on. Point by point John Brown beat down their objections. Again he described the details of his campaign. With a small body of trusty men he proposed to occupy a place in the mountains of Virginia. He would make incursions down into the cultivated districts to liberate slaves. As they were freed, he would arm them. He would subsist on the enemy, fortify himself against attack, and raise the standard of revolt until his name was terror to all through the South. As his adherents might increase to great numbers, he had prepared a scheme of provisional government. At worst he would have a retreat open through the North to safety. Some of this his friends did not understand, but they understood or thought they understood John Brown's recurring argument: "If God be for us, who can be against us?"[4]

While the remote winter sun was setting, Smith and Sanborn walked for an hour in the snow-covered woods and fields. At last Gerrit Smith spoke: "You see how it is. Our old friend has made up his mind to this course, and he cannot be turned from it. We cannot give him up to die alone; we must stand by him now. I will raise so many hundred dollars for him and you must lay the case before your friends in Massachusetts."[5] They walked slowly back to the house in the diminished light.

Sanborn returned immediately to Boston where he placed the plan before Higginson and Theodore Parker. The latter was not too hopeful: "I doubt whether things of that kind will succeed. But we shall make a great many failures before we discover the right way of getting at it." Higginson was more militant and sanguine. Dr. Samuel Gridley Howe, enthusiast in the cause of humanity, and Stearns made promises of aid.[6]

The tall farmer-like old fellow with his neat rural dress, his talk about bayonets and bullets and God's will, his immense awkward dignity, his white beard and glittering grey-blue eyes, moved impressively about the albums and pleasant china of New England parlors. He met all types. He spent one pleasant Sunday evening in Theodore Parker's parlor arguing with Garrison on the subject of resistance and non-resistance. Garrison talked of peace and quoted the New Testament. Captain Brown talked of war and repeated his favorite text: "Without the shedding of blood, there is no remission of sins."[7] At another time he attended the convention of the New England Anti-Slavery Society and said as he went away: "These men are all talk; what is needed is action—action."[8]

The Massachusetts State Kansas Committee two years before had voted to turn over to Brown, as agent of the Committee, money and guns to help redeem Kansas. But when he returned to Kansas, he had found both parties disposed to have recourse to ballots instead of bullets, and he thus developed his new and daring plan.[9]

After his meeting with Gerrit Smith, Brown made a secret visit to Boston. There in a room of the American House, the old Puritan, direct descendant of one of the pilgrims of the Mayflower, and his Massachusetts friends plotted together. A fund of one thousand dollars was raised. In communicating with each other, the conspirators used cipher. Brown assumed the name of Hawkins. He called his followers scholars and their work, going to school. The enterprise was spoken of as the wool business and Sanborn wrote that Hawkins "has found in Canada several good men for shepherds, and if not embarrassed by want of means, expects to turn his flock loose about the 15th of May." Parker, whose failing health had driven him to Europe, wrote from Rome: "Tell me how our little speculation in wool goes on, and what dividend accrues therefrom." But the immediate execution of the plan was checked.[10]

A former associate, a Garibaldian adventurer, named Colonel Hugh Forbes, made disclosures to Senators Sumner, Seward, Wilson, and possibly others. Nobody believed the scoundrel though he told the truth. But on account of his revelations, the attack was postponed a year. Brown appeared in Kansas, and under the pseudonym of Shubal Morgan resumed his raids into slave territory. A reward was offered for his arrest and he made his way East.

In the early summer of 1859 the mobilization of weapons and forces began. More than four thousand dollars had been contributed in aid of the Virginia enterprise. For arms Brown had 250 Sharp's rifles, 200 revolvers, and 950 pikes. The pikes were to arm the slaves who should fly to his standard. "Give a slave a pike," said Brown, "and you make him a man."[11]

He wanted Frederick Douglass. Giving Douglass a fraternal embrace he said, "Come with me, Douglass: I will defend you with my life. I want you for a special purpose. When I strike, the bees will begin to swarm, and I shall want you to help hive them." Douglass flatly refused. He combated the design with the strongest of arguments. "You not only attack Virginia," he urged, "but you attack the federal government, and you will array the whole country against you. Furthermore you are going into a perfect steel trap. Once in, you will never get out alive. You will be surrounded and escape will be impossible." But Douglass failed to shake the old man's purpose.[12]

Many of his followers remonstrated with him when his plan was disclosed. One of his sons said: "You know how it resulted with Napoleon when he rejected advice in regard to marching with his army to Moscow." But in the end by persuasion and by threatening to resign as their leader, Brown silenced all objections.[13]

2

"Good morning, gentlemen, how do you do?" John Unseld, a resident of the neighborhood of Harper's Ferry, regarded four men in the road before him with an easy, half kindly curiosity. One was an old fellow, stooped and bearded, and the other three were young men. The old fellow introduced himself and his companions. He was a Mr. Smith; two of the young men were his sons, Oliver and Watson, and the last was named Anderson. "Well, gentlemen," the planter said, "I suppose you are out hunting mineral, gold and silver?" "No, we are not; we are looking for land; we have a little money but we want to make it go as far as we can. What does land sell for about here?" "It runs in price," Unseld answered, "from fifteen to thirty dollars in the neighborhood." "That's high. I thought I could buy land here for about a dollar or two the acre." "No, sir," the planter replied emphatically. After some desultory conversation, they parted, Unseld going on into Harper's Ferry. On returning from the town, he met the party again, and Brown expressed satisfaction with what he had seen and asked whether there was any farm for sale in the neighborhood. Unseld informed him that the heirs of a Dr. Kennedy had one for sale, five miles from Harper's Ferry. Brown then expressed the opinion that it would be better for him to rent rather than to buy, and after declining an invitation to dinner at Unseld's, he went on towards the farm. He was not long in making up his mind to take it. To Unseld he stated also that his real business was buying fat cattle and driving them on to the State of New York for disposal there. Others in the neighborhood retained the impression that the newcomers were really mineral prospectors. To assist in the disguise Brown's daughter and daughter-in-law joined the community.[14]

Late in August Secretary of War Floyd received an anonymous letter from Cincinnati. "Sir," the letter ran, "I have lately received information of a movement of so great importance that I feel it my duty to impart it to you without delay. I have discovered the existence of a secret organization, having for its object the liberation of the slaves of the South by a general insurrection. . . ." Floyd thought the letter had been sent by a crank. A scheme of such wickedness and outrage could not be entertained by any citizen of the United States. Furthermore, the writer said that one of the leading conspirators was in an armory in Maryland, and there was no arsenal in Maryland. And so easy going Floyd pigeonholed the letter and banished it from his thoughts.[15]

Sunday night, October 16, was dark and chill and damp.[16] Brown called his men together and after giving them final instructions said—"Now, gentlemen, let me press this one thing on your minds. You all know how dear life is to you, and how dear your lives are to your friends, and in remembering that, consider that the lives of others are as dear to them as yours are to you. Do not, therefore, take the life of anyone if you can possibly avoid it. But if it is necessary to take life in order to save your own, then make sure work of it." With the command, "Men, get on your arms; we will proceed to the Ferry," they started from Kennedy Farm, John Brown leading the men down the road. The wagon with its load of pikes, sledge, crowbar, and fagots, creaked down the grade. Behind it marched eighteen members of the Provisional army, two by two with their rifles hidden under their coats and shawls.[17]

They seized the armory and arsenal. By midnight they were masters of Harper's Ferry. The lights in the town were put out and the telegraph wires cut. To secure hostages and to make a beginning of conferring freedom on the slaves, they sent out a party to bring in prominent citizens of the surrounding country with their Negroes. They stopped the mail train. News of the foray spread far and wide.

When the people of Harper's Ferry aroused themselves in the morning, they found a hostile force in possession of the strongholds of their town and holding most of the available fire-arms. Men on their way to work, citizens passing through the streets, were taken prisoners. Already the bell of the Lutheran Church was tolling the alarm. The inhabitants got out their squirrel rifles and shotguns. In Charlestown the bells were ringing furiously, and before the high pillared court house, the Jefferson Guards, ununiformed, were falling into line. The bells tolled on—insurrection—civil war. Beyond the militia, other men and boys were forming into line. They carried all sorts of weapons—flintlocks, hunting rifles, shotguns—but they were in earnest. At ten o'clock both companies boarded a train for the Ferry.

But by the time the train from Charlestown was on the way, telegrams were already in the hands of the President of the United States, the Governor of Virginia, and the Major General of Maryland Volunteers.

The fighting began. Men fell on both sides, among them the Mayor of Harper's Ferry. Brown and his followers might have retreated to the mountains. But influenced by sympathy for his prisoners and their distressed families, he refused to move and at last found himself surrounded by opposing forces. His retreat was cut off; his men were killed, captured, or dispersed. At midday he withdrew the remnant of his force with his hostages into the engine house in the armory yard. The door and windows were barred, and portholes were cut through the brick wall. The firing from the outside now became terrible.

When an assailant could be seen, the shots were returned by
the besieged. Brown would not allow his men to fire on non-
combatants outside. "Don't shoot," he would say; "that man is
unarmed."

He was cool and firm. With one son dead at his side and
another, Oliver, shot through, he felt the pulse of his dying
son with one hand and held his rifle with the other, and commanded his men with the utmost composure. Again and again
Oliver Brown begged in agony to be shot. "No, my son, have
patience. I think you will get well," his father replied. When that
comfort failed, he said what was left to be said—"If you die,
you die in a good cause, fighting for liberty. If you must die,
die like a man."[18]

At two o'clock on the morning of October 18 Colonel Robert
E. Lee arrived from Washington with a company of marines
and prepared to begin the assault at dawn. Colonel Lee offered
the privilege of attack to Colonel Shriver of the Maryland Militia who declined for a sound reason—"These men of mine have
wives and children at home. I will not expose them to such
risks. You are paid for doing this kind of work." Colonel Baylor,
senior Virginia officer, likewise passed by the opportunity for
distinction to get a court martial in the end. Colonel Lee had
made his gestures of courtesy; it was now business. "Lieutenant
Green," he inquired, "would you wish the honor of taking those
men out?" Lieutenant Israel Green was paid for such work; he
took off his cap and thanked the Colonel.[19]

Colonel Lee in civilian clothes stood on a little rise of ground
within pistol range of the engine house.

It was dawn. Lieutenant Green held twelve marines in readiness for the expected assault and another twelve with fixed
bayonets for support if necessary. Lieutenant Jeb Stuart had
orders to approach the engine house and make a final demand
for surrender. Under the gaze of several thousand spectators,
Lieutenant Stuart walked up to the engine house. John Brown
opened the door a hand's breadth and blocked the crack with
his body. In his hand he held a cocked carbine. The officer was
greatly surprised. "Why, aren't you old Osawatomie Brown of
Kansas, whom I had there as my prisoner?" "Yes," came Brown's

answer, "but you did not keep me." Stuart presented his demand for surrender. John Brown would have none of it. "I prefer to die just here."[20]

Every point of vantage was crowded by people who wanted to see the show. No shouting, no tumult now; everywhere was the silence of waiting.

Jeb Stuart stepped smartly back from the door and gave the signal by waving his cap. Green gave the order instantly and the marines came on the double. No one was hit in the rush and the marines were at the doors trying to beat an opening with sledge hammers. The stout timbers, though ripped and shattered by rifle balls, held. The prisoners huddled in the back part of the room. The five men inside kept blindly firing at the swaying doors. Suddenly the battering at the doors ceased. One of the men turned to John Brown: "Captain, I believe I will surrender." "Sir, you can do as you please," was the answer. The hostages shouted to the attackers, "One man surrenders!" Their voices were lost in a terrific blow low down on the doors which split and buckled with the shock. The marines were using a ladder as a battering ram.

Another shock. A ragged hole was burst in the right hand door. On the instant, Lieutenant Green plunged through, blade in hand, and rising, rushed to the rear of the building between two engines to command a better view. Colonel Lewis Washington, one of the prisoners, pointing to Brown, said, "This is Osawatomie." Green sprang at Brown with an upward thrust of his sword which seemed to lift Brown from his feet. But the light blade caught on the belt or bone and bent double, and Green seizing it by the middle brought the hilt down time and time again on the old man's head until he lay still. In the meanwhile the marines came rushing in; the first two to follow Green fell at the breach; the others jumping over their fallen comrades, like tigers, caught one man skulking beneath the engine and pinned another clean to the wall with a single thrust. All resistance now ceased, the door was pulled down, and amidst intense excitement, the dead, wounded, and dying were dragged out and laid on the grass.[21]

Of the nineteen men who had left the Kennedy farm, ten were killed, five taken prisoners, and four escaped.

"Mr. Brown," said Congressman Vallandigham, "who sent you here?"

"No man sent me here; it was my own prompting and that of my Maker, or that of the Devil, whichever you please to ascribe it to. I acknowledge no master in human form."

John Brown lay on his miserable pallet in the paymaster's office of the armory. Reporters, Lieutenant Jeb Stuart, Colonel Lee, Senator Mason and others were present.

The questioners persisted. Again Brown was asked: Who furnished the money? How many were engaged with him in the movement? When did he begin the organization? Where did he get the arms? Brown had one reply: "I will answer anything I can with honor, but not about others."

"How do you justify your acts?" asked Senator Mason.

"I think, my friend," said Brown, "you are guilty of a great wrong against God and humanity,—I say it without wishing to be offensive—and it would be perfectly right in any one to interfere with you so as to free those you wilfully and wickedly hold in bondage. I do not say this insultingly."

"I understand that," said Mason.

The prisoner continued: "I think I did right, and that others will do right to interfere with you at any time and at all times. I hold that the golden rule, 'Do unto others as you would others should do unto you,' applies to all who would help others to gain their liberty."

He considered his enterprise, he said, "a religious movement" and "the greatest service man can render to God." He regarded himself as "an instrument in the hands of Providence." "I want you to understand, gentlemen," he said, turning to the reporter of the *Herald*,—"and you may report that—I want you to understand that I respect the rights of the poorest and weakest of colored people, oppressed by the slave system, just as much as I do those of the most wealthy and powerful. That is the idea that has moved me and that alone. We expected no reward except the satisfaction of endeavoring to do for those in distress and greatly oppressed, as we would be done by. . . . I wish to say, furthermore, that you had better, all you people of the South, prepare yourselves for a settlement of this question, that must come up for settlement sooner than you are prepared for it. . . . You may dispose of me very easily. I am nearly disposed of now, but this question is still to be settled—this Negro question, I mean; the end of that is not yet."[22]

Brown had attacked with eighteen men a village of 1400 people. The accessibility of Harper's Ferry to Washington and Baltimore doomed him to destruction.

But his plan seemed to him no greater folly than was the attempt of Joshua to take a walled city by the blowing of trumpets and by the shouts of people. Not more foolish than Gideon who went out to encounter a great army with three hundred men, bearing only trumpets and lamps and pitchers. Yet the walls of Jericho had fallen flat at the noise, and Gideon had put to flight amidst great confusion the Midianites and Amalekites, who were like the grasshoppers for multitude. And as the old Puritan was doing God's work, he felt that God would not forsake him.

To Emerson, he seemed "transparent," a "pure idealist." Gerrit Smith thought of all men in the world he was "most truly a Christian."[23] But to the South he had "whetted knives of butchery for our mothers, sisters, daughters, and babes." It was reported that Governor Wise had made a requisition on the Governor of New York for Gerrit Smith. Smith's house was guarded and his friends said that nothing less than a regiment of soldiers would suffice to take him from his home. The nervous tension on the philanthropist was so great that his mind gave way and he was taken to a lunatic asylum.[24]

On the day after the marines entered the engine house, Frederick Douglass left for Canada and only a little later sailed for England. Sanborn promptly followed Douglass's example. Higginson remained firm in the general panic and Parker wrote from Italy—"I could not help wishing I was at home again to use what poor remnant of power is left to me in defence of the True and the Right." Dr. Howe repudiated his connection with John Brown. Higginson retorted with savage directness: "Is

there no such thing as *honor* among confederates?" Howe was
deeply grieved.[25]

Incriminating papers existed, but they could not be found.
Phillips brought a batch of them from Brown's house which for
safe-keeping he promptly placed in the hands of Governor John
A. Andrew. At a later date the Governor returned the papers
to the respective writers.

A week following the assault, John Brown was indicted. On
Monday, October 31, the fifth day of the trial, the jury after
deliberating three quarters of an hour brought in a verdict of
"Guilty of treason and conspiring with slaves and others to rebel,
and murder in the first degree." Two days afterwards Brown
was brought into court to receive his sentence. The Judge asked
him whether he had anything to say, why sentence should not
be pronounced upon him. John Brown got slowly to his feet,
put his hands on the table before him, and leaned slightly forward over it. He spoke without hesitation.

"I have, may it please the court, a few words to say. In
the first place, I deny everything but what I have all along
admitted—the design on my part to free the slaves. . . . I
never did intend murder, or treason, or the destruction of
property, or to excite or incite slaves to rebellion, or to make
insurrection.

"I have another objection; and that is, it is unjust that I
should suffer such a penalty. . . . Had I interfered in behalf
of the rich, the powerful, the intelligent, the so-called great,
or in behalf of any of their friends—either father, mother,
brother, sister, wife, or children, or any of that class—and
suffered and sacrificed what I have in this interference, it
would have been all right; and every man in this court
would have deemed it an act worthy of reward rather than
punishment.

"This court acknowledges, as I suppose, the validity of the
Bible. That teaches me that all things whatsoever I would
that men should do to me, I should do even so to them. It
teaches me, further, to 'remember them that are in bonds,
as bound with them.' I endeavored to act up to that instruction. I say I am yet too young to understand that God is any
respecter of persons. I believe that to have interfered as I

have done—as I have always freely admitted I have done—
in behalf of His despised poor was not wrong, but right.
Now, if it is deemed necessary that I should forfeit my life
for the furtherance of the ends of justice, and mingle my
blood further with the blood of my children and with the
blood of millions in this slave country whose rights are disregarded by wicked, cruel, and unjust enactments—I submit;
so let it be done!" . . .[26]

The Judge then pronounced the sentence of death by hanging.
The date for the public execution was fixed for Friday, December 2, one month from the day of sentence. One man clapped
his hands, but he was promptly suppressed. The spectators remained in their seats until John Brown was led away to his cell
and then they rose and quietly departed.

The coolness and bravery of "Old Osawatomie," his self-
sacrifice for a despised race, his tenderness, made him the hero
of the hour.

On November 1, 1859, Phillips lectured in Plymouth Church,
Brooklyn, and took "Harper's Ferry" for a text. He began with
a gay and graceful compliment to Thomas Corwin, an old statesman of the Henry Clay school who was seated on the platform,
but he soon became intensely serious.

" 'The Lesson of the Hour?' I think the lesson of the hour
is insurrection (Sensation.). . . . Harper's Ferry is the Lexington of today. . . .

"Has the slave a right to resist his master? I will not argue
that question to a people hoarse with shouting ever since
July 4, 1776, that all men are created equal, that the right
to liberty is inalienable, and that 'resistance to tyrants is
obedience to God.' But may he resist to blood—with rifles?
What need of proving that to a people who load down
Bunker Hill with granite, and crowd their public squares
with images of Washington; ay, worship the sword so blindly
that, leaving their oldest statesmen idle, they go down to the
bloodiest battlefield in Mexico to drag out a President? But
may one help the slave resist, as Brown did? Ask Byron
on his death-bed in the marshes of Missolonghi. Ask the
Hudson what answer its waters bring from the grave of

Kosciusko. I hide the Connecticut Puritan behind Lafayette, bleeding at Brandywine, in behalf of a nation his rightful king forbade him to visit.

"But John Brown violated the law. Yes. On yonder desk lie the inspired words of men who died violent deaths for breaking the laws of Rome. Why do you listen to them so reverently? Huss and Wickliffe violated laws; why honor them? George Washington, had he been caught before 1783, would have died on the gibbet, for breaking the laws of his sovereign. Yet I have heard that man praised within six months. Yes, you say, but these men broke *bad* laws. Just so. It is honorable, then, to break *bad* laws, and such law-breaking history loves and God blesses! Who says, then, that slave laws are not ten thousand times worse than any those men resisted? Whatever argument *excuses* them, makes John Brown a saint."[27]

Phillips delivered the same speech in New York City. A portion of the hall was filled with pro-slavery roughs who hooted and cursed and threw missiles at him. A stone which struck a chair near him on the platform might have done him serious injury. Nothing dismayed, Phillips continued his speech, and taking his text from the insults of his enemies, hurled defiance back in their teeth. Friends who accompanied him were ready to defend him from personal violence, but Phillips, they said, surpassed anything they had known of him before, and fairly quelled the rioters by his courage, address, and personal magnetism. Attempts to mob him were also made at Troy and Staten Island, but failed.

While Brown lay in prison, a meeting was held in Tremont Temple, Boston, to raise funds for his impoverished family. The hall was packed. John A. Andrew presided and said—"Whether the enterprise of John Brown and his associates in Virginia was wise or foolish, right or wrong, I only know that John Brown himself is right."[28] The Reverend J. M. Manning of the Old South Church remarked that if John Brown had consulted him in regard to inciting a slave insurrection, he should certainly have advised him not to do it, but he was far from regretting that the attempt had been made.[29] And Emerson and

Thoreau asserted that when a government becomes so bad
that honesty and virtue cannot endure, revolution is imminent.[30]
Phillips was the last speaker and treated the subject in a bold
manner. Before he had finished, the applause was deafening.
A Judge of the Superior Court sat on the front bench clapping
his hands like the noise of pistol shots.

"It seems to me," said Phillips, "that in judging lives,
this man, instead of being a failure, has done more to lift
the American people, to hurry forward the settlement of a
great question, to touch all hearts, to teach us ethics, than a
hundred men could have done, living each on to eighty
years old. Is that a failure? . . .

"Men say it is flinging away his life. That is for him to
judge. Men say that the result is not worth the sacrifice.
Suppose I could carry you back to Boston streets, on the
evening after the Bunker Hill fight. I will carry you into
Hutchinson's House, I will carry you into the parlors of
any of the old Colonial families. You will hear them saying,
'What a pity! Warren's dead; Hancock and Adams have fled;
there is a warrant out against them; those deluded soldiers,
how can these men answer it to the widows and children?
What fools! a few farmers to fling themselves against the
embattled phalanx of the British government!' It seemed
so to the men who were accustomed to look up to England.
Doubtless the Tories strengthened themselves, and many a
heart sank. But . . . was Warren's life worth giving? What
did he establish? He established the example of resistance.
He bade the colonies try their strength. He showed them
that blood was equal to blood, and that right was right the
world over."[31]

This was John Brown's position, continued Phillips. Dr.
Channing said in one of his last essays: We have given the sword
to the white man; now give our tongues to the black. But John
Brown reasoned differently. He was a Calvinist of the old
stamp. He said: For sixty years we have given the sword to the
white man; the time has come to give it to the black. What
right had we to give it to oppression?

"John Brown has taught the slave at Harper's Ferry that there is hope for him amid the millions of the North. He has sent him this message: 'There are friends for you working—bide your time, and help us!' He has sent the gleam of a hopeful sun into the hovels of Carolina; he has taught the heart of the bondman to leap up and thank God for the Mayflower.

"I think, therefore, he has taught us a great lesson. He has exemplified a great moral; he has released us from a servility to forms; he has taught us to pierce down to the essence of things. We deify intellect, till we fancy every man mad who cannot give three reasons for every act, and cite seven statutes to justify raising his right hand rather than his left. But every now and then some sublime mad-man strikes the hour of the centuries; straightway fossil pedants and bloodless attorneys insist on proving how the world ought not to admire. Still the million hearts will melt, and looking back over centuries, bathed in the sunlight of that great deed, posterity wonders at the blindness which could not see in it the very hand of God himself."[32]

3.

The prisoner remained dignified and impressive, and visitors left his cell with a strange respect for his veracity and courage.[33] To ministers he was very direct: He "would not insult God by bowing down in prayer with anyone who had the blood of slaves on his skirts." When Samuel Pomeroy of Kansas was admitted to his cell, he asked: "You remember the rescue of John Doy. Do you want your friends to attempt it?" John Brown answered: "I am worth now infinitely more to die than to live."[34]

Brown's letters were published in the *Tribune* and *Liberator*. To his wife he wrote—"My mind is very tranquil, I may say joyous." To a cousin he expressed self content with his fate—"When I think how easily I might be left to spoil all I have done or suffered in the cause of freedom, I hardly dare wish another voyage, even if I had the opportunity."[35] To his younger children, to take from them the thought that the manner of his death was ignominious, he wrote—"I feel just as content to die for God's eternal truth on the scaffold as in any other way." And on the same day he assured his older children that "a calm peace seems to fill my mind by day and by night." To a clergyman he wrote—"I think I feel as happy as Paul did when he lay in prison. He knew if they killed him, it would greatly advance the cause of Christ; that was the reason he rejoiced so. On that same ground do I rejoice . . . Let them hang me. I forgive them, and may God forgive them, 'for they know not what they do.' I have no regret for the transaction for which I am condemned. I went against the laws of men, it is true, but 'whether it be right to obey God or men, judge ye.'"[36] More than once as Sheriff Campbell read those letters in his duty as censor, he wiped the tears from his eyes before he folded the sheets and passed them on to do their work.

On November 30, John Brown wrote his last letter to his family—

"I am waiting the hour of my public murder with great composure of mind and cheerfulness, feeling the strongest assurance that in no other possible way could I be used to so much advance the cause of God and of humanity, and nothing that either I or all my family have sacrificed or suffered will be lost. The reflection that a wise and merciful as well as just and Holy God rules not only the affairs of this world but of all worlds, is a rock to set our feet upon under all circumstances. . . . I have now no doubt but that our seeming disaster will ultimately result in the most glorious success.

"So my dear shattered and broken family, be of good cheer and believe and trust in God 'with all your heart and with all your soul,' for he doeth all things well. Do not feel ashamed on my account, nor for one moment despair of the cause, or grow weary of well doing. I bless God I never felt stronger confidence in the certain and near approach of a bright morning and a glorious day than I have felt, and do now feel since my confinement here."[37]

And he urged his sons and daughters to study the Bible with a childlike, honest, and teachable spirit, to love the stranger still, and to love one another.

This was his final admonition: "John Brown writes to his children to abhor with undying hatred that 'sum of all villainies' —Slavery."[38]

'If they hang John Brown," remarked Amos A. Lawrence, a backer of John Brown's company, "Virginia will be a free State sooner than they expect. He has played his part grandly, though the plot of the play is a poor one."[39]

Rebecca Buffum Spring, who visited John Brown in jail, gave him a rose which he put on his pillow.[40]

On December 2, Longfellow wrote in his diary—"This will be a great day in our history; the date of a new Revolution— quite as much needed as the old one. Even now as I write they are leading old John Brown to execution in Virginia for attempting to rescue slaves. This is sowing the wind to reap the whirlwind, which will come soon."[41]

Early that morning the prisoner was awake and reading his Bible. He wrote a last note of some three or four lines to his wife, enclosing a codicil to his will and epitaphs of his dead sons and himself which he wished chiselled on the old tombstone of his grandfather John. Then the guard came and escorted him to say goodbye to the other prisoners. As he left the jail he handed a piece of paper to one of the attendants, his last message to his country and the world—

"I, John Brown, am now quite certain that the crimes of this guilty land will never be purged away but with blood. I had as I now think vainly flattered myself that without very much bloodshed it might be done."[42]

They led him out to the porch of the jail. A common wagon with a team of white horses and a black coffin in it waited in the roadway. Before it three companies of infantry held their regular files. Brown climbed into the wagon and seated himself on the coffin. The escort received the order to march and the driver spoke to the horses.

As they rode along, someone asked Brown if he felt any fear. He replied: "It has been a characteristic of me from infancy not to suffer from physical fear. I have suffered a thousand times more from bashfulness than from fear." The day was bright and clear. Brown looked across toward the Blue Ridge with the sunlight falling upon it and said—"This is a beautiful country. I have not cast my eyes over it before, that is, in this direction." When he got in sight of the militia in the field, he said—"You have quite a military display." Arriving at the gallows he remarked: "I see no citizens here; where are they?" "None but the troops are allowed to be present" was the reply. "That ought not to be," said Brown. "Citizens should be present as well as others." Then he bade goodbye to some acquaintances and mounted the scaffold.[43]

Around the scaffold 1500 Virginia troops were massed in a great hollow square. Howitzers were placed to command the field, a force of cavalry was posted as sentinels, while scouts and rangers were on duty outside the enclosure. A brass cannon loaded with grape shot was close to and pointed at the gallows.

Behind the scaffold could be seen the red and grey uniforms of the Virginia Military Institute and at their head a bearded, preoccupied man—Professor T. J. Jackson. He had prayed that John Brown might be spared and now in fulfillment of duty, he witnessed the rejection of his prayer. In company F of Richmond, a little farther back, a militiaman held a musket and waited. The militiaman was John Wilkes Booth.[44]

John Brown stood a few moments on the scaffold in his loose fitting old clothes and carpet slippers. Asked if he had anything to say, with an expression of weariness on his face, he only responded—"No, I have nothing to say. I shall not detain you. Whenever you are ready, go ahead." The sheriff then pulled the black cap over his face, placed the hangman's noose about his neck and adjusted the knot under the left ear. Brown waited for death. "Captain Brown," suddenly said the sheriff, "you are not standing on the drop, will you come forward?" "I can't see," was his answer. "You must lead me." The sheriff led him forward to the center of the drop. "Shall I give you a handkerchief and let you drop it as a signal?" "No, I am ready at any time, but do not keep me needlessly waiting!"[45]

Brown stood upright and motionless. The sheriff's hatchet flashed in the sunlight. The trap was released, the rope spun through, jerked heavily with its weight below and vibrated for a moment. Colonel Preston broke the awful silence around him—"So perish all such enemies of Virginia! All such enemies of the Union! All such foes of the human race!"[46]

The new hinges gave forth a startled metallic sound.

It required twenty minutes for the old man to choke to death. Twelve minutes longer the body hung and then was cut down, laid into a walnut coffin, and this screwed up in a white poplar box. The corpse was delivered to the widow.

Louisa Alcott set down in her diary: "December, 1859: the execution of St. John the Just took place on the second."[47] "Old Brown, Esq. is supposed to have been strangled today for obeying the Golden Rule," remarked the Wood County (Wis.) *Reporter*.[48] The American Anti-Slavery Society in its calendar of events designated 1859 as "the John Brown year," and when Brown was led to the gallows, black crepe was hung on Abolitionist doors.[49] "There he hangs and will hang," said Karl Heinzen, "until revenged. The Mason and Dixon line no longer divides the nation. A gallows now separates North from South. That gallows will be the signpost for the politics of this land. It will move down towards South Carolina or up to Massachusetts."[50]

Political leaders condemned the deed. Jefferson Davis called it "the invasion of a state by a murderous gang of Abolitionists . . . to incite slaves to murder helpless women and children . . . and for which the leader has already suffered a felon's death." Douglas intimated that Brown was a horsethief and spoke of him as "a notorious man who has recently suffered death for his crimes upon the gallows." Lincoln, speaking at Cooper Institute, referred to Brown in cold and measured words: "John Brown's effort was peculiar. It was not a slave insurrection. It was an attempt by white men to get up a revolt among slaves, in which the slaves refused to participate. In fact it was so absurd that the slaves, with all their ignorance, saw plainly enough it could not succeed. That affair in its philosophy corresponds with the many attempts related in history at the assassination of kings and emperors. An enthusiast broods over the oppression of a people until he fancies himself commissioned by Heaven to liberate them. He ventures the attempt which ends in little else than in his own execution." To Seward the attempt was "an act of sedition and treason and criminal in just the extent that it affected the public peace and was destructive of human happiness and life." The National Republican Convention meeting in May following, resolved that the Harper's Ferry invasion was "among the gravest of crimes."[51]

But men who lived in the spirit, who were not obliged to count "the votes of Pennsylvania and company" had already spoken.

Motions to adjourn in honor of Brown were defeated in both houses of the Massachusetts legislature. That night, however, Tremont Temple was filled to the doors by one of its greatest meetings. Three thousand were turned away. When the doors were opened men and women were swept in, some without touching their feet to the ground. The meeting, held under the auspices of the American Anti-Slavery Society, was presided over by Samuel E. Sewall. A picture of John Brown was on the speaker's desk surrounded by a cross and a wreath of evergreen and amaranth. Large printed placards were placed around the hall bearing sentences of John Brown, quotations from Washington, Lafayette, Henry, Jefferson, etc. One read—"I don't know what weakness may come over me, but I don't believe I shall ever deny my Lord and Master, Jesus Christ, and I should deny Him if I denied my principles against Slavery—John Brown."[52]

Garrison declared that the meeting was called to witness John Brown's resurrection, and read Brown's speech to the Court when he was sentenced. The Abolitionist leader said in the course of his speech:

"Nevertheless I am a non-resistant. . . . Yet as a peace man—an ultra peace man—I am prepared to say: 'Success to every slave insurrection, at the South and in every slave country.' Rather than see men wearing their chains in a cowardly and servile spirit, I would, as an advocate of peace, much rather see them breaking the head of the tyrant with their chains. Give me, as a non-resistant, Bunker Hill, and Lexington, and Concord, rather than the cowardice and servility of a Southern Slave plantation."[53]

When the train which bore Brown's body and its guardians arrived at Philadelphia, it was met by a reception committee. The coffin was placed in a furniture wagon and carried to the Walnut Street wharf whence it was taken by boat to New York on the way to North Elba. There Wendell Phillips and J. Miller McKim, a leading Philadelphia Abolitionist, as well as Mrs. Brown, escorted the body. At every town they tarried, bells were tolled, and the citizens appeared to express their sympathy for the widow. At Elizabethtown, the last resting place for a night, a guard of honor watched the coffin in the court house until dawn. Thence over almost impassable roads for twenty-five miles, the funeral party journeyed all day of Wednesday, December 7. It was a cold, bitter day. After sundown the little party approached North Elba. Lanterns were lit and the whole family waited out on the lonely hillside in sad expectation. By them they were conducted in silence to the house. Not a word was spoken.

Next day in the early afternoon they laid all that was mortal of John Brown in a grave at the foot of a huge boulder in his dooryard. As the coffin was lowered into the winter earth, members of a neighboring colored family sang some of the hymns for which he cared.

> Blow ye the trumpet, blow—
> The gladly solemn sound;
> Let all the nations know,
> To earth's remotest bound,
> The year of jubilee has come, etc.[54]

Back in the unfinished drafty house, Wendell Phillips spoke the funeral address.

"Marvelous old man! He has abolished slavery in Virginia. You may say this is too much. Our neighbors are the last men we know. The hours that pass us are the ones we

appreciate the least. Men walked Boston streets, when night
fell on Bunker's Hill, and pitied Warren, saying, 'Foolish
man.' Thrown away his life! Why didn't he measure his
means better?' Now we see him standing colossal on that
blood-stained sod, and severing that day the tie which bound
Boston to Great Britain. That night George III ceased to rule
in New England. History will date Virginian Emancipation
from Harper's Ferry. True, the slave is still there. So, when
the tempest uproots a pine on your hills, it looks green for
months,—a year or two. Still, it is timber, not a tree. John
Brown has loosened the roots of the slave system; it only
breathes,—it does not live,—hereafter . . .

"Men say, 'Would he had died in arms!' God ordered
better, and granted to him and the slave those noble prison
hours,—that single hour of death; granted him a higher than
the soldier's place, that of teacher. God make us all worthier
of him whose dust we lay among these hills he loved. Here
he girded himself and went forth to battle. Fuller success
than his heart ever dreamed God granted him. He sleeps
in the blessings of the crushed and the poor, and men believe
more firmly in virtue, now that such a man has lived. Standing here, let us thank God for a firmer faith and fuller
hope."[55]

CHAPTER THIRTY-FOUR

FEARLESS LIPS

On May 10, 1860, Theodore Parker died of consumption in Florence, Italy. That home in the rear of Phillips's own residence was now broken up. That light in the study overlooking Phillips's garden was quenched at last.

A memorial service was held in Music Hall when the sad news came from Italy. Phillips spoke with great sweetness and beauty.

"The lesson of this desk is truth! That your brave teacher dared to speak, and no more. It is only two or three times in our lives that we pause in telling the whole merit of a friend, from fear of being thought flatterers . . . I find myself hesitating to speak just all I think of Theodore Parker, lest those who did not know him should suppose I flatter, and thus I mar the massive simplicity of his fame . . .

"There is one thing every man may say of this pulpit.— it was a live reality and no sham. Whether tearing theological idols to pieces at West Roxbury, or here battling with the everyday evils of the streets, it was ever a live voice, and no mechanical or parrot tune; ever fresh from the heart of God, as these flowers over which when eyesight failed him, with his old gesture he passed his loving hand, and said, 'How sweet!'

"Yes, his diocese is broader than Massachusetts; his influence extends very far outside these walls. Every pulpit in Boston is freer and more real today because of the existence of this. The fan of his example scattered the chaff of a hundred sapless years. . . .

"There are men whom we measure by their times,—content, and expecting to find them subdued to what they work

409

in. They are the chameleons of circumstance; they are Aeolian harps, toned by the breeze that sweeps over them. There are others who serve as guideposts and landmarks; we measure their times by them. Such was Theodore Parker.

"Say that his words won doubt and murmur to trust in a loving God,—let that be his record! Say that to the hated and friendless, he was shield and buckler,—let that be his epitaph! The glory of children is the fathers. When you voted 'that Theodore Parker should be heard in Boston,' God honored you. Well have you kept the pledge. In much labor and with many sacrifices he has laid the cornerstone. His work is ended here. God calls you to put on the topstone. Let fearless lips and Christian lives be his monument!"[1]

The congregation of Theodore Parker turned to Phillips. Through the fall and winter of 1860-61, the orator frequently occupied their platform, having on it some of his most thrilling experiences. On November 18, he spoke on "The Pulpit," giving his conception of its function and scope. The Gospel, he declared, should be applied to daily life. The silence of the ministry on living questions was fatal to its permanent influence and usefulness. He then proceeded—

"Theodore Parker did not fill these walls because of his unmatched pulpit talent. It was because all that he thought, all that he planned, all that he read, all that he lived, he brought here. All the great topics that made the court, the street, the caucus,—life—interesting to you, he brought here. All that makes your life a life he brought here . . .

"Mark me, I am not speaking in any bitterness towards the pulpit. I have no more bitterness than the municipality of Paris has when it cuts down an old street in order to make a new thoroughfare. My opinion is, that the age, in order to get all its advantage from the pulpit, needs a new type of the pulpit.

"Politics takes the vassal and lifts him into a voter. The press informs him concerning the happenings of the day. The school gives him elementary instruction. We need in addition a pulpit—moral initiative. I value the Sunday for this: it gives opportunity for such instruction. The pulpit should use the day and opportunity for the training of the community in the whole encyclopedia of morals—social questions, sanitary matters, slavery, temperance, labor, the condition of women, the nature of the Government, responsibility to law, the right of a majority, and how far a minority may yield, marriage, health,—the entire list. For all these are moral questions and they are living questions, not metaphysics, not dogmas. Hindostan settled these thousands of years ago. Christianity did not bury itself in the pit of Oriental metaphysics; neither did it shroud itself in the hermitage of Italian doctrine. The pulpit, as seen in the North of Europe and in this country, is not built up of mahogany and paint and prayers. It is the life of earnest men, the example of the community; a forum to unfold, broaden, and help mankind. That is the pulpit. If this were recognised and acted upon, people would not desert the Church, as they tend to do; or go, if at all, from a mere sense of duty; but would be drawn to the pulpit as they are to the press and theatre, by a felt want."[2]

The splendid homage that Phillips paid to Parker might as easily be paid to Phillips himself. Like Parker he was an honest man who must and would speak out the truth, a man whose every word was "fiercely furnaced" in the blast of an iron will. What he saw to be false, he proclaimed on the housetops, and as fast as he saw the truth, he declared the word. But like Parker too his love was greater than men knew, and his faith in mankind heartening and sublime. Finally like Parker he was meant not to flatter and please, but to instruct and serve, to raise and inspire.

As an orator, he was remarkable and rare. He could not only arouse a common audience to the pitch of enthusiasm but could lift the clod weight of their dull intelligence to the rarefied plane of Ideas, could transmute the base metal of their emotions into the wings of finer impulses. To listen to him was an experience—the drossy business of fixed and menial duties was obliterated or cleansed and washed away. To follow him—but how many in this world of ours are dedicated spirits?

He had said, in praising Garrison's *Liberator*, that the best test of a book's value was the mood of mind with which one rose from it. Could we not apply the same test to his speeches? Could we not say the same of him as he so generously said of Garrison? One did not leave the sound of his quiet, reserved, earnest voice without feeling his coldness rebuked, his selfishness shamed, his hand strengthened for awhile for any good purpose, without feeling lifted from his ordinary life and made to hold communion with higher thoughts and loftier aims, and without being moved—even the coldest—for a moment at least with an ardent wish that he, too, might be privileged to be coworker with God in noble purposes for his brother's welfare.

This has been said in effect before. It is repeated now. It can bear repetition. To the damage of our country we have been neglectful of those sturdy arms like Phillips's, been blind to the gleam which they upheld above the morass of our material accomplishment. If this vast wealth of ours is an accomplishment, it is an accomplishment for whom and for what? asked Phillips. And he replied: for man, for man's liberty, for man's happiness, for man's good.

CHAPTER THIRTY-FIVE

ELECTION OF 1860—

"WHO IS THIS HUCKSTER IN POLITICS?"

Friday, May 18, 1860. Republican Convention: The Wigwam, Chicago. A brawny man jumps on the platform and pulling his coat sleeves up to the elbow shouts—"I can't stop. Three times three more cheers for our next President, Abe Lincoln!" The hall goes wild. Ten thousand throats take up the cry. The city hears it. Whistles on the river and lake front, on locomotives and factories, and bells in the steeples break forth. Guns boom. The Chicago *Press* and *Tribune* declare that the earth has heard no such tumult since the walls of Jericho fell.[1]

Down at Springfield, fifteen minutes later, while Lincoln is sitting at the editor's desk of the *Journal,* he is handed a telegram from one of his staunch supporters; "We did it. Glory to God."[2]

The plea, Succcess rather than Seward, had won. The shock of surprise at Lincoln's nomination was tremendous. Seward's failure filled his friends with gloom and bitterness. Boss Thurlow Weed shed tears. The East knew Lincoln by report as abominably uncouth. Emerson heard the result coldly and sadly: "It seemed too rash, on a purely local reputation, to build so great a trust in such anxious times."[3] "Who is this country court advocate? Who is this who does not know whether he has got any opinions? What is his recommendation? It is that nobody knows bad or good of him. His recommendation is that his past is a blank, and the statesman of New York who has done as much as any man in politics has done to marshal the North on the political anti-slavery platform, is unavailable because of those efforts—nothing else."[4] And Phillips added: "The ice is so

413

thin that Mr. Lincoln standing six feet four inches cannot afford to carry any principles with him on to it! (Laughter.)"[5]

Chase proclaimed as his motto for the Republican party: "Freedom Throughout This Country's Wide Domain." Sumner described the issue thus—"On one side slavery, just, divine, permanent; on the other, unjust, barbarous, and to be abolished."[6] Lincoln had little to say, but little of leadership was expected of him. However, the platform was "piously worded" to conceal the thought of the party. Less than one third of the new platform concerned slavery, whereas five-sixths of the document of 1856 had touched upon the subject. The offensive phrase, "twin relics of barbarism" (slavery and polygamy) was now omitted, and for "the right and duty of Congress" to prohibit slavery in the territories, there was substituted the colorless statement: "We deny the authority of Congress, of a territorial legislature, or of any individuals to give legal existence to slavery in any territory of the United States."[7]

All this truckling dismayed the Abolitionists. They also searched in vain for condemnations of the Dred Scott Decision, the Fugitive Slave Law, or of the existence of slavery in the District of Columbia. Indeed the Republican party of 1860 was the unwilling instrument of Time in striking off the shackles of the slaves.

"One of my predecessors on the platform," remarked Wendell Phillips in the Melodeon, "said the Republicans had meanly sneaked off from the post. What could they do better? An empty bag cannot stand on end! (Laughter and applause.) Do not ask them for bricks—they have no straw, nor hay either! (Renewed merriment.) They are looking to the election, and to see whether the national anthem shall run, 'tweedle-dum' or 'tweedle-dee!' (Laughter.) They cannot defend us, they cannot help us, and you ask too much when you expect it. Lament it as much as you please. It is very hard measure when we see our idols all clay, breaking to pieces before our eyes."[8]

After his nomination Lincoln remained quietly at home in Springfield, Illinois, made no important political utterances, and wrote no letters on political topics that found their way into the papers.

In July, Phillips launched a bitter though hasty attack on him in the *Liberator*:

> "*Abraham Lincoln, the Slave Hound of Illinois.* We gibbet a Northern hound today side by side with the infamous Mason of Virginia. Mason's Slave Bill is based on that clause of the United States Constitution, which provides for the surrender of slaves escaping from one State into another State of the Union.
>
> "The Supreme Court of the United States has decided that the District of Columbia is not a State within the meaning of the Constitution. . . . The District of Columbia is not, therefore, included in the terms of the Fugitive Slave clause. Whoever tries to extend the dominion of that clause over the District of Columbia, exhibits only his own voluntary baseness, can have no pretence of constitutional obligation, out Masons Mason, and stamps himself a hound of special 'alacrity.'
>
> "This deed Abraham Lincoln, Republican candidate for President, has done!"[9]

"Here are the facts," added Phillips. On January 10, 1849, Lincoln had introduced a bill requiring the municipal authorities of Washington and Georgetown "to arrest and deliver up to their owners all fugitive slaves escaping into said District."

Lincoln had proposed the bill, however, as a concession in the scheme of ridding the District of both the slave trade and slavery. Whether the scheme was a good or bad one was not the point in the discussion. But when answered in this manner by Joshua R. Giddings, Phillips replied, consistently enough—

> "It is the nature of the compromise with which I find fault. Compromise is only trading. We give so much for so much. No honest man will trade in infamy. The life, liberty, and happiness of ourselves, or of others, are never to be compromised away for any seeming good. . . . Some things are too sacred to be made counters of, to be traded

in or compromised away. My charge is, that in 1849 Mr. Lincoln did not know that slavehunting was one of these."[10]

There were four parties in the field: the Republican, the Douglas wing of the Democratic Party, the Buchanan wing of the Democratic Party (with the Northern backing of August Belmont and Tammany Hall), and the Constitutional Party.

The main driving force of the Republican campaign was thrown behind the homestead issue in the Northwest, the tariff issue in Pennsylvania, New Jersey, and New England, the Pacific Railroad in the Mississippi Valley, and internal improvements everywhere. A call went up for a campaign of education—with this result: no less than ten thousand set speeches for the Party in New York alone, and fifty thousand in the Union.[11]

The campaign was surprisingly tame. Republican wide awake clubs provided the only novelty. Wide awakes with oil cloth cloaks (cut ample and long as a protection against rainy weather) on which the words "wide awake" were painted in tall white letters, marched in nightly procession carrying lanterns or swinging torches. They paraded in New York, and Fifth Avenue was a blaze of light from torches, lanterns, and fireworks, and crowded with 50,000 people to witness the parade. When to the music of the bands, tens of thousands of marchers took up the chorus of the song, "Ain't You Glad You Joined the Republicans?" the effect was tremendous.

The Democrats, aping the Republicans, had marching clubs under various names: "Ever Readys," "Little Giants," "Invincibles," "Douglas Guards," etc.[12]

The Southerners contented themselves with indiscriminate abuse of the "black Republican" candidate. Some called Lincoln a "nigger lover," others spoke of him as a "nigger," and some newspapers said his father was a gorilla imported from Mozambique.[13] The Charleston *Mercury* described him as "a horrid looking wretch—sooty and scoundrelly in aspect; a cross between the nutmeg dealer, the horse swapper, and the nightman—a creature 'fit,' evidently, for petty treason, small stratagems, and all sorts of spoils. He is a lank-sided Yankee, of the uncomeliest visage, and one of the dirtiest complexion and the most indecent comparisons. Faugh! After him what decent white man would be President!"[14]

But despite the mud slinging and vituperation, North and South alike conceded the election of Lincoln. Seward gulped down his defeat and devoted himself to Lincoln's cause. Wendell Phillips said, "See what magnificent speeches William Henry Seward has been making in the Northwest! When a politician ceases to be a candidate for the Presidency, he becomes a man again."[15]

The election returns were amazing. Breckinridge carried the South and had 72 electoral votes. Bell and Everett carried the border states with an electoral vote of 39. Douglas with a popular vote almost as large as that of Bell and Breckinridge together received only twelve electoral votes. Lincoln had 180 and was overwhelmingly elected.[16]

"Babylon is fallen, is fallen" remarked the *Liberator* of the election.[17] And on November seventh while the streets were noisy with paraders, Wendell Phillips lectured in Boston.—

"Ladies and Gentlemen: If the telegraph speaks truth, for the first time in our history the *slave* has chosen a President of the United States. (Cheers.) We have passed the Rubicon, for Mr. Lincoln rules today as much as he will after the 4th of March. It is the moral effect of this victory, not anything which his administration can or will probably do, that gives value to this success. Not an Abolitionist, hardly an Anti-Slavery man, Mr. Lincoln consents to represent an anti-slavery idea. A pawn on the political chessboard, his value is in his position; with fair effort, we may soon change him for knight, bishop, or queen, and sweep the board. (Applause.). . . .

"In 1760 what rebels felt, James Otis spoke, George Washington achieved, and Everett praises today. The same routine will go on. What fanatics now feel, Garrison prints, Lincoln will achieve, and at the safe distance of half a century, some courtly Everett will embalm in matchless panegyrics. You see exactly what my hopes rest upon. Growth! The Republican party have undertaken a problem the solution of which will force them to our position."[18]

Phillips's speech was confident and ungrudging. The people he believed, had reached the foothills and were beginning to set their faces towards the mountain tops.

But not all of them. On December 2, 1860, the anniversary of John Brown's execution, a meeting was announced in Tremont Temple to discuss the question: "How can American Slavery be abolished?" The meeting was broken up by a howling, jeering, and hissing mob, and after three hours of pandemonium, the Mayor ordered the police to clear the hall. A number of business men had gained control of the meeting, passed resolutions condemning John Brown and declared the assemblies of certain "irresponsible persons and political demagogues" of Boston "a public nuisance which, in self defence, we are determined shall henceforward be summarily abated."

The discussionists adjourned to Joy Street Church where Phillips spoke. The street in front was filled with angry and yelling rioters. At the conclusion of his address, Phillips, guarded by his friends, left through a rear passageway and proceeded uphill to Myrtle Street on the way to his residence. When the mob heard that Phillips had escaped, they rushed uphill and overtook his escort just as it descended the stone steps leading to Beacon Street Mall. They found a cordon of about forty young men who with locked arms in close formation had Phillips in the center of their circle and were safely bearing him home. Believing an assault fruitless, the mob stood back and yelled taunts.[19]

Two weeks later Theodore Parker's church invited the orator to fill their pulpit. Even before the subject of his discourse was announced, a rumor spread about the city that the rioters who had broken up the John Brown meeting had sworn that Phillips should not speak. Phillips concluded that he would. And he selected for his theme the men who had attempted to muzzle free speech—"Mobs and Education." The hall was crowded. Phillips was calm. As he poured out his blistering anathemas several of his friends sat trembling lest they should hear the snap of a pistol. But no violence was attempted, though Phillips was frequently interrupted by shouts and hisses. The Mayor had stationed policemen in plain clothes in the anterooms and

hall.[20] At the conclusion of his address, Phillips's friends flocked
upon the platform to congratulate him. After a while he withdrew and was joined in the lower entry by a squad of twenty
young men. As the party merged into the street, the baffled
rioters, numbering about a thousand, cried out—"There he is!"
"Crush him out!" "Down with the Abolitionist!" "Bite his head
off!" "All up!" "Damn him! he has depreciated stocks three million dollars by his slang."[21] etc.—and surged towards Phillips.
But his friends, aided by the police, finally forced the crowd
to give way and he proceeded up Washington Street, followed
by the yelling and booing mob until he reached his house in
Essex Street. As he entered, three cheers were given by his friends
which were answered by hisses from the other side. Deputy
Chief of Police Ham then ordered the mob to disperse which
they did sullenly and slowly. Two hundred policemen in all
were needed to get Phillips home alive through the crowd of
merchants and clerks whose very living, they thought, compelled
them to trample him down in the streets.[22]

The volunteer bodyguard which had protected Phillips to
his home was composed of German Turners. The Turn Verein
had heard of the attempt to throttle free speech and resolved to
defend its champion. For weeks members of the Verein kept
watch day and night over Phillips's house in the neighboring
printing office of Karl Heinzen's *Der Pionier*.[23]

The Boston *Courier* declared Phillips's speech "a mass of poisonous and malignant trash—a thorough jail delivery of bad
temper, vituperation, and hatred." Adding: "Mr. Phillips thinks
like a Billingsgate fisherwoman, or a low pot house bully, but
he speaks like Cicero. It is a jewelled hand flinging filth."[24]

A few days later Phillips was invited to Watertown to deliver
his lyceum lecture on Toussaint L'Ouverture. Again rumors were
circulated that a riotous demonstration was to be made, and
fifty friends went to Watertown with the expressed determination
to protect him. Phillips made a few introductory remarks—

"Now what we want to decide at this hour and this year
is, not whether the North will back down or stand up, but
whether New England keeps her right of discussing freely

all things. (Applause.) And that is the main Gibraltar that
we should see to it that we defend . . .

"This is, to be sure, but a Lyceum lecture—nothing but
an ordinary literary lecture. But when a man says it shall not
be delivered, it is of inestimable importance that it should
be. As Luther said of the Sabbath, when the priests charged
upon him at that day,—'I don't care what I do on that day,
but if you say I shall not play upon the violin, I will, to
show that I had a right to.' So I am here tonight to show
that we can meet in peace, selecting our own time and our
own subject."

Then Phillips proceeded to deliver his lecture. At the conclusion he remarked—

"There! Watertown still lives! (Laughter and applause.)
And I don't think any harm has been done either. I wish
I could say something worthy of the occasion. It is a pity
that so many good men should come out here tonight to hear
nothing better. But coming here was the thing, the sitting
here one hour and going away our masters. State Street
has not bought these acres, nor got title deeds of Yankee
tongues yet. (Applause.) While we keep the English language and this glorious Saxon tongue of ours, we mean to
use it, wherever we choose, as did the Sidneys, the Adamses,
the Hancocks, the Otises of that day when it was treason
to preach free speech. But they preached it if they broke
an empire asunder, and we will sustain it and practise it,
even if the Canada line goes down to Mason and Dixon's.
God speed the day—let it travel fast." (Great applause.)[25]

CHAPTER THIRTY-SIX

THE ERRING SISTERS

Late one December day in 1860 a Southern gentleman hastened to the White House. On the steps he met an old friend who had just left President Buchanan. Waving his hat he shouted, "This is a glorious day! South Carolina has seceded!" That night an impromptu banquet was held in Washington at which Southern leaders drank to the success of the slave empire to be founded and talked about a Southern army, a Southern navy, the annexation of Mexico and the West India Islands. Then swiftly followed the secession of Mississippi, Florida, Alabama, Georgia, Louisiana, and Texas.[1] The Charleston (S.C.) *Mercury* issued an extra edition bearing the headline in large black type —"THE UNION IS NO MORE."[2]

President Buchanan, pale with fear, divided his time between praying and crying. He shut his eyes and did nothing. South Carolina's representatives called on him and asked him not to strengthen Fort Sumter without at least giving notice to the state authorities.

He sent a message to Congress on December 4 in which he showed his bewilderment and evasion. He denied the constitutional right of secession but also denied his own right to oppose such a course. As Seward wrote to his wife—Buchanan showed "conclusively that it is the duty of the President to execute the laws—unless somebody opposes him, and that no State has a right to go out of the Union—unless it wants to."

For a few weeks the issue hung in the balance. Then there appeared at Washington commissioners from South Carolina "empowered to treat for the delivery of forts . . . and other real

421

estate" held by the Federal Government within their State. On the day following their arrival, Buchanan was informed by telegraph that Anderson had dismantled Fort Moultrie, spiked its guns, and removed his garrison to the island fortress Sumter which was supposed to be more defensible. At Charleston, this action was interpreted as preparation for war, and all South Carolina saw in it a violation of the pledge which they believed President Buchanan had given their congressmen three weeks previous. Greatly excited the South Carolina commissioners held two conferences with the President on the 27 and 28 of December. They believed he had broken his word and told him so. When Senator Jefferson Davis added, "And now, Mr. President, you are surrounded with blood and dishonor on all sides," the President standing by the mantelpiece, crushed up his cigar in the palm of one hand, sat down, and exclaimed— "My God! are calamities never to come singly? I call God to witness. You gentlemen, better than anybody, know that this is not only without but against my orders. It is against my policy." He continued to reiterate that Anderson had acted on his own responsibility, but refused to order him back to the now ruined Fort Moultrie. "You are pressing me too importunately," exclaimed the unhappy president. "You don't give me time to consider; you don't give me time to say my prayers. I always say my prayers when required to act upon any great state affairs."[3]

The President turned at last to implore divine guidance and proclaimed January 4 a day of fasting and prayer. "God helps those who help themselves," snapped the New York *World*. "He is the most pitiable object in the country."[4]

Buchanan was ready to give way to the demands of the commissioners. He drew up a paper to that effect and showed it to his cabinet. Then the turning point came. Secretary of State Jeremiah S. Black threatened to resign and Attorney General Stanton said he would go with him. The idea of losing the support of these strong personalities terrified the President who immediately fell into a panic. He handed the paper drawn up to Black and begged him to retain office and alter the paper as he saw fit. To this Black agreed. The demand for the surrender of the forts was refused; Anderson was not ordered back to Moultrie.

2.

An early spring day in Montgomery, Alabama. An excited and jubilant crowd milled about the state Capitol. It was a typically Southern Capitol, rather small and dingy, but with an imposing front of tall, white columns, which seen from the river below looked classic. Around the Capitol women in hoop skirts, men in black swallow tailed coats, light trousers, and broad brimmed hats, Negroes in homespun or tatters waited voluble and expectant.

The doors of the Capitol opened creakingly. The crowd rushed into the building and flooded up the narrow stairways into the galleries, filling them to overflowing. They were narrow, uncomfortable, dirty galleries, but people in their intense interest took no note of discomfort. Eyes and ears were for only what was passing below.

The presiding officer, Howell Cobb of Georgia, late Secretary of the Treasury, spoke out clearly and deliberately. "The next matter before the Convention is the election of a provisional president of the Confederate States."

The vote was by states—one vote for each state. Tellers rose and visited one group of delegates after another, collecting scraps of paper. A single piece of paper was given them by each group. There were six ballots in all. The tellers, after studying the papers a moment, made a brief report to the presiding officer in low tones.

A tense silence fell on the hall as Howell Cobb rose to his feet and spoke slowly with a certain painful emphasis. "It is my duty to announce that the Honorable Jefferson Davis of Mississippi has been unanimously elected provisional President of the Confederate States of North America."

A first handclap came from the gallery, and then there was a loud burst of applause.[5]

Jefferson Davis was cutting roses in his garden when a messenger rode in on horseback delivering a telegram. There were a few minutes of silence while Davis read and reread the message. Then he told Mrs. Davis its contents: at Montgomery, Alabama, a group of gentlemen had selected him President of the Confederate States.[6]

That night Jefferson Davis assembled all his slaves, bade them an affectionate farewell, and next morning started for Montgomery.

Crowds flocked to the stations to hear him in the daytime and in the glare of torchlight at night. He told the clamorous throngs that a long war lay ahead of them. It was springtime in the land of magnolias and people laughed at him and did not believe him.

At Montgomery he was met with wild enthusiasm. He was driven from the Exchange Hotel in a carriage drawn by four white horses and at the suggestion of a young lady the band played "Dixie." The Southern anthem had been found.[7]

Around the state Capitol crowded statesmen, jurists and senators, soldiers and sailors, officers and office seekers, farmers, artisans, women with streamers and tri-colored cockades. At exactly one o'clock the spare, thoughtful figure, with broad forehead and high cheek bones, heavy square chin, and thin lips, appeared upon the platform with the Vice President, Alexander H. Stephens of Georgia, and when the mighty wave of applause had subsided, Howell Cobb administered to him the oath of office. Then in a musical voice Davis delivered his inaugural address.

Few people in the South expected that the North would care or dare to fight for the preservation of the Union, and if it should was not one Southerner a match for five Yankees! Was not cotton King?

" 'Yes, the North,' sez Colquitt,
  'Ef we Southerners all quit,
    Would go down like a busted balloon,' sez he."[8]

Oliver Wendell Holmes wrote a pleasant little poem to "Caroline, Caroline, child of the sun," promising to kiss the naughty child when she came home again.[9]

In the North there was a widespread desire for peace. The watchword of the Abolitionists was: "Let the erring sisters go in peace." "Let there be no Civil War," demanded the *Liberator,* "but a separation between the Free and Slave States in the spirit of Abraham and Lot." Phillips, also against war, would approve of no compromise. "You may as well dam up Niagara with the bulrushes as bind our anti-slavery purpose with Congressional compromise."[10] Whittier put the same feeling in verse:

> "They break the links of Union, shall we light
> The fires of Hell to weld anew the chain
> On that red anvil where each blow is pain?
> Pity, forgive, but urge them back no more."[11]

Northern papers called coercion wrong and impossible. Horace Greeley said in an editorial of the New York *Tribune,* chief molder of Republican opinion—"If the cotton states shall decide that they can do better out of the Union than in it, we shall insist on telling them go in peace. . . . We hope never to live in a republic where one section is pinned to the residue by bayonets."[12] Even Lowell thought the South "not worth conquering back."[13]

Democratic papers and leaders were violently opposed to preventing the Southern States from going out of the Union. Ex-Governor Horatio Seymour asked: "The question is simply this: Shall we have compromise after war or compromise without war?" The Indianapolis *Journal* added: "How long would this war last, think you? Ten years? Yes—fifty-forever—for the enmity begotten of it would never die."[14]

In striking contrast to these views were the views of men of the type of Oliver P. Morton, representing the Radical wing of the Republican party. "If South Carolina gets out of the Union," he remarked in Indianapolis, November 22, 1860, "I trust it will be at the point of the bayonet after our best efforts have failed to compel her submission to the laws." "This twaddle about the Union and its preservation," commented the Erie (Pennsylvania) *True American,* "is too silly and sickening for any good effect. We think the liberty of a single slave is worth more than all the Unions God's universe can hold." Senator Wade of Ohio exclaimed before an audience—"And after all this to talk of a Union! . . . Sir! the only salvation to your Union is that you divest it entirely from all taints of slavery. If we can't have that, then I go for no Union at all, but I go for Fight. (Great applause.) If there is any man here possessing a weaker spirit, let him show himself, for I want to see his meek face."[15]

No power was arrayed more zealously on the side of peace than the power of money. Two hundred million dollars were owed by the South to Northerners. War, it was argued, would cause cancellation of these debts. The moneyed interests joined with the Abolitionists to let the erring sisters go in peace. The stock market of New York was in a panicky condition, went up and down with feverish uncertainty. Banks suspended payment in Washington, Baltimore, and Philadelphia. There loomed the spectre of unpaid Southern accounts. One Harvard student whose father was connected with Southern trade asked for a delay in the payment of his tuition.

August Belmont spoke of "the reaction which has already taken place among thousands who voted for Lincoln. . . . I meet daily now with men who confess the error they have been led into, and almost with tears in their eyes they wish they could undo what they helped to do."[16]

New York merchants were outspoken in their demands for peace. On January 18, 1861, a memorial with forty thousand names attached praying for a peaceable solution of the pending difficulties was endorsed by a meeting held in the Chamber of Commerce and forwarded to Washington. Fernando Wood, Mayor of New York, went so far as to suggest that the city declare its independence and thus save its trade. The Common Council thought so well of this message that they ordered 3,000 copies printed for general circulation.[17]

Politicians fell on their knees and besought the South to forgive the rebellious conduct of the North and return, offering immense concessions as the price. Anxious saviors of the Union dashed to and fro in an eager haste to be doing something. If Henry Seward and Charles Francis Adams moved in favor of compromise, the Republican Party swayed like a field of grain beneath the breath of either of them. When Congress assembled in December, 1860, the rush to be first to placate the South began. The Senate appointed a Committee of Thirteen, and the House a Committee of Thirty-Three for conciliation. Senator Crittenden of Kentucky submitted to the Senate a resolution providing for six constitutional amendments all favorable to slavery. One of these divided the country on the Missouri Compromise line: in the territory North of 36°30′ slavery was prohibited; South of that line slavery was to be recognized and protected.

The conservatives were delighted. Edward Everett wrote— "I saw with great satisfaction your patriotic movement, and I wish from the bottom of my heart it might succeed." And August Belmont spoke for the money interest—"I have yet to meet the first Union-loving man, in or out of politics, who does not approve your compromise proposition."[18]

The Senate submitted Crittenden's Compromise to the Committee of Thirteen. Southern leaders were willing to accept the compromise if a majority of the Republican members would agree. But Lincoln refused point blank to accept the compromise (he distrusted Crittenden as a compromiser anyway) and put his refusal in writing. The party would have to go along with him. "Entertain no proposition for a compromise in regard to the extension of slavery," he wrote on December 11 to a member of the Committee of Thirty-Three. "The instant you do, they have us under again: all our labor is lost and soon or late must be done over. . . . The tug has to come, and better now than later." Lincoln was inflexible on the territorial question and the Crittenden Compromise was killed.[19]

The Committee of Thirty-Three was more fortunate in being able to arrive at a series of conclusions. Charles Francis Adams was so transported by devotion to the Union as to propose a security for slavery such as no Southern man, during the long agitation of slavery from 1820-1860, had ever ventured to demand. He moved to enact that "no amendment of the Constitution, having for its object any interference with slavery, should originate with any state that did not recognize that relation within its own limits, or be valid without the assent of every one of the states composing the Union." This proposition was opposed by only three members of the House Committee. An amendment to the Constitution which would have made slavery perpetual in the United States was actually passed by the House by a majority of 133 to 65 and by the Senate by 24 to 12, precisely the necessary two thirds.

This joint resolution was listed as the Thirteenth Amendment to the Constitution. It was unnecessarily signed by Buchanan and was accepted by Lincoln himself in his inaugural, but in the upheaval received no attention from the states.[20]

A Peace Congress called by Virginia, made a last desperate attempt to save the Union. Twenty-one states accepted the invitation. Entreaty not menace was the underlying idea. As a member from Connecticut expressed it—"Let us be gentle and pleasant. Let us love one another. Let us not try to find out who is smartest or keenest. Let us vote soon and without any feeling or quarreling."[21]

The proposals did not differ markedly from the Crittenden scheme. But the Peace Convention ended in thin smoke. In a letter read in the Senate on the report of the convention, one Senator remarked: "Without a little blood letting this Union will not, in my estimation, be worth a rush."[22]

The Colonel of the Second Regiment, United States Cavalry, arrived at San Antonio from Fort Mason. The Federal garrison was leaving the town with the band playing Union airs and Union colors flying. San Antonio was swarming with Secessionist rangers. The whole place was at sixes and sevens and anything might have happened.

As the tall and handsome Colonel came up to the hotel, he was warmly greeted by Mrs. Darrow, the anxious wife of a clerk in the pay and quartermaster service. "Who are those men?" he asked pointing to the rangers who wore red flannel shoulder straps. "They are McCulloch's," she answered. "General Twiggs surrendered everything to the State this morning." The Colonel looked astonished, his lips trembled, and his eyes filled with tears. "Has it come so soon as this?" he exclaimed.[23]

In a short time Mrs. Darrow saw him cross the plaza on his way to headquarters and noticed particularly that he was in citizen's dress. He returned at night and shut himself into his room which was over hers, and she heard Colonel Lee's footsteps through the night and sometimes the murmur of his voice, as if he were praying.

CHAPTER THIRTY-SEVEN

MOBBING PHILLIPS

Compromise, said Phillips, was wrong, demoralizing, suicidal. Disunion was gain, liberty, justice. On January 20, 1861, he occupied Theodore Parker's pulpit and his subject was "Disunion."[1]

He spoke calmly. A bloodthirsty mob as before occupied the hall and the approaches to it. And as before he was escorted home by a self-appointed bodyguard assisted by the police. There were a few wild rushes, but the police held good. The mob kept them company, oozing and surging slowly on, cursing all the way.

During these days Phillips walked the streets of Boston with a hand on his revolver. A friend said one day: "I am more afraid now they will try injury rather than insult." "Don't trouble about that!" replied Phillips. "I can see over my shoulder and before a man can touch me, I shall shoot."[2]

The annual meeting of the Massachusetts Anti-Slavery Society at Tremont Temple on January 24 was the occasion for wild disorder and uproar. The Mayor, a Democrat named Wightman, refused the Society's request for police protection, and the rioters, discovering that the dozen policemen sent by the Mayor were for ornament merely, grew bold. The first speaker of the morning was the Reverend James Freeman Clarke, who made a forcible speech and was interrupted only by occasional hisses. But soon the mob came tumbling in by the hundreds, and when Phillips rose to speak, all hell broke loose. Rowdies in the gallery cried out, "All up!" but the noise was drowned in a burst of applause. Cheers for "Mayor Wightman,"

"Bell and Everett," "Clay" were punctuated by groans and hisses, the audience yelling, screeching, stamping, bellowing. The tumult was deafening. For fifteen minutes the infernal scene continued, Phillips uttering a sentence now and then in a lull which even then was not audible beyond a few feet from the speaker.

"We come here today to let Washington see what Boston thinks of this crisis, and we want her to declare that, Constitution or no Constitution, Union or no Union, against the law or with it, the Southern States, so long as they be slave states, shall be shovelled out of this Union. (Loud applause and hisses.) We not only accept the crisis but thank God it has come. (Applause and hisses.) I am sorry for every merchant whose ledger balances on the wrong side. I am sorry for every laborer who has lost a week's or a month's wages; and if his Daniel Webster and his Caleb Cushing, and his Edward Everett, had listened to us thirty years ago, this trouble never had come on the country. (A voice— 'Never!' and applause. Then the gallery screamed itself hoarse for Webster and Everett and other idols of their worship.) O, Mr. Chairman, we have plenty of time! We have this session, this afternoon and evening, and three to-morrow. No occasion to hurry in the least. South Carolina is waiting to hear from us. (Cheers for South Carolina.) . . . . The Southern States say that when they have organized their confederacy, they mean to leave New England out in the cold. Well, we shall be glad to be there. I am only sorry that my friends there (pointing to the rioters) are out in the cold. Now ladies and gentlemen, this is a very momentous question—"

Here the reprobates in the gallery flung their cushioned seats upon the floor and struck up the song—

> We are going home,
> We are going home,
> We are going home,
> To die no more.

A declaration which they repeated again and again, but they did not go. Instead of that they struck up another tune—

Tell John Andrew,
Tell John Andrew,
Tell John Andrew,
John Brown's dead.[3]

Followed by three groans for General Scott, screeches and yells: "Sit down," "Blow your horn," "Throw a bucket at him," "Your house is afire, don't you know your house is afire?" "The Union"—

Phillips.—"I just now heard three cheers for the Union. I think the dead ought to be allowed to rest."

Hisses and howl from the gallery. An amateur whistler struck up "Yankee Doodle," and the gallery gods joined in noisily.

At one time they all rose up and clattered downstairs and surged towards the platform. But Phillips's friends who were armed were stationed at every door and in the middle of every aisle. They formed a firm wall which the mob could not pass.

A message went from Tremont Temple to the State House where Governor Andrew sat waiting. An answer came back by word of mouth and was misunderstood. In a lull Phillips's voice could be heard in a direct appeal to the mob:—"We have a message from the Governor. The State Militia is on its way to the Temple and will sweep that rabble where it belongs— into the calaboose." The rabble thought it over for a while in silence, but began again.[4]

Phillips spoke a few more sentences, then by a clever stroke, stooped forward and quietly addressed his speech to the reporters stationed directly below him. This tantalized the mob and they began to call out—"Speak louder. We want to hear what you're saying."

"Abolitionists! Look here!" said Phillips. "Friends of the slave, look here! These pencils (pointing to the reporters) will do more to create opinion than a hundred thousand mobs. While I speak to these pencils, I speak to a million of men. What, then, are these boys? (Applause.) We have got the press of the country in our hands. Whether they like us or not, they know that our speeches sell their papers. (Applause and laughter.) With five newspapers we may defy five hundred boys. Therefore, just allow me to make my speech to these gentlemen in front of me, and I can spike all those cannon. (Applause.) My voice is beaten by theirs but they cannot beat out types. . . ."[5]

"Now, those fellows cannot last but one morning," continued Phillips in a louder voice, "while the Abolitionists can talk till doomsday. They have an unending gift of free speech." (Groans for the Abolitionists.)

"They say one man is a majority, when he has right on his side; I have got three thousand on my side. (Tumult in the gallery, during which Phillips paused, and then said:) Do not be impatient, ladies and gentlemen, it is only ten minutes to twelve; there is time enough. Time will do everything. It will bring South Carolina back into the Union a free State. (Applause.) We are not going to lose one of the old thirteen. We are going to conquer them all to freedom. . . .

"We will have free speech yet. Massachusetts is not conquered; the Capitol is not owned by State Street (Cheers), and whoever is Mayor of Boston, John A. Andrew is Governor of the Commonwealth. (Prolonged cheers.) I do not despair of the Commonwealth."[6]

Three groans for Governor Andrew by the crowd in the gallery, followed by three cheers for Mayor Wightman. Then someone called out—"Three cheers for Wendell Phillips," which were given with emphasis.

Phillips.—"An Abolitionist is a happy man to have such a cheer as that, and a mob besides. (Laughter and applause.) I hope all my blessings won't come at once.

A Voice.—"Go ahead! We've got them where the hair is short." (Uproarious laughter from both sides.)

Phillips continued his speech with occasional interruptions. But as soon as he sat down the mob began to yell again to prevent any more speaking. When adjournment came, Phillips said to a friend—"I am going to Governor Andrew. Come."

They found the Governor, a bulky man with blue eyes and curly brown hair, in his room at the golden domed State House. He greeted them cordially and listened while Phillips stated his case. Phillips urged that the Anti-Slavery Society had a right to meet, a right to transact business, a right to the free use of that free speech which was a right attaching to citizenship in Massachusetts, and a right to be protected when that right was denied. Primarily, he said, it was the business of the police to keep order and give protection, but the police acting under orders of Mayor Wightman, refused to do their duty.

"Therefore," said Phillips, "I come to the Governor of the State to safeguard the citizens of the State in the exercise of their rights."

"Mr. Phillips, what do you wish me to do?"

"Send a sufficient force of troops to Tremont Temple to put down the rioters and protect law abiding citizens in the legal exercise of their legal rights."

The Governor sat behind a table on which lay a copy of the Revised Statutes of Massachusetts. He opened it, handed it to Phillips, and said—"If you wish me, as Governor, to act, show me the statute which gives me the power."

But Phillips was not to be turned aside. He answered in tones less cool than before:

"Free speech is a common law right. The power to which I appeal is a common law power, inherent in the Governor, as the chief magistrate of the State."

But Andrew said again:

"Show me the statute."

And again:

"Show me the statute."

And from that he was not to be moved. Seeing that Andrew's mind was made up, Phillips turned away abruptly, saying to his friend, "Come," and they departed. As he went downstairs, he remarked—"I will never again speak to Andrew as long as I live."[7]

In the afternoon session the mob, counting on the sympathy of the Mayor, became violent. The hall was crowded to overflowing. As soon as the doors were thrown open, the crowd—

"Breckinridgers, Negroes, Douglas men, Garrisonians, Bell men, North streeters, Beacon streeters, John Brown men, ministers of the Gospel, pickpockets, reporters, teamsters, dry goods jobbers, loafers, brokers, rum sellers, ladies, thieves, gentlemen, State officers, boys, policemen," said the *Traveller*, rushed the doors. A number of people remained outside too curious to go away inspecting all who entered. One gentleman seemed anxious to enter, yet still very reluctant to run the gauntlet of curious eyes. At last he spasmodically passed the threshold, and turning round, took off his hat and said—"Gentlemen, I wish my presence here may not be misconstrued. I am neither an Abolitionist, a rioter, nor a pickpocket. I'm going to see a man." (Silence broken by a slight tittering.)

A number of policemen entered the galleries and were greeted with hisses by the rowdies. The mob had complete possession of the hall. One corner of the hall cheered and hissed and was lustily answered by cheers from the opposite corner. The President called upon the police, but his voice was drowned in the uproar. Then the mob began hurling cushions from the gallery seats to the floor below. First they would sing, then cheer, then hiss, then sway one way, and then the other. Hats were thrown in the air.

Scarcely a word could be heard that was uttered on the platform. Just then a movement was noticed in one of the aisles, and presently it was seen that the Mayor with the Chief of Police and a large posse of officers, was slowly forcing his way to the platform. Arrived there, he stepped to the centre, in front of the President and said—

"Silence! SILENCE! SILENCE! in the gallery! Fellow citizens—fellow citizens—I am sure that you, who are the citizens of Boston, will listen to the voice of its chief Magistrate. (Gallery —'Good'—'Good'—'Three cheers for Mayor Wightman.'). . . . I am requested, inasmuch as this meeting has been disturbed by tumultuous and riotous proceedings—I am requested by the trustees of this building to disperse the meeting."

The rowdies screamed, "Good"—"Good" and cheered at the top of their lungs.

Deacon Gilbert, one of the Trustees, pressed forward and exclaimed: "It isn't so. Will you let me see the letter?" The Mayor declined.

Mr. Quincy—"Will you allow the agent of the building, Mr. Hayes, to see it? We doubt its authenticity."

The Mayor—"I will not, sir. I will settle that tomorrow, not now. (Turning to the audience.) Fellow citizens, having thus announced my purpose, under the written order of the Trustees, (voices—"False"—"False") I have now simply to say to you that I am sure you will respect me enough to leave this place quietly and peaceably." ("No"—"Yes"—"Read the letter!")

The confusion was tremendous—that of the platform rivalling the gallery, everybody crowding forward to the desk, amid excited cries of "It's false."—"It's a lie!" "Read it." etc. At length the Mayor was forced to read the letter which he did, first remarking—"I am requested to read the document which has been placed in my hands, and I regard it is sufficiently authentic for this purpose."

The letter read—"Honorable J. M. Wightman, Mayor of the City of Boston:—We hereby notify you that a tumultuous and riotous assembly of more than thirty persons is now engaged in disturbing a meeting of the Massachusetts Anti-Slavery Society at Tremont Temple, and we hereby request you, in your official capacity, to quell the riot and protect the property where the meeting is now being held—to wit, Tremont Temple." And the letter was signed by the trustees.

Shouts of derisive laughter were heard on all sides, for everybody saw that the request was one totally different from that stated by the Mayor. The Mayor in confusion turned meekly to Quincy, the acting President, and asked. "What do you want me to do?"

"Clear the galleries," Quincy replied, and it was done. "Give us fifty policemen this evening to protect the meeting," he continued. "You shall have them," responded the Mayor. But returning to City Hall he straightway issued an order to close up the hall to "prevent any meeting being held there" that evening.[8]

The crowds in the street before the hall constantly increased and joined in a riotous procession. By eight o'clock the more turbulent portion took refuge in the Tremont House barroom. A chair served as the rostrum for various speakers. Finally a young man mounted the chair and proposed that all friends step up to the bar and drink, then adjourn to Johnny Gallagher's arbor in Howard Street and there organize and go up to Phillips's house to carve him out. He was answered by cries of "Hoe him out! Carve him out." etc. From Tremont House the mob hooting and halloing, rushed down the street. They turned out of Howard Street, shouting "To Wendell Phillips's." "To Wendell Phillips's" and all started for that point.

Upon arriving in front of Phillips's residence, the mob started singing "Tell John Andrew," etc. Shouts, groans and hootings. The Chief of Police Ham with a large detachment of police suddenly made his appearance upon the steps of Phillips's house, addressed the mob, and gave them the choice of either retiring quietly to their homes or being taken to the station house. Then the officers began to clear the streets.[9]

Phillips could not be silenced—he could be neither coaxed, hired, nor driven to hold his tongue. On February 17, he re-entered Parker's pulpit and spoke on "Progress,"[10] still uncompromisingly, still with the mob for his audience and a phalanx of armed friends. In the end the hall broke into wild applause. While he was speaking, a string of fifty or more rioters pushed into the hall and surged towards the desk. But they were stopped by a protecting cordon in front of the orator. One of them addressed a bystander, supposing him to be a malcontent. Pulling a noosed rope half out of his overcoat pocket, he said in a whisper—"See! we are going to snake him out and hang him with this on the Common." The person addressed drew out a revolver, pushed it into the eyes of the ruffian and cried—"God damn you, if you don't get out of this hall, I'll blow your brains out." He got out in a hurry.[11]

At the close of his address Phillips was spirited away in a waiting buggy and driven home. For days his house was an arsenal: friends encamped within, well armed, the police stood guard without, while the mob paraded noisily in the vicinity.

"If those fellows had broken in would you have shot them, Mr. Phillips?" asked a lady friend.

"Yes," was the quiet answer, "just as I would shoot a mad dog or a wild bull!"[12]

CHAPTER THIRTY-EIGHT

SIMPLE SUSAN—FRESH SEED

Abraham Lincoln left Springfield February 11, 1861, to be inaugurated at Washington on March 4, and all the way he sprinkled gay little speeches while the South was seceding State after State, drilling and organizing its armies. Party feeling was belligerent, business demoralized, the press voicing and increasing the perplexity of the people.

At Columbus, Ohio, he remarked in his shrill, piping voice: "There is nothing going wrong. . . . There is nothing that really hurts anybody."[1] At Pittsburgh he explained: "Notwithstanding the troubles across the river (the speaker pointing southwardly across the Monongahela and his features lighting up with a smile) there is no crisis but an artificial one."[2] At Cleveland he reiterated: "Why all this excitement? Why all these complaints? As I said before, this crisis is all artificial. . . . Let it alone and it will go down of itself."[3] ("The time for compromise has passed," said Jefferson Davis to an audience a few days before at Montgomery, Alabama, "and those who oppose us will smell powder and feel Southern steel.")[4]

At Utica, New York, his remarks were reported in full: "Ladies and gentlemen, I have no speech to make to you, and no time to speak in. I appear before you that I may see you and that you may see me; I am willing to admit that so far as the ladies are concerned, I have the best of the bargain, though I wish it to be understood that I do not make the same acknowledgment concerning the men."[5]

The ridiculous was reached when this man proceeding to grave duties stopped at the town of Westfield, Ohio. At the station

439

he took occasion to say that during the campaign he had received a letter from a young girl of this place, Grace Bedell, in which he was kindly admonished to do certain things and among others to let his whiskers grow, and that as he had acted upon that piece of advice, he would now be glad to welcome his fair correspondent, if she was among the crowd. In response to his call, a little lassie made her way through the crowd, was helped to the platform and kissed by the President who said, "You see, I have let these whiskers grow for you, Grace. (The whiskers were of the blacking brush variety, coarse, stiff, and ungraceful.) The next day's journal headed the account—"Old Abe kissed by a Pretty Girl."[6]

The inaugural journey was a painful disappointment. The country stood aghast. Some supporters were discouraged, others exasperated. One angry partisan went so far as to write—"Lincoln is a Simple Susan."[7]

The fourth of March arrived: the inaugural contained three main propositions. Lincoln pledged himself not to interfere directly or indirectly with slavery in the States where it then existed, promised to support the enforcement of the fugitive slave law, and declared he would maintain the Union. Addressing the South he said—"In your hands my dissatisfied fellow country men, and not in mine, is the momentous issue of civil war. The government will not assail you. . . . We are not enemies but friends."[8]

James Gordon Bennett of the New York *Herald* wrote in an editorial that the address would have been "as instructive if President Lincoln had contented himself with telling his audience a funny story and let them go."[9]

The olive branch was lost upon the South. The Richmond *Enquirer* declared, "No action of our convention can now maintain the peace and Virginia must fight." The Charleston *Mercury* declared it to be their wisest policy "to accept it as a declaration of war."[10]

Senator John Sherman came to the President with his brother, Colonel William Tecumseh Sherman. Colonel Sherman had been for two years professor at Louisiana College, but on January 10, the Confederates had taken the United States arsenal at Baton

Rouge, and Sherman declaring that "these were acts of unjustifiable war," resigned and returned North. Brother John took Brother William to the White House to give the new head of the nation information about conditions in the South. "Ah, how are they getting along down there?" asked the President easily. "They think," began Colonel Sherman, bursting with inside information, "they are getting along swimmingly—they are preparing for war—" "Oh, well," broke in Lincoln carelessly, "I guess we'll manage to keep house."

Colonel Sherman's fount of information was frozen. All he could get out was an offer of his services. Lincoln smilingly pushed that off with—"We shall not need men like you; the affair will soon be over." That ended the conversation and Brother William spoke no more till he got outside the White House. Then he turned on Brother John and stormed him with curses on all politicians. "You have got things in a hell of a fix," he roared; "and you may get them out as best you can." He went to St. Louis and became President of a street railroad.[11]

2.

Cannons were booming over Charleston. People came out on the water front of the lovely old city and watched the duel far down the harbor and spoke joyously of the great event. They applauded every telling shot with the clapping of hands and the waving of shawls and handkerchiefs. Reckless observers even put out in small boats and roamed about almost under the guns of the fort whose brick walls rose sheer from the midst of the harbor. They saw shells of the shore batteries mount high, curve through the air, and crash within the fort. They watched the fire of the defenders slacken and cease. At last the flag of the Union fluttered down from above the fort. Early Sunday morning, April 14, the news flashed over the North: "Fort Sumter has surrendered."

The tension broke. In a moment the current of popular feeling changed. The old flag had been fired on, and Democrats vied with Republicans in the sentiments of patriotism and loyalty. "Since they will have it so," declared Governor Andrew—

"in the name of God—amen! Now let all the governors and chief men of the people see to it that war shall not cease until emancipation is secure."[12]

Lincoln called for 75,000 men to serve three months. "Why," snorted Sherman, "you might as well attempt to put out the flames of a burning house with a squirt gun."[13]

Soon after three o'clock on the afternoon of Wednesday, April 17, the Fourth Massachusetts Regiment appeared at the State House. It received its equipments, the Governor spoke a few sentences—"You cannot wait for words," he said—and the regiment hurried away to take train for Fall River and then to Fortress Monroe. They were the first armed troops to move anywhere in the North.[14]

A great mass meeting was held in Union Square, New York City, on April 20. Mayor Fernando Wood in an eloquent speech declared with Jackson that "the Union must and shall be preserved."[15] The air was surcharged with military ardor. Fife, drum, and bugle corps, troops mustering in the armories, parading on the square, tenting in the parks, marching rank on rank through the streets were familiar sights and sounds. Bryant, honored poet of New York, urged

> Lay down the axe, fling by the spade
> Leave in its track the toiling plough.
> The rifle and the bayonet blade
> For arms like yours are fitter now.[16]

In a passionate plea Richard Henry Stoddard called upon the men of the North and West to fight for their country if they loved freedom better than slavery—

> Men of the North and West
> Wake in your might
> Prepare, as the rebels have done,
> For the fight!
> You cannot shrink from the test;
> Rise! Men of the North and West!

"They have torn down your banner of stars,
    They have trampled the laws,
They have stifled the freedom they hate,
    For no cause!
Do you love it or slavery best?
Speak! Men of the North and West.

They strike at the life of the State:
    Shall the murder be done?
They cry: 'We are two!' And you: 'We are one!'
You must meet them, then, breast to breast!
    On! Men of the North and West!

Not with words; they laugh them to scorn,
    And tears they despise;
But with swords in your hands and death
    In your eyes!
Strike home! leave to God all the rest;
Strike! Men of the North and West."[17]

The Abolitionists were quiet for a time. Garrison wrote on the 23—"Let us stand aside when the North is rushing like a tornado in the right direction." But he declared that it was the duty of the government to suppress the rebellion. Soon he forgot that he was a non-resistant and made the *Liberator* over from a quaker gun into a Columbiad. When taunted about his new political views, he replied wittily—"You remember what Benedick in the play says: 'When I said I would die a bachelor, I did not think I should live till I were married.' And when I said I would not sustain the Constitution because it was a covenant with death and an agreement with hell, I had no idea that I should live to see death and hell secede."[18]

Another Abolitionist, Dr. Samuel Gridley Howe, wrote militantly: "If I can be of any use, anywhere, in any capacity (save that of spy), command me."[19]

Phillips veered with the rest. All winter he had been advising the North to let the South go in peace. Now he too favored war and wished to save the Union. He changed not his principles, but his methods. War would mean the emancipation of the Negro race and the liberation of the North from slave-holding domination. Two ideas therefore took possession of him: free the blacks as a war measure and then enfranchise them. This policy he urged throughout the war and throughout the period of reconstruction. To those who accused him of inconsistency, he replied:

"People may say this is strange language for me,—a Disunionist. Well, I was a Disunionist, sincerely, for twenty years. I did hate the Union, when union meant lies in the pulpit and mobs in the streets, when union meant making white men hypocrites and black men slaves. (Cheers.) I did prefer purity to peace,—I acknowledge it. The child of six generations of puritans, knowing well the value of Union, I did prefer disunion to being the accomplice of tyrants. But now—when I see what the Union must mean in order to last, when I see that you cannot have union without meaning justice, and when I see twenty millions of people, with a current as swift and inevitable as Niagara, determined that this Union shall mean justice, why should I object to it? I endeavored honestly, and am not ashamed of it, to take nineteen States out of this Union, and consecrate them to liberty, and twenty millions of people answer me back, 'We like your motto, only we mean to keep thirty-four States under it.' Do you suppose I am not Yankee enough to buy union when I can have it at a fair price?"[20]

Having gone over, Phillips took his whole heart with him. There was no compromise, no transition. He knew what he was about. Learning of his conversion, Theodore Parker's society invited the orator to occupy their desk on Sunday, April 21, nine days after the firing on Fort Sumter. Charles Follen asked whether Phillips would like the Music Hall platform hung with the American flag. "Yes," said Phillips, "deck the altar for the victim." And decked it was—a forest of flags. The flags told the story long before Phillips opened his mouth.[21]

The tremendous audience sprang up and cheered. The hall was a furnace seven times heated. The only unmoved man in it was Wendell Phillips. Abolitionists imagine, he said, that the age of bullets was over and that the age of ideas had come, that thirty million people were able to take a great question and decide it by the conflict of opinions, that without letting the ship of state founder, they could lift four million men into liberty and justice. But a great mistake had been made. They counted too much on the intelligence of the masses, on the honesty and wisdom of statesmen as a class. Again they did not give enough weight to the fact that the nation was made up of clashing ideals, different ages: serfdom and freedom, the age of barbarism (the South) and the age of civilization (the North). Such a struggle could be settled only by arms. In a splendid peroration Phillips closed:

"The war, then, is not aggressive, but in self defence, and Washington has become the Thermopylae of Liberty and Justice. (Applause.) Rather than surrender that Capital, cover every square foot of it with a living body. (Loud Cheers.) Crowd it with a million of men and empty every bank vault at the North to pay the cost. (Renewed cheering.) Teach the world once for all, that North America belongs to the Stars and Stripes, and under them no man shall wear a chain. (Enthusiastic cheering.) In the whole of this conflict, I have looked only at Liberty,—only at the slave. Perry entered the battle of the Lakes with 'Don't Give Up The Ship!' floating from the masthead of the Lawrence. When with his fighting flag he left her crippled, heading North, and mounting the deck of the Niagara, turned her bows due west, he did all for one and the same purpose,— to rake the decks of the foe. Steer north or west, acknowledge secession or cannonade it, I care not which, but 'Proclaim Liberty throughout all the land unto all the inhabitants thereof.'" (Loud cheers.)[22]

Not one of the Boston papers printed a word of Phillips's speech save the *Advertiser,* and this only by accident. The reason alleged was that it was feared Phillips's advocacy of the war would render it unpopular elsewhere! The *Liberator* published the address in an extra and sold nearly twenty thousand copies by newsboys in the streets.[23] Later when urged to explain Garrisonianism, Phillips replied: "I feel no wish to explain. . . . Besides *qui s'excuse, s'accuse* has always been my motto. . . . Then I'm no longer exclusively a Garrisonian. I'm a citizen and prefer so to address my fellows just now."[24]

He entered heart and soul into the movement to educate public opinion and made a personal canvass of the country. In December he visited New York and spoke on "The War for the Union." His aim was to explain the essential nature of the strife and the futility of compromise. The North could pledge, compromise, guarantee what it pleased. But the South feared one thing—the nature of Northern institutions, the perilous freedom of discussion, the flavor of Northern ideas, the sight of Northern growth. The very neighborhood of such states constituted the danger. This the South felt. Hence the imperious necessity that she should rule and shape the government or sail out of it.

"And the struggle is between these two ideas. Our fathers, as I said, thought they could safely be left, one to outgrow the other. They took gunpowder and a lighted match, forced them into a stalwart cannon, screwed up the muzzle, and thought they could secure peace. But it has resulted differently; their cannon has exploded, and we stand among the fragments."[25]

At the Independence Day celebration he sounded a rallying cry:

"Today we plant fresh seed. The furrow is opened. The guns are shotted to the lips. They are to be pointed—where? At a miserable rattlesnake flag? At a bankrupt and fugitive cabinet. No! Your two hundred and fifty thousand muskets, shotted by thirty years of anti-slavery agitation, are to be pointed at the Slave Power. (Applause.) Demolish it. (Renewed applause.) Shame England, waken France, summon Europe to our side by proclaiming that the cause of the North is liberty, and our end justice; that no flag, no parchment, is worth shedding a drop of blood, but that four millions of slaves, whom we have outraged for seventy years, claim of us this atonement; and whether in money or in blood, it is to be laid cheerfully on the altar."[26]

THE PEACE OF JUSTICE

More and more Phillips made himself the whip and spur of the Administration. In season and out of season, he urged Congress, the Cabinet, the President to proclaim Emancipation—to hurl the bolt that could save the Union or make it worth saving. The cabinet was but a pine shingle upon the rapids of Niagara, borne which way the great popular heart and natural purpose directed. It was in vain now to create public opinion. Phillips's object was to concentrate, to manifest, to make evident, to make intense the matured purpose of the nation.

Lincoln was riding two hobbies—that of compensated emancipation in the Border States and that of Colonization. Touching the second Phillips said—

> "Colonize the blacks! A man might as well colonize his hands; or when the robber enters his house, he might as well colonize his revolver. . . . We need the blacks even more than they need us. They know every inlet, the pathway of every wood, the whole country is mapped at night in their instinct. And they are inevitably on our side, ready as well as skilled to aid: the only element the South has which belongs to the nineteenth century. Aside from justice, the Union needs the blacks. . . . We are none of us, as a nation, fit for the lunatic asylum, and until we are, we never shall colonize four million of workers. I believe in Yankee common sense, and therefore I do not fear colonization."[1]

He wrongly thought the hesitation of the Administration arose from its aristocratic Whig antecedents, which had no trust in the

447

masses and looked upon the world as a probate court in which the educated and the wealthy were the guardians. And so when the men in power entered on the great work of defending the nation in its utmost peril, they dared not trust the country to the hearts of those that loved it.[2]

As for the spirit of the great battle, he complimented the South upon its earnestness and sincerity—

> "No man can fight Stonewall Jackson, an honest fanatic on the side of slavery, but John Brown, an equally honest fanatic on the side of freedom. They are the only chemical equals, and will neutralize each other. You cannot neutralize nitric acid with cologne water. William H. Seward is no match for Jefferson Davis. We must have what they have— positive convictions. Otherwise the elements of the struggle are unequal."[3]

The war was a death grapple of irreconcilable ideas. Concerning the problem, he said—

"We have not only an army to conquer, but we have a state of mind to annihilate. . . .[4]

And he added—

> "I do not think we have any claim to govern this country on the ground that we have more cannon, more men, and more money than the South. That is a bald, brutal superiority. The claim of the North to govern must be founded on the ground that our civilization is better, purer, nobler, higher than that of the South. Our civilization is ideas, rights, education, labor. I hold that the South is to be annihilated. I do not mean the geographical South, but the intellectual, social, aristocratic South—the thing that represented itself by slavery and the bowie knife, by bullying and lynch law, by ignorance and idleness, by the claim of one man to own his brother, by statutes existing on the books of Georgia today, offering five thousand dollars for the head of William Lloyd Garrison. That South is to be annihilated. (Loud Applause.)"[5]

He stated and answered a common taunt—"But men say, 'This is a mean thing; nineteen millions of people pitched against eight millions of Southerners, white men, and can't whip them, and now begin to call on the Negroes.'" Was that the right statement? asked Phillips. Look at it. What was the South's strength? She had eight million whites; she had the sympathy of foreign powers; she had the labor of four million slaves. What had the North? "Divided almost equally—into Republicans and Democrats, the Republicans willing to go but halfway and the Democrats not willing to go at all." (Laughter.)[6]

However much others doubted and hesitated, Phillips and the Abolitionists did not. They banded together in an Emancipation League to arouse the nation and annihilate slavery. "We are willing to accept the challenge now made to us," he said, "a Union for slavery, or a Union without it; and we abide the issue, no matter at what cost of fire, and blood, and treasure. We will make no peace but the peace of Justice." (Applause.) And he drew the distinction between a statesman and a politician. A statesman is one who is ready to do all the people allow. He drags public sentiment up to its utmost possible efficiency. A politician is one who does all the people demand. He yields, he does not lead. He submits, he does not initiate. The administration was ready. It stood looking to the North and West and saying, "What shall I do?" Like Barkis, it was "willing."[7]

"We want more," added Phillips. "We want an indication that shall ripen public sentiment. We want a proposal—an opening of the channel that shall guide the public thought. The chiefs of the administration propose nothing. They merely cry with the people, 'The stars and stripes.' They merely respond to this war cry of an insulted nation. It seems to me that they should show us how we are to be got out of this difficulty. . . .
"I put my faith in the honesty of Abraham Lincoln as an individual, in the pledge which a long life has given of Chase's love for the anti-slavery cause; but I do not believe either of them, nor all their comrades, have the boldness to

declare an emancipation policy, until, by a pressure which we are to create, the country forces them to it. . . ."[8]

Again the insistent prodding, again the demand for action, for a summary and ruthless execution of the "vile" system: "I don't believe there will be any peace until 347,000 slave holders are either hung or exiled. (Cheers.) History shows no precedent of getting rid of an aristocracy like this, except by the death of a generation."[9] (In this instance Phillips was as rabid as any frothing Southern slaveowner.)

He thought Lincoln blind to the significance of events, and profoundly distrusted Seward. "If we fail," he said, "we shall be under the harrow. I expect that—but those poor contrabands!" He uttered the last words in a low tone with an intense expression of sympathy and pity and clenched his hands as he spoke.[10] The administration had been six months in office and what had it done? Had it set forth any principle? Any avowal of purpose? Not a line, not a word. "The world speculates upon the purposes of the United States. It seems to me so far that the hour has come, but not the man." (Applause.)[11]

Sumner was bombarded with letters, flattering his vanity, steeling his purpose:

> "Never fear that the masses, the hearts are all with you and you'll see your enemies at your footstool. . . (October 3, 1861)."
>
> "I tell all that 'you and Resolutions never go back'—that there's no white feather in you. . . . You came into politics defiant. Holding to it has put hitherto all your enemies under your foot and made the people regard you as the incarnation of a principle and as one without fear—with no personal ends to serve. . . . I know your feeling will agree with me and only fear some may try to inoculate you with their fears, and ask you to do the only thing that can harm you, i.e., seem to give an inch to the yelling curs at your heels. . . . I don't ask you to trust me too much but only *consider* what I urge."[12] (October 12, 1861.)

When the Confederate envoys, Mason and Slidell, were surrendered to England, Phillips's anger flamed. "I must say these ten months have exhausted my patience with the cabinet at Washington. (Applause.) I call it the Apology Cabinet." The contemptible root of bitterness, American bondage, had poisoned the future of the Republic. Let the nineteen States, urged Phillips, say to the world that the struggle was one betwixt Freedom and Slavery and the Government announce that it was a war for Liberty. If McClellan put that upon his banner so broad that it could be seen in London, Earl Russell would write no more haughty notes to Seward.[13]

The Boston *Post* ran a headline: "Treason Rampant in Boston," and added—"Wendell Phillips attacked the Generals for making no advance, he attacked the Cabinet for being an Apology Cabinet, he attacks the President for not being a man, he attacks the men in power for giving up Mason and Slidell, he attacks the North for being as bankrupt in character as in money."[14]

In the Mason and Slidell case Phillips was plainly wrong. The act of Captain Wilkes was contrary to the laws of nations and our own precedents. Great Britain had been wronged and the injury could be atoned only by the surrender of Mason and Slidell. Had they not been surrendered, England would have ordered her minister to leave Washington and prepared for war.[15]

After the flight of the Union forces at Bull Run, the New York *Herald* titled an article—"How to retrieve the Bull Run Defeat Immediately—Let Garrison, Greeley, Brownson, Wendell Phillips, Beecher, Cheever, be arrested by order of the government, sent to Fort Lafayette and boarded there for six months. These Abolitionists are traitors to the Constitution and deserve to be imprisoned."[16] To the Nashville *Union,* organ of Andrew Johnson, Governor of Tennessee, Phillips was a "flashy, blasphemous incendiary and half-crazed Jacobin, as vile a disunionist as Jefferson Davis or William L. Yancey."[17]

Phillips's attacks on the timid administration[18] became so annoying that George Livermore finally wrote Sumner: "Cannot you have influence with some of Wendell Phillips's friends and have him sent to a madhouse? . . . If he is sane, the prison is too good for him; if crazy, have him gently treated but not suffered to go at large."[19]

According to the New York *Tribune,* probably fifty thousand people heard, and hardly less than five millions read Phillips's lectures and speeches during the winter of 1861-62.[20] No wonder, then, the hysterics and anger of the loyal Lincoln supporters!

Compelling, insistent, fierce, denunciatory, often extreme, Phillips's message was always the same:

> "I want somebody to occupy the Presidential chair who will act without casting his eyes over his shoulder to see how far the people will support him. We want leaders that initiate.
>
> "We shall never succeed until we slough off everything that believes in the past and bring to the front everything that believes there is but one purpose—that is, to save the Union on the basis of Liberty."[21]

CHAPTER FORTY

HOBBY HORSES

Yes, Lincoln was in favor of abolishing slavery but on two
conditions: 1.) that abolition be gradual; 2.) that compensation
be made to the owners. To which he added a condition nearest
to his heart: that the Negroes be colonized.

He never heeded nor respected the cries of the Abolitionists.
He deemed them a small sect of visionaries without influence,
scorned and laughed at by the people. "That Abolition Sneak,"
Mrs. Lincoln once said of Seward.[1] So convinced was he that
the country was not for Abolition that he bided his time. He
could not restore the Union on the old basis because as he said,
"the longer the basket that holds the eggs is being shaken,
the more eggs will break."[2] He would have sacrificed immediate emancipation for the sake of preserving the Union.[3] Garrison and Phillips would have sacrificed the Union for the sake
of immediate emancipation. If told when he entered the Presidency that before his term of office expired, he would be
hailed as the "Great Emancipator," he would have treated the
remark as equal to one of his best jokes.

Indeed, if we take his official action from first to last, it is
a question whether he was not more of an obstructionist than
a promoter of the Anti-Slavery cause.

His democracy was a white man's democracy. It did not con-
tain Negroes. He could not conceive of the two races enjoying
the same political and social privileges. His attitude towards
the slave and the Negro was opportunistic and compromising.

Soon after the inauguration, his Secretary of State sent minister Dayton at Paris a dispatch that he might use with foreign

453

officials in which, speaking of the Rebellion, he said: "The condition of slavery in the several states will remain just the same whether it succeeds or fails. . . ."[4]

On the evening of May 24, 1861, Major General Butler, commandant of Fortress Monroe, was informed that three Negro men had been brought into camp at their own request, having voluntarily surrendered to one of his pickets. The Negroes said they had belonged to Colonel Mallory who was on the point of sending them to North Carolina to work on the relief forts, but they objected to being separated from their families. General Butler reflected a moment. Here was a great question to be solved. Colonel Mallory was a rebel. And if his horses or any ordinary property belonging to him had fallen into Butler's hands, he would not have hesitated about using it in the service of the country. Then why not his slaves? They were regarded as property by their masters, and if so, why not like other property, subject to confiscation?

"The South," said Wendell Phillips, "fought to sustain slavery, and the North fought not to have it hurt." Here was a conundrum. And General Butler solved it by pronouncing the magical word —*contraband*. Yes, these Negroes were according to the rules of war, contraband, and he ordered them set to work.

The news spread among the slave population, and Negroes flocked in from every quarter daily. By the first of August, Butler had not less than nine hundred usefully employed in and around the fort.

A rebel officer, Major Carey, sent Butler a note asking an interview on the high road. It was granted at once and the General accompanied by his staff rode out to meet some of their old Democratic friends. After a polite but rather stately greeting, Major Carey said—

"I wish to know, sir, upon what principles you propose to conduct the war. I am agent for Colonel Mallory, and having learned that three Negroes belonging to him have escaped within your lines, I wish to ask what you mean to do with them."

"I propose to keep them, and make them useful to the government."

"Do you mean, then, to set aside your constitutional obligations?"

"I mean to abide by the decision of Virginia, as expressed in her ordinance of secession passed day before yesterday. I am under no constitutional obligations to a foreign country which Virginia now claims to be."

"But you say we can't secede, and you can't consistently claim them."

"I shall hold them as contraband of war. You were using them against the government; I propose to use them in favor of it. If, however, Colonel Mallory will come in and take the allegiance to the United States, he shall have his Negroes."

At this point the conversation ended.[5]

Butler's order the president did not immediately dispose of, but left it to be treated as a question of the camp and local police in the discretion of each commander. Under this theory some commanders excluded, others admitted fugitives to camp. And the terse formula of General Orders: "We have nothing to do with slaves. We are neither Negro stealers nor Negro catchers" was easily construed by subordinate officers to justify the practise of either course.[6]

Many called Butler the Yankee Danton since he lived by the Frenchman's rule—"l'audace, encore l'audace, toujours l'audace." They wished he were President, "for though he would make millions for himself during the first three months, he would finish the war in three months more."[7]

On August 30, 1861, Fremont, commander of the department of the West, issued a proclamation establishing martial law in Missouri and declaring all property of the enemy confiscated and their slaves freemen. The effect was instantaneous. That proclamation of freedom was echoed from plantation to plantation all along the Mississippi, Tennessee, and Red Rivers. To a certain extent it was an act of insubordination, but it was right in principle and sound in policy. Its adoption by the Federal Government would have saved four years of contention and turmoil in Missouri.

But the first straight blow at the fiend was revoked. The President did not at that time want slavery interfered with and asked Fremont to modify the order—"I think there is great danger that the closing paragraph . . . will alarm our Southern Union friends and turn them against us; perhaps ruin our fair prospect for Kentucky. . . . This letter is written in a spirit of caution." When Fremont remained obdurate and refused to modify the proclamation, Lincoln ordered him to do so.

Garrison commented sharply on the President's course. Then printing the letter of Lincoln between heavy black rules, he declared the President "guilty of a serious dereliction of duty."[8] In a private letter to a friend in Washington, Governor Andrew remarked: "The President has never yet seemed quite sure that we are in a war at all. As to Mr. Seward . . . he has always regarded the case about as a police justice would an assault and battery between two loafers in a pot house—or else he has worn a well contrived mask for the last six months."[9]

Finally Fremont was removed. Mismanagement and fraud in government contracts at St. Louis created a public scandal and the reputation of the government had to be saved. Fremont had showed reckless favoritism to a number of speculators. The corruption, however, did not involve him personally and the situation could have been remedied without his removal.

The story of Fremont's fall was best told by Whittier in four lines:—

"Thy error, Fremont, simply was to act
    A brave man's part without the statesman's tact,
    And, taking counsel but of common sense,
    To strike at cause as well as consequence."[10]

The Pathfinder rose to heroic stature. People considered him a martyr.

"Do you mean to let your servants defy you in that way? foil your wish in that triumphant method?" wrote Phillips to Sumner urging him to speak to Stanton about several officers dismissed from service for having refused to obey orders to return slaves.

"If you do—excuse me—you're a caitiff Senate and that's a milk-livered Administration—and God grant soon the Cromwell that will clear such Essex and Manchesters out. . . . Don't, my dear fellow, throw this aside—put it in your pocket as a reminder and go see Stanton about it." When Colonel Cowdin and Jones returned to their masters slaves found in camp, Phillips earnestly requested Sumner to have them reprimanded from the floor of the Senate. "This much is due to the hope held out that this Government means freedom by this war and through it."[11] (The bare fact remains, though, that Colonels Cowdin and Jones who returned slaves were obeying military orders while the Union officials who refused to return slaves were plainly disobeying them. Phillips's attitude would have worked havoc with army discipline.)

In November the President proposed to Delaware a scheme for gradual emancipation with the assistance of the Federal government. By the census of 1860 that little state was accredited with 1,798 slaves which, valued at $400. each, would be worth $719,000. It was suggested that Delaware take the amount in six per cent bonds of the United States payable in thirty-one annual installments and free all her slaves in thirty-one years or by New Year's Day, 1893, a difficult problem satisfactorily solved. The pro-slavery men in the Delaware legislature indignantly rejected the "Abolition bribe," as they called it, and declared that when they wished to extinguish the institution, they would do it upon their own motion and in their own way.[12]

The President's annual message in December, 1861, again stated the three cardinal points of his theory of emancipation: 1) that it should be voluntary on the part of the loyal slave states. 2) that compensation should be made to the slave owners, and 3) that the freed Negroes be colonized. In addition the President made the suggestion: "It might be well to consider too, whether the free colored people already in the United States could not, so far as individuals may desire, be included in such colonization." Congress received the recommendation with such seriousness as to appropriate one million dollars for compensation and $100,000 to assist in the colonization of the freedmen of the District of Columbia.[13]

"What a wishy washy message from the President!" wrote Garrison to Oliver Johnson. "He has evidently not a drop of anti-slavery blood in his veins."[14]

On March 6, 1862, Lincoln urged the passage of a joint resolution by both Houses to this effect—"Resolved, That the United States ought to cooperate with any state which may adopt gradual abolishment of slavery, giving to such state pecuniary aid. . . ."[15] Thaddeus Stevens called the resolution, "the most diluted milk and water gruel proposition ever made to the American nation."[16] The *Liberator* commented: "The cabinet should help the President to mend his phraseology. . . . The President is culpable for keeping up the old delusion of 'gradualism.' Away with it! President Lincoln, delay not at your peril! 'Execute judgment in the morning—break every yoke—let the oppressed go free.'"[17]

The policy of compensation to owners Emerson condemned—

> "Pay ransom to the owner,
> And fill up the bag to the brim,
> But who is the owner? The slave is owner
> And ever was, pay him!"[18]

Phillips in a lecture before the Emancipation League of Boston welcomed the special message with his "whole heart" as one more sign of promise. "If the President has not entered Canaan," he declared, "he has turned his face Zionward." He interpreted the message as saying in effect—"Gentlemen of the Border States, now is your time. If you want your money, take it, and if, hereafter I should take your slaves without paying, don't say I did not offer to do it."[19]

And he added later:

> "I observe that the cautious, and careful, and amiable, and good natured President, in his message to the Border States, did not speak of the 'abolition' of slavery—that is Garrison's phrase; he talked of 'abolishment.' Well, it is no matter, if he likes that way of spelling it better." (Laughter.)[20]

In March Phillips went to Washington. He took the town by storm. The Vice President left the chair of the Senate to greet him, when introduced on the floor, and Speaker Grow entertained him at a dinner party. He was no longer the despised Abolitionist, the crazy Disunionist, the "nigger stealer," but the distinguished anti-slavery advocate. The ostensible object of his visit was the delivery of two lectures, one literary, the other political. He spoke on successive evenings to immense audiences: "Every cannon fired by Halleck," he remarked, "or heard by McClellan (he never fired one) is a better anti-slavery lecturer than a thousand such as I. The end is sure."[21]

He also had an interview with Lincoln: "I told him that if he started with the experiment of emancipation, and honestly devoted his energies to making it a fact, he would deserve to hold the helm until the experement was finished—that the people would not allow him to quit while it was trying." At the same time he urged Lincoln to dismiss Seward from the Cabinet as an obstructionist.[22] But Phillips was not welcome in Abraham's bosom and Lincoln refused.

From the capital Phillips went westward. He spoke generally to sympathetic audiences. But at Cincinnati, a gang of pro-slavery rioters poured into Pike's Opera House and fusilladed the "damned Abolitionist" with missiles. He commenced by avowing himself a Disunionist. "I have labored nineteen years to take sixteen states out of this Union." Persons in the gallery jumped up and threw rotten eggs and stones at him, some of them hitting him. One jagged flint came near to cracking his skull. It grazed his head and came crashing down among the footlights like a cannon shot. The eggs were accompanied with a series of yells: "Down with the traitor." "Egg the nigger Phillips." Phillips stood calm and collected, without moving a muscle. When the tumult subsided, he resumed his discourse. He proceeded until something objectionable was again said, and again eggs were thrown at him. He persevered and a third time was stoned and egged. The mob now moved downstairs crying —"Put him out," "Tar and feather him," "Lynch the traitor," (We omit the profanity.) They proceeded down the aisle towards the stage and were met by Phillips's friends. A fight en-

sued—some ladies screaming and fainting, others scrambling un-
gracefully over benchtops; the men jumping on chairs and shouting. During the melee someone turned off the gas and Phillips
was conducted in darkness off the stage to an exit on the back
street.[23]

"I really imagined I was back in Boston," commented the
orator with a laugh. "The Cincinnati Opera House suggested
Tremont Temple, and the rats of the West closely resembled
those of the East. These and those alike nibble and gnaw—and
run."[24] Yet to Sumner he wrote: "You see Cincinnati mobbed
and pelted with eggs me whom Washington cheered. So it
goes."[25]

An attempt to reproduce in Chicago the Cincinnati outrage
failed utterly. "You have no idea how the disturbance has
stirred the West," asked Phillips. "I draw immense houses, and
could stay here two months, talking every night, in large towns,
to crowds."[26]

Speaking of the state of mind of Lincoln and his cabinet,
he said: "I view them as milestones, showing how far the great
nation's opinion has travelled."[27]

On Monday, April 14, 1862, Congress passed a bill abolishing
slavery in the District of Columbia. Lincoln signed it but not
with full approval. At night Senator O. H. Browning went to
see him to lay before him the bill. Lincoln said he would sign
the bill though he regretted it had been passed in its present
form—that it should have been for gradual emancipation. He
further told Browning that he would not sign before Wednesday
as he wished to give old Governor Wickliffe of Kentucky time
to send two old slaves back to Kentucky before the bill became
law.

It was said: "Abraham Lincoln hopes that he has God on his
side but thinks he must have Kentucky."[28]

The poet Whittier rejoiced over the emancipation of slaves
in the District of Columbia, rejoiced even though it came by a
method other than that which he had hoped for—

"Not as we hoped; but what are we?
Above our broken dreams and plans

> God lays, with wiser hand than man's
> The corner stones of liberty.
>
> I cavil not with Him; the voice
> That freedom's blessed gospel tells
> Is sweet to me as silver bells,
> Rejoicing! yea, I will rejoice.[29]

Over the battlefields of old Virginia floated the black man's song—

> "Brudder, God is takin' vengeance
> For de darkeys' wrong!
> Shout, shout for God and Freedom!
> Sing, darkies, sing!
> Ole Massa Cotton's dead foreber;
> Young Massa Corn am King!
> *Jubilate* God and Freedom,
> Sing, Americans, sing!
> Tyrant Cotton's dead foreber,
> Honest Corn is King.[30]

Less than a month after the passage of the District of Columbia Bill, General David Hunter, commanding the Department of the South, issued an order proclaiming: "Slavery and martial law in a free country being altogether incompatible, the slaves in Georgia, Florida, and South Carolina are therefore declared forever free."

The first knowledge of Hunter's order came to Lincoln through the newspapers one week earlier. Chase urged him to let the order stand. "No commanding general shall do such a thing upon my responsibility without consulting me," the President replied. Three days later, May 19, before he had official notice, Lincoln published a message declaring Hunter's order unauthorized and null and void.[31]

"Canst thou draw out Leviathan with a hook?" Garrison asked.[32] And Phillips remarked: "The President is still disposed to treat the dragon of slavery as though it was only a wayward colt. . . . The President is a very slow man; an honest man, but a slow moving machine. (Laughter.) I think if we can nudge him a little, it will be of great advantage. (Merriment.)"³³

But at a Republican meeting in Boston called to express disgust at the conduct of the government, Phillips in a bitter mood said: "President Lincoln, with senile lick-spittle haste runs before he is bidden to revoke the Hunter proclamation. The President and the Cabinet are treasonable. The President and the Secretary of War should be impeached."

In countermanding Hunter's order, Lincoln made another futile and unrealistic overture to the Border States, renewing his plea for gradual and compensated emancipation—a plea humane but unrealistic because founded on wishful thinking.

"I do not argue—I beseech you to make arguments for yourselves. You cannot, if you would, be blind to the signs of the times. I beg of you a calm and enlarged consideration of them, ranging, if it may be, far above personal and partizan politics. This proposal makes common cause for a common object, casting no reproaches upon any. It acts not the Pharisee. The change it contemplates would come gently as the dews of heaven, not rending or wrecking anything. Will you not embrace it?"³⁴

Lincoln pulled his ardent generals back behind him. Then like an auctioneer he cried to the Davis cabinet, "Going, going," but before he said, "Gone!" he called for three hundred thousand men in response to the plea of nearly all the governors of the loyal states.

Phillips denounced the President's habitual caution.

"Mr. Lincoln is not a leader. . . . His theory of Democracy is that he is the servant of the people, not the leader. Like an Indian trapper on the prairie, his keen ear listens to know what twenty million of people want him to do.

"We are paying today the enormous penalty of millions of dollars of lives for that bad system of government, miscalled 'democracy,' which necessarily gives us second-rate, noncommittal men for Presidents and Senators. We pay dear today for having as President a man so cautious as to be timid—and so ignorant as to fear the little near danger more than the danger farther off."[35]

Again Phillips bitterly and intemperately remarked—but so many other anti-slavery advocates at the time deeply felt as he did: "As long as you keep the present turtle at the head of affairs, you make a pit with one hand and fill it with the other. I know Mr. Lincoln. He is a first rate, second rate man —that is all of him. He is a mere convenience and is waiting like any other broomstick to be used." (Caution and moderation to Abolition eyes when principles of freedom were involved partook of damning evil. Dr. John Jebb, member of the Society for Constitutional Reform in England, was impatient of men who paraded their moderation. "Don't tell me of a moderate man," he used to say to Cartwright; "he is always a rascal.")

Phillips because of his criticism ran into a storm of abuse. "Wendell Phillips Spouting Foul Treason," the New York *Herald* shouted to its readers. "The Coryphaeus of the Abolition faction —the foul-mouthed traitor—delivered a speech which in treason and sedition has outstripped anything he has yet uttered."[36] "Arrest him. He is a nuisance, a pest, and should be abated," yelled the Boston *Post.* The New York *Tribune*, basing an attack on the garbled extracts and lying versions of the New York papers misrepresented Phillips as discouraging enlistments.[37] Phillips replied heatedly: Yes, he believed in the Union. But Government and the Union were one thing; this Administration was quite another. Whether the Administration would ever pilot the nation through its troubles, he had serious doubts; that it never would unless it changed its policy, he was quite certain. Where, then, was his place under a Republican government which only reflected and executed public opinion? Where, then, was his post, especially under an Administration that avowedly sat waiting, begging to be told what to do?

"I must educate, arouse, and mature a public opinion which shall compel the Administration to adopt and support it in pursuing the policy I can aid. This I do by frankly and candidly criticising its present policy, civil and military. . . . Such criticism is always every thinking man's duty. War excuses no man from his duty. . . . My criticism is not, like that of the traitor presses, meant to paralyze the administration, but to goad it to more activity and vigor."[38]

2.

Lincoln when eulogizing the dead Henry Clay already seemed to be in love with the idea of restoring the poor African to that clime from which he had been rudely snatched by the rapacious white man. "The enterprise is a difficult one," he said, "but where there is a will there is a way, and what colonization needs most is a hearty will. . . . The children of Israel, to such numbers as to include four hundred thousand fighting men went out of Egyptian bondage in a body."[39]

On August 14, 1862, he called a deputation of Washington Negroes to him. He made them a long speech telling them that he had found what seemed to be a suitable location for a colony in Central America and appealing to them to supply the colonists.

"Your race is suffering, in my judgment, the greatest wrong inflicted on any people. But even when you cease to be slaves, you are yet far removed from being placed on an equality with the white race. . . . I do not propose to discuss this, but to present it as a fact with which we have to deal. I cannot alter it if I would. . . . See our present condition—the country engaged in war—our white men cutting one another's throats . . . and then consider what we know to be the truth. But for your race among us there could not be war, although many men engaged on either side do not care for you one way or the other. . . . It is better for us both, therefore, to be separated.

"The practical thing I want to ascertain is, whether I can get a number of able-bodied men, with their wives and children, who are willing to go when I present evidence of encouragement and protection. Could I get a hundred tolerably intelligent men, with their wives and children, and able to 'cut their own fodder,' so to speak? Can I have fifty? If I could find twenty-five able-bodied men, with a mixture

of women and children,—good things in the family relation,
I think,—I could make a successful commencement. I want
you to let me know whether this can be done or not. This
is the practical part of my wish to see you."[40]

The Negroes, not anxious for exile, diplomatically said they
would think the matter over. Garrison heaped scorn upon it as
"puerile, absurd, illogical, impertinent, untimely." In the end it
was discovered that Central America did not want the Negroes
and that the Negroes did not want Central America.

Nevertheless Lincoln did not give up his pet idea. At his
instance Congress appropriated several large sums of money for
colonizing experiments. One sharper by the name of Bernard
Koch got them to buy from him an island in the West Indies
called Ile à Vache, which he represented as an earthly paradise.
Several hundred Negroes were collected, the poor refugees flock-
ing on board ship, shouting hallelujahs and falling on their knees
in thanksgiving for the promised blessings in store for them.
The Negroes, however, were not well cared for on the voyage,
small pox broke out, and about thirty died. The rest were dumped
upon the unknown island during the rainy season. They found
no houses and but little timber with which to construct them.
Agent Koch brought no supplies, no seeds, and no implements,
but being charged with the discipline of the colony, brought
handcuffs, leg chains, and stocks. He proved to be despotic
and incompetent. The situation was deplorable, the inhabitants
poisoned by malaria, stung by venomous insects and reptiles,
having scarcely anything to eat, and dying like cattle with the
murrain. In the end Lincoln reluctantly abandoned his second
serious attempt at colonizing the blacks: he requested Stanton
to send a ship to bring the Cow Island survivors back to the
District of Columbia. To Lincoln the failure of this enterprise
was a bitter disappointment.[41]

But he kept on with his experiments—even going so far as to
discuss with a Mr. Bradley, a Vermont contractor, the prospect
of removing the whole colored population to Texas, there to
establish a republic of its own.[42] Toward the end of the war,
he called in General Butler and discussed with him a plan for

exporting Negro soldiers to Liberia or South America or Demerara. "General Butler," he said, "I am troubled about the Negroes. We have got some one hundred and odd thousand Negroes who have been trained in arms. When peace shall come, I fear lest these colored men shall organize themselves in the South into guerilla parties, and we shall have down there a warfare between the whites and the Negroes. Would it not be possible to export them to some place, say Liberia, or South America and organize them into communities to support themselves?"

General Butler recommended that the black soldiers when war ended should be sent to Panama under his command to dig an isthmian ship canal. "There is meat in that, General Butler, there is meat in that," remarked the President. "Go and see Seward." But unforseen events occurred.[43]

On the nineteenth of August, 1862, Horace Greeley in the New York *Tribune* published an open letter to the President entitled "The Prayer of Twenty Millions," calling upon the President for "a frank, declared, unqualified, ungrudging execution of the laws of the land, more especially of the Confiscation Act," denouncing him for his "mistaken deference to rebel slavery," for bowing to the influence of certain fossil politicians hailing from the Border States," and declaring "that all attempts to put down the Rebellion and at the same time uphold its inciting cause, are preposterous and futile—that the Rebellion if crushed out tomorrow would be revived within a year if slavery were left in full vigor and that every hour of deference to slavery is an hour of added and deepened peril to the Union."[44]

Unexpectedly to Greeley, President Lincoln three days later replied to "the Prayer of Twenty Millions" by telegraph—an unusual proceeding then for an Executive to reply to the criticism of a purely private citizen.

"My paramount object in this struggle is to save the Union, and is not either to save or to destroy slavery.
If I could save the Union without freeing any slave, I would do it; and if I could save it by freeing all the slaves, I would do it; and if I could save it by freeing some and leaving others alone, I would also do that.

What I do about slavery and the colored race, I do because I believe it helps to save the Union; and what I forbear, I forbear because I do not believe it would help to
save the Union.

I shall do less whenever I shall believe what I am doing
hurts the cause, and I shall do more whenever I shall believe
doing more will help the cause."[45]

Greeley was dissatisfied with Lincoln's explanation and as the
Tribune was still teeming with complaints and criticisms of the
administration, Lincoln requested Greeley to come to Washington. The editor of the *Tribune* came. Lincoln said: "You complain of me. What have I done, or omitted to do, which has
provoked the hostility of the *Tribune?*" Greeley replied, "You
should issue a proclamation abolishing slavery." Lincoln answered: "Suppose I do that. There are now twenty-thousand of
our muskets on the shoulders of Kentuckians who are bravely
fighting our battles. Every one of them will be thrown down
or carried over to the rebels." The reply was: "Let them do it.
The cause of the Union will be stronger if Kentucky should secede with the rest than it is now." Lincoln answered: "Oh, I
can't think that."[46]

To some clergymen from Chicago who told him on September
13 that it was God's will that he adopt a policy of emancipation,
Lincoln replied, "I hope it will not be irreverent for me to say
that, if it is probable that God would reveal His will to others
on a point so connected with my duty, it might be supposed He
would reveal it directly to me. Is it not odd that the only
channel He could send it by was the roundabout route by that
awfully wicked city of Chicago."[47]

But as Lincoln was feeling his way carefully towards general
emancipation, he added more seriously:

"What good would a proclamation of emancipation from
me do, especially as we are now situated? I do not want to
issue a document that the whole world will see must necessarily be inoperative, like the Pope's bull against the comet.
Would my word free the slaves, when I cannot even enforce
the Constitution in the rebel States? . . ."[48]

This cautious attitude towards emancipation angered Phillips. And the latter's strident urgency was a logical and stern result: it may be deplored, but it can always be extenuated. As Lincoln himself stated in his reply to Greeley's "Prayer of Twenty Millions," his paramount object in the struggle was to save the Union and not either to save or destroy slavery. To an ardent Abolitionist like Phillips it seemed that Lincoln's letter came perilously close to the position of Douglas whom Lincoln denounced for saying that he didn't care whether slavery was voted up or down. Emancipation to Lincoln, a Westerner, was not an immediate right but a practical war measure to be decided on according to the advantages or disadvantages it might offer to the suppression of the rebellion. Granted that the Union was a precious boon to be preserved, that freedom must wait on political wisdom and necessity, one must grant, too, that Lincoln's attitude towards the slave was essentially opportunistic and compromising.[49] Political wisdom? Political necessity? Such dull weapons found no scabbard in Phillips's armory of God. Instead freedom came first, freedom always, freedom as an immediate and moral necessity, though the superstructure of revered Union fall.

But in due time even political necessity, which had kept the gates of mercy shut, now swung them open on colored mankind.

CHAPTER FORTY-ONE

"GLORY! HALLELUJAH!"

Wednesday, the seventeenth of September, 1862, was a day when the cannon roared for fourteen hours at Antietam and thousands upon thousands went down to death. By the end of the week, it was known that the Confederate Army was in retreat. On Monday Lincoln summoned his cabinet.

As the members came in, they found the President deep in a humorous book. When they had taken their seats, and after some general talk, the President turned to the members and said, "Gentlemen, did you ever read anything from Artemus Ward? Let me read you a chapter that is very funny." He then proceeded to read the "High-Handed Outrage at Uticy." He seemed to enjoy it very much, moving his rugged hands up and down his legs with an habitual motion, and having finished, laughed heartily. The members of his cabinet except Stanton laughed with him. Laying the book aside, he assumed a graver tone. "Gentlemen, I have got you together to hear what I have written down. I do not wish your advice about the main matter for that I have determined for myself. This, I say, without intending anything but respect for any one of you. But I already know the views of each on this question." He then began reading the Emancipation Proclamation. . . .[1]

There were limitations to the Day of Jubilee. The Proclamation, a politic and conciliatory measure, was not intended to cover all the slaveholding territory. Both Missouri and Maryland were left out of the proclamation, as were Tennessee, Kentucky, and Delaware, and parts of Virginia, Louisiana, and the Carolinas, in which excepted parts slavery was to be left "pre-

cisely as if the proclamation were not issued." It reached only
such sections as were in rebellion. Thus slavery continued legal
in almost half of all the slave states and prevailed in all the
others, despite the proclamation.

Freedom under it was decreed not as a boon but as a penalty.
No recognition of the principles of justice or humanity surrounded the act with a halo of glory. The Proclamation was
issued in two parts separated by one hundred days. The first
part gave the Rebels warning that the second would follow on
January 1, 1863, if in the meanwhile they did not give up their
rebellion. All they had to do to save slavery was to cease from
their treasonable practices and return to the Union.

"The Proclamation of Emancipation by the President is out,"
Governor Andrew wrote to Albert Browne. "It is a poor document
but a mighty act, slow, somewhat halting, wrong in its delay
till January, but grand and sublime after all. 'Prophets and
Kings have waited for this day, but died without the sight.' "[2]

"It is a step in the right direction," said Garrison. "A step!"
exclaimed Phillips, "it's a stride."[3] But later he added—"It does
not annihilate the system. In the Gospel the devils came back
to the swept and garnished chambers. Unless free institutions
are put in the South, the old order will return in some form.
Confiscate the lands and colonize them with Northern men and
schools, ploughshares and seeds. Send a new government there.
Organize the South anew."[4]

The South answered with a hiss of scorn. Beauregard hoped
that all Abolition prisoners taken after the first of January would
be garrotted. The Richmond *Enquirer* recalled the horrors of
Nat Turner's insurrection in 1831 and said this was the kind
of work Lincoln desired. General Butler was, by common consent,
called the Beast, but "bad as he is, he is a saint compared with
the Master. What shall we call him? Coward, assassin, savage,
murderer of women and babies? or shall we consider him Lincoln
the Fiend?" The Proclamation, added the *Enquirer*, was not
worth the paper it was written on.[5]

In Richmond "An Address to the Christians throughout the
World" was issued and signed by ninety-six clergymen of all
denominations. Among other things it said: "The recent Procla-

mation . . . is, in our judgment, a suitable occasion for solemn protest on the part of the people of God throughout the world."

As a practical measure the Proclamation was more than a bull against the comet. The Negroes hailed it as their liberation from generations of bondage and flocked to the armies in embarrassing numbers. As a way of weakening the enemy, slaves were encouraged to come within the Union lines. Thousands were used as soldiers, many were put to labor for wages, either for the government or for loyal employers; the women and children and infirm became wards of the nation. Camps for freed Negroes were established. In general throughout the Confederacy, the slaves remained quiet and loyal to their Southern masters, but it was also true that where the Federal armies advanced, thousands came within Union control.

The moral influence of the Proclamation was great. It helped hasten the movement that had by that time become practically irresistible. Its political results were far more marked and important. It prevented an open rupture with the Abolitionists. The latter interpreted the President's Proclamation as a concession and abandonment of his previous policy, which it was more in appearance than in actuality. At all events it was splendid politics. The somewhat theatrical manner in which it was worked up and promulgated in installments, thus arousing in advance widespread interest and curiosity, showed no little strategic ability.

To Governor Curtin of Pennsylvania, Lincoln said—"You see, Curtin, I was brought to the conclusion that there was no dodging this Negro question any longer. We had reached the point where it seemed that we must avail ourselves of this element or in all probability go under,"[6]—a significant remark to be kept in mind when one judges extremists like ·Phillips and the Abolitionists.

When Secretary Seward brought the President the official copy of the Proclamation for his signature, he had been shaking hands with callers all morning and his right arm was almost paralyzed. He was fearful lest it affect the steadiness of his signature. "If my name ever goes into history," he said to the Secretary, "it will be for this act, and my whole soul is in it. If my hand trembles when I sign the Proclamation, all who

examine the document hereafter will say, 'he hesitated.'" With
that he took pen in hand and very painstakingly wrote "Abraham
Lincoln." It stood out strong and it satisfied him. "That will do,"
he commented.

He reinspected it later. He said to a friend on New Year's
Eve: "The signature looks a little tremulous, for my hand was
tired, but my resolution was firm. I told them in September, if
they did not return to their allegiance and cease murdering our
soldiers, I would strike at the pillar of their strength. And now
the promise shall be kept, and not one word of it will I ever
recall."[7]

In his second annual message two months after the Emancipation Proclamation, Lincoln proposed to Congress the submission
of a constitutional amendment that would work universal liberation. There were conditions, however. One was that the slaves
should be paid for by the government; another that the masters
might retain their uncompensated services until January 1, 1900
—that is, for a period of thirty-seven years—unless they were
sooner emancipated by the grave as most of them would be.

The fantastic proposition was not claimed by him for the
bondman's benefit. He urged it as a measure of public economy:
it would shorten the war, perpetuate peace, insure the increase
of wealth and population (103,200,000 by 1900; 251,680,000
by 1930 he predicted), and lessen the expenditure of money and
blood. And he pointed out "the great advantage of a policy by
which we shall not have to pay until we number 100,000,000
what by a different policy we would have to pay now, when we
number but 31,000,000."[8]

The public did not take to the President's plan. They no more
favored the buying of men by the government than by anybody
else. They held that if the master had no right to the person of
a bondman he had no right to the payment for him. And as for
the arrangement that might prolong slaveholding for thirty-
seven years, they saw in it not only an injustice to the Negroes
but a possible plan for sidetracking a genuine freedom movement. And so Lincoln's "tinkering off" policy, as he called it,
failed.

On the evening of January 1, 1863, an immense throng gathered in Tremont Temple, Boston, to await the first flash of the electric wires announcing the final Emancipation Proclamation. Eight, nine, ten o'clock came and went and still no word. A shadow was falling on the expectant crowd which the confident utterances of the speakers sought in vain to dispel. Then suddenly a man with hasty step advanced through the crowd and with face illumined with the news he bore, exclaimed—"It is coming! It is on the wires!" A great shout shook the building and a colored preacher led all voices in the anthem—

"Sound the loud timbrel
    O'er Egypt's dark sea,
Jehovah hath triumphed,
    His people are free."[9]

Four hundred miles away, in the capital of the nation, the hands of the clock stole on to midnight. Thousands of Negroes, who had gathered for the occasion, kneeled and began to sing—

"Oh, go down Moses,
    Way down to Egypt's land;
Tell King Pharaoh
    To let my people go.
Oh, Pharaoh said he would not cross—
    'Let my people go!'
But Pharaoh and his hosts were lost—
    'Let my people go.'"

The song ceased. The church bell slowly tolled the hour. There was silence for a moment, and then shouts—"Glory! hallelujah! we are free! we are free!"

"O dark, sad millions, patiently dumb,
Waiting for God, your hour at last has come,
    And freedom's song
Breaks the long silence of your night of wrong."[10]

"Our rejoicing today is," said Phillips to an audience at Music Hall, Boston, "that at last the nation unsheathes its sword, and announces its determined purpose to be a nation. . . ."

The Proclamation, he added, was no sidelong appeal to a nuisance, a burden, an intrusive race to take itself away from the center of the conflict. No, it was the act of a great nation, linking its cause to the throne of the Almighty, proclaiming Liberty as an act of Justice, and abolishing a system found to be inconsistent with the perpetuity of the Republic.

"But let me open for you the huts of three million of slaves, and what is that Proclamation there? It is the sunlight scattering the despair of centuries. . . . It is a word that makes the prayers of the poor and the victim the cornerstone of the Republic. Other nations since Greece have built their nationality on a Thermopylae or a great name—a victory or a knightly family. Our cornerstone, thank God, is the blessings of the poor."[11]

2.

On Sunday evening, January 25, 1863, a delegation of Boston citizens, including Wendell Phillips, Dr. S. G. Howe, George L. Stearns, and others, was ushered into the President's business room accompanied by Senator Wilson of Massachusetts. They called to protest against military governor Stanley who had been appointed by the President for as much of North Carolina as the Union forces occupied. Stanley was denouncing the Abolitionists as strenuously as if the President's proclamation had been a pro-slavery document. This and similar facts determined the anti-slavery people in Boston to send a delegation to the President.

The President entered the room laughing and said that in the morning one of his children told him the cat had had kittens, and as he was entering, another told him that the dog had had pups, so the White House was in a prolific state. His hilarity disturbed the delegation, but it was pathetic to see the change in the President's face when he resumed his burden. Senator Wilson began introducing the visitors severally, but the President said he knew perfectly who they were and requested them to be seated.

The conversation was begun by Wendell Phillips who with characteristic courtesy expressed joy at the Proclamation and asked the President how it seemed to be working. The President said he had not expected much from it at first, and so far had not been disappointed. He hoped something would come of it after a while. "My own impression, Mr. Phillips," said the President, "is that the masses of the country generally are only dissatisfied at our lack of military successes. Defeat and failure in the field make everything seem wrong." His face clouded and the next words were bitter: "Most of us here present have been long working in minorities and may have got into a habit of being dissatisfied." Several of the delegation protesting, the President said, "At any rate, it has been very rare that an opportunity of 'running' this administration has been lost." To this Phillips answered in his sweetest voice: "If we see this administration earnestly working to free the country from slavery and its rebellion, we will show you how we can run it into another four years of power."

The President's good humor was restored and he said, "Oh, Mr. Phillips, I have ceased to have any personal feeling or expectation in that matter,—I do not say I never had any—so abused and borne upon have I been." "Nevertheless what I have said is true," replied Phillips who then went on to submit the complaint against military governor Stanley. The President said Stanley could stand the Emancipation Proclamation. "Stand it!" exclaimed one of the delegation. "Might the nation not expect in such a place a man who can not merely stand its President's policy but rejoice in it?" This vexed the President a little and he said, "Well, gentlemen, I have got the responsibility of this thing and must keep it." "Yes, Mr. President," interposed Phillips, "but you must be patient with us, for if the ship goes down, it doesn't carry down you alone. We are all in it."

"Well, gentlemen," said the President, bowing pleasantly to Phillips, "whom would you put in Stanley's place?" Someone suggested Fremont. "I have great respect for General Fremont and

his abilities," said the President slowly, "but the fact is that the
pioneer of any movement is not generally the best man to
carry that movement to a successful issue. It was so in old times
—wasn't it?" he continued with a smile. "Moses began the
emancipation of the Jews but didn't take Israel to the Promised
Land after all. He had to make way for Joshua to complete the
work. It looks as if the first reformer of a thing has to meet
such a hard opposition and gets so battered and bespattered,
that afterwards, when people find they have to accept this reform, they will accept it more easily from another man."

The humor and philosophy of the remark was appreciated by
the delegation. The discussion continued.

The President said he did not believe his administration would
have been supported by the country in a policy of emancipation
at an earlier stage of the war. He reminded the delegation that
he had been elected by a minority of the people. "All I can
say now is that I believe the Proclamation has knocked the
bottom out of slavery though at no time have I expected any
sudden results from it. . . ."

There were a few moments of silence and the delegation rose.
Phillips expressed their thanks for the kindly reception accorded
them. The President bowed graciously at this and said he was
happy to have met the gentlemen known to him by their distinguished selves, and was glad to listen to their views, adding,
"I must bear this load which the country has entrusted to me
as well as I can, and do my best." He then shook hands with
each of the delegation.[12]

3.

The American Anti-Slavery Society through its British agents
started a campaign to enlighten England on American affairs.
An Emancipation Society was organized in London in the interest of the Union with George Thompson as its animating
spirit. Among its members were John Stuart Mill, John Bright,
Richard Cobden, Goldwin Smith, Justin McCarthy, Thomas
Hughes, Professor Cairnes, Herbert Spencer, Newman Hall—
the brainiest leaders of British thought and life. Every one of

these worked day and night in behalf of the Union. They fortified the sentiment of the cotton spinners, operatives, and small
tradesmen of England against slavery.

The spinners of Lancashire were being starved to death by
the blockade of our Southern ports. Nearly one million people
in the manufacturing districts were wholly dependent upon
charity. *Punch* put the question squarely—

> The South enslaves those fellow men
> Whom we all love so dearly:
> The North keeps commerce bound again,
> Which touches us more nearly.
> Thus a divided duty we
> Perceive in this hard matter:
> Free trade or sable brother free?
> O, won't we choose the latter?[13]

At first the factory owners were really glad of an excuse to
close down for some months because they were overstocked
with manufactured goods. But by 1863 the lack of raw cotton
began to be a serious matter, and pressure was brought upon
the ministry by the capitalists to intervene.

The English masses, however, took a different course. They
listened not to Palmerston, Russell, or Gladstone, but to John
Bright and Richard Cobden. They felt the Union was fighting
slavery (even while the Unionists denied it loudly) and therefore gave the North heroic support. On one occasion Southern
sympathizers thought it a good time to hold a meeting in Roch-
dale at which a lecture was delivered showing the British
workers that their interests lay with the Confederacy. They
listened and when the orator finished, they passed resolutions
censuring him for making such a speech.[14]

The attitude of the Lancashire spinners was solely altruistic.
They had nothing to gain and everything to lose, but they could
not think of selfish interests when Bright said as he did to
cheers—

"The leaders of this revolt propose this monstrous thing—
that over a territory forty times as large as England the

blight and curse of slavery shall be forever perpetuated. I cannot believe, for my part, that such a state will befall that fair land, stricken, though it now is, with the ravages of war. I cannot believe that civilization, in its journey with the sun, will sink into endless night to gratify the ambition of the leaders of this revolt who

'Wade through slaughter to a throne,
And shut the gates of mercy on mankind.' "[15]

Carlyle, whose early books had no sale in England, and who wrote Emerson that he had received the first money to keep him from starvation from Boston and New York, "when not a penny had been realized in England," had no sympathy with liberty and the North. Carlyle called the war "a smoky chimney that had taken fire. No war ever waged in my time was to me more profoundly foolish looking. . . . Neutral I am to a degree." And he again remarked—"The South says to the nagur, 'God bless you! and be a slave,' and the North says, 'God damn you and be free.' "[16]

The aristocracy of England and the upper middle class were in the main sympathetic to the South. Four-fifths of the House of Lords were "no well wishers of anything American," and most of the House of Commons voted in sympathy with the South.[17] When Lincoln washed his hands of slavery, the moral issue evaporated in the eyes of foreign observers. The war became like any other war—a mere effort to settle political and economic questions by brute force.[18] "The Yankees are, after all, only fighting for the tariff and hurt vanity," declared some. And it seemed immoral that thirteen millions should hold ten millions in subjection against their will.

The expansion of America also was watched with alarm and presaged the rise of a dangerous state. Both parties entertained a suspicion that the United States, once she had beaten the South, might turn on Canada.[19] Then again the democratic influence of the United States on European institutions would be greatly lessened if the United States broke into two parts. But despite Southern sympathizers, the government was honestly endeavoring to maintain a policy of strict neutrality. There were strong economic forces bidding her to do so.

India became the chief source of British supply of cotton. While the cotton imports from the South declined from 2,580,700 bales in 1860 to 72,000 bales in 1862, the imports from the other countries rose from 785,000 bales in 1860 to 2,755,000 bales in 1865. During the cotton famine, the farmers of India received more money for a year's crop than they had received in all their lives before. They squandered it buying such absurd and useless things as silver ploughshares and silver tires for their cart wheels.

Most of the cotton obtained was the kind called surat, which is coarse and hard to spin. The Lancashire operatives disliked this cotton very much and in their prayer meetings, they were often heard to say—"Oh, Lord! send us more cotton, but preserve us from surat."[20]

Northern wheat, however, was the decisive factor counterbalancing the influence of cotton in keeping the British government from recognizing the Confederacy. In 1861-62 there was one of the worst crop failures in the history of the country, and England was confronted with a huge deficit in its wheat supply. To provide the usual amount of food for the nation, it required the importation of wheat. But the European harvests were exceedingly poor, and the other countries could not supply Great Britain in her hour of need. The North alone could supply the deficiency.[21]

The Lancashire operatives suffered but made no sign and stood by the Union. The Emancipation Society labored to arouse and direct the mass of public opinion. George Thompson urged Phillips to go to England and cooperate with the Abolition leaders. Phillips wanted to go but was held at home by his wife's illness. Subsequently Henry Ward Beecher, abroad for a vacation, found what he sought in endless battles with hostile audiences. Wherever he appeared and spoke, he aroused, intensified, unified, and made effective the great force of English popular feeling.[22]

When the Emancipation Proclamation reached England, the reception there was only slightly less enthusiastic than here. The Proclamation, followed as it was by the smashing victories of

Grant and Meade, dealt the forces of intervention a stunning and decisive blow.

4.

The government was loath to arm the Negroes. It distrusted them and feared to excite antagonism by such a step. When a brigadier of General Butler's army announced his purpose to organize Negro troops, Lincoln disapproved. "What is all this itching to get niggers into our lines?" he said once.[23]

Some Senators called upon the President urging him to take the step. "Gentlemen," he said, "I have put thousands of muskets into the hands of loyal citizens of Tennessee, Kentucky, and Western Northern Carolina. They have said they could defend themselves if they had guns. I have given them the guns. Now these men do not believe in mustering in the Negro. If I do it, these thousands of muskets will be turned against us. We should lose more than we should gain."

There was further urging. "Gentlemen, I can't do it. I can't see it as you do. You may be right and I may be wrong, but I'll tell you what I can do; I can resign in favor of Mr. Hamlin. Perhaps Mr. Hamlin could do it."

The Senators were amazed. They hastened to assure the President they could not consider such a step on his part. He must do what he thought right. In any event he must not resign.[24]

The Confederates furiously denounced the arming of Negroes. In the spring of 1862 General David Hunter began to organize South Carolina regiments of colored infantry. The Savannah *Republican* reviled Hunter as a "cold blooded Abolition miscreant engaged in executing the bloody and savage behests of the imperial gorilla who, from his throne of human bones in Washington, rules, reigns, and riots over the destinies of the brutish and degraded North." Hunter soon came to be known as "Black" David Hunter and was compelled to assign his own nephew to the new contingent.[25]

Butler infused his wonted energy into a similar attempt. Early in September, 1862, he reported with his usual biting sarcasm: "I shall also have within ten days a regiment, one thousand strong, of native guards (colored), the darkest of whom will be about the complexion of the late Mr. Webster."[26]

No one could be found to command the Negroes after they were accoutred. Officers in command of black troops were branded as outlaws. If captured, they were to be treated, not as prisoners of war, but as common felons to be hanged to trees and telegraph poles. The Confederate Secretary of War suggested that they "be dealt with redhanded on the field of war or immediately after."[27]

To be killed by a Negro was to Southern cavaliers the most opprobrious of deaths. The fire of the enemy was likely to be concentrated upon the black battalions, and Negroes taken on the field suffered indignities and cruelties. In some instances, as at Fort Pillow, they were killed in cold blood.

With the rebel yell of "No Quarter," the enemy assaulted the exhausted garrison and carried the fort. As rapidly as the men surrendered, they were murdered. The Negroes ran down hill to the river, but the rebels kept shooting them as they were running. Several were shot after they were wounded. As they were crawling around, a rebel would step out and blow their brains out. Some of the colored troops jumped in the river, but were shot as fast as they were seen. Others on the bank were shot, and their bodies kicked into the water, many of them still living but unable to save themselves from drowning. The Mississippi was red with blood for thirty yards. Women and children were deliberately shot down, beaten, and hacked with sabres. Some of the rebels stood on top of the hill and called to the Union soldiers to come up to them, and as they approached, shot them down in cold blood; if their guns or pistols missed fire, forcing them to stand there until they were again prepared to fire. All around were heard the cries of "No Quarter! No Quarter! Kill the damned niggers! Shoot them down!" The huts and tents in which the wounded sought shelter were set on fire. The carnival of murder continued until dark.[28]

On July 17, 1862, a bill authorizing the employment of Negroes as soldiers, and conferring freedom on all who should render military service became law. The movement, slow at first, gained headway steadily. Finally Lincoln reversed himself and gave earnest encouragement to the proposal. In May, 1863, a special bureau was established to supervise the recruitment of colored troops. In December, 50,000 Negroes were under arms, and when the war closed nearly 186,097, employed in different branches of the service, were in Federal uniform. After the process had been on trial for a year, Lincoln remarked that there was apparently "no loss by it in our foreign relations, none in our home popular sentiment, none in our white military force— no loss by it anyhow or anywhere."

In fact Negro military labor was indispensable to the Union armies. Negroes built most of the fortifications and earthworks for General Grant in front of Vicksburg, and the general, testifying before a Congressional Committee on the siege of Petersburg, remarked, "General Burnside wanted to put his colored troops in front. I believe if he had done so, it would have been a success." Black men were repeatedly and deliberately used as shock troops where there was little or no hope of success. They took part in 198 battles and skirmishes, and their losses during the war numbered 36,847. The mortality rate among Negro colored troops was 35% greater than among other troops, notwithstanding the fact that the former were not enrolled until some eighteen months after the fighting began. The stereotype of the Negro as a passive onlooker during the Civil War is a damning fiction that will not bear the light of investigation.[29]

To the demand that the Negro regiments be disbanded (which was incorporated in the Democratic platform of 1864), Lincoln responded: "You say you will not fight to free Negroes. Some of them seem willing to fight for you." Should these soldiers be returned to slavery, he remarked with some force, "I should deserve to be damned in time and eternity."[30] And he was induced to issue an order commanding "that for every soldier of the United States killed in violation of the laws of war, a rebel soldier shall be executed."[31]

Singularly enough, even Jefferson Davis at last became docile to the stern teachings of events. In a message of November, 1864, he recommended the employment of 40,000 slaves in the Confederate army. Judah P. Benjamin, bolder and more realistic, remarked: "We have 680,000 blacks capable of bearing arms who ought now to be in the field. Let us now say to every Negro who wishes to go into the ranks on condition of being free, go and fight—you are free."[32]

In the North where the draft was being resorted to and men were taken off to war unwillingly, there was a diminishing disposition to inquire who was wearing the uniform and carrying Federal guns. Private Miles O'Reilly gave expression to the thought that had taken hold of large numbers of men.

> Some say it is a burnin' shame
> To make the naygars fight,
> An' that the thrade o' bein' kilt
> Belongs but to the white.

> But as for me upon me sowl!
> So liberal are we here,
> I'll let Sambo be murthered in place o' meself
> On every day in the year.[33]

"Every race," said Governor Andrew, "has fought for liberty and its own progress. The colored race will create its own future by its own brains, hearts, and hands."[34]

Andrew sent agents through the loyal states of the North to recruit Negroes for the 54th Massachusetts regiment. To fill the ranks the agents even penetrated beyond the Mississippi. Officers were obtained not only "in whom the men put faith," but "who would put faith in the men."[35]

On the day when the regiment was to receive the colors, extra trains from Boston carried the crowds of people who were eager to be spectators. The lines of dark skinned soldiers, the handful of white officers, the young Colonel, Robert Gould Shaw, married three weeks before, the Governor and his uniformed staff and the four banners—a national flag, a state flag, an emblematic flag of white presented by the society of colored women, and a flag having a cross upon a blue field with the motto, *In hoc signo vinces* (By this sign thou shalt conquer)—presented a memorable scene. The modest young Colonel thought the Governor made "a beautiful speech" and that his own reply was "small potatoes."

"I know not, Mr. Commander," said Andrew, "when in all human history, to any given thousand men in arms, there has been committed a work at once so proud, so precious, so full of hope and glory as the work committed to you."[36]

The Colonel planned to have the regiment march down Broadway—"all America looks on at a Broadway procession"— but the plan had to be abandoned as offering too great a temptation to New York rowdies and toughs. Instead, the blacks marched proudly down the streets of Boston to embark directly for the front. Throngs lined the sidewalks and bands played the stirring music of John Brown's hymn. Startling memories came back—Garrison dragged through the streets by a mob, Anthony Burns and Thomas Sims being carried back to bondage.[37]

There were contemptuous glances from the club windows of Beacon Street, but the regiment was received with cheers from the business men who packed the steps of the exchange.

The Abolitionist leaders viewed the parade from Phillips's study. There was a bust of John Brown, and Garrison got permission to take it out on the balcony where it was held firm by Garrison's daughter. Phillips was in the room above with his wife, watching the soldiers. Some of the officers lifted their hats as they passed by.[38]

Doubt in these days touched the capacity of the blacks—their courage, their humanity, their ability for improvement. To disabuse the popular mind of this prejudice, Phillips delivered far and wide his lecture on Toussaint L'Ouverture, the creator of Hayti. His estimate of Toussaint, great Negro that he was, is purely rhetorical, but he made Toussaint as familiar to the American Lyceum as John Brown or Washington.

Above the lust of gold, pure in private life, generous in the use of his power, Toussaint stood as a symbol of the finest type of ruler and warrior. Against such a man Napoleon sent his army. To save his liberty and the liberty of his people the

Negro exhausted every means, seized every weapon, and turned back the hateful invaders with a vengeance as terrible as their own, though he ever refused to be cruel. Phillips's passionate tribute could not but stir the hearts of his audience and awaken their generous impulses:

"I would call him Napoleon, but Napoleon made his way to empire over broken oaths and through a sea of blood. This man never broke his word. 'NO RETALIATION' was his great motto and the rule of his life; and the last words uttered to his son in France were these: 'My boy, you will one day go back to St. Domingo; forget that France murdered your father.' I would call him Cromwell, but Cromwell was only a soldier, and the state he founded went down with him into his grave. I would call him Washington, but the great Virginian held slaves. This man risked his empire rather than permit the slave-trade in the humblest village of his dominions.

"You think me a fanatic tonight, for you read history, not with your eyes, but with your prejudices. But fifty years hence, when Truth gets a hearing, the Muse of History will put Phocion for the Greek, and Brutus for the Roman, Hampden for England, Fayette for France, choose Washington as the bright, consummate flower of our earlier civilization, and John Brown the ripe fruit of our noonday (thunders of applause), then dipping her pen in the sunlight, will write in the clear blue, above them all, the name of the soldier, the statesman, the martyr, TOUSSAINT L'OUVERTURE." (Long continued applause.)"³⁹

In the spring of 1863 Phillips gave his attention to another matter. State laws, even city laws, were flouted when they ran counter to the prejudices or interests of influential classes in the centers of population. Accordingly he pleaded for and secured in Boston a Metropolitan or state-controlled Police.⁴⁰

With the delivery of the President's annual message in December, Phillips returned to the troubled waters of slavery and politics. Lincoln proposed to establish State governments in the South wherever there should be found a population loyal to the Union sufficient to cast a vote equal to one tenth of that cast at the presidential election in 1860. Opponents in Congress referred to Louisiana and Arkansas as Lincoln's 10% States. Phillips in a speech at Cooper Institute on the "lick-spittle" administration attacked the President's plan as "neither wise, safe, nor feasible," ending in shame and defeat. Why criticise the President? True, Lincoln was a growing man with his face Zionward. But how did he learn? Why did he advance? Because the nation pushed him on. "The President never professed to be a leader. The President is the agent of public opinion. He wants to know what you will allow and what you demand that he shall do,"—which was what many sincere people wanted a President of a democracy to be. Phillips denied he was doing a harsh injustice to Lincoln. "Mr. Lincoln has done such service in this rebellion, has carved for himself a niche so high in the world's history, that he can well afford to have his faults told."

But the President's plan according to Phillips was radically wrong. The Union was to be reconstructed with a cement that laughed all interference to scorn. Daniel Webster had said that the cement of the Union was the Fugitive Slave Bill. Sin, however, never cemented anything. "The cement of the Union is to be the mutual respect of the sections, bred of that blood which has mingled on bravely contested fields . . . and out of that mutual respect is to grow a Union as indestructible and indivisible as the granite that holds up a continent."

One question remained: how far would the North go? All civil wars ended by compromise. The question was: what would the North compromise on? Once launched on the stormy, turbid waters of politics no one could tell. "Today the helm is in our hands, and you and I, if faithful, can say this to the nation, and the future: You may compromise when and where you please, with one exception, and that is, that the tap root of slavery shall be cut." (Applause.)

And Phillips went on to urge that land owned by the defeated slave oligarchy should be confiscated and put into the hands of the Negroes and white men who fought for it. The nation owed the Negro after such a war, not technical freedom but substantial protection in all his rights. Indeed more than

that. It owed him land and it owed him education also. It was
a debt that had to be paid.

> "What I ask of Mr. Lincoln in his behalf is, an amend-
> ment of the Constitution which his advice to Congress would
> pass in sixty days, that hereafter there shall be neither
> slavery nor involuntary servitude in any State of this Union.
> (Prolonged applause.) Mr. Seward wants the Mississippi
> chairs—the Senate chamber filled. So do I. He is for having
> them filled as they are. I am for making them so hot that
> a slaveholder cannot sit in them."[41]

"We pollute our columns, this morning, with a speech of
Wendell Phillips" said the New York *World*. "Emancipation,
Abolition, confiscation, Southern lands for landless Negroes!
This is the programme. The *Tribune* will, as usual, wait six
months, and then follow Wendell Phillips's lead face foremost.
The *Times* will wait about ten months, and then follow, as
usual, back foremost."[42]

Phillips, ahead of the general sentiment, was demanding still
more. That which he had demanded the year previous had been
accomplished, but in that year he too had gone forward. At a
meeting of the American Anti-Slavery Society he asked the vote
for the Negro.

> "The moment a man becomes valuable or terrible to the
> politician, his rights will be respected. Give the Negro a
> vote in his hand, and there is not a politician from Abraham
> Lincoln down to the laziest loafer in the lowest ward of this
> city, who would not do him honor. . . . Give a man his
> vote, you give him tools to work and arms to protect himself.
> The ballot is the true standing ground of Archimedes, planted
> on which a man can move his world.
>
> "It is not slaveholders we fight, but it is the system—that
> system for which the Southerner undertakes to battle, to
> kill democracy and plant an institution of caste. That system
> is our enemy, no matter whether on the banks of the Ohio,
> or on the banks of the Mississippi; and wherever the nation
> strikes, it must strike slavery, not slaveholders, and not only
> slavery in the Gulf States, but slavery in Tennessee and
> Kentucky."[43]

"There stands the black man," said Phillips at the Massachusetts Anti-Slavery Society, "naked, homeless; he does not own a handful of dust; he has no education; he has no roof to shelter him. You turn him out like the savage on the desert, to say to Europe, 'Behold our magnanimity!'

"Honestly! I believe that if the President's blood could be analyzed you would not find one drop in him, from head to foot, which was not resolved that the Negro in the end shall be free." (Applause.)[44] But there, unfortunately, the President stopped. He did not recognize the Negro as a man; he did not talk of rights, he talked of benefits.

In the autumn of 1863 Phillips's collected *Speeches and Lectures* was first published. The orator took a copy to his wife in which he had written on the title page: "*Speeches and Lectures—By Ann Phillips.*"[45]

CHAPTER FORTY-TWO

"DON'T SWAP HORSES"

A skirmish was fought in the Abolition societies over the question of supporting Lincoln for reelection. Phillips and others distrusted the President's treatment of the freedman. They spoke of the danger of premature reconstruction of the seceded states and demanded suffrage for the Negroes. Garrison, on the other hand, came to believe in the righteousness of Lincoln's intention, and regarded support of him as a moral obligation upon Abolitionists. Hence, when Phillips at the Massachusetts Anti-Slavery Society proposed to declare "that the government is ready to sacrifice the honor and interest of the North to secure a sham peace and have the freedmen under the control of the late slaveholders,"[1] Garrison took exception and offered the amendment that "the government was only *in danger* of doing so." He was unwilling to follow Phillips in charging the President with perfidy. The vote taken was a test of the new factions in the Massachusetts Anti-Slavery Society. Garrison's views were defeated by a small majority.[2]

Again at the meeting of the New England Anti-Slavery Society the two clashed. Parker Pillsbury urged the adoption of a series of resolutions denouncing the administration. Garrison substituted others of a laudatory nature, but they were lost. Phillips spoke an hour, but his argument was still incomplete when suddenly Garrison stood up and complained that Phillips was taking up all the time and that it was late. Phillips sat down and Garrison came forward. The audience began to shout, "Phillips!" "Phillips!" "Free Speech," etc. Garrison tried in vain to be heard. Phillips came forward and stilled the people by a few quiet words. Garrison then made a speech in favor of Lincoln.[3]

Enemies made as much as they could of the schism in the church of Abolition. It caused no little disturbance of mind in some of the faithful followers. But both Garrison and Phillips protested vigorously that the difference was one of opinion and judgment, and not of fundamental principles. Garrison defended Phillips against some of the sharp criticisms of the press and warmly praised him—"The honesty of his conviction is not to be impeached, while its soundness may be questioned without any personal feeling."[4]

Garrison visited the White House and was warmly welcomed. "I have just come from Baltimore," said Garrison. "I have been searching for the old jail which I once had the honor of occupying, but have not been able to find it."[5]

"Well," said Lincoln, "times have changed. Then you couldn't get out, and now you can't get in."

Throughout 1864, Phillips kept up an attack on Lincoln for his readiness to reconstruct the States without Negro suffrage. "My charge against the administration, as an Abolitionist, is that it seeks to adjourn the battle from cannon shot to the forum, from Grant to the Senate House, and to leave the poisoned remnants of the slave system for a quarter of a century to come.

"I contend that the government has shown a willingness to let the white race and the black race remain, after this war, as nearly what they were before as possible. That is really the philosophy of the administration. What McClellan was on the battlefield—'Do as little hurt as possible!'—that Lincoln is in civil affairs—'Make as little change as possible!' 'Touch slavery the last thing; touch it the least possible.' "[6]

Expressing sorrow for Garrison's course, Phillips declared he would sooner have severed his right hand than taken the responsibility which his dear and faithful friend had assumed in favoring Lincoln's reelection: "A million dollars would have been a cheap purchase for the administration of the *Liberator's* article on the Presidency." On May 11, at Cooper Institute, he renewed his avowal of hostility to Lincoln, the day of whose election, he said, "I shall consider the end of the Union in my day, or its reconstruction on terms worse than Disunion."[7]

Phillips went so far as to become a delegate from his ward to the Massachusetts State Republican Convention in order that he might oppose the election to the National Convention of delegates in favor of Lincoln. He spoke against the resolution endorsing the President's policy, but the convention swept over him and adopted the resolution by acclamation.

The rank and file of the Abolitionists supported Lincoln. Lydia Maria Child voiced their position when she said—"I suppose taking all things into consideration, we can have no better president than 'honest Abe,' with his slow mind and legal conscience forever pottering about details and calculating chances. . . . But he obviously lacks sympathy for the wrongs and sufferings of the colored race, and religious-minded as he seems to be, his fear of God is, unfortunately, secondary to his fear of the Democratic party. Still I wish him to be reelected."[8]

Phillips would not alter his opposition to Lincoln and continued unsparing. "Lincoln is doing twice as much today to break this Union as Davis is," he remarked to Sumner. "We are paying thousands of lives and millions of dollars as penalty for having a timid, ignorant President all the more injurious because honest."[9] Lowell wrote sarcastically: "Mr. Lincoln seems to have a theory of carrying on the war without hurting the enemy."[10] Other followers called Lincoln "a man of very small calibre" and said he had "better be at his old business of splitting rails than at the head of the government." Richard H. Dana expressed the same judgment—"He likes rather to talk and tell stories . . . than to give his mind to the manly and noble duties of his great post. He has a kind of shrewdness and common sense and mother wit and slipshod, low-level honesty that make him a good Western jury lawyer. But he is an unutterable calamity where he is."[11]

A movement in support of Fremont started in Missouri, a hotbed of Republican radicalism. It spread to Illinois, and Fremont circles were formed by Germans in various places.

Many Germans were ardent Fremont men,[12] and half of the Abolitionists were following in his standard.

A call was sent out for a mass convention to meet on May 31. The Convention opened formally in Cosmopolitan Hall in Cleveland with a motley body of about four hundred Radicals, Germans, and War Democrats. Many delegates had no credentials, though they represented various political organizations. The Cleveland *Herald* declared that the convention was made up of "sly politicians from New York, impetuous hair-brained Germans from St. Louis, Abolitionists, and personal friends and parasites of Fremont." Thurlow Weed characterized the movement as a "slimy intrigue."[13]

Everything went like clockwork. Fremont was nominated by acclamation, General John Cochrane of New York named for Vice President, and a platform adopted which expressed radical ideas from beginning to end. It called for uncompromising prosecution of the war, constitutional prohibition of slavery, for free speech, free press, for a one term presidency, for leaving reconstruction exclusively to Congress and for confiscation of rebel lands to be divided among soldiers and actual settlers. The convention adopted as its slogan, "Anything to beat Lincoln."

> Rise up Fremont and go before . . .
> Put on the hunting shirt once more,
> And lead in Freedom's van.[14]

Phillips, an ardent Fremont supporter, wrote a long and severe letter to the convention in which he charged that the administration had been "a civil and military failure." It had thought more of conciliating rebels than of subduing them.

"We had three tools with which to crush the rebellion—men, money, and the emancipation of the Negro. We were warned to be quick and sharp in the use of these, because every year the war lasted hardened the South from a Rebellion into a nation, and doubled the danger of foreign interference. For three years the administration has lavished money without stint, and drenched the land in blood, . . .

meanwhile slavery was too sacred to be used; that was saved lest the feelings of rebels should be hurt. . . .

"Mr. Lincoln's model of reconstruction puts all power into the hands of the unchanged white race, soured by defeat, hating the laboring class, plotting constantly for aristocratic institutions. . . . To reconstruct the rebel States on that model is only continuing the war in the Senate chamber after we have closed it in the field. . . . Such reconstruction makes the freedom of the Negro a sham, and perpetuates slavery under a softer name. . . . There is no plan of reconstruction possible within twenty years unless we admit the black to citizenship and the ballot, and use him with the white, as the basis of States. . . .

"The administration I regard as a civil and military failure, and its avowed policy ruinous to the North. Mr. Lincoln may wish the end—peace and freedom—but he is wholly unwilling to use the means which can secure that end.

"Fremont is my choice."[15]

The Pathfinder's pluck, dash, energy, self-reliance appealed to popular fancy. His slender, well built frame, handsome weather browned face with its high forehead, deep blue eyes and aquiline nose, his full beard and long curling brown hair were a familiar picture throughout the nation. He spoke French and Spanish fluently, was courtly in demeanor and fascinating.

Enthusiastic meetings were held at many places. At a great mass meeting at Concord where Fremont was supposed to deliver an address, more than twenty thousand people gathered. The German population rallied to his standard. Reports came from St. Louis that the Germans would stick to him thick and thin. The entire German population of the United States in 1860 was 1,301,136 and the movement for Fremont was becoming formidable.[16]

Lincoln, though, did not seriously consider Fremont's candidacy. When he heard of the nomination, he turned to a Bible and opening the book, dryly read a verse from First Samuel: "And every one that was in distress, and everyone that was in debt, and every one that was discontented, gathered themselves unto him and he became a captain over them; and there were with him about four hundred men."[17]

Fremont to Lincoln was like Jim Jell's little brother. Jim used to say that his brother was the biggest scoundrel that ever lived, but in the infinite mercy of Providence, he was also the biggest fool.[18]

The National Convention of the Republican or "Union" party was held at Baltimore on June 8, 1864.[19] Although the report of the convention showed the nomination of Lincoln to have been unanimous, and although not one word was spoken publicly against him within the Convention Hall, there was much silent opposition. Lincoln himself was aware that he really was not the unanimous choice of the party. In an address at the National Union League he commented: "I do not allow myself to suppose that either the Convention or the League have concluded to decide that I am either the greatest or the best man in America, but rather they have concluded it is not best to swap horses while crossing the river, and have further concluded that I am not so poor a horse that they might not make a botch of it in trying to swap."[20]

The fear of disunion was almost a mania among members of the convention. Andrew Johnson of Tennessee was selected as vice-president to gain the support of a large number of war democrats and to make a favorable impression upon observers abroad by the selection of a vice-president from a reconstructed state in the heart of the Confederacy. "Why should they take a man from that damned little rebel territory?" snarled Thaddeus Stevens, stamping his club foot.[21]

Overtures were made to General Butler, but that canny and self conscious general had the pleasure of declining. "Tell, Mr. Lincoln," Butler remarked to the emissary, Simon Cameron, "I would not quit the field to be vice-president even with himself as president, unless he will give me bond with sureties in the full sum of his four years salary, that he will die or resign within three months after his inauguration. Ask him what he thinks I have done to deserve the punishment at forty-six years of age, of being made to sit as presiding officer over the Senate to listen for four years to debates, more or less stupid, in which I can take no part, nor say a word, nor even be allowed a vote upon any subject which concerns the welfare of the country."[22]

The New York *Tribune* cited the Richmond *Enquirer* as having said—"The only merit we can discover in this Baltimore ticket is the merit of consistency; it is all of a piece; the tail does not shame the head, nor the head shame the tail. A rail splitting buffoon and a boorish tailor, both from the backwoods. Both growing up in uncouth ignorance, they would afford a grotesque subject for a satiric poet."[23]

2.

The summer of '64 was a period of intense gloom throughout the country. The Union reverses, the draft riots, the sluggish character of the war, the open vaunting of the Copperheads, the dissension in the President's cabinet, the opposition to his plans of reconstruction, the rabid attacks printed in the New York *World*,[24] which led to the temporary suspense of its publication, all weakened the support of the administration. Gold was at a premium. On a summer morning $2.60 in paper money was required to purchase $1.00 in gold. The credit of the government was at the lowest ebb.

A mob rose in New York, shot Negroes, hanged them to lampposts, hunted them down, maltreated them, threw them into the river, burned a colored orphan asylum to the ground and sacked the Colored Sailors' Home. Troops called to quell the uprising shot a thousand rioters down. The country was aghast at the terrific slaughter on the battlefields. In a month's Wilderness campaign Grant lost 60,000 men—as many as Lee had in his entire army. In one hour at Cold Harbor he lost 7,000. And what advantage had he gained? "None, whatever," admitted Grant. "For thirty-six days now," said one of Grant's corps commanders, "there has been one unbroken funeral procession past me." The morale of the troops was broken, the rank and file of the army was on the verge of mutiny. Before the assault at Cold Harbor thousands of men pinned to their coats little strips of paper bearing their names and addresses so that their bodies might not lie unidentified.[25] The spectacular raid of General Early at the beginning of July brought Washington within an inch of capture—so close that the Navy Department hastily prepared a vessel to carry the President down the Potomac.

Lincoln issued a call for half a million more men. The call staggered the country. The nation was plunged into an abyss of despair. Even such a conservative Democratic paper as the Columbus *Ohio Statesman,* emphasized that a vote for Lincoln was a vote for the draft.[26] Among the most vehement opponents of conscription were the workers who resented exemption from service of those paying $300. They sang, "We are coming Father Abraham $300 more" or shouted, "A poor man's blood for a rich man's money."[27] "Everything now is darkness and doubt and discouragement," one of Lincoln's secretaries recorded in his diary.

The people were eager for peace and dissatisfied with Lincoln. "Mr. Lincoln is already beaten," wrote Greeley. "He cannot be elected."[28] "The people," said the Cincinnati *Gazette,* "regard Mr. Lincoln's candidacy as a misfortune."[29] A disillusioned Ohio statesman remarked, "Anybody can begin a war, but a statesman can conduct a war, and especially does it require the highest wisdom to terminate a war."[30] It is now scarcely credible that in the early days of August, the New York *Herald* could have carried editorial sentences such as these:

> "The Republicans are still in a muss. The feeling against Old Abe is daily increasing."

> "Abraham Lincoln has been weighed in the balance and found wanting. His election was a rash experiment, his administration is a deplorable failure."[31]

"I write a few words to say that I am in Buffalo," Arthur Brisbane informs Greeley," and that I have been inquiring into the state of political feeling. Among the masses of the people, a strong reaction is setting in in favor of the Democrats and against the war. I have been among the mechanics, and the high prices of provisions are driving them to wish a change. . . . I write mainly today to say that I am alarmed. . . ."[32]

It was customary among Republican leaders to insult the President publicly. Mrs. Lincoln showed to a friend more than eighty declinations to attend a White House reception, and

Senator Ben Wade worded his declination in this fashion: "Are the President and Mrs. Lincoln aware that there is a civil war? If they are not, Mr. and Mrs. Wade are, and for that reason decline to participate in feasting and dancing."[33]

The striking thing was the absence of personal and party loyalty to the President. He had no admirers, no enthusiastic supporters, none to bet on his head. A majority of the Republicans in Congress were hostile to him. Probably not one member in ten favored his reelection.

A newspaper editor who warmly supported the President came to Washington during the winter of '64 and said to Thaddeus Stevens: "Introduce me to some member of Congress friendly to Mr. Lincoln's renomination." "Come with me," was the reply, and going to the seat of Representative Arnold of Illinois, who was a personal friend of the President, Stevens remarked: "Here is a man who wants to find a Lincoln member of Congress. You are the only one I know and I have come over to introduce my friend to you."[34]

The radicals in Congress lost no time in preparing to knife the President's plan of reconstruction. Thad Stevens exploded that he was tired of hearing damned Republican cowards talk about the Constitution, and that he would give the rebels "reconstruction on such terms as would end treason forever."[35] A measure was framed and passed by both branches of Congress, demanding that not one tenth of the voters of 1860 should constitute the electoral vote, but a majority of the male population, and that they should prohibit slavery in their constituencies. The bill was sent to the President on the last day of the session. The President permitted the bill to fail by use of the pocket veto. A few days later Wade and Davis, chagrined at the action of the President in not signing the bill, gave vent to their anger by issuing a joint manifesto. The President's veto, they declared, was a rash and fatal act, a usurpation, "a blow at the rights of humanity. . . . The President holds the electoral votes of the Rebel States at the direction of his personal ambition. . . . A more studied outrage on the legislative authority of the people has never been perpetrated."[36]

The Wade-Davis manifesto was like a bomb thrown into the city of Washington, and Lincoln's friends spoke of the two men as public enemies comparable to the Confederates. When asked if he had read the manifesto or any of Phillips's speeches, the President replied: "I have not seen them, nor do I care to see them. I have seen enough to satisfy me that I am a failure, not only in the opinion of the people in rebellion, but of many distinguished politicians of my own party."[37]

It was urged that all this opposition must be embarrassing to his administration as well as damaging to the party. Lincoln replied: "Yes, that is true, but our friends, Wade, Davis, Phillips, and others are hard to please. I am not capable of doing so. . . . I accord them the utmost freedom of speech and liberty of the press, but shall not change the policy I have adopted, in the full belief that I am right. I feel on this subject as an Illinois farmer once expressed himself while eating cheese. He was interrupted in the midst of his repast by the entrance of his son, who exclaimed, 'Hold on, dad! there's skippers in that cheese you're eating!' 'Never mind, Tom,' said he as he kept on munching his cheese; 'if they can stand it, I can.' "[38]

William Cullen Bryant of the *Evening Post* declared that he was "so disgusted with Lincoln's behavior that he could not muster enough courage to write to him."[39]

Chase learned that the people at Cincinnati were more and more satisfied that "Honest Abe" was a "trixter."[40] Youthful Whitelaw Reid of the *Gazette* declared that the President was ready to "surrender the cause of human freedom to the masters of slave plantations."[41] Senator Sherman said that if the Democrats should select a candidate who had "any particle of patriotism or sense," they would sweep the Republicans out of office like an "avalanche."[42] People in New York State thought the President should resign because he was "fickle, careless, and totally unqualified" to lead the government.[43] "The simple truth," said William P. Fessenden, "is that never was such a shambling half and half set of incapables collected in one government before since the world began." He believed that the King of Siam had more understanding of the situation than the

President. These were the private thoughts of Fessenden. Publicly he supported Lincoln because it was politically expedient.[44]

Even the New York *Times* burst forth in violent criticism of the government. "Gold at 175, and Congress with tax bills, tariff bills, bank bills, and every financial measure lifeless and shapeless, engaged in putting down debate in the national capital. In the name of loyal people we protest. It is a disgrace and an outrage . . ."[45]

The general conviction gained hold throughout the nation that the President did not possess "energy, dignity or character to either conduct the war or to make peace."[46] "Your reelection," wrote Thurlow Weed, "is an impossibility."[47]

Time and the myth-making proclivities of our nation have put a halo around Lincoln, and any criticism is like an arrow in his side. The extreme urgings of the Abolitionists are dubbed the fulminations of madmen, the whisper of dissent from idolatry treason—treason to democratic moderation, democratic compromise. As if the Declaration of Independence and our freedoms stemmed from such debilitating and passive qualities. But the people of 1864, before Lincoln's martyrdom, judged the President as an individual, as an executive in crisis, and found him wanting. Because the Abolitionists came to the same conclusion, are they alone spouters of venom or folly, inciters of hateful emotions?

Lincoln was reported to have said: "You think I don't know I am going to be beaten, but I do, and unless some great change takes place beaten badly."[48]

Just before the cabinet entered the executive chamber on August 23, the day assigned for the weekly meeting, the President wrote the following words—"This morning, as for some days past, it seems exceedingly probable that this administration will not be reelected. Then it will be my duty to so cooperate with the President-elect as to save the Union between the election and the inauguration, as he will have secured his election on such ground that he cannot possibly save it afterward." The writing was placed in an envelope and sealed. The members of the cabinet entered the room. Cheerful as ever the

President greeted them. "Gentlemen, may I ask a favor—will you please write your names upon this envelope?" They did not know why he asked it. He made no explanation. They had no knowledge of its contents. They wrote their names and the package was laid away.[49]

The leading men of the party, Greeley and Whitelaw Reid, Charles Sumner, Andrew and others, started a movement to compel the withdrawal of Lincoln and the nomination of a new candidate. "We must have another ticket to save us from utter overthrow," said Greeley on August 18. On that very day a committee met in New York and arranged to send out a petition for a new convention to be held at Cincinnati.[50]

A definite movement was started to nominate Chase, Secretary of the Treasury. Supporters were at work day and night laying mines, stringing wires, and planning to make Chase president. They went so far as to produce a circular which declared that the reelection of Lincoln was "practically impossible," and that the cause of human liberty and the dignity of the nation suffered from his "tendency towards compromises and temporary expedients."[51] When this circular became public, Chase sent in his resignation, but Lincoln refused to accept it. Chase clubs began to spring up all over the North, but Old Abe had the inside track.

The time seemed ripe for the Democrats to select a leader who would give dignity to the opposition. Among the available military men none stood out like George McClellan. Numerous soldiers of his old command in the Army of the Potomac staunchly supported him and Democratic leaders believed the soldier vote would carry their candidate to victory.

The Democrats met on August 29 at Chicago. The task of providing the platform was left chiefly to the Peace Democrats headed by Clement L. Vallandigham of Ohio. August Belmont of Rothschild's Banking House called the delegates to order. "Four years of misrule," he said, "by a sectional, fanatical, and corrupt party have brought our country to the verge of ruin."[52] Governor Seymour of New York was soon chosen permanent chairman. In his opening address, Seymour delivered a polished jeremiad against Lincoln's administration. With no difficulty

McClellan was nominated as the Presidential candidate. George H. Pendleton was selected to be McClellan's running mate.

The Democratic program toward war was summed up by leader Vallandigham—"The war for the Union is in your hands a most bloody and costly failure. War for the Union was abandoned, war for the Negro openly begun. With what success? Let the dead at Fredericksburg make answer. Ought this war to continue? I answer, 'No, no, no!' Stop fighting. Make an armistice."[53]

The Vallandigham plank placed General McClellan in a most embarrassing position. Gideon Welles remarked: "There is fatuity in nominating a general and a warrior in time of war on a peace platform."[54] McClellan was not prepared to accept the platform without qualification. Moreover he was not willing to speak of war as "four years of failure." Less than three months before this convention, the general had delivered a finished oration at West Point in which he gave expression to his steadfast devotion to the Union and asked—"Shall it be said in after ages that we lacked the vigor to complete the work thus begun? That, after all these noble lives freely given, we hesitated, and failed to keep straight on until our land was saved? Forbid it, Heaven, and give us truer hearts than that."[55]

"The platform," someone remarked to Lincoln, "has not yet been accepted by McClellan. He seems to be as slow as he was in taking Richmond." "Perhaps he is intrenching," said the President laughingly.[56]

A number of friends suggested to McClellan that he repudiate the Chicago platform. But "Little Napoleon" did not want to take such drastic action. His letter of acceptance indicated that he was not entirely in agreement with the Chicago platform. In any event he did not follow Vallandigham's advice not "to insinuate even a little war" into his letter of acceptance.[57]

It is a rule in American politics, long remarked in Europe, that you should "never accuse your adversary of ignorance or error; declare boldly that he murdered his grandmother or stole clocks." The Democrats were well agreed as to the sentiments to be entertained of "Abraham I." One of the delegates at Chicago declared that "for less offenses than Mr. Lincoln had been guilty of, the English people had chopped off the head of the first Charles." Another arose and asserted—"Ever since that usurper, traitor, and tyrant has occupied the presidential chair, the party has shouted war to the knife, and knife to the hilt. Blood has flowed in torrents and yet the thirst of the old monster is not quenched. His cry is for more blood."[58]

The Reverend Henry Clay Dean, Iowa Copperhead, centered his campaign fire against the President's character: "With all his vast armies, Lincoln has failed, failed, Failed, FAILED!" screamed the Dominie. "And still the monster usurper wants more victims for his slaughter pens."[59]

"The reelection of Lincoln," declared the Honorable J. G. Abbott in Faneuil Hall, "means war for the next four years. It means drafts, drafts, drafts, till there is nothing more to be drawn. It means debt that is threatening us every day with national bankruptcy. It means starvation prices. It means grinding and vexatious taxation, so that a man from the time he is born into the world, can do nothing—can't get married and can't even die—without being taxed."[60]

Copperhead songs were spread broadcast. The first song in the official pamphlet did not scruple to rehearse the falsehood about Lincoln's telling dirty stories on the battlefield of Antietam—

"Abe may crack his jolly jokes
O'er bloody fields of stricken battle,
While yet the ebbing life-tide smokes
From men that died like butchered cattle."[61]

The same official collection related that—

"There was an old joker in Springfield did dwell
He wandered all over his stories to tell,
He joked irrepressibly by night and by day,
Till his smutty jokes drove decent people away."[62]

The freedmen came in for their full share of attention and the soldiers were reminded of what they were fighting for. Thus to the popular tune *Wait for the Wagon*, the soldier was admonished—

"Each soldier must be loyal and his officers obey,
Though he lives on mouldy biscuit and fights without
his pay;
If his wife at home is starving, he must not be discontent,
Though he waits six months for greenbacks worth forty-five
percent.

CHORUS:

Fight for the nigger
The sweet scented nigger,
The wooly-headed nigger
And the Abolition crew.

Guard well the Constitution, the government and laws,
To every act of Congress don't forget to give applause;
And when you meet the rebels, be sure and drive them back
Though you do enslave the white man, you must liberate the
black.

CHORUS:

Fight for the nigger, etc."[63]

In the songs everything was included that would encourage
the soldiers to scorn their task and everything that could discourage enlistments and the progress of the war.

Phillips denounced the Copperhead platform. "My motto is
the Country, and I welcome any man's aid to save it. If Chicago
comes to Cleveland, I shall welcome its aid. If any of us quit
Cleveland and go to Chicago, I shall not follow."[64] The New
York *Anti-Slavery Standard* titled an editorial: "Richmond at
Chicago—A Conference of rebels to finish up the work of the
Rebellion."[65]

"It was astonishing," remarked P. T. Barnum, "when the
first men and the first scholars and the first newspapers in the
country were striving to do justice to the Negro, the poor, pur-
blind copperheads could not see 'the signs of the times,' turn
from their miserable delusions, and bow to the logic of events."[66]

"This fratricidal war
    Grows on the poisonous tree
That God and men abhor—
    Accursed Slavery.
And God ordains that we
    Shall eat this deadly fruit
Till we dig up the tree
    And burn its every root."[67]

The campaign was carried on with great vigor. Never had there been so many marching clubs, such torchlight parades, such fireworks, such crowds at mass meetings, such enthusiasm. Night and day young men without cessation stood in halls, upon street corners, and from carttails, haranguing, pleading, sermonizing, orating, arguing, and extolling their cause and their candidate and denouncing their opponents. A good deal of oratory, elocution, rhetoric, declamation, and eloquence was hurled into the troubled air.

But it was of little use. The flashing of Sherman's guns at Atlanta and of Farragut's in Mobile Bay did more than all their oratory and cleared the atmosphere. The war was won on the battlefield and not in diplomatic armchairs. In the slangy words of Seward: Sherman and Farragut knocked the bottom out of the Chicago platform.

"The fall of Atlanta," declared one writer, "puts an entirely new aspect upon the face of affairs. The McClellan party is in check—God be praised." By September 12 the idea of a new convention to select a candidate superseding Lincoln was abandoned.[68]

There was an equally sudden change in the Administration's attitude towards Fremont. His candidacy might be disastrous. His followers were intensely in earnest. He would poll a large vote and would poll it in states likely to be close. Some Bostonians were so alarmed that they published a letter proposing that Fremont and Lincoln withdraw in favor of a compromise candidate.

Leading politicians appealed to Fremont in the interest of party unity. He would be given active service with high command, and those who had long persecuted him—that "nest of

Maryland Serpents," the Blairs—would go. (General Frank Blair had exposed Fremont's maladministration of the West and Fremont clapped him in jail for it. Montgomery Blair, Postmaster General, was Frank's brother) Fremont, after a week of consideration declined these rewards. He wished no further command so late in the war; he felt that the worst his enemies could do had been done. However, as an act of pure patriotism, he would withdraw. His withdrawal, he said, was not because he approved of Lincoln's policies, but because General McClellan had declared, in effect, for restoration of the Union with slavery, and the Democrats must hence at all costs be defeated. Between the two sides no liberal man could hesitate, but the Chief Executive was simply the lesser of two evils. "I consider," he stated, "that his administration has been politically, militarily, and financially a failure, and that its necessary continuance is a cause of regret for the country."[69]

Phillips's position was the same. On October 20, at Tremont Temple he again spoke of "Abraham Lincoln's halting, halfway course, neither hot nor cold, wanting to save the North without hurting the South," not "from want of brains, but want of purpose, of willingness to strike home. Observe how tender the President has been towards the South, how unduly and dangerously reluctant he has been to approach the Negro and use his aid. Vigorous, despotic, decisive everywhere else, he halts, hesitates, delays to hurt the South or help the Negro." And Phillips continued by affirming—"I mean to agitate till I bayonet him and his party into justice."

"Let me allow that he is the only candidate in the field. As for that Confederate gunboat which anchored off Chicago, August 29, and invited G. B. McClellan to be Captain, my only wish is may she soon meet her Kearsarge, and join her sister pirate Alabama in the ocean's depths.

"Reconstruction will be a matter of bargain. In a bargain, neither party ever gets all he sets out with asking. We must expect, therefore, that when the bargain is made, one or the other of the two claims made at Niagara (Union and Abolition) will be wholly or in part surrendered. This is inevitable. Which is it like to be?

"In the first place remember he is a politician, not like
Mr. Garrison, a reformer. Politicians are like the foreleg and
shoulder of a horse—not an upright bone in the whole
column. Reformers are Doric columns. Weight may crush
them, but can neither bend nor break. But our politician,
whose function is to bend—how much will he bend, and to
which side,—the Union side or the Abolition side? Look at
his life and judge."[70]

Lincoln was willing to use diplomacy to bring about his
reelection. He removed Blair to propitiate Chase and Fremont,
tendered Blair's office to Horace Greeley, wrote a letter in
his own hand to James Gordon Bennett, critical editor of the
New York *Herald,* and gave his presidential endorsement to
Roscoe Conkling, his avowed enemy. Overtures regarding the
Vice-Presidential nomination were made to Henry Winter Davis
on the promise that he would support Lincoln. This was indignantly refused. Horace Greeley, however, was made of different stuff. A few days after he received the offer of the
Postmaster General's job, he responded bravely in a two column editorial in the *Tribune* of September 6—"Henceforth we
fly the banner of Abraham Lincoln for the next President."[71]

Bennett declined the proffer of a French mission but soon
came forth with the suggestion in his paper that an entirely
new nomination was needed. "Lincoln has proved a failure,"
he said. "Fremont has proved a failure. Let us have a new
candidate." As was expected, a new candidate could not be
found and the *Herald* announced itself openly in favor of
Lincoln.[72]

The President continued to work in his own behalf. Indiana
and Missouri were doubtful states and the German vote was
important, so Lincoln promoted Hovey and Osterhaus to be
Major Generals. Sherman's indignation boiled over at those
military leaders who left in the midst of bullets to go to the
rear in search of personal advancement.

Pennsylvania was also doubtful. Some Republican politicians
went to Lincoln to say that if 15,000 or more Pennsylvania
soldiers were granted furloughs and would come home to vote
in their uniforms at their separate polling places, they would

be an important influence in creating enthusiasm for the Union. Grant was suggested to do this for him, but Lincoln did not know whether the General-in-Chief would be his friend in such matters. Then it was urged that he might ask Meade or Sheridan. "Oh," said Lincoln, as his face suddenly lighted up with a smile—"I can trust Phil. He's all right."[73] Thus it was that several thousand Pennsylvania soldiers left their commands and returned home to help carry the State for Lincoln and the Union party.

The Democrats claimed that the army was weakened by sending soldiers home to vote the Republican ticket. The New York *Journal of Commerce* said: "Several thousand more soldiers arrived from Washington Friday. They were pouring through some of the streets from morning to night, making their way to the railroad, depots, and steamboat landings, where they could take passage home to vote. When asked how many are on the route, they laugh and say that 'It's only begun to sprinkle yet, but a smart shower may be looked for on Saturday, Sunday or Monday.' A sergeant on the way through Albany boasted he had brought on sixty-nine soldiers—all Republicans—on their way to Utica to vote and had left every damned Democrat behind to take charge of the battery and horses."[74]

The election came off on the 8 of November. Lincoln carried enough states to give him 212 electoral votes out of 233 and a popular majority of 411,428. New Jersey, Delaware, and Kentucky voted for McClellan. The vote stood: Lincoln—2,213,665; McClellan—1,802,237.

"I give you joy of the election," wrote Emerson to a friend. "Seldom in history was so much staked on a popular vote, I suppose never in history."[75] Lincoln received the news quietly sitting in Stanton's office studying the telegraphic returns. When there was a lull in reports, he read aloud the writings of a contemporary humorist, "Petroleum V. Nasby."

Reelection saved the name of Abraham Lincoln from ignominy and covered him with lasting glory.

CHAPTER FORTY-THREE

A KING'S CURE-ALL

The Thirty-Eighth Congress was in session. Senator Trumbull, from the Joint Judiciary Committee, reported the Thirteenth Amendment to the Constitution,

SECTION I. Neither slavery nor involuntary servitude, except as a punishment for crime whereof the party shall have been duly convicted, shall exist within the United States, or any place subject to their jurisdiction.

SECTION II. Congress shall have power to enforce this article by appropriate legislation.

Mr. Voorhees, a member from Indiana, thought the time had not come for such an amendment and opposed it. Such was not the opinion of Mr. Rollins of Missouri. "I have been a slaveholder," he said, "but I am no longer an owner of slaves, and I thank God for it." Thaddeus Stevens, who had the amendment in charge, came limping down the aisle with his club foot. "We have suffered for slavery more than all the plagues of Egypt," he remarked. "If the gentleman opposite will yield to the voice of God and humanity and vote for it, I verily believe the sword of the destroying angel will be stayed, and this people be reunited."

Two thirds of those voting must favor the amendment to secure its passage. The bill though passed in the Senate had failed at the last session of the House. It was known that some of the Democratic members, in view of the results of the presidential election in 1864, were now ready to vote for the measure. But would there be a sufficient number?

Breathless and silent the crowd waited as the clerk called the roll—so breathlessly silent that the sound of a hundred pencils keeping tally as the names were called and recorded could be heard. The most intense anxiety was felt. The silence was broken by a low murmur of approval when Mr. English, Democratic member from Connecticut, responded "Aye." The applause was repeated with increasing emphasis as other Democrats followed his example. The last name was called. One hundred and nineteen ayes, fifty-six noes—two more than the requisite number. A tumult of joy broke forth. Representatives on the floor, soldiers, spectators in the gallery, Senators, Supreme Court Judges, women and pages jumped on seats, or mounted desks, waved handkerchiefs and hats and cheered. Members were dancing and pulling each other around and performing all kinds of antics.[1]

Thereupon the House adjourned "in honor of this immortal and sublime event," guns were fired from batteries guarding the city, and the president so often serenaded was again called to the window at the White House for a speech to the jubilant crowd. When the cheering and band playing had subsided, the President, raising his arm slowly, said—"The great job is ended. The occasion is one of congratulation, and I cannot but congratulate all present, myself, the country, and the whole world upon this great moral victory!" His proclamation, he added, might be objected to as unconstitutional and partial in its operation. "But this amendment is a King's cure-all for all the evils. It winds the whole thing up."[2]

Less than a week later, on the evening of February 5, the President called his cabinet together and read to them the draft of a resolution designed as a peace offering to the States in rebellion. It empowered the President to pay four hundred million dollars to the Southern States for their slaves on condition that hostilities cease by the first of April, 1865, and the Thirteenth Amendment be ratified. The cabinet unanimously vetoed the document. Folding up the paper with a sigh, the President put it away. "You are all opposed to me," he sadly uttered.[3]

The 13th Amendment proposed a revolution in federalism. To the theorists, the Amendment brought about a fundamental change: it took from the states what hitherto had been constitutionally reserved to them, the power to protect or promote slavery. It abolished slavery throughout the land, nationalized the right of freedom, and made the National Congress the organ of enforcement. In the eyes of the Abolitionists Congress now had a constitutional mandate to enforce not just the liberty of blacks, but the liberty of whites as well. It included not merely freedom from personal bondage, but protection in a wide range of natural and constitutional rights.[4]

The war was near its end. Sherman marched through the Confederacy to the sea—Lee was pushed back, stubbornly but vainly contesting each step—Richmond was captured—Appomattox was reached—and on April 9, 1865, the Rebellion collapsed.

On April 14, exactly four years after the surrender of Fort Sumter, the stars and stripes were raised again on that very stronghold. Major General Anderson was there, Henry Ward Beecher, Senator Henry Wilson, and by special invitation of the national government, George Thompson (who had crossed the Atlantic to be "in at the death" of slavery) and Garrison.

The day was clear and beautiful. Vessels in Charleston Harbor were dressed up with flaunting flags, the artillery of the forts and warships thundered solemn salutes, and the banner of the Union floated everywhere except over Sumter. Anderson, who as a Major had hauled down the flag, had the privilege of raising again the same shot-torn banner. Henry Ward Beecher delivered the principal address. In a brief speech, Garrison declared, "I hate slavery as I hate nothing else in the world. It is not only a crime, but the sum of all criminality."

Early next morning, on April 15, Garrison visited a small cemetery opposite St. Phillip's Church. He stopped at a monument of brick, covered with a large plain slab of marble inscribed with the single name Calhoun. Laying his hand on the monument before him, he said impressively: "Down into a deeper grave than this slavery has gone, and for it there is no resurrection."[5]

Even as Garrison uttered these words, miles away in the capital of the nation, Lincoln lay dead.

Good Friday, always the worst night of the year in the theatre, was one of the best in 1865. Ford's Theatre in Washington was full to the doors as the curtain went up and the play, "Our American Cousin," began. The box overlooking the stage had been decorated with flags for the President's party. A little after eight o'clock, the President, Mrs. Lincoln, and two young guests, Miss Cora Harris and her fiancé, Major Rathbone, came in. Down on the stage Laura Keene, the star, stopped the dialogue to curtsy towards the arriving party. A roar went up from the crowd, the orchestra crashed into "Hail to the Chief," and the President, his huge sallow face relaxing, bowed and bowed until the tumult died.

Along in the third act, a shot rang out through the house. A moment later the President was observed to lurch forward in his box. A man from behind jumped down from the box on to the stage. But a flag caught in his spur and brought him with a crash to the floor. He scrambled to his feet, waving a bloody knife, then turned and shouted—"*Sic semper tyrannis*"—and vanished into the wings.

A woman screamed and all eyes turned to the draped box. Major Rathbone, blood gushing from his arm, shouted, "Stop that man! Stop him! He has killed the President!" Then there was tumult and a rush for the doors.

The wounded President was borne from the theatre to a nearby residence, and there surrounded by relatives and friends, he died without regaining consciousness.[6]

At a mass meeting in Tremont Temple on April 23, "to consider the great question of our country and its perils," Phillips paid a glowing but frank and consistent tribute to Lincoln.

"The Martyr sleeps in the blessings of the poor whose fetters God commissioned him to break. Give prayers and tears to the desolate widow and the fatherless; but count him blessed far above the crowd of his fellow men. (Fervent cries of "Amen!") He has sealed the triumph of the cause he loved with his own blood. Who among living men may not envy him? leaving a name immortal in the sturdy pride of our race and the undying gratitude of another, withdrawn at the moment when his star touched its zenith, and the nation needed a sterner hand for the work God gives it to do.

"With prejudices hanging about him, he groped his way very slowly and sometimes reluctantly forward: let us remember how patient he was of contradiction, how little obstinate in opinion, how willing, like Lord Bacon, 'to light his torch at every man's candle.' With the least possible personal hatred, often forgetting justice in mercy, tenderhearted to any misery his own eyes saw,—recollect he was human, and that he welcomed light more than most men, was more honest than his fellows, and with a truth to his own convictions such as few politicians achieve. With all his shortcomings, we point proudly to him as the natural growth of democratic institutions. (Applause.) Coming time will put him in that galaxy of Americans which makes our history the day-star of the nations—Washington, Hamilton, Franklin, Jefferson, and Jay. History will add his name to the bright list, with a more loving claim on our gratitude than either of them. For not one of those was called upon to die for his cause."[7]

2.

The two prophets of Abolition came to a parting of the ways. The end of the war showed an irreconcilable difference between them. Garrison held that the work of Abolition was ended. Phillips said it had just begun. Garrison wished to disband the American Anti-Slavery Society; Phillips insisted that its functions were never greater nor more important.[8] At the annual meeting in May, 1865, the clash came.

Garrison moved to disband. "The point is here," he said. "We organized expressly for the abolition of slavery; we called our Society an *Anti-Slavery* Society. The other work (Negro suffrage) was incidental. Now, I believe, slavery is abolished in this country, abolished constitutionally, abolished by a decree of this nation, never, never, to be reversed, and, therefore, that it is ludicrous for us, a mere handful of people with little means, with no agents in the field, no longer separate, and swallowed up in the great ocean of popular feeling against slavery, to assume that we are of special importance, and that we ought not to dissolve."

Garrison was sure that the North in reconstructing the Southern States would insist on "guarantees for the protection of the freedmen"—that is, would give them the vote and protect them by force of arms. The more radical Abolitionists could not share his faith.[9]

Phillips vehemently opposed Garrison's motion. He maintained that the Thirteenth Amendment was not yet legally ratified and he declared that he was not going to haul down the flag.

"The Anti-Slavery Amendment has torn that weapon from the hands of the leaders, but the purpose remains the same. The South is not converted. You cannot kill off all the white men who cherish a hatred toward democratic institutions. You can only flank them, as Grant flanked Lee—flank them by democratic elements—Yankee commerce, black suffrage, divided lands.

"We came together to abolish the system of slavery. That system was a legal matter; it existed in the parchment; it was laid up in the statute book. Well, it lies there still. In the eye of the law, we have not touched it.

"Now we accepted the Constitution of the American Anti-Slavery Society; we all came under it, and labored under it. It has one harmonious, indivisible idea; it is the safety beyond peril and the equality without a doubt of the colored race in this country. (Applause and cries of 'Hear, hear.') If Garrisonianism means anything, it means that, and in all prior time, we have claimed it. . . . Well, we stand today not only with technical and substantial slavery. We stand with the black race on the heights of Canaan, it is true, but by no means in it. Prejudice is very rife. All over the country, the colored man is a Pariah. Now, friends, my abolitionism, when I pledged my faith to that Declaration of Sentiments and Constitution of the American Anti-Slavery Society, was, 'Absolute equality before the law; absolute civil equality.' (Loud applause.); and I never shall leave the Negro until, so far as God gives me the power, I achieve it."

Garrison.—"Who proposes to do so?"[10]

The discussion was heated and bitter. George Thompson quoted Phillips's earlier speeches against him (an inconsistency which was rather to Phillips's credit) and exclaimed: "I appeal from Phillips drunk to Phillips sober." Nor was this the worst of it. Phillips argued his case with all the ardor and energy of his nature, but there escaped from him not one resentful sentence towards his former associates. Emerson said:—"How handsomely Mr. ♦Phillips has behaved in his controversy with Mr. Garrison. In fact Phillips was the same we have always known him." But the wound went deep into him and seven years later when he said at the Radical Club, "I have known cases in which it only took one to make a quarrel," they all recognised what he was thinking of.[11]

At one time Phillips was a guest in Quaker Mrs. Chace's house. As he was preparing to ascend the staircase, he broke into sudden speech—"Oh, I don't think that there is much satisfaction to be gotten out of this life."

"Thee shouldn't feel so," said Mrs. Chace.

Tears came into his eyes as he answered,—"Half the men I worked with for thirty years will not speak to me when they meet me in the street."

"That is hard, I know," she half answered.[12]

"We don't see any of them," wrote Ann dejectedly to Henry C. Wright about the Garrisons, "for they feel very unkindly towards us."[13] Higginson once saw Edmund Quincy deliberately turn his back on Phillips in the Ticknor building. Higginson said—"It seemed to me the saddest thing I ever saw."[14]

True the force of habit was strong with many old friends of the cause to whom annual meetings and festivals and conventions had been the meat and drink of life for many years, and who were reluctant to break up old and delightful associations. But the majority evidently felt that discontinuance of the society was tantamount to abandoning the Negro, and proposing to do so treachery to the cause of freedom. On a vote Garrison's resolution to disband was rejected by 118 to 48. Phillips was elected President and Garrison withdrew from the movement. Aaron M. Powell took editorial charge of the society's organ, the *Anti-Slavery Standard*, replacing Edmund

Quincy and Oliver Johnson, who also withdrew. A new executive committee was chosen. Then an adjournment was carried amid great rejoicing.

Two weeks later, at the annual meeting of the Massachusetts Anti-Slavery Society, the discussion was continued. Garrison and Phillips were again on different sides of the fence. Some of the speakers bluntly intimated that Garrison had fallen behind and being no longer the man for the crisis, should now yield the leadership to •Phillips. Garrison repudiated the claim to leadership, declaring that he had been "one of a multitude of noble men and women," and Phillips protested against being extolled at the expense of his friend—"There is nothing more unpleasant to me than any allusion to him and myself as antagonists. Whatever may have been the immediate cause of my anti-slavery life and action, he is in so true and full a sense the creator of the anti-slavery movement that I may well say I have never uttered an anti-slavery word which I did not owe to his inspiration. I have never done an anti-slavery act of which the primary merit was not his. More than that: in my experience of nigh thirty years, I have never met the anti-slavery man or woman, who had struck any effectual blow at the slave system in this country, whose action was not born out of the heart and conscience of William Lloyd Garrison."[15]

The two men never lost respect for each other, but their temperamental differences were so strong that probably only the great bond of their mutual affection had previously kept them together. Garrison was a humanitarian, Phillips a militant democrat. Besides Garrison was the elder and had suffered more from the terrible strain of thirty-five years of fighting; his nature was to seek peace and pursue it. The intensity of his feeling against slavery had not only worn him down, but at the same time had circumscribed his views.

He bid an affectionate farewell to the American Anti-Slavery Society—

"Friends of the American Anti-Slavery Society, this is no 'death bed scene' to me! There are some in our ranks who seem to grow discouraged and morbid in proportion as light abounds and victory crowns our efforts. (Applause.) . . . We have had something said about a funeral here today. A funeral because Abolitionism sweeps the nation! A funeral? Nay, thanks be to God who giveth us the victory, it is a day of jubilee, and not a day to talk about funerals or deathbeds! It is a resurrection from the dead, rather, it is an ascension and beatification! Slavery is in its grave, and there is no power in this nation that can ever bring it back.[16]

While Garrison was in Philadelphia engaged in delivering a lecture, the final ratification of the Thirteenth Amendment was announced. Instantly he hastened home to get the proclamation into the *Liberator*. He wrote his valedictory editorial with the printers standing at his elbow for copy which he doled out to them a few lines at a time. When all but the final paragraph had been set up and adjusted in the chase, he himself took up the composing stick, finished the work, and set his take in the space left for it. Evening had come and the little group in the printing office gathered about and watched silently as the form was locked and the last number of the *Liberator*, bearing the date of December 29, 1865, went to press.

"Most happy am I," said Garrison, "to be no longer in conflict with the mass of my fellow countrymen on the subject of slavery. For no man of any refinement or sensibility can be indifferent to the approbation of his fellow men if it be rightly earned."[17]

The last number of the *Liberator* contained the valedictory but the preceding number had contained the paean—

"Rejoice, and give praise and glory to God, ye who have so long and so untiringly participated in all the trials and vicissitudes of that mighty conflict! Having sown in tears, now reap in joy. Hail, redeemed, regenerated America! Hail, North and South, East and West! Hail, the cause of Peace, of Liberty, of Righteousness, thus mightily strengthened and signally glorified! Hail, the Present, with its transcendent claims, its new duties, its imperative obligations, its sublime opportunities! Hail, the Future, with its pregnant hopes, its glorious promises, its illimitable powers of expansion and development! Hail, ye ransomed millions, no more to be chained, scourged, mutilated, bought and sold in the market, robbed of all rights, hunted as partridges upon the mountains in your flight to obtain deliverance from the house of bondage, branded and scorned as a connecting link between the human race and the brute creation! Hail, all nations, tribes, kindreds, and peoples, made of one blood, interested in a common redemption, heirs of the same immortal destiny! Hail, angels in glory and spirits of the just made perfect, and tune your harps anew, singing, 'great and marvelous are thy works, Lord God Almighty; just and true are thy ways, thou King of Saints! Who shall not fear thee, O Lord, and glorify thy name? for thou only art holy: for all nations shall come and worship before thee: for thy judgments are made manifest.' "[18]

CHAPTER FORTY-FOUR

" 'JOY MY FREEDOM!"

All over the South the Negroes held jubilee. The topsy-turvy world had been righted and they as God's chosen children were to be proprietors of the land and favored of paradise:

> "We's nearer to de Lord
> Dan to de white folks an' dey knows it
> See de glory-gates unbarred,
> Walk in, darkies, past de guard.
> Bet yer a dollar he won't close it.
>
> Walk in, darkies, troo de gate
> Hark de kullered angels holler
> Go 'way, white folks, you're too late.
> We's de winnin' kuller. Wait
> Tell de trumpet blows to foller . . .
>
> No more Lards with auburn locks,
> Kullered Shepherd—wooly flocks—
> We's de bressed Lord's relashins.[1]

At all hours of the day they could be seen laying down their implements and sauntering singing from the fields. If freedom did not mean surcease from back-breaking labor, where was the boon? Hundreds of thousands could not rest content until they had tasted this freedom. Jubilant and happy, multitudes swarmed into the towns and gathered in noisy groups in the streets, or tramped aimlessly about the country. "What did you leave the old place for, Auntie?"—"What fur? 'Joy my freedom!"[2]

"Walk up hyer, and buy cheap!" shouted a Negro huckster in a Richmond market. "I don't say niggers. I say ladies and gentlemen. Niggers is played out; they're colored people now, and as good as anybody."[3]

If called "nigger," the freedman responded with "Secesh," "reb," or "po' white trash." As a sign of his new status he acquired a hat, which he was generally denied in slavery and which thus came to be the symbol of freedom. He wore his hat indoors and outdoors, in season and out of season and offended the whites. In addition the ex-slave began to acquire surnames and middle initials, and demanded to be called "Mister." Before the Civil War the slave as a rule had only a given name. He added his mother's name or father's name, or in some instances the name of his former master. But he now felt that John Hatcher or Hatcher's John was not the proper title to denominate a freedman, and in many cases John Hatcher was changed to John S. Sherman. The initial S stood for no name, it being simply a part of what the colored man proudly called his "entitles."

One new Negro said: "We're free now, but when our masters had us, we was only change in their pockets."[4]

Their gratitude was profound, childish, but touching. In Georgia, it is said, they prayed in this manner to their Savior—

> "Now I lay me down to sleep,
> I want to be a Republican.
> I pray the Lord my soul to keep,
> Because I am a Republican.
> If I should die before I wake,
> I want to be a Republican.
> I pray the Lord my soul to take,
> If I have been a Republican.
> And this I ask for Jesus' sake,
> Because I am a Republican.[5]

The notion got abroad that each Negro family would receive "forty acres and a mule." White sharpers reaped a rich harvest by selling to freedmen the painted stakes or "preemption rights" with which each must be provided if he expected to obtain his share on the day of division. The deed sold to one credulous Negro read as follows—"Know all men by these presents, that a nought is a nought and a figure is a figure; all for the white man and none for the nigure. And whereas Moses lifted up the serpent in the wilderness, so also have I lifted this d—d old nigger out of four dollars and six bits. Amen! Selah!"[6] Other swindlers sold painted red, white and blue pegs which, it was asserted, came from Washington and could be used by the purchaser to mark out homesteads. It was a common experience to meet a black fellow who had come a hundred miles to get a barrel of flour sent him by the Queen of England, or a free railway ticket to Washington that he might see the President. The Freedman's simplicity was imposed upon at every hand. "When is de land goin' fur to be divided? One say dis, an' one say dat, an' we don' know an' so hol' off till Janerwery."[7]

On foot, on horses and mules, in rough oxcarts and sumptuous carriages taken from their master's stables, the Negroes had followed the conquering hosts. "I'se hope de Lord will prosper you Yankees and Mr. Sherman," said the spokesman of a large number of refugees to an aide-de-camp, "because I tinks and we all tinks, dat youse down here in our interests." Another gray-haired "uncle" told Sherman that he had been looking for the "angel of the Lord" since he was knee high.[8]

The Yankee teacher entered the South on the heels of the soldier. Of the 9503 teachers in freedmen's schools in the South, possibly 5,000 were natives of the Northern states. Many had been Abolitionists; all were profoundly religious, of a missionary spirit. Most would have heartily agreed with the teachers who said, "Our work is just as much a missionary work as if we were in India or China." No hardship was too great, no inconvenience too irritating, no religion too remote for these consecrated missionaries. The educational work of the Freedmen's Bureau was carried out in cooperation with the benevolent and philanthropic associations of the North.[9]

Major Plumly in Louisiana, after working a year and a half, opened 126 schools with 230 teachers giving instruction to 15,000 children in day classes and 5,000 adult freemen at night and on Sundays. General Howard said in 1865 that more than

200,000 persons in the South learned to read in the past three years.[10] And one officer of the Freedmen's Bureau reported that in a school in North Carolina he saw sitting side by side four generations: a child six years old, her mother, grandmother, and great grandmother, the last over seventy-five years old— all studying their letters and learning to read the Bible.

CHAPTER FORTY-FIVE

THE GREENEVILLE TAILOR—

POLITICAL GOTHS

In a dingy hotel room a man stood with hand uplifted. He had been roused early to take the oath as President. He was a short man with harsh, definite features: a tension of muscles between the eyes that was almost a scowl, straight black Indian-like hair, swarthy skin and eyes full of intense light. Lines of decision ran from the corners of his nose to the corners of a large mouth. A firm chin had a combative cleft in it.

Chief Justice Chase in the presence of cabinet officers and others administered the oath. Andrew Johnson impressively kissed the book and the ceremony was ended. The Greeneville tailor was President of the United States.

Chase noted that the new President pressed the twenty-first verse of the eleventh Chapter of Ezekiel—"But as for them whose heart walketh after the heart of every detestable thing and their abominations, I will recompense their weight upon their own hands, saith the Lord God."[1]

April 15, 1865, was a day of cheer and hope to the Republican leaders in Congress. President Lincoln had died at 7:22 that morning and Johnson took the oath of office at 11. Republican leaders felt that Lincoln's death was a providential occurrence. They held a caucus that afternoon at which the feeling was nearly universal that because of Lincoln's known policy of tenderness to the rebels, the change in the •Presidency "would prove a godsend to the country." The caucus thought the time opportune "to get rid of the last vestige of Lincolnism."[2]

Johnson was breathing fire and hemp. The President, remarked the New York *Tribune*, knew the rebellion "egg and bird."[3] Lincoln "would have dealt with the rebels," said Senator Doolittle of Wisconsin, "as an indugent father deals with his erring children." Johnson "would deal with them more like a stern and incorruptible Judge. Thus in a moment," continued the Senator, "has the sceptre of power passed from a hand of flesh to a hand of iron."[4]

Senator Ben Wade declared to the President: "Johnson, we have faith in you. By the Gods, there will be no trouble now in running the government." To which Johnson replied: "Treason is a crime and crime must be punished. Treason must be made infamous and traitors must be impoverished."[5] "I shall go to my grave," he wrote, "with the firm belief that Davis, Cobb, Toombs, and a few others of the arch conspirators and traitors should have been tried, convicted, and hanged for treason. . . . If it was the last act of my life, I'd hang Jefferson Davis as an example. I'd show coming generations that while the rebellion was too popular a revolt to punish many who participated in it, treason should be made odious and arch-traitors should be punished."[6] "By the eternal God, I would execute them," he added in the Senate. The spectators stood upon their seats, swung their hats in the air, and cheered wildly.

Even his radical friends feared Johnson would be too vindictive. Soon, however, Johnson amazed and disappointed them. When the excitement caused by the assassination of Lincoln moderated, Johnson saw before him a task so great that the desire for violent measures chilled. Sobered by responsibility, the influence of moderate advisers, the fervent pleadings of Seward, ("Seward entered into him," explained Stevens, "and ever since they have been running down steep places into the sea.")[7] and the judicious flattery of the Southern leaders, he rather quickly adopted Lincoln's policy. He recognized early in May the Lincoln 10% governments of Louisiana, Tennessee, Arkansas, and Virginia, and to bring the other seven states back to the Union, inaugurated a plan like that of Lincoln but not quite so liberal.

In April, May, and June, Johnson had been the "drunken tailor," the "bloody minded tailor," the "vulgar renegade." Now the South spoke of his "wise measures" and his "mode of pacification," of his generous sentiments" and of his "liberality and magnanimity." Now, the Jackson (Mississippi) News nominated him as the South's candidate for President in 1868. All South Carolina reposed confidence in him. His policy, said Governor Orr in his inaugural address, would attach the South to the Union by cords "stronger than triple steel."[8]

Even the World and Daily News, which appealed to the masses of New York, experienced a change of heart. They did not regard Vice-President Johnson and President Johnson in the same light. While Lincoln lived, the Daily News saw in "Andy" Johnson "a debauched demagogue," a member of the heinous Republican Party, and a man without political principles, but one who "could bellow his bastard 'loyalty' loudly." The World maintained that Mr. Johnson lacked the sentiments and bearing of a gentleman. "And to think that only one frail life stands between this insolent, clownish drunkard, and the presidency. Should this Andrew Johnson become his (Lincoln's) successor, the decline and fall of the American public would smell as rank in history as that of the Roman Empire under such atrocious monsters in human shape as Nero and Caligula."[9] But after Johnson took over the office of President, the two newspapers flattered and cajoled this anti-aristocrat and pro-Unionist until his policy of revenge was transformed into one of conciliation and "tenderness."

Like Lincoln, Johnson did not like slavery; like Lincoln, he recognized the constitutional rights of slavery; like Lincoln, he was more interested in the preservation of the Union with or without slavery, and like Lincoln he thought the war was waged for the preservation of the Union and for no other purpose.

The Union he loved fiercely and the Constitution he revered. "We do not intend that you shall drive us out of this house that was reared by the hands of our fathers. It is our house . . . the Constitution house."[10] Turning to those of the South who had run away because Lincoln was elected—"I voted against him, I spoke against him, I spent my money to defeat him, but

still I love my country; I love the Constitution; I intend to
insist upon its guarantees."[11] He always scouted the idea that
slavery was the cause of the trouble or that emancipation could
ever be tolerated without immediate colonization. Speaking
in the Senate on John Brown: "John Brown stands before the
country as a murderer," he said. "The time has arrived when
these things ought to be stopped, when encroachments on the
institutions of the South ought to cease . . . when you must
either preserve the Constitution or you must destroy the Union."
John Brown compared to Christ? What blasphemy! "I once
heard it said that fanaticism always ends in heaven or in
hell. . . . I believe it true." John Brown a God? "Those may
make him a God who will, and worship him who can—he is
not my God and I shall not worship at his shrine."[12]

"I would chain Massachusetts and South Carolina together,"
he once said in Congress, "and I would transport them to some
island in the Arctic Ocean, the colder the better till they cool
off and come to their senses."[13]

He disliked slavery not because of its moral wrong, but because of its degrading effect on white labor—he was always
thinking of that. Emancipation would break down "an odious
and dangerous aristocracy" and free more whites than blacks.[14]
"I want to see slavery broken up, and when its barriers are torn
down, I want to see industrious, thrifty immigrants pouring in
from all parts of the country. Come on! We need your labor,
your skill, your capital."[15]

Like many Americans he was proud of his humble origin, but
unlike many others, he never sloughed off his backwoods crude-
ness. He continually boasted of himself and vilified the aristocrats who in return treated him badly. He hated a gentleman
by instinct. "Governor," said Bailie Peyton to him one day,
"the anti-slavery men of the North oppose slavery because it
is unjust, and hope by abolishing it to make free citizens of
those human chattels." He answered: "Damn the Negroes; I
am fighting these traitorous aristocrats, their masters!"[16] His
dislike of them was so open and marked that a rival politician
said that "If Johnson were a snake, he would lie in the grass
to bite the heels of rich men's children."[17]

He devoutly believed in the common people. "I am a Democrat now," he had said in '62. "I have been one all my life. I expect to live and die one . . . they shall never divert me from the polar star by which I have ever been guided from early life—the great principles of Democracy upon which this government rests."[18]

He was ruggedly honest. He declined a fine equipage with a span of horses proffered by a New York City group on the ground that he had always made it a practise to refuse gifts while in public station. Handling millions as military Governor of Tennessee, he was poorer on leaving than on taking office. This was considered intolerably stupid by not a few patriots of the time. Nothing depressed and alarmed him more than moral laxity in public life, and he foresaw that railroad giants mean "nothing but a series of endless corrupting legislation."[19] Thus he was thought vulgar in the house of Cooke. It was bad enough to be a plebeian and the champion of labor; it was intolerable that he should be the enemy of favor-seeking capital.

He struck back at his enemies, at "the god forsaken and hell deserving, money-loving, hypocritical, backbiting, Sunday praying scoundrels of the town."[20] He seldom whined; he was too combative for that. He gave no love taps in battle, but used a battle axe. He was utterly without fear. When there was every likelihood that he would be shot from ambush if he tried to take office as Governor of Tennessee, he refused the offer of friends to form a bodyguard for him. "No," he said, 'If I am to be shot at, I want no man to be in the way of the bullet." And he walked to the State Capitol alone—and slowly.[21]

No wonder George Atzerodt, who had been assigned by Booth to kill Johnson while he was killing Lincoln, and had gone to Johnson's hotel with his gun, looked Johnson over, and then thought better of it.

Time and again, he spoke at the peril of his life and never faltered or moderated his tone. More than once his speaking was interrupted by the cocking of pistols. Once he was warned that the repetition of his speech would injure his party. "I will make that same speech tomorrow," he replied, "if it blows the Democratic party to hell."[22]

A difficult orator, but an honest one. Told that he would be assassinated if he spoke in one community that teemed with his enemies, he appeared upon the platform with the comment that he understood shooting was to be one of the preliminaries and that decency and order dictated that these be dispensed with first. "I have been informed that part of the business to be transacted is the assassination of the individual who now has the honor of addressing you. I beg respectfully to propose that this be the first business in order. Therefore, if any man has come here tonight for the purpose indicated, I do not say to him, Let him speak, but let him shoot." Drawing a pistol from his pocket, and looking the crowd over, he paused expectantly. There was a dead silence. "Gentlemen, it appears I have been misinformed," he said quietly returning the pistol to his pocket. "I will now proceed to address you on the subject which has called us together," and he launched forthwith into an uncompromising speech.[23]

He was never a demagogue. Nor were his prepared speeches frothy and unsubstantial things—they were packed with substance. In the session he haunted the Congressional Library in search of facts; he had a passion for evidence. When preparing for the stump, his office had the appearance of a factory at the close of day. It was filled with pamphlets, works on economics, speeches, histories,—and always at hand a copy of the Constitution.

When calm and collected he was able to state his opinions impressively. Faced with skilful heckling, he was unbridled, relentless, undignified. At such times he gave foundation to the popular concept of him as a vulgar drunken tailor, a soap box ranter, an illiterate, ill-mannered, intemperate fellow, stubborn, quarrelsome, intolerant, and a fool.

"But Andrew Johnson was a drunkard." He was nothing of the sort. The slander arose out of an unfortunate incident at the time of his inauguration as Vice-President. He had just recovered from typhoid fever and had not wanted to come to Washington, but Lincoln had insisted. On the morning of the inauguration, Johnson still felt weak from his illness. While waiting to go into the Senate Chamber for the ceremony, he complained of feeling faint and asked for a stimulant. A messenger was despatched for some brandy and Johnson drank a glass, and in the course of conversation, two more. When he rose to enter the Senate Chamber, he was perfectly sober, but the heat of the crowded room had its effect, and when sworn in, he was in a befuddled state of mind. He made a rambling and strange harangue listened to with pain and mortification by his friends. Several Senators on the Republican side began to hide their heads. Sumner covered his face with his hands and bowed his head down on the desk. Up in the press gallery some reporters were too ashamed to write the news. "The man is certainly deranged," said Speed, the new Attorney General. And Gideon Welles whispered to Stanton on his right: "Johnson is either drunk or crazy."[24]

Lincoln sat facing Johnson with an expression of "unutterable sorrow," but did not join in the condemnation of the others. He sent an emissary to Nashville to report on Johnson's habits. "It has been a severe lesson for Andy," he said, "but I do not think he will do it again." Another talked with Lincoln about the incident. "I have known Andy Johnson for many years," he said. "He made a bad slip the other day, but you need not be scared. Andy ain't a drunkard."[25]

However, Johnson's "slip" gave a handle to the radicals and within two weeks of his accession to the Presidency, a London paper referred to him as "a drunken mechanic."[26] The truth is, he never took wine or liquor with a meal, never drank a cocktail in his life, never was in a barroom, and did not care for champagne. He did, however, take two or three glasses of Robertson County whiskey some days—some days less and some days and weeks no liquor at all. While the White House cellars were always stocked with fine wines and liquors which were served to the guests, Johnson (according to a veteran White House attache of five administrations) "never drank to excess."[27]

Aside from politics his only game was checkers, which he played indifferently. He looked on all sorts of gambling as wrong. He liked circuses and minstrels but seldom attended them, for he "never had much time for frivolity." He wore neat black clothes,—a black broadcloth frock coat and waistcoat,

black doeskin trousers, and a high silk hat. He was scrupulously
clean, almost dainty about his linen.

His industry was amazing. He kept six secretaries busy, and
except for an hour or so in the afternoon and at meal times,
he rarely left his desk from six in the morning until midnight.
All day long he received throngs of office hunters, pardon seekers,
advice givers, petitioners, well-wishers who crowded the anterooms. He read long reports, formulated policies, handled the
routine of the administration, held frequent cabinet meetings,
and wrote letters, telegrams, and orders to subordinates all over
the country. He worked in ill health under the strain of abuse
and weighty problems, month after month without a vacation
or recreation. His devotion to duty was tireless. As an old man,
Henry Adams, recalling his youthful prejudices, was "surprised
to realize how strong the Executive was in 1868—perhaps the
strongest he was ever to see."[28]

Unfortunately the Executive lacked tact. It was to curse him
through life and—on this all were agreed—cause his downfall.

2.

Before the close of 1865 President Johnson's so-called reconstructed states gave evidence of the spirit in the South following the Rebellion. That spirit was the spirit of the old South
plus the hatred and animosity engendered by the war.

The Negro who had wandered whistling at noonday from the
field was told to work as formerly he had worked. He would
"stand no sech treatment from no white man nohow" and gave
his employer insulting answers. Then likely he was whipped
or hung by the thumbs. When the Freedmen's Bureau officer
or commandant failed to satisfy the Negro's employer, the latter
took things into his own hands—paddling, flogging, drowning,
shooting, or burning the recalcitrant. A crime storm of devastating fury swept over the South. Negro school houses and churches
were burned. Ears were cropped and throats cut. Men and
women were stabbed, maimed, outraged, shot and hanged.
Others were hunted and killed by dogs. In North and South
Carolina alone, within a period of eighteen months, General

Canby reported 197 murders and 548 cases of aggravated assault. In Alabama corpses dangled for months from trees to poison the air and make the traveler sick with horror.

It was feared, in fact, that the Negro would take things in his own hands; hence the need to show him his place. "This is a white man's country," was the doctrine to which all the conventions subscribed.

"As to recognizing the rights of freedmen to their children," remarked a rich planter in a letter to General Fish, "I will say there is not one man or woman in all the South who believes they are free, but we consider them as stolen property—stolen by the bayonets of the damnable United States government."[29]

The Yankee teachers, abolitionist in sentiment and equalitarian in practice, represented a philosophy which was anathema to the Southern white. The program which they introduced met with hearty and active opposition. As the political controversy progressed from bitterness to violence, they became the object of social ostracism, persecution, and physical assault. Many were visited by the Ku Klux Klan, many were severely beaten, some tarred and covered with cotton.[30]

"Wherever I go," Carl Schurz summed up in his report, "the street, the shop, the house, the hotel, or the steamboat, I hear the people talk in such a way as to indicate that they are yet unable to conceive of the Negro as possessing any rights at all. Men who are honorable in their dealings with their white neighbors will cheat a Negro without feeling a single twinge of their honor. To kill a Negro they do not deem murder; to debauch a Negro woman, they do not think fornication; to take the property away from a Negro, they do not consider robbery. The people boast that when they get freedmen's affairs in their own hands, to use their expression, 'the niggers will catch hell.' "[31]

The South was paralyzed for want of labor. To force the Negroes to settle down to work and to hold to their contracts, "Black Laws" were enacted. The cruelty and injustice of these laws were great. Laws making it almost impossible for freedmen to secure a just return for their labor were followed by laws punishing him for his poverty. Almost every act, word, or gesture of the Negro, not consonant with good taste, good manners, good morals was made a crime or misdemeanor, for which he could be fined by the magistrates and then consigned to a condition almost of slavery for an indefinite time if he could not pay the bill. The Negro became something better than a serf, something less than a citizen.

Mississippi with her harsh and impolitic codes led the way. Negroes were to become lessees of lands or tenements nowhere in that state except in towns and cities. They must make annual contracts for their labor in writing. If they should run away from their tasks, they forfeited their wages for the year. Whenever required of them, they must present licenses citing their places of residence and authorizing them to work. Fugitives from labor were to be arrested and carried back to their employers. Five dollars a head and mileage were allowed for such Negro catchers. It was made a misdemeanor, punishable with fine or imprisonment, to "entice" a freedman to leave his employer, or to feed a runaway. Minors were to be apprenticed: if males until they were twenty-one, if females until eighteen years of age. Vagrants were to be fined heavily, and if they could not pay the sum, they were to be hired out to service until the claim was satisfied.

The system of pains and penalties in the South remained barbarous as measured by the standards of the North. The whipping post, the pillory, the stocks, treadmills, and chain gangs were words often seen in the Southern codes and aroused a great revulsion of feeling in the North.

A Southern writer was amazed at the stupidity of the Southerners. They acted as though they had been asleep during the war. Upon waking they had begun to legislate for the Negroes at a point "just where the Code of 1857 had left off." "The men who had brought this reproach upon Mississippi," said the Columbus (Miss.) *Sentinel,* were "as complete a set of political Goths as were ever turned loose to work destruction upon a State. The fortunes of the whole South have been injured by their folly."[32]

Friends of the Negro heard the rattle of chains and took alarm. It was of no avail to say that Northern states had vagrant laws and laws for masters and apprentices. These were the "slave codes" revived for the freedmen. "We tell the

white men of Mississippi," said the Chicago *Tribune,* "that
the men of the North will convert the State of Mississippi
into a frog pond before they will allow any such laws to
disgrace one foot of soil over which the flag of freedom
waves." "The moment we remove the iron hand from the
rebels' throats," said Greeley, "they will rise and attempt the
mastery." The denial of the right of the Negro to testify in
court was "an outrage against civilization."[33] Wendell Phillips in Steinway Hall, New York, suggested that the way to
handle the South was "to march thirty million men to the
Gulf" irrespective of men, women, and children, and "hang
a few generals."[34]

In Congress Sumner and Thaddeus Stevens took up the
cry. The "Black Codes" were represented as a deliberate attempt by the South to nullify the results of the war and to re-
establish slavery. Public opinion in the North therefore demanded that "Presidential" reconstruction be undone.

Besides, the success of Johnson's plan threatened to wreck
the Republican party, and by restoring the Democrats to
power, bring back Southern supremacy and Northern vassalage.
The humanitarian ideas of the North harmonized too well with
the political ideas of Congress.

Four men were responsible for the Congressional policy
of Reconstruction: Andrew Johnson by his obstinacy and bad
behavior; Thaddeus Stevens by his revengefulness and parliamentary tyranny; Charles Sumner by his vigilant persistence;
and Wendell Phillips by his fiery speeches.

The Seceded States, declared Sumner, had virtually committed
suicide: they had abdicated all rights under the Constitution
and were now practically territories under the exclusive jurisdiction of Congress. Congress should punish the rebels by
abolishing slavery, by giving civil and political rights to the
Negroes, and by educating them with the whites.

Not essentially different but harsher was Thaddeus Stevens'
plan. This dark-eyed, savage-faced, lame old man of seventy-three
bluntly declared that the South was a conquered province, having
no constitutional rights the victor was bound to respect. Con-

gress, not the President, was the only power competent to "revive, create, and reinstate these provinces into the family of States." "Strip a proud nobility of their bloated estates; reduce them to a level with plain republicans; send them forth to labor and teach their children to enter the workshops or handle a plow, and you will thus humble the proud traitors. . . . The foundations of their institutions, both political, municipal, and social, *must* be broken up and *relaid*, or all our blood and treasure have been spent in vain."[35]

The thunder rolled and the floods descended; it was the doom of reconstruction by the President's method. The Thirty-Ninth Congress met on Monday, December 4. Whittier speaking for the Abolitionists apostrophized its members in verse—

> O people—chosen! Are ye not
> Likewise the chosen of the Lord
> To do His Will and speak His word?
>
> Say to the pardon-seekers: Keep
> Your manhood; bend no suppliant knees,
> Nor palter with unworthy pleas;
>
> Make all men peers before the law,
> Take hands from off the Negro's throat,
> Give black and white an equal vote.[36]

Edward McPherson, clerk of the House, presided. Floor, galleries, anterooms were packed with people. The hour of twelve struck and the middlesized, smoothfaced young man with blue eyes and light sunny hair, rapped for order. He called the roll. Kentucky finished, he proceeded to Indiana. Tennessee with its eight members, at least five of them firmly loyal, was passed over. Horace Maynard of the second district of the State, armed with a certificate of election, rose and addressed the clerk. He was called to order. "Does the clerk decline to hear me?" The clerk did decline though Maynard rose twice. One hundred and seventy-six representatives were present; it was a quorum for the transaction of business without calling one

Southerner's name. The majority desired to proceed at once to the election of Schuyler Colfax to the speakership.

But first James Brookes of New York, minority leader, gained the floor. "If Tennessee is not in the Union," said he, "and has not been in the Union, and is not a loyal state, and the people of Tennessee are aliens and foreigners to this Union, by what right does the President of the United States usurp his place in the White House?" He asked that Mr. Maynard be allowed to be heard. But Thaddeus Stevens and others effectually interposed. And the House was soon listening to Schuyler Colfax's periods in an address of thanks about "a Republican form of government," "the men who had died that the Republic might live," "the fires of civil war" which had "melted every fetter in the land and proved the funeral pyre of slavery."

"The door had been shut in the rebel faces; it was still to be bolted." In a few minutes, Thaddeus Stevens, his old wig awry, reared his venerable frame and moved the appointment of a Joint Committee of Fifteen, nine members from the House and six from the Senate, to "inquire into the condition of the States which formed the so-called Confederate States of America and report whether they or any of them are entitled to be represented in either house of Congress." He had driven his scheme through the caucus on Saturday night and the resolution was passed by a vote of 129-35.[37]

The Radical majority having the whip hand proceeded to wield it. It divided the Old Confederacy into five military districts and over each district placed an army general. The Reconstructed States had to ratify the Fourteenth and Fifteenth Amendments. It also passed two bills: the Freedmen's Bureau and the Civil Rights Act, the latter making citizenship a United States and not a state affair and guaranteeing certain civil rights to Negroes. Both of these bills President Johnson vetoed, but the radical majority was strong enough to pass them over his veto. "For the first time," said Phillips of the Reconstruction Bill, "Congress proposes action to which it does not ask Southern assent. It orders. Like a conqueror it dictates terms—terms to which it orders submission. This is a great step, an immense gain."[38]

Radical Reconstruction had positive benefits. State constitutions as drawn up by the carpet baggers were so harmonious with progressive tendencies that they have substantially survived to the present day. These constitutions achieved reforms in the organization of the courts, in the codes of judicial procedure, in the systems of county government and school administration, in the manner of electing public officials and in methods of taxation. Through them the Southerners learned of the equality of all men before the law, the right of all children to attend state-supported schools.[39] Even a partisan-minded historian generously admits that the Radicals by their lip service and laws elevated education into a position of first importance. They provided on paper for elaborate school systems calling for appropriations shocking to Southerners. They established the principle of an obligation to levy taxes for education. And they set up the rights of the Negroes to be educated. These were genuine contributions.[40]

But the South trampled upon many features of the democratic concept. For Radical Reconstruction was an assault upon the theory of white supremacy. This explains why it seemed that the whites "had gone crazy with anger or were obsessed with some fearful mania" when confronted with "gibbering, louse-eaten, devil-worshipping barbarians from the jungles of Dahomey" in legislative halls. Even if these regimes had shown exemplary statesmanship, they would have been unacceptable to white Southerners as long as Negroes comprising any part of them were regarded as political equals.[41]

As the sociologist Gunnar Myrdal remarks: the schoolbook histories, as well as the more scholarly histories, perpetuate the myths about the Reconstruction period. They still give, for the most part, undue emphasis to the sordid details of the Reconstruction governments but avoid mentioning their accomplishments. "They exaggerate the extent of 'black domination' and deprecate the Negro politicians even more than they deserve while they give subtle excuses for the cruelty and fraud employed in the restoration of white supremacy. They usually make all the errors found in the scholarly histories and omit all the complicating qualifications that make the scholarly histories have a semblance of objectivity."[42]

Perhaps the Reconstruction, in a sense, can be characterized as "a prolonged race riot." The Ku Klux Klan and a dozen similar organizations which sprang up over the South were as inevitable as a chemical reaction. Their purpose was punitive and regulatory—the restoration of absolute white supremacy. "They flogged, intimidated, maimed, hanged, murdered, not only for actual attacks and crimes against whites, but for all sorts of trivial and imagined offenses. Every Negro was assumed to be 'bad' unless he proved by his actions that he was 'good.' . . . The number of Negroes killed during Reconstruction will never be known. Five thousand would probably be a conservative estimate."[43]

The bloody riots at New Orleans advanced the Radical cause tremendously. While some Negroes were marching to a political convention in New Orleans, they became engaged in brawls with white spectators. Shots were exchanged, and the Negroes took refuge in the convention hall. Bells of the city were rung. Immediately work ceased in the saw mills and shops, and the Mayor's police, the firemen with their iron wrenches, bands of ex-Confederate soldiers, and the rabble generally, ran into the streets and rushed pell mell for the convention hall. Whites and blacks inside and outside the building were stabbed, clubbed, and shot. The wounded, pleading for mercy, were cruelly beaten with brickbats. Disorder spread to the far parts of the city. Negroes fell in the general massacre and their dwellings were burned to the ground. Sheridan hurried back from Texas, but before he came fifty persons had been killed and one hundred and fifty more wounded. It was not a riot, he telegraphed to Grant, but "an absolute massacre by the police which was not excelled in its murderous cruelty by that of Fort Pillow."[44]

"The hands of the Rebels are again red with loyal blood; Rebel armies have once more begun the work of massacre," wrote the *Tribune*. It mourned "brothers and friends . . . butchered by a Rebel mob" and held Andrew Johnson responsible.[45] "Charles IX of France," Sumner thundered, "was not more completely the author of the massacre of St. Bartholomew than

Andrew Johnson is the author of those recent massacres which now cry for judgment . . . and a guilty •President may suffer the same retribution which followed a guilty king." Carl Schurz, a new citizen and a hot Republican patriot, whose adverse report on the South was circulated widely, pronounced that Johnson ought to be hanged, and that he was worse than Judas Iscariot or Benedict Arnold. Congressman Logan declared that the only way to treat the Southerners was to "take the torch in one hand and the sword in the other . . . and sweep over the territory."[46]

"Let us hear no more of Andrew Johnson's sufferings in Tennessee," said Wendell Phillips. "The Andrew Johnsons of Louisiana he shot and stabbed in the streets of New Orleans. . . . This is all idle. The whites of the South are our enemies. If the Union is ever reconstructed, it must be reconstructed from the blacks. What New Orleans is today, Washington will be in December, ruled by the President and his mob,—unless the people prevent!"[47]

CHAPTER FORTY-SIX

HUSSAR JACKETS

At first Phillips turned expectantly to Johnson. "I believe in him," he said. But when Johnson revealed his hand, Phillips denounced the President's policies in a blistering lecture. "The South Victorious," he tauntingly called it.

"They come into the Union as they went out, an aristocracy. The same men, with the same theories are to put their hands on the helm of state.

"The South is victorious today, and victorious for a dozen years to come. (Tremendous and continued cheering.) Slavery is being reestablished by Congress and there is a spectre walking over the country in its shroud. . . . If the President succeeds, he shall write his name higher than Burr or Arnold."[1]

Friends asked Phillips to repeat his lecture in New York, but he refused. He was sickened by the pro-slavery attitude of men of that city and he would "rather not breathe the same atmosphere with them." But he did come in a few days and spoke in Cooper Institute.

"Jefferson Davis Johnson," he dubbed the President. "This mobocrat of the White House," "tipsy mountebank," "vagabond brawler," "pardoner of murderers," Phillips called him,[2] "this St. Michael whose resistless sword was to mow down the Satan of the fallen hosts."[3]

Congress too felt the whiplash of Phillips's tongue. He complained bitterly of "the dawdling Congress," "the surrender of Congress," "its truck and bicker policy." "It may be bought, bul-

538

lied, or deceived. We wish to put on record our affirmation that the trimmers and hucksters of today, who counsel a new order of things in which knaves and honest men shall stand just equal, all these milk and water statesmen are to be reminded that this is not a game of jackstraws but a war. . . ."[4]

"It was this policy of conciliation which betrayed Hamlin . . . and went down to the grocery corners of Tennessee to dig up this drunken nightmare which rides us today.

"Henceforth let our bugle call be: *No State admitted at present, and none ever admitted which has the word 'white' or the recognition of race in its Statute Books.*"[5]

"You and half a dozen others redeem Congress," •Phillips wrote to Sumner in one of his commanding or cajoling notes. "Your arguments have been grand and exhaustive." Again:

"Now at the risk of boring you let me offer one suggestion. Remember these are not times of *ordinary* politics; they are formative hours: the national purpose and thought grows and ripens in thirty days as much as ordinary years bring it forward. We radicals have all the elements of national education in our hands—pressure of vast debt—uncertainty of it—capital unwilling to risk itself in the South but longing to do so—vigilant masses—every returned soldier a witness—every defeated emigrant to the South a witness and weight. . . .

"Now this is not the time to consult harmony. Harmony purchased at any sacrifice of the absolute need of the hour is dangerous. To do nothing is infinitely better and safer than to do half what we need. . . . Plant yourselves on the bare claim: no state readmitted without impartial suffrage—live and die by that vote alone, if necessary, against everything short of it. . . . Disclaim all coming down to the level of dead Whiggery (Fessenden), cowardly Republicanism (Wilson), disguised Copperhead (Doolittle), unadulterated treason (Raymond) stolid ignorance of this epoch at least (Trumbull)—and stand for what every clear-sighted man sees and confesses as *indispensable* for safe settlement. . . . Secure as many 'civil rights' as you

can, bolster up as many Bureaux as you please, but never
open your doors to any State unless on *avowed* principle
of Negro suffrage. But I weary you—you *get* my idea—trust
it and the coming years very soon will justify it."[6]

(One cannot escape the impression that throughout this
period Phillips's influence on his friend was formative and
tremendous.)

When Phillips felt that an alliance offensive and defensive
had been made between the Supreme Court and the President,
he advocated the abolition of the court. "The nation must be
saved," said he, "no matter what or how venerable the foe
whose existence goes down before that necessity."[7]

The first public blast against Johnson had been sounded
by Phillips at the New England Anti-Slavery Convention, Boston, May 31, on a resolution offered by himself: "The reconstruction of the rebel states without Negro suffrage is a practical
surrender to the Confederacy . . .

"Better, far better, would it have been for Grant to have
surrendered to Lee than for Johnson to have surrendered to
North Carolina."[8]

In May, 1866, at the annual meeting of the American Anti-
Slavery Society Phillips reiterated his stand—

> "The rebellion has not ceased; it has only changed its
> weapons. Once it fought, now it intrigues; once it followed
> Lee in arms, now it follows President Johnson in guile and
> chicanery; once it had its headquarters in Richmond, now
> it encamps in the White House.
> "I hold that the American Anti-Slavery Society meets
> to say this to the American people: that those who repre-
> sented the black race in this struggle of two generations,
> are not content; that they protest against every settlement
> that has been proposed, either by Congress or the President,
> of the national crisis. . . . The Society announces today
> the only cure that is possible for the national hurt is uni-
> versal amnesty and universal suffrage, wherever the na-
> tional flag floats. (Applause.)"[9]

Phillips denied that the Civil War (which he called the revolution)[10] was ended. Slavery was not ended. The black codes ruled the South. Mississippi had her vagrant laws. South Carolina had her lash. Louisiana had the power of contract given to the blacks for ten days in January and denied to them three hundred and fifty-five days in the year. Slavery was not ended: the slave oligarchy was still ruling; the South was unconverted; she was only smothered by force, crowded down by strength. She had not given up her theory, insisted Phillips. "Withdraw the troops and she will throw our Bureau and our teachers out of her limits. She will neither allow a Yankee schoolmaster nor a Federal officer to dictate between her and her subjects. . . ."

But the South was a conquered section, said some. In a sense, yes, remarked Phillips. Its idea was conquered. It was a fight between democratic impartial manhood and the government of classes. The democratic principle conquered and had a right to dictate—not to dictate in the sense in which England would dictate in the conquered territory of Denmark if she dared, or as Prussia would dictate in Holstein, but in this sense only: when a civil war had been waged for an idea and when in the conflict one of the opposing ideas has vanquished the other, that idea had a right to dictate relating to the issues involved in the strugggle.

"We have conquered, not the geographical South but the ideal South; its thumb-screws and slavery, its no-schools, its white men born, booted, and spurred, and its black men born, saddled and bridled for them to ride; the South which imprisons teachers, which denies Bibles, which raises up half its population in concubinage and ignorance, which denies the right of marriage between men and women— that South we have conquered, and we have a right to trample it under the heels of our boots. (Applause.) That is the meaning of the war. Whenever a question relating to such issues comes before Congress, its power over it is the war power, omnipotent until the end is secured. . . .

"The whole North should ring out its protest. Every congressman should feel himself leaning back upon constituency all aglow with resistance to the treason of the White House. There should ring out such a protest against the betrayal of the issues of the war, as would make even Andrew Johnson turn his footsteps back to honest courses."[11]

In speaking on the resolutions before the Society, Phillips told a story.

"I have a great delight in taming animals. Rarey is a hero of mine. The other day I read of the taming of a lion in Paris. They took a stuffed hussar jacket, covered with a hundred brass buttons, and they put it in the den. He tore it to pieces and devoured it and had an awful fit of indigestion—lay a sick lion for a week. Afterward, whenever a man clad in a hussar jacket came into the cage, the lion lay silent and submissive before him. He would never touch a hussar jacket, whatever it had in it. Now America devoured one hussar jacket with 'John Tyler' written on it, and another with 'Fillmore' written on it, and now another in Andy Johnson. Not as wise as the brute, in spite of political indigestion, this nation goes on devouring hussar jackets."[12]

At Cooper Institute Phillips again struck the same insistent note: Root up the old South, permeate her channels and make her over, cover her with a rich and prosperous growth of Northern emigration, brains, and money. "That is the right which victory has given to the better and dominant idea." And he added: "Depose the President."

Phillips kept on stressing his point. (The art of propaganda was an art Phillips had learned and practiced well. He was never in fear of repeating himself; repetition made dominant and indelible the impression he wished to make.) At the evening session of the American Anti-Slavery Society he remarked: "What I say to the American people is, that we want absolute control over the Southern territory until the seeds are planted. I want the nineteenth century carried down there."[13] And his speech before the New England Anti-Slavery Society emphasized the same idea:—

"When once the nation is absolutely, irrevocably pledged
to the principle that there shall be no recognition of race by
the United States or by State law, then the work of the great
anti-slavery movement which commenced in 1831 is accomplished."

Phillips did not mince terms. Just what the South had intended for the North, he wanted to mete out to her. She had
intended to take the northern belt of the continent and consecrate it to slavery. If she had conquered, she would have done
it and have had the right to do it by the rules of war.

> "She would have called the roll of her slaves on Bunker
> Hill and put her flag over Faneuil Hall. As she did not con-
> quer, we have a right to crowd Faneuil Hall down the
> throat of every one of those millions. (Applause.) We have
> a right to carry the civilization against which they re-
> belled down there. Our victory means, ought to mean,
> Bunker Hill in the Carolinas and Faneuil Hall in New
> Orleans. . . ."[14]

These are militant words, but typical of Phillips when he
saw the freedom of the slave endangered. Then he became a
fanatical and relentless Puritan warrior hewing at the serpent.
But again he was back in the calm and peaceful sunshine of
ideas.

> "The cry at the South is 'Keep out the Yankees!' What
> does it mean? It does not mean the individual, palpable
> Yankee. The individual Yankee who goes down there is
> received as kindly as need be, in many cases. It is the ideal
> Yankee—the Yankee of small farms—the Yankee of New
> England—the Yankee who represents Northern civilization,
> against which the South rose. If you had asked Jefferson
> Davis, Alexander Stephens, at Montgomery, 'What are you
> warring against?' the answer would have been,—'We are
> warring against the North overwhelming the South'—mean-
> ing by 'the North,' not the geographical North, but the ideal
> North—the North of enterprise and energy, the North of
> education and equality, the North of toleration and free
> education, the North of books and brains, the North of the

Declaration of Independence. It was in the service of that North that we conquered, and the war will be ended when that North goes down to the Gulf, and not sooner."[15]

"What we ask for the Negro," added Phillips, "is justice; not charity, not patronage, but justice."

"I can never forget—I never wish to forget, the long years I have been permitted to serve the Negro race. The poor, poor Negro, who never yet leaned on the word of a white man without finding it a broken reed, the thread of whose fate never mingled with ours without painting a picture of wretchedness, though of honor to him and infamy to us. (Applause.). . . .
"We never repudiate money debts. That is dangerous. Money kings can hit back. The Negro has no friends. Let him go to the wall, starve, or be shot. Who cares?"[16]

Phillips wrote a letter to the *Anti-Slavery Standard* urging a constitutional amendment authorizing Congress to establish common schools in any state destitute of them, at the State's expense, and another amendment securing universal suffrage. Suffrage was "opportunity, education, fair play, the right to office, and elbow room."[17]

The Ballot and Education were but two great steps in the right direction. Phillips demanded a third: Land. Confiscate the large estates, he declared, and divide them with the Negro. "Confiscation is mere naked justice to the former slave. Who brought the land into cultivation? Whose sweat and toil are mixed with it forever? Who cleared those forests? Who made those roads? Whose hand reared those houses? Whose wages are invested in those warehouses and towns? Of course, the Negro's. . . . Why should he not have a share of his inheritance?"[18]

"The angry South," "the reluctant South," was stonehearted, untrustworthy, and irreconcilable, on the alert to defraud and enslave the Negro. Phillips considered it time that the South was told that Northerners put no confidence either in oaths or parchments, that they left no guarantee untouched, that they

would believe the Negro safe when they saw him with forty
acres under his foot, the schoolhouse behind him, a ballot in his
right hand, and the sceptre of the Federal Government over his
head.

"I will tell you my faith. I do not believe God ever converted an adult generation. I do not believe in the efficacy
of battle or a few cannon on the wrong side in changing
the lifelong opinions of a man like Jefferson Davis or Wade
Hampton. I believe, as all history shows, that adult men
in the mass go to their graves with the opinions to which
they have been wedded during most of their lives. Believing
that, I want no evidence today but that of the general principle that one half at least of the white men of the Southern
States are rebels today in heart and in purpose."[19]

Revenge? "We still hold that treason and murder ought to
be punished, and that it is a most unsound as well as disgraceful 'policy' to treat murderers like honest men in order
to conciliate other murders. . . . Jefferson Davis is one of the
vilest and guiltiest men of the century." And Phillips went on
in extreme and intemperate fashion (but with a voice, quiet,
serene, composed):—

"A thousand men rule the rebellion—are the rebellion.
A thousand men. We cannot hang them all. We cannot hang
men in regiments. What! cover the continent with gibbets!
We cannot sicken the nineteenth century with such a sight.
It would sink our civilization to the level of Southern bar-
barism . . .
"Banish everyone of these thousand rebel leaders—every
one of them, on pain of death if they ever return! (Loud
applause.) Confiscate every dollar and acre they own.
(Applause.) These steps the world and their followers
will see are necessary to kill the seeds of caste, dangerous
States rights and secession.
"Banish Lee with the rest. (Applause.) No government
should ask of the South which he has wasted, or of the
North which he has murdered such superabundant Christian
patience as to tolerate in our streets the presence of a wretch

whose hand upheld Libby Prison and Andersonville, and whose soul is black with 64,000 deaths of prisoners by starvation and torture."[20]

Again he sounded the call to the radicals in Congress:— "Hang out the banner of impartial suffrage and rebel disfranchisement on the outmost wall. Throttle the President. Clean out that nest of unclean birds—the Cabinet. Rally patriotism to the front. Every other policy is death!"[21]

"Wendell Phillips does not dislike the Republican party," said the New York *World*, "for it is his creature; but the Republican party dislikes Wendell Phillips for he is its master. He whips up the host. The bummers are exasperated by the bugle which summons them up and urges them onward."[22]

The New York *Daily News* held the same view:—

> "Mr. Wendell Phillips is perhaps a little ahead of his party, but they are traveling the same path and making for the same goal. Where Mr. Phillips stood a few months ago, the Radicals stand today; where he stands today they will doubtless be a few months hence. He is apparently the pilot fish of the political sharks.
>
> "We like to deal with Wendell Phillips. He is plain spoken. There is no misunderstanding him. He reveals his political self with the unblushing absence of apparel of Venus rising from the sea. . . . He tells us plainly that Radicalism is determined to rule or ruin."[23]

Phillips was indeed the real leader, "the enfant terrible,"[24] "the great war horse" of the Republican party.[25] "What does Phillips say?" was the first query regarding each new phase of the struggle. Every word he spoke or wrote had the weight of an oracle. His articles were regularly copied from the *Anti-Slavery Standard* to the pages of the leading newspapers of the country. He became special contributor to the *Standard* and when its editor, Aaron Powell, was ill, wrote the editorials. He was in touch with Sumner, Wilson, Wade in the Senate, with Kelley, Stevens, Colfax in the House. He was recognized as the most prominent figure in unofficial life.

At no other period since their formation did the American Anti-Slavery Society, the New England Anti-Slavery Society, and the Massachusetts Anti-Slavery Society possess the influence they now wielded. They were so many multiplications of Wendell Phillips worked by his friends, vitalized by his spirit. Crowds jammed their meetings. Statesmen in Washington recognized their services. "Hold the societies together," wrote Sumner to Phillips. "The crisis is grave. You and they are doing indispensable work; in this I express the conviction of every Senator and every Representative on our side of pending questions."[26]

In the summer of 1866 Phillips was urged to accept the nomination for Congress by the workers of his district. It was felt that he might be what John Bright was in Parliament. Journals in Boston and New York strongly favored the project. But the agitator refused even to consider a nomination. He believed he could serve the Radical Cause better out of Congress than in it. His position now was unique, made so by his perfect independence. "The proper leader of the Radical Republican platform does better," said the editor of the New York *Times* "as a faithful and impartial critic of men and measures outside of legislative halls and independent of all party alliances. By virtue of his position he can proclaim in advance unwelcome truths which other men hesitate to speak."[27] Phillips remained untrammelled.

Using the old agencies he went up and down instructing, warning, denouncing, inspiring. His text was constantly, persistently this—

"Better a renewal of the war than a surrender of the Negro to the control of his old master. The real basis of reconstruction should be to concentrate all power exclusively in the hands of our friends, the loyal white men and the Negro. . . .[28]

"It is a struggle between the nation and traitors, between the Conqueror and the conquered, between men of property and swindlers, between justice and infamy. Shame on us if the scale of treason and infamy do not kick the beam! Shame on us if the struggle be no immediately ended!"

From the close of the war onward, Phillips was in enormous demand. No lecture course was deemed complete without him. His name was a magnet, and months in advance his dates were filled. "Dear Sir—I have looked through my book and am sorry to find that I have no evening to offer you. . . . I must be excused."[30] Again: "Do not suppose from your not having any answer to your interesting and welcome note that I forgot you. The truth is . . . I have lectured almost every day since I saw you. . . ."[31] Or: "All my days are taken"; "The tyrant has not yet relaxed his hold—even the engagements I made I have sometimes been forced to break."[32]

The season of 1866-67 opened in Boston with a lecture on "The Swindling Congress" (the 39th) which put juggles for justice. In this lecture he said:—

> "There have never been any friends of the Southerner in the Northern States but the Abolitionists. The Democrats deluded him; the Whigs cheated him; the Abolitionists stood on his border and said: 'It is in vain for you to fight against the thick bosses of Jehovah's buckler. You are endeavoring to sustain a system that repudiates the laws of God and the spirit of the nineteenth century; put it away, or you will make blood and bankruptcy your guests.' But the maddened South closed its eyes and rushed on to destruction. Now we say, 'Come into line with the age, found your economy on righteousness, and then spindles will make vocal every stream and fill every valley.'"[33]

From Boston, Phillips proceeded westward and was welcomed everywhere with enthusiasm. During the day and on Sundays he spoke on Temperance; in the evenings on the crisis.

At St. Louis the *Daily Despatch* printed his lecture in full and remarked editorially: "Wendell Phillips has exercised a greater influence on the destinies of the country as a private man than any public man, or men, of his age."[34]

From Alton, Illinois, he wrote to the *Standard* describing the grave of Lovejoy:—

"The gun fired at him was like that at Sumter—it scattered a world of dreams. Looking back, how wise as well as noble his course was. Incredible that we should have been compelled to defend his 'prudence.' What world-wide benefactors these 'imprudent' men are! How 'prudently' most men creep into nameless graves; while now and then one or two forget themselves into immortality."[35]

The orator returned to Boston in April after giving sixty lectures and traveling more than 12,000 miles.

In this period needy friends seeking office constantly importuned him for aid. His correspondence with Sumner is sprinkled with earnest appeals in their behalf:

"Happy New Year, Dear Sumner—You are a magnanimous man—so I (in strict confidence, without any one's *knowledge*) write to give you the opportunity you wish.

"Your once friend A. G. Browne has lost all his means—cheated out of the remnant of his fortune by one whom he too much trusted (his usual fault—too generous) . . . asks some position as Appraiser by which he can get bread while he turns round to help himself. . . ." (Jan. 1, 1870.)

Or: "My friend Sigismund Lasar, a German radical, a real good fellow, active in all right things—wants to be appointed Commissioner to the Hamburg Exhibition. He asks no pay—wishes no appropriation—only desires the official mantle. . . . Now for his sake, for the nation's, and for mine, name him Commissioner." (May 21, 1869-?)

A nudging note: "Excuse my importunity—But your generous efforts for Browne has resulted in nothing yet. Of course he makes no complaint. But I feel disappointed as well as surprised." (May Day, 1870.)[36]

Or—to George W. Julian:—"A friend wishes to study the land question. May I trouble you," etc.[37] Later to James G. Blaine:—"Do you know anyone likely to be interested in an effort made by the bearer of this, Mr. E. A. Hutchins . . . to introduce to public notice . . . Heliotype copies of Hogarth? If so," etc. etc.[38]

About this time an event occurred which caused Phillips much pain. Francis Jackson, dying in Boston some years before, had left a will bequeathing $10,000. to the Anti-Slavery cause. Phillips, Garrison, Quincy, and others were the executors with Phillips as chairman. The Thirteenth Amendment abolished slavery before the money became available and the question then arose: What should be done with the fund? The majority agreed with Phillips that it ought to go toward the support of the *Anti-Slavery Standard*. The minority composed of seceders from the American Anti-Slavery Society wished to hand over the bequest to the Freedman's Union for educational purposes. The court urged the executors to agree. They could not agree, and the money went by decision of the court to the Freedman's Union. At first an agreement had been reached, but Garrison, on the eve of departing for Europe, withdrew his assent to it. His excuse was flimsy. It is impossible to avoid the conclusion that the conduct of the minority of the trustees was dictated by pique and grudge. The immediate effect was to throw upon Phillips a financial burden which the fund would have helped him to bear. He thought this conduct was unkind and unworthy and felt it keenly.

In the course of his lectures Phillips addressed the Lyceum at Gloucester, Massachusetts. Returning home by train the next morning, he fell in with a lady who got on at a way station. She was a Southern refugee who had been reduced to poverty and was supporting herself and her children by giving an occasional lecture before a country audience. It was a terrific struggle, for the field was full and she was unknown and friendless. Phillips saw her get into the car and asked her to take a seat beside him. It was a winter day and she was thinly clad and shivering from the cold. Observing this, Phillips asked:

"Where did you speak last night?"

She told him it was at a town about ten miles distant from the railway.

"And—I wouldn't be impertinent—how much did they pay you?"

"Five dollars, and the fare to and from Boston."

"Five dollars!" he exclaimed; "why I always get one or two hundred; and your lecture must be worth more than mine,—you give facts, I only opinions."

"Small as it is, I am very glad to get it, Mr. Phillips," she replied. "I would talk at that rate every night during the winter."

He sat for a moment in silence; then he put his hand into his pocket, drew out a roll of banknotes, and said in a hesitating way:

"I don't want to give offence, but you know I preach that a woman is entitled to the same as a man if she does the same work. Now, my price is one or two hundred dollars; and if you will let me divide it with you, I shall not have had any more than you, and the thing will be even."

She at first refused; but after a little gentle urging, she put the banknotes into her purse. At the end of her journey, she counted the roll, and found it contained one hundred dollars. The lady was a niece of Jefferson Davis.[39]

CHAPTER FORTY-SEVEN

"IMPEACH THE REBEL!"

At the Radical Republican Convention held in Philadelphia, a resolution was offered requesting President Johnson to resign. The delegates rose to their feet cheering lustily. "Good! good!" they cried. A voice was heard amidst the confusion:—"No need for him to resign; Chicago will save him the trouble. They'll throw him in the lake. They'll poison the waters of Lake Huron with his carcass."[1]

Thaddeus Stevens was the grand master of invective:—

"A Congress elected by the people to resist armed traitors were not disposed to cower before the usurped sceptre of a single apostate. . . . You all remember that in Egypt the Lord sent frogs, locusts, murrain, and lice, and finally demanded the blood of the first born of all the oppressors. Almost all of these have been sent upon us. More than the first-born has been taken from us. We have been oppressed with taxes and debts, and He has sent us more than lice, and has afflicted us with Andrew Johnson."[2]

"We will march once more," shouted Butler, "and woe to him who opposes us. What! six millions of Rebels who have renounced the Constitution, who have murdered 500,000 of our citizens, who have loaded the nation with debt and drenched it with blood, when conquered have forfeited no right, have lost no jurisdiction or civil authority!"[3]

Passions were stirred. The Radicals played upon every fear and every hatred that might serve their purpose. They did not dare raise economic issues for they would have lost half of their party. In the East economic issues were insinuated into the campaign; in the farming West, when conservatives raised them, they were shouted down as non-political and irrelevant. If the South could be excluded or admitted only with Negro suffrage, the new industrial order which the Northeast was developing, was safe. Intentionally, then, economic issues were befogged.

If the Southern representatives were returned, the tariff would be lowered, the debt repudiated, government bonds taxed and payable in greenbacks. The South was traditionally opposed to national banks; hence Eastern bankers dreaded to see the South return. Hard money men, deflationists, business men who wished federal protection, land speculators who sought confiscated lands, and new corporations, shared their dread.

Congress was spending money lavishly—squandering the national revenues through extravagance and corruption. They voted themselves a "salary grab," increasing their own pay from three to five thousand dollars, and gave the soldiers only $100. Retrenchment would have been a cry popular with taxpayers all over the country. The New York *Herald* took it up. Editors pleaded with Johnson privately as well as editorially to force the issue into the Congressional Campaign. Radicals, said that paper, "think that they can raise enough noise about Negro riots, restoration, and other side topics to keep the financial question out of the coming canvass and carry all the Northern States. But they forget that every voter is a taxpayer." The *Herald* calculated the cost of "reckless squandering" of the public treasure at $250,000,000.

Johnson failed to advertise the extravagance of Congress. By training and instinct, however, he was the enemy of the bondholders, national banks, monopolies, and a protective tariff. Had he, then, followed his bent and launched into the campaign an attack upon the economic views of the Eastern wing of the Radical party, he would have aroused the West and split the Radical party at one blow. Instead he maintained strict silence.

The Congressional Campaign of 1866 resulted in Johnson's downfall. The victory of the radicals was due not only to adroit tactics on their own part, but to the mistakes, bad judgment, and bad manners on part of the President. His violent language and undignified bearing cost him the support of thousands.

On Washington's birthday, a surging crowd of wildly excited partisans—a fighting crowd—gathered at the White House to cheer and encourage the President. There was music and shouting and a great demonstration. Andrew Johnson was the second Andrew Jackson—"a man not to be bullied or intimidated."[4] Calls went up for a speech. Emerging from the North door on to the White House terrace and looking into the faces of these cheering people, the man caught their spirit and forgot he was the ruler of millions. He was in Tennessee again. He was fighting the battles of the Union, standing for the Constitution and the old flag. He threw discretion to the winds.

Girding up his loins and addressing the excited crowd, he asked:—

"What usurpation has Andrew Johnson been guilty of? What is his offence? His only usurpation has been standing between the people and the encroachments of power. . . . Though I am opposed to the Davises, the Toombs, the Slidells and the long list of such, yet when I perceive on the other end of the line men still opposed to the Union, I am equally against them, and I am free to say I am still with the people."

(Voice from crowd): "Name three of the men you allude to."

"The gentleman calls for three names and I will give them to him. I say Thaddeus Stevens of Pennsylvania, I say Charles Sumner of Massachusetts, and I say Wendell Phillips of Massachusetts. (Applause.)"

Throughout Johnson's speech there was wild cheering, laughter, and applause. Someone asked about Forney—once the President's friend, now his worst detractor. "Forney?" the President replied. "I do not waste my fire on dead ducks."

The President grew more personal. He declared the American people by instinct knew who their friends were and that Andrew Johnson in all his positions from alderman to president had been their friend.

"I have occupied many positions in the government, going through both branches of the legislature—" (Interruption: "And was once a tailor.")

"Some gentleman here behind me says that I was once a tailor. Now that don't affect me in the least. When I was a tailor, I always made a close fit, was punctual to my customers, and did good work."

A Voice.—"No patchwork!"

The President.—"No, I did not want any patchwork. But we pass by this disgression."

And so on in the same manner. Concluding the President declared that he wished the thirty million American people "could sit in an amphitheatre and witness the great struggle now going on to preserve the Constitution of our Fathers in which struggle I am but your instrument."[5]

The maundering speech was condemned or defended according to the political sympathies of him who judged it. The New York *Herald* found the speech to be "bold, manly, and outspoken." Seward gave it the seal of his approval. "It is all right and safe," he telegraphed from New York. It was a "glorious speech," Thurlow Weed wrote to the President. "Traitors will seek hiding places."[6]

"The nation held its nose ez one man," wrote Petroleum V. Nasby (David R. Locke). "The Ablishnists who had previously sworn that he wuzn't drunk when he was inoggerated, admitted that they might hev bin, and ondoubtedly wuz mistaken." It was an "appalling picture." It would suffuse "every honest brow with shame," said Dead Duck Forney in his two newspapers.[7] James Russell Lowell speaking for the North asked—"Shall we descend to a mass meeting?"[8]

In the summer the President started on a speech making tour of the West which was called "Swinging Around the Circle," and thereby wrote his political death warrant. Every time he made a speech, heckled by persons in the crowd, he lost his temper, fulminated against Congress and the Radical leaders, and conducted himself like the drunken soap box ranter he was reputed to be.

Dead Duck Forney in the Philadelphia *Press* headed an account of Johnson's progress from town to town with, "I," the next day with "Me," again with "I, Me, My," or with "Myself." Johnson's policy for the peaceful and immediate restoration of the Southern States came to be known everywhere as "My Policy." It was "My Policy" in Philadelphia, "My Policy" in New York, "My Policy" in Albany, Auburn, Buffalo, and Chicago.[9]

The organized partisan mobbing of the President began. Town after town turned out its ruffians. He was greeted with insulting placards and shouts for Grant and Custer, hooting and groaning. At Steubenville there was such noise that Johnson did not respond. Custer, furious, hurled defiance at the mob, and Johnson in one sentence paid his compliments to the decent part of the crowd and "in a cat-o'-nine-tails" paid his respects to the "blackguards," and retired.[10] At Pittsburgh, he was denied a hearing, the mob shouting insults for an hour until Grant appeared and ordered the rowdies home. At Indianapolis, while the President was at dinner, a riot broke out in the lobby of his hotel and several persons were killed or wounded.

The press correspondents hated the President. Like Grant, he dealt with them brusquely when they interfered with the efficient administration of the war. In Tennessee he had no time for interviews; he was indifferent to their favor, often curt. The correspondents bided their time and bore their grudges. Now on the President's tour they saw their chance and wreaked all the accumulated grievances of years upon his head.

Radicals spoke of Johnson's special train as a traveling barroom and called him a demagogue, a trickster, a drunken, perjured and usurping traitor, a culprit with a "bloodstained and cowardly hand," an "insolent, drunken brute in comparison with whom Caligula's horse was respectable."[11] Petroleum V. Nasby regaled the public with a farcical life of "Androo Johnson includin' his infancy, his boyhood and his dimocrisy and abolishunism, separate and mixed"—by Nasby, "a democrat uv thirty years standin' who never skratched his ticket and allaz tuk his likker strate. . . . Nacher intended him for a Democrat, but circumstances hev somewhat spiled him."[12] Nasby's pamphlets ran speedily through many editions. *Harper's* had blood curdling cartoons by Thomas Nast, sometimes covering two pages. One of these was labeled "Andrew Johnson's Record—How it works." Skeletons of starving Union soldiers at Andersonville were depicted. Negro men and women were seen tied to a stake while the bull whip was being applied on their naked backs. Nast's drawings reached hundreds of thousands of voters.[13]

As Johnson read these attacks upon himself he hurled back the charges. Congress was a "subsidized gang of hirelings and traducers," "bloodsuckers and cormorants," "diabolical and nefarious." And he promised to "kick them out just as fast as I can."

There was hatred and passion and unadulterated abuse on both sides. But the conduct of Johnson helped the radicals undermine his cause with the people. It was a gross breach of dignity for the President of the United States to engage in a wordy political brawl or to bandy remarks with heckling toughs.

At Cleveland Johnson spoke from the portico of the Kennard House before a throng which filled the adjacent streets. The crowd had been waiting impatiently for many minutes to catch a glimpse of the President and when they saw his stocky form emerge from the hotel, a great shout went up. Crowds excited Johnson's itch for public speaking.

> "I came here as I was passing along," he said, "and have been called upon for the purpose of exchanging views, and ascertaining if we could, who was wrong. (Cries of 'It's you'). That was my object in appearing before you tonight and I want to say this, that I have lived among the American people, and have represented them in some public capacity for the last twenty-five years, and where is the man or woman who can place his finger upon one single act of mine deviating from any pledge of mine or in violation of the constitution of the country? (Cheers.) Who is he? What language does he speak? What religion does he profess? Who can come and place his finger on one pledge I ever violated, or one principle I ever proved false to? (A voice, 'How about New Orleans?' Another voice, 'Hang Jefferson Davis.') Hang Jefferson Davis, he says. (Cries of 'No,' and 'Down with him.') Hang Jefferson Davis, he says. (A voice, 'Hang Thaddeus Stevens and Wendell Phillips.') Hang

Jefferson Davis, Why don't you hang him? (Cries of 'Give us the opportunity.') Have not you got the Court? Have not you got the Attorney-General? (A voice, 'Who is your Chief Justice who has refused to sit upon the trial?' (Cheers.) I am not the Chief Justice. I am not the prosecuting attorney (Cheers) I am not the jury. . . .

Let me ask this large and intelligent audience if your Secretary of State who served four years under Mr. Lincoln, and who was placed upon the butcher's block, as it were, and hacked to pieces and scarred by the assassin's knife, when he turned traitor? (Cries of 'Never'.) If I were disposed to play the orator and deal in declamation tonight, I would imitate one of the ancient tragedies, and would take William H. Seward and bring him before you and point you to the hacks and scars upon his person. (A voice, 'God bless him!') I would exhibit the bloody garments saturated with gore from his gushing wounds. Then I would ask you why not hang Thaddeus Stevens and Wendell Phillips? I tell you, my countrymen, I have been fighting the South, and they have been whipped and crushed, and they acknowledge their defeat, and accept the terms of the Constitution; and now, as I go around the circle, having fought traitors at the South, I am prepared to fight traitors at the North. (Cheers.) God willing, with your help, we will do it. (Cries of 'We won't.'). . . . I will tell you one other thing. I understand the discordant notes in this crowd tonight. He who is opposed to the restoration of this government and the reunion of the states, is as great a traitor as Jefferson Davis or Wendell Phillips. (Loud cheers.) I am against both. (Cries of 'Give it to them!'). . . . The courageous men, Grant, Sherman, Farragut and the long list of the distinguished sons of the Union, were in the field and led on their gallant hosts to conquest and to victory, while you remained cowardly at home. (Applause, 'Bully!') Now, when these brave men have returned home, many of whom have left an arm or a leg or their blood, upon many a battlefield, they find you at home speculating and committing fraud on the government. (Laughter and cheers.)

"You pretend now to have great respect and sympathy for the poor brave fellow who has left an arm on the battlefield. (Cries, 'Is this dignified?'). . . .

"There is a portion of your countrymen who will always respect their fellow citizens when they are entitled to respect, and there is a portion of them who have no respect for themselves, and consequently have no respect for others. (A voice, 'Traitor'.) I wish I could see that man. I would bet you now, that if the light fell on your face, cowardice and treachery would be seen in it. Show yourself. Come out here where I can see you. (Shouts of laughter.) If you ever shoot a man you will do it in the dark, and pull the trigger when no one is by to see you. (Cheers.) I understand traitors. I have been fighting them at the South end of the line, and we are now fighting them in the other directions. (Laughter and cheers.) . . .

"I tell you, my countrymen, that though the powers of hell and Thaddeus Stevens and his gang were by, they could not turn me from my purpose except you and the God who spoke me into existence."[14]

The New York *Post* said that Johnson's speeches had "driven people's blood to their heads and aroused a storm of indignation throughout the country." No matter what the people might think of his principles, said the President's friend, Henry J. Raymond, in the New York *Times*, they were "startled and bewildered" by the manner in which he advocated these principles. Americans could never see the dignity of the President forgotten or laid aside "without profound sorrow and solicitude."[15]

Many said that Johnson had "sunk the presidency to the level of a grog house."

The election was an overwhelming defeat for the President. When the record was complete, it revealed that the House like its predecessor had a two thirds majority that could override any veto.

"The people have spoken and uttered their veto on Johnson, his policy, and his adherents," said Phillips. . . . They believe with Landor, that 'a king should be struck but once, a mortal blow.' They mean that slavery, with all its roots, branches, suckers, parasites and dependents, shall die utterly and forever."[16]

Victory emboldened the Radicals. They redoubled their attacks on Johnson. "Let us pray to God," urged Phillips, "that the President may continue to make mistakes, that he may continue to speak, and that his text may be furnished by the people of the South."[17]

A clamor arose for Johnson's impeachment. The *Standard* sent out impeachment petitions. The question was not whether the President was guilty of any crime, but whether he should be deposed from office because of his opposition to the majority in Congress.

The conspirators were soon ready to slaughter Johnson politically. Moneybearers prepared to buy Senators as swine. "Tell the damn scoundrel," later said Ben Butler of a Senator (after the first vote), "that if he wants money there is a bushel of it to be had." Butler was hobnobbing with jailbirds in an attempt to manufacture a case of murder against the President. As Butler said—"If any man stands in the way of the great march of the country . . . he must be taken out of the way."[18]

Accordingly, the articles of impeachment were voted by the House and the trial began before the Senate, the Chief Justice of the United States presiding. "The usurping President has been impeached," declared Wendell Phillips, "we heartily congratulate the loyal people of the nation. . . . All hail! at the prospect of its speedy triumph."[19]

At meetings of the managers of the impeachment, Thaddeus Stevens, a sick old man, long a teetotaler, kept himself stimulated with dosages of brandy or strong wine. Johnson said Stevens was like Vesuvius, which became quiescent at times only to burst forth again with more lava and flames. James A. Garfield, one of the listeners, was moved to remark that the impeachers had been "wading knee deep in words, words, words," and not the least prolix had been Stevens, "reeling in the shadow of death, struggling to read what could not be heard twenty feet off."[20]

Heaven and earth were moved to whip the weak-kneed Republicans into line. Grimes, Fessenden, Trumbull, and other Senators were denounced as "recreants, apostates, and Judases."[21] A Congressional committee was raised and sent out appeals for help. Loyal men hastened to Washington to badger and coerce. Senator Henderson of Missouri, threatened and bull-dozed by Missouri congressmen, in person offered to resign, but it was not his resignation, it was his vote that was wanted. Senator Trumbull was told he was in danger of being hanged to the nearest lamppost if he should be seen on the streets of Chicago. Senator Ross of Kansas, browbeaten and tricked, replied to the telegraphed threats of State leaders: "I have taken an oath to do impartial justice," and received this answer by wire: "Kansas repudiates you as she does all traitors and skunks."[22] Three days before the court voted, Senator Grimes of Iowa was stricken with paralysis. The Methodist Church took a hand. High were the hopes of the Radicals. Butler wired: "Wade and prosperity are sure to come with the apple blossoms."[23]

The fateful day, May 16, arrived. Crowds filled the Senate chamber, galleries, and corridors. Chief Justice Chase came in from a side door, his robes rustling, took a seat in a stately chair, and nervously twirled an eyeglass. A crier intoned the usual command, and the crisis of impeachment was at hand. Hundreds of women fluttered with fans and ribbons. After the Chief Justice admonished the galleries to silence, he directed the secretary to read the crucial eleventh article, which was to be voted on first and would settle the whole thing. There was a hush after the reading, and Chase directed, "The clerk will now call the roll." The clerk called, "Mr. Senator Anthony!" Mr. Anthony rose in his place. "Mr. Senator Anthony, how say you?" the Chief Justice asked. "Is the respondent Andrew Johnson, President of the United States, guilty or not guilty of a high misdemeanor as charged in this article?" Mr. Senator Anthony answered, "Guilty."

The roll call proceeded. Bazard, Buckalew, Cameron, Cattell, Chandler. The breathing in the gallery could be heard at the announcement of each Senator's vote. The members grew sick and pale. Suddenly Senator Grimes was borne through the excited crowds and lifted into his seat. "His coming on that day is one of America's inspiring acts of heroism."

How would Senator Ross vote? So far he was non-committal. "Mr. Senator Ross?" the clerk called. "Not guilty," was the response. "Mr. Senator Van Winkle?" "Not guilty." The roll call was finished, and the clerk announced the result. Thirty-five Senators had voted for conviction and nineteen for acquittal. The President was acquitted by one vote. The news was rushed to the White House. The President received it with composure. The Radicals were wild with rage.

"Three cheers for the Union and for Andy Johnson of Tennessee!" shouted Grinnell of Iowa. The galleries joined in the demonstration. Another Senator demanded that the galleries be cleared. The presiding officer pounded his desk and ordered the arrest of the offenders. Charles Aldrich, a spectator in the galleries, jumped to his feet and yelled back, "Arrest and be damned!"[24]

Democrats heaved a sigh of relief, Europe applauded the verdict, the stock market rallied, and old Thaddeus Stevens, broken hearted, issued his valedictory to the American people: "No chief executive will be again removed by peaceful means," he sorrowfully asserted and went home to die.[25]

Ross was the special object of Radical savagery. It was the irony of Fate that the Republican party should so be served by a Kansas man. None had thought, Sumner said, that a Kansas man could quibble against his country! His had been "shameless treachery," and it was too bad that the case had been lost through the vote of such "a miserable poltroon and traitor." Ross complained that he was passed in the streets and in the hall of Congress "like a leper with averted face and every indication of hatred and disgust." "When I voted not guilty," he added, "I felt that I was literally looking into my open grave."[26]

All seven Republicans who had voted for acquittal had "sorely disappointed the country and disgraced themselves," said the Philadelphia *Inquirer*. They had tried, convicted, and sentenced themselves.[27]

"No matter what Mr. Justice Chase announces," Phillips remarked in the *Standard*, "thirty-five out of every fifty-four have pronounced President Johnson guilty. Poll the nation and seven out of every ten say Amen to that ver-

dict. A technical rule of the Constitution requiring a 2/3
vote may save him his office; but the judgment of the
Nation is recorded against him as a criminal."
And Phillips printed on the second page:

THE ROLL OF INFAMY
Salmon P. Chase

William Pitt Fessenden, Lyman Trumbull, James W. Grimes,
Joseph S. Fowler, Peter G. Van Winkle, John B. Henderson,
Edmund G. Ross.[28]

CHAPTER FORTY-EIGHT

"TO YOUR TENTS, O ISRAEL"

The President was not impeached out of office, but his power was extensively curtailed. The important question just now was: who should succeed Johnson? General Grant was the coming man. Phillips opposed his nomination for two reasons: first, because he lacked civil experience; second, because he failed to take a stand on the issues of the day. He contended that a civilian, not a soldier, was needed in the White House— that the standard-bearer should be a man of frank convictions, not a sphinx. Through the campaign of 1868 this was his constant and unpopular plea: "Friends, I am treading on hot ashes when I touch the great soldier. But it is a land of graves, it is a land of orphans, it is a land of widows, and I say to you, you have no right, standing on such sod, and under such a harvest, to risk the harvest which this great lavish martyrdom gained, by your hapless confidence in any man, however beloved."[1]

In the *Standard* Phillips chided the American public on a harmful characteristic.

"Hasty, reckless, unreasoning hero worship is one of our national faults—a chief one. Let a man stumble on one good action, and we credit him with all the cardinal virtues at once. Every five years produces its own Admiral Crichton, the possessor of all the merits and virtues of the Seven Worthies. This heedless, blind enthusiasm has cost us hundreds of millions, and brought the nation again and again into fearful peril. To pronounce the single word McClellan ought to disenchant Americans of such folly for a century to come."[2]

The glare of Grant's military success, argued Phillips, had been just enough to dazzle men. Zealots turned the nation deaf with Grant's "discretion," "balance," "statesmanship" "straitforward independence," and the nation ached for the chance to risk everything once more on an untried man, if only that man were Grant. "Our best hope is in free, fearless discussion of every man's fitness. Swallow no man with closed eyes. Never be dazzled by his merits—*scrutinize his defects.*"[3]

When the convention at Chicago nominated Grant and Colfax for President and Vice President, Phillips was skeptical. Conservatism had gone to Chicago and won a victory, he remarked. The men who wished to get possession of the government without being definitely pledged to anything had availed themselves of General Grant's popularity to effect their object. "Every politician must now wear a gag until November. Expect no truth from any man until the vote is declared. We might multiply signs. Everything shows that the era of toadies and place hunters, of blacklegs, charlatans and gulls has begun."[4]

Still there was but one choice. Phillips listed the shortcomings of the Republican party: shuffling, evasive, unprincipled, corrupt, cowardly, and mean. But "the heart of the nation beats in the Republican Party," he added. "A vote for Grant means the Negro suffrage recognized; a vote for Seymour means the Negro disenfranchised. Seymour's election is Lee's triumphing at Appomattox. Thus success of the Republican party is the continuance of our opportunity."[5]

When Grant rolled up his majority, Phillips declared: "The loyal party has triumphed. . . . The blood and treasure of the last seven years have not been spent in vain."[6]

Under Radical prodding, Congress had passed the Fourteenth Amendment, giving guarantee of citizenship and equal civil rights to freedmen. Now Congress halted on the brink. Phillips urged it to take the final plunge.

Cold facts spoke more incisively than altruistic fervor. In the election of '68 Grant had received 3,000,000 votes and Seymour 2,700,000. This gave the Radicals cause for alarm, for it showed that the Democrats had more white votes than the Republicans whose total included nearly 700,000 blacks. To insure the continuance of the Radicals in power, the Fifteenth Amendment was framed and sent out to the States in February, 1869. This amendment appeared not only to make safe the Negro majorities in the South, but also gave the ballot to Negroes in a score of Northern states and thus assured for a time at least 900,000 Negro voters for the Republican party.

In April Phillips turned aside to advocate a kindred cause. With Julia Ward Howe he went before the legislature of Massachusetts to plead for female suffrage. During the war the country had been so engrossed in its bloody struggle that the woman's movement could make no headway. "Never mind," said Phillips, "it is the Negro's hour." "No, no!" the women replied, "this is the time to press our claim. We have stood with the black man in the Constitution for half a century and it is fitting that we should pass through the same door now opened to his political freedom."[7]

Phillips's words rankled in the memory of some of the ladies. They accused their champion of favoring one reform at the expense of another, of preferring Negro suffrage to woman suffrage. He hastened to clarify his position. There had never been an hour, he asserted, in which he had denied the natural right of woman to the ballot. But it was a question of *where*, it was a question of *when*. In ten years, in five years, perhaps in three, it might be the woman's hour. But Gettysburg and Atlanta had not been fought on the woman question.[8] Again in the *Woman's Advocate* he declared:

> "I have always given, spoken, and printed for the cause, and am doing so now. When I said, in 1861, 'This is the Negro's hour,' I meant in the sense of ripeness. When we mow our grass in July, and dig our potatoes in September, but put off gathering Baldwin apples till October, it is economy and good sense—but no injustice to the apples. July is the 'grass's hour;' October is the 'Apple's Hour'."[9]

When the ladies persisted in their clamor against the Fifteenth Amendment, Phillips wrote another article for the same journal, reproaching them and defending his course.—

"The fact does not surprise us. It is sad indeed. For the Woman's Rights movement is essentially a selfish one; not disinterested as the Anti-Slavery cause was. It is women contending for their own rights; the Abolitionists toiled for the rights of others. When women emphasize this selfishness by turning aside to oppose the rights of others, it is, in truth, no generous spectacle."[10]

Friends said it was not wise to recognize these rights piecemeal; the Amendment was faulty because it did not cover the whole ground, woman's vote too and all that related to voting. But Phillips replied:

"Shall we wait till the whole country gets educated up to all these ideas and make no change till we can settle the subject in its whole breadth? Absurd. Man goes forward step by step, the recognition of half a truth helping him to see the other half.

"In the present instance this great rule holds. We have drawn the weight so far up; fasten it there; and thus get a purchase to lift it still higher.

"Let ignorance believe that the only way to improve the world is to do everything at once—'I shall never get to the top of the hill by single steps; the only way is to wait till I can leap the whole way at one bound.' Let selfishness cry— 'He shall not have his rights till I get mine.' The true reformer will say, 'Let every class have its rights the very moment the world is ready to recognize them. Thus and thus only will every other class get one step nearer to the recognition of its own. First the blade, then the ear, after that the full corn in the ear.' "[11]

Susan B. Anthony met Phillips and Theodore Tilton to discuss plans for immediate work. Susan was indignant. Walking closer to the group, she thrust out her arm at full length. "Look at this," she said, "all of you! And hear me swear that I will cut off this right arm of mine before I will ever work for or demand the ballot for the Negro and not the woman." She walked out of the room hearing as she passed through the door

Tilton's smooth voice, "Why, whatever is the matter with Susan? I never before knew her to be so unreasonable or so rude."[12]

In Congressional circles the phrase, "The Negro's Hour" was cast aside and immediately forgotten. In its place came a new slogan, "A Political Necessity." Once Mrs. Stanton, lecturing in California, met Senator Bingham of Ohio stumping the State on behalf of the Fourteenth and Fifteenth Amendments which that State had declined to ratify. Mrs. Stanton gently charged him with insincerity, since every argument he was presenting applied equally to woman suffrage. With a cynical smile he replied that he was not the puppet of logic, but the slave of practical politics.[13]

April and May were busy months for Phillips: a week after his plea for woman suffrage, he addressed the legislature of his native state in behalf of Labor Reform. Then he turned aside to speak before a Sunday audience in Horticultural Hall, Boston, on a religious theme: "Christianity is a Battle—not a dream." Rousing speeches and editorials followed in defence of the pariahs of our population: the Indians and Chinese.

"I am an ingrained Democrat," he declared in May at the anniversary of the American Anti-Slavery Society. "I believe in the equality of race. I do not believe a man was ever found so irredeemably ignorant, that if he was fit to be hung he was not fit to vote. Irishman, black man, Chinaman —no matter where he was born, the American people are strong enough to absorb them all. (Applause.)"[14]

This government never would be safe, he continued, never would be just, never would be founded on the true faith until as Grant said in his inaugural, the Indian was made a citizen and then let alone.

"I blush today at the swords of the Republic crimsoned and disgraced by blood better than theirs. Sheridan—*Sheridan* sends Custer out, with his sword ready drawn against the Indians, and Custer sends a letter to Sheridan—'I have had a glorious victory;' and Sheridan heads a dispatch, 'A brilliant victory.' You read on, and Custer says,—'I came on a Cheyenne Village, silent as night, careless as children, unheeding danger. I descended on the sleeping group, and slew men and women; and when the sun rose, I found myself in possession of 875 head of cattle, and as I could not carry them, I shot them.' Oh, the American soldier descended on a peaceful village, filled with agriculture and industry and property, sleeping in peace under the flag of the Republic, and like a ruthless savage, he trod it out in blood! ('Shame,' 'shame.') You send your generals, fresh from the great war that taught the nation that we had no eye to see race, to herald that victory to Washington as a brilliant success! Oh, it was a cold blooded butchery. And on the statute books on the other slope of the mountains are now planted the seeds of the same enmity against China. Thank God, I know no Empire that is not large enough to embrace in its liberal bosom all bloods, all creeds, all tongues, all races, under one common law. (Applause.)"[15]

The distinctive anti-slavery pledge would be fulfilled, Phillips granted, when the keystone of the Fifteenth Amendment was in its place. But the essential principle of the anti-slavery crusade would not be reached and satisfied until the American race got bold, and brave, and high, and intelligent enough to believe with Jefferson that "All men are created equal."

"I want it done; I want it out of the way; and the reason why I trouble you with it tonight is, because, hanging over the horizon, claiming a hearing, demanding our attention, are just as great, and some of them just as angry questions.

"There is woman claiming the ballot. There is labor, claiming leisure and education. There is finance, that is destined one day to conciliate the quarrel between capital and labor. They all claim the field. They never can either of them have it until this element of discord, hatred of race, is banished from the statute books of the Republic. Why I am interested in that question is because I want the epoch finished; I want the seal put on the idea . . .

"I remember, when I was in Rome, I saw the colossal pillar of Trajan, and upon it was engraved, in obedience to the orders of the Emperor, the figure and the uniform of every tribe that he had gathered under his sceptre; and the whole world is represented, in one great sweeping procession, moving up to his statue, under the imperial rule of impartial Rome, worthy the name of an Empire. When I see that Capitol at Washington, with its pillared halls crowded with black and white, Indian and Saxon, Christian, Pagan, and Jew, looking up with the same gratitude to the same banner, and uttering the same shibboleth of nationality in a hundred tongues, I shall feel that the American Anti-Slavery Society has done its work, and that the epoch is ended." (Loud applause.)[16]

Again in a striking editorial, Phillips took up the cudgels in defense of the despised races: "The Indians will soon have a new ally. We shall feel them, as the Quaker advised his friend, 'in our pockets.' Twenty thousand Indians on the warpath will cost us more than Boutwell can save." This nation never did anything yet from pure principle, declared Phillips. It has always been lashed to its duty by necessity. America freed the Negro because only so could we save our Nationality. America would soon do justice to the Indian because it costs too much to wrong him.

Phillips wished he could see the same bright hours ahead for the Chinese. The codes of the West were stained with laws against them. "Charles Francis Adams likens the immigration of the Chinese to an immigration from Sodom. The Adams family always means to stand just as far ahead as it is respectable and *useful* (to themselves) to stand."[17]

Phillips foresaw another racial conflict to prevent the emigrants of Chinese blood from sharing the privileges of American citizenship. (What happened later in California bore out his predictions.) He urged his friends to be on vigilant guard. The next generation, he insisted, need not put off their armor, need not imagine that the heroic days of the Republic were over, that there was no necessity for martyrdom. Some there were who had borne the standard of reform for many years who felt as if they would like to

> Wrap the drapery of their couch about them
> And lie down to pleasant dreams.

But there was no rest for reforming spirits. They must still work on. They owed it to the age in which they lived, to the ideas they upheld, and to all the nations of the earth.[18]

Victory was in the air. The Fifteenth Amendment was in the process of ratification by the States. The veterans were jubilant. But Phillips merely intensified his agitation. From platform and editorial chair he reiterated his message—pointed, inflexible, stirring: "The great struggle between Equality and Caste, between Free Institutions and a government founded on Race,—is not, by any means, ended. The Rebellion was only a preliminary skirmish. To your tents, O Israel."[19] If the Union lasted, its cornerstone must rest on three things for the Negro people: Education, Land, the Ballot. And now was the time to grant and rivet them firm and deep in the constitution itself.

Phillips took courage from the fall elections. They showed "the soundness of the people's heart." And he struck a note which he was to magnify into a rallying call later on:

"The public debt, repudiation, and the Fifteenth Amendment have really been the questions at issue. Repudiation we have never feared. The country is too honest for that. Our danger lies in quite another direction. We shall never cheat the moneyed class. We shall rarely be able to defeat them in any of their plans. The real danger of the future is, that combined and incorporated wealth will rule the land; that our laws will be made not in Congress, but in the gambling Hells of Wall Street, in Bank parlors and by railroad cliques. It will be a new sight in history when a working class repudiates its contracts. . . .[20]

The lecture season Phillips spent as usual, mostly on railroad trains, going to and from his Lyceum appointments. He thought that he and John B. Gough were the great American travelers. "I know," said he, "every locomotive, every conductor, and the exact depth of the mud in every road in the country."[21]

March 30, 1870, was a memorable date: President Grant proclaimed the adoption of the Fifteenth Amendment: Neither the nation nor any of the States shall deny or abridge the right of any citizen to vote on account of race, color, or previous condition of servitude. The struggle was ended. Phillips read the proclamation in Leroy, New York. Sitting down, he dashed off a few jubilant lines to the Reverend John T. Sargent of Boston.

> "Leroy, N.Y., March 30, 1870
> Dear John: Let me exchange congratulations with you. Our long work is sealed at last. The nation proclaims Equal Liberty. Today is its real 'Birthday.'
> 'Io! Triumphe!'
> Thank God.
>
> Affectionately,
> WENDELL PHILLIPS."[22]

> Our nation's free! Our nation's free!
> All hail! the land of liberty!
> Loud swell the trump that sounds its fame,
> No longer now an empty name. . . .

> The oppressor's power at last is broke,
> And millions, freed from slavery's yoke,
> Their thankful hearts and voices raise,
> To speak their great Deliverer's praise.

> Our nation's free! Our nation's free!
> How bright its future destiny!
> Within its bounds no clanking chains
> Shall bind the human form again.[23]

Statutes never turn sinners into saints. Prejudice dies hard. It must be lived down and shamed out. Phillips was aware that the Negroes would have to face prejudice and discrimination for generations. The remedy for this, he felt, could be found only in time and achievement. Meanwhile the arena was open. "Slavery is dead. We have not only abolished slavery, but we have abolished the Negro. We have actually washed color out of the Constitution."

The mission of the American Anti-Slavery Society was fulfilled.[24] What remained save to meet once more and disband? On April 9, 1870, the Abolitionists held their commemoration at Steinway Hall in New York City. The streets were alive with

Negroes marching in joyous procession. The attendance at the hall was immense. Phillips, as President of the Society, was in the chair. Letters were read from a host of coworkers, and the "Old Guard" sat on the platform. "Wolfe died," wrote Sumner, "in the arms of victory; and such is the fortune of your noble society."

As Phillips rose to say the last word, he received the most tremendous ovation of his life.

"I go out of this thirty years of agitation," he said "with no faith whatever in institutions. The only faith that is left me is the faith in human nature. Two of the speakers this morning have spoken of the deep gratitude each one of us owes to this cause. It has given us much. It has refined our hearts. It has lifted us to a more Christian atmosphere. We owe to it also a revelation of human nature. It has brought me to know the noblest men and women of my day, and elevated my conception of the capacity of human nature. . . .

"Why, some men say, do you disband this Society? Have you never seen a long boat, with twenty men bending their muscles to the oar, surmounting wave after wave, until they at last reached the great frigate? Then the idle oars were balanced on the boat side, the rowers and the boat were both taken on the mighty mass, and, fore-sail, main-sail, and mizzen-sail spread to the breeze, it moved onward. The American Anti-Slavery Society for thirty years with straining oars and hard labor, has at last reached the level of the great nation's frigate. We won't disband; she takes us on board. (Applause.) We have no constitution left under which to exist. The Constitution of the United States has absorbed all. (Applause.). . . .

"And so, friends, we will not say 'Farewell,' but we will say, 'All hail, welcome to new duties.' We sheathe no sword. We only turn the front rank of the army upon a new foe."[25]

At the business meeting which followed, the Society adjourned *sine die*.

CHAPTER FORTY-NINE

THE CITADEL OF STATE STREET

When slavery fell, Wendell Phillips was in his sixtieth year. He was still in the prime of life, mentally and physically alert, steady, vigorous. Time had ripened his faculties at every point.

Friends thought that after his fierce struggle of thirty-three years, he was now entitled to a victor's rest. Edmund G. Quincy, acting on this principle, had reverted to a life of ease and leisurely enjoyment. Like a tired steed, Quincy had merely shaken himself and dropped the reformer's equipment entirely. He utterly denied that there was anything left to fight for. He simply became a reformer emeritus, in the university phrase, and was for the rest of his life a brilliant and delightful flaneur. This desperate fanatic of former years went to theatre with the constancy of a Parisian and could be found exchanging graceful jests with men from whose company he had long been excluded.

Phillips disdained such a pleasant existence. He always seemed to be crying like Shakespeare's Hotspur, "Fie upon this idle life!" and always to be seeking for some new tournament. Accordingly he said to a friend:—"Now that the field is won, do you sit by the camp fire, but I will put out into the underbrush."[1]

He meant what he said: he "put out." Temperance had from the start a warm place in his heart and he gave the question increasing prominence in his speeches. But the great cause which enlisted his eloquence was Labor Reform. Slavery abolished, this was the next inevitable step.

Here many of the Abolitionists balked. They saw plainly enough the enormity of Negro slavery. They could not see the enormity of wage slavery. Coming from families "of the best New England stock," "of pilgrim descent," "of a serious, pious household," Abolition leaders steered clear of the wage controversy. The factory worker represented an alien and unfamiliar system towards which they felt no kinship or response.[1a] Even Garrison scorned the labor movement. When in England, he combated the idea that a single workman there, however much oppressed, was a slave. "You express the conviction that the present relation of capital to labor is hastening the nation to its ruin," he wrote, "and that if some remedy is not applied, it is difficult to see how a bloody struggle is to be prevented. I entertain no such fears. Our danger lies in sensual indulgence, in a licentious perversion of liberty, in the prevalence of intemperance, and in whatever tends to the demoralization of the people."[2]

The Old Guard followed their leader and accused Phillips of "preaching crusades on difficult problems which he had never seriously studied." But the truth is that Phillips had begun to study the labor question as far back as the late 1840's.[3] To his mind the slavery question was but one part of a still greater labor question that must be settled if society was to endure. Wage slavery was as truly slavery as chattel slavery and as much a thing to be abolished. Nevertheless there was this difference, that whereas chattel slavery was confined to a few regions in a few countries, wage slavery was universal, and while chattel slavery involved some millions, wage slavery involved and degraded the entire working class of the world. In other words he had been thinking along economic lines. He had a clear view of things as they were in his time and as they were to be after him.

In a speech on Lincoln's election he had said: "Caesar crossed the Rubicon borne in the arms of a people trodden into poverty and chains by an oligarchy of slaveholders, but that oligarchy proved too strong even for Caesar and his legions."[4] Phillips had taken a hand in suppressing one American oligarchy and saw another rising in our midst from the iron kings and other industrial magnates whose gigantic combinations controlled the forces of government.

As early as November 2, 1865, he made a speech at Faneuil Hall in which he unequivocally declared himself in favor of an eight hour day.

> "It is twenty-nine years this month since I first stood on the platform of Faneuil Hall to address an audience of the citizens of Boston. I felt then that I was speaking for the cause of the laboring man, and if tonight I should make the last speech of my life, I would be glad that it should be in the same strain,—for laboring men and their rights."[5]

Phillips's labor for twenty-nine years had been in behalf of a race bought and sold. That struggle for the ownership of labor was now near its end. Another struggle had commenced for him: to define and arrange the true relations of capital and labor.

> "Today one of your sons is born. He lies in his cradle as the child of a man without means, with a little education, and with less leisure. The favored child of the capitalist is borne up by every circumstance as on the eagle's wings. The problem of today is how to make the chances of the two as equal as possible; and before this movement stops, every child born in America must have an equal chance in life."[6]

Eight hours a day and political action were then the goals of Phillips's program of reform:

> "We have a government resting on the masses. I undertake to say that when a government rests on the people, government is bound to seek, at least, so to arrange labor and capital that the laboring class may have time to understand matters of government and vote intelligently. (Applause.) Shut a man up to work ten, eleven, sixteen hours a day, he comes out the fag end of a man, (Applause) with neither brain nor heart rightly to discharge the duties of citizenship. Capital, for its own security, seeing that labor holds the majority at the ballot box, is bound, moved only by its own selfishness, to see that labor has leisure to look

calmly into and patiently comprehend the great questions of politics. Therefore I say it is a fair division of a man's day—eight hours for sleep, eight hours for work, eight hours *for his soul*—his own to idle if he pleases.

"I defy a million of men, having got leisure and comfort not to improve. . . ."

It would be a disgrace to New England if any class could bully any other class into submission. The only reason why the laboring class had apparently been threatened into submission was that the laboring class in its ignorance, its divisions, and its indifference allowed the other class to have its own way.

"You will never get the journals, you will never get public men, you will never get the brain of the country to think for you, crumbled and divided as you are, resolved on nothing, united on nothing, demanding nothing. How will you make the *Advertiser*, the *Journal*, the *Traveler*, the *Transcript*, the Springfield *Republican* and the Worcester *Spy* discuss your question and not have the agitation confined to the *Daily Voice?* I'll tell you. Go into the political field, and by the voice of forty thousand working men in this State, say, 'We mean that eight hours shall be a working day; we mean that no man shall go into municipal, federal, or state office, who does not support that measure. (Applause.) We don't care for Democrat; we don't care for Republican: we are going at last to attend to our own concerns.'

"When, with one practical point at a time before you, united in one party, you make journals, statesmen and colleges discuss your question, you will convert the State and stereotype your idea into a statute. Until, laying aside all differences, you so unite, your cause will lie wind-bound and sunk in shallows.[7]

"Your challenge cannot be made in words. It cannot be printed in the *Voice*; it cannot be announced here. A mass meeting is a flaming meteor—seen today and gone tomorrow; but a political movement behind which stand ten thousand men, saying, 'This is our right: we'll have it, if we grow gray in fighting for it'—that never adjourns. It is an everlasting session."[8]

Such blunt words alienated Phillips's friends. In a few years
for the sake of his position on labor and for no other reason,
he was back again in the old situation, facing hatred and incessant attacks. The banker's exploitation of the national currency and the manufacturer's exploitation of factory labor—
these were the issues that a cautious man who was careful of his
good name would not meddle with. But Phillips was never
cautious and his good name had long since been flung to the
wolves. And so in the evening of his days, he embarked on
a campaign that had for its ultimate objective the impregnable
citadel of State Street.

2.

The history of labor organizations after the close of the
Civil War was a record of ebb and flow, agitation, organization,
disintegration. A public meeting in the interest of labor at that
day was a novelty and the man who had the temerity to address
such a gathering was sure to meet a storm of abuse and ridicule.
It made no difference what was said or done at a meeting
of workingmen, the report of the proceedings in the papers of
the following day would be the same. The meeting was characterized as a "gathering of the rag-tag and bob-tail of the
community;" "the worst element was out last night to hear a
kid-gloved, oily-tongued, sleek-faced demagogue hold forth
in an incendiary, blood curdling speech on the rights of horny-
handed workingmen." Labor speakers were called communists,
socialists, Molly Maguires, incendiaries, blood and thunder
spouters, blatherskites, hungry looking loafers, sinister faced
wretches, fellows who violently gesticulated and frothed at
the mouth for half an hour without saying anything.[9]

It was a time too when working men could not tolerate the
idea of defiling labor by bringing it into contact with politics.
Politics meant corruption and fraud. Why should workingmen
have anything to do with politics except as members of a party?

Despite the prevailing sentiment, the National Labor Union
determined to organize an independent political party. A radical
platform was adopted at the Congress held in Cincinnati in
August, 1870. In substance the party announced itself as "a

rallying ground for the people to fight Monopolies and every
species of Thieving, Corruption, and Rascality. A Party for the
People, and not the People for a Party."

Local units sprang up in the states. In Massachusetts labor
was militant. The champions in the eight hour fight hailed
from the Commonwealth and a majority of the intellectuals
were in sympathy with the movement. In 1869 workingmen
without newspaper support and political skill had, with an organization but three weeks old, succeeded in electing twenty-
one representatives and one Senator and had polled a vote of
more than 13,000 in the State. Now with Phillips as their
champion enthusiasm was pitched high.

At a state convention of the Labor Reform Party they made
Phillips their standard bearer by acclamation on the first ballot. Three weeks earlier the Prohibitory Party had conferred
on him the same honor.[10] Phillips knew that his chances for
election were hopeless. The canvass would be simply a protest
and an education.

Four parties were in the field, exclusive of the woman's suffrage movement: Labor Reform, Prohibitory, Republican, and
Democratic.

The Republican Party took note of the existence of the
Labor Party in its platform: "The Republican Party, which in
the ten years of its history, has accomplished more for the
elevation of the laborers of America than had been accomplished
before since the government was framed, hears with surprise
and indignation the claim of any other organization to arrogate
to itself the title of 'labor party.' "[11] Efforts were made to secure from the Republican and Democratic conventions pledges
in favor of woman suffrage, but the resolutions were defeated.

Phillips rallied his parties in a lively campaign. His language
was sharp, intense, incisive. In October he spoke on "Temperance
and Labor Reform," the second lecture in the Parker Fraternity
Course. The parts on Labor, said the Boston *Daily Advertiser*,
drew applause "from the queer, sporadic persons with long
hair who haunt the galleries on Fraternity nights."

"The Democratic party proposes nothing," said Phillips.

"What does the Republican party propose? Nothing!

"Temperance and the claim of the workingmen. These are the only two live issues today in Massachusetts. The Republican Party is an honorable party, but as the old critic said of the man who was praising his ancestors, 'If you judge it by the present canvass, its great merit rests, like the potato, underground.' (Laughter and slight applause.) Its past is all its claim. It puts forth no effort for the future. . . .

"There are only two forces in politics; only two. One is a sublime faith, a sublime, undoubting faith in a great principle, which gathering a score or two of men under its banners, forces its triumphant way against majorities and wealth. That is one force, and the other is a majority of votes.

"The Republican party today has no faith. . . . The soul is dead. It announces to the world that it waits. It tells the woman: I wait till you show me that a majority of the women of the Commonwealth want it. (Faint platform applause.) It says to temperance: 'Prove to me that you have got a working majority.' It says to labor: 'Rally your forces and make it safe for me to act.' Well, we are doing it." (Applause.)[12]

A great blunder was made in the matter of strikes. The National Labor Union had publicly criticised strikes as detrimental to the workers themselves. Phillips defended the right to strike and attacked the oppressive conduct of employers.

"The whole world is blaming Fall River for its strikes. When Fall River proposed to reduce her wages ten per cent, the operators said: 'Condescend to show me why.' 'Take it, or move your wife into the street from the tenement which I own. Submit, or move out of my house; submit or put your family into the street.' Well, the men did it. They walked out of the tenement; they walked into the street. They reduced their pay. They went to Valley Falls and said: 'Can I have employment?' 'Sign the register.' He signs it. 'We know you; no use for you.' He goes to another mill. 'Sign the register.' 'Why, we don't want you.' He goes to Providence. 'Can I have work?' 'Yes, sign the register.' 'We don't want you;' and so, having taken the man by the throat, dictated to him the worth of his labor, turned his family into the street, and then followed him with the ban of exclusion, the capitalist then sends up to the legislature and says: 'Am I not all right? Is there any slavery in New England?'"[13]

Phillips simply spotlighted a common practice. A typical note of a Lowell concern read: "Bearer————has been employed by the Middlesex Company and has the liberty to work elsewhere." A more subtle method than the certificate system, as Phillips mentioned in his speech, was the blacklist. Massachusetts employers planned such a scheme in 1861; in New Britain, Connecticut, two firms circulated secret lists of names of molders with the comment: "If any of the above named have obtained employment in your establishment we trust you will act in the premises as you would wish us to do." In Cincinnati, Philadelphia, Louisville, Boston, Syracuse, Detroit, and other cities, "struck molders" were catalogued and driven from pillar to post. William Sylvis, labor leader and pioneer, accused employers of using "every means which grovelling minds could invent, avarice suggest, malice dictate, or unprincipled men execute."[14]

At a meeting held under the auspices of the Eight Hour League, Phillips dealt with various aspects of the Labor Problem. The main weakness of the laboring movement, claimed Phillips, was not in the lack of leaders from its own ranks. The defect lay in another direction: that long lack of leisure which left the mass of the working men indifferent. Was it hard criticism to say of a mass of men wronged that they were indifferent to their wrongs? he asked. But one of the gravest perils of a wrong was that it demoralized a man out of the sensibility to his wrongs. "When you have made a contented slave," said Burke, "you have made a demoralized man." Were this claim of eight hours for a day's labor mentioned to the State Street man, he would remark: "Well, if you are to work eight hours a day, we cannot make seven and ten per cent on the cotton capital of the commonwealth." "I tell him, in the first place," said Phillips "I don't care whether you can or not."

Yards of cotton, tons of coal, ingots of metal, are not the measure of a civilization; men and women are; and if you told me that the method we are about introducing, or hoping to introduce, would strike down capital to one-half the amount employed today, but would lift the men and women of Massachusetts forty per cent above their present level, I should say, 'All hail the change! (Loud applause.) That is a true civilization.'

"State that in State Street, and you would be considered a fanatic; state it from a pulpit on Sunday, and it is considered trite. It is so much of an axiom and a truism that the hearer says, 'Bless us, can't he tell us something new?' (Laughter.) When a man puts on his Sunday coat and his Christian creed, and his character as a Christian man, and goes to church, he expects to have that doctrine preached to him; but when he puts on the guise of a broker, then he votes that to be fanaticism. (Laughter.)[15]

Phillips approached the question from two points. He maintained that it was possible to plan a Christian civilization where the mass of the human race would not stand in danger of crime and starvation, death or pollution. And he claimed that it was possible so to arrange the relations of labor to capital that the thirty millions of voters would be intelligent, educated men. That was his goal.

"I do not want any fewer Stewarts, worth forty millions. I am willing to have a dozen Vanderbilts instead of one; I am willing to have a score of Astors instead of one. That is not the danger I see. What I claim is that no man has a right to be a Stewart in a Christian civilization while there is a Five Points starving within two miles of his residence. (Loud applause.)

"It is the inequality I complain of—the monstrous inequality. We have got to invent our way out of it. I do not care for these temporary owners of mills, these temporary possessors of capital. They may be cruel, they may be

heartless or they may be ignorant; I do not care in which
category they stand. All I know is, the world gropes its
way onward to a better civilization and this is one of the
gropings. They may laugh at it, they may deride it, they
may endeavor to smother it, but it is the tendency of the
times, and it will certainly conquer. How soon it will conquer
rests with you. I say this eight hour movement is the first
step toward this good. There are other questions beyond
it. . . ."16

One of the great values of this question, added Phillips, was
that out of it was to come the redemption of the timber out
of which the Republic was built. Already the dry rot of a money
aristocracy that was far more dangerous than that of blood was
invading the Republic.

"There is not one of us, *not one,* that even in this Commonwealth of Massachusetts, can get his rights in a railroad car. There is not a Judge in the Commonwealth who
will administer the ordinary common law between a railroad corporation of the State and a single offended and
wronged passenger. Such is the power of wealth.
"The recognized corporations of this country have established the power to construe their own contracts and execute
them in their own way. It has grown up in a night. Everybody submits. There is not common law enough to hinder
it. It is eating out individual liberty."17

To Phillips the education of the masses was their only hope.
The interest of millions of men, the keen, everyday, selfish,
bread and butter interest of millions of men was in this cause.
And Phillips urged them to take that interest and organize, for
organization was strength.

"My friend (Mr. McLean) said, rightfully, strikes are only
the last resort. True, but after all, strikes are an admissible
and a defensible remedy. (Applause.) Don't let us give up,
even if we have the ballot, the right to strike.
"There is a man who walks down into State Street and
issues his orders all over the country by the telegraph wire,
buys up all the flour, and makes a million of dollars in a

day. He walks out on State Street and men congratulate him: 'Clever fellow' 'adroit boy.' (Laughter.) What has he done? Struck!—nothing else. He has bought up all the flour and fixed his own price. What is a strike? A million of men who have got all the labor there is in the community to sell have got together and fixed a price, made a corner in the market, done exactly what the flour merchant does— nothing more. The same thing made a Vanderbilt. Everybody makes a bronze statue of him and puts it over the depot: The magnificent striker, who struck a railroad, and cornered New York. Nothing but a strike in principle. And so long as it is honorable to go down into State Street and strike on flour, or strike on stocks, or strike on coals, labor can say, 'In this same civilization, I can make a corner wherever I choose.' Perfectly defensible. Never let a man say a word against strikes, therefore. Always insist that in the last resort of self defense that is your power."[18]

But at the same time, added Phillips, there was a better way, a manlier way, a more American way.

"Write over the ballot box, 'Here we never forgive! (Applause.) Inscribe it in letters of gold over every ballot box, 'Here labor never forgives!' . . .
"There are 600,000 of you. You could not be smothered with 600,000 statutes. Go to work faithfully at the ballot box, and you can change the legislation of Massachusetts. You can go up to that legislature and say, 'When you give capital corporate privileges, we claim that you shall affix to the charter labor conditions, and the first one is, eight hours.' (Applause.)"[19]

Again on November 3, Phillips urged organization of political action.

"You see a party is not an agitation. An agitation cares only for an individual conscience, and with one man and an idea it can outweigh the stupid millions. But politics has one level. It counts noses, cannot count anything else, and unless you can offer it a working majority, of course it would be idle to ask it to come out and show its banner

and risk itself. Why, a politician, of course, is not a man
with his eye fixed on the polar star of duty; he is a man
who rushes into the market place with a war cry and a
banner over his head, but he always has one eye over his
shoulder to see who is following him, and when nobody
follows him he stops. It is his function . . .

"Wealthy men combine, until there is not a spot for the
hunted victim in which to earn his bread this side of the
Connecticut River, and it is God-like civilization; but let
poverty combine: 'Did you ever see such nasty Crispins?' "[20]

A friend taunted Phillips with being ambitious. Phillips proudly
replied—"Born of six generations of Yankees, I knew the way
to office and turned my back on it thirty years ago."[21]

During the campaign Boston experienced a slight earthquake.
The earthquake was generally voted to be "no great shakes,"—
some windows were rattled and a few of the more sensible bells
were rung. But the rattling of types produced by Phillips's
campaign speeches beat the earthquake hollow. For days papers
printed them in full. The New York dailies copied them and a
number of weekly papers gave large extracts from them.[22]

Despite the stir and eloquence, the result was forecast. At
the election on November 15, the Republicans won. Phillips
made a splendid showing, but came out at the tail end of the
list: William Claflin, Republican, 79,549; John Q. Adams, Democrat, 49,536; Wendell Phillips, Labor Reform and Prohibitory,
21,946.[23]

CHAPTER FIFTY

THE BATTLE OF LABOR

In 1871 Phillips intensified the feeling against him in the better classes by giving his support to General Benjamin Butler who was making an active canvass for the governorship on a mixed Republican and Labor platform. Boston Brahmins were outraged by Phillips's conduct. They believed that he had lost his head or "was gone crazy." But he was used to such insinuations. The truth is that Phillips applied to Butler the same standard he applied to every other public man. What ideas did he stand for? For justice to labor, for the plain people, and for the cause of temperance. That was enough. Phillips supported him.

Butler was the bugaboo of American politics. Ejected from the Democratic party and booted out of the Republican, he now threatened to start a new party of his own. He cannot be dismissed as a mere demagogue. He gave an impetus to the radical movement.

Only two charges against Butler's administration at New Orleans have any foundation in facts. He gave orders that women who emptied slop buckets on the soldiers should be treated as prostitutes and arrested; and he hanged a respectable citizen of New Orleans who hauled down the American flag after the city was captured by United States sailors and soldiers. He never stole silver spoons.

The act for which Butler was held in particular horror was his famous woman order. Disloyal women of the city continually insulted Union officers and soldiers. The outrages were not occasional, but constant and almost universal. For example:

586

one woman deliberately spat in the face of an officer in full uniform as he was on his way to church; a woman emptied from the balcony a pail of dirty water on Admiral Farragut in full uniform as he was walking along one of the principal streets. There were other minor instances: they wore rebel flags in their bonnets; they pulled their skirts away when passing Union soldiers as though to avoid contamination by contact with them; they would jump out of a street car if a Yankee got into it. Butler thereupon issued his order that if any female should insult in any manner a Union officer or soldier, "she should be regarded and held liable to be treated as a woman of the town, plying her avocation."[1]

The South resented the order, and the North professed to be ashamed of it. General Butler was vilified as brute, beast, tyrant, thief, robber. Beauregard ordered the document read on dress parade for the information of the army and thus addressed his followers: "Men of the South, shall our mothers, wives, daughters, and sisters be thus outraged?. . . . Arise, friends, and drive back from our soil these infamous invaders."[2] In England it afforded an opportunity for eloquence on the floor of the House of Commons and almost became the subject of an official protest to the Ambassador Adams on the part of the British ministry. Lord Palmerston got up in Parliament and denounced the order as unfit to be written in the English language.[3] In *Punch* the following stanza appeared—

Haynau's lash tore woman's back,
When she riz his dander,
Butler, by his edict black,
Stumps that famed commander, . . .

Yankee doodle, doodle doo,
Yankee doodle dandy;
Butler is a rare Yahoo,
As brave as Sepoy Pandy.[4]

However, there was not a single claim that any Southern woman was ever insulted or outraged under the order.

With all Butler's severity and crudity and tactlessness, it must be said that he restored order, controlled his soldiers, and, though he had no patience with those whom he considered traitors, conducted himself decently and even kindly towards those who were willing to admit defeat and to repent.[5]

A cloud of suspicion hung over Butler's administration. His policy was energetic and immensely effective, but corruption was rampant. An enormous speculative trade was carried on with the enemy and those close to Butler profited. Though nothing was proved against the general, the taint followed him. He kept about him a class of persons that would have damaged any man.

It was always Butler's strenuous assertion that his aims were of the highest and his acts not far behind them. As he aptly expressed it, "I have done nothing but good and that *continually*."[6] His impetuous, insolent temper revelled in hostility and he thought it fun to be hated. In fact he made enemies from the start and kept on making them. As a young lawyer in Lowell and as a Massachusetts legislator, he became obnoxious to those in position and power by speaking and arguing for radical measures. Decorous newspapers decried him, professors and well groomed people despised him. When after repeated efforts he won the governorship of Massachusetts, Harvard College for the first time in its history refused him the degree of Doctor of Laws.

Sometime in the fifties when he made a political speech at Lowell, a local newspaper printed an account of it with the following headline: "BEN BUTLER: This notorious demagogue and political scoundrel, having swilled three or four extra glasses of liquor, spread himself at whole length in the City Hall last night. . . . The only wonder is that a character so foolish, so grovelling and obscene, can for a moment be admitted into decent society anywhere out of the pale of prostitutes."

The editor of the paper was indicted for criminal libel. But Judge Ebenezer R. Hoar, a conservative who presided at the trial and disliked Butler, charged the jury that the government was bound to prove beyond a doubt that the article in the paper was intended for the Ben Butler whose name was "Benjamin F. Butler," and went on to say: "I am at a loss to see that there is any evidence upon this point to make it sufficient." The jury acquitted the editor.[7]

Sumner said of Butler: "He is a gallant fellow. What a splendid man he would be if he had more of the moral in him."[8] Grant said: "I like Butler and have always found him not only, as all the world knows, a man of great ability, but a patriotic man and a man of courage, honor, and sincere convictions."[9] And Charles A. Dana, who fought him on innumerable occasions: "His intellectual resources were marvellous, his mind naturally to the cause of the poor and the weak. . . . He was no pretender and no hypocrite."[10]

Unfortunately Butler's appearance was against him. He was fat and ungainly, with a drooping moustache and scanty looks, a domed forehead and big, bulging eyes. A low turned-down collar revealed a Danton-like throat, and one of his eyelids drooped so as to make him look more like a pirate than a statesman.

His vigor, his energy were astounding, but his belligerent manner antagonized. He had a shrewd, coarse wit which got him often into trouble. He remarked of New Orleans women who turned their backs upon Northerners: "Those women evidently know which end of them looks the best."[11] He took delight in a lavish bestowal of bitter epithets upon those who had offended him. Badeau was "the French for 'dirty water.'" Halleck was a "lying, treacherous hypocritical scoundrel with no moral sense." Porter was "a reckless, consciousless [sic], impudent liar." And so on.[12] He had an illimitable flow of language, a terrible power of speech. He fired the laborers of Lowell to fury. His voice rang out: "As God lives and I live, by the living Jehovah! if one man is driven from his employment by these men because of his vote, I will lead you to make Lowell what it was twenty-five years ago—a sheep pasture and fishing place, and I will commence by applying the torch to my own house!" The effect was marvelous. The place was a bedlam. Someone yelled "Let us do it now," and applause broke out all over the hall.[13]

"God made me in only one way," he said. "I must be always with the underdog in the fight! I can't help it; I can't change, and upon the whole I don't want to."[14]

A friend happened to be along with Phillips and said without preface. "Mr. Phillips, how the papers have been pitching into you lately. You are not very popular just now."

Phillips answered good humoredly but with emphasis, "No, I am not in the least popular."

"Why are you so intimate with Butler?" the friend inquired.

"Well," he said, "there is an old saying that you must fight fire with fire, and sometimes, when you are struggling with very savage forces, the best man you can use for the purpose is one whose original nature is a little like that of the enemy. Butler is that man today in the country. He is just the one to fight those fellows on the other side."[15]

The campaign was an exciting one. Phillips spoke often on the "twins," as he called them, Labor and Temperance. His most notable utterance was at a vast assembly on Salisbury Beach with the Atlantic for a background and a September sky as a sounding board. He called his speech, "The People Coming to Power."

"Fellow citizens," Phillips began, "General Butler told you this was a gathering, on the seaside, of all parties and all classes of man, and that he hoped his remarks would not offend the prejudices of any class or of any party. Gentlemen, I recognize, as he does, the duty we owe to the harmony of this occasion; but if I thought, fellow citizens, that I should leave Salisbury Beach without treading on somebody's toes, I would regret I ever came here."[16]

What was the use, added Phillips, of a thousand men meeting together to compare notes, to exchange ideas one with the other if they did not leave, after they had separated, some hint, some seed, some suggestion that would bear fruit, that would clear up the doubts, cut away the underbrush, and enable men to see clearer and act more nobly?

"I came here on purpose to offend your prejudices; I did not come for any other reason; because, fellow citizens, if you stood here, and I was one of the crowd now before me, I should hope that you would drop some salt, or endeavor to stir the waters of the public mind, for the health and life of us all."[17]

Phillips launched into an attack on the Republican Party and the unjust distribution of wealth.

"Gentlemen, the Republican party is dead; the only mistake is that it fancies itself alive, and resists burial. As Edmund Burke said seventy years ago, there is a man walking this earth, who supposes himself to be alive. So the Republican party supposes itself to be alive and denies its grave clothes. It is a mill without any grist. The party has nothing to do and proposes nothing. It has achieved all it was organized to achieve. It is no fault of the honorable men whose names have been put before the public as candidates, that they represent nothing."[18]

The party insisted Phillips, "lagged superfluous on the stage." The country teeming with men and forces that were struggling for a place to mould the age and benefit the world, was no cabinet chamber where laurelled men scrambled for office. It was the field where the tools ever offered themselves to him who could use them and where, through respected men or over them, the work had to be done. In that stage of affairs such a man as Butler was flung—representing a new idea: the protection of labor, North and South, labor everywhere.

"The meaning of the labor question in Europe and in this country is this: Whether you on these acres, on yonder waves, or in the mills shall work honestly, industriously, soberly, for seventy long years, and then die worth a thousand or two thousand dollars, a small house, forty acres of land, or nothing, while some financial sponge sucks up millions.

"Do you know that out of one hundred men, the record is that there are not more than seven that leave any estate to be administered. Now, what I say is, I find no fault that Vanderbilt is worth fifty millions of dollars; I find no fault that Stewart is worth $100,000,000. What I say is this: that this system of finance by which one man at sixty years old has gathered $50,000,000, and of the ten thousand men that work for him, seven thousand get up every morning not knowing where dinner is coming from,—that system of finance belongs to the bottomless pit, and the sooner it goes home the better.

"The system is unjust, cruel, and fatal to any true republic. The safety of our institutions, justice and Christianity dictate that out of the common profits, capital should have less and labor should have more than it now does. I do not blame anybody; but I am determined, as far as I am concerned, that the brains of this generation shall try to tear that system open and let the light into it, and the readiest way I know is by political action."[19]

"What was General Butler's offence?" asked Phillips. He revealed the dry rot of the Republican party. He called the roll call of his party on its own camping ground—man. Immediately, said Phillips, every sword turned on him, betrayed the secret that its leaders were planning to make it only a brotherhood of officeholders and a tool of capital.

"But 'such personality'—see every journal arraigning him. Yes if it were not so I would not have given a sixpence for him. If I go into an orchard, wanting pears, I naturally go to the tree that has been the most pelted with brick-bats. If I get into the Commonwealth and want to know the man that represents the radical ideas of his time, give me the man that has made enemies by thousands every time that he has put his foot down. I went into one of the burying grounds in the next country to this, and I read an epitaph. 'Here lies a man who never had an enemy.' Well, I said to myself, then here lies a man who never had an idea. If you find a man in politics of whom everybody speaks well, I will tell you that his soul is made up of soft-soap; he is a 'mush of concession'; you cannot feel him in a dark night if you run against him. . . ."[20]

Without mincing words Phillips went on to say: "I have given thirty years of my life—and I rejoice to have been permitted to give them to the redemption of a race. If I am spared another ten years, I hope I shall be permitted to give them to the redemption of every man who works with his hands. (Applause.) For gentlemen, the great danger that threatens in the future is the money power." And Phillips confessed that though he had studied democratic institutions for forty years, he still did not see the means by which the independence of the legislature of Massachusetts was to be saved from the hands of its capital and corporations. What held true for Massachusetts held true for the legislature in Pennsylvania, asserted Phillips. The set of men that went up to Harrisburg were bought and paid for by the Pennsylvania Central Railroad.

"At the end of the late session, a member rose and said, 'If Tom Scott (President of the Pennsylvania railroad) has no more business for this legislature, I move we adjourn.' You laugh, as though it was only true of Pennsylvania. Why, gentlemen, you have a legislature in Boston. You have three railroad commissioners. They are to guard your railroads, in order that you may travel safely. There is a railroad that runs down to this point, and the President of the road has been laboring for one object for the last fifteen years—that is, to raise its stock from 45 to 120; and by his parsimony, he has accomplished it, not spending a single dollar for your safety or comfort.

"Last winter the railroad commissioners suggested certain needed reforms in the railroads of Massachusetts. They said, 'The people are not safe,' and the reply of the railroads was, 'It will cost too much to make them so. If we make improvements, we cannot make a dividend.' The reply of the commissioners was that 'the first interest of a railroad was the safety of its passengers; the second interest its dividends.'

" 'Now listen,' said the railroad agents to your servants, the railroad commissioners, appointed by Governor Claflin, 'if you don't hold off and shut your mouths and forbear pressing the necessity of this measure, we will abolish the Board of Commissioners.' Thus you see which rules the

State, your legislature or your money corporations, with a capital of $100,000,000.

"Everyone knows that the laws of the State of New York are not made at Albany; they are made in Vanderbilt's counting room . . .

"The great question of the future is money against legislation. My friends, you and I shall be in our graves long before that battle is ended; and unless our children have more patience and courage than saved this country from slavery, republican institutions will go down before money corporations. Rich men die, but banks are immortal, and railroad corporations never have any diseases. In the long run with the legislatures they are sure to win."[21]

The great battle which General Butler represented, added Phillips, was the battle of labor. True, he supported Butler for Governor because he represented that element of disturbance in the Republican party. But the moment he ceased to represent it, labor would clasp hands to trample him under its feet.

"Gentlemen, I am very frank to say that I don't want that convention at Worcester merely to nominate General Butler; that will not satisfy me. Neither will it satisfy me if General Butler's friends go there and put a small plank labelled 'labor' in one part of the platform. I want king's post and girder, wallplate and ridgepole, every plank and joist carved, moulded, stamped and labelled, 'Justice to MAN'—'Man first—MONEY, the week after.' . . .

"People say, General Butler is not a temperance man; I know that. General Butler drinks his champagne; I know that. Governor Claflin does not; I know that. I have been a teetotaler for thirty-four years, and it is a cause nearest my heart. Yet I had rather, twice rather, that General Butler should be governor of the State, with his champagne in his right hand, than a sober man that does not execute it. I had rather have a man that looks in my face and says, 'I shall drink Madeira, but if you have that statute which forbids the Parker and Tremont Houses from selling, I will inexorably execute it.' I would rather have him than a prohibitionist like Governor Claflin, whose friends claim that he executes the law in a *reasonable way*."[22]

What was that *reasonable way?* asked Phillips. It was to
pick up some petty vendor down on North Street that had
two gallons of whiskey hidden in her back room, and then put on
double-refined black spectacles and walk by the Parker House.
That sort of *sensible* way of executing the law Phillips did
not like. "Give me a man, no matter what his private habits,
who will shut up every grog shop in Boston, and I will risk the
future."

"Look at the journalism of the last six weeks," continued
Phillips. "I think General Butler has been charged with
about every sin that can be imagined; but there is one
thing, I watched very carefully,—I put my ear down to
the earth like an Indian listening,—he never has been
charged, ever since 1861, of not doing what he said he
would do. You cannot find a newspaper correspondent so
utterly reckless that he will charge Butler with having
broken his promise.
"For one, I have nothing against him. He has done a
great many things that I should not have done; he has done
a great many things that I would ask him to do differently;
but I will tell you a secret, friends. If I was Pope today,
there is not a man among all the candidates, Butler included, whom I would make a saint of; not one. If I was
Pope tomorrow, there has not been a governor for fifty
years that I would make a saint of. The difficulty is, saints
do not come very often, and when they do come, it is the
hardest thing in the world to get them into politics. I don't
believe that if you could import a saint brand new and
spotless from heaven, that he could get a majority in the
State of Massachusetts for any office that has a salary."[23]

The contest was for the Republican nomination. Butler marched
over the state "with the stride and voice of a braggart," rallying
the voters of his party. But when the delegates gathered at
Worcester, another candidate, William B. Washburn, finally got
the nomination.
Butler's defeat was a moral victory.

"He came so near to succeeding," declared Phillips, "that no men were more surprised than those who whipped him. (Laughter and cheers.) The reason why he led 464 men up to Worcester is not that he exercised any fraud. It's because the people of the Commonwealth of Massachusetts had been living on a set of potato governors for a long time, and they wanted some roast beef. (Great and continued applause.) Called by journals equally a knave and a fool; they didn't know which predominated. The truth is, take the Butler men out of the Republican party, and there isn't enough of vigor left in it to digest its meals." (Applause.)[24]

The state convention of the Labor Reform party of Massachusetts met at South Framingham on October 4. Phillips made the keynote speech.

"Under all flags, there is one great movement. It is for the people *peaceably* to take possession of their own. (Cries of 'Good,' 'Good,' and applause.). . . .

"I look upon this convention as the great insurance society of civilization. (Applause.) No more riots in the streets; no more disorder and revolution; no more arming of defiant bands. Today the people have chosen a wiser method. They have the ballot in their right hands and they say we come neither to attack nor to injure capital. (Applause.) We come by the right of numbers to take possession of the governments of the earth. (Applause.). . . .

"Gentlemen, I say so much to justify myself in styling this the grandest and most comprehensive movement of the age."[25]

Shorn of its numbers and with a grim determination to survive, the Labor Reform Party became still more militant. Phillips drew up and read the platform—

"We affirm as a fundamental principle, that labor, the creator of wealth, is entitled to all it creates.

"Affirming this, we avow ourselves willing to accept the final results of the operation of a principle so radical, such as the overthrow of the whole profit-making system, the extinction of all monopolies, the abolition of privileged classes, universal education and fraternity, perfect freedom of exchange, and, best and grandest of all, the final obliteration of that foul stigma upon our so-called Christian civilization, the poverty of the masses. Holding principles as radical as these, and having before our minds an ideal condition so noble, we are still aware that our goal cannot be reached at a single leap. We take into account the ignorance, selfishness, prejudice, corruption, and demoralization of the leaders of the people, and, to a large extent, of the people themselves; but still, we demand that some steps be taken in this direction: therefore,—

"*Resolved,* That we declare war with the wages system, which demoralizes alike the hirer and the hired, cheats both, and enslaves the workingman; war with the present system of finance, which robs labor, and gorges capital, makes the rich richer, and the poor poorer, and turns a republic into an aristocracy of capital; war with these lavish grants of the public lands to speculating companies, and, whenever in power, we pledge ourselves to use every just and legal means to resume all such grants heretofore made; war with the system of enriching capitalists by the creation and increase of public interest-bearing debts. . . ."[26]

A clamor arose when this platform and Phillips's speech appeared. Newspapers called Phillips a Nihilist and a dangerous person. From this time his reputation steadily declined. Many persons viewed with sorrow the sad failure of the promise of the war period. He might have been sensible and successful, he might have gone to Congress or been a Senator or a judge. Instead he insisted upon casting in his lot with this handful of "rag-tag and bobtail."

The party had declared war, but unfortunately, the party did not have an army to go to war with and its candidate Chamberlain received in that year only 6,848 votes.[27] The heart was taken out of his followers. The National Labor Union was by this time crumbling.

Unmindful of the defeat, Phillips intensified his agitation. In his address before the Reform League, in Steinway Hall, he presented resolutions urging Congress to strangle the Ku Klux

Klan, "this rebellion of assassins," and to curb the power of moneyed corporations to secure the safety of the people. A corporation doubled its power, he warned, but decreased its responsibility. It was a power by which a dozen men put their fortunes together and wielded the aggregated power, beyond their capital, without risk. Such power could enter into a jealous battle with the people. It could defy public opinion, could resist public resistance, and still fold its arms and say, 'If my corporation is annihilated, I have ten millions left.'

Pointing a warning finger at the bloody Paris *Commune* he remarked:

"Take heed of the sore discontent, consult the masses, make your law to be respected because it is respectable. There is your choice. Adopt the labor movement into the grand platform of Republicanism and you are wisely imitating England. Sneer at it, trample it under foot, ignore it, and New York will be Paris. Choose—you stand at the dividing way. It is almost by the skin of your teeth that we have evaded open war in the coal regions of Pennsylvania. Let it come again in a dozen years hence and the muskets will be actually loaded. We cannot afford it. This is the question that is to be settled in 1872.

"If you want secession to stay in the grave, if you want law and order to reign in the great commonwealths of the North, crush the Ku Klux with one hand and the corporation tyranny with the other. (Great applause.)"[28]

Pulpit and press and parties were all doing obeisance to this modern nobility, to this baronetage of millions, to this peerage of wealth.

"The question was now," added Phillips in Union League Hall, New York, "should the people fight up against it? "All we see at the present time is the substratum of society, heaving and tossing in angry and aimless and ignorant struggle, not knowing what it wants, nor why it suffers, nor how it can be remedied, and daily becoming angrier and more soured, and more embittered. The question is, who shall speak to it, who shall educate these conflicting interests, who shall hold them and cram down their reluctant throats the facts which they ought to know and don't want to know, and never will be told by those that seek to gain something by conciliating them."[29]

Phillips turned aside to defend "an uprising against ignorance and despotism" in the Paris *Commune*. "The men who led the *Commune*, were among the foremost, the purest and the noblest patriots of France," he declared in the *Standard*.[30] And he added on the platform: "I have not a word to utter against that grand record of popular indignation which Paris wrote on the pages of history in fire and blood—not a word. (Applause.) In spite of the column of Vendome shattered and the palace of the Tuilleries in ruins, I honor Paris as the vanguard of the masses of the world. (Applause.)" The conspiracy of emperors was to put down what? Not the Czar, not the Emperor William, not Thiers, not the English Navy or the armies of United Germany. "But when the emperors come together in the centre of Europe what plot do they lay? To kill the Internationals. (Applause.) And France is the soul of the Internationals."[31]

Capitalism in America must take the lesson of the Paris Commune to heart. If we looked at Churches, Caucuses, the Exchange, or the College, he added, one would infer that Christ had died to save property. Labor would be peaceful and patient whenever the same means were used to find and cure her ills that were exhausted to help capital. She ought not, he insisted, to be patient longer. He urged not war on capital, he preached no materialism. He wanted simply that cooperation which, born of Christianity, killed the angry system of competition and wages, and brought in brotherhood. "One thing I know; if wealth wants a safe and quiet land to dwell in thirty years hence, it must wake soon to remember that Property has Duties as well as Rights!"[32]

("Wendell Phillips's political economy," said the Boston *Evening Traveller* was "richly ridiculous," "Crazy.")

As Phillips clearly revealed, his socialism was a homespun Yankee product. In a strict modern sense he was not a Socialist at all, for he never advocated ownership and operation of industry by the government. His knowledge of the Marxian philosophy was rudimentary. And he was "vague regarding the economic system that was to supplant Capitalism—a loose confederation of cooperative enterprise such as W. H. Sylvis and other labor leaders had been advocating for some time."[33]

His ideal of society was Jeffersonian. Although he was a city man, he had been born at a time when Boston was hardly more than an overgrown village. He never accepted urban life or industry and never squared his socialist theories with the mass growth of cities in the Industrial Revolution.[34]

On October 31, he delivered in the Music Hall, Boston, the most elaborate of his Labor speeches. In it he replied to certain criticisms:

"We are asked, Why hurry into politics? We see the benefit of going into politics. If we had not rushed into politics, had not taken Massachusetts by the four corners and shaken her, you never would have written your criticisms. We rush into politics because politics is the safety-valve. We could discuss as well as you if you would only give us bread and houses, fair pay and leisure, and opportunities to travel: we could sit and discuss the question for the next fifty years. It's a very easy thing to discuss, for a gentleman in his study, with no anxiety about tomorrow. Why, the ladies and gentlemen of the reign of Louis XV and Louis XVI, in France, seated in gilded saloons and on Persian carpets, surrounded with luxury, with the products of India and the curious manufactures of ingenious Lyons and Rheims, discussed the rights of man, and balanced them in dainty phrases, and expressed them in such quaint generalizations that Jefferson borrowed the Declaration of Independence from their hands. There they sat, balancing and discussing sweetly, making out new theories, and daily erecting a splendid architecture of debate, till the angry crowd broke open the doors, and ended the discussion in blood. They waited too long, discussed about half a century too long. You see, discussion is very good when a man has bread to eat, and his children all portioned off, and his daughters married, and his home furnished and paid for, and his will made; but discussion is very bad when

'Ye hear the children weeping, O my brothers!
Ere the sorrow comes with years;'
discussion is bad when a class bends under actual oppression. We want immediate action."[35]

He thus described his ideal.

"My ideal of civilization is a very high one; but the approach to it is a New England town of some two thousand inhabitants, with no rich man and no poor man in it, all mingling in the same society, every child at the same school, no poor-house, no beggar, opportunities equal, nobody so proud as to stand aloof, nobody so humble as to be shut out."[36]

To break up colossal fortunes, the State ought to graduate taxes, ought to tax land, ought to tax incomes. The labor of yesterday, capital, was protected sacredly. Not so the labor of his day. The labor of yesterday got twice the protection and twice the pay that the labor of today got. Why was he not entitled to an equal share? asked Phillips. And he was not quite certain that capital—the child of artificial laws, the product of society, the growth of social life—had a right to only an equal burden with labor, the living spring. He doubted it so much that he devised a "little" plan (not unlike that favored by the New Deal) by which he thought to save the nation and Congress from the moneyed corporations.

"When we get into power, there is one thing we mean to do. If a man owns a single house, we will tax him one hundred dollars. If he owns ten houses of like value, we won't tax him one thousand dollars, but two thousand dollars. If he owns a hundred houses, we won't tax him ten thousand dollars, but sixty thousand dollars; and the richer a man grows, the bigger his tax, so that when he is worth forty million dollars he shall not have more than twenty thousand dollars a year to live on. We'll double and treble and quintuple and sextuple and increase tenfold the taxes, till Stewart out of his uncounted millions, and the Pennsylvania Central out of its measureless income, shall not have anything more than a moderate lodging and an honest table. The corporations we would have are those of associated labor and capital,—cooperation."[37]

Phillips repeated the substance of his address in Steinway Hall, New York, on December 6 and at various other places during the winter. The New York *Daily Tribune* remarked—

"Wendell Phillips delivered a characteristic lecture on 'The Labor Movement, the Sheet Anchor of the Republic' at Steinway Hall last evening, before a large audience. The accommodations for the reporters were, as usual, inexcusably incomplete, the janitor of Steinway Hall being distinguished for his impoliteness on all occasions to the press."[38]

After advising his audience to "go down into the very slums of existence, where human beings by the thousands live year in and year out in dwellings which no man in Fifth Avenue could trust his horses in for twelve hours" Phillips went on to relate an experience and point a moral:

"I had once, at the request of some operatives who waited upon me in Boston, to discuss the relations of capital and labor in a manufacturing town of Massachusetts. When we came to the hall, and the door was opened for me to face the audience, I said to eight or ten workingmen who escorted me, 'Which of you will introduce me?' They all looked down and asked me if it were necessary that I should be introduced. 'No,' said I, 'it is customary.' Then they said if I had no objection they would rather not show themselves on the platform. They did not dare to be seen by the capitalists seated in front of them, where I was to discuss the cotton operations of New England. (Applause.) I don't believe in the safety of the existence of such classes in a republic. . . ."[39]

It was money that riveted the chains of labor, he continued; only by grappling with the organizations of power in the nation could the ultimate view which he aimed at: cooperation, be attained. There would be no labor as such, no capital as such: every man would be interested proportionately in the results.

"I have another proposition. I think when a man has passed five years in the service of a corporation, though he may not have bought a dollar of its stock, he is in a certain sense a stockholder. He has put his labor and persistency there, and I think every man who has been employed in a corporation for a year or two should have a voice in its financial management. In Japan when a man dies his land is left to the State. Do you not think that is a wiser plan than ours? The land becomes more valuable through the labor of the whole country, and not by that of the man who eats off of it. Our great hope in the future is in the education of the masses, for they will yet be our rulers."[40]

In April, 1872, Phillips made another important speech before the International Grand Lodge of St. Crispin. He was interested, he said, in the Labor question, not simply because of the long hours of labor, not simply because of a specific oppression of a class. He sympathized with the sufferers; he was ready to fight on their side. But he looked out upon Christendom with its three hundred millions of people and he saw that out of this number of people, one hundred millions never had enough to eat.

"Physiologists tell us that this body of ours, unless it is properly fed, properly developed, and carefully nourished, does no justice to the brain. You cannot make a bright or good man in a starved body; and so this one third of the inhabitants of Christendom, who have never had food enough, can never be what they should be. Now, I say that the social civilization which condemns every third man in it to be below the average in nourishment God prepared for him, did not come from above: it came from below; and the sooner it goes down the better. . . .

"I take, for instance, one of the manufacturing valleys of Connecticut. If you get into the cars there at 6:30 o'clock in the morning, as I have done, you will find, getting in at every little station, a score or more of laboring men and women, with their dinner in a pail; and they get out at some factory that is already lighted up. Go down the same valley about 7:30 in the evening, and you will again see them going home. They must have got up about 5.30; they are at their work until nigh upon eight o'clock. There is a good, solid fourteen hours. Now, there will be a strong, substantial man, like Cobbett, who will sit up nights studying, and who will be a scholar at last among them, perhaps; but he is an exception. The average man, when he gets home at night, does not care to read an article from the *North American*, nor a long speech from Charles Sumner. No; if he can't have a good story, and a warm supper, and a glass of grog, perhaps, he goes off to bed. Now, I say that the civilization that has produced this state of things in nearly the hundredth year of the American Republic did not come from above."[41]

Again he urged the vital importance of organization which could stereotype just reforms into statutes and bring pressure to bear on Legislatures which counted votes. Above all organization brought stamina and strength.

"Now, let me tell you where the great weakness of an association of workingmen is. It is that it cannot wait. It does not know where to get its food for next week. If it is kept idle for ten days, the funds of the society are exhausted. Capital can fold its arms and wait six months; it can wait a year. It will be poorer, but it does not get to the bottom of the purse. It can afford to wait; it can tire you out. And what is there against that immense preponderance of power on the part of capital? Simply organization. That makes the wealth of all the wealth of every one.

"So I rejoice at every effort working men make to organize; I do not care on what basis they do it. Men sometimes say to me: 'Are you an Internationalist?' I say, I do not know what an Internationalist is; but they tell me it is a system by which the working men from London to Gibraltar, from Moscow to Paris, can clasp hands. Then I say 'Godspeed. Godspeed, to that or any similar movements.' "[42]

CHAPTER FIFTY-ONE

SUMNER'S HUMILIATION—"OLD WHITE HAT"—ENLIGHTENING JONATHAN

A strange thing happened in Washington. Sumner repudiated Grant and the Republican party. "The slave of principles, I call no party master" was the proud slogan with which he had begun his service in the Senate. Now after twenty years, he still clung tenaciously to that motto. His action sprang from a quarrel with the President.

Grant's pet scheme included the annexation of San Domingo. But the country was in no mood for annexing a hotbed of revolution with a population like that of San Domingo and Sumner's opposition to the plan was bitter and unyielding. Besides Grant believed that Sumner had been detected in a falsehood in having promised at first to support the bill. With Grant's ideas of military discipline, this was like rank insubordination. He conceived a violent hatred for Sumner and his detestation overcame his reticence. Someone remarked that Sumner did not believe in the Bible: "Oh, no, he wouldn't," said the President; "he didn't write it." George F. Hoar was taking a walk with the President one day on Pennsylvania Avenue and the President was talking in a quiet, friendly manner when they turned the corner near Sumner's house in Lafayette Square. Grant shook his closed fist at the house and said, "That man who lives up there has abused me in a way which I never suffered from any other man living."[1]

On his side Sumner's hostility grew so acrimonious that he finally declared: "Among the foremost purposes ought to be the downfall of this odious, insulting, degrading, aide-de-campish, incapable dictatorship. At such a crisis, is the country to be left at the mercy of barrack counsels and mess room politics?"[2] And the Senator "roared like the Bull of Bashan" when he got to discussing the President with his friends.[3]

However, there were many ways of showing Sumner his proper place. He had friends in official positions and the President could wound him by wounding his friends and allies. One of Sumner's close adherents was John Lothrop Motley, Phillips's boyhood friend, who was now American minister to England. When in the Alabama claims Motley had glaringly disregarded his instructions, Grant had angrily wished to dismiss him. But he was retained out of courtesy to Sumner. Now that Sumner openly flouted the President, the latter believed Motley should be ousted.[4]

The day after the San Domingo treaty was rejected, Grant directed Hamilton Fish, Secretary of State, to recall Motley at once. He wanted Fish to send Motley a cablegram telling him to get out of the embassy immediately. Fish said such a procedure would not be dignified, and he urged Grant to let Motley remain until the next winter.

"That," Grant replied with set jaw, "I will not do. I will not allow Mr. Sumner to ride over me."

"But it is not Mr. Sumner but Mr. Motley at whom you are striking."

"It is the same thing."[5]

Finally Fish persuaded him to let Motley receive his dismissal through the formality of a State document.

"I thought myself entirely in the confidence of my own government," wrote Motley, "and I know that I had the thorough confidence of the leading personages in England." Then all at once had come the letter requesting him to resign. This gentle form of violence is well understood in diplomatic service. Horace Walpole says, speaking of Lady Archibald Hamilton: "They have civilly asked her and grossly forced her to ask civilly to go away, which she has done with a pension of £1200 a year."[6]

Besides Sumner was ignored by the party which so long had idolized him and which he had done so much to create and inspire. He was deposed from the chairmanship of the Committee of Foreign Relations, humiliated in committee assignments, and denounced by his own state. In the interest of "national unity and good will among fellow citizens," he had introduced a bill providing that "the names of battles with fellow citizens shall not be continued in the Army Register, or placed on the regimental colors of the United States. It is contrary to the usages of civilized nations to perpetuate the memory of civil war." The lawmakers of Massachusetts condemned Sumner's gesture of conciliation, "as an insult to the loyal soldiery of the nation," and "meeting the unqualified condemnation of the people of the Commonwealth."[7] It was this rebuke from his own people that hurt Sumner most. "I know I never deserved better of Massachusetts than now," he wrote. "It was our State which led in requiring all safeguards for liberty and equality. I covet for her that other honor of leading in reconciliation."[8]

Phillips took up the cudgels in defense of his old friends, Sumner and Motley. He denied vehemently that the removal of Sumner as Chairman of the Committee on Foreign Relations was proper and justified because Sumner had been negligent of public duty. When did Grant first find out this negligence? he asked. Why had he not uttered it sooner? Because the charge was an afterthought, said Phillips.

"But General Grant says that Mr. Sumner lied." Phillips remembered the occasion and recited the circumstances. Sumner received the treaty of San Domingo from the hands of the President who drove up to his door while he was sitting with some friends at the dinner table. Sumner said to Grant: "I will look at the bill. I trust I shall have the pleasure of supporting the administration."[9] These were the words of politeness, of courtesy merely, said Phillips. When Sumner went home and examined the treaty, he found he could not support it. The next day he saw President Grant and pointed out the objection to the document, laid before him the impossibility of his supporting it, and urged a reconsideration of the action of the administration. Grant listened in sullen silence. "If Grant never heard that Sumner took back that courteous pledge in the chamber of the White House," remarked Phillips, "it was because his brain refused to perform its office. He is no judge of the veracity of the Senator from Massachusetts. . . ."[10] As for the removal of Motley: Fish was a tool of the President and this removal was out of spite.

Then came the rebuke by the lawmakers of Massachusetts of Sumner's gesture of good-will towards the soldiery of the South. Phillips disliked the resolution, wanted it expunged from the records. In defense he sent a militant letter to J. B. Smith of the Legislature:

> "The flags our national Regiments march under belong as much to South Carolina as to Massachusetts. Georgians will be called to defend them as much as we are. Is it generous, is it wise, to ask them to pour out their blood for a flag which is written all over with the disgrace of their fathers? Do men say the South never will defend our flag? Such men despair then of our ever being one Nation. I do not.
>
> "Show me the community or the nation that has ever inflicted an insult on any of its people. Greece repudiates it —France and Germany scorn it. England allows no name on any of her flags which can pain a Cavalier or a Roundhead—a Scotsman or an Irishman. When in 1758, I think, William Pitt took the ban off conquered Scotland and called the Highlanders into the army, he gave them back their tartans, before illegal. How utterly inconsistent would he have been had he required them to march under banners where every man saw written their great disaster, Culloden?
>
> "All history is full of this chivalrous respect for the feelings of the conquered—long before, the Black Prince, English Edward, acted as servant to his Royal captive, and often since Washington rebuked his men's cheer over Cornwallis's surrendering his sword, with the words, 'Let posterity cheer for us.' If we attempt such an outrage in these insolent flags, we shall set the world the first example of it. . . .
>
> "I should despise a Southerner who would march under such a flag. Only I should despise yet more heartily a North that could ask him to do so. A North that could expect—and a South that could submit to—such indignity, would make up a Nation of which the age ought to be ashamed. . . . Let

such a disgraceful bunting be once more borne by Carolinians and Yankees over one Victorious field and the men themselves would fitly celebrate the victory by tearing such a flag to pieces and clasping generous and brave hands over its rags. . . .

"Censures have been rare, very rare, in the history of our State. I hardly recollect one. Whom then are we lifting first to this bad eminence? A man whose term in the Senate has been longer than that of any other Massachusetts Senator; one who in ability is equalled by Dexter and Webster, and perhaps by George Cabot among his predecessors, and of whom it may be said that he has been put into office by the votes of two generations. But with whom no other man Massachusetts ever sent to the Senate deserves to be named. A Senator who has been privileged to do more for the honor of the Commonwealth and the safety of the Nation than any one ever commissioned by Massachusetts. . . .

"I would not speak disrespectfully of the Legislature, but I seem to hear the jeers of all honorable men the world over when, in such a Washington as men have seen the past twelve months, Massachusetts singles out Charles Sumner and sets him apart for censure. I hope this legislature will erase that record of intemperate haste. . . . Expunge the mistaken assertion from your records. I ask it for the honor of the Old Commonwealth."[11]

In time, the resolution was rescinded, but the scar of the wound remained. And there were other wounds that still bled, especially that inflicted by Sumner's wife, and he was bitter. As Bryant remarked: "A wife is not content with a husband who is exclusively occupied with himself and his own greatness."[12] It was simply another instance of a woman marrying a man because he is devoted to all mankind and leaving him because he is not devoted to her. Sumner read in the press of his wife's activities in Europe where she was "occupying her time . . . chiefly in doing good to others." But she had done no good to him and that spring he secured a divorce in Boston on the ground of desertion. He was deserted everywhere—by Massachusetts, by the Republican party, by his wife. His physical condition was poor. He kept himself alive by taking drugs. One night in the house on Lafayette Square with its pictures and books Phillips lingered with the lonely man till after midnight and even then Sumner clung to him and would not let him go. When Sumner was reminded that he was to take a footbath, he replied, "Well, I will take it if you don't go." And so with Phillips looking on, the fallen idol bathed his feet and his friend remained to solace him.[13]

2.

The Liberal Republican movement of 1872 was a revolt against privilege and corruption. An increasing band of sympathizers urged civil service and tariff reform and an end of Northern misrule of the South. But when the convention met at Cincinnati[14] and nominated for President Horace Greeley who had opposed every tenet of the Liberal platform, a bombshell burst which nearly blew up two parties. Bryant of the New York *Evening Post* thought it incredible that such a blunder could be made by men in their right senses and said that the convention had surrendered "stock and fluke to the wire pullers." The Cincinnati group which had been the source of so much strength to the movement left the scene in disgust. General Brinkerhoff "swore the ticket blue." The Germans said they would bolt the ticket and fight Greeley to the bitter end. Gratz Brown, the politician, was denounced by the rank and file as a "red-headed, red-bearded scoundrel."[15] The New York *Times,* which had been calling the party "a combination of malcontents and guerillas," "a little faction of grumble and fuss," declared: "If any one man could send a great nation to the dogs that man is Mr. Greeley. There is no department of business he would not disorganize and unsettle."[16]

Two months after the Liberal Republicans met, the Democracy, setting its jaw a bit stupidly, also chose Greeley as its leader. No contrast could be so absurd as that which brought to the denouncer of the South the support of the party of the South.

The day before the Convention met at Cincinnati Greeley was out for national unity. "The biggest thing before the people is the question of honest men against thieves. What the country needs and imperatively demands is a reform in the administration of government. That is not to be attained by combinations of worn-out political hacks." His chief appeal was to put the peace of the nation above the resentments of a war that was over. "Peace to the nation, power to the people, purity to the government" was his proclaimed platform."[17]

General Sherman wrote his brother in a laughing mood: "Grant, who never was a Republican, is your candidate, and Greeley, who never was a Democrat, but quite the reverse, is the Democratic candidate."[18] "We have been singing Democratic hymns for forty years down here," exclaimed a gentleman from North Carolina, "and since the Baltimore Convention puts Greeley in our hymn book, we'll sing it through if it kills us."[19]

It is hard to think of a type more incompatible with the presidential chair than the queer, fiery, versatile, garrulous, emotional, whimsical editor. When the Civil War broke out, it was too much for him. He was distracted between humanity, love of the Union, hatred of slavery, hatred of war, and his general disposition to dictate to everybody in everything. First he was zealous to let the States go: "No War! No War!" he shouted. Then he was for prosecuting the war and emancipating the slaves. "On to Richmond! On to Richmond!" he nagged and vociferated day after day on the editorial page. When an advance was made and the disaster of Bull Run followed, he was beside himself with horror and had a violent attack of brain fever.[20] The extent of his panic was so great that on July 29, 1861, at midnight, he addressed a letter to the President, begging for peace with the rebels and later offering to pay them $400,000,000 or more to get it. Then after all was over, he was for forgiving everybody, especially Davis whose bail bond he signed. Sometimes he pleaded with Lincoln, sometimes he bullied him, sometimes he rejected him as a poor creature. His flighty inconsistencies were bewildering.[21]

He was consciously and affectedly grotesque. His pink baby face surrounded up to the ears by silken throat whiskers, his dull blue eyes gazing behind heavy lensed spectacles, his white hat and rumpled white overcoat, the pockets bulging with newspapers, his shapeless trousers often stuck in his boot tops, his shambling gait and fat cotton umbrella and his absent minded manner were as well known as his squeaky voice and inde-cipherable handwriting. He had a way of closing his eyes when listening to any speech. Caricaturists cruelly exaggerated his child-like naiveté and Pickwickian appearance.

"I shall carry every Southern State but South Carolina" he said bruskly, and plunged into the campaign.[22] It was a cam-paign of personalities and not much else. "Old Horace," "Our Uncle Horace," "the Household Farmer," "Old White Coat," "Old White Hat," "Old Tree Chopper," "the Sage of Chappaqua" or "Sore Head," "Renegade," "Apostate," "Rebel,"—such designa-tions abounded.[23] Campaign songs besmeared Greeley with "free love and free farms and all that," and Liberals had Grant arm in arm with Tom Murphy "shouting the battle cry of plunder."[24] It was strange enough to see Beauregard, Braxton Bragg and other rebel chiefs declaring for Greeley, but to see the leaders of Tammany, lately convicted and condemned in the courts of law, cheering for the old editor of the *Tribune* was truly amazing. Never before has such a "miscellaneous coalition" made its appearance in American politics.

Multitudes of pamphlets appeared, ridiculing Greeley's foi-bles, inconsistencies and absurdities. Partisans remorselessly searched the files of the *Tribune,* and the editor emerged as little short of traitorous to the North and as a brute to the South. Day after day the Republican press reprinted from pages of his paper what he had earlier said of those whose cause he now led.

"There are several hundred thousand mulattoes in this coun-try, and we presume that no one has any serious doubt that the fathers of at least nine-tenths of them are white Democrats. . . ."

"When the rebellious traitors are overwhelmed in the field and scattered like leaves before an angry wind, it must not be to return to peaceful and contented homes. They must find poverty at their firesides and see privation in the anxious eyes of mothers and the rags of children. . . ."

"Everyone who chooses to live by pugilism or gambling, or

harlotry, with nearly every keeper of a tippling house, is politically a Democrat. . . .[25]

"May it be written on my grave that I was never its (the Democratic party's) follower, and lived and died in nothing its debtor. . . ."

"It is a glorious ticket," he had cried in 1868 of the Republican candidates. "Grant never has been defeated and never will be."[26]

Thomas Nast, a young German cartoonist, visited Washington in winter and was beside himself with droll ecstasy over the flattery of the great. "It certainly is funny the way the Senators know me, everyone is glad to see me, from the President down. They are trying to keep me as long as they can." And Nast went back to try to do his best for *Harper's Weekly* and it was savage and brutal.[27]

He caught Greeley's expression of fatigue and made him look strained, slow witted, slow footed. In one cartoon Greeley appeared fat, sagging at the knees, his mouth stupidly open, holding out an instrument called the New York Trombone and maintaining that whoever called this instrument an organ was a "liar, a villain, and a scoundrel." In another, he was seen painfully eating from a bowl of uncomfortably hot porridge labeled, "My own words and deeds." In still another he was pictured at his country home at Chappaqua sitting well out upon a Grant limb which he was gravely sawing off between himself and the tree. Other cartoons represented him as whitewashing Tammany, covering with his old white coat and hat a monument of infamy across whose base Ku Klux was sculptured, gloating over the ruin of Southern firesides, and extending a friendly hand towards the South across the graveyards of Andersonville, and as old Honesty marshalling an army of jailbirds, thugs, and crooks. Finally Nast drew Greeley clasping hands with the shade of Wilkes Booth over the grave of Lincoln. "Horrors Greeley" was one of Nast's favorite designations.[28] People roared with laughter at his savagery.

In early summer the Old Man of the White Hat took to the stump and his friends trembled. But not for long. He drew enormous crowds, spoke well, and his listeners fairly liked him.

None the less he appeared as an innocent silly old sheep on the way to a terrible slaughter.

Grant stayed out of the canvass—"I am no speaker," he wrote, "and don't want to be beaten."[29]

Dana, now editor of the *Sun,* was unsparing in bombasting his old chief. Godkin of the *Nation* was chilly.[30] "The difficulty," he remarked, was "that men who are enthusiastic about Mr. Greeley are not apt to care much for reform, while ardent reformers cannot be enthusiastic about Mr. Greeley."[31] Neither could Henry Ward Beecher stomach his old friend: "Mr. Greeley and his friends are fighting General Grant and we refuse to join them."[32]

Charles Sumner, however, urged the Negro to support Greeley: Grant had voted for Buchanan; Greeley had wanted Negro suffrage, Grant had opposed it. Instantly Sumner's old comrades were deep in ink-horns, and Garrison in a bitter reply excoriated Greeley, shamed Sumner and praised the "illustrious administration of Grant."

Thus bewildered the colored people appealed to the gentle poet Whittier who replied in a letter that could be read either way. Finally they turned to Phillips to resolve their doubts.

Though smarting under the injustice done to his friends Sumner and Motley, Phillips nevertheless supported Grant and opposed Greeley. Neither the Republican candidate nor his policies suited him but like Garrison he felt that Greeley was "the worst of all counsellors, the most unsteady of all leaders, the most pliant of all compromisers in times of great public emergency."[33]

In August Phillips wrote a letter to the Negroes of Massachusetts analyzing the situation and giving his views—and they were harsh and one-sided, embittered by the memories of past years, but they were also long-sighted in pointing out an avenue for the discussion of a great national problem—Labor.

"I think every loyal man, and especially every colored man, should vote for General Grant.

"If General Grant is set aside, who is offered us in his place? Horace Greeley. I need not tell you, my friends, what Horace Greeley is: we Abolitionists knew him only too well in the weary years of our struggle. He had enough of clear, moral vision to see the justice of our cause; but he never had courage to confess his faith. . . . A trimmer by nature and purpose, he has abused even an American politician's privilege of trading principles for success. As for his honesty—for twenty years it has been a byword with us that it would be safe to leave your open purse in the same room with him; but, as for any other honesty, no one was ever witless enough to connect the idea with his name.

"Gentlemen, I have another interest in Grant's re-election. The Anti-Slavery cause was only a portion of the great struggle between Capital and Labor. . . . If Grant is elected, that dispute, and all questions connected with it, sink out of sight. All the issues of the war are put beyond debate, and a clear field is left for the discussion of the Labor movement . . .

"If Greeley is elected, we shall spend the next four years in fighting over the war-quarrels, constitutional amendments, Negroes' rights, State rights, repudiation, and Southern debts. And we shall have besides a contemptuous ignoring of the Labor question. Its friends were at Cincinnati. The Convention scorned their appeals, and Mr. Schurz himself affirmed that Labor was 'not a live issue.' President Grant means peace, and opportunity to agitate the great industrial questions of the day. President Greeley means the scandal and wrangle of Andy Johnson's years over again, with secession encamped in Washington. . . .

"Workingmen, rally now, to save your great question from being crowded out, and postponed another four years.

"Soldiers, at the roll-call in November, let no loyal man fail to answer to his name."[34]

At last came the deluge. Greeley carried only six states. New York went against him by more than 50,000 votes, Massachusetts by 75,000, Pennsylvania by 137,000. He was the worst beaten candidate who had ever sought the Presidency. And Nast's efforts were not over. On the day following the election, the cruelest of his cartoons appeared, showing Greeley distraught, abject, ragged and dirty, with stark horror looking out of his eyes, dancing on one foot, his hand clutching the air. "I have been assailed so bitterly," he wrote to a friend in New Hampshire, "that I hardly know whether I was running for the Presidency or the penitentiary."[35]

He was a sadly broken man. Returning from his Western tour, he had kept a sleepless vigil at the bedside of his dying wife who passed away before the election. After the election he resumed the editorship of the *Tribune,* but his own race was run. The strain of campaigning, the mortification of defeat, the crippled financial condition of the journal (stockholders were blaming him for the interruption in their dividends and wanted him ousted) and the death of his wife were more than he could bear. His nerves gave way completely and he died on November 29, but little more than three weeks after the election.[36]

In a solemn and impressive funeral all antagonisms were forgotten. The New York papers, which a month before had been ready to put him in jail, united in eulogy, and the President and Vice President, and the Vice President-elect rode in one carriage behind the hearse.

The political experiment of the Laborites and currency reformers in the election was unfortunate. Their convention, held in February, started off auspiciously enough, announcing itself as "a rallying ground for the people to fight Monopolies and every species of Thieving, Corruption, and Rascality. A Party for the people and not the People for a Party."[37] Three candidates were spoken of: Judge David Davis of the United States Supreme Court, Governor John W. Geary of Pennsylvania, and Wendell Phillips. Phillips was the only one identified with the labor or reform movement in any sense, but the delegates went ahead and nominated Davis. After the Liberal Republican Party nominated Greeley, Davis wrote to the Labor men declining the nomination. He did not want to lead a lost cause; he wanted to run for President with a chance to win. The candidate for Vice President, Joel Parker, informed the Laborites that he had "always been a member of the Democratic party" and presumably intended to remain one.[38]

A meeting of the Executive Committee was held in August,

but the Committee decided it was too late to nominate candidates.

The fiasco of '72 put the finishing touches on the brief existence of the National Labor Union.

3.

James A. Froude, professor of the University of Oxford and noted historian, landed in America in 1872 to deliver a series of lectures on England and America.

He undertook to justify the conduct of his countrymen before the "Yankees" and to persuade them that England had provocation for her treatment of Ireland. He believed that false views of the Irish question prevailed in America, and that he could set them right. He did not underrate the magnitude of his enterprise: "I go like an Arab of the desert," he said. "My hand will be against every man, and therefore every man's hand will be against me."[39]

Froude explained his mission by stating that the judgment of America had more weight in Ireland than twenty batteries of English cannon.[40] When the Irish managed their own affairs, the result was universal misery. They could not govern themselves in the sixteenth century; therefore they could not govern themselves in the nineteenth. If American opinion would only tell the Irish that they had no longer any grievances which legislation could redress, the Irish would believe it, and all would be well. God had left the Irish unfinished; no wit of man could make citizens of them. They were unfit for independence. "The Irishman requires to be ruled. . . . It was that very leaving Ireland to herself which she demands so passionately that was the cause of her wretchedness."[41]

It was hopeless to expect an impartial hearing for Froude. Every Irishman understood that the lecturer was an enemy and was prepared to smite him. The New York *Tribune* remarked: "We have had historical lecturers before, but never any one who essayed with such industry, learning, and eloquence to convince a nation that its sympathies for half a century at least have been misplaced."[42]

Froude was not a man to be put down by clamor. His lectures all had been carefully prepared and he went steadily on with them. He never consciously defended injustice or tampered with the truth. But his personal likes and dislikes were violent and arbitrary. In religious matters he could not be neutral. Where Catholicism and Protestantism came into conflict, he took instinctively the Protestant side. Catholicism, Roman or Anglican, *voilà l'ennemi.* The Catholic side was the side of Ireland, and Cromwell was the minister of divine vengeance upon the murderous and idolatrous Papists. He did not spare the English. But he said Gladstone did not know what he was talking about, the Irish were superstitious and treacherous, and the papal cause in the sixteenth century was the cause of stake and gibbet, the inquisition, dungeons, and political tyranny.[43] And he preached the gospel of force: "I say frankly that I believe the control of human things in this world is given to the strong, and those who cannot hold their own ground with all advantage on their side, must bear the consequences of their weakness."[44] Froude seldom did things by halves, and his apology for Cromwell was not half-hearted. He applauded his celebrated pronouncement:—"I meddle with no man's conscience, but if you mean by liberty of conscience, liberty to have the mass, that will not be suffered where the Parliament of England has power."

The historian's lectures not only stung the Irish to the quick, but harassed his friends. The servants of George Peabody in Boston, who were Irish Catholics, threatened to leave if Froude remained as a guest in their master's house. The Irish found a champion in Father Burke, a Dominican Friar, who dissected Froude with the utmost savagery.[45] But the knell of the British historian was rung when the greatest orator in America rushed to the defence of an oppressed people. Phillips had always a profound sympathy for the wrongs and sufferings of Ireland under the English misrule. In a lecture entitled, "Inferences from Froude," he challenged the fantastic statements of the historian.

"I believe, that instead of England's having conquered Ireland, Ireland has conquered England! She has summoned her before the bar of the civilized world, to answer and plead for the justice of her legislation. . . ." Phillips thanked Froude for painting the Irishman as a chronic rebel. It showed that at least the race knew that they were oppressed, and gathered together all the strength that God had given them to resist. They never rested contented. It was by no means, therefore, a surprise that a patriotic Englishman, looking back on the last three centuries, should long to justify his nation and his own race, after having conceived that it had all the brains, and two-thirds of the heart of the world.

"It volunteered to be the guardian of this obstinate Ireland. It volunteered to furnish a government to the distracted, ignorant, poverty-stricken, demoralized millions of Ireland. It has been three hundred years at the experiment; and Mr. Froude told us the other evening, that, rather than let Ireland go,—weary of their long failure,—rather than let Ireland go, they would exterminate the Irish race! What a confession of statesmanship! 'We have tried for three hundred years to manufacture a government, and at the end of it our alternative is extermination!'

"Well, you see, the world asks, whence comes this result? Was the English race incapable? Did it lack courage? Did it lack brains? Did it lack care? Did it lack common sense? Did it lack that discriminating sagacity which knows time and place? What is the meaning of this failure? And, of course, the only answer of an Englishman who is unwilling to tear down the great splendor of his flag, is, to find the cause in the dogged incapacity of Ireland, and not in any lack of his own country. Mr. Froude is obliged to prove that the Irish were left by God *unfinished,* and that you cannot, by any wit of man, manufacture a citizen out of an Irishman. He is shut up to this argument: for unless he proves the Irishman a knave, he is obliged, from the facts of the case to confess England a fool; that is the grand alternative.

"He comes, therefore, to us with that purpose. He comes to excuse England on the ground of Irish incapacity. Well, it was a marvelously bad choice of a jury: for there were a number of logical, middle aged gentlemen, who met in

Philadelphia, on the Fourth day of July, 1776, and asserted God created every man fit to be a citizen; that he did not leave any race so half made up and half finished, that they were to travel through the cycle of three hundred years under the guardianship of any power. And on that fourth day of July, they established the corner-stone of American political faith, that all men are capable of self government; while the whole substratum of this course of lectures, by this eloquent British scholar was the claim that God left Ireland so unfinished that a merciful despotism was necessary."[46]

Surprised and discomfited by the fierce attacks made upon him, Froude was compelled to abandon his Western tour. A preposterous rumor that he received payment from the British ministry obtained circulation in New York. His life was in danger and he was put under the special protection of the police. Finally he embarked for England, having failed either to enlighten or "amuse Jonathan."

Phillips took a fancy to Swampscott by the sea, and there Ann and he spent the summer of '73. He enjoyed this breathing spell before the rush of lecture engagements caught him up and whirled him away again.

CHAPTER FIFTY-TWO

THE LOUISIANA EPISODE

The people of New Orleans were rioting in the streets, and two factions, one composed of white democrats of the South and the other made up of carpet baggers from the North combined with Negro voters, were at each other's throat. An illegal returning board had given victory to the defeated Republicans without the formality of canvassing the votes and a drunken Federal judge had written a midnight injunction against the legal board. Against this abuse the citizens rose up, erected barricades of stones, horse cars, and boxes, and opened fire on the advancing metropolitan police.

Grant ordered the "turbulent people" to disperse. To enforce his order three men of war and Federal troops were hurried to New Orleans. The Democratic Governor McEnery surrendered the public buildings under protest and the Republican nominee Kellogg emerged from hiding to resume his office at the State House.

Bitterness was at white heat. Grant sent General Sheridan to assume command in the South as he saw fit. No officer was less fitted for the task or more execrated by the people of New Orleans. Entering the breakfast room of his hotel each morning, he was greeted by loud groans and hisses. Abusive articles were marked and handed to him by the waiters which he received with smiles and bows as if he were accepting pleasant compliments.[1]

Events moved swiftly. The Democrats in the legislature, catching their enemy napping, elected one of their number Speaker, and organized the House. Then General de Trobriand suddenly appeared with soldiers bearing an order from the Republican Governor Kellogg to clear the hall of all persons not returned as legal members by the returning board. If the five members from disputed parishes were ejected, the quorum would be broken. With fixed bayonets the soldiers approached one by one each of the five members sitting in his place and forced him to leave the hall. The conservative speaker withdrew; The Republicans returned and organized as best they could.

Soldiers guarded the State House with cannon, and Sheridan spurred himself into the picture with the clatter of a cavalry-man. He sent a telegram to Grant suggesting that if Grant would proclaim the protesting people banditti "no further action need be taken except that which would devolve upon me." Belknap, Secretary of War, replied: "The President and all of us have full confidence in and thoroughly approve your course."[2]

Opposition newspapers in the North thundered against Sheri-dan, against de Trobriand, against Grant. "If this can be done in Louisiana," cried Schurz, "and if such things be sustained by Congress, how long will it be before it can be done in Massa-chusetts and Ohio? . . . How long before a soldier may stalk into the National House of Representatives and pointing to the Speaker's mace, say 'Take away that bauble!' "[3] Vast indigna-tion meetings were held in many cities. Resolutions denouncing government by bayonets were adopted. A protest meeting, claim-ing to speak for Boston, was held in Faneuil Hall at noon on Friday, January 15, 1875.

The house was packed to the doors, the floor with men standing solid together and the galleries with people seated and standing. The day was cold and the hall was so chilly that none could be comfortable without an overcoat.

Phillips, greatly interested in the Louisiana question, sat quietly in the gallery. Resolutions were read denouncing Grant and Sheridan. As each speaker concluded, long cries for Phil-lips rang through the hall. Neither the chairman nor Phillips paid any attention to these calls until the program was ended. Then the demand became so loud and persistent that it could not be ignored. At last the chairman said, "Fellow Citizens: We are assembled in Faneuil Hall to discuss great public questions. The meeting is open to any citizen who wishes to give us his advice. (Cries of 'Good.') Whoever chooses to speak shall be heard."

Phillips stood up in his place in the gallery. "Mr. Chairman," he said, and was about to continue, when there were loud cries of "Platform." Phillips hesitated, but the Chairman having beckoned to him, he descended to the platform in the midst of tremendous applause. As he stepped upon the platform three cheers were given for him and there were some hisses. Then in the old place a familiar scene was enacted—a masterful artist playing at will with his audience.

He came to Faneuil Hall that morning, he said, because he had seen in the journals that the voice of Boston was to be uttered on a great national question. He looked over the list of gentlemen who had summoned the people of Boston, asking himself, if this were the voice of Boston, who were the Boston men that voted and paid taxes in Boston that summoned the meeting?

"The first named is Charles Francis Adams of Quincy (Tremendous applause), a very worthy gentleman, but he votes in Quincy. (Great confusion here prevailed.) If you will only hear me, you will see that I mean no disrespect to Mr. Adams or any other signer. (Cries of 'You can't,' and 'Hear him.') I say that Mr. Adams—allow me to speak— that Mr. Adams—(Applause and confusion.)—if you will only hear me gentlemen, we shall save time. I have no intention—"[4]

Here the noise was so great that Phillips could not be heard and the President rose to restore order. The words "Question," and "Free Speech," were being shouted on all sides, and for some time the President could say nothing. At length the noise subsided to a certain extent, and the President said: "Fellow citizens, hear Mr. Phillips; hear anybody and everybody who wishes to speak in Faneuil Hall. Be patient and give them your ears, and finally, vote according to your own judgment." The words were received with great applause and Phillips continued.

"I observed on this list, gentlemen, the names of worthy citizens from Salem, and Plymouth, and Quincy, and Worcester, and Cambridge. . . .—(A voice, 'You agree with Grant') —all I ask is this. When gentlemen come here to express the voice of Boston and have not the name of a leading clergyman or lawyer—(Cries of 'Beecher,' 'Infidel,' 'Question' 'Who wrote the letter for Boston?' 'Free Speech', etc.) Because in the absence of Dana, and Abbott, and Bigelow, and Bartlett and their fellows, the legal profession is not here, in the absence of the merchants of State Street, with half a dozen exceptions, the commerce of Boston is not here; in the absence of every clergyman who votes in this city, the pulpit is not here ('That's so'), therefore I say (Hisses), gentlemen, that it becomes you to exercise extraordinary caution (cries of 'Free Speech' in the midst of noisy demonstrations) that the facts which you state in such a position, and the inferences which you make, are careful and guarded.

"Now gentlemen—(a voice, 'Give us your opinion, quick').[5]

Phillips urged his listeners to silence then proceeded to dissect their arguments and reshape their opinions. At one point he took off his overcoat which act caused a great deal of noise and enthusiasm. In concluding he cast doubt on the testimony of General Quincy the first speaker of the meeting. General Quincy had said that though he left firebrands, turmoil, and bloodshed in New Orleans, he didn't believe they were there any longer. Sheridan was there with him, said Phillips, and saw these firebrands and Sheridan went back to New Orleans. Which would the audience believe? asked Phillips. Was not the man on the spot a better witness than the man a thousand miles off?

"Men of Boston, I am not here to praise the administration. If these resolutions are passed, they will carry consternation and terror into the house of every Negro in Louisiana. (Applause, hisses, and groans.) They will carry comfort to every assassin in New Orleans. (Hisses and applause.) My anxiety is not for Washington. I don't care who is President. My anxiety is for the hunted, tortured, murdered population, white and black, of the Southern States, whom you are going to consign to the hands of their oppressors. If you pass these resolutions (Cries of 'We will,' 'we will.')—if you pass these resolutions (cries of 'We will,' 'we will')—if you pass these resolutions (cries of 'We will,' 'we will,')—I say it in the presence of God Almighty (cries of 'Sh!' 'Sh!') the blood of hundreds of blacks and hundreds of whites will be on your skirts before the first day of January next. (Loud laughter.)"[6]

"I know why I came here," continued Phillips. A voice: "You came here to make a row." (Laughter, applause, and hissing.) Here there was so much hissing and confusion that Phillips could not be heard. The President stepped to his side and said: "Hear him, hear him! Order! Order! Order." And a voice replied: "Mesmerize him." To cries of "Played out!" "Sit down!" "Hear, hear!" Phillips went on. The resolution offered in Faneuil Hall would take from the President the power to protect the Negroes. What more contemptible object than a nation which, for its own selfish purpose, summoned four million Negroes to liberty and then left them endangered and defenceless. What more pitiable object than the President of such a nation if he yielded to the contemptible clamor and refused to protect these colored citizens.

"I have done all I intended to do. I only wanted to record the protest of one citizen of Boston (uproarious applause) against that series of resolutions. Other men recorded it by their absence, and their refusal to sign the call. (Renewed applause.) I chose to record mine in your presence in this very hall, and under this very roof, where I have so often labored to bring these colored men into the very condition which makes them the object of the White League's fear and hatred, and doubles their trouble and perils for the present. (Cries of 'Yes, that's it' and laughter.)"[7]

A great deal of noise and confusion here ensued, during which three cheers were given for Wendell Phillips. The resolutions were put to the audience. The vote against them was manifestly heavier than that for them, though, of course, the President had to declare them carried, as that was what the meeting was for. But the back of the protest was broken.

In the Louisiana difficulties Phillips appeared more on the side of the oppressor than for the oppressed.

The upshot of the question was: A Congressional Committee visited New Orleans and after a full inquiry agreed that the returning board had wrongfully applied an erroneous rule of law. A compromise was effected: the Democrats took the lower House while the Republicans kept the Senate and governorship.

CHAPTER FIFTY-THREE

THE MONEY QUESTION—DANIEL
O'CONNELL—OLD SOUTH CHURCH

A question of deeper interest than the Louisiana muddle related to the currency. When the Rebellion broke out, the government, in order to conduct its stupendous operations, issued bonds to raise money, and notes, called greenbacks from their color, as a circulating medium. The situation was desperate. Money leaders would not buy the bonds save at a heavy discount; and though the greenbacks were legal tender, it took two or three dollars in currency to make a gold dollar. With the success of the Union, the greenbacks appreciated, but gold continued to command a fluctuating premium. The constant endeavor of the government was to resume specie payments, that is, make the greenbacks worth their face value. Meanwhile through these years trade was disturbed, financial panics were frequent, and gold remained in Europe.

Numerous remedies for these evils were proposed. Phillips had his plan. He decried the position of bondholders that debts against the United States were more sacred than any other and that they be paid in specie. He took the position that there was no difference between legal tender notes of the United States and gold and silver as money. He first stated his views in public at a meeting of the American Social Science Association in Boston on March 3, 1875. Briefly his suggestions were:

(1) Take away from the banks the right to issue bills, and call in those now in circulation.

(2) Let the government supply a national currency ample to meet the demands of business—its issue being secured by the wealth of the country.

(3) Reduce the heavy rates of interest by calling in out-standing interest-bearing bonds.[1]

The results of such a policy, he contended, would be fourfold, namely, to redeem and destroy the present greenbacks, and thus silence the complaint that the government had not kept faith in their redemption: to put the currency on a basis as stable as the national resources, and thus avoid the danger of inter-ference by the gold rings here and abroad; to make the bonds a good permanent investment for capitalists; and to develop the country by making it possible for individual borrowers to get money at a low rate from the government by placing collateral in its hands.

This would make the new greenbacks as good as gold. It would bring about practical resumption of specie payments. Before long the government bonds would command a premium.

"Three times within a dozen years, capitalists with their knives on the throat of the Government, have compelled it to cheat its largest creditor, the people; whose claim, Burke said, was the most sacred. First, the pledge that greenbacks should be exchanged with bonds was broken. Secondly, debts originally payable in paper, as Sherman confessed in the Senate, were made payable in gold. Thirdly, silver was demonetized, and gold made the only tender. A thousand millions were thus stolen from the people."[2]

These beliefs Phillips embodied in a lecture on "Finance," which he delivered widely for several years. In the fall of 1875 he exchanged shots with Carl Schurz on the same question.

"Here he complains" said Schurz, "that the banks do not accommodate the whole mass of business men with their favors, and what remedy does he propose? His system of greenbacks and incontrovertible bonds. Now, what in the name of common sense does he mean? That the government under his system is to discount the notes of business men, who cannot get their notes discounted at a bank, and to make time loans to them and to buy and sell their bills of exchange? . . . You see the thing is too childish to be discussed among serious men."[3]

The Boston *Daily Globe* aided Schurz by a little denunciation.

"O no!," it remarked, "Wendell Phillips is not a demagogue. He sincerely believes what he says for the time being. He is merely a fanatic, that's all. There is a wide difference."[4]

Phillips never claimed originality for his financial theories. He held them in common with a host of others. The originator of greenbackism was Edward Kellogg, a merchant of New York. His book *Labor and Other Capital* was practically contemporary with Marx's *Communist Manifesto,* Proudhon's *What is Property?* and also Louis Blanc's *L'Organization du Travail.* After 1861 several reprints of Kellogg's book were published. The greenback theory was the American counterpart of the radicalism of Europe.

"Who shall rule us?" asked Phillips. "Money or the people?" The first question in an industrial nation is, where ought the control of the currency to rest? In whose hands can this almost omnipotent power be trusted? Whom can we trust with this despotism? The banks and the money kings wielded this power, answered Phillips. They owned the yardstick and could make it shorter or longer as they pleased and when they willed. This explained the riddle, so mysterious to common men, why those who traded in money always grew rich while those who traded in other things went into bankruptcy. "This is the issue today: WHO SHALL MAKE THE YARDSTICK?"

"Today we are fighting to secure what Jefferson in 1813 advised, that the circulation be restored to the nation to whom it belongs. This is the reason why the banks and money kings hate this movement so bitterly, and pour out their money like water to kill it. They feel and know it is a hand-to-hand fight between themselves and the people—one of the last battles between aristocracy and democracy."

The most cunning weapon the money men used was that of confusing the question. They fooled their dupes and instructed their agents to drag in the questions of paper money, inflation, bonds, and a score of others in order to hide the real issue. "Shall the nation make its own currency or put itself under the guardianship of capital—sheep in the keeping of wolves?"

"If corruption seems rolling over us like a flood, mark, it is not the corruption of the humbler classes. It is millionaires who steal banks, mills, and railways; it is defaulters who live in palaces and make way with millions; it is Money Kings who buy up Congress; it is demagogues and editors in purple and fine linen who bid fifty thousand dollars for the Presidency itself; it is greedy wealth which invests its thousand millions in rum to coin money out of the weakness of its neighbor. These are the spots where corruption nestles and gangrenes the State. If humble men are corrupted, these furnish the overwhelming temptation. It is not the common people in the streets, but the Money Changers who have intruded in the temple that we most sorely need some one to scourge. If the hills will cease to send down rottenness, the streams will run clean and clear on the plains."[5]

A heretic in finance, Phillips was a conservative in the matter of tariff—a strict protectionist.

"National lines—artificial lines—" he said, "trip up fine theories sadly. If all the world were under one law, and every man raised to the level of the Sermon on the Mount, free trade would be so easy and so charming! But while nations study only how to cripple their enemies,—that is, their neighbors,—and while each trader strives to cheat his customer and strangle the firm on the other side of the street, we must not expect the millennium."[6]

The centennial of the birth of Daniel O'Connell occurred on August 6, 1875. A world wide celebration was held. In Boston Phillips observed the occasion by eulogizing the Irish agitator before a vast throng at Music Hall.

"Ireland was a community impoverished by five centuries of oppression,—four millions of Catholics robbed of every acre of their native land: it was an island torn by race-hatred and religious bigotry, her priests indifferent, and her nobles hopeless or traitors. In this mass of ignorance, weakness and quarrel, one keen eye saw hidden the elements of union and strength. With rarest skill he called them forth, and marshalled them into rank. Then this one man, without birth, wealth, or office, in a land ruled by birth, wealth, and office, moulded from those unsuspected elements a power, which overawing the king, senate, and people, wrote his single will on the statute-book of the most obstinate nation in Europe. Dying, he left in Parliament a spectre, which, unless appeased, pushes Whig and Tory ministers alike from their stools.

"To show you that he never took a leaf from our American gospel of compromise; that he never filed his tongue to silence on one truth, fancying so to help another; that he never sacrificed any race to save even Ireland,—let me compare him with Kossuth, whose only merits were his eloquence and his patriotism. When Kossuth was in Faneuil Hall, he exclaimed, 'Here is a flag without a stain, a nation without a crime!' We Abolitionists appealed to him, 'O eloquent son of the Magyar, come to break chains! have you no word, no pulse-beat, for four millions of Negroes bending under a yoke ten times heavier than that of Hungary?' "

O'Connell never said anything like that, claimed Phillips. When Phillips was in Naples, he asked Sir Thomas Foxwell Buxton, a Tory, "Is O'Connell an honest man?"—"As honest a man as ever breathed," said Buxton and then told Phillips this story. When, in 1830, O'Connell entered parliament, the Anti-Slavery cause was so weak that it had only Lushington and Buxton to speak for it; and they agreed that when O'Connell spoke Buxton should cheer O'Connell and when Buxton spoke O'Connell should cheer Buxton; and these were the only cheers they ever got. O'Connell came, with one Irish member to support him. A large number of members (Buxton said twenty-seven), who were called the West-India interest, the slave party, went to him, saying, "O'Connell, at last you are in the House, with one helper. If you will never go down to Freemason's Hall with Buxton and Brougham, here are twenty-seven votes for you on every Irish question. If you work with those Abolitionists, count us always against you."

It was a terrible temptation. How many so-called statesmen would have yielded! O'Connell said, "Gentlemen, God knows I speak for the saddest people the sun sees; but may my right hand forget its cunning, and my tongue cleave to the roof of my mouth, if, to save Ireland,—even Ireland,—I forget the Negro one single hour!"—"From that day," said Buxton, "Lushington and I never went into the lobby that O'Connell did not follow us."

"Learn of him, friends, the hardest lesson we ever have set us, that of toleration. The foremost Catholic of his age, the most stalwart champion of the Church, he was also broadly and sincerely tolerant of every faith. His toleration had no limit, and no qualification.

"I scorn and scout the word 'toleration.' It is an insolent term. No man, properly speaking, *tolerates* another. I do not tolerate a Catholic, neither does he tolerate me. We are equal, and acknowledge each other's right: that is the correct statement.

"It is natural that Ireland should remember O'Connell as her *Liberator*. But, strange as it may seem to you, I think Europe and America will remember him by a higher title. I said in opening, that the cause of constitutional government is more indebted to O'Connell than to any other political leader of the last two centuries. What I mean is, that he invented the great method of constitutional agitation. *Agitator* is a title which will last longer, which suggests a broader and more permanent influence, and entitles him to the gratitude of far more millions, than the name Ireland loves to give him. The 'first great agitator' is his proudest title to gratitude and fame. Agitation is the method that puts the school by the side of the ballot box. The

Fremont canvass was the nation's best school. Agitation prevents rebellion, keeps the peace, and secures progress. Every step she gains is gained forever. Muskets are the weapons of animals: agitation is the atmosphere of brains. The old Hindoo saw, in his dream, the human race led out to its various fortunes. First, men were in chains which went back to an iron hand; then he saw them led by threads from the brain, which went upward to an unseen hand. The first was despotism, iron, and ruling by force. The last was civilization, ruling by ideas."[7]

Later in the year Phillips dealt with the question of Temperance, Labor, and Women, and defended the Indian who had been vilely abused. He contrasted our conduct with the English attitude in Canada, and hailed Grant's Indian policy as the first sane one since the days of William Penn. Uprisings on the frontier such as the Madoc War and the victory of the Sioux over General Custer at Little Big Horn gave timeliness and point to his utterances. Indeed, Phillips seldom wasted his ammunition on dead issues. His aim was always to

Shoot folly as it flies.

Again in 1875 Phillips was drawn into the political struggle. The Labor Reformers in Massachusetts nominated him for governor and General William F. Bartlett (who was also nominated by the Democrats) for Lieutenant Governor. Attendance at the convention was small but there was a big wrangle.[8]

The political labor movement in Massachusetts had dwindled down to two small mutually hostile groups: the Labor Union led by Phillips and the Eight Hour League led by Ira Stewart and George E. McNeill. The latter, however, united with Phillips to bring about the establishment of a Massachusetts Bureau of Labor Statistics. The bone of contention was the eight hour question. To Steward this was the only question, but Phillips advocated a broader program with money reform at the head of the list. Personal criminations and recriminations became frequent.

Steward was an "eight hour monomaniac." For this one idea he lived, worked, and fought with almost fanatical zeal. He contributed to nearly every reform paper then published, but each article emphasized his one thought. "Meet him any day, as he steams along the street (like most enthusiasts he is always in a hurry)," said a writer in the *American Workman,* "and although he will apologize and excuse himself if you talk to him of other affairs, and say that he is sorry, that he must rush back to his shop, if you only introduce the pet topic of 'hours of labor,' and show a little willingness to listen, he will stop and plead with you till nightfall."[9] The major point stressed by Steward was that the reduction of working hours could be effected without any cut in wages. This idea was popularized by a jingle attributed to his wife—"whether you work by the piece or work by the day—Decreasing the hours increases the pay."[10]

At the Labor Convention the forces backing Phillips won. A platform was adopted defending the governor's right to refund its bonded debt by issuing new bonds, calling for a currency of legal tender, and resolving "that the national bank system is one of the greatest swindles ever perpetrated on a patient people." The manufacturers of Fall River were roundly denounced: "They are earning the execrations of all mankind; they are treasuring up wrath against a day of wrath, and their success is demonstrating the fact that between them and their workingmen is a slave and master relation, which means war, and a justification of all that will follow sooner or later, when an oppressed people find themselves able to overthrow their oppressors."[11]

Phillips's advocacy of inflation lost him many supporters. Little enthusiasm could be aroused to bolster a tottering party. A card to the public, therefore, was addressed through the columns of the *Weekly Globe,* "giving three good reasons" why citizens of all parties should vote for Wendell Phillips: first— the two great parties had outlived the issues which gave them existence, and were now nothing but names on the gravestones of the dead past; second—the spirit of reform was in the air, and Wendell Phillips was the living embodiment of that idea; third —the spirit of distrust was in the air. Men knew not whom or what to trust. Wendell Phillips had a life record of political and moral honesty, courage, and patriotism—and everybody knew it. "He can't be bought and he can't be sold. He will do all that one man can do to make the administration of public affairs pure."[12]

At the election on November 2, Phillips received a few hundred scattered votes.[13]

At home it was a year of "weariness and great pain." Ann suffered more than during all their married years and was given doses of laudanum. To Mrs. Garrison: "Ann tells me to send you her kindest love and best thanks for the memory of her and the fruit (jelly) you sent. The poor child has only memories left to live on—weakness and pain and weariness make up the days now—so old memories are the pleasantest and she lives in the past—though we hope on. . . ."[14]

The great revolutionary leaders Phillips held in peculiar reverence. He argued that what they were to the King of their day, the real American ought to be to the money barons of his. There should be no such thing as contentment with what had been inherited from the past. Every age should have its Samuel Adams and James Otis and its Patrick Henry.

The places that these men had made famous were sacred to him. In his walks about the city of Boston he was fond of visiting them and recalling the memories enshrined in each. None was dearer to him than the Old South Meeting House. None of the city's churches was so rich in historical associations as this. Here Lovell, Church, Warren, and Hancock had delivered orations on the anniversary of the Boston Massacre. In the Old Church Benjamin Franklin had been baptized. In the new, the famous Tea Party meeting was held after being adjourned from Faneuil Hall.

In 1876 the Old South was threatened with destruction. The religious society which owned it had sold the building and as the property had a high value for business purposes, the new owners decided to raze the building and occupy the site. The alarming prospect aroused the citizens of Boston who protested against it. Phillips took part in the movement that raised a fund large enough to preserve the historic edifice. On June

14, 1876, he spoke in the Old South itself on behalf of this movement.

"These arches will speak to us, as long as they stand, of the sublime and sturdy religious enthusiasm of Adams; of Otis's passionate eloquence and single-hearted devotion; of Warren in his young genius and enthusiasm; of a plain, unaffected but high-souled people who ventured all for a principle, and to transmit to us, unimpaired, the free life and self-government which they inherited. Above and around us unseen hands have written, 'This is the cradle of Civil Liberty, child of earnest religious faith.' I will not say it is a nobler consecration; I will not say that it is a better use. I only say that we come here to save what our fathers consecrated to the memories of the most successful struggle the race has ever made for the liberties of man. Think twice before you touch these walls. We are only the world's trustees. The Old South no more belongs to us than Luther's or Hampden's or Brutus's name does to Germany, England, or Rome. Each and all are held in trust as torchlight guides and inspiration for any man struggling for justice and ready to die for the truth."[15]

Although Phillips refused a nomination for Congress in 1878, he vigorously entered the political campaign. In the summer he headed a petition of 51,700 citizens asking General Butler to become an independent candidate for Governor on the issue of State reform. The people were rising against party dictation and ring rule. Phillips also addressed a letter to the *Globe* giving his reasons for voting for Butler. "No party," said Phillips in speaking of the Republicans, "has ever existed in this country that has made itself more the tool of capital or that has manifested a more determined purpose to get rid of universal suffrage and enslave the masses to the Money Kings. I shall vote for General Butler because he represents the determination of the *People to Take the Currency out of the Control of Money Kings,* 'the Cannibals of 'Change Alley,' as Lord Chatham called them—and keep possession of it themselves."[16]

The General made a forceful canvass. He delivered one hundred speeches to immense audiences in various cities and villages of the State. But Democratic and Republican hard money orators literally swarmed over the land like the locusts and frogs of Egypt. Butler's personal character was slandered. The Republican party issued a circular letter to the clergy of the State urging them to come to the rescue. Another circular was printed and sent secretly to all manufacturers, urging them by the authority they exercised over their employees "to maintain the honor of Massachusetts, and keep it out of the hands of spoilers and political knaves who have selected General Butler as their candidate. His election would disgrace our State and ruin our standing at home and abroad."[17]

The manufacturers resorted to the method of bulldozing. Laborers were terrorized with hints of the coming winter with no employment. The Boston *Herald,* giving the anti-Butler men their cue, remarked—

> "The Laborers employed by General Butler in his various enterprises—mills, quarries, etc.—will be expected to vote for him or give up their situations.
> "The same rule will hold good on the other side. There will be no shotguns or threats. Everything will be managed with decorum adorned by noble sentiments. But the men who oppose Butler, employ three quarters, if not seven-eighths of the labor of the State. They honestly believe that Butler's election would injure their prosperity. They know that idle hands are waiting to do their work. It is not to be expected that they will look on indifferently and see their employees vote for a destructive like Butler."[18]

With such methods of intimidation it is not surprising that the Republicans won. Butler, however, received the largest number of votes polled (110,000) for a defeated candidate. "The treatment of General Butler by the press of Massachusetts," said Phillips, "is a foul disgrace to the State. Men not worthy to unloose the latchet of his shoes are cheered while they load him with all manner of abuse."[19]

In 1882 Butler secured the undivided support of the Democratic party and was elected. The story of his administration is the story of a bitter struggle between the executive and legislature. He urged better civil service laws, a constitutional amendment to allow women to vote, and supported radical and far reaching labor legislation. In 1884, however, he was defeated for reelection.

Phillips turned aside from politics to advocate other causes; the treatment and care of the insane, financial aid to Negroes who wished to emigrate from the South, the vindication of his friends Sumner and Motley. On the first question, he had felt strongly for half a century. Indeed there had been a time when his own family entertained the idea of shutting him up in a madhouse as an Abolitionist. Without doubt, scores of men and women whom relatives wished to get out of the way were being thrust into straightjackets. Crooked physicians and loose laws produced such rascalities. Taking his cue from a flagrant case in the neighborhood, Phillips called a public meeting. As a result the legislature of Massachusetts was petitioned to pass stringent laws regarding the committal of persons alleged to be insane and securing for them the right of frequent and fair examinations and timely release.

After the deaths of Sumner and Motley, Phillips began to deliver a eulogy on "Charles Sumner" in which he courageously defended his friends.[20] But soon he was called upon to mourn the loss of another friend, his coworker in the fight against slavery—William Lloyd Garrison.

Yielding to the persuasions of his daughter, Mrs. Villard, who visited him in the spring of 1879 and saw how ill he was, Garrison returned with her to New York to be cared for at her home on Union Square. But the kidney disease from which he was suffering had gone too far for a cure. On May 10, he took to his bed completely prostrated. He was "weary" and expressed a desire to "go home." Two weeks later his children gathered about him and in his last hours of consciousness sang to him the hymns of which he was so fond—"Lenox," "Coronation,"

"Hebron"—   Thus far the Lord hath led me on,
                             Thus far His power prolongs my days,
                        And every evening shall make known
                            Some fresh memorial of His grace.

"Christmas"—   Awake, my soul, stretch every nerve,
                              And press with vigor on;
                              A heavenly race demands thy zeal,
                              And an immortal crown.

and "Amsterdam"—   Rise, my soul, and stretch thy wings,
                              Thy better portion trace,
                              Rise from transitory things
                              To heaven, thy native place.

Though he could no longer speak, he took part by beating the tune with his foot and hand. He died on May 24, 1879.[21]

Funeral services were held at Roxbury on May 28. Garrison lay in the spacious church of the First Religious Society on Eliot Square. In accordance with his views of death, everything was done to avoid the appearance of mourning. Blinds were opened to admit the cheerful light of a perfect spring day and the pulpit was tastefully decorated with flowers.

The body was interred beside that of Mrs. Garrison in the beautiful cemetery at Forest Hills in the presence of a large number of friends. The Reverend Samuel May who conducted the services read some passages from the Old and New Testament. Then as a shower of arrows from the setting sun pierced the trees and the voices of a quartette of colored friends sang his favorite hymns, the last remains of the great reformer were laid to rest.[22]

Phillips delivered a moving tribute.

"Serene, fearless, marvellous man! Mortal, with so few shortcomings!

"Farewell for a very little while, noblest of Christian men! Leader, brave, tireless, unselfish! When the ear heard thee, then it blessed thee; the eye that saw thee gave witness to thee. More truly than it could ever heretofore be said since the great patriarch wrote it, 'the blessing of him that was ready to perish' was thine eternal reward."[23]

CHAPTER FIFTY-FOUR

THE CHAMPION OF ORTHODOXY

In an old fashioned, roomy mansion in the aristocratic section of Boston gathered the most gifted and progressive people in America. For here under the roof of the Reverend John T. Sargent the famous Radical Club met. It had its origin in the growing desire of certain ministers and clergymen for a larger liberty of faith, fellowship, and communion. In this respect it closely resembled the Transcendentalist movement of an earlier date.

At the meetings in Sargent's home one might find almost any day Henry Wadsworth Longfellow with his white head and patriarchal beard, George William Curtis with his refined face, Oliver Wendell Holmes, a boy in the midst of his white headed contemporaries, Emerson, John Weiss, Julia Ward Howe, Henry James, and a host of other celebrities. Much of the talk was excellent—bright, inspiring, hopeful. There was never a mean sentiment or offensive word.

Phillips was a frequent guest of the club. Friends observed how the radical instantly assumed, when religion was the topic under consideration, the garb of exemplary conservatism. Against iconoclasts and liberals, he was the champion of orthodoxy.

On one occasion the Reverend W. H. Channing read a paper on "The Christian Name." When the discussion began Phillips remarked:

"Christianity is a great moral power, the determining force of our present civilization, as of past steps in the same direction. Jesus is the divine type who has given His peculiar

640

form to the modern world. Speculations as to why and how may differ, but we see the fact. We cannot rub out history.

"The battle for human rights was finally fought on a Christian plane. Unbelief has written books, but it never lifted a million men into a united struggle. The power that urged the world forward came from Christianity."[1]

At another sitting John Weiss spoke on "Heart in Religion," and contended that Jesus was effeminate. Whereupon Phillips said:

"You speculate as to whether Jesus was a masculine character. Look at the men who have learned of Him most closely,—at Paul and Luther and Wesley. Were they effeminate? Yet the disciple is but a faint reflection of his Master. The character from which came the force which has been doing battle ever since with wrong and falsehood and error was nothing less than masculine, but sentiment is the toughest thing in the world,—nothing else is iron."[2]

One day Quakerism was discussed. Phillips said—

"Quakerism showed the limitations of human nature. A religious genius arises, and bears the precise testimony needed by the world at that time; but if he tries to organize or perpetuate himself, he fails. George Fox was a great religious genius. William Penn was a trimmer, who, if he had lived in New England of our time, would have been a doughface . . .

"Fox shows us how little we owe to colleges. The great religious ideas of modern Europe all came from the people. Intellect led by scholars opposes progress. If Fox were here among us, he would be as radical now as he was then, and would be again imprisoned as a disturber of society."[3]

Phillips was now on familiar ground. In a discussion of the American Rebellion, on whether Boston would act with the same spirit as it did a century ago, he remarked—

"I believe the pictures of that Boston a hundred years ago are highly colored. . . . That 'brace of Adamses' were then men of no repute, vulgar fanatics heading a crowd of workingmen, scoffed at and scorned by the respectables of the day. The marvel is that the middle well-to-do and commercial classes headed the rebellion. . . . That is explained by the fact that every successful merchant in Boston was obliged to be a smuggler. England crippled our trade to save her own as she has been doing with Ireland for the last century. So the traders, angered by self interest, calculated it would pay to join the mob and rise. But Toryism had the fashion, the old wealth, and the prestige, as it has always had."[4]

David A. Wells read a paper on economic laws and in the discussion that followed, Phillips replied—

"The greenback system (using the credit of the government as the basis of currency) will be the first work needed by a true Democratic party. For this greenback question only means whether we shall trust the Declaration of Independence that all men are equal in money matters, as in everything else. Hitherto we have been Tories in money questions and trusted the people only in other matters. In those, capitalists, bank directors, and a select class have been thought to be the only safe guides. The people now claim that they can and will decide these as wisely and honestly as they do all other matters. This is the last fight between wealth and the people,—not between the noble and serf, but between money bags and the workingmen, between the men who create wealth and those who steal a living by the hocus-pocus of banking and the nonsense of coin. The people will now carry the Declaration of Independence into Wall Street, where it has never yet penetrated, and we shall have a more honest finance than the world has yet seen."[5]

To one who doubted this popular virtue, Phillips replied—

"Never expect heaven in Boston. I never said that a democracy was a good government. A thing may be the best we can get, and yet not be good. Democracy is not a good government, but it is the best we can get while we have only this poor, rotten human nature to work with. Governments created by the people have always been more honest and less corrupt than those originating with the aristocracy, and revolutions made by the people have generally been more merciful and less bloody than the victories of the upper classes."[6]

Phillips's enthusiastic advocacy of his scheme of abolishing all coin and issuing two billion dollars (an amount equal to the national debt), based on the thirty billions of property of the country, so that interest should never be more than five percent, was welcomed with much good natured laughter.

CHAPTER FIFTY-FIVE

LECTURING

Phillips was on the road more than any other speaker in the country. The lecture season which began in November and lasted until April took him on long tours through every state of the North. Western rural travel was something formidable. Along the old "corduroy" roads, one had to cling vigilantly to his seat to keep from being thrown from the wagon into the apparently bottomless mud.

But Phillips adjusted himself to the hardships of a lecturer's life. He was in the habit of carrying a large shawl which he always spread between the sheets of his bed in various hotels to avoid rheumatism and prevent colds. As he was fond of tea he carried his own English breakfast tea in his traveling bag and had tea made everywhere. Before speaking he usually ate a light meal—three raw eggs and as many cups of tea.

The orator's repertoire was vast,[1] but such was the magnetism of his manner that his audience felt he could talk long and entertainingly about the handle of a broom. Men and women went to hear him, determined to dislike him and sat breathless through the hour.

He never spoke merely to amuse. His main purpose was to instruct. According to his view, influence was a trust to be exerted in Lord Bacon's phrase, "for the glory of God and the relief of man's estate."

During the anti-slavery period when invited to lecture and asked to name his price, his habitual response was—"If you want a literary lecture, the price is so and so—a high one. But if you will let me speak on slavery, I will come for nothing and pay my own expenses!"[2]

Through his lectures on science and biography, however, he often won a hearing for the cause which lay nearest his heart. They were introductions to a hostile audience which would not permit him to discuss slavery at first, but which, once under his spell, gave him carte blanche. It was in this way that he was led to prepare his famous lecture on "The Lost Arts." He began to deliver it in 1838. Thenceforth and for forty-five years, he gave it again and again to fascinated crowds from Portland to St. Louis. No doubt it was an exaggeration to say he gave it over two thousand times and that it netted him $150,000. He was inclined to make fun of the lecture and to wonder at the continued demand for it. "These hard times," he writes to McKim, "will probably make it impossible to get much of an audience at either lecture. Don't worry about netting anything from the Lyceum one—It's of no consequence whatever—I come to keep my old promise to you and convince you that the 'Lost Art' is not worth hearing."[3]

The press of his lectures worked havoc with his correspondence. He was always excusing the lateness of his replies —absence from home, unavoidable engagements, etc. "Unresponding correspondent," he confessed himself to Sumner. "I received your welcome note ten days ago—but running 'round the country have had no time to reply." Again: "Excuse the scrawl—it's the 11th letter I've written this evening."[4] (A fact, for after 1865 Phillips's letters are often nothing but illegible scrawls dashed off in spare moments between tending Ann and entraining for a lecture.) "Do you know why I send such horrid writing," he wrote guiltily to Mrs. Garrison. "On the same principle with Sheridan's reply to the Scottish orator in the House of Commons who wanted to get rid of his brogue. 'Don't, my dear fellow. Now folks think you eloquent because they don't understand you. Get rid of your brogue and it's all up'— so you, perhaps, will fancy this letter would be good if you could read it."[5]

Life on the road was hard. From Illinois he writes "in the cars," and with a lead pencil, to a protegé of whom Ann was fond—

"The weather is dull—only two days since I left that I have seen the sun. Rain, clouds, damp, mud, and grim heavens. Still the audiences are large.

"Since my letter from Chicago, I have been shaken in omnibuses and hacks to a terrible degree. The mud has been fearful. And then the sudden quick freeze, and it is iron in deep ruts—horrible to ride on. I rejoice that dear old Boston (how I love those streets!) has no such inflictions."[6]

To the same friend he sends a description of an oil town in Pennsylvania,—

"Here I am in an oil town—mud over the hubs of the wheels; literally, one horse was smothered in it: the queerest crowd of men, with trousers tucked in their boots; no privacy—hotels all one crowd—chambers mere thoroughfares, —everybody passing through at will. And here I must be all Sunday, unless some train will carry me on in the direction I wish.

"I find some of the Boston people. Everybody here is making money: the first place I have found where this is the case. Explanation—they have just struck oil!"[7]

From Davenport, Iowa, he writes the Reverend Mr. Sargent:

"Dear John:

"I, the traveller, the 'elderly gentleman,' have been— kissed! in Illinois! Put that in your pipe and smoke it. Yes, kissed!! on a public platform, in front of a depot, the whole world envying me. 'Who did it?' do you ask. It was an old man of seventy-three years—a veteran Abolitionist, a lovely old saint. In the early days of the cause we used to kiss each other like the early Christians; and when he saw me he resumed the habit."[8]

He lectured one night in a New England town on "The Lost Arts." When he finished, a lady said:

"I was interested in the lecture, but it didn't seem to have much relation to the origin of law."

"What do you mean, madam?" he asked.

"Why," said she, "weren't you to lecture on 'The Law Starts'?"[9]

In the old anti-slavery days he lectured several times in Cincinnati. Once at the same time there was a convention of ministers in session. The next morning he took the train, seating himself near the door. The car was full of white cravats, so that it looked like an adjourned session of the convention. Presently a sleek, well fed clergyman, bustled on the platform, and addressing the brakeman, asked—

"Is Mr. Phillips on board?"

"Yes," was the reply, "there he sits back of the door."

The man came into the car, and in a loud voice cried, pointing his finger at Phillips—

"Are you Mr. Phillips?"

"I am, sir."

"Are you trying to free the niggers?"

"Yes, sir, I am an Abolitionist."

"Well, why do you preach your doctrines up here? Why don't you go there?" pointing toward Kentucky, just across the Ohio River."

"Excuse me," said Phillips, "are you a preacher?"

"I am, sir."

"Are you trying to save souls from hell?"

"Yes, sir, that is my business."

"*Well, why don't you go there?*"

There was a roar of laughter, and the minister vanished to the next car.[10]

Phillips was fond of telling the following anecdote on his tour.

"Hung Fung was a Chinese philosopher well-nigh a hundred years old. The Emperor once said to him:

" 'Hung, ninety years of study and observation must have made you wise. Tell me, what is the great danger of a government?'

" 'Well,' quoth Hung, 'It's the rat in the statue.'

" 'The rat in the statue!' repeated the Emperor. 'What do you mean?'

" 'Why,' retorted Hung, 'you know we build statues to the memory of our ancestors. They are made of wood, and are hollow and painted. Now, if a rat gets into one you can't smoke it out—it's the image of your father. You can't plunge it into the water—that would wash off the paint. So the rat is safe because the image is sacred.' "[11]

"Some people's idea of agitation," Phillips used to say, "is like the clown in the classic play, two thousand years ago, who seeing a man bring down with an arrow an eagle floating in the blue ether above, said: 'You needn't have wasted that arrow —the fall would have killed him.' "[12]

One Everett O. Foss, an ardent admirer of Phillips, once undertook on his own responsibility when he was a very young man to have his idol deliver a lecture in his town of Dover, New Hampshire. The town was deluged by a terrific storm that night and only one person appeared at the hall. Instead of lecturing, Phillips invited Foss across the street to the old American House where he ordered a pot of tea and sat and talked until late at night. Later Foss induced Phillips to return to Dover and again attempt a lecture. For some reason it was poorly attended, but Phillips spoke with his accustomed force and brilliancy, for the size of his audience never made any difference with him. After he had finished, he and Foss once more adjourned to the hotel for tea.

"Mr. Foss," said Phillips suddenly, "how much have you lost on this lecture engagement?"

Foss tried to evade the subject, but Phillips persisted until the young man named the approximate amount.

"You must let me share it," said Phillips, and produced bills to half the amount which he insisted that Foss accept.

They drank their tea and talked for a time and then Phillips said suddenly—

"Mr. Foss, do you know, I have a partner in this business and one that holds me to a very strict account for everything I do? It is my wife. Now she will want to know all about this affair and she will not like it. I don't dare to go home and tell her of it as the case now stands. I shall have to make a little change in our arrangements in order to satisfy her. I shall

have to ask you to take the rest of this money, or I shall never
be able to make my partner think that I have done right."

And he made Foss accept the proffer.[13]

To the Reverend Samuel May in the same spirit:

> Dear May—You know your check struck me as a little
> too generous when you gave it to me—on looking at it tonight
> the feeling returns—and it strikes me that if I reduce it by
> sending back a few dollars—(which I propose you should
> give to the cause by paying your own expense to Albany
> where you cheered us if not the public)—the balance would
> be about my share under the circumstances—as some of our
> friends say in horrid English—so gratify me by taking back
> the inclosed $10. . . ."[14]

Wherever Phillips went, autograph hunters, album in hand,
lay in wait for him. Phillips "made his mark" as he said, in a
thousand places. Among his favorite autographs were:

> "John Brown taught these lines to each of his children:
> Peace if possible.
> Justice at any rate."[15]

Or this:

> I slept and dreamt that life was beauty.
> I woke and found that life was duty.
> Was my dream then a shadowy lie?
> Toil on, sad heart, courageously,
> And thou shalt find thy dream to be
> Noonday light, and truth to thee.[16]

One day when William D. Brigham was quite a young boy,
he came into the store and said, "Mr. Phillips, would you give
me your autograph?" Phillips replied, "With pleasure, young
man," and he wrote the lines from John Brown. Then he said,
"Let me add a sentiment which De Tocqueville wrote to my
friend Charles Sumner: 'Life is neither pain nor pleasure, but
serious business to be entered upon with courage in the spirit
of self-sacrifice.'"[17]

CHAPTER FIFTY-SIX

TIMID SCHOLARSHIP

Phillips redoubled his efforts for the causes of Temperance and Irish Freedom. He made a vigorous speech before a committee at the State House against the liquor license system, flayed Dr. Crosby, then Chancellor of New York University, who had argued against total abstinence, and took the stump for the Land League of Ireland. Cut the knot that binds the two islands together, he declared. Separation from England was the only solution of the Irish problem. Not long afterwards he was invited to Ireland itself to advocate the cause of the Land League, but was forced to refuse on account of ill health.

In the summer of 1881 he received another invitation: to deliver the centennial Phi Beta Kappa oration at Harvard. He accepted and on June 30 spoke on "The Scholar in a Republic." Never seemed he more at his ease, more colloquial and more extemporaneous.

He had two opportunities. He could deliver a grand but ineffectual academic discourse, leaving behind personalities, forgetting for the hour his hatreds and enmities, and meeting all his old opponents peacefully in the still air of delightful studies. Or he could, face to face with that recreant Cambridge scholarship which had been hostile to all his past labors, tell them how backward they had been in the old anti-slavery contest, and how reluctant to take part in other reforms. If he had been bitter before, he could be ten times as bitter now. He could make this the day of judgment for the sins of half a century. He chose the latter course.

Into the midst of cold and aristocratic dons, he hurled the unadorned truth. He tempered no words, disguised nothing, drove home his point.

He arraigned and condemned all scholarship as essentially timid, selfish and unheroic.

"I urge on college-bred men that as a class they fail in republican duty when they allow others to lead in the agitation of the great social questions which stir and educate the age. . . .

"Timid scholarship either shrinks from sharing in these agitations or denounces them as vulgar and dangerous interference by incompetent hands with matters above them. A chronic distrust of the people pervades the book-educated class of the North; they shrink from that free speech which is God's normal school of educating men, throwing upon them the grave responsibility of deciding great questions and so lifting them to a higher level of intellectual and moral life. Trust the people—the wise and the ignorant, the good and the bad—with the gravest questions, and in the end you educate the race. At the same time you secure not perfect institutions, not necessarily good ones, but the best material to build with. Men are educated and the state is uplifted by allowing all—everyone—to broach all their mistakes and advocate all their errors. The community that will not protect its most ignorant and unpopular member in the free utterance of his opinions, no matter how false or hateful, is only a gang of slaves!. . . .

"Wycliffe was, no doubt, a learned man. But the learning of his day would have burned him, had it dared, as it did burn his dead body afterwards. Luther and Melanchthon were scholars, but they were repudiated by the scholarship of their time, which followed Erasmus, trying 'all his life to tread on eggs without breaking them;' he who proclaimed that 'peaceful error was better than tempestuous truth.' Hence, I do not think the greatest things have been done for the world by its bookmen."[1]

Phillips gave a list of the leading reforms of the previous forty years in none of which Cambridge scholarship had taken any share. What had it done against chattel slavery? Next to nothing. In fact the greatest scholar New England had sent to Congress quoted the original Greek of the New Testament in support of slavery and offered to shoulder a musket in its defence. What had it done for woman suffrage, for temperance, for political regimentation? In all these its attitude had been one of cold disdain or hostility. What educated man had ever lifted his voice against the oppression of the Irish people? And yet their cause was the cause upon which the American nation had been founded.

> "We ought to clap our hands at every fresh Irish 'outrage,' as a parrot press styles it, aware that it is only a far-off echo of the musket-shots that rattled against the old State House on the fifth of March, 1770, and of the war whoop that made the tiny spire of the Old South tremble when Boston rioters emptied the three India tea ships into the sea."[2]

Phillips wound up the catalogue by denouncing as disgusting all condemnation of Russian Nihilism and its methods. Colonel Higginson said that "many a respectable lawyer and divine felt his blood run cold."

> "Note the scorn and disgust with which we gather up our garments about us and disown the Sam Adams and William Prescott, the George Washington and John Brown of St. Petersburg, the spiritual descendants, the living representatives of those who made our history worth anything in the world annals."[3]

Nihilism he urged, was the righteous and honorable resistance of a people crushed under the iron rule of the Czar. Nihilism was evidence of life—the last weapon of victims choked and manacled beyond all other resistance. "When 'order reigns in Warsaw,' it is spiritual death." Here again Phillips was advocating a familiar principle, one which he advocated as an Abolitionist: when the State becomes oppressive, and the people enslaved, it is the right and duty to rebel. "Success to the first insurrection of slaves in Jamaica" declared Dr. Johnson in a standing toast. That sentiment Phillips consistently echoed and upheld.

"In Russia there is no press, no debate, no explanation of what government does, no remonstrance allowed, no agitation of public issues. Dead silence, like that which reigns at the summit of Mont Blanc, freezes the whole empire, long ago described as a despotism tempered by assassination. . . .

"Machiavelli's sorry picture of poor human nature would be fulsome flattery if men could keep still under such oppression. No, no! in such a land dynamite and the dagger are the necessary and proper substitutes for Faneuil Hall and the *Daily Advertiser*. . . .

"Born within sight of Bunker Hill, in a commonwealth which adopts the motto of Algernon Sydney, *sub libertate quietem* ('accept no peace without liberty'); son of Harvard, whose first pledge was 'Truth'; citizen of a republic based on the claim that no government is rightful unless resting on the consent of the people, and which assumes to lead in asserting the rights of humanity,—I at least can say nothing else and nothing less; no, not if every tile on Cambridge roofs were a devil hooting at my words!"[4]

Before the Civil War, he continued, American men were like the crowd in that terrible hall of Beckford's Eblis—each man with his hand pressed on the incurable sore in his bosom and pledged not to speak of it. "Compared with other lands, we were intellectually and morally a nation of cowards."

"At last that disgraceful seal of slave complicity is broken. Let us inaugurate a new departure, recognize that we are afloat on the current of Niagara, eternal vigilance the condition of our safety, that we are irrevocably pledged to the world not to go back to bolts and bars,—could not if we would, and would not if we could. Never again be ours the fastidious scholarship that shrinks from rude contact with the masses. Very pleasant it is to sit high up in the world's theatre and criticise the ungraceful struggles of gladiators, shrug one's shoulders at the actors' harsh cries, and let every one know that but for 'this villainous saltpetre you would have been a soldier.' But Bacon says, 'In the theatre of man's life, God and his angels only should be lookers-on.' 'Sin is not taken out of man as Eve was out of Adam, by putting him to sleep.' 'Very beautiful,' says Richter, 'is the eagle when he floats with outstretched wings aloft in the clear blue; but sublime when he plunges down through the tempest to his eyry on the cliff, where his unfledged young ones dwell and are starving.' Accept proudly the analysis of Fisher Ames: 'A monarchy is a man-of-war, staunch, iron-ribbed, and resistless when under full sail; yet a single hidden rock sends her to the bottom. Our republic is a raft hard to steer, and your feet always wet; but nothing can sink her.' If the Alps, piled in cold and silence, be the emblem of despotism, we joyfully take the ever-restless ocean for ours,—only pure because never still."[5]

"It was a delightful discourse," said one Harvard gentleman, "but preposterous from beginning to end."[6]

Friends said Phillips was unjust to Cambridge scholarship in remembering only its lapses and forgetting its examples of courage: Sumner and Lowell, Channing and Emerson, Parker and Palfrey, Adams and Quincy. Admirers felt that he himself was a living refutation of the charge against the cowardice of scholarship.[7] To comments at the time he replied—"Well, I suppose they wanted me to bring myself."[8]

"I thought they might hiss me," he added. "But they showed their true education by bearing it well. Indeed, I seldom have had such cheers, and such a warm reception."[9]

For the most part, however, his audience listened in silence to his paradoxes, his denunciations of scholarship, his defence of Nihilism. Their disapproval of many of his opinions was marked and apparent. It was evident that they approved of the man, and disapproved of most of his opinions. One striking incident occurred when he described the man who would not equivocate, would not retreat an inch and at last would be heard. Phillips was thinking of Garrison, but the audience applied it to himself. They received the sentence with repeated thunders of applause. This touched him deeply and when he spoke again, there were tears in his voice.[10]

Learning that his admirers proposed to celebrate his seventieth birthday, Phillips hastened to nip the project in the bud. Writing to one of the sponsors of the movement, he said.

"Please understand that any such thing would be *very disagreeable* to me. I particularly request that you have no hand in it. And should you hear of any one intending such a notice of the day, please let him understand my wishes."[11]

However, Bronson Alcott in the vale of years (it was his eighty-third year) surveying the whole career of Phillips gave his outline of it.

Wendell Phillips at Three Score and Ten

People's Attorney, servant of the Right,
Pleader for all shades of the solar ray,—
Complexions dusky, yellow, red, or white,—
Who, in thy country's and thy time's despite,
Hast only questioned, 'What will Duty say?'
And followed swiftly in her narrow way! . . . .

The scorn of bigots and the worldling's flout,
If Time long held thy merit in suspense,
Hastening repentant now, with pen devout,
Impartial History dare not leave thee out.[12]

CHAPTER FIFTY-SEVEN

LAST DAYS

Phillips assisted countless people. He selected for his motto the Latin sentence which he had translated while at school, "Phocian always remained poor, though he might have been very rich."[1]

From the years 1845 to 1875 he gave personal gifts aggregating over $65,000. Not a few well known names figure among his beneficiaries. Page after page of his memorandum book reads like this:

John Brown	$10.00
A poor Italian	2.00
Mrs. Garnaut	10.00
Poor man	1.00
Refugee	5.00[2]

Although Phillips inherited some money from his parents and Ann from hers, their joint fortunes never exceeded $100,000. He made large sums from lectures, his income from this source ranging from $10,000 to $15,000 a year. But when he died he left almost nothing. "As to politics," he once wrote to a friend, "I wish I had funds to help you labor in that field as I know you have seen so much of the Southern spirit that I can trust your teachings. But my means are so crippled that I have nothing to contribute. . . ."[3] To another friend he said that he had no wish to leave a fortune to anybody or anything, that his idea of living was to walk with open heart and open hand from day to day, and that he had done all he could in this way—he had been his own executor. Before his death he cancelled every note he held.[4]

His philanthropy was local as well as cosmopolitan. For years he spent a large part of each morning in court, at the jail, or in some home, looking up needy causes or defending some poor fellow who had run afoul of the law.

He haunted the streets of Boston. "They are a good place for the study of human nature," he said, "better than the theatre, for here both tragedy and comedy are real—and so are the actors." His friend Bowditch discovered him one morning, when the pavement was thronged with people, leaning against the granite wall of a bank on State Street like a beggar. "Wendell," he said, "if you want these people to give you money you must take off your hat and hold it in your hand."[5]

He liked to steal up to children whom he saw gazing wistfully into shop windows and slip money into their hands.[6]

All Bostonians have a local pride; Phillips loved the very stones of his native city. No one, said Higginson, could ever forget the thrilling modulation of his voice when he said at some crisis of the anti-slavery agitation: "I love inexpressibly these streets of Boston, over whose pavements my mother held up tenderly my baby feet; and if God grants me time enough, I will make them too pure to bear the footsteps of a slave."[7]

In the spring of 1882 Phillips was forced to move from number 26 Essex Street, in which he and his wife had lived so comfortably for forty years.[8] The city had decided to widen the adjacent Harrison Avenue, and the work necessitated the demolition of the house. Phillips had for his old home a very great attachment; to leave it was genuine hardship. He found new quarters at number 37 Common Street. To make it more homelike, he transferred the old mantel and open grate and had the furniture similarly arranged. But the charm was broken; they never felt quite at home again. To Caroline H. Dall:

"Mrs. Phillips for the last eleven months has been very much more ill than usual—indeed I think the shock of being flung out of our forty years' home is one she will never rally from. She has not stood or lifted herself from her pillow without help since—so I have given up lecturing

—am a good boy and stay at home—cleaning up and giving away my books and pamphlets—acting as my own executor and getting ready to go."[9]

Once after the Essex Street house had been demolished, he went back and stood for a time looking at the vacant spot. "It was hard," he said, "that the city would not let me stay till the end." Then, after a pause, he turned away with the remark, "It is no matter. I am almost through with it all."[10]

One who knew him well recalled his habit about this time of walking slowly up Beacon Hill and examining all the sights of the place with as much interest as a stranger. His tall figure was perfectly erect, his hair white and there was an air about his movement, of dignity and grace. At the top of the hill he would stand for a long time carefully observing the State House as if he had never seen it before. Then he would turn, look out over the city, and go home.

Nora Perry, the poetess, met him once in the street and he asked where she was going; "To see a friend," she replied. "Ah," he said, "you remind me of the Frenchman who received the same answer and said, 'Take me along. I never saw one.'"[11]

Phillips had friends, but a man, though he have many friends, may sometimes feel like that.

He was so quiet and gentle and beautiful in his manners and conversation and whole presence that when he breakfasted with Sallie Holley, she said, "It seems as if we had breakfasted with an angel."[12]

In April he was invited with Amos A. Lawrence by the University of Kansas and the authorities of the city of Lawrence to be a guest at commencement.[13] The fall and winter of 1882-1883 found him out lecturing as usual. At the end of the season he went with Ann to Belmont for the summer. "Nothing is changed here," he wrote to a friend on August 17, "we plod on as usual. . . . I go in town twice a week and sometimes thrice; reading and dozing the other days. Boston is crowded notwithstanding our absence! I don't think I could live all the time in the country. It would make me a Rip Van Winkle in ten months."[14]

Two weeks later he was again in town. "We are at 37 Common Street," he informed the same friend, "Ann was so uncomfortable that we were obliged to run in; and here we are —dust, noise, heat!"[15]

On December 3, 1883, with William Lloyd Garrison, Jr., he spoke in the Old South Church at the unveiling of Ann Whitney's statue of Harriet Martineau. When his well known form appeared, the assembly broke into hearty applause.

"Webster once said, that 'In war there are no Sundays.' So in moral questions there are no nations. Intellect and morals transcend all limits. When a moral issue is stirred, then there is no American, no German. We are all men and women. And this is the reason why I think we should indorse this memorial of the city to Harriet Martineau, because her service transcends nationality. There would be nothing inappropriate if we raised a memorial to Wickliffe, or if the common-school system of New England raised a memorial to Calvin; for they rendered the greatest of services. So with Harriet Martineau, we might fairly render a monument to the grandest woman of her day, we, the heirs of the same language, and one in the same civilization; for steam and the telegraph have made, not many nations, but one, in perfect unity in the world of thought, purpose, and intellect. . . ."[16]

This was Phillips's last address. The serious illness of Ann kept him in through January. He hardly left her room. On Saturday, the 26, he was suddenly seized with a pain in the chest. His father and three of his brothers had died after a similar warning. The family physician, Dr. Thayer, was summoned, and diagnosed the case as angina pectoris, and prescribed some remedies. Phillips lay on the couch self possessed and smiling.

A friend called and conversed with him. She asked him about his faith. He said it was absolute, later adding that nothing but the spirit of Christ had enabled him to suffer and endure what he had. "Then you have no doubt about a future life?" she asked. His answer was: "I am as sure of it as I am that there will be a tomorrow."[17]

On Sunday the pain returned. He was treated again and seemed to be better. On Tuesday he was quite himself. But on Wednesday he suffered a relapse and his condition grew steadily worse. The doctor and his assistants remained in constant attendance. On Saturday he was again relieved. When Dr. Thayer, at his request, told him the probable result, he smiled and said—

"I have no fear of death. I have long forseen it. My only regret is for poor Ann. I had hoped to close her eyes before mine were shut."[18]

He had once said to Susan B. Anthony—"I remember seeing my grandfather look out of the window at my grandmother's funeral, and hearing him say, 'I thank God I have lived to see her go first!' I did not understand his feeling then, but I know now what it was. I have lived to have every hope and desire merge itself and be lost in the one wish that I may outlive Ann."[19] That wish was not granted.

He lay quietly through the day in the full possession of his faculties. At fifteen minutes past six o'clock Saturday evening, February 2, he sighed gently, closed his eyes, and passed away as calmly as though going to sleep.

In every home in Boston the death of Wendell Phillips was discussed on Sunday and clergymen alluded to it from the pulpits.

On Monday the Legislature and Common Council adopted tributes to the character of the "fearless, uncompromising reformer." At the same time the Labor Reformers in session at the Tremont House arranged for a public memorial meeting on Tuesday night in Faneuil Hall, while opposite in Tremont Temple the lecturer, Joseph Cook, speaking on the dead orator, declared: "Fifty years hence it will not be asked, 'What did Boston think of Wendell Phillips?' but 'What did Wendell Phillips think of Boston?'"

The funeral took place on Wednesday, February 6. As the old clock in the belfry struck the hour of eleven, the remains of Wendell Phillips were borne up the center aisle of the Hollis Street Church in the presence of a vast throng. In accordance with Phillips's known wishes the services were most simple—

a brief prayer by the Reverend Samuel Longfellow, brother of the poet, and a faltering word by the Reverend Samuel May. May read Longfellow's "Funeral Hymn" which was also sung, the large audience rising and joining in the singing.[20]

From the church the body was borne, escorted by colored troops, through the crowded streets to Faneuil Hall. Here for three hours the body lay in state, and a long procession of the poor, and almost the entire colored population of the city, passed the coffin. Thousands upon thousands of people struggled for a place in line eager for a last look at the noble countenance.[21]

Finally the doors were clanged to, the casket removed, and the line of march retaken through massive lines of uncovered and silent spectators. The old Granary Burial ground on Boston Common was reached. Here, beside his father and mother in the family vault, Wendell Phillips was laid to rest.[22]

In the life of Wendell Phillips, as one of his biographers[23] states, there is nothing that tarnishes. In public and private life he walked without deviation from the loftiest standards. Cautious friends sometimes deplored what they called the violence of his utterances; they never had the slightest cause to regret a lapse in his conduct, not one surrender to temptation, not one instance of faltering in duty. I know not where shines another such character, nor any other study so rich in satisfaction as the record of his life. For in the words that he himself applied to Washington he was "the bright consummate flower of our civilization and in all ways the incarnation of the highest American ideal."

Three months after his death, George William Curtis paid to him at the memorial meeting in Tremont Temple a fitting and splendid tribute.

"As we recall the story of that life, the spectacle of to-day is one of the most significant in our history. The memorial rite is not a tribute to official service, to literary genius, to scientific distinction; it is a homage to personal character. It is the solemn public declaration that a life of transcendent purity of purpose, blended with commanding powers, devoted with absolute unselfishness, and with amazing results, to the welfare of the country and of humanity, is, in the American Republic, an example so inspiring, a patriotism so lofty, and a public service so beneficent, that, in contemplating them, discordant opinions, differing judgments, and the sharp sting of controversial speech, vanish like frost in a flood of sunshine."[24]

The golden trumpets blow, and Wendell Phillips rises and stands before the Judgment Seat as Defender of the Poor and Oppressed, Seeker of the Common Good, Knight Errant of Unfriended Truth, and Prophet of Liberty.

REFERENCES

CHAPTER ONE
The Revolutionary Tradition

1. Octavia Roberts, *With La Fayette in America* (Boston, 1919), p. 263.

2. Brand Whitlock, *La Fayette* (New York, 1929), II, 223.

3. Josiah Quincy, *Figures of the Past* (Boston, 1926), p. 89. See also Gilbert J. Hunt, *The Tour of General La Fayette* (New York, 1825), p. 6. Even the Boston *Recorder* interrupted its religious discussion to devote almost three tall columns to the nation's guest. Boston *Recorder*, Aug. 28, 1824.

4. Wendell Phillips, "Address to the Boston School Children," *Speeches, Lectures, and Letters,* Second Series (Boston, 1894), p. 226; A. A. Parker, *Recollections of General La Fayette on His Visit to the United States* (Keene, N. H., 1879), p. 20.

5. Whitlock, II, 224.

6. Quincy, pp. 92–93; Henry D. Sedgwick, *La Fayette* (Indianapolis, 1928), pp. 395–396.

7. John T. Morse, Jr., *Thomas Jefferson* (Boston, 1898), pp. 306–307; James Parton, *Life of Thomas Jefferson* (Boston, 1874), pp. 734–735.

8. George L. Austin, *Wendell Phillips* (Boston, 1888), pp. 29–31.

CHAPTER TWO
A New England Boyhood

1. Henry Bond, *Genealogies of the Families and Descendants of the Early Settlers of Watertown, Massachusetts* (Boston, 1855), II, 872–875; James Savage, *A Genealogical Dictionary of the First Settlers of New England* (Boston, 1861), pp. 409–410; Albert M. Phillips, *Phillips Genealogies* (Auburn, Mass., 1885), pp. 2–3.

2. *The New England Historical and Genealogical Register,* XXXIX, 110–111; Albert M. Phillips, pp. 15–20.

3. He had been public prosecutor, a member of the House of Representatives, President of the Senate of Massachusetts, a Judge of the Court of Common Pleas, a member of the Corporation of Harvard College, and had sat in the Convention for the Revision of the Constitution of the State. Two candidates were named for the mayoralty—Harrison

Gray Otis and Josiah Quincy. When a deadlock ensued, John Phillips was unanimously chosen as the compromise candidate. In the election the total number of votes returned was 2650, of which John Phillips received 2500, and was accordingly chosen. "There can be no doubt he will give stability and permanence to such a government," said the Boston *Commercial Gazette.* "It gives us pleasure to perceive that the choice of the electors has fallen upon this gentleman, and especially at a time when the public mind was so much disturbed by conflicting opinions, growing out of the claims of different candidates." For the nomination and election of John Phillips see the Boston *Commercial Gazette,* April 8, 1822, April 15, 1822, April 22, 1822; *Columbian Centinel,* April 10, 1822, April 13, 1822, April 17, 1822; Boston *Recorder,* April 13, 1822, April 20, 1822. For accounts of his career see the *New England Historical and Genealogical Register* (October, 1866), XX, No. 4, 297–299; John G. Palfrey, *A Sermon after the interment of the late John Phillips* (Boston, 1823), pp. 13–15. James S. Loring calls John Phillips a "clear, forcible, conciliatory, and judicious" speaker. (James S. Loring, *The Hundred Boston Orators,* (Boston, 1853), p. 251.)

4. T. W. Higginson, "Other Days and Ways in Boston and Cambridge" in *Days and Ways in Old Boston,* ed. William S. Rossiter (Boston, 1915), p. 36. In a letter to Justin Winsor, Wendell Phillips says that his father built in 1804–1805 the first *brick* house that was built on Beacon Street. This street Beacon was *then* considered *out of town* (Justin Winsor, (Editor), *The Memorial History of Boston* (Boston, 1881), 4 vols., III, 225.)

5. Albert M. Phillips, pp. 30–35; Henry Bond, II, 885–886. See Note I in Appendix.

6. John Phillips, faithful and devout, in his inaugural address, expressed this sentiment most familiar to his mind: "Purity of manners, general diffusion of knowledge, and strict attention to the education of the young,—above all, a firm practical belief of that divine revelation which has affixed the penalty of unceasing anguish to vice, and promised to virtue rewards of interminable duration, will counteract the evils of any form of government." (Boston *Commercial Gazette,* May 2, 1822; *Columbian Centinel,* May 4, 1822; Boston *Recorder,* May 11, 1822; Josiah Quincy, *A Municipal History of the Town and City of Boston* (Boston, 1852), pp. 42–43, Appendix, pp. 373–374.)

7. Carlos Martyn, *Wendell Phillips, the Agitator* (New York, 1890), p. 30. Martyn was a friend of Phillips and his testimony at times is the only evidence we have. Attempts to locate his descendants and relatives who might have inherited his primary source material proved fruitless.

8. Josiah Quincy says that the elder Phillips hesitated to venture on changes of which the result was uncertain. This tendency of his mind was increased and strengthened by his precarious state of health. (Josiah Quincy, p. 55.) Justin Winsor calls John Phillips "a man of rather pliable disposition but of strict integrity and general good judgment." (Justin Winsor, III, 224.) Harrison Gray Otis in his inaugural address of 1829 says: "The novel experiment of city government was commenced by your first lamented mayor with the circumspection and delicacy which belonged to his character. He felt and respected the force of ancient and honest

prejudices. His aim was to allure and not to repel, to reconcile by gentle reform, not to revolt by startling innovation." (Ibid., III, 226.) The policy of the new administration to keep things substantially as they were, however, disappointed people. (Ibid., III, 225; Josiah Quincy, pp. 54–55.)

But all his associates agreed that John Phillips was a good man—disinterested, considerate, candid. He was trusted because he was trustworthy. (Palfrey, pp. 7, 14–16; *New England Historical and Genealogical Register*, XX, No. 4, p. 299.)

Neither inclination nor health permitted him to become a candidate for reelection. (Josiah Quincy, p. 56; *Columbian Centinel*, April 12, 1823; Boston *Weekly Messenger*, April 17, 1823.)

9. Testimony of Theodore D. Weld in Martyn, p. 27.

10. *New England Historical and Genealogical Register*, XX, No. 4, p. 298.

11. Thomas G. Appleton's tribute to Wendell Phillips. (*Book of Clippings on Wendell Phillips*, Boston Public Library.)

12. Oliver W. Holmes, *Ralph Waldo Emerson and John Lothrop Motley* (Boston, 1892), pp. 332–333.

13. "The high reputation of the Latin . . . School continues undiminished." (Boston *Commercial Gazette*, March 7, 1822.)

14. Edward Everett Hale, *A New England Boyhood and Other Bits of Autobiography* (Boston, 1920), pp. 23–24, 27, 31–33.

14ᵃ. John William Sattler, *Wendell Phillips: Speaker and Agitator*, Unpublished Doctoral Dissertation, Northwestern University, June, 1943, pp. 21–23, 544. Sattler's dissertation is an able and thoroughgoing technical or rhetorical analysis of Phillips's oratory: his speeches and his speaking.

15. Martyn, p. 35.

16. Hale, p. 64.

17. James D' Wolf Lovett, *Old Boston Days* (Boston, 1906), pp. 29–33; Mark A. De Wolfe Howe, *Boston Common* (Boston, 1921), p. 55.

18. Boston *Daily Advertiser*, Jan. 22, 1820.

19. Samuel Barber, *Boston Common* (Boston, 1916), p. 174.

20. Howe, p. 56.

21. Lovett, p. 9.

22. Advertisements in the newspapers open up magic casements or are quaint: Ads of Russian Diapers and Gunpowder elbow "The Actress of All Work" (a play); Shagbarks, Ivica Salts, Superfine Mustard Mix with Molasses, Rum, Pimento. "A certain cure for a certain Disorder—In common cases one bottle effects a cure—$5" is followed by Ipecacuanbia, Aloes, Annatto, and Genuine Lemon Syrop. (Boston *Commercial Gazette*, Feb. 28, 1822, March 7, 1822, March 11, 1822, July 8, 1822.)

23. The Tenth Annual Report of the Committee of Finance, for example, listed expenses as $249,170.15. Included were these items: For City Watch, $9,000; Oil, Lamps, etc., $10,000; Bells and Clocks, $500. It is pleasant to report that the schools came in for their share of the expenditure: Apparatus for Classical Schools, $3,000; a new school house at the North part of the city, $19,000. (Boston *Weekly Messenger*, Sept. 19, 1822; *Columbian Centinel*, Sept. 11, 1822.)

24. An "1801-er" remarks that there was not a single Irish servant girl in Boston in 1808. Wages were one dollar a week. (James W. Hale, *Old Boston Town By an 1801-er*, New York, [1883?], p. 34.)

25. Thomas G. Appleton, *A Sheaf of Papers* (Boston, 1875), pp. 335–336.

26. Daniel Webster, "The First Settlement of New England," *The Writings and Speeches of Daniel Webster,* National Edition, (Boston and New York, 1903), I, 221–222.)

CHAPTER THREE

Harvard Days

1. He died of angina pectoris on May 29, 1823. The House and Senate of Massachusetts adjourned in token of respect for his memory. See obituary notices in the *Columbian Centinel,* May 31, 1823: "One of the most eminent, worthy, and useful citizens. . . . We scarcely remember an instance of mortality, the annunciation of which made so deep an impression of sorrow throughout the city as this. . . . He appeared born to serve the public and advance their interests:" *New England Galaxy,* May 30, 1823.

2. Arthur Stanwood Pier, *The Story of Harvard* (Boston, 1913), pp. 137–138, 140–141.

3. Samuel Eliot Morison, *Three Centuries of Harvard, 1636–1936* (Harvard University Press, 1936), p. 260.

4. Pier, pp. 137–138, 142–143; Morison, pp. 246–247.

5. But President Quincy's policy towards the students, an alternate cuffing and caressing, ended in making him the most unpopular President since Hoar. In his conferences with them he was abrupt and tactless, often committing the unpardonable sin of criticizing their dress or their whiskers which (greatly to his disgust) began to sprout towards the end of his administration. (Morison, pp. 251–253.)

6. George F. Hoar, *Autobiography of Seventy Years,* 2 vols. (New York, 1903), I, 87, 97, 123.

6ᵃ. Sattler, pp. 32, 34, 35.

7. Martyn, p. 48.

8. Lindsay Swift, *Garrison,* (Phila., 1911), p. 168.

9. "Clubs fairly pullulated," says Morison. (Morison, p. 202.)

10. A newspaper clipping in one of the scrapbooks of the Boston Public Library mentions Phillips's presidency of the Porcellian Club at Harvard, adding, "He was the leader of the element which adopted the rule that no student could belong to that and the Hasty Pudding Club at the same time." (Note to author from Miss Elizabeth L. Adams of the Boston Public Library.) Sattler, p. 46.

11. Frank Preston Stearns, *Sketches from Concord and Appledore* (New York, 1895), p. 182; Sattler, pp. 48–50, 52–53.

12. Higginson, p. 29.

13. Religious revivals came and went with the seasons. The drought in revivals at the close of 1829 was followed by plentiful showers at the turn of the year. "The number of places now refreshed," said the Boston *Recorder and Religious Telegraph* of Feb. 10, 1830, "is so great as distinctly to mark a new and more joyful season. The indications are such at

this moment as to excite in some bosoms the humble hope that 1830 will be 'a year of the right hand of the Most High' and a 'set time to favor Zion.'" The following year witnessed a veritable flood of religious revivals. (See Boston *Recorder and Religious Telegraph,* Oct.–Dec. 1829, passim, and issues of 1830 and 1831, especially with reference to Boston, Dec. 29, 1830, April 6, May 11, June 29, 1831.)

"A powerful revival of religion is now progressing in this city. It commenced about two months ago in Dr. Beecher's congregation, and has since spread in other congregations. The work goes on silently, but with great power." (Article in the St. Johnsbury, Vt., *Herald* of May 9, reprinted in the Boston *Recorder and Religious Telegraph,* June 9, 1830.)

14. Paxton Hibben, *Henry Ward Beecher* (New York, 1927), pp. 24, 35.

15. Martyn, p. 41.

16. Lyman Beecher, *Autobiography, Correspondence, Etc.,* ed. Chas. Beecher, 2 vols. (New York, 1865), II, 113, 115–118.

17. Constance M. Rourke, *Trumpets of Jubilee* (New York, 1927), pp. 37–38.

18. Lyman Beecher, II, 75–76.

19. Evidence of personal friend, Rev. O. P. Gifford, cited in Martyn, p. 42.

20. George L. Austin, *Wendell Phillips,* pp. 36–38.

21. Included in the order of exercises was No. 18: "A Deliberate Discussion. Will the present proposed Parliamentary Reform endanger the Monarchial and Aristocratical Portion of the British Constitution?" Those taking part in the discussion were Charles George Clinton Hale of New York and Wendell Phillips of Boston.

Among other items were: "No. 9. A Colloquial Discussion: The Influence of the Multiplication of Books upon Literature" (discussed by Caleb F. Abbott and John Lothrop Motley); "No. 2. A Conference: Heraclitus, Democritus, Epicurus, and Diogenes;—No. 11. A Dissertation. The Infirmities of Men of Genius, etc."

It is ironic that the Phi Beta Kappa oration was delivered by James T. Austin. *Columbian Centinel,* Aug. 31, 1831; Boston *Recorder,* Sept. 7, 1831.

CHAPTER FOUR

A Judge, an Actress, a Corsair, and a Conspirator

1. Before 1829 the Harvard Law School, which had been established in 1817, was in a precarious state. It offered so few advantages in comparison with apprenticeship to a leading member of the bar that the students dwindled away to but one or two a year. Besides neither Professor Isaac Parker nor Professor Asabel Stearns was able to give his full time to the institution. The classes of 1828 and 1829 had an enrollment of 9 and 5 students respectively. (Morison, p. 239; *Catalogue of the Officers and Students of the Law School of Harvard University, 1817–1887* (Cambridge, 1888), p. 4.)

In 1829 when the Law School most needed it, Nathan Dane donated $10,000. Joseph Story accepted the Dane Professorship and John H. Ashmun succeeded Judge Parker. The class number jumped to 32 in 1830 and 37 in 1831. (*Catalogue of the Officers and Students of the Law School at Harvard University*, pp. 5–6; Morison, p. 239.)

It is interesting to note that students of the first ten years of the Law School were obliged to undergo a written examination in order to qualify for the degree. (Charles Warren, *History of the Harvard Law School* (New York, 1908), I, 338–339.)

2. *Life and Letters of Joseph Story*, ed. William W. Story (Boston, 1851), II, 601–602, 611–612; see also Charles Warren, I, 458.

3. Samuel F. Batchelder, *Bits of Harvard History* (Cambridge, 1924), pp. 216–217.

4. Story, II, 52.

5. Warren, I, 434.

6. Ibid., I, 435.

7. Ibid., I, 436. It was in the vastly elaborate list of text books that the instruction differed from that of Ashmun's predecessor, Professor Stearns.

8. Batchelder, pp. 231, 232.

9. Dorothie Bobbé, *Fanny Kemble* (New York, 1931), p. 85.

10. Ibid., p. 87.

11. *Catalogue of the Officers and Students of the Law School of Harvard University, 1817–1887*, p. 7. Phillips was one of a class of 37; see Note 2 in Appendix on rift with Story.

12. F. B. Sanborn, *Recollections of Wendell Phillips*, Ms. quoted in Martyn, p. 52.

13. H. J. Massingham, *The Friend of Shelley* (New York, 1930), p. 298; Frances Ann Kemble, *Records of a Girlhood* (London, 1878), III, 308–312.

14. F. B. Sanborn, quoted in Martyn, p. 53.

15. Hopkinson was of the class of 1832. He was in turn a member of the State Legislature, 1838–45, 1846, Senator, Chairman of the Commission of Railroad Laws, Judge of the Court of Common Pleas, and in 1849, after resigning his Judgeship, President of the Boston and Worcester Railroad Co. (*Catalogue of the Officers and Students of the Law School of Harvard University*, p. 6; Warren, III, 7.)

16. Ms. letter of Judge Hopkinson, quoted in Martyn, p. 54.

17. Austin, *Wendell Phillips*, pp. 43–44.

CHAPTER FIVE

The Martyr Age

1. *Papers Relating to the Garrison Mob*, ed. Theodore Lyman (Cambridge, Mass., 1870) and *Proceedings of the Anti-Slavery Meeting on the Twentieth Anniversary of the Mob of Oct. 21, 1835* (Boston, 1855) give a full account of the episode. See also the *Liberator*, V:42–47, Oct. 17,

1835 through Nov. 21, 1835.—Only one newspaper in the city did not attempt to incite mob action—Hallett's *Daily Advocate.*

2. Austin, *Wendell Phillips,* pp. 65–66.

3. Wendell P. and Francis J. Garrison, *William Lloyd Garrison* (New York, 1885), II, 35.

4. Archibald H. Grimké, *William Lloyd Garrison* (New York, 1891), p. 226.

5. Ibid., p. 230; *Papers Relating to the Garrison Mob,* p. 45.

6. Swift, p. 137.

7. *Proceedings of the Anti-Slavery Meeting on the Twentieth Anniversary of the Mob of Oct. 21, 1835,* p. 21.

8. W. P. and F. J. Garrison, II, 4.

9. *Papers Relating to the Garrison Mob,* p. 14; *Proceedings of the Anti-Slavery Meeting on the Twentieth Anniversary of the Mob of Oct. 21, 1835,* p. 24; W. P. and F. J. Garrison, II, 5–9.

10. For the fullest and most varied newspaper accounts of the Garrison mob and opinions expressed on it, see the *Liberator,* V, 44–47, October 31, 1835 through November 21, 1835.

11. As Alice Dana Adams (*The Neglected Period of Anti-Slavery in America 1808–31,* Boston and London, 1908) shows, immediate emancipation had been advocated before Garrison although not with equal vehemence. Again the attitude of Garrison did not "break up" Lundy's *Genius of Emancipation.* Garrison's advocacy of immediate emancipation was not the first in the paper; the trouble in finding subscribers existed long before the partnership of Lundy and Garrison, and the *Genius* continued for more than six years after the connection of Garrison with the paper had ceased.

"To preach distant reform is very cheap philanthropy—the cheaper in proportion to the distance. The feeling of self-satisfaction exists without the necessity of personal sacrifice." (Julius Pringle, quoted in Dwight L. Dumond, *Anti-slavery Origins of the Civil War in the United States,* Ann Arbor, Mich., 1939, p. 51.)

12. Most of the twenty-five subscribers to the first issue of the *Liberator* were Negroes and one enthusiastic (and affluent) black Abolitionist sent Garrison a gift of fifty dollars. (John H. Franklin, *From Slavery to Freedom,* New York, 1947, p. 247.)

In 1831 out of 450 subscribers to the *Liberator* 400 were Negroes, and in 1834, of the whole number of subscribers, 2300, only about one fourth were white. (Herbert Aptheker, *Essays in the History of the American Negro,* New York, 1945, p. 153.)

13. Quoted in Jesse Macy, "Anti-Slavery Crusade," *Chronicle of America Series* (New Haven, 1919), XIII, part 2, p. 65.

14. Fanny Garrison Villard, *Garrison on Non-Resistance* (New York, 1924, pp. 10–11.

15. Grimké, p. 202; Swift, p. 104.

16. John J. Chapman, *William Lloyd Garrison* (Boston, 1921), pp. 80–81.

17. Quoted in George S. Eddy and Kirby Page, *Makers of Freedom* (New York, 1926), p. 23.

18. W. P. and F. J. Garrison, I, 335–336.

19. Ibid., I, 235, 238.

20. Ibid., I, 449.

21. Clement Eaton (*Freedom of Thought in the Old South*, Durham, N. C., 1940), discussing the rise of intolerance in the Old South blames the Abolitionists: "Extremes tend to produce extremes. The violent attacks of the Abolitionists built up a war psychosis in the South. . . . The ceaseless agitation of the slave question by politicians, by fireeaters, and by political-minded editors must be put down as one of the major causes for the decline of liberal thought and free speech in the Old South. . . ." (p. 161.)

Yet another Southern historian, Charles S. Sydnor (*The Development of Southern Sectionalism, 1819–1848*, Baton Rouge, 1948) cogently argues: "Although the Abolition movement was followed by a decline of anti-slavery sentiment in the South, it must be remembered that in all the long years before that movement began, no part of the South had made substantial progress towards ending slavery. . . . The trends are not clear enough to warrant prophecy as to what the South would have done about slavery had it not been disturbed by the Abolitionists, but it is at least certain that before the crusade began, Southern liberalism had not ended slavery in any state." (p. 243.) The Southern defense of slavery antedated the organization of the American Anti-Slavery Society. (p. 243.)

And Kenneth M. Stampp ("The Fate of the Southern Anti-Slavery Sentiment," *Journal of Negro History*, January, 1943, XXVIII, No. 1, 10–22) firmly denies that the decline of Southern Anti-Slavery sentiment was due to the rise of Abolition in the North or that Southern anti-slavery men were apparently alienated by the intolerance of their Northern associates. The bulk of anti-slavery advocates was found in the yeomen farmers. The weakening of their opposition can be better explained by the decimation of their numbers through migration to the West and the spread of the slave system into the Piedmont. Many yeomen in Western Virginia abandoned their anti-slavery views in anticipation of joining the ranks of the slaveholding planters. "Precisely in proportion as slavery has become more profitable," observed a contemporary, "attachment to it has increased, and the number of those, where it exists, who seek to abolish it, has diminished."

In addition force, political manipulation, and repressive legislation supplemented propaganda in removing the threat of anti-slavery sentiment from this group. Legislation prohibiting slavery agitation and mob action against the emancipationists provided additional reasons for the dissolution of Southern anti-slavery societies. Further, uneven representation in state legislatures held in check the political power of the small farmer.

22. W. P. and F. J. Garrison, I, 249. The Committee of Savanah, Ga., offered $10,000 for Amos A. Phelps; East Feliciana, La., $50,000 for Arthur Tappan; Mount Meigs, Ala., $50,000 for Arthur Tappan or any other prominent Abolitionist; New Orleans, $100,000 for Tappan and La Roy Sunderland, the editor of Zion's *Watchman*. (Russell B. Nye, *Fettered Freedom, Civil Liberties and the Slavery Controversy, 1830–1860*, East Lansing, Mich., 1949, pp. 143–144.)

23. Swift, p. 69.

24. *Liberator,* Jan. 1, 1831.

25. Adin Ballou, *American Slavery* (Boston, 1837), p. 27.

26. W. L. Garrison, *The New Reign of Terror* (New York, 1860), Anti-Slavery Tracts, No. 4, New Series, p. 40.

27. Nye, p. 141; Elizabeth Merritt, *James Henry Hammond* (Baltimore, 1923), pp. 32–33.

28. *The Emancipator* (Oct. 12, 1837), II, No. 24, Whole No. 76, p. 92.

29. Oswald G. Villard, "Anti-Slavery Crisis in Massachusetts, 1830–1850," in *Commonwealth History of Massachusetts,* ed. Albert B. Hart (New York, 1930), IV, 332.

30. Nye, p. 141; *Niles' Weekly Register* (Sept. 26, 1835), XLIX, Whole No. 1, p. 49.

31. Albert Mordell, *Quaker Militant, John Greenleaf Whittier* (Boston, 1933), pp. 94–96.

32. Garrison clearly analyzed the reasons underlying the formation of Northern mobs. They were backed by several groups: 1) by men who believed Abolitionism was a threat to peace and order, men who simply disliked agitation; 2) by men who for business reasons believed Abolitionism a threat to Southern trade connections; 3) by those who believed Abolitionists to be infidels, anti-Biblical, religiously unorthodox; 4) by those who feared radical equality and amalgamation; 5) by those who believed the controversy, if unchecked, might break up the Union. He might have added, as a sixth group, those "drunken and deceived mobocrats whose arguments consist of vulgar blackguardism, brickbats, and rotten eggs." (Nye, p. 157.)

33. John F. Hume, *The Abolitionists* (New York, 1905), pp. 77–78.

34. Ibid., p. 35.

35. Swift, p. 155.

36. John H. Barrows, *Henry Ward Beecher* (New York, 1893), p. 193.

37. Oliver Johnson, p. 269. In Congress John Quincy Adams noted of Henry A. Wise: "his tartness, his bitterness, his malignity, and his inconsistencies." One wrote of Wise: "He speaks excessively loud and twists his face into all kinds of shapes. The blood rushes to his face, and he has the appearance of a man who is strangling." In the election of 1856 he stumped for the Democrat Buchanan against Fremont. Once he shouted to a Richmond crowd: "Fremont is nothing . . . an adventurer, born illegitimately . . . a Frenchman's bastard." (Reinhard H. Luthin, "Some Demagogues in American History," *American Historical Review,* Oct. 1951, LVII, No. 1, 35–36.

38. Oliver Johnson, p. 186. A modern historian, Arthur Y. Lloyd (*The Slavery Controversy, 1831–1860,* Chapel Hill, N. C., 1939) may not be as desperate as the Rev. Witherspoon but is no less "violent," "vitriolic," "vituperative," "rabid," and "extreme" than the moral agitators whom he belabors with these terms. "As Calhoun pointed out in 1837: 'Abolitionism originated in that blind fanatical zeal which made one man believe that he was responsible for the sins of others,' the same fanaticism that two hundred years before had 'tied the victim that it could not convert to the stake.'" "Slavery was magnified by their distorted perspective until it reached the proportions of a devastating evil that would gradually extend itself, crushing all good before it. . . . The entire galaxy of mob

riots, killings, lynchings, burnings, and other atrocities published can be
compared only with the waving the bloody shirt type of propaganda in
the years of Reconstruction or to the more recent crusade of certain
Northern elements to turn attention to the *alleged* political and judicial
discrimination against the Negro in the South." (Amazing! Italics mine.)
"The South . . . largely desired to be left alone and was not aggressively
seeking to extend the system of bondage as charged by the Abolitionists.
Or in the words of Edmund Rhett, 'the Southern people merely wished
the opportunity of rearing their children for some other purpose than
to make them vulgar, fanatical, cheating Yankees.'" (pp. 70–71, 76, 123.)
The comment above needs three exclamation points.

39.   Thomas E. Drake (*Quakers and Slavery in America*, New Haven,
1950) lucidly analyzes the split in Quaker ranks on slavery. Gradualism
particularly characterized their approach to the problem of emancipation.
Yet even here the Society of Friends split between the cautious and
conservative and the radicals. Rural Friends took more readily to Abolitionism than the Quakers in commercial centers such as Baltimore, Philadelphia, and New York. (pp. 114, 141, 153–155, 165.) "What a paradox,"
adds the author, "that the Society of Friends—the first important Christian
group in America to see the evils of slaveholding and the first to renounce
it without regard to cost—the Quakers who had faithfully guarded the
anti-slavery flame in the years when it burned so low, should now divide
over the issue of Abolition." (p. 166.)

The Quaker majority decided finally that their religious society
must follow a quiet way in opposing slavery. Friends might do what they
could, but they must shun activities that would stir up violence. Abolitionists damned the "modern Quakers." Foster lumped the Quakers with
the rest of the American Church and clergy in a "brotherhood of thieves."
(p. 176.) The orthodox Philadelphians protested to the London Friends
more than once that the slavery question in America had a "very exciting
tendency." (p. 179.) Quaker opinions on the Underground, as on radical
Abolitionism, differed extremely. Some joined wholeheartedly in the
dangerous work; many helped quietly when help was needed, but did
not go out of their way to violate the law; a conservative few believed
that Quakers should abhor and abstain from all such illegal activity. (pp.
186–187.)

40.   E. W. Small and Miriam R. Small, "Prudence Crandall," *New
England Quarterly* (Dec. 1944), XVII, No. 4, pp. 513–516, 520, 524–526.
In 1886 the Connecticut legislature at the instigation of Andrew
Clark, the nephew of Andrew T. Judson, who had brought about the
enactment of the Black Law, granted Prudence an annuity of $400. At
the age of eighty-six she was alert and vivid and still cared more for
causes than profits. She did not want charity since she would rather dig
than beg. She did not want the house given back to her, as had been
suggested, since she was happy and well in her "little pioneer box house
of three rooms." But she would be grateful for a yearly sum as payment
for the "just debt" owed her by the state for destroying her "hopes and
prospects" by an unjust and unconstitutional law. She named gratefully
the particular men who had advocated her cause with the legislature—
including Mark Twain. (pp. 527–528.)

41. Harriet Martineau, *The Martyr Age* (New York, 1839), p. 13.

42. Samuel Brooke, *Slavery and the Slaveholder's Religion* (Cincinnati, Ohio, 1846), p. 59.

43. When President Jackson in his message to Congress in December of 1835 called attention to the advisability of a Federal law prohibiting the circulation of "incendiary publications intended to instigate the slaves to insurrection," the Abolitionists were able to put their complete case before the public. The Reply of the American Anti-Slavery Society, addressed to Jackson, was a splendid piece of propaganda. The Abolitionist case, the Society reminded Jackson, had not yet been heard; the Society had been condemned on charges that were vague, indefinite, and untrue. The accusation that the Society intended to foment revolt was, they said, absurd in the light of the facts. First the Society had long been on record as opposed to violence in abolishing slavery. Second, Abolitionists mailed nothing to slaves, who usually could not read. Last, the Society threw all its publications open to inspection—let a special Congressional Committee attempt to discover a single inflammatory passage in any of them. "To repel your charges and to disabuse the public was a duty we owed to ourselves, to our children, and above all to the great and holy cause in which we are engaged." (Nye, pp. 60–61; "Protest of the American Anti-Slavery Society," *A Collection of Valuable Documents* (Boston, 1836), pp. 41–53.)

44. Leverett Street Jail was demolished in 1852. (W. P. and F. J. Garrison, II, 28; Oliver Johnson, pp. 199–200.)

CHAPTER SIX

Ann Greene

1. Martyn, pp. 78–79, gives this version of the episode.

2. Ibid., p. 79.

3. See announcement of engagement in gossipy letter of C. H. Parker to Amos A. Lawrence, Dec. 14, 1836 (Lawrence Manuscript Collection, Massachusetts Historical Society.)

4. Memorial Sketch of Ann Phillips (Boston, 1886), p. 5.

5. Manuscript letter to Elizabeth Pease, Sept. 17, 1841. (Boston Public Library).

6. Manuscript letter to R. D. Webb, June 29, 1842. (Boston Public Library.)

7. W. P. and F. J. Garrison, II, 128–129.

8. Martyn, pp. 82–84.

9. So Phillips told Martyn, p. 427.

10. *Liberator*, XXI:48, Nov. 28, 1851.

CHAPTER SEVEN

"Those Pictured Lips"

1. For accounts of Lovejoy's martyrdom see N. Dwight Harris, *The History of Negro Servitude in Illinois* (Chicago, 1904), pp. 68–98; Henry Tanner, *The Martyrdom of Lovejoy* (Chicago, 1881); Henry Wilson, *History of the Rise and Fall of the Slave Power in America* (Boston, 1874–77), I, 374–382; Oliver Johnson, pp. 222–226; *Liberator*, VII: 48, 49, Nov. 24 and Dec. 1, 1837; *Dictionary of American Biography*, XI, 434; Harrison A. Trexler, *Slavery in Missouri, 1804–1865* (Baltimore, 1914), pp. 117–119; John M. Krum, "Death of Elijah P. Lovejoy, A Voice from the Past," *Journal of the Illinois State Historical Society* (Jan. 1912), IV, No. 4, 499–503.

2. An article in the *Records of the American Catholic Historical Society of Philadelphia* (Sept. 1951), LXII, No. 3, speaks of Lovejoy's blind spot: religious prejudice: his intense dislike of Roman Catholicism, his condemnation of Catholic Church observances and clergy. He feared foreign influences were infiltrating the United States through the Jesuits, and alluded to conditions of Catholics in other countries as a warning of what might happen in the United States if Catholic immigration continued. (pp. 173, 175, 176, 180.)

3. N. Dwight Harris, pp. 73–74; Nye, pp. 115–116.

4. N. Dwight Harris, p. 76. Judge Lawless was an Irish Catholic.

5. H. A. Trexler believes Lovejoy's expulsion from St. Louis was occasioned as much by his vitriolic attacks on the Catholics and Judge Lawless as by his views on slavery. (pp. 117–119.) Lawless called Lovejoy "a sanctimonious enthusiast." (p. 117.)

6. Tanner, pp. 123–124, 145–147; Henry Wilson, I, 377–379.

7. *Liberator*, VII:48, Nov. 24, 1837.

8. Ibid., VII:48, Nov. 24, 1837.

9. Nye, p. 121. "The contest," said Francis Jackson, "is therefore substantially between liberty and slavery. As slavery cannot exist with free discussion—so neither can liberty breathe without it. Losing this, we, too, shall not be freemen indeed, but little, if at all, superior to the millions we now seek to emancipate." (*The Legion of Liberty and Force of Truth*, New York, 1842, pages unnumbered.)

The American Anti-Slavery Society asserted in its Declaration of Sentiments that its primary aim was the practical realization of the preamble to the Declaration of Independence, a position rooted essentially in the natural rights philosophy, and a position it never changed. (Nye, pp. 179–180.)

10. *Liberator*, VII:50, Dec. 8, 1837.

11. Ibid., VII:49, Dec. 1, 1837.

12. As Quoted in the *Liberator*, VII:53, Dec. 29, 1837.

13. *Independent Messenger*, Dec. 22, 1837. For agitation prior to meeting see also *Liberator*, VII:49, Dec. 1, 1837.

14. Frank P. Stearns, *Sketches from Concord and Appledore*, pp. 187–188.

15. For a detailed account of the meeting and speeches see the *Liberator*, VII:51, Dec. 15, 1837.

16. Austin's speech was printed in the *Liberator* with caustic notes appended by the reporter present: "This statement is palpably false," "Crocodile tears!" etc. (*Liberator*, VII:51, Dec. 15, 1837.)

17. H. H. Hagan, "Wendell Phillips," *Sewanee Review* (New York, 1913), XXI, 337; Martyn, p. 94.

18. Wendell Phillips, "The Murder of Lovejoy," *Speeches, Lectures, and Letters*, First Series, pp. 1–10.

19. Ibid., pp. 1–4.

20. Ibid., pp. 5–9.

21. Ibid., p. 10.

22. As quoted in the *Liberator*, VII:53, Dec. 29, 1837.

23. Samuel T. Pickard, *Life and Letters of John G. Whittier* (Boston, 1894), I, 197–198.

24. *Independent Messenger*, Dec. 22, 1837.

25. Austin, *Wendell Phillips*, p. 86; Stearns, *Sketches from Concord and Appledore*, pp. 189–190. Phillips justifies Dostoievski's observation that "an aristocrat is irresistible when he goes in for democracy." (Arthur M. Schlesinger, *The American Reformer*, Cambridge, Mass., 1950, pp. 34–35.)

CHAPTER EIGHT

Whipmaster and Scouts

1. W. P. and F. J. Garrison, II, 168.

2. Lewis A. Dexter, "The Legend of William Lloyd Garrison," reprinted from *The Social Studies* (Feb. 1939), XXX, No. 2.

3. W. P. and F. J. Garrison, II, 89–90; Albert B. Hart, *Slavery and Abolition* (New York, 1906), pp. 197–198; Swift, p. 142.

4. Swift, p. 142.

5. Ibid., p. 186.

6. William Birney, *James Birney and His Times* (New York, 1890), p. 311.

7. Archibald H. Grimké, p. 320.

8. Goldwin Smith, *The Moral Crusader, William Lloyd Garrison* (New York, 1892), pp. 81–82.

9. Josiah P. Quincy, "Memoir of Edmund Quincy," *Proceedings of the Massachusetts Historical Society*, (Boston, 1905), XVIII, Second Series, 403.

10. Birney, p. 316.

11. W. P. and F. J. Garrison, III, 22.

12. Ibid., I, 423. A touching note from Garrison to the Rev. W. H. Ward, March 24, 1876: "Though she was an invalid for many years, the blow at last came very suddenly, and the bereavement is keenly felt by me and my dear children. But all is of God:

Angels of Life and Death alike are His;
Without His leave they pass no threshold o'er;
Who, then, would wish or dare, believing this,
Against His messengers to shut the door?"

(Manuscript letter, New York Public Library, 135th Street Branch.)

13. Fanny Garrison Villard, p. 8.

14. James Russell Lowell, "Letters from Boston," *The Complete Poetical Works of James Russell Lowell* (Boston and New York, 1896), p. 111.

15. Hart, p. 183; W. P. and F. J. Garrison, II, 70.

16. W. P. and F. J. Garrison, II, 271.

17. Arthur B. Darling, *Political Changes in Massachusetts* (New Haven, 1925), p. 151.

18. James E. Cabot, *A Memoir of Ralph Waldo Emerson* (Boston and New York, 1887), II, 430; James Ford Rhodes, *History of the United States* (New York, 1902–1907), I, 67.

19. Lillie Buffum Chace Wyman, *American Chivalry* (Boston, 1913), p. 81.

20. Ibid., p. 81.

21. Ibid., p. 76.

22. Lowell, p. 112.

23. Wyman, p. 70.

24. Ibid., p. 71.

25. Swift, p. 229.

26. Wendell Phillips to Samuel Brooke, Dec. 4, 1845: "How gloriously matters seem to be going on in Ohio—Victory seems to have taken up her permanent abode on Abby's brow." (Manuscript letter, New York Historical Society.)

27. Louis Filler, "Parker Pillsbury: an Anti-Slavery Apostle," *The New England Quarterly* (Sept. 1946), XIX, No. 3, 315, 320, 322.

28. Ibid., pp. 318, 323.

29. Lowell, p. 112.

30. Danvers Historical Society, *Old Anti-Slavery Days* (Danvers, Mass., 1893), p. 86.

31. Louis Filler, p. 334.

32. *Dictionary of American Biography* (New York, 1931), III, 285.

33. Ibid., XII, 448.

34. John J. Chapman, p. 29.

35. Samuel J. May, *Some Recollections of Our Anti-Slavery Conflict* (Boston, 1869), p. 254.

36. Theodore C. Smith, *The Liberty and Free Soil Parties* (New York, 1897), p. 11.

37. Gilbert H. Barnes, *The Anti-Slavery Impulse, 1830–1844* (New York, 1933), p. 80.

38. Ibid., p. 81; Benjamin P. Thomas, *Theodore Weld, Crusader for Freedom* (Rutgers University, 1950), pp. 103–104.

39. Barnes, p. 82.

40. Thomas, pp. vii, 73.

41. Ibid., p. 73.

42. Weld's golden voice was silenced and his labors had ceased by 1843, long before the slavery agitation became bitter and strident. Gilbert H. Barnes greatly contributes to our knowledge of Abolition, but unfortunately grinds one axe: for adulation of Garrison, adulation of Weld. But why the childish and meticulous allocation of laurel wreaths? Weld and Garrison were both unselfish men passionately devoted to a great cause.

At Garrison's funeral Weld remarked: "We cannot speak his name, but it is the highest praise that can be given him. Who does not recognize that? . . . See how the whole land is strewn with his deeds! . . . The fact is, nothing that he has done can be spoken of that is not a eulogy. . . . Those words ["I am in earnest. I will not equivocate, etc."] were the passwords of Liberty. They were the keynote struck by him so loud that they startled the nation. Thank God that there was one man in those times who could utter them, who had a soul large enough, deep enough, strong enough, fired enough, God-like enough, to utter them." (Letter of Oswald Garrison Villard, April 19, 1949, to author.)

43. Barnes, p. 34.

44. Benj. Thomas, p. 5, foreword.

45. Barnes, p. 34. Theodore Weld to Lewis Tappan, May 21, 1836: "The brethren in New York feel as though I had not treated them kindly in staying away from the anniversary meeting. . . . I am sorry and grieved. Dear brother, I kept in the country because I felt it my duty to be there—I felt that I could do more good—I believe I have—Besides I am sure more of our agents are doing little in comparison with what they might do—and would have done if instead of having spent so much time in posting from anniversary to anniversary they had kept in their respective fields and worked day in and out." (Manuscript letter, New York Historical Society.)

"I never heard Weld in the full vigor of that eloquence which every one tells has never been equalled." (Extract from letter printed in *James Mott* by Mary Grew, p. 23. Moorland Foundation, Howard University.)

46. Benj. Thomas, p. 5, foreword.

47. Josiah P. Quincy, pp. 407–408.

48. Hart, p. 187.

49. Swift, p. 122.

50. Ibid., p. 121.

51. Phillip S. Foner, *The Life and Writings of Frederick Douglass*, 2 vols. (New York, 1950), I, 15, 17.

52. Benjamin Quarles, *Frederick Douglass* (Wash., D. C., 1948), pp. 9–10; George Shepperson, "Frederick Douglass and Scotland," *Journal of Negro History* (July, 1953), XXXVIII, No. 3, p. 313.

The name was not ill-fixed. As Douglass stood on platform after platform, spoke from street corner to street corner throughout Scotland, and was feted by rich and poor alike in his fight against acceptance by the Free Church of Scotland of slave money, especially from Charleston, to ,aid the Church, he made a deep impression on the Scottish people. His physical presence was noted by an anonymous witness in 1846, this time in broad Scotch: "On Munonday nicht our Jock gat me to gang down an' hear that chiel Douglass. I had came away wanting ma specks, but fraie the luik I gat o' him, he seemed a burly fellow, ane I shouldna like to hae a tussle wi him either feeseecally or intellecktually." A song to the tune of Ballenomoro Oro declared that "Nae Douglass has blown sic 'a flame/ That we winna hae peace till the siller's sent hame." But the "siller" was never sent home, for the Free Church was intransigent. (Shepperson, pp. 313–314, 317.)

Douglass writes to Franklin B. Sanborn in a postscript on Sept. 14, 1879: "Forty-one years today I became a freeman. It is my birthday though I am more than forty-one years old." (Jos. A. Borome, "Some Additional Light on Frederick Douglass," *Journal of Negro History*, April, 1953, XXXVIII, No. 2, p. 219.)

53. W. P. and F. J. Garrison, III, 19, footnote; Swift, pp. 233–234.

54. Foner, *Frederick Douglass*, I, 46.

55. Ibid., I, 49–50.

56. Ibid., I, 50–51.

57. Quarles, *Frederick Douglass*, p. 5.

58. Foner, *Frederick Douglass*, I, 53.

59. Ibid., II, 100.

60. "Letter to W. H. Prescott," George Ticknor, *Life, Letters, and Journals*, 2 vols. (Boston and New York, 1900), I, 479; Cabot, I, 105; Rhodes, I, 64–65.

61. William E. Channing, *Slavery* (Boston, 1836), pp. 63–64.

62. *Dictionary of American Biography*, IV, 68.

63. Manuscript letter to her brother, Oct. 25, 1857. (New York Public Library, 42nd Street.)

64. Manuscript letter to the Rev. C. Waterson, Aug. 27, 1844. (New York Historical Society.)

65. Lydia Maria Child, *Letters* (Boston, 1883), p. 266.

66. Ibid., p. 268.

67. Lowell, p. 111.

68. Angelina E. Grimké, *Appeal to the Christian Women of the South* (New York, 1836), p. 26.

69. Catherine H. Birney, *Sarah and Angelina Grimké* (Boston, 1885), pp. 188–191.

70. Sallie Holley, *A Life for Liberty* (New York, 1899), p. 107.

71. Catherine H. Birney, p. 170.

72. Samuel J. May, pp. 243–244.

73. *Dictionary of American Biography*, VII, 635.

CHAPTER NINE
The Armory of God

1. Says Kenneth M. Stampp: "Abolitionists have suffered severely at the hands of historians during the past generation. They have been roundly condemned for their distortions and exaggerations. But are historians really being objective when they combine warm sympathy for the slaveholders' point of view with cold contempt for those who looked upon the enslavement of four million American Negroes as the most shocking social evil of their day?" ("The Historian and Southern Negro Slavery," *The American Historical Review*, (April, 1952, LVII, No. 3, pp. 623–624.

The Dutch historian, Pieter Geyl, in "The American War and the Problem of Inevitability" *New England Quarterly*, June, 1951, XXIV, No. 2) pays a glowing tribute to the Abolitionists: "Their ultimate success shows that it is not sufficient to count noses. It shows the incalculable influence which may be exerted by an idea, by conscience, by individual moral strength, by passion in the service of an ethical cause. . . . Lincoln was not an Abolitionist. He loathed slavery, but in Abolitionism he perceived the defiance of the South and unconstitutionality. I admire that mentality and that temperament, but I wonder if with that alone the spiritual revolution in the North and the abolition of slavery in the South could have been achieved." (pp. 161, 162.)

Drawing an analogy between the Calvinists and William the Silent, and Lincoln and the Abolitionists, Prof. Geyl says: "One has to begin by accepting their convictions as a profound historic reality and their dynamic strength as an element in the situation, from which it cannot be eliminated even in the imagination." (p. 162.)

2. Arthur B. Darling, p. 151.

3. Octavius B. Frothingham, *Theodore Parker* (New York, 1880), pp. 158, 347.)

4. Rev. Samuel Longfellow, *Life of Henry Wadsworth Longfellow,* 2 vols. (Boston, 1886), II, 127, 194–195.

5. Samuel J. May, *Some Recollections of Our Anti-Slavery Conflict,* pp. 173–174.

6. Danvers Historical Society, p. xxi.

7. *Commonwealth History of Massachusetts,* IV, 320.

8. Hazel C. Wolf, *On Freedom's Altar* (Madison, Wisconsin, 1952), pp. 49, 61, 143. "Their concept of slavery as a national sin," says the author, "led them to adapt to their own crusade the techniques of the religious evangelists." (p. ix, preface.) Americans developed a concept of martyrdom which embraced certain essential ingredients. By 1830 they expected martyrs to be men who, like St. Paul, were indifferent, prior to sudden conversion, to the truth of the cause for which they later suffered. Prospective martyrs like St. Peter led ascetic lives; martyrs prayed forgiveness for their prosecutors. Most characteristic of the martyr was his willingness, even his intense desire, to suffer persecution and death. (pp. 7–8.) "Martyrdom was a revered American tradition. Every American believed that persecution sent the earliest settlers to the continent. All remembered colonial suffering from British despotism, and the willingness with which the signers of the Declaration of Independence pledged their lives, their fortunes, and their honor in support of the great precepts set forth in that document. So in the three decades before the Civil War, Abolitionists demonstrated time after time the truth of Jesus's teaching that no greater love existed than that of the man who would lay down his life for his friends." (pp. 146–147.)

9. Danvers Historical Society, p. 17.

9[a] Professor David Donald's analysis in "Towards a Reconsideration of the Abolitionists" is acute, but his conclusions are dubious. He implies that Abolitionist hatred of slavery was an unconscious hatred of the new industrial system. "An attack on slavery was their best, if quite unconscious, attack upon the new industrial system" and agitation allowed the only chance for personal and social self-fulfillment. "Their appeal for reform was a strident call for their own class to re-exert its former social dominance. . . . Reform gave meaning to the lives of this displaced social élite." Abolition was a double crusade, seeking freedom for the Negro in the South and a restoration of traditional values of their class at home. *"Basically* abolitionism should be considered the anguished protest of an aggrieved class against a world they never made" (Italics mine).

When Professor Donald begins to analyze "unconscious" motives of past leaders, he is standing on shaky foundations. The last sentence cuts away even those wobbly underpinnings from most of the structure of his remarks. I have retained in the text what I consider the solid part. (David Donald, *Lincoln Reconsidered,* New York, 1956, pp. 33–36.)

10. Ibid., p. 9.

11. Letter of Dec. 2, 1841, *Liberator,* XI:53, Dec. 31, 1841.

12. John F. Hume, *The Abolitionists* (New York, 1905), p. 27.

13. Oliver Johnson, *William Lloyd Garrison and His Times* (Boston, 1881), p. 321.

14. Manuscript poem by Eliza Lee Follen. To be sung at Faneuil Hall by the Friends of Freedom at the Anti-Slavery Fair. (New York Historical Society.)

15. Henry Wilson, I, 205.

16. See Constitution of the American Anti-Slavery Society, Note 3, Appendix.

17. Nye, p. 7; *Correspondence between the Hon. F. H. Elmore and James G. Birney* (New York, 1838), p. 7.

18. Benjamin Quarles, "Sources of Abolitionist Income," *The Mississippi Valley Historical Review* (June, 1945), XXXII, No. 1, p. 63.

During the first six years of existence the American Anti-Slavery Society collected a total of $158,849.43. A typical year during the mid-fifties, 1855, resulted in a total of $34,466.69. The Massachusetts Anti-Slavery Society collected approximately $6,000 annually; the Pennsylvania Society from 1850–1854 averaged $5935; other anti-slavery societies ranged from $3,000 downward to the sum of $221.62, reported in 1859 by a society in Ohio. (Quarles, "Sources of Abolitionist Income," pp. 75–76.)

Quarles remarks: "The conclusion is inescapable that in proportion to the scope of their program, the funds of the Abolitionists were smaller than those of any other reform enterprise in the history of our country." (p. 76.)

19. Nye, pp. 36–37, 55. In 1837 the American Anti-Slavery Society, under the direction of Henry B. Stanton, Weld, and Whittier, evolved an efficient organization for the circulation of petitions through the more than thousand anti-slavery societies in the country. Printed petitions or directions for drawing them up went from the society's presses to the local and state group, which in turn distributed them, solicited signatures, and returned them to the societies for transmission to state legislatures and Congress. The petitions themselves were mere sentences, brief and to the point. The potent reason was that under the gag rules petitions could be presented by subject only, and anything more than the simple statement of their prayer never would be heard.

The number of petitions submitted to Congress during the first eighteen months of the campaign increased from 23 to 300,000. A breakdown of the total of 412,000 petitions to the House gives these results: 130,200 for the abolition of slavery in the District of Columbia; 182,400 against annexation of Texas; 32,000 for repeal of the gag rule; 21,200 for legislation forbidding slavery in the territories; 22,160 against admission of any new slave state, and 23,400 for the abolition of the interstate slave trade. (Nye, pp. 36–37; William Chauncey Fowler, *The Sectional Controversy*, New York, 1862, pp. 128–132; Austin Willey, *The History of the Anti-Slavery Cause in State and Union*, Portland, Me., p. 83; Gilbert H. Barnes, *The Anti-Slavery Impulse*, pp. 130–145; Janet Wilson, "The Early Anti-Slavery Propaganda," *More Books*, The Bulletin of the Boston Public Library, Nov. 1944, pp. 352–355.

As for the plan to publish different periodicals each week of the month: in the first week the Society planned a folio paper, *Human Rights* (25 cents a year); in the second, a magazine, the *Anti-Slavery Record* ($1.50 a thousand); in the third, the *Emancipator*, an enlarged sheet (50 cents a year), and in the last, *The Slave's Friend*, a juvenile (1 cent a copy). Until it changed its policy in 1840 it flooded the nation with such publications. The million pieces (1,095,800) printed and circulated included: *Human Rights* (240,000), the *Anti-Slavery Record* (385,000), the *Emancipator* (210,000), *The Slave's Friend* (205,000), bound volumes (5,000), quarterly anti-slavery magazines (5,500), miscellaneous (45,300). The totals do not include publications of state or local societies.

Publications reached the following figures:

May,	1836–37	161,000
May,	1837–38	646,500
May,	1838–39	724,000

Until a traveling agent system was developed in 1837 distribution was primarily by mail to names on file in the New York offices. Congressmen, ministers, theological students, state officials and legislators, newspaper editors, justices of the peace, and prominent citizens in all states received copies of the Society's publications gratis. A subscription list was built up, but none of the publications operated at a profit. (American Anti-Slavery Society, *Second Annual Report*, New York, 1835, pp. 48–53; *Third Annual Report*, New York, 1836, pp. 35–36; Janet Wilson, pp. 353–355; Nye, p. 55; the *Emancipator*, Oct. 12, 1837, II, No. 24, Whole No. 76, p. 92.)

20. *Commonwealth History of Massachusetts*, IV, 331. As a rule the top salary for an agent with a family was $600 a year and traveling expenses. The National Society offered Weld a yearly salary of $416. (Quarles, "Sources of Abolitionist Income," p. 70.)

21. Manuscript letter from Phillips to J. Miller McKim, Oct. 31, 1844. (Cornell University Library.)

22. Frederick Douglass, *Life and Times* (Boston, 1895), p. 277.

23. Moncure D. Conway, *Autobiography* (Boston, 1904), I, 284.

24. James Freeman Clarke, *Anti-Slavery Days* (New York, 1883), p. 114.

25. John H. Franklin, *From Slavery to Freedom* (New York, 1947), pp. 247–249.

26. The grand jury of Tuscaloosa, Alabama, indicted R. G. Williams, publishing agent of the American Anti-Slavery Society for publishing and circulating the *Emancipator*. When Gov. Gayle of Alabama requested his surrender from Gov. Marcy of New York, he raised the interesting

legal question of whether or not a person in one state could commit a
crime in another state without leaving his own. Marcy refused to allow
Williams' extradition on the obvious ground that he had never been in
Alabama. (Nye, p. 59.)

27. Black Abolitionists wrote as well as spoke for the emancipation
of Negroes. Perhaps the outstanding journalist was Samuel Cornish, who
with John Russwurm established the first Negro newspaper, *Freedom's
Journal* in 1827. Subsequently Cornish published *Rights of All*, the *Weekly
Advocate*, and with the help of others edited *Colored American*. Other
Black Abolition newspapers were the *National Watchman*, edited by
William G. Allen and Henry Highland Garnet, the *Mirror of Liberty*, a
quarterly issued by David Ruggles, and of course the *North Star* of Fred-
erick Douglass. (John Hope Franklin, p. 249.)

28. Quarles, "Sources of Abolitionist Income," p. 64.

29. "Every secret society is at war with the genius of republicanism.
That genius calls for open and impartial dealings amongst all and everywhere." (Manuscript, New York Public Library.)

30. Quarles, "Sources of Abolitionist Income," p. 64.

31. "Gerrit Smith Homestead, Abolition Shrine, Burns. The homestead was to have become the property of the State to be used as a
museum." (New York *Times*, March 3, 1936.)

32. The New York Anti-Slavery Society, organized in 1833, adopted
the modified version, "immediate emancipation gradually accomplished."
In the West the Lane Seminary group, led by Theodore Weld, redefined
the term as "gradual emancipation, immediately begun," meaning "the
slaves be at once delivered from the control of arbitrary and irresponsible
power, and like other men, put under the control of equitable laws,
equitably administered." The Lane doctrine did not mean simply turning the freed slave loose, and investing him at once with political rights.
It meant that legal control of the master over the slave should cease,
that he was free to sell his labor in open market, and that he should be
placed under "a benevolent and disinterested supervision" (presumably
that of the state or federal government) until he was ready for "intellectual
and moral equality with whites." Despite its vagueness the Lane doctrine remained the popular version of immediatism for some years in
non-Garrisonian circles. (Nye, pp. 5–6.)

Nye sensibly remarks: "However, despite the plurality of alternate
schemes of emancipation and the obvious faults of immediatism, no remedy
for the evil of slavery was suggested which was any more practicable
or any more acceptable to the South than that of the immediate Abolitionists, a fact which accrued to their advantage." (p. 10.)

And Nye adds: "Though the South generally came to feel that 'the
impertinent interference of Abolitionists . . . provoked us to argument
and investigation' [the *Richmond Enquirer*, Oct. 17, 1857], there is
good reason to believe that if Garrison and his Northern followers had
never existed, the pro-slavery philosophy would have developed no differently though perhaps more slowly and with less unity." (p. 18.)

33. Jesse Macy, part 2, pp. 46–47.

34. Manuscript letter. (Sumner Collection, Harvard College Library.)

35. In a typical year, 1853, the British sent by packet ships a total of fifteen boxes; in the peak year of 1857 the bazaar received twenty-four cases from across the Atlantic. Receipts from the Boston Fairs ranged from $360 in 1834 to $5,250 in 1856. From twenty-three of the twenty-four Fairs held, the total amount received was $65,826.23. But measured against the effort expended, so meager was the return in dollars and cents that after 1857 the Boston ladies abandoned the bazaar. They asked their supporters to send money, not merchandise. The leading figure in the movement, Anne Weston, had come to the conclusion that "fairs are like an excise: good only if no other mode is practicable." (Quarles, "Sources of Abolition Income," pp. 72–75.)

36. Manuscript letter to R. D. Webb, Aug. 12, 1842. (Boston Public Library.)

37. Ralph Waldo Emerson, "West India Emancipation," *The Complete Works of Ralph Waldo Emerson*, Centenary Edition, (Boston and New York, 1932), XI, 139; see also the *Liberator*, XIX:21, May 25, 1849; Danvers Historical Society, p. 16.

38. *A Selection of Anti-Slavery Hymns* (Boston, 1834), p. 23.

39. Ibid., p. 28.

40. Samuel J. May, *Some Recollections of Our Anti-Slavery Conflict*, p. 260.

41. *Liberty Bell*, By the Friends of Freedom (Boston, 1842), pp. 64–66. See Note 4 in Appendix.

CHAPTER TEN

A Melancholy Tour

1. Lorenzo Sears, *Wendell Phillips* (New York, 1909), p. 67; see also Massachusetts Anti-Slavery Society, *Sixth Annual Report*, (Boston, 1838), p. 48, and *Seventh Annual Report* (Boston, 1839), p. 15.

2. See lithograph circular of May 13, 1839, signed among others by Wendell Phillips, in the Boston Public Library.

3. Manuscript letter, Feb. 23, 1839. (Boston Public Library.)

4. Newell D. Hillis, *The Battle of Principles* (New York, 1912), p. 92.

5. Octavius B. Frothingham, *Theodore Parker* (Boston, 1874), pp. 96–99.

6. Ibid., p. 97; John W. Chadwick, *Theodore Parker* (Boston, 1900), p. 85.

7. Lorenzo Sears, p. 77; Massachusetts Anti-Slavery Society, *Eighth Annual Report* (Boston, 1840), pp. 32–35.

8. Manuscript letter, July, 1939. (Boston Public Library.)

9. Ibid.

10. Ibid.

11. *Memorial Sketch of Ann Phillips*, p. 7.

12. See Note 5 in Appendix.

13. *History of Woman Suffrage*, ed. by Elizabeth C. Stanton, Susan B. Anthony, and Matilda Joslyn Gage, 3 vols. (Rochester, N. Y., 1889), I, 54.

14. Harriet J. Robinson, *Massachusetts in the Woman Suffrage Movement* (Boston, 1881), p. 14.

15. *History of Woman Suffrage*, I, 55.

16. Robinson, p. 194.

17. *History of Woman Suffrage*, I, 56. For debate in convention see W. P. and F. J. Garrison, II, 369–373.

18. George L. Austin, *Life and Times of Wendell Phillips*, pp. 98, 99.

19. *Memorial Sketch of Ann Phillips*, p. 8.

20. Swift, p. 198.

21. W. P. and F. J. Garrison, II, 375.

22. *History of Woman Suffrage*, I, 61–62.

23. Ibid., I, 62.

24. W. P. and F. J. Garrison, II, 374–375.

25. Ibid., II, 375–376.

26. *Correspondence of John Lothrop Motley*, ed. by George W. Curtis, 2 vols. (New York, 1889), I, 277–278.

27. Goldwin Smith, p. 127.

28. "Daniel O'Connell," Phillips, *Speeches, Lectures, and Letters*, Second Series, p. 412.

29. New York *Morning Herald*, July 20, 22, 1840.

30. W. B. Duffield, "Daniel O'Connell," *The Cornhill Magazine* (London, 1899), New Series, Jan.–June, 1899, VI, 35.

31. Michael MacDonagh, *Daniel O'Connell and the Story of Catholic Emancipation* (London, 1929), p. 118.

32. William J. O'N. Daunt, *Personal Recollections of Daniel O'Connell*, 2 vols. (London, 1848), I, 287–288.

33. Manuscript letters, Oct. 19, Nov. 5, 1840. (Sumner Collection, Harvard College Library.)

34. Manuscript letter, Nov. 19, 1840. (Boston Public Library.)

35. Letter from Naples to Garrison, April 12, 1841, in the *Liberator*, XI:22, May 28, 1841.

36. Austin, *Wendell Phillips*, pp. 103–104; Ralph Korngold, *Two Friends of Man* (New York, 1950), pp. 158–159.

37. Manuscript letter, July 3 (?), 1841. (Boston Public Library.)

38. They arrived on the Caledonia. (*Bay State Democrat*, July 17, 1841.) At the reception Phillips expressed happiness on finding himself once more in the field of anti-slavery conflict surrounded by those who had continued "faithful among the faithless" during his absence. In his opinion, the anti-slavery artillery was now to be leveled mainly against a pro-slavery priesthood and church as the greatest obstacles to the overthrow of the slave system. (*Liberator*, XI:30, July 23, 1841; XI:31, July 30, 1841; and for the reception, XI:32, Aug. 6, 1841.)

39. Manuscript letter, July 27, 1841. (Boston Public Library.)

40. Manuscript letter to Eliz. Pease, Oct. 1846. (Boston Public Library.)

41. Manuscript letter, Sept. 17, 1841. (Boston Public Library.)

42. Manuscript letter, Nov. 25, 1841. (Boston Public Library.)

43. *Memorial Sketch of Ann Phillips*, p. 13.

44. Manuscript letter, July 27, 1841. (Boston Public Library.)

CHAPTER ELEVEN

Ultraism Afloat—"Cling by the Abolitionists"

1. W. P. and F. J. Garrison, II, 264.
2. Macy, p. 58.
3. Letter of Jan. 11, 1839 in W. P. and F. J. Garrison, II, 263–264; *Liberator*, XI:7, Feb. 15, 1839.
4. W. P. and F. J. Garrison, II, 265.
5. See Note 6 in Appendix.
6. W. P. and F. J. Garrison, II, 347; Goldwin Smith, p. 124.
7. Swift, p. 195.
8. Henry Wilson, I, 415.
9. Ibid., I, 420.
10. Oliver Johnson, p. 293.
11. Hart, p. 201.
12. "Divisions," *The Liberty Bell*, 1842, pp. 46–50.
13. John T. Morse, *John Quincy Adams* (Boston, 1882), p. 249.
14. "The Right of Petition," Phillips, *Speeches, Lectures, and Letters*, Second Series, pp. 1–6.
15. Nye, p. 218; *Letters of James Gillespie Birney, 1831–1857*, 2 vols., ed. Dwight L. Dumond (New York and London, 1938), I, 243.
16. Nye, p. 251.
17. Ibid., p. 250.
18. *Eighteenth Annual Report of the Massachusetts Anti-Slavery Society* (Boston, 1850), pp. 107–108; see also Lewis Tappan, *A Sidelight on Anglo-American Relations, 1839–1858*, ed. A. H. Abel and F. J. Klingsberg, (Lancaster, Pa., 1927), p. 30.
19. Phillips, *Speeches, Lectures, and Letters*, Second Series, pp. 19–23.
20. Manuscript letter to relative, so quoted in Martyn, p. 157.
21. Manuscript letter from George Thompson, Ibid., p. 157.
22. Sears, p. 99.
23. Madeleine H. Rice, *American Catholic Opinion in the Slavery Controversy* (New York, 1944), pp. 100, 103, 109, 156. As Madeleine H. Rice reveals, there was a fairly unanimous agreement among Catholics and Churchmen that the principles and methods of Garrisonian Abolitionism were not only a threat to the safety of the country but also in conflict with Catholic ethics and ideals. Throughout the entire period, Catholic hierarchical leaders adhered in their national councils to their policy of silence on the critical issues of slavery. Both scriptural and Church tradition were interpreted as recognizing that its existence was compatible with the practice of religion. As emancipation came closer, Catholic hostility mounted. The press, with one or two exceptions, attacked it with a vigor that led them virtually to endorse the perpetuation of slavery for an indefinite time. It must not be overlooked that most of the editors were of Irish ancestry and their subscribers belonged mainly to the immigrant body. Emancipation raised the spectre of mass migration of black workers.

According to its long established teaching, human bondage was not morally wrong per se provided the conditions laid down by theologians as necessary for a "just servitude" were observed.

The belief that Catholics were pro-slavery in sentiment was apparently fairly widespread in the North and South. Alexander Stephens wrote of Catholics: "They have never warred against us or our peculiar institutions. No man can say as much of New England Baptists, Presbyterians, or Methodists; the long roll of Abolition petitions, with which Congress has been so agitated for past years, come not from the Catholics; their pulpits at the North are not desecrated every Sabbath with anathemas against slavery. And of the three thousand New England clergymen who sent the anti-Nebraska memorial to the Senate, not one was a Catholic. . . ." (pp. 85, 89–90, 123–126, 157.)

Chester F. Dunham (*The Attitude of the Northern Clergy towards the South, 1860–1865.* Toledo, Ohio, 1942) says Bishop Hughes during the Civil War was "a neutral really rather than an ardent patriot." (pp. 16–17.) Generally the Northern Protestant clergy was in the middle of the road position, swinging momentarily to the right or left as events became intensely emotionalized.

24. Manuscript letter, March 30, 1842. (Boston Public Library.)

25. Manuscript letter to R. D. Webb, June 29, 1842. (Boston Public Library.)

26. Manuscript letters, June 29, 1842 to R. D. Webb; June 29, 1842 to Elizabeth Pease; Aug. 12, 1842 to R. D. Webb. (Boston Public Library.)

27. Manuscript letter, Oct. 1846. (Boston Public Library.)

CHAPTER TWELVE

King of the Lyceum

1. Oliver W. Holmes, *The Autocrat of the Breakfast Table* (Boston and New York, 1891), pp. 140–141.

2. Thoreau in a letter dated March 12, 1845, remarks: "We have now, for the third winter, had our spirits refreshed and our faith in the destiny of the Commonwealth strengthened by the presence and the eloquence of Wendell Phillips, and we must wish to tender him our thanks and our sympathy. . . . We must give Mr. Phillips the credit of being a clean, erect, and what was once called a consistent man. . . . He stands so distinctly, so firmly, and so effectively alone, and one honest man is so much more than a host that we cannot but feel that he does himself injustice when he reminds us of the American Society, which he represents. It is rare that we have the pleasure of listening to so clear and orthodox a speaker, who obviously has so few cracks or flaws in his moral nature . . . and aside from the admiration at his rhetoric secures the genuine respect of his audience. . . . Here is one who is at the same time an eloquent speaker and a righteous man." Thoreau goes on to say that he considers Phillips "one of the most conspicuous and efficient champions of a true Church and State," and he calls the orator a Red Cross Knight. Henry David Thoreau, *The Writings of Henry David Thoreau* (Boston and New York, 1893), X, 76–80.

3. Quoted in Katherine H. Porter, *The Development of the American Lyceum* (Chicago, 1914), p. 34.

4. "The admission of this gentleman into the Lyceum has been strenuously opposed by a respectable portion of our fellow citizens . . . and in each instance the people have voted they *would hear him*." (Thoreau, X, 76.)

5. Martyn, p. 159.

6. Quoted in Martyn, pp. 160–161.

7. Thoreau, X, 78.

8. Recollections of Miss Mary Grew (Ms.) in Martyn, pp. 162–163. See also James Freeman Clarke, pp. 117–118.

CHAPTER THIRTEEN

A Covenant with Death and an Agreement with Hell—Dumb Dogs That Dare Not Bark

1. Martyn, p. 164.

2. *Liberator*, XII:44, Nov. 4, 1842.

3. Quoted in the *Liberator*, XII:44, Nov. 4, 1842.

4. Ibid., XII:44, Nov. 4, 1842.

5. Ibid., XII:45, Nov. 11, 1842.

6. Ibid., XII:45, Nov. 11, 1842.

7. John G. Whittier, "Massachusetts to Virginia," *The Complete Poetical Works of John Greenleaf Whittier* (Boston and New York, 1904), pp. 356–359.

8. *Liberator*, XII:47, Nov. 25, 1842; XII:3, Jan. 20, 1843; XII:5, Feb. 3, 1843.

9. Any officer violating this act was to forfeit a sum not exceeding $1,000 or be imprisoned not exceeding one year. ("An Act further to protect Personal Liberty," General and Special Statutes of Massachusetts, Chap. LXIX, in *Acts and Resolves passed by the Legislature of Massachusetts*, 1843 (Boston, 1844), p. 33.

10. Martyn, p. 165.

11. George William Curtis, *Wendell Phillips* (New York, 1884), pp. 20–21; see also Phillips's *Review of Webster's Speech on Slavery* (Boston 1850), p. 6.

12. James Russell Lowell, "The American Tract Society," *The Complete Writings of James Russell Lowell*, Elmwood Edition (Boston and New York, 1904), VI, 12.

13. Oliver Johnson, p. 344.

14. Nye handles concisely the divergent attitudes towards the Constitution: One group of Abolitionists contended that the Constitution was in reality an anti-slavery document, and slavery therefore was unconstitutional, illegal, and immediately to be abolished. Paramount in this argument was the contention that the Declaration of Independence, a prior document, and one carrying with it the principles of the national government-to-be, was anti-slavery. The Declaration, part of the nation's constitutional law, made slavery illegal; the Constitution did not establish it or recognize it. Since slavery was abolished by the Declaration, and thus had no legal existence in 1783, it was therefore manifestly im-

possible for the Constitution to sanction it. The whole point rested upon the belief that the Declaration was an accepted portion of constitutional law.

Variations on this scheme were common. Horace Mann believed that the Constitution simply acquiesced in slavery, but neither legalized nor protected it. Cassius Clay of Kentucky thought it was neither pro-slavery or anti-slavery, but neutral. Others felt that the framers intended to make slavery unconstitutional after 1808 or that they did not intend it to spread but instead to die a natural death.

This disagreement among Abolitionists, Nye acutely points out, was of vital importance to the movement. If the Constitution was a neutral or anti-slavery document, the most efficient and proper method of abolishing slavery was therefore by political action, retaining the Constitution as an article of government but ensuring its proper interpretation by political means—a view adopted by the Liberty Party. But if the Constitution was a pro-slavery document, it must be by-passed or violated. The fundamental disagreement split the Abolitionists into a political action group and an anti-constitutional group.

Less direct was the position taken by the proponents of the higher law doctrine. The principle itself stated that a law higher than human enactment existed in the laws of God. Since slavery deprives a man of his most fundamental human right, it is therefore a violation of both natural and divine law. The laws which sustain slavery are not laws but outrages. "The fact that a law is constitutional amounts to nothing, unless it is also pure. It must harmonize with the laws of God or be set at naught by upright men."

If the Constitution was a pro-slavery document and the "self-evident truths" of the Declaration of Independence were only meaningless generalities, then the nationalization and extension of slavery seemed inevitable. But by adopting as a general platform, as Nye concludes, the principles of the Declaration, and by shifting the basis of the argument to the Higher Law, the divine law, the Abolitionists changed the tone of the controversy. Their movement became a holy crusade, a battle for the divine and natural rights of man. (Nye, pp. 189–192, 194, 196.) Says the anonymous author of *The Higher Law Tried by Reason and Authority* (New York, 1851): "In the hands of a subtle lawyer, working for a fee, the Constitution and the laws are as elastic as India rubber, but when the voice of humanity cried out for justice suddenly, they are found to be stereotyped in steel." (p. 53.)

15. See *Liberator*, 1842, *passim;* Massachusetts Anti-Slavery Society, *Eleventh Annual Report;* and W. P. and F. J. Garrison, III, 99–101.

16. W. P. and F. J. Garrison, I, 307–309; *Liberator*, II, 52, Dec. 29, 1832.

17. *Liberator*, XII:19, May 13, 1842.

18. James Russell Lowell, "The Biglow Papers," No. 1, *The Complete Poetical Works of James Russell Lowell* (Boston and New York, 1896), Cambridge Edition, p. 182.

19. Massachusetts Anti-Slavery Society, *Eleventh Annual Report*, 1843, p. 94; see also Swift, p. 246.

20. James Russell Lowell, "Letter to C. F. Briggs, *"The Complete Writings of James Russell Lowell*, Elmwood Edition, XIV, 173.

21. Manuscript letter, May 24, 1848. (Harvard College Library.)

22. Manuscript letter, Feb. 17, 1845. (Sumner Collection, Harvard College Library.)

23. John F. Hume, p. 13.

24. Oliver Johnson, p. 314.

25. William Birney, *James G. Birney and His Times* (New York, 1890), p. 185.

26. Grimké, p. 287.

27. George W. Julian, *Political Recollections, 1840–1872* (Chicago, 1884), p. 33.

28. Theodore C. Smith, "The Liberty and Free Soil Parties," *Harvard Historical Studies* (New York, 1897), VI, 72.

29. Julian, p. 33.

30. William C. Cochran, *The Western Reserve and the Fugitive Slave Law* (Cleveland, Ohio, 1920), p. 82.

31. *Liberator*, XIV:1, 2, 3, 5, Jan. 5, 12, 19, Feb. 2, 1844.

32. Wendell Phillips, *The Constitution, a Pro-Slavery Compact* (New York, 1856).

33. Ibid., Introduction, ix.

34. Manuscript letter, Feb. 25, 1845. (Boston Public Library.) When McKim requested a batch of pamphlets, Phillips could send at first but eight. (Manuscript letter to J. Miller McKim, March 2, 1845, Cornell University Library.)

35. *Can Abolitionists Vote or Take Office under the United States Constitution?* (New York, 1845), p. 29.

36. Ibid., pp. 32–33.

37. Ibid., p. 37.

38. Ibid., p. 5.

39. Ibid., pp. 5–6.

40. *Liberator*, XVIII:5, Feb. 4, 1848.

41. Ibid., XVIII:5, Feb. 4, 1848.

42. Swift, p. 227.

43. Massachusetts Anti-Slavery Society, *Tenth Annual Report*, 1842, Appendix, p. 8.

44. *Liberator*, XX:32, Aug. 9, 1850.

45. Speech at Broadway Tabernacle, May 8, 1849, *Liberator*, XIX:20, May 18, 1849.

46. Ibid.

47. Ibid.

48. Wendell Phillips Stafford, *Wendell Phillips* (New York, 1911), p. 18.

CHAPTER FOURTEEN

Of Martyr Build—Father Mathew

1. Herbert Aptheker (*American Negro Slave Revolts*, New York, 1943) finds that a widespread fear of slave rebellion was characteristic of the South. "Many people never lay down at night without fears that their throats might be cut in their sleep." The meekness and docility of the Negro, Aptheker indisputably points out, are a delusion. The fundamental

factor provoking rebellion against slavery was the social system itself, the degradation, exploitation, oppression, and brutality which it created and with which indeed it was synonymous. The author found records of approximately 250 revolts and conspiracies in the history of American Negro slavery. The evidence points to the conclusion "that discontent and rebelliousness were not only exceedingly common but, indeed, characteristic of Negro slaves." It must be added, too, as an historical fact that in the Turner cataclysm twice as many Negroes were indiscriminately slaughtered as the number of white people who had fallen victims to the vengeance of the slaves. (pp. 39, 52, 139, 162, 374.)

Even a Southern partisan, Clement Eaton, agrees substantially with Aptheker's contention. The Southerners were racked at intervals by dark rumors and imagined plots—the fear was contagious. Olmsted, "perhaps the most capable observer who traveled in the pre-war South," says Eaton, reported that though Southerners did not fear any successful general uprising of the slaves, yet there was no part of the South where the slave population was felt to be quite safe from the contagion of insurrectionary excitement. "The perfected slave code contained many Draconic regulations indicating fear of insurrection." The Southern people suffered at times and in certain sections from a pathological fear of their slaves, not at all justified by actual danger. But "the stringent slave codes, the patrol system, the efforts to get rid of the free Negro, the prevalence of alarming rumors, the savage severity with which Negroes accused of plotting insurrection were punished, the flimsy evidence of the existence of plots which was credited, all indicate a certain current of uneasiness in Southern society, a feeling that stern precautions should be taken against possible slave revolt." (pp. 107, 110, 112–114, 116.) See also Raymond A. Bauer and Alice H. Bauer, "Day to Day Resistance to Slavery," *Journal of Negro History*, Oct. 1942, XXVII, No. 4, 388–419.

2. Hart, p. 278.

3. Henry Wilson, I, 580–582.

4. Ralph Waldo Emerson, *Journals of Ralph Waldo Emerson*. Edited by Edward Waldo Emerson and Waldo Emerson Forbes (Boston and New York, 1912), VII, 14; Arthur B. Darling, *Political Changes in Massachusetts* (New Haven, 1925), pp. 326–327. For comments on expulsion of Squire Hoar see also *Liberator*, XIV:52, Dec. 27, 1844, XV:1, 2, 3, Jan. 3, 1845 through Jan. 17, 1845.

5. For resolutions against insult to Massachusetts and for disunion see meeting of the Massachusetts Anti-Slavery Society described in the *Liberator*, XV:5, Jan. 31, 1845.

6. "His presence was an action; his look was a testimony." But it was also admitted that "his voice could not be heard beyond the platform." (*Liberator*, XVI:40, Oct. 2, 1846.) "It is thought that 5,000 persons were present, and every eye was turned with indignant reprobation upon the man at whose instance the slave was taken back to slavery—John H. Pearson, Merchant, Long Wharf." (Ibid., XVI:40, Oct. 2, 1846.)

7. Ibid., XVI:40, Oct. 2, 1846; Austin, pp. 129–130.

8. Martyn, p. 214.

9. Manuscript letter. (Sumner Collection, Harvard College Library.)

10. Manuscript letter to R. D. Webb, Jan. 13, 1848. (Boston Public Library.)

11. *Liberator*, XII:7, Feb. 18, 1842.

12. James Schouler, *History of the United States of America* (Wash., D. C., 1889), IV, 206–207.

13. Phillips replied in an extended letter to the City Solicitor, P. W. Chandler, who had affirmed the decision of the Committee. Said Phillips: "The post of persecuting the colored children, of sacrificing their rights to a cruel and eminently vulgar prejudice, became too hot for the School Committee to maintain it alone. . . . If it be a fact that the best interests of the white and colored children can only be secured by separate schools, then their best interests cannot be secured under any system of public state instruction. We must give up the theory, and they must, from the nature of the case, resort to private schools." Finally in a parting shot at Chandler: "Mr. Chandler has said and done many things which as a wise, if not an honest man, he will have ample cause to regret, but the weakest act of all was when he suffered himself to be made the tool of a few narrow-minded and prejudiced men." (*Liberator*, XVI:35, Aug. 28, 1846.)

14. Massachusetts Anti-Slavery Society, *Proceedings*, 1856, pp. 66–67.

15. *Liberator*, XI:36, Sept. 3, 1841.

16. Frederick Douglass, *Life and Times of Frederick Douglass* (Hartford, Conn., 1882), p. 226; Martyn, p. 203.

17. Wendell Phillips, *Review of Lysander Spooner's Essay on the Unconstitutionality of Slavery* (Boston, 1847), pp. 3, 5.

18. Martyn, p. 215.

19. Richard A. Armstrong, *Latter Day Teachers* (London, 1881), p. 60.

20. Ibid., pp. 60–61.

21. Ibid., pp. 61–62; John W. Chadwick, *Theodore Parker* (Boston, 1900), pp. 237–238.

22. Armstrong, pp. 62–63.

23. Edwin D. Mead, *Emerson and Theodore Parker* (Boston, 1910), pages unnumbered.

24. Ibid.; Chadwick, p. 200.

25. Ibid., p. 202.

26. Mead, *Emerson and Theodore Parker*.

27. Ibid.; Conway, I, 261.

28. Mead, *Emerson and Theodore Parker*.

29. Chadwick, pp. 98–99.

30. Daniel D. Addison, *The Clergy in American Life and Letters* (London, 1900), p. 252.

31. Mead, *Emerson and Theodore Parker*.

32. Armstrong, p. 66.

33. Henry Steele Commager, *Theodore Parker, Yankee Crusader* (Boston, 1947), pp. 185, 168–196.

34. Mead, *Emerson and Theodore Parker*.

35. Addison, p. 248.

36. Rhodes, I, 289.

37. Mead, *Emerson and Theodore Parker*.

38. Lowell, "A Fable for Critics," *Complete Poetical Works*, p. 131.

39. Addison, p. 247.
40. John F. Maguire, *Father Mathew* (New York, 1864), p. 465.
41. W. P. and F. J. Garrison, III, 250–253; *Eighteenth Annual Report of the Massachusetts Anti-Slavery Society* (Boston, 1850), Appendix B, pp. 103–104.
42. Maguire, pp. 470–471.
43. *Liberator,* XIX:34, Aug. 24, 1849.
44. Ibid.
45. W. P. and F. J. Garrison, III, 254.
46. *Liberator,* XIX:34, Aug. 24, 1849.
47. Maguire, p. 482.
48. W. P. and F. J. Garrison, III, 260–261.
49. *Liberator,* XXI:47, Nov. 21, 1851.

CHAPTER FIFTEEN

Plunder of Mexico—The Free Soil Party

1. For general material on subject of war with Mexico, Texas annexation, and Free Soil Party, see William Birney, pp. 332–356; W. E. Dodd, *Expansion and Conflict* (Boston, 1915), passim; W. P. and F. J. Garrison, II, III, passim; Daniel W. Howe, *Political History of Secession* (New York, 1914), pp. 104–110, 143–158; Robert McNutt Elroy, *The Winning of the Far West* (New York, 1914), pp. 53–85, 130–148, and passim; Schouler, IV, passim; T. C. Smith, *The Liberty and Free Soil Parties,* pp. 69–159; Henry Wilson, I, 587–651, II, 7–17; Alfred H. Bill, *Rehearsal for Conflict* (New York, 1947).

2. The Legislature of Massachusetts resolved in 1843: "That under no circumstances whatsoever can the people of Massachusetts regard the proposition to admit Texas into the Union in any other light than as dangerous to its continuance in peace, in prosperity, and in the enjoyment of those blessings which it is the object of a free government to secure. (*Acts and Resolves Passed by the Legislature of Massachusetts,* Chap. XX, 1843, pp. 68–69.)

In the following year the state took a militant stand: "1. Resolved, That the power to unite an independent foreign state with the United States is not among the powers delegated to the general government by the constitution of the United States. 2. Resolved, That the Commonwealth of Massachusetts, faithful to the compact between the people of the United States, . . . is sincerely anxious for its preservation, but that it is determined, as it doubts not the other states are, to submit to undelegated powers in no body of men on earth: That the project of the annexation of Texas, unless arrested on the threshold, may tend to drive these states into a dissolution of the Union, and will furnish new calumnies against republican governments by exposing the gross contradictions of a people professing to be free, and yet seeking to extend and perpetuate the subjection of their slaves." (Ibid., Chap. LXXXVII, 1844, p. 319.)

3. Manuscript letter, Jan. 23, 1846. (Boston Public Library.)

4. William Ellery Channing, *A Letter to the Hon. Henry Clay on the Annexation of Texas to the United States* (Boston, 1837), p. 37.

5. W. P. and F. J. Garrison, II, 130; III, 134–149.

6. *Liberator*, XV:45, Nov. 7, 1845.

7. Henry Wilson, I, 485.

8. Manuscript letters, Feb. 24, Feb. 25, 1845. (Boston Public Library.)

9. Joshua R. Giddings, *History of the Rebellion* (New York, 1864), pp. 326–327.

10. For meeting see *Liberator*, XV:45, Nov. 7, 1845; for speech, ibid., XV:49, Dec. 5, 1845.

11. Webster, "Speech on the Oregon Question, Nov. 7, 1845," XIII, 322–323.

12. Hermann E. Von Holst, *John C. Calhoun* (Boston, 1900), p. 276; James D. Richardson, *Messages and Papers of the Presidents* (Wash., D. C., 1896–1899), IV, 442.

13. John W. Chadwick, *Theodore Parker*, pp. 237–238.

14. Lowell, "The Biglow Papers, No. 1," *Complete Poetical Works*, pp. 181–182.

15. *Commonwealth History of Massachusetts*, IV, 337; see also Massachusetts Anti-Slavery Society, *Fifteenth Annual Report*, 1847, pp. 9, 17–19.

16. Hume, p. 44.

17. Henry Wilson, II, 153.

18. *Congressional Globe*, 29th Congress, 1st Session, 1845–46, Aug. 8, 1846, XV, 1214, 1217.

19. McElroy, p. 317; Carl Schurz, *Life of Henry Clay* (Boston, 1899), II, 344.

20. *Congressional Globe*, Appendix, 29th Congress, 2nd Session, Feb. 8, 1847, XVI, 315, passim.

21. W. P. and F. J. Garrison, III, 216–217; John Caldwell Calhoun, *Works*, ed. Richard K. Crallé (New York, 1857), IV, 343–344.

22. Wendell Phillips, "Everything Helps Us," *Liberty Bell*, 1849, p. 284.

23. *Liberator*, XVIII:12, March 24, 1848.

24. Ibid., XVIII:22, June 2, 1848.

25. Ibid., XIX:20, May 18, 1849.

26. Ibid., XIX:33, Aug. 17, 1849.

27. Ibid., XIX:22, June 1, 1849.

28. Theodore C. Smith, p. 126.

29. Ibid., p. 128.

30. Macy, p. 93; T. C. Smith, p. 140.

31. Allan Nevins, *Ordeal of the Union*, 2 vols. (New York, 1947), I, 207.

32. "Campaign of 1848," *Free Soil Songs for the People* (Boston, 1848) front cover.

33. Nevins, *Ordeal of the Union*, I, 209–210.

34. *Liberator*, XIX:3, Jan. 19, 1849.

35. See manuscript letter of J. G. Whittier, Note 7 in Appendix. (New York Public Library, 42nd Street.)

36. *Liberator*, XVIII:38, Sept. 22, 1848.

37. Ibid., XVIII:22, June 2, 1848.

38. Ibid., XXIII:21, May 27, 1853.
39. Copy of letter to Mrs. F. H. Drake of Leominster, Oct. 11, 1849. (Boston Public Library.)
40. Marion G. McDougall, *Fugitive Slaves* (Boston, 1891), pp. 59–60.
41. *Liberator*, XIX:24, June 8, 1849.
42. Ibid., XIX:33, Aug. 17, 1849.
43. New York *Tribune*, Aug. 11, 1848. The report of this speech of Aug. 10 is more emphatic than a similar passage in Webster's speech of Aug. 12 entitled, "Exclusion of Slavery from the Territories" (Webster, X, 44.)

CHAPTER SIXTEEN

Five Bleeding Wounds

1. Theodore H. Hittell, *History of California* (San Francisco, 1885), II, 682, 689–700.
2. *The Seventh Census of the United States: 1850* (Wash., D. C., 1853), I, 972; *The Eighth Census: 1860* (Wash., D. C., 1864), I, 27.
3. Hittell, II, 712, 756–759, 784.
4. James D. Richardson, *Messages and Papers of the Presidents*, V, 18–19.
5. Richard M. Johnston and William H. Browne, *Life of Alexander H. Stephens* (Phila., 1878), p. 237.
6. Herbert D. Foster, *Collected Papers* (Hanover, N. H., 1929), p. 195.
7. See Note 8 in Appendix.
8. Carl Schurz, I, 352–353; Thomas Hart Benton, *Thirty Years' View* (New York, 1866), II, 749.
9. Brainerd Dyer, *Zachary Taylor* (Baton Rouge, 1946), p. 383. Only on the basis of personal pride and jealous hatred of Clay, says Dyer, can Taylor's firm stand be explained. Threats but stirred his fighting spirit. (pp. 390–391.)
10. George Ticknor Curtis, *Life of Daniel Webster* (New York, 1870), II, 473.
11. Schouler, V, 185–186; Franklin B. Sanborn, *Dr. Samuel G. Howe* (New York, 1891), pp. 233–234; Frederick W. Seward, *Reminiscences of a War Time Statesman and Diplomat* (New York, 1916), p. 72. See harsh treatment of Taylor in Allan Nevins' *The Ordeal of the Union*, I, 330-332, and chapters on the Compromise of 1850. One wonders whether that judgment has been influenced by the notion of some historians that the Civil War was an avoidable war and that the Compromise of 1850 was an absolute necessity. In answer to that view see my "Ignoble Ease and Peaceful Sloth, Not Peace," *Phylon*, Fourth Quarter, 1948.
12. Holman Hamilton, *Zachary Taylor* (Indianapolis, 1941), pp. 229–230.
13. Carl Schurz, *Henry Clay*, II, 335.
14. Schouler, V, 164–165.
15. Henry Clay, *Speech of the Hon. Henry Clay delivered in the Senate, Feb. 5 and 6, 1850* (New York, 1850), pp. 4, 11.

16. Christopher Hollis, *The American Heresy* (London, 1927,), pp. 105–106.

17. John C. Calhoun, *Works*, IV, 542–573; Margaret L. Coit, *John C. Calhoun* (Boston, 1950), p. 490.

18. McElroy, p. 336; Rhodes, I, 127; Coit, pp. 491–495.

19. *Congressional Globe*, 31st Congress, 1st Session, March 4, 1850, XIX, Part I, 451–455. In a profoundly interesting article, "John C. Calhoun, Philosopher of Reaction," (*"The Antioch Review,* June, 1943, No. 2, 223–234), Ricard N. Current reveals a startling trend in Calhoun's thought. Historians, Current states, have completely overlooked the key to Calhoun's political philosophy. That key is a concept of the class struggle. He used a terminology and treatment which in many respects anticipated the later "scientific approach of Friedrich Engels and Karl Marx." He started, as Marx and Engels were also to do, with John Locke's so-called labor theory of values. From that assumption he deduced that in all contemporary and historical societies except the most primitive there existed a system of exploitation of a working class. He anticipated a number of other Marxist doctrines: 1) the eventual division of society into only two classes, capitalist and proletarian; 2) the gradual expropriation of the bulk of the population by the capitalists so that the propertied would become fewer and fewer and the property-less more and more numerous; and 3) the ultimate impoverishment of the masses to a bare subsistence level. All this would come through capitalist control and use of the powers of the state. As a result of the exploitation and expropriation of the working class, according to Calhoun, there would follow an inevitable social conflict until it must eventuate in a revolutionary crisis. Calhoun even predicted, Current adds, the defection from the bourgeoisie of leaders to aid the proletariat in its revolutionary struggle. This was an idea to which Marx and Engels attached a great importance in the Communist Manifesto.

Unlimited democracy, according to Calhoun, would be followed by anarchy and then an appeal to force, and finally dictatorship, "monarchy in its absolute form."

On behalf of the planter class he appealed again and again to fellow conservatives among the bankers and manufacturers of the North. "A very slight modification" of the arguments used to attack property in slaves "would make them equally effectual against property of all kinds."

Not only American capitalists but also the British ruling class had a stake in the preservation of Southern slavery. To Calhoun there was no real difference between the subjection of one man to another, as in the South, and the subjection of one class to another, as in the British Isles, or the subjection of one nation to another, as in the British Empire.

"Calhoun's appeal to the Northern capitalist before the Civil War was like Marx's appeal to the Northern workingman after the war had begun: both the great reactionary and the great revolutionary contended that the destruction of capitalism would come only after the destruction of the slave economy."

20. Calhoun, Works, IV, 578; Coit, p. 495.

21. Von Holst, pp. 348–349. As W. E. Dodd stated: "He died the

greatest reactionary of his time." (Quoted in Nevins', *Ordeal of the Union*, I, 157.)

22. *Congressional Globe*, 31st Congress, 1st Session, Part I, 1849–1850, March 7, 1850, XXI, 476; Albert J. Beveridge, *Abraham Lincoln, 1809–1858*, 2 vols. (Boston, 1928), II, 94.

23. Claude M. Fuess, *Daniel Webster*, 2 vols. (Boston, 1930), II, 212.

24. See unfavorable version of Webster's speech in Julian, pp. 86–87.

25. Webster, "The Constitution and the Union," Speech of March 7, 1850, *Writings and Speeches*, X, 57, 58, 82, 84.

26. Ibid., X, 86, 87, 89.

27. Schouler V, 167–169.

28. *Congressional Globe*, 31st Congress, 1st Session, March 7, 1850, Appendix, XIX, part 1, pp. 269–276; Coit, p. 499.

29. Beveridge, II, 124.

30. Claude M. Fuess, "Daniel Webster and the Abolitionists," *Massachusetts Historical Society Proceedings, 1930–32* (Boston, 1932), LXIV, 37.

31. Ralph Waldo Emerson, *The Complete Works of Ralph Waldo Emerson* (Boston and New York, 1918), IX, 399.

32. Ibid., XI, 203–204.

33. Theodore Parker, *Collected Works,* ed. Frances Power Cobbe (London, 1863), V, 115.

34. Wendell Phillips, *Speeches, Lectures, and Letters,* First Series, pp. 260–261.

35. Ibid., p. 167.

36. *Letters on American Slavery* (Boston, 1860), p. 18.

37. Whittier, "Ichabod," *Complete Poetical Works*, p. 230.

38. *Liberator*, XX:30, March 29, 1850.

39. Wendell Phillips, *Review of Webster's Speech on Slavery* (Boston, 1850), pp. 26–30, 42–44.

40. Frederick Bancroft, *The Life of William H. Seward* (New York, 1900), I, 241.

41. *Congressional Globe*, 31st Congress, 1st Session, March 11, 1850, XIX, Appendix, pp. 262–265.

42. Schouler, V, 170–171.

43. *Congressional Globe*, 31st Congress, 1st Session, March 11, 1850, Appendix, XIX, pp. 262–265.

44. Bancroft, *Life of William H. Seward*, I, 252.

45. Ibid., I, 253.

46. Ibid., I, 253.

47. *Congressional Globe*, 31st Congress, 1st Session, April 17, 1850, XIX, Part I, pp. 602–604, 762–764; July 30, 1850, XIX, Part II, pp. 1480–1481.

48. Ibid., XIX, Part I, pp. 762–764; Julian, pp. 91–92.

49. Julian, p. 92; Coit, p. 498.

50. Elbert B. Smith, "Thomas Hart Benton, Southern Realist," *The American Historical Review* (July, 1953), LVIII, No. 4, p. 806.

51. Ibid., p. 796.

52. Rhodes, I, 169.

53. Julian, pp. 92–93.

CHAPTER SEVENTEEN
Bowery Toughs

1. New York *Herald,* May 7, 1850. See also issues of May 6, 8, 9.
2. *Liberator,* XX:20, May 17, 1850.
3. Swift, p. 284.
4. For report of speeches and disturbances at meeting see *Liberator,* XX:20, May 17, 1850.
5. New York *Daily Tribune,* May 9, 1850. Though unfriendly to the Abolitionists, this paper, unlike the *Globe* and the *Herald,* took a splendid stand on the rights of free speech. Its language was studded with the blackest plums of denunciation. Rynders was "a notorious pimp and gamblers' decoy duck, who seems to have pretty much run out here," and his followers "simply knaves who plot the overthrow of the Right of Free Speech and Opinion as coolly as a Malay pirate would fire a vessel containing five hundred human beings, in the hope of possessing himself of a back-load of copper sheathing from her ruins. . . . Our Authorities have not done their duty in the premises. . . . Whoever goes into a building so hired, a meeting so called, to disturb, interrupt, and arrest the proceedings of those rightfully in possession, is morally a burglar and thief, essentially a tyrant and a scoundrel, who should be ornamented with ruffles on his wrists and sent to prison before he could utter a second cry."
6. Barrows, p. 192.
7. Hibben, p. 151.
8. *Liberator,* XX:21, May 24, 1850.
9. Henry W. Beecher, *Wendell Phillips* (New York, 1884), p. 421.
10. *Liberator,* XX:21, May 24, 1850.
11. Ibid., XX:21, May 24, 1850.
12. Ibid., XX:21, May 24, 1850.
13. Ibid., XX:21, May 24, 1850.
14. Ibid., XX:24, June 14, 1850.
15. Ibid., XX:24, June 14, 1850; XX:26, June 28, 1850.
16. Ibid., XX:25, June 21, 1850.
17. Ibid., XX:25, June 21, 1850.
18. Ibid., XX:30, July 26, 1850.
19. Philip S. Foner, *Business and Slavery* (Chapel Hill, N. C., 1941), pp. 1–5.
20. Ibid., pp. 5, 6, 7, 88, 105.
21. Ibid., pp. 148, 161, 168.

CHAPTER EIGHTEEN
"Hush, don't agitate!"

1. Dyer, 406; Rhodes, I, 176–177.
2. Dyer, p. 408. Said the British minister in Washington: "His intentions were always good, his word could always be relied upon; his

manners were downright, simple, and straightforward. . ." (Dyer, pp. 408–409.) A desideratum in political circles. Of how many leading politicians could the same be said?

3. Rhodes, I, 184.

4. *Congressional Globe*, 31st Congress, 1st Session, Sept. 12, 1850, XXI, Part II, pp. 1806–1807.

5. See, for example, Emmett D. Preston, "The Fugitive Slave Acts in Ohio," *Journal of Negro History* (Oct. 1943), XXVIII, No. 4, pp. 422–477.

6. Richardson, V, 629, Dec. 3, 1860. As Prof. Nevins remarks: "Later events clearly demonstrated that it was impossible to enforce the Fugitive Slave Law in communities which universally regarded it as improper and wicked. No enactment, as men learned again in prohibition days, can be made valid in a district whose people regard it as morally indefensible and materially injurious." (Nevins, *Ordeal of the Union*, I, 302.)

7. Wilbur Henry Siebert, *The Underground Railroad* (New York, 1918), p. 246.

8. Ibid., p. 249.

9. Allen Chamberlain, "Old Passages of Boston's Underground Railroad," *Magazine of History* (Tarrytown, N. Y., 1926), Extra No. 124, XXXI, No. 4, p. 37.

10. Manuscript letter to J. Miller McKim, Feb. 8, 1858. (Cornell University Library.)

11. Chamberlain, p. 39.

12. Daniel Dulany Addison, *The Clergy in American Life and Letters* (London, 1900), pp. 253–254.

13. Cochran, p. 187.

14. Wendell Phillips, *Speeches, Lectures, and Letters*, First Series, p. 91.

15. Charles Sumner, *His Complete Works* (Boston, 1910), III, 129–130.

16. Beveridge, II, 134–135.

17. Webster, "Speech at Capon Springs, Va., June 28, 1851," *Writings and Speeches*, XIII, 435.

18. "Letter to Franklin Haven, Sept. 5, 1850," Ibid., XVI, 561.

19. Fuess, "Daniel Webster and the Abolitionists," *Massachusetts Historical Society Proceedings* (Boston, 1932), LXIV, 38.

20. Webster, "Remarks at Boston, April 29, 1850," *Writings and Speeches*, XIII, 387. For other examples of the same sentiment see "Letter to the Citizens of Medford" (XII, 237–238), "Letter to the Citizens on the Kennebec River" (XII, 241–242). Speeches and Letters throughout 1850 and 1851 constantly stress the note: "*Union, Union, Union*, now and forever!" (Speech in Front of the Revere House, April 22, 1851, XIII, 407.)

21. Johnston and Browne, p. 254.

22. Webster, "Letter to Francis Brinley, April 19, 1850," *Writings and Speeches*, XVI, 609–610.

23. *Exercises at the Dedication of the Statue of Wendell Phillips* (Boston, 1916), p. 21.

24. Fuess, Daniel Webster, II, 288–289.

25. Theodore Parker, *A Discourse Occasioned by the Death of Daniel*

Webster, Oct. 31, 1852 (Boston, 1853), pp. 66, 69, 70, 81, 97; Fuess, "Daniel Webster and the Abolitionists," LXIV, 39.

26. *Liberty Bell,* 1853; see also *Liberator,* XXII:52, Dec. 24, 1852.
27. Phillips is giving a free translation of the French.
28. *Liberty Bell,* 1853; see also *Liberator,* XXII:52, Dec. 24, 1852.

CHAPTER NINETEEN

Stealers of Men

1. *Liberator,* XX:27, Nov. 22, 1850.
2. "Welcome to George Thompson," *Speeches, Lectures, and Letters, Second Series,* pp. 24–39.
3. Manuscript letter to Elizabeth Pease, March 9, 1851. (Boston Public Library.)
4. Proceedings of the soirée in W. P. and F. J. Garrison, III, 318–320; Goldwin Smith, pp. 157–158.
5. Henry Wilson, II, 330–331; Richardson, V, 104–105. President Fillmore condemned the rescue in angry tones: "Nothing could be more unexpected than that such a gross violation of law, such a high-handed contempt of the authority of the United States should be perpetrated by a band of lawless confederates at noonday in the city of Boston and in the very temple of justice. (Ibid., V, 101.)
6. Austin Bearse, *Reminiscences of Fugitive Slave Days* (Boston, 1880), pp. 17–18.
7. Rhodes, I, 220; John Weiss, *Life and Correspondence of Theodore Parker,* 2 vols. (New York, 1864), II, 103; Frothingham, *Theodore Parker,* p. 412.
8. Charles P. Greenough, "The Rendition of Thomas Sims," *Massachusetts Historical Society Proceedings, 1921–1922* (Boston, 1923), LV, 342.
9. *Twentieth Report of the Massachusetts Anti-Slavery Society* (Boston, 1852), pp. 20, 22.
10. *Liberator,* XXI:15, April 11, 1851.
11. Rhodes, I, 212; Weiss, II, 104; Frothingham, pp. 413–414.
12. Austin Bearse, p. 26.
13. Austin, *Wendell Phillips,* p. 140.
14. Vincent Y. Bowditch, *The Life and Correspondence of Henry Ingersoll Bowditch* (Boston, 1902), I, 221–222; Bearse, pp. 27–28.
15. Bearse, p. 29.
16. Ibid., p. 26.
17. *Liberator,* XXI:18, May 2, 1851.
18. Ibid., XXI:18, May 2, 1851.
19. Theodore Parker, *A Discourse to Commemorate the Rendition of Thomas Sims* (Boston, 1852), p. 48.
20. Henrietta Dana Skinner, *An Echo from Parnassus* (New York, 1928), p. 154.
21. *Liberator,* XXI:23, June 6, 1851.
22. Ibid., XXI:33, August 15, 1851.
23. Ibid., XXI:33, August 15, 1851.

CHAPTER TWENTY

Twin Reforms: Woman Suffrage and Teetotalism

1. Robinson, p. 25.
2. Manuscript letter to Miss May, Feb. 3, n.d. (New York Historical Society.)
3. Lillie Buffum Chace Wyman, *American Chivalry* (Boston, 1913), p. 91.
4. Alice Felt Tyler, *Freedom's Ferment* (Minneapolis, Minn., 1944), pp. 434–435.
5. *The Southern Literary Messenger* (Richmond, Va.), vols. XXXIV–XXXV, July–August, 1862, p. 511.
6. Manuscript letter, Jan. 1866. (Dall Collection, Massachusetts Historical Society.)
7. "Woman's Rights," *Speeches, Lectures, and Letters*, First Series, pp. 15–16.
8. The discussion of the "sphere" of woman now seems, to put it mildly, dated—in the opinion of women today, prehistoric.
9. "Woman's Rights," pp. 29–31.
10. Ibid., pp. 31–34.
11. Aaron Macy Powell, *Personal Reminiscences* (New York, 1899), pp. 90–91.
12. Story told by Mrs. Lucy Stone. Quoted in Martyn, pp. 247–248.
13. George F. Clarke, *History of the Temperance Reform in Massachusetts* (Boston, 1888), p. 35.
14. Ibid., pp. 45–46.
15. Ibid., p. 52.
16. Alice Felt Tyler, p. 344.
17. Rheta C. Dorr, *Susan B. Anthony* (New York, 1928), p. 62.
18. Ibid., p. 63.
19. John Allen Krout, *The Origins of Prohibition* (New York, 1925), pp. 253–255.
20. *Liberator*, II:32, Aug. 11, 1832.

CHAPTER TWENTY-ONE

Guest of the Nation

1. *Liberator*, XXI:45, Nov. 7, 1851.
2. Rhodes, I, 233; P. C. Headley, *The Life of Louis Kossuth* (Auburn, 1852), pp. 246–247.
3. Rhodes, I, 231–236.
4. Ibid., I, 237; John W. Oliver, "Louis Kossuth's Appeal to the Middle West," *The Mississippi Valley Historical Review* (Cedar Rapids, Iowa. 1928), XIV, No. 4, 481.
5. Oliver, p. 495.
6. Jane Gray Swisshelm, *Half a Century* (Chicago, 1880), p. 96.
7. Phillips, *Speeches, Lectures, and Letters*, Second Series, p. 44.

8. Ibid., pp. 46, 48.

9. Ibid., pp. 52–53, 68.

10. Manuscript letter, April 27, 1852. (Sumner Collection, Harvard College Library.)

11. Lajos Kossuth, *Kossuth in New England* (Boston, 1852), p. 86.

12. *Congressional Globe*, 32nd Congress, 1st Session, July 8, 1852, XXI, part 2, p. 1692.

CHAPTER TWENTY-TWO

A Best Seller

1. Phillips, "Public Opinion," *Speeches, Lectures, and Letters,* First Series, p. 36.

2. Today that statement needs drastic qualification. For radio and television have definitely undermined the power of the press and usurped the throne.

3. Phillips, "Public Opinion," *Speeches, Lectures, and Letters,* First Series, pp. 41, 46.

4. Ibid., I, 44–45, 51–52.

5. Phillips, "Surrender of Sims," *Speeches, Lectures, and Letters,* First Series, p. 59.

6. Ibid., pp. 63–64.

7. *Liberator*, XXII:6, Feb. 6, 1852.

8. Harriet Beecher Stowe, *The Life of Harriet Beecher Stowe,* compiled from her letters and journals by her son, Charles Edward Stowe (Boston and New York, 1891), p. 327.

9. Florine T. McCray, *The Life and Work of the Author of Uncle Tom's Cabin* (New York, 1889), p. 12.

10. New York *Independent,* Aug. 26, 1852. "Will it not make also in time," asked the *Independent,* "two million of emigrants?"; McCray, p. 117.

11. Ibid., p. 109.

12. Rhodes, I, 282.

13. Hillis, pp. 144–145.

14. Beveridge, II, 138.

15. Charles E. Stowe and Lyman B. Stowe, *Harriet Beecher Stowe* (Boston, 1911), p. 173.

16. Rhodes, I, 284.

17. Beveridge, II, 139–140.

18. McCray, p. 106.

19. Grimké, p. 351.

20. Jesse Macy, p. 132.

21. Phillips, "Sims Anniversary," *Speeches, Lectures, and Letters,* First Series, pp. 79–82.

22. Ibid., pp. 82, 84.

23. Ibid., pp. 85–86.

24. Ibid., pp. 90–92.

25. Samuel J. May, *The Fugitive Slave Law and Its Victims* (New York, 1861), pp. 23, 49.

CHAPTER TWENTY-THREE

Horace Mann and Phillips—"Infidels" and "Female Pests"

1. Phillips, "The Philosophy of the Abolition Movement," *Speeches, Lectures, and Letters,* First Series, I, 107.
2. Ibid., pp. 109–110.
3. Ibid., pp. 114–115.
4. Ibid., p. 138.
5. *Liberator,* March and April, 1853; see also George A. Hubbell, *Horace Mann* (Phila., 1910), pp. 159–160.
6. Hubbell, p. 220.
7. *Liberator,* XXIII:18, May 6, 1853.
8. Ibid., XXIII:18, May 6, 1853.
9. Ibid., XXIII:21, May 27, 1853.
10. Ibid., XXIII:21, May 27, 1853.
11. Ibid., XXIII:21, May 27, 1853.
12. Ibid., XXIII:21, May 27, 1853.
13. Ibid., XXIII: issues of Sept. 1853.
14. New York *Daily Times,* Sept. 8, 1853. See also issues of Sept. 6, 7.
15. New York *Herald,* Sept. 7, 1853. See also issues of Sept. 3, 4, 5, 6 for tart editorial comments.
16. Martyn, p. 262.

CHAPTER TWENTY-FOUR

Philosopher of Agitation

1. Phillips, "Public Opinion," *Speeches, Lectures, and Letters,* First Series, p. 54.
2. Ibid., p. 45.
3. Phillips, "Daniel O'Connell," Ibid., Second Series, p. 397.
4. Phillips, "Public Opinion," Ibid., First Series, p. 45.
5. Phillips, "Daniel O'Connell," Ibid., Second Series, pp. 398–399.
6. Martyn, p. 183.
7. Phillips, "Daniel O'Connell, "*Speeches, Lectures, and Letters,* Second Series, pp. 399–400.
8. *Liberator,* XXIX:18, May 6, 1859.
9. Ibid., XXVIII:22, May 28, 1858.
10. Ibid., XIX:20, May 18, 1849.
11. Phillips, "Public Opinion," op. cit., First Series, pp. 52–53.
12. Ibid., pp. 53–54.
13. *Liberator,* XXVII:33, Aug. 14, 1857, speech of Aug. 1, 1857.
14. Speech of July 4, 1855, at Framingham, *Liberator,* XXV:32, Aug. 10, 1855.
15. *National Standard,* May 27, 1871.
16. *Liberator,* XXX:23, June 8, 1860.
17. Phillips, "Daniel O'Connell," op. cit., Second Series, pp. 401–402.
18. Ibid., pp. 401–402.

CHAPTER TWENTY-FIVE

Animated Conversation

1. Thomas W. Higginson, *Wendell Phillips* (Boston, 1884), p. 12.
2. *Liberator*, XXVII:12, March 20, 1857.
3. Martyn, p. 500.
4. *Andover Review*, March, 1844, in *Memorials of Wendell Phillips*, book of clippings. (Boston Public Library.)
5. Wyman, p. 15.
6. *Andover Review* in op. cit.
7. Lowell, "Letter from Boston," *Complete Works*, p. 112.
8. Higginson, pp. 12–13.
9. Wyman, p. 4.
10. Martyn, p. 497.
11. Phillips, "Idols," *Speeches, Lectures, and Letters*, First Series, pp. 253–254.
12. Powell, p. 83.
13. Stafford, p. 19.
14. Stearns, *Sketches from Concord and Appledore*, pp. 202–203.
15. Ibid., p. 203.
16. Ralph Waldo Emerson, *Journals of Ralph Waldo Emerson*, Edited by Edward Waldo Emerson and Waldo Emerson Forbes (Boston and New York, 1912), 1844, VI, 542. Emerson goes on to say: "The first and the second and the third part of art is to keep your feet always firm on a fact. They (Webster and Everett) talk about the Whig Party. There is no such thing in Nature. They talk about the Constitution. It is a scorned piece of paper. He feels after a fact, and finds it in the money-making, in the commerce of New England, and in the devotion of the Slave States to their interest which enforces them to the crimes which they avow or disavow, but do and will do. He keeps no terms with sham churches or shamming legislatures, and must and will grope till he feels the stones. Then his other and better part, his subsoil, is the morale which he solidly shows. Eloquence, poetry, friendship, philosophy, politics, in short all power must and will have the real, or they cannot exist. (Ibid., 1844, VI, 542–543.) See also IX, 250 (1859) and IX, 455 (1862): "When Phillips speaks, Garrison observes delighted the effect on the audience and seems to see and hear everything except Phillips, is the only one in the audience who does not hear and understand Phillips." See also Note 9 in Appendix; Stafford, p. 20.
17. Paul R. Frothingham, *Edward Everett* (Boston, 1925), pp. 394–395.
18. Claude M. Fuess, *Rufus Choate* (New York, 1928), p. 231.

19. Prentiss' addresses were show pieces in a florid style then acceptable to people everywhere. But he was able to deliver the most purple of passages naturally and sincerely. To the question of his friend Judge George Winchester as to how he was able to express so many figures of speech and flights of fancy, Prentiss replied—"When I get to speaking and become excited, I am like a little boy walking through a meadow when he sees a beautiful butterfly, with its fancy wings of gold, and starts in pursuit eager to capture his glittering prize; then in the race up jumps another, and still another until the whole sky is filled with beautiful butterflies, each a new one, capable of attracting the boy's attention. So with me, each fancy starts a new one till in the pursuit my whole mind is filled with beautiful butterflies." (Dallas C. Dickey, Seargent S. Prentiss, Whig Orator of the Old South, Baton Rouge, La., 1945, pp. 342–346.) (Today we demand a mind filled with something more substantial and significant than butterflies.)

20. James Bryce, The American Commonwealth (New York, 1901), II, 807.

CHAPTER TWENTY-SIX

"We are one, you know,"

1. Statement of Dr. Samuel A. Green, an old friend of Phillips and quoted in Martyn, p. 190.

2. Memorial Sketch of Ann Phillips, p. 15.

3. Martyn, p. 191. So Martyn was told by a Mrs. Bannard of Long Branch, New Jersey.

4. Ibid., p. 513. We may assume that Martyn is relying on personal reminiscences or again on statements made to him by personal friends of Ann and Wendell Phillips.

5. Ibid., p. 192.

6. Manuscript letter, Jan. 31, 1846. (Boston Public Library.)

7. Manuscript letter to Elizabeth Pease, Jan. 31, 1846; Jan. 31, 1847. (Boston Public Library.)

8. Manuscript letters: Oct. 1846 to Elizabeth Pease; June 29, 1842, to the Rev. Samuel May; Aug. 20, 1847, to Mrs. Garrison; Sept. 25, 1874, to Frank Garrison; Dec. 1842, to R. D. Webb. (Boston Public Library.)

9. Wyman, p. 10.

10. Manuscript letter, n.d. (Boston Public Library.)

11. From statements made to Martyn by Mrs. John T. Sargent, Dr. David Thayer (Phillips's family physician), and others. Martyn, p. 197.

12. Manuscript letter, Oct. 24, 1867. (Massachusetts Historical Society.) This writer must confess his eyes have suffered considerably from Phillips's parsimony.

13. Higginson, p. 15.

CHAPTER TWENTY-SEVEN

On Freedom's Southern Line

1. Roy F. Nichols, *Franklin Pierce* (Phila., 1931), pp. 234–236;
Schouler, V, 270–271.
2. Renzo D. Bowers, *The Inaugural Addresses of the Presidents* (St.
Louis, Mo., 1929), pp. 223–224.
3. Richardson, V, 222.
4. Schouler, V, 280.
5. Rose Strunsky, *Abraham Lincoln* (New York, 1914), p. 85.
6. *Congressional Globe*, 33rd Congress, 1st Session, Jan. 4 and Jan.
23, 1854, XXVIII, Part I, pp. 221–222; Strunsky, p. 85.
7. *Congressional Globe*, 1st Session, Speech of Jan. 30, 1854, XXVIII,
275–280, and the debate of March 3, 1854, XXX, New Series, 327–328,
Appendix, especially, p. 338.
8. Moorfield Storey, *Charles Sumner* (Boston, 1900), pp. 105–106;
Nevins, II, 105–106.
9. For heated remarks on Chase's address, see *Congressional Globe*,
33rd Congress, 1st Session, Jan. 30, 1854, XXVIII, Part I, pp. 275–276.
10. New York *Evening Post*, Jan. 7, 1854.
11. Rhodes, I, 429.
12. Samuel E. Morison, *The Oxford History of the United States* (London, 1928), II, 124.
13. W. E. Dodd, *Expansion and Conflict*, p. 240.
14. Henry Wilson, II, 393.
15. Speech of March 7, 1854 in the Tabernacle reported in the New
York *Evening Post* of March 8, 1854.
16. Rhodes, I, 500.
17. Washington Correspondent, New York *Daily Times*, Feb. 2, 1854.
18. James Redpath, *The Roving Editor* (New York, 1859), p. 37.
19. As Professor Nevins in effect states: Douglas's leading arguments
rested on unsound foundations or were streaked with half truths. "It was
not a fact that in laying down a certain line the Missouri Compromise
had established a 'geographical' principle which should later have been
applied to the area wrested from Mexico," nor had the Utah-New Mexico
legislation in the Compromise of 1850 established a new "principle"
which must be extended to all other Territories. If the Compromise of
1850 had been regarded as repealing the Missouri Compromise, it would
have been defeated. By no means was it evident, as Douglas maintained,
that climate, soil, and other physiographic conditions made Kansas an
impossible ground for slavery. Parts of it were not manifestly less suited to
a slave economy than Delaware, Maryland, Kentucky, or Missouri where
slavery existed. Again: "When Douglas said he supposed no man in
Congress believed that Kansas could be made permanently slave soil, he
gave an erroneous view of the facts. The fact was many so believed."
(Nevins, *Ordeal of the Union*, II, 108, 115–117.)

20.   Theodore Parker, *The New Crime against Humanity* (Boston, 1854), pp. 39–40.

21.   Rhodes, I, 469–470.

22.   Ibid., I, 470.

23.   Charles Sumner, *Recent Speeches and Addresses* (Boston, 1857), pp. 321–322.

24.   *Congressional Globe*, 33rd Congress, 1st Session, XXX, New Series, Appendix, pp. 331, 337. For Douglas's speech see pp. 325–338; Daniel W. Howe, pp. 206–213; Rhodes, I, 473–474; Beveridge, II, 206–207, 209.

25.   Rhodes, I, 476.

26.   Ibid., I, 495.

27.   As Granville D. Davis points out in "Douglas and the Chicago Mob," (*American Historical Review*, LIV, No. 3, April, 1949, pp. 553–556), he did not say: "It is Sunday morning; I have to go to Church, and you may go to hell!" for the meeting was held on Friday evening, Sept. 1, 1854.

28.   Carl Wittke, *Refugees of Revolution* (Phila., 1952). p. 196.

29.   S. D. Carpenter, *Logic of History* (Madison, Wisc., 1864), p. 91.

30.   Eli Thayer, *A History of the Kansas Crusade* (New York, 1889), p. 15; Frank W. Blackmar, *The Life of Charles Robinson* (Topeka, Kansas, 1902), p. 94.

31.   Ibid., p. 162.

32.   Whittier, "The Kansas Emigrants," *Complete Poetical Works*, pp. 391–392.

33.   Thayer, p. 282; Hill Peebles Wilson, *John Brown, Soldier of Fortune* (Boston, 1918), p. 65.

34.   Wilson, p. 65), Thayer, p. 187.

35.   Lyman Abbott, *Henry Ward Beecher* (Boston and New York, 1903), pp. 211–212; Paxton Hibben, *Henry Ward Beecher*, p. 159.

36.   Manuscript subscription list. See list in Note 10 in Appendix. (Massachusetts Historical Society.)

37.   Addison, p. 257. Prof. Nevins clearly states the social and economic factors in the Kansas crisis: "Indeed it may be said that the battle for Kansas was fought and won years before any settler put foot on her soil or Atchinson and Thayer began to rally their respective camps. It was won when the population of the Ohio Valley and the middle country generally accepted the principle that slavery injures a pioneering race of small farmers growing mixed crops." (Nevins, *Ordeal of the Union*, II, 304–306, 382.)

38.   *Liberator*, XXIV:20, May 19, 1954.

39.   Ibid., XXIV:20, May 19, 1854.

40.   Ibid., XXIV:20, May 19, 1854.

41.   But the Union made possible, by the dominance of law and order, that wheat could be grown in Illinois and the West settled.

42.   *Liberator*, XXIV:20, May 19, 1854.

43.   Ibid., XXIV:21, May 26, 1854.

CHAPTER TWENTY-EIGHT

Sons of Otis and Hancock

1. Charles F. Adams, *Richard Henry Dana* (Boston, 1891), I, 262–263.
2. Henry Steele Commager, *Theodore Parker* (Boston, 1936), pp. 232–233; Rhodes, I, 500.
3. Rhodes, I, 500, 501.
4. John Weiss, *Life and Correspondence of Theodore Parker* (New York, 1864), II, 134.
5. Ibid., II, 134; see also *The Boston Slave Riot and Trial of Anthony Burns* (Boston, 1854), p. 40.
6. *The Boston Slave Riot and Trial of Anthony Burns*, p. 7; Charles E. Stevens, *Anthony Burns* (Boston, 1856), p. 33.
7. *Liberator*, XXIV, June 2, 1854.
8. Ibid., XXIV:22, June 2, 1854; see also *The Boston Slave Riot and Trial of Anthony Burns*, p. 9; Stevens, pp. 289–295.
9. *Liberator*, XXIV:22, June 2, 1854; Stevens, p. 295; *The Boston Slave Riot and Trial of Anthony Burns*, p. 9.
10. *Liberator*, XXIV:22, June 2, 1854; Stevens, pp. 40–41; *The Boston Slave Riot and Trial of Anthony Burns*, pp. 9–10.
11. Ibid.
12. *The Boston Slave Riot and Trial of Anthony Burns*, pp. 9–10.
13. Ibid., pp. 10–11; Skinner, p. 162.
14. Dr. Frederick L. Willis, *Alcott Memoirs* (Boston, 1915), pp. 73–74.
15. Rhodes, I, 501–503; Weiss, II, 128.
16. See Manuscript letter to Higginson, Note 11 in Appendix. (Boston Public Library.)
17. Mark A. De Wolfe Howe, *Boston* (New York, 1907), p. 216.
18. Commager, pp. 236–238.
19. Manuscript letter, May 30, 1854. (Boston Public Library.)
20. Willis, p. 75.
21. Rhodes, I, 503–506.
22. Commager, pp. 240–242.
23. *Liberator*, XXIV:23, June 9, 1854.
24. George W. Smalley, *Anglo-American Memories*, First Series (London, 1911), pp. 33–34.
25. Commager, p. 240.
26. W. P. and F. J. Garrison, III, 410–411.
27. Rhodes, I, 506.
28. Manuscript letter to Higginson, June 14, 1854. (Boston Public Library.)
29. Swift, pp. 306–307.
30. *Liberator*, XXIV:28, July 14, 1854.
31. Manuscript letter to Wendell Phillips, quoted in Martyn, p. 274.
32. Weiss, II, 147.

CHAPTER TWENTY-NINE

"Sir, I am a Fanatic"

1. Quoted in Bearse, p. 13.
2. Phillips, "Removal of Judge Loring," *Speeches, Lectures, and Letters*, First Series, pp. 154–212. See also *Liberator*, XXV:8, 9, 10, 11, 12, Feb. 23, March 2, 9, 16, 23, 1855.
3. *Liberator*, XXV:8, 9, Feb. 23, March 2, 1855.
4. See *Report of the Joint Committee of Federal Relations of the House of Representatives on the Removal of Judge Loring* (Massachusetts Historical Society). The reasons assigned in the Address of the two branches of the Legislature for the removal of Loring were: "1. Because he consented to sit as United States Commissioner in definance of the moral sentiment of Massachusetts as expressed in the Legislative Resolves of 1850; 2. Because now, in defiance of the provisions contained in section 13 of Chapter CDLXXXIX of the Acts of 1855 (an act which the Legislature had adopted, declaring that certain offices under the government of the United States were incompatible with offices of honor, emolument, and trust in this Commonwealth), Edward G. Loring continues to hold the office of judge of probate, under a Massachusetts commission, and at the same time hold in defiance of law a commission under the United States which qualifies him to issue warrants and grant certificates under the acts of Congress." (Massachusetts *Statutes, Acts and Resolves*, 1855, pp. 924–929; ibid., 1857, pp. 766–772.)

The Attorney General declared the Act of 1855 "obnoxious . . . and clearly repugnant to the provisions of the Constitution of the United States." (Ibid., 1855, pp. 1011–1012.) And Governor Gardner in his veto was equally forthright: "To the allegation that Judge Loring has shocked the popular sentiment of Massachusetts, it may be pertinent to ask what the duty of judges is. Are they to expound the laws as made by the law-making power; or are they to construe them in accordance with popular sentiment? When the time arrives that a judge so violates his oath of office as to shape his decisions according to the fluctuations of popular feeling, we become a government not of laws but of men. . . . The error, if error it be considered, was a mistake. Is a judge then to be removed from one office because in another capacity he made an erroneous decision?" (Ibid., 1856. p. 333. For message see pp. 325–335.) Governor Gardner contended if the removal was to be effected, it should be only by impeachment. (Ibid., 1857, pp. 766–772.) For removal by Governor Banks see Ibid., 1858, pp. 186–191.
5. *Liberator*, XXVIII, 13, March 26, 1858.
6. *Acts and Resolves*, 1855, pp. 924–929.
7. *Liberator*, XXVI:32, Aug. 8, 1856
8. Phillips, "Capital Punishment," *Speeches, Lectures, and Letters*, Second Series, p. 97.
9. It is a paradox that the most humane of criminal law reformers are *logically* the most cruel. For if life imprisonment is severer than capital punishment, why advocate the former? If duration is more important than punishment of death, why criticize punishment of death?

See Beccaria, *An Essay on Crimes and Punishments,* with a commentary by M. de Voltaire (Edinburgh, 1778), pp. 167–168.

10. Phillips, "Capital Punishment," in op. cit, pp. 99–101.

11. G. T. Garratt, *Lord Brougham* (London, 1935), pp. 78–80, 341.

12. Phillips, *Speeches, Lectures, and Letters,* Second Series, pp. 107–109.

13. New York *Daily News,* May 12, 1855.

14. *Liberator,* XXV:21, May 25, 1855.

15. Ibid., XXV:23, June 8, 1855.

16. Ibid., XXV:33, Aug. 17, 1855.

17. Phillips, "The Boston Mob," *Speeches, Lectures, and Letters,* First Series, pp. 219–220, 226–227.

18. Phillips, "The Pilgrims," ibid., First Series, pp. 235–236.

CHAPTER THIRTY

Barbarism at the Capitol—The Mother of Isms

1. Hillis, p. 104.

2. John S. Barry, *A Historical Sketch of the Town of Hanover* (Boston, 1853), pp. 319–335. Nicholas Jacob (or Jacobs) migrated from England to America in 1633.

3. Howe, p. 265.

4. Ibid., p. 266; *Congressional Globe,* 34th Congress, 1st Session, Appendix, XXV, 534.

5. Ibid., 34th Congress, 1st Session, Appendix, XXV, 530; Howe, pp. 266–267.

6. *Congressional Globe,* Appendix, XXV, 545.

7. Ibid., Appendix, XXV, 544–545; Howe, pp. 268–269.

8. *Congressional Globe,* 34th Congress, 1st Session, Appendix, XXV, 547.

9. Storey, pp. 145–146; Howe, p. 271; George W. Haynes, *Charles Sumner* (Phila., 1909), p. 204.

10. *Congressional Globe,* 34th Congress, 1st Session, Part 2, pp. 1306, 1304–1305; Howe, pp. 271–272.

11. *Congressional Globe,* 34th Congress, 1st Session, July 14, 1856, Appendix, XXV, 831–833.

12. Ibid., 34th Congress, 1st Session, Speech of June 21, 1856, Appendix, XXV, 656.

13. Howe, pp. 273–275.

14. Ibid., p. 275.

15. T. C. Smith, p. 158.

16. Howe, pp. 275–276.

17. Charles Sumner, *His Complete Works* (Boston, 1910), V. 257.

18. Haynes, p. 214.

19. Howe, pp. 276–277.

20. *Liberator,* XXVI:22, May 30, 1856.

21. Ibid., XXVI:23, June 6, 1856.

22. Phillips, "Charles Sumner," *Johnson's New Universal Cyclopaedia* (New York, 1881), IV, 656.

23. Manuscript letters, Aug. 13, 1856, June 2, 1858. (Sumner Collection, Harvard College Library.)

24. Frank A. Flower, *History of the Republican Party* (Springfield, Ill., 1884), pp. 147–168; Howe, p. 281.

25. Flower, pp. 160, 168.

26. Ibid., p. 535, Appendix; Proceedings of the First Three Republican National Conventions of 1856, 1860, 1864 (Minneapolis, Minn., 1895), p. 43.

27. Manuscript poem by Lydia M. Child (New York Public Library, 42nd Street).

28. *Liberator*, XXVIII:22, May 28, 1858; see also Note 12 in Appendix.

29. Ibid., XXVI:28, July 11, 1856.

30. Ibid., XXVI:28, July 11, 1856.

31. Ibid., XXVI:28, July 11, 1856.

32. Ibid., XXVI:32, Aug. 8, 1856.

33. Ibid., XXVI:32, Aug. 8, 1856.

34. Rhodes, II, 191.

35. See Phillips's views on marriage and divorce, Note 13 in Appendix.

36. *History of Woman Suffrage*, I, 637, et seq.

37. Ibid., I, 638.

38. Ibid., I, 640–641.

39. *Liberator*, XXVII:2, Jan. 9, 1857.

40. Ibid., XXVII:8, Feb. 20, 1857.

41. Ibid., XXVII:43, Oct. 23, 1857.

42. Ibid., XXVII:21, May 22, 1857.

CHAPTER THIRTY-ONE

Nine Old Men

1. For informative and revealing accounts see Charles Warren, *The Supreme Court in United States History* (Boston, 1922), III, 1–41; Beveridge, II, 443–498; Frank H. Hodder, "Some Phases of the Dred Scott Case," *Mississippi Valley Historical Review* (June, 1929–March, 1930), XVI, 13–21; Vincent C. Hopkins, *Dred Scott's Case* (New York, 1951): Allen Nevins, *The Emergence of Lincoln*, 2 vols. (New York, 1950), including Appendix.

2. Warren, II, 154–156.

3. Ibid., III, 83–84.

4. Hopkins, p. 2. Hopkins can give no satisfactory answer how Dred obtained his celebrated and euphonious name. (vi, pref.)

5. Ibid., pp. 6, 23–24; Nevins, *The Emergence of Lincoln*, I, 184–185.

6. Carl B. Swisher, *Roger B. Taney* (New York, 1935), pp. 505–506.

7. Hodder, pp. 13–14.

8. Ibid., pp. 14–15. Prof. Nevins feels too that Taney, old and feeble, his patriotism alloyed by sectionalism, wished the Court to bulwark his own people and their institutions. Now was the time to strike a blow

for Southern rights in the territories. At the time, too, Grier's family affairs were embarrassed. (*The Emergence of Lincoln*, I, 104, II, 474–475.) Prof. Nevins argues against the idea that Curtis sought to curry favor—that his legal eminence would have given him a lucrative practice no matter what his political views, that his lifelong integrity makes such a charge absurd. (Ibid., II, 475, 476.)

9. United States, *Reports of Cases Argued and Adjudged in the Supreme Court of the United States, December Term, 1856.* By Benjamin C. Howard (Wash., D. C., 1859), XIX, 399–454. For quotation see XIX, 407.

10. For general analysis of decision see Swisher, pp. 505–506; Howe, pp. 320–321; Hopkins, op. cit., and Allan Nevins, *The Emergence of Lincoln.*

11. Manuscript letter to Theodore Parker, quoted in Martyn, p. 287.

12. *Liberator*, XXVII:22, May 29, 1857.

13. New York *Independent*, March 26, 1857. See also issues of March 12, 19.

14. New York *Daily Times*, May 15, 1857.

15. Beveridge, II, 488–499.

16. G. S. Merriam, *The Negro and the Nation*, p. 149.

17. Hodder, p. 21.

18. Dodd, *Expansion and Conflict*, p. 257.

19. Beveridge, II, 496; Hopkins, p. 176.

20. Hopkins, p. 182.

21. Beveridge, II, 457–458. Speaking of the mystery of the case, Vincent C. Hopkins remarks: ". . . Why Mrs. Emerson refused to allow him [Scott] to buy his and his family's freedom—why the Blows, the sons of his first master, took such a deep interest in him—why the young lawyer, Edmund La Beaume [whose sister Eugenie had married Peter E. Blow, son of Scott's former owner] approached Roswell Field to find out how the case decided against the Scotts by the Missouri Supreme Court could be carried to the Federal Courts—these are but some of the interesting questions which receive in the present study but tentative and, consequently, unsatisfactory answers." (Hopkins, vi, preface.) Hopkins feels if the motives of La Beaume could be ascertained a great deal of the mystery about the Scott case would be cleared up. (Ibid., p. 29.) Governor Reynolds stated that "Scott's case was backed by people interested in testing the question . . . whether a slave taken into the Northwest territory became free, and when brought back to a slave-holding state, if he still remained free." (Ibid., p. 31.)

After a year of freedom, on Sept. 17, 1858, Dred succumbed to a rapid consumption, and his wife Harriet followed soon after. (Ibid., pp. 176–177.)

22. Swisher, p. 97.

23. Warren, III, 115–116, 117–118. Prof. Nevins, however, quoting E. S. Corwin, states that no man is as impartial as he thinks he is, and Taney was shaped by a special environment and a distinct set of allegiances. (Nevins, *The Emergence of Lincoln*, I, 117.)

24. Frederick Bancroft, *Seward*, I, 458–461.

25. *Liberator*, XXVII:23, June 5, 1857.

26. Ibid., XXVII:23, June 5, 1857.
27. Ibid., XXVII:23, June 5, 1857.
28. Ibid., XXVII:23, June 5, 1857.

CHAPTER THIRTY-TWO

The Impending Crisis

1. Hinton R. Helper, *The Impending Crisis* (New York, 1860), pp. 32–33. Just as Helper said, not all the white population of the South made their living out of the sweat and blood of Negro slaves. In 1850 the situation was as follows:

Owners having		1	slave each				68,820
”	”	1	slave and less than		5		105,683
”	”	5	slaves	”	”	10	80,765
”	”	10	slaves	”	”	20	54,595
”	”	20	slaves	”	”	50	29,733
”	”	50	slaves	”	”	100	6,196
”	”	100	slaves	”	”	200	1,479
”	”	200	slaves	”	”	300	187
”	”	300	slaves	”	”	500	56
”	”	500	slaves	”	”	1000	9
”	”	1000	slaves and more				2

Aggregate number of slaveholders in the United States   347,525

Total white population in South   6,125,000

Total number of slaves   3,200,000

United States, *Statistical View of the United States. Being a Compendium of the Seventh Census* by J. D. B. De Bow, Superintendent of the United States Census (Washington, D. C., 1854), Table XC, p. 94. As Bernard Mandel points out in *Labor: Free and Slave. Working Men and the Anti-Slavery Movement in the United States* (New York, 1955): The propertyless white class in the South was in "a deplorable state of degradation," because of slavery. The slaves were given preferential employment and the white mechanics of "Egyptland" could not win jobs from the slaves. There was a growing tendency to replace white workers with slave labor in many branches of employment, for slaves were cheaper, provided a steadier labor force without the hazards of "fluctuations," for they could neither quit, nor strike, nor organize unions. As one emigrant said, "There is no chance for the poor white man among the slaves—he cannot get work and he is treated like a dog." (pp. 28, 31, 34, 43.)

2. Helper, pp. 120–121. Although they did not forget moral issues, Southern Abolitionists directed their appeals and propaganda primarily to the working men and farmers. William S. Bailey, a machinist of Newport, Ky., edited an anti-slavery newspaper in Kentucky in which he said, "We plead the cause of WHITE MEN and WHITE WOMEN in the South—We ask for their sake a patient and candid hearing." Two sections of the working class in the South were thoroughly and actively anti-slavery: the free Negro

mechanics and the German American laborers (including the German American Communists). (Mandel, pp. 50, 53–54.)

As Mandel states: "The ruling class understood much more clearly than the [Southern white] workers that the interests of the latter were in opposition to slavery and that to maintain their subjection, it was necessary to keep them down, keep them ignorant, keep them weak and keep them divided from their natural allies." (p. 55.)

3. Helper, p. 328.

4. Ibid., p. 183.

5. Ibid., pp. 186–187.

6. *Liberator*, XXX:6, Feb. 10, 1860.

7. W. J. Cash, *The Mind of the South* (New York, 1941), pp. 66–68. Clement Eaton states that the poor white voters were more bitterly hostile to the Abolitionists than the owners of hundreds of slaves. Fanatical devotees of a "White America," they were easy victims for the politicians who agitated the slavery question. (Eaton, p. 87.) See also Mandel, pp. 57–59.

8. *Liberator*, XXVII:33, Aug. 14, 1857.

9. Sears, pp. 188–189.

10. Ibid., p. 189.

11. *Congressional Globe*, 35th Congress, 1st Session, Feb. 5, 1858, XXVII, part 1, p. 603.

12. *Punch*, March 6, 1858, XXXIV, 100.

13. Thompson, p. 81.

14. New York *Herald*, May 12, 1859. See also issue of May 11, 1859.

15. New York *Times*, May 11, 1859.

16. New York *Evening Express*, May 11, 1859.

17. *Liberator*, XXIX:21, May 27, 1859.

18. *History of Woman Suffrage*, I, 674.

19. Ibid., I, 674.

20. Ibid., I, 675.

21. Ibid., I, 273.

22. Phillips, "Idols," *Speeches, Lectures, and Letters*, First Series, pp. 254–255.

CHAPTER THIRTY-THREE

St. John the Just

1. The latest research, often anti-Brown, can be found in James C. Malin's *John Brown and the Legend of Fifty-Six* (Phila., 1942). But Brown, like Abraham Lincoln, has become the Myth or Symbol.

In the John Brown matter Prof. Nevins leaves one with the impression that he cannot make up his mind—or rather his heart affirms but his head denies. The reasonableness of the first few statements do not mix well with the bitter stricture that follows: "Usually rigidly honest, he sometimes showed a financial irresponsibility that approached dishonesty; a man of principle he could be a provoking opportunist; kindly and philanthropic he had a vein of harsh cruelty." (*The Emergence of Lincoln,* II, 5.) "It was thus as a failure, a man who had lost part of his early integrity as well as his faith in organized Christianity, a soured, hardened reformer who took refuge from his own deficiencies in fighting the wrongs of others." (Ibid., II, 8.) "He [James C. Malin] tells us that Brown's murder of five men on Pottawatomie Creek in May, 1856, probably had nothing to do with slavery, but was an act of political assassination. This may be true, and yet not all the truth. Brown probably remained a convinced hater of slavery who had steeped himself in Abolitionist literature and who regarded slaveholders as criminals. He remained, also, a man with a sense of mission. . . . The old veins of Puritan idealism and reformative zeal were still to be found in his nature, but a vein of the ruthlessness peculiar to fanatics, and especially fanatics gnarled by failure, had asserted a dominant place." (II, 8.) "Psychogenic disorders amounting to mental disease," (II, 10), "the paranoic flaw in John Brown's mind," "his paranoia" (II, 77). Finally (and somewhat inconsistently: "In his last weeks moving as a man who fulfilled a mighty destiny, he impressed all observers by his unshaken courage and serene equanimity." (II, 95.) "He was heroic—but not blameless." (II, 90.)

2. Robert Penn Warren, *John Brown, The Making of a Martyr* (New York, 1929), p. 273; Octavius B. Frothingham, *Gerrit Smith* (New York, 1878), pp. 237, 239.

3. Warren, p. 274; Franklin B. Sanborn, *Recollections of Seventy Years,* 2 vols., (Boston, 1909), I, 145–146.

4. Warren, p. 274; Sanborn, I, 146.

5. Rhodes, II, 387; Warren, p. 274; Sanborn, I, 147; Frothingham, *Gerrit Smith,* pp. 239–240.

6. Warren, p. 276.

7. Ibid., p. 230.

8. Swift, p. 312.

9. R. P. Warren, p. 231.

10. Rhodes, II, 388; Frothingham, *Theodore Parker,* p. 462.

11. Rhodes, II, 391; James Redpath, *The Public Life of Capt. John Brown* (Boston, 1860), p. 206.

12. Quarles, *Frederick Douglass,* pp. 170–171, 177–179.

13. Frederick Douglass, *Life and Times* (Boston, 1895), p. 390; Rhodes, II, 390; Sanborn, I, 183.

14. Episode based on material in R. P. Warren, pp. 320–323.

15. Ibid., pp. 335–336.

16. For raid see Oswald Garrison Villard, *John Brown* (Boston, 1911), pp. 426–455; Rhodes, II, 393–397; R. P. Warren, 347–381.

17. R. P. Warren, pp. 347–348, 351.

18. Ibid., p. 375.

19. Ibid., pp. 377–378.

20. Ibid., p. 378.

21. Ibid., pp. 380–381.

22. Rhodes, II, 397–398; Hillis, pp. 155–156; R. P. Warren, pp. 382–384.

23. Rhodes, II, 399; Frothingham, *Gerrit Smith,* pp. 237, 258; Ralph Waldo Emerson, *The Complete Works of Ralph Waldo Emerson* (Boston and New York, 1932), XI, 268.

24. Rhodes, II, 400; Frothingham, *Gerrit Smith,* pp. 243–245.

25. R. P. Warren, pp. 422–423.

26. Rhodes, II, 405; Hillis, p. 157; R. P. Warren, pp. 410–411.

27. Phillips, "Harper's Ferry," *Speeches, Lectures, and Letters,* First Series, pp. 263, 274, 279–280.

28. R. P. Warren, p. 431.

29. Stearns, *Sketches from Concord and Appledore,* pp. 206–207.

30. Emerson, *Complete Works,* XI, 267–273; Henry David Thoreau, *The Writings of Henry David Thoreau,* X, 197–236.

31. *Liberator,* XXIX:48, Dec. 2, 1859.

32. Ibid., XXIX:48, Dec. 2, 1859.

33. One of the visitors was Governor Henry A. Wise. Wise gave public credence to absurd rumors of further Northern invasions, deployed bodies of militia, and temporarily suspended travel on railroad trains. The Governor became a temporary idol. Songs were composed in his honor.

In Harper's Ferry there was an insurrection,

John Brown thought the Niggers would sustain him;

But old Massa Wise put his spectacles on his eyes,

And landed him in the happy land o' Canaan." (Luthin, p. 37.)

34. R. P. Warren, p. 427.

35. Manuscript letter to Rev. Luther Humphrey. (New York Public Library, 42nd Street.)

36. Rhodes, II, 406–408.

37. O. G. Villard, *John Brown,* pp. 551–553.

38. R. P. Warren, p. 436.

39. Ibid., p. 430.

40. Elizabeth B. Chace and Lucy B. Lovell, *Two Quaker Sisters* (New York, 1937), p. 175.

41. Rhodes, II, 410; Samuel Longfellow, *Life of Henry Wadsworth Longfellow,* 2 vols. (Boston, 1886), II, 347.

42. William E. Barton, *President Lincoln* (Indianapolis, 1933), I, 32.

43. Elijah Avey, *The Capture and Execution of John Brown* (Elgin, Ill., 1906), p. 39.

44. Barton, I, 32–33.

45. Avey, pp. 40–41.

46. R. P. Warren, p. 439.

47. Rhodes, II, 409–410; Louisa M. Alcott, *Her Life, Letters, and Journals* (Boston, 1889), p. 105.

48. Carpenter, p. 69.

49. Elizabeth B. Chace, *Anti-Slavery Reminiscences* (Central Falls, R. I., 1891), p. 41.

50. Carl Wittke, *Against the Current—The Life of Karl Heinzen, 1809–1880* (Chicago, Ill., 1945), p. 175.

51. Abraham Lincoln, *Complete Works,* ed. by John G. Nicolay and John Hay (New York, 1905), V, 318–319; William H. Seward, *The Works of William H. Seward,* ed. by George E. Baker, 5 vols. (Boston, 1884), IV, 637; *Congressional Globe,* 36th Congress, 1st Session, XLIX, 553–554; *Jefferson Davis, Constitutionalist, His Letters, Papers, and Speeches* (Jackson, Miss., 1923), IV, 99; Rhodes, II, 411–412.

52. *Liberator,* XXIX:49, Dec. 9, 1859.

53. Wilson, *John Brown*, p. 560.
54. *Liberator*, XXIX:50, Dec. 16, 1859.
55. Phillips, "Burial of John Brown," *Speeches, Lectures, and Letters*, First Series, pp. 289, 290, 293.

CHAPTER THIRTY-FOUR

Fearless Lips

1. *Liberator*, XXX:25, June 22, 1860; see also Phillips, "Theodore Parker," *Speeches, Lectures, and Letters*, Second Series, pp. 428, 431–432, 434, 439.
2. Phillips, "The Pulpit," Ibid., Second Series, pp. 259–260, 263–264. See also Martyn, pp. 301–302.

CHAPTER THIRTY-FIVE

"Who Is This Huckster in Politics?"

1. For proceedings see Flower, pp. 229–241. *Proceedings of the First Three Republican National Conventions*, pp. 83–169.
2. Raymond Warren, *The Prairie President* (Chicago, 1930), p. 405.
3. Emerson, *Complete Works*, XI, 330–331.
4. *Liberator*, XXX:23, June 8, 1860.
5. Ibid., XXX:23, June 8, 1860; see also Raymond Warren, p. 411; W. P. and F. J. Garrison, III, 503.
6. J. G. de Roulhac, "Lincoln's Election and Slavery," *American Historical Review* (July, 1932), XXXVII, No. 4, pp. 707–708.
7. *Proceedings of the First Three Republican National Conventions*, pp. 130–133.
8. *Liberator*, XXX:24, June 15, 1860; see Note 14 in Appendix.
9. Ibid., XXX:28, July 13, 1860.
10. Ibid., XXX:34, Aug. 24, 1860.
11. Nevins, *The Emergence of Lincoln*, II, 301–302, 305.
12. John B. McMaster, *A History of the People of the United States* (New York, 1885–1913), VIII, 459–461; Emerson D. Fite, *The Presidential Campaign of 1860* (New York, 1911), pp. 226–227; Nevins, *The Emergence of Lincoln*, II, 305.
13. *Liberator*, XXX:34, Aug. 24, 1860. See also Albert B. Moore, *Southern Contemporary Opinion of Abraham Lincoln to July, 1861* (Chicago, 1915), p. 19.
14. *Liberator*, XXX:34, Aug. 24, 1860; see also Albert B. Moore, p. 19.
15. Frank P. Stearns, *True Republicanism*, pp. 160–161.
16. Fite, p. 233. The vote was:

Candidate	Popular Vote	Electoral Vote
Lincoln	1,857,610	180
Douglas	1,365,967	12

| Breckinridge | 847,953 | 72 |
| Bell | 590,631 | 39 |

17. *Liberator*, XXX:46, Nov. 16, 1860.

18. Phillips, "Lincoln's Election," *Speeches, Lectures, and Letters*, First Series, pp. 294, 314.

19. See manuscript letter to A. A. Lawrence (Massachusetts Historical Society), Note 15 in Appendix.

20. Phillips, "Mobs and Education," *Speeches, Lectures, and Letters*, First Series, pp. 319–342.

21. Edith E. Ware, "Political Opinion in Massachusetts during the Civil War and Reconstruction," *Studies in History, Economics, and Public Law* (New York, 1916), LXXIV, No. 2, p. 89.

22. *Liberator*, XXX:51, Dec. 21, 1860.

23. For manuscript tribute to Karl Heinzen, see Note 16 in Appendix, *Wendell Phillips Scrapbook*.

The German refugees looked upon slavery as the blackest stain on the banners of the new land. Besides, German refugees wanted farms and free homesteads and could not accept with equanimity a policy which would open still unoccupied territories to slavery. A powerful economic interest reinforced the humanitarian motive to abolish slavery. "In the conflict between liberty and slavery, civilization and barbarism, loyalty and treason, the Germans will play not a subordinate but a leading role. The spirit of 1848 is abroad again." Thus wrote Belletristisches, the editor of the *New Yorker Criminal Zeitung und Belletristisches Journal*, April 26, 1861. (Carl Wittke, *Refugees of Revolution*, pp. 191–192, 221.

Garrison called Heinzen's *Pionier* "the ablest, most independent, and highest toned of all the German papers in the country. (Quoted in Ibid., p. 276.)

Heinzen was an uncompromising, unbending, militant radical republican, a crusader against censorship, bureaucracy, a radical Abolitionist, and a champion of equal rights for women and many other political, economic, and social reforms. To Heinzen the United States was a great experiment in liberty and human culture and a process forever unfinished. On his monument is the inscription: "His life work—the elevation of mankind." "It is hard," said Heinzen, "to swim against the current, but it is upstream that one finds the source and the clear, fresher water"—words that apply to Wendell Phillips. (Wittke, *Against the Current—The Life of Karl Heinzen*, pp. v. pref., 101, 307.)

Heinzen's program of social reform would classify him with modern socialists, but he was not a communist. He believed that communists wished to make people happy without making them free. He accused Marx of wanting "to break window panes with cannon" and of using his "whole artillery of logic, dialectic, stylistic, and learning" to annihilate those who could not see eye to eye with him. He rejected as the devil's philosophy that the end justifies the means. (Ibid., pp. 239, 240, 243.) Marx's program, he prophesized, led to a "barrack's state," "a jailhouse for individual liberties." (*Refugees of Revolution*, p. 167.)

24. *Liberator*, XXX:52, Dec. 28, 1860.

25. Ibid., XXX:52, Dec. 28, 1860.

CHAPTER THIRTY-SIX

The Erring Sisters

1. Hillis, p. 189.

2. Rose Strunsky, *Abraham Lincoln* (New York, 1914), p. 133.

3. Nathaniel W. Stephenson, *Abraham Lincoln and the Union in the War of Secession* (New Haven, 1919), pp. 84–88; French E. Chadwick, *Causes of the Civil War* (New York, 1906), p. 212.

4. Kenneth M. Stampp, *And the War Came* (Baton Rouge, La., 1950), p. 61.

5. Hamilton Eckenrode, *Jefferson Davis* (New York, 1923), pp. 1–3; Allen Tate, *Jefferson Davis* (New York, 1929), pp. 16–18, 22–23.

6. Elisabeth Cutting, *Jefferson Davis, Political Soldier* (New York, 1930), p. 144.

7. Ibid., pp. 145–146.

8. Lowell, "The Debate in the Sennit," Biglow, No. V, *Complete Poetical Works*, p. 199.

9. Morison, II, 153.

10. *Liberator*, Jan. 25, 1861.

11. Whittier, "A Word for the Hour," op. cit., p. 412.

12. Stephenson, p. 90.

13. West, p. 597.

14. D. W. Howe, pp. 558–559.

15. Carpenter, pp. 92–93.

16. Rhodes, III, 144.

17. Charles B. Todd, *The Story of the City of New York* (New York, 1895), p. 446.

18. Stephenson, p. 92.

19. Abraham Lincoln, *Complete Works*, I, 657–658; Chadwick, p. 176.

In *The Emergence of Lincoln*, Prof. Nevins dents the armor of the "repressible conflict" historians (or has he wisely changed camps?): "The South was further from a just solution of the slavery problem in 1830 than it had been in 1789. It was further from a tenable solution in 1860 than it had been in 1830. Why was it going from bad to worse? Because Southern leaders refused to nerve their people to pay the heavy price of race adjustment. . . . A heavy responsibility for the failure of America in this period rests with this Southern leadership which lacked imagination, ability, and courage." ((II, 468.)

"All hope of bringing Southern majority sentiment to a better attitude would have been lost if Lincoln and his party had flinched on the basic issue of the restriction of slavery, for by the seventh decade of the nineteenth century history, the time had come when that demand had to be maintained. . . . Evasion by the South, evasion by the North was no longer possible." (II, 469, 470, 471.)

Kenneth M. Stampp in his *And the War Came* (Baton Rouge, La., 1950) adopts a balanced and judicious point of view: there was no basis for sectional harmony as long as Negro slavery survived and dominant groups on neither side were willing to yield. Alfred Iverson of Georgia, addressing his senatorial colleagues a month after the election of Lincoln, clearly prophesied to the impending conflict—"Sir, disguise the fact as you will, there is an enmity between the Northern and Southern people that is deep and enduring and you never can eradicate it—never!" (p. 1.)

Prof. Stampp, analyzing the statement that the propaganda of Northern and Southern agitators was one of the prime causes of the Civil War, repeatedly and wisely, I think, emphasizes that beneath all the propaganda there was the fact of Negro Slavery. Without the peculiar institution there could have been no pro-slavery or anti-slavery agitators. Enmeshed with slavery were other economic differences which engendered sectional hate. The South was a static, agrarian, debtor section; the North was a dynamic, commercialized, industrializing creditor section. The South was exploited and the North was the exploiter. "These matters, together with slavery, were always back of the tirades of the agitators. And these matters, rather than the tirades, were at the roots of things. Without them there could have been no sectional agitation and no Civil War." (Ibid., pp. 2–3.) Besides the author feels that the great mass of Republicans were unalterably opposed to compromise. Not more than a hundred thousand of the 1,866,000 voters who supported Lincoln were willing to follow the retreatists. Lincoln, unable to devise an original solution, was being guided by, and was not controlling, public opinion. The majority of the people of the North opposed the expansion of slavery and looked upon the institution as a disgrace. (Ibid., pp. 141, 153–154, 183, 189, 251.) See also the article by Stampp, "The Historian and Southern Negro Slavery," (*The American Historical Review*, April, 1952, LVII, No. 3, 613–624): "Perhaps historians need to be told what James Russell Lowell once told the South: 'It is time . . . to learn . . . that the difficulty of the Slavery question is slavery itself,—nothing more, nothing less.'" (LVII, 624.)

Roy F. Nichols in *The Disruption of the American Democracy* (New York, 1948) spotlights agitation as the cause of the Civil War, but not that of the Abolitionists. "Why a Civil War? Most of the principal 'causes' —ideological differences, institutional differences, moral differences, cultural differences, sectional differences, physiographic differences have existed in other times and places without necessarily causing a war. Then why should they set the people of the United States to killing one another in 1861? . . . . Why was emotion in the United States in 1861 supercharged?

"Fundamentally the process was an illustration of what Machiavelli describes as the 'confusion of a growing state'"—the growth of population, partly by natural increase and partly by foreign immigration, deep-seated enjoyment of political activity by Americans—so many elections and such constant agitation. "This constant agitation certainly furnishes one of the primary clues to why the war came. . . . The constant heat generated in the frequent elections brought an explosion. . . . The social, economic, and cultural differences had been so used by the political operators as to produce secession and civil war." (pp. 513, 515–517.)

A Southern historian, Henry H. Simms in *A Decade of Sectional Controversy, 1851–1861* (Chapel Hill, N. C., 1942) feels political factors more than any other produced the hostile feeling which resulted in war.

Pieter Geyl pertinently remarks: "Here, there, and everywhere peace was what men wanted and the war came. . . . Name-calling, shibboleths, epithets, tirades,"—the question remains whether one is justified in labeling these extra-rational factors with contemptuous terms and deny to them, as Randall does, a rightful role in the drama of history. "A blundering generation" works up passions. But "must one not wilfully blindfold one's historical imagination in order to avoid seeing that the excitement was natural?" Randall's vision of "'a blundering generation' does not do justice to the past . . . it ignores the tragedy of that struggle with an over-whelming moral problem, slavery. . . . Neither with the one-sided atten-tion to economic aspects of the Beards nor with Randall's determination to reduce everything to exclusively practical and reasonable terms can the importance of the moral problem be done justice." (Pieter Geyl, pp. 155, 161, 167, 168.)

The books by Avery Craven deserve a section by themselves, spotlighted in the intensity of their amazing assertions and antiquated and reactionary point of view.

It is preposterous to talk of building up a moral wall against the encroachments of communistic slavery when the architects and masons of that wall, our historians, have gone over lock, stock, and barrel, to appeasing or apologizing for the peculiar institution and speak of the "repressible" conflict, the "needless" war. Even a Wilsonian liberal like J. G. Randall talks of the slaves of the North as no better off than the slaves of the South. In a letter to the author, Prof. Randall stated that I misjudged his position—that he was a liberal, etc. Unfortunately I judged, perhaps too uncompromisingly, but too well. Yes, the American historians will construct that wall, but it will be one sixteenth of an inch thick and an eighth of an inch tall.

In a chapter on "The Peculiar Institution" in his *The Repressible Conflict, 1830–1861* (Baton Rouge, La., 1939) Prof. Craven speaks of slavery with a particular and peculiar tenderness or partiality. That a leading *modern* historian could write such a slanted chapter is shocking to the moral sensibilities of any liberal *American*. It is also a tragic commentary on the decline of that precious sentiment handed down by Revolutionary forefathers, expressed in gist in the Declaration of Independence, the early years of our Republic, and the Bill of Rights in our Constitution—and I am not spluttering off into molten and glittering generalities. The tragedy of our modern situation is that just the mere sound of those bene-ficient things in our heritage tastes like ashes in the mouth—they have be-come a bitter memory—and whereas, formerly, they were contemptuously dismissed as wearisome platitudes fit only for cheap politicians in the arena of soapbox oratory—what politician today pays them, not glowing tribute, but even lip service? No, not for fear! And what historians? No, for thin blooded moral conviction, unimbued with the spirit of freedom, writes what?—*The Repressible Conflict.*

For both scholarship and analysis, judiciousness and candor in the interpretation of the slavery issue consult Kenneth M. Stampp. At least in my frankly partisan "Ignoble Ease and Peaceful Sloth, Not Peace" (*Phylon*, Dec. 1948), an answer to Prof. Randall, I plant my banner firmly on rock: Christian imperatives: the moral evil of slavery, and cherished

American rights: freedom and equality. What is Prof. Craven's stand?—
if shifting sands of appeasement and apology for tyranny can be called a
stand: "William Lloyd Garrison had the gift of making everyone mad—
including himself. He had an unusual capacity for hating." (p. 79.) Un-
called for moves and irresponsible leadership were the very things which
lifted the crusade of a band of *"crackpot reformers in the North* and an
extravagant group of fire-eaters in the South" to the proportions of a
national conflict. (p. 94. Italics mine.) Sane men on both sides were
helpless before fanatics armed with holy weapons. (p. 96.) (For answers
see Pieter Geyl, Allan Nevins, and my article mentioned above.) Or to put
the answer another way: War is caused by extremes, but the problem of
despotism and slavery kept on raising extremes. War is abnormal, despotism
is psychopathic. You cannot say: "See, there were peaceful adjustments
in the controversy of "54–40 or Fight," the Venezuela trouble, the Alabama
Claims, etc. For here whatever would have been adjusted, the canker
at the core—slavery—would have remained, remained after the frenzy of
war agitation had passed to stir up and poison the blood again. The irreconcilable forces of slavery would never have been reconciled, the intransigent remained uncompromising. The man of despotism knows no
surfeit, gluts on all—or gets nothing. And precious blood is spilled in consequence. Said Phillips: "We have not only an army to conquer, but we have
a state of mind to annihilate."

Even had the material condition of the Negro been as good as apologists
were (and are) in the habit of asserting (the slave was supported "for
the whole of life and against possible misfortune") the eagerness of nearly
every Negro for freedom would have been a grave indictment of the system.

Prof. Craven's *The Coming of the Civil War* (New York, 1942) advances a step further in proffering the olive branch to the irreconcilable
South. Craven remarks he is viewing the institution as a scientist, not a
partisan. To twist the phrase, he is partisan, not scientific. I wonder what
Prof. Craven thinks science or the scientific method is. He should hook his
historical eye to the fact, not let his gaze wander in nostalgic (and fan-
cied) recreations of ante-bellum nirvanas. He should first investigate the
attitude of the slaves themselves, how "enraptured" they were about the
"glories" or "paternalism" of bondage, classed as property with cattle,
horses, and swine. The pathological fear of insurrection, the flights to
freedom are blasting rejoinders to Prof. Craven's jerry-built argument.
We must confess he writes with languid charm, with grace and glow, with
vividness, but these stylistic virtues are enlisted not for the cause of
freedom, but, unfortunately, to enchant readers, under the guise of historical and scientific objectivity, in an obsolescent and tyrannical cause.
(Cf. B. A. Botkin, *Lay My Burden Down,* Chicago, Ill., 1945; Herbert
Aptheker, *American Negro Slave Revolts,* New York, 1943; Clement Eaton,
Freedom of Thought in the Old South, Durham, N. C., 1940.)

"The great tragedy of the ante-bellum South," adds Craven, "lies
in the fact that this group [the middle class] failed to assert itself or to
greatly influence trends in the section." (p. 32.) Cash's *The Mind of
the South* may have the answer to Prof. Craven's perplexing problem.

But nothing can be more brazen or naive or insulting to one's intelligence than the comparison of the resentment and resistance of the

slaves to the "solemn columns of girls [in a Northern town] marching down the streets waving their kerchiefs to the girls in the other mills to join them." (p. 80.) We can suppose (not imagine) the columns of slaves marching down the streets of Atlanta or Charleston protesting against their bondage. The last straw, I should say, the real howler is when Prof. Craven remarks of the slave: "Even then his life partner was often selected for him. His plight in this respect was as bad as that of European royalty. . . . (p. 82.) (We are tempted to emit one devastating WHEW!) But we may reply: were families of European royalty broken up or sold on the auction block? Or the mother rewarded with "a white dress"? No doubt Northern factory conditions were properly the targets of social criticism, but at least freedom moved in the direction and along the open highway of treating men as human beings, not merchandise. Randolph of Roanoke called Whittier's "Farewell of a Virginia Slave Mother" with its haunting refrain, "Gone, gone, sold and gone, etc." mere Abolition cant. Yet when he who listened to Patrick Henry, Clay, Calhoun, Webster, was asked to name the greatest orator he had ever heard, the old Virginian snapped out—"A slave. She was a mother and her rostrum was the auction block." (See Mandell, pp. 122–123.)

Yes, I am frankly (and honestly) partisan about slavery. Frederick Douglass had a rude and awakening response to the brutal realities of bondage. Love was Henry Ward Beecher's remedy for slavery—love and Christian piety. But as Douglass, who was unimpressed with Beecher's high sounding rhetoric, and, no doubt, would have exploded at Prof. Craven's syrupy apologies, said: "With a good cowhide, I could take all that out of Mr. Beecher [or Mr. Craven] in five minutes."

20. Chadwick, pp. 179–180; James G. Blaine, *Twenty Years of Congress* (Norwich, Conn., 1884–1886), I, 260; Wilbur, pp. 45–46.
21. Henry Wilson, III, 89.
22. Chadwick, p. 273.
23. Douglas S. Freeman, *R. E. Lee* (New York, 1934–1935), I, 427.

CHAPTER THIRTY-SEVEN

Mobbing Phillips

1. Phillips, *Speeches, Lectures, and Letters*, First Series, pp. 343–370.
2. Smalley, p. 87.
3. Henry G. Pearson, *The Life of John A. Andrew* (Boston, 1904), I, 150.
4. Smalley, pp. 89–90.
5. W. P. and F. J. Garrison, IV, 5–6.
6. Ibid.
7. Smalley, pp. 89–90; Pearson, I, 150–152.
8. W. P. and F. J. Garrison, IV, 7.
9. Report of meeting in the *Liberator*, XXXI:5, Feb. 1, 1861.
10. Phillips, *Speeches, Lectures, and Letters*, First Series, pp. 371–395.

11. Recollection of Dr. Thayer, Phillips's family physician, in Martyn, p. 310.
12. Told by Mrs. Eleanor F. Crosby, ibid., p. 310.

CHAPTER THIRTY-EIGHT

Simple Susan—Fresh Seed

1. Abraham Lincoln, *The Writings of Abraham Lincoln* (New York, 1906), V, 212–213; see Note 17 in Appendix.
2. Ibid., V, 215–219.
3. Ibid., V, 219–220.
4. Thompson, p. 129.
5. Lincoln, *Writings*, V, 224.
6. Rhodes, III, 303; Barton, *Lincoln*, I, 515–517.
7. Stephenson, *Abraham Lincoln and the Union,* p. 99.
8. Ibid., p. 101.
9. James T. Adams, *March of Democracy* (New York, 1932–1933), II, 13.
10. Henry Wilson, III, 183.
11. Thompson, pp. 129–130.
12. Pearson, I, 176.
13. Thompson, p. 130.
14. Pearson, I, 185–186.
15. Todd, p. 447.
16. W. C. Bryant, "Our Country's Call," in *Poems of American History* (Boston, 1922), pp. 410–411.
17. Richard H. Stoddard, "Men of the North and West," in Ibid., p. 409.
18. W. P. and F. J. Garrison, IV, 40–41.
19. Pearson, I, 176.
20. Phillips, "The War for the Union," *Speeches, Lectures, and Letters,* First Series, p. 440.
21. Smalley, p. 98.
22. Phillips, "Under the Flag," *Speeches, Lectures, and Letters,* First Series, pp. 398–400.
23. *Liberator,* XXXI:19, May 10, 1861; see also W. P. and F. J. Garrison, IV, 20, footnote.
24. Manuscript letter, Aug. 28, 1862. (New York Historical Society.)
25. Phillips, "The War for the Union," *Speeches, Lectures, and Letters,* First Series, pp. 418, 426, 428.
26. *Liberator,* XXXI:28, July 12, 1861.

CHAPTER THIRTY-NINE

The Peace of Justice

1. Phillips, "The State of the Country," *Speeches, Lectures, and Letters,* First Series, pp. 545, 546. See also Martyn, p. 326.
2. Phillips, "The State of the Country," op. cit, p. 529.
3. Ibid., p. 540; Martyn, p. 327.
4. Phillips, "The State of the Country," op. cit., p. 544; Martyn, p. 327.
5. *Liberator;* XXXII:21, May 23, 1862; also *Speeches, Lectures, and Letters,* First Series, pp. 534, 538.
6. Phillips, "The State of the Country," ibid., p. 553.
7. Though gradualism came to express the dominant anti-slavery temper, it does not follow that the Northern conscience would have been aroused to this pitch except for the non-gradualists. Even Lincoln admitted: "I have been only an instrument. The logic and moral power of Garrison and the anti-slavery people of the country and the army have done all." (Arthur M. Schlesinger, *The American as Reformer,* p. 40.)
8. *Liberator,* XXXI:28, July 12, 1861.
9. Carpenter, p. 105.
10. Wyman, pp. 2–3.
11. *Liberator,* XXXI:35, Aug. 30, 1861.
12. Manuscript letters. (Sumner Collection, Harvard College Library.)
13. *Liberator,* XXXII:3, Jan. 17, 1862.
14. Ibid., XXXII:4, Jan. 24, 1862.
15. Rhodes, III, 410, 412–413.
16. *Liberator,* XXXII:6, Feb. 7, 1862. For attacks on Phillips see the New York *Tribune,* Aug. 11, 1861, Jan. 12, 13, 15, 16, 1862.
17. Ellis P. Oberholtzer, *Abraham Lincoln* (Phila., 1904), p. 265.
18. But Lincoln was far from timid and shilly-shallying in his interpretation of emergency executive powers and his abrogation of civil rights. The government was more industrious than ever in hustling off to prison without regard to civil law men who were regarded as obstacles in the prosecution of the war. Arbitrary arrests were frequent and unpopular. Most arrested were kept in prison without opportunity to hear charges against them. Arrests were often unjust and always haphazard in their application and stirred up resentment among unquestioned supporters of the war. (Wood Gray, *The Hidden Civil War, The Story of the Copperheads,* New York, 1942, p. 97.)

Even Lincoln's ablest and staunchest defender, J. G. Randall (*Lincoln, the Liberal Statesman,* New York, 1947), admits that Lincoln earnestly believed that the rights of war were vested in the President and that as President he had extraordinary legal resources which Congress lacked. "As commander-in-chief . . . I suppose I have a right to take any measure which may best subdue the enemy." Says Randall: it argued a curious commingling of legislative and executive functions for a President to perform an act which he adjudged to be within the competence of Congress and then when the measure had been irrevocably taken, to present Congress with a fait accompli for subsequent sanction. "No President," concedes Randall, "has carried the power of presidential edict and executive order (independently of Congress) so far as he did. . . . Most of the executive powers under Wilson and under Franklin D. Roosevelt were conferred by Congress." Besides exercising extraordinary executive authority, he took over legislative and judicial functions—for instance, suspension of the habeas corpus privilege, presidential conscription of 1862, special war courts created by the President with sweeping powers. The commissary general of prisoners reported 13,535 citizens arrested and confined in military prisons from February, 1863, to the end of the war. Randall affirms Wood Gray's charge: in the vast majority of cases, persons had no trial, not even a military one. They were arrested, held in prison irregularly with no charge or indictment, and then released just as irregularly. There was a striking contrast between the great number of arbitrary arrests and the negligible amount of completed judicial action for such matters as treason, conspiracy, and obstructing the draft. Lincoln's suspension of the habeas corpus was, as Randall suggests, regrettable. Indeed the precedent was not followed under Wilson or Franklin D. Roosevelt. But the actual treatment of the prisoners was mild. (pp. 121–133.)

In stark contrast Jefferson Davis followed constitutional channels. Says William M. Robinson, Jr. (*Justice in Grey*, Cambridge, Mass., 1941), "Taken as a whole, the government's answer to disloyal conditions was within constitutional limitations. Its restricted use of martial law and its limited suspension of the writ of habeas corpus, only when authorized by the Congress, stand in marked contrast to Lincoln's unrestrained use of extra-constitutional measures." (p. 628. See also Rembert W. Patrick, *Jefferson Davis and His Cabinet,* Baton Rouge, La., 1944, pp. 32–35, 306–309, 315–317.)

19. Ware, p. 113, footnote.

20. New York *Tribune,* April 4, 1862.

21. *Liberator,* XXXIII:23, June 5, 1863.

CHAPTER FORTY

Hobby Horses

1. Rose Strunsky, "The Truth about Lincoln and the Negro," *The New Review* (May, 1914), II, No. 5, p. 264.

2. Ibid., p. 265.

3. "His love for the Union was great, but that it was as impelling as his hatred of slavery I cannot believe." (Dwight L. Dumond, p. 114.) It is the purpose of this chapter to prove that the opposite was true. Fortunately hatred of slavery and love of the Union later became fused or commingled in one—freedom of the slave.

4. Hume, p. 140.

5. T. A. Bland, *Life of Benjamin F. Butler* (Boston, 1879), pp. 50–52; Robert S. Holzman, *Stormy Ben Butler* (New York, 1954), pp. 41–42.

6. John G. Nicolay, *A Short Life of Abraham Lincoln* (New York, 1906), p. 223.

7. Rhodes, V, 310.
8. W. P. and F. J. Garrison, IV, 33.
9. Pearson, II, 3.
10. Whittier, "To John C. Fremont," op. cit., p. 413.
11. Manuscript letters, April 29, 1862; July 15, 1861. (Sumner Collection, Harvard College Library.)
12. Oberholtzer, *Abraham Lincoln,* p. 274.
13. Wilbur, p. 55.
14. W. P. and F. J. Garrison, IV, 133.
15. Oberholtzer, *Abraham Lincoln,* p. 275.
16. Isaac N. Arnold, *Abraham Lincoln* (Chicago, 1885), p. 249; Samuel W. McCall, *Thaddeus Stevens* (Boston and New York, 1899), p. 216; Lincoln, *Complete Works,* II, 129–130.
17. *Liberator,* XXXII:11, March 14, 1862.
18. Emerson, "Boston Hymm," *The Complete Works,* IX, 204.
19. *Liberator,* XXXII:11, March 14, 1862.
20. Ibid., XXXII:20, May 16, 1862.
21. Ibid., XXXII:12, March 21, 1862.
22. Martyn, p. 325; Rhodes, IV, 204. The conciliatory attitude of Seward antagonized Phillips. Seward had heeded the protest of Great Britain in the Mason and Slidell case, despite hotheaded Northern opinion, and was urging Lincoln to postpone action on Emancipation until a Federal victory was achieved. A caucus of Republican Senators, assuming to speak for the Party, gave as a formal opinion that the failure of a vigorous and successful prosecution of the war was due to the fact that the President was badly advised by cabinet ministers. Most thought that the clog to the administration was Seward, and at their first meeting passed a resolution declaring that the welfare of the country required his withdrawal from the cabinet.
23. *Liberator,* XXXII:14, April 14, 1862.
24. Quoted in Martyn, p. 326.
25. Manuscript letter, March 27, 1862. (Sumner Collection, Harvard College Library.)
26. *Liberator,* XXXII:15, April 11, 1862; see also New York *Tribune,* April 1, 1862.
27. *Liberator,* XXXII:20, May 16, 1862.
28. Barton, II, 132.
29. Whittier, "Astraea at the Capitol," op. cit., pp. 417–418.
30. Lorenzo D. Turner, pp. 115–116.
31. Nicolay, p. 327; Richardson, VI, 91–92.
32. Swift, p. 324.
33. *Liberator,* XXXII:21, May 23, 1862.
34. Lincoln, *Complete Works,* II, 156.
35. *Liberator,* XXXII:28, July 11, 1862. Prof. Richard Hofstadter intelligently states the problem of historical judgment regarding agitators: "With the single exception of V. L. Parrington the standard writers have been handling him [Phillips] roughly for over forty years. Finding him useful chiefly as a foil of Abraham Lincoln, historians have stereotyped him as the wrongheaded radical of the Civil War crisis. . . . But conventional historians in condemning men like Phillips have used a double

standard of political morality. Scholars know that the processes of politics normally involve exaggeration, mythmaking, and fierce animosities. . . . Somehow the same historians who have been indulgent with men who exaggerated because they wanted to be elected have been extremely severe with men who exaggerated because they wanted to free the slaves." (Richard Hofstadter, *The American Political Tradition and the Men Who Made It.* New York, 1948, p. 135.)

Sitting in the quiet sunshine of judicial calm almost a century later, historians too have obstinately refused or blindly failed to comprehend the strident and fevered passions that agitated the slavery period. It seems they can comprehend (or surrender to) the urgency of contemporary compulsions only. Ralph Korngold aptly remarks: "One who had battled against slavery for a quarter of a century could hardly be blamed for looking with some suspicion upon a man who while claiming to have been opposed to human bondage all his life had remained virtually silent on the question until through the efforts and sacrifices of others, it had become a promising political issue." (Ralph Korngold, *Two Friends of Man,* New York, 1950, p. 266.)

36. New York *Herald,* Aug. 7, 1862. See also issue of Aug. 12, 1862.

37. New York *Daily Tribune,* Aug. 13 and 15, 1862, and letter by "Philo," Aug. 16, 1862. The charge was made in contrasting Phillips and Vallandigham.

38. *Liberator,* XXXII:35, Aug. 29, 1862; also Phillips, *Speeches, Lectures, and Letters,* First Series, pp. 465–467.

39. Pickett, p. 315.

40. Strunsky, "The Truth about Lincoln and the Negro," p. 267.

41. Hume, pp. 133–134; Paul J. Scheips, "Lincoln and the Chiriqui Colonization," *Journal of Negro History,* October, 1952, XXXVII, No. 4, p. 450. Scheips states that Negro opposition can well be given as a reason why no plans for large scale resettlement of Negroes could be executed or could be executed only with difficulty. Large scale colonization of Negroes could only have succeeded, if it could have succeeded at all, if the nation had been willing to make the gigantic propaganda, diplomatic, administrative, transportation, and financial effort that would have been required. As it was, "in a way nobody cared." (pp. 451, 453.)

42. Strunsky, "The Truth about Lincoln and the Negro," p. 267.

43. Pickett, p. 328; Oberholtzer, *Lincoln,* p. 289; Strunsky, "The Truth about Lincoln and the Negro," pp. 267–268; Holzman, p. 157.

44. Wilbur, pp. 75–77.

45. Ibid., p. 78.

46. Oberholtzer, *Lincoln,* p. 280.

47. Hollis, p. 198.

48. Wilbur, p. 81.

49. One man's meat is another man's poison. Though Prof. David Donald's conclusion differs from mine, the elements constituting it are the same, and he honestly remarks: "Lincoln's renowned sense of humor was related to his passion for secrecy. Again and again self-important delegations would descend upon the White House, deliver themselves of ponderous utterances upon pressing issues of the war and demand point blank what the President proposed to do about their problems. Lincoln

could say much in few words when he chose, but he could also say nothing at great length when it was expedient. His petitioner's request, he would say, reminded him of a 'little story' which he would proceed to tell in great detail, accompanied by mimicry and gestures, by hearty slapping of the thigh, by uproarous laughter at the end—at which time he would usher out his callers, baffled and confused by the smoke screen of good humor, with their questions still unanswered.

"Akin to Lincoln's gift for secrecy was his talent for passivity. Repeatedly, throughout the war, Lincoln's passive policy worked politically. Because any action would offend somebody, he took as few actions as possible. . . . Outright Abolitionists demanded that he use his war time powers to emancipate the Negroes. Border state politicians insisted that he protect their peculiar institutions. Lincoln needed the support of both groups, and therefore he did nothing. . . .

"Along with secrecy . . . Lincoln brought to his office an extraordinary frank pragmatism—some might call it opportunism. . . .

"A pragmatic politician . . . as President he could only do his best to handle problems as they arose and have a patient trust that popular support for his solutions would be forthcoming . . . ! My policy is to have no policy." (David Donald, pp. 68–70, 131, 138, 143. See also pp. 133, 135–136.)

CHAPTER FORTY-ONE

"Glory! hallelujah!"

1. Rhodes, IV, 161; Seitz, p. 335; Lincoln, *Complete Works*, II, 237–238.
2. Pearson, II, 51.
3. Martyn, p. 329.
4. Sears, p. 242; W. P. and F. J. Garrison, IV, 62, footnote.
5. McMaster, pp. 260–261.
6. Oberholtzer, *Lincoln*, p. 286.
7. Seitz, p. 348.
8. Richardson, VI, 136–142.
9. Douglass, p. 429.
10. Charles Coffin, *Abraham Lincoln* (New York, 1893), pp. 358–359; Whittier, "The Proclamation," op. cit., p. 419.
11. *Liberator*, XXXIII:2, Jan. 9, 1863.

"By his [Lincoln's] effective actions against slavery," says Professor Donald, "he left the Abolitionists without a cause. . . . For them Abraham Lincoln was not the great Emancipator; he was the killer of the dream." (p. 36.) But how does Prof. Donald explain Abolitionist support of the Emancipation Proclamation and Garrison's support of Lincoln in the election of 1864?

12. Conway, I, 336–339.
13. West, p. 619.
14. Thompson, p. 264.
15. John Bright, *Speeches of John Bright, M. P., on the American Question* (Boston, 1865), p. 128.

16. Hollis, pp. 236–237; Rollo Brown, p. 308.

17. Rhodes, IV, 358.

18. Wilbur D. Jones, "The British Conservatives and the American War," *American Historical Review* (April, 1953), LVIII, No. 3, p. 529. According to Jones both the extent and intensity of Southern sympathy among the Conservatives have been greatly exaggerated. During her years of struggle and need the South received "only the most illusory solace from British aristocrats, a detached innocuous sympathy which was quickly lost amid practical concerns." The life or death struggle in America, Jones insists, did not excite or hold Conservative interest to any appreciable extent. America was far away, and its affairs were not nearly so important as a division on a domestic issue or the troubles of Poland and Denmark. Besides the Conservatives were out of power and had little or nothing to do with the direction of foreign affairs. In fact their course during the period was aimed at gaining some sympathy from the British masses. But Jones weakens his argument by admitting uncertainty as to what, beneath the surface conciliation, were the prejudices and hopes of the Conservatives. (pp. 527, 540, 542–543.)

19. Ibid., p. 540.

20. Turpin, pp. 112–113.

21. Louis B. Schmidt, "Wheat and Cotton during the Civil War," *Iowa Journal of History and Politics* (Iowa City, Iowa, 1918), XVI, 418–419, 425–427, 437–438.)

22. Hillis, p. 212.

23. Hosmer, p. 208.

24. Seitz, p. 347.

25. Oberholtzer, *Lincoln*, pp. 270–271.

26. Nicolay, p. 349.

27. Strunsky, *Abraham Lincoln*, p. 193.

28. Macartney, pp. 76–77; George D. Williams, *A History of the Negro Troops in the War of the Rebellion* (New York, 1888), p. 259.

29. William E. B. DuBois, *Black Reconstruction* (New York, 1935), p. 111; Herbert Aptheker, "Negro Casualties in the Civil War," *Journal of Negro History* (Jan., 1947), XXXII, No. 1, p. 16; see also Aptheker, "The Negroes in the Union Navy," *Journal of Negro History* (April, 1947), XXXII, No. 2. Of the total deaths 2870 were killed in action or mortally wounded; 29,756 died of disease. As for the loss of life, the ratio for white volunteers was 94.32 per thousand (35.10 killed in action plus 59.22 died of disease) while that of the United States colored troops equaled 157.50 per thousand (16.11 killed in action plus 141.39 died of disease). (Aptheker, pp. 12–13, 15.)

The greatest single cause of death for all troops was disease, and this was particularly true among Negro troops. The explanation for the high mortality from disease in Negro regiments rested on many factors: the difficulty to find qualified surgeons to serve with Negro troops; the harsh treatment meted out to them, the menial duties assigned (they were used excessively for fatigue and labor details). But a host of other factors made for a high mortality rate: poor equipment, poor arms, poor leadership, poor training, poor and heedless and criminally careless employment in combat, and brutal orders among several Confederate officers of no quarter for Negro prisoners.

Until equalization of pay, the pay of the Negroes (regardless of rank) was $10 a month plus $3 for clothing, which was $3 less than that paid to white privates. The discriminatory wage aroused hostile and bitter feeling. The 54th Massachusetts Regiment served a year without pay rather than accept discriminatory wages and went into battle in Florida in 1864 singing, "Three cheers for Massachusetts and seven dollars a month." After many protests the War Department, beginning in 1864, paid the Negroes as much as the whites. (Aptheker, passim; J. H. Franklin, pp. 286–290.)

In the Navy, of the total reported battle casualties one fourth was suffered by Negroes, or of the 3220 men listed as killed, wounded, and missing, approximately 800 were Negroes. Of course, as in the army, disease was a major mortality factor, and conjectural figures of Negroes who died from disease, on the basis of army percentages of battle casualties to casualties from disease, totaled 2400. (pp. 70, 76.)

The Negroes constituted 25% of Navy personnel and performed all duties required of sailors aboard mid-nineteenth century men of war. They behaved well and at all times with conspicuous gallantry under fire. (Aptheker, "The Negroes in the Union Navy," p. 200 and passim.)

30. Strunsky, *Abraham Lincoln,* p. 216.

31. Ibid., p. 193.

32. Du Bois, p. 117; Robert D. Meade, *Judah P. Benjamin* (New York, 1943), pp. 289–292, 306, 307–308; Rembert W. Patrick, pp. 199–200.

Even without impressment the Confederate and state governments were able to secure the services of thousands of slaves who performed many important tasks. Most of the cooks in the Confederate army were slaves; there were also slave teamsters, mechanics, hospital attendants, ambulance drivers, and common laborers.

The Confederate Congress in 1864–65 openly debated arming the slaves. A representative from Mississippi deplored any suggestion that slaves should be armed and cried out, "God forbid that this Trojan horse should be introduced among us." A bill was introduced in the Confederate Senate in 1865 providing for the enlistment of 200,000 Negroes and their emancipation if they remained loyal through the war. General Lee said the measure was not only expedient but necessary. On March 13, 1865, a bill was signed by President Davis which authorized him to call on each state for her quota of 300,000 additional troops, irrespective of color, on condition that the slaves recruited from any state should not exceed 25% of the able-bodied male slave population between eighteen and forty-five. But it was too late. (John H. Franklin, pp. 283–286.)

33. Oberholtzer, *Lincoln,* pp. 272–273.

34. Pearson, II, 70.

35. Ibid., II, 85.

36. Ibid., II, 87.

37. Ibid., II, 88.

38. Wyman, p. 5.

39. Phillips, "Toussaint L'Ouverture," *Speeches, Lectures, and Letters,* First Series, pp. 484–489; 491–494.

40. Phillips, "A Metropolitan Police," ibid., pp. 495–523.
41. *Liberator*, XXXIV:1, Jan. 1, 1864.
42. New York *World*, Dec. 23, 1863.
43. *Liberator*, XXXIII:22, May 29, 1863.
44. Ibid., XXXIV:6, Feb. 5, 1864.
45. So stated by Martyn, p. 335.

CHAPTER FORTY-TWO

"Don't Swap Horses"

1. *Liberator*, XXXIV:6, Feb. 5, 1864.
2. W. P. and F. J. Garrison, IV, 95–97.
3. *Liberator*, XXXIV:24–26, June 10–24, 1864.
4. W. P. and F. J. Garrison, IV, 97.
5. Coffin, p. 415.
6. *Liberator*, XXXIV:21 May 20, 1864.
7. Ibid., XXXIV:22, May 27, 1864.
8. Ware, pp. 139–140.
9. Manuscript letter, June 29, 1862. (Sumner Collection, Harvard College Library.)
10. Ware, p. 112; Horace E. Scudder, *James Russell Lowell*, 2 vols. (Boston and New York, 1901), II, 29.
11. Hillis, p. 205.
12. "Without doubt the idea that the existence of slavery degraded labor and that new slave territory tended to limit opportunity for poor immigrants who could not purchase slaves had considerable appeal to the German population." Ruhl J. Bartlett, *John C. Fremont and the Republican Party* (Columbus, Ohio, 1930), pp. 28–29. Bartlett makes the statement above of the German support of the Republican Party in 1856, but the Germans still advocated that slavery be abolished and that the Confederate states be treated as territories. (Ibid., pp. 97–98.) In Boston the German group was led by Heinzen, Phillips's friend and protector. (Ibid., p. 100.)
13. Bartlett, pp. 104–105.
14. Whittier, "The Pass of the Sierra," op. cit., p. 396.
15. *Liberator*, XXXIV:23, June 3, 1864.
16. *United States Census Report, 1860.* Introduction, lii–liii. The German population of New York State was 150,000, and Lincoln's majority in New York State was only 6,749. The entire Lincoln majority throughout the country was only about ten per cent of the voters. (Bartlett, pp. 12–13.)
17. Oberholtzer, *Lincoln*, p. 313.
18. Barton, *The Life of Abraham Lincoln*, II, 285.
19. *Proceedings of the First Three Republican National Conventions,* 1864, pp. 175–247.
20. Harold M. Dudley, "The Election of 1864," *Mississippi Valley Historical Review* (1931–1932), XVIII, 509; Lincoln, *Complete Works*, II, 531–532.

21. Winston, p. 257.
22. Allen Thorndike Rice, Reminiscences of Abraham Lincoln by Distinguished Men of His Time, New York, 1886, pp. 158–159.
23. Dudley, p. 510.
24. See, for example, issues of July 19, Aug. 3, 1864. (The New York World.)
25. Thompson, p. 190; Arnold, pp. 374–375.
26. Wood Gray, p. 191.
27. Jonathan Grossman, William Sylvis, Pioneer of American Labor (New York, 1945), p. 50.
28. New York Sun, June 30, 1889; Rhodes, IV, 518.
29. Rhodes, IV, 519.
30. Dudley, pp. 500–501.
31. Ibid., p. 516.
32. Manuscript letter. (New York Public Library, 42nd Street.)
33. Thompson, p. 142.
34. Arnold, p. 385, footnote.
35. Nevins, Fremont, II, 647.
36. Coffin, p. 431; Bartlett, p. 117.
37. Barton, Life of Abraham Lincoln, II, 292–293.
38. Ibid., II, 293.
39. Forbes, II, 101.
40. Bartlett, p. 117.
41. Nevins, Fremont, I, 651.
42. Bartlett, p. 118.
43. Ibid., p. 84.
44. Fessenden, I, 265–266.
45. Bartlett, p. 86.
46. Ibid., pp. 118–119.
47. Coffin, p. 431.
48. Bartlett, p. 119.
49. Strunsky, Abraham Lincoln, p. 224; Coffin, pp. 431–432.
50. Dudley, p. 511.
51. Strunsky, Abraham Lincoln, p. 218.
52. Coffin, p. 439.
53. Hollis, p. 203; Wood Gray, p. 184.
54. Dudley, p. 513.
55. Ibid., p. 514.
56. Coffin, p. 443.
57. Dudley, p. 514.
58. Oberholtzer, Abraham Lincoln, pp. 312–313.
59. Lloyd Lewis, Myths about Lincoln (New York, 1929), p. 24.
60. Ware, p. 137.
61. Barton, President Lincoln, I, 656.
62. Ibid., I, 656.
63. Ibid., I, 657.
64. National Anti-Slavery Standard, July 9, 1864.
65. Ibid., Sept. 10, 1864.
66. Manuscript letter, May 29, 1865. (New York Historical Society.)

67. Manuscript poem by John Pierpont, Dec. 1863. (New York Historical Society.)
68. Bartlett, p. 126.
69. Nevins, *Fremont*, I, 667.
70. *Liberator*, XXXIV:44, Oct. 28, 1864.
71. Dudley, pp. 511–512.
72. Strunsky, *Abraham Lincoln*, pp. 229–230.
73. Allen T. Rice, p. xliii.
74. Carpenter, pp. 79, 279.
75. Emerson, *Letters*, Nov. 16, 1864, V, 387.

CHAPTER FORTY-THREE

A King's Cure-All

1. Coffin, pp. 472–473.
2. Ibid., p. 473; Arnold, p. 366.
3. Strunsky, *Abraham Lincoln*, pp. 268–269.
4. Jacobus Ten Broek, *The Antislavery Origins of the Fourteenth Amendment* (Berkeley and Los Angeles, 1951), pp. 147–148, 154–155). Ten Broek perceptively states that it was as a culmination of the Abolition movement that the clauses of section 1 of the 14th Amendment were made a part of the Constitution and their accepted meaning was the meaning which the Abolitionists gave them on the hustings, in revival meetings, in pamphlets, and in the thousand other outlets to their moral ardor. (pp. 94–95.) The Abolitionists emphasized the concept of the equal protection of the laws, accepted as axiomatic the notion that governments were instituted to protect man in his inalienable rights to life, liberty, and property, and that the standard by which this protection was to be meted out was that of equality, that the equal protection of the laws was made explicit in the Declaration of Independence and in the Early Republic, that the due process of law was not merely a restraint on governmental power but an obligation imposed upon government to supply protection against private action, and that the privileges and immunities of a citizen were not to be abridged by the states. Slavery destroyed "a man's inalienable right to his own body," his ownership of himself. The slave was transformed from a man into a thing. All these inalienable rights were invaded, destroyed, or denied by slavery. So was one other—the right to be protected equally in these various rights —to prevent one class of men from seizing upon another class and robbing them of their liberty and the ownership of their own persons. (Ibid., pp. 94–105.)

After the passage of the 13th Amendment doubts about the adequacy of the Amendment became so serious that it seemed advisable to try to do the same job over again through another amendment to make the provisions constitutionally secure. (Ibid., p. 185.)
5. W. P. and F. J. Garrison, IV, 144.
6. Lloyd Lewis, pp. 53–54; Wertenbaker and Smith, *The United States of America* (New York, 1931), p. 414.

7. Phillips, "Abraham Lincoln," *Speeches, Lectures, and Letters, Second Series,* pp. 447–449.

8. Phillips, "The Immediate Issue," in *The Equality of All Men before the Law,* pp. 32, 33–35.

9. W. P. and F. J. Garrison, IV, 157–161.

10. *Liberator,* XXXV:21, May 26, 1865.

11. Stearns, *Sketches from Concord and Appledore,* p. 212.

12. Wyman, pp. 13–14.

13. Manuscript letter, Dec. 7, 1868. (Boston Public Library.)

14. Wyman, pp. 12–13.

15. W. P. and F. J. Garrison, IV, 155–157.

16. *Liberator,* XXXV:22, June 2, 1865.

17. Goldwin Smith, p. 183.

18. *Liberator,* Dec. 29, 1865.

CHAPTER FORTY-FOUR

"'Joy My Freedom!"

1. New York *World,* Aug. 2, 1865.

2. Rhodes, V, 557.

3. *Journal of Negro History,* XVIII, 17.

4. Ibid., p. 17.

5. Ibid., p. 22.

6. Paul L. Haworth, *Reconstruction and Union* (New York, 1912), p. 9.

7. Rhodes, V, 558.

8. Haworth, p. 7.

9. Henry Lee Swint, *The Northern Teacher in the South, 1862–1870* (Nashville, Tenn., 1941), pp. 5, 26, 35–36, 42, 77.

10. Ellis P. Oberholtzer, *History of the United States Since the Civil War* (New York, 1917–1937), I, 89–90.

CHAPTER FORTY-FIVE

The Greeneville Tailor—Political Goths

1. George F. Milton, *The Age of Hate* (New York, 1930), p. 164.

2. Ibid., p. 169.

3. Oberholtzer, *History of the United States,* I, 21.

4. New York *Daily Tribune,* April 24, 1865.

5. Fleming, p. 73; Edward McPherson, *Political History of the United States during the Period of Reconstruction* (Wash., D. C., 1880), p. 47, footnote.

6. Maj. Gen. Benj. C. Truman, "Anecdotes of Andrew Johnson," (1913), *The Century Magazine* LXXXV, 440.

7. Du Bois, p. 252.

8. Oberholtzer, *A History of the United States,* I, 149.

9. Marguerite H. Albjerg, "The New York Press and Andrew Johnson," *The South Atlantic Quarterly* (Durham, N. C., 1927), XXVI, 409.

10. *Congressional Globe,* 36th Congress, 2nd Session, Dec. 18, 19, 1860, pp. 117–119, 134–143, especially p. 141.

11. Ibid., p. 142.

12. Ibid., 36th Congress, 1st Session, Part 1, Dec. 12, 1859, pp. 100–107, especially pp. 105–107.

13. Winston, p. 145.

14. Claude G. Bowers, p. 33.

15. Du Bois, pp. 244–245.

16. Clifton R. Hall, *Andrew Johnson, Military Governor of Tennessee* (Princeton, N. J., 1916), p. 221.

17. Fleming, p. 72.

18. *Congressional Globe,* 32 Congress, 2nd Session, 1862, p. 586.

19. Claude G. Bowers, p. 41.

20. Ibid., p. 42.

21. Thompson, p. 341.

22. Claude G. Bowers, p. 39.

23. Ibid., p. 40.

24. Milton, *The Age of Hate,* p. 147.

25. Hugh McCulloch, *Men and Measures,* New York, 1888, p. 373; Milton, p. 145.

26. Bowers, p. 37.

27. Ibid., pp. 37–38.

28. Henry Adams, The Education of Henry Adams, Boston and New York, 1918, p. 246.

29. Du Bois, p. 142.

30. Swint, pp. v, 107. The majority of these men and women went South with the idea that the whole people of the South were defeated sinners who refused to repent. What the sword had conquered the school must now make secure. Their aim was to urge the Negro to support with his ballot the party of his friends and to assume his place as a social and political equal of the Southern white man. That underlying purpose caused ill feeling among the Southerners. (Swint, pp. 57, 59, 82–83, 90.) Swint contends that the South was not against Negro education but was opposed to education of the Negro by radical Abolitionists from the North. Yet the sentiment did not result in the adoption of any definite program. (Ibid., pp. 115 et seq.)

31. 39 Congress, 1st Session, Senate Executive Document No. 2, Report of Carl Schurz, *Condition of the South,* p. 81.

32. James W. Garner, *Reconstruction in Mississippi* (New York, Macmillan, 1901), p. 116.

33. New York *Daily Tribune,* Nov. 15, Oct. 3, 1865.

34. Claude G. Bowers, p. 344.

35. Fleming, pp. 59–60.

36. Whittier, "To the Thirty-ninth Congress," op. cit., pp. 427–428.

37. Oberholtzer, *A History of the United States,* I, 151–152.

38. *National Anti-Slavery Standard,* March 23, 1867.

39. Francis B. Simkins, *The South, Old and New* (New York, 1947), pp. 198–199, 223.

40. E. Merton Coulter, *The South during Reconstruction* (Baton Rouge, La., 1947), p. 322.

41. Simkins, p. 199. Simkins pertinently remarks: Reconstruction was an era of unhealthy politics which called forth the evil in men that under happier conditions would have been suppressed. "It is an error, however, to treat those years as an example of isolated evil. If Reconstruction was a time of rampant corruption in Southern history, this was also true of the same period in the Northern States. The contemporary scandals of the Grant Administration in Washington and the Tweed Ring in New York were fully as regrettable as events in Southern capitals. Conservative governments of the Southern States which preceded and followed the Radical regimes were not spotless; for example, numerous Democratic land agents stole public lands in the time of President Van Buren, and the Brown-Gordon-Colquitt coalition after Reconstruction behaved unscrupulously. All these examples of corruption and extravagance, including those of the Radical legislatures, may be construed as part of a national era of expansion. . . . Even the attempt of South Carolina's legislature to endow blacks with homesteads—sometimes cited as a prime example of radical folly—was not an act of madness, but an effort to supplement political with economic enfranchisement, an experiment not without precedent among progressive European nations."

Although Simkins believes the expenditures of the Southern Radicals were high, they were still not great enough to stifle the significant agricultural and commercial progress of the Reconstruction period. "That reputed Utopia, the Old South, was responsible in a sense for the ignorance and incompetence of the Negro voters and office-holders of the antebellum period. For if the Radicals in Congress were unwise in conferring political and social privileges upon ex-slaves, the rulers of the Old South were equally short-sighted in keeping down these unfortunate people." (pp. 197–198.)

Finally:"It is doubtful whether Reconstruction essentially changed the beliefs of the South. Left to itself the region could not have accorded the Negro the vote or other manifestations of equality. After Reconstruction, when the South was free from Northern interference, it deprived the Negro of his rights." (p. 223.)

Gunnar Myrdal in *An American Dilemma, The Negro Problem and American Democracy* (New York, 1944) finds the explanation for the economic backwardness of the South in the rigid institutional structure of the economic life of the region which, historically, is derived from slavery and, psychologically, is rooted in the minds of the people." (I, 221.) "The South is a stubbornly lagging American frontier society with a strong paternalistic tinge inherited from the old plantation and slavery system. . . . Paternalism . . . fits ideally into the individualistic and romantic temper." (I, 459.)

W. J. Cash (*The Mind of the South*) expressed a similar sentiment: ". . . the extent of the change and of the break between the Old South that was and the South of our time has been vastly exaggerated. The South, one might say, is a tree with many age rings, with its limbs and trunks bent and twisted by all the winds of the years, but with its tap roots in the Old South. . . . If this war had smashed the Southern world, it had left the essential Southern mind and will . . . entirely unshaken." (pp. x, 103.)

42. Gunnar Myrdal, I, 448.
43. Ibid., I, 450.
44. Oberholtzer, *A History of the United States*, I, 382.
45. Ibid., I, 384; Beale, pp. 353–354.
46. James T. Adams, *March of Democracy*, II, 119–120.
47. *National Anti-Slavery Standard*, Aug. 18, 1866.

CHAPTER FORTY-SIX

Hussar Jackets

1. *National Anti-Slavery Standard*, Oct. 28, 1865.
2. Ibid., June 6, 1868; Aug. 28, 1869.
3. New York *World*, Sept. 7, 1867.
4. *National Anti-Slavery Standard*, May 11, 1867.
5. Ibid., April 21, 1866; May 30, 1868.
6. Manuscript letters, March 17, April 30, March 24, 1866. (Sumner Collection, Harvard College Library.)
7. Albert B. Hart, *Salmon P. Chase* (Boston and New York, 1899), p. 346; see Note 18 in Appendix.
8. Horace White, *The Life of Lyman Trumbull* (Boston, 1913), p. 239.
9. *National Anti-Slavery Standard*, May 19, 1866.
10. Ibid., May 19, 1866.
11. Ibid., May 19, 1866.
12. Ibid., May 19, 1866.
13. Ibid., May 18, 1867.
14. Ibid., June 8, 1867.
15. Ibid., June 8, 1867.
16. Ibid., Oct. 28, 1865.
17. Ibid., March 20, 1869.
18. Ibid., June 15, 1867.
19. Ibid., May 18, 1867.
20. Ibid., June 8, 1867.
21. Ibid., Oct. 19, 1867.
22. New York *World*, Oct. 29, 1866.
23. *National Anti-Slavery Standard*, Nov. 24, 1866.
24. Ibid., June 1, 1867.
25. Carpenter, p. 105.
26. Manuscript letter from Sumner, March 17, 1866, quoted in Martyn, p. 353.
27. *National Anti-Slavery Standard*, Sept. 15, 1866. See unfavorable editorial, however, in the New York *Times* of July 21, 1866. The truce between Phillips and the newspapers was never long lasting.
28. *National Anti-Slavery Standard*, Sept. 29, 1866.
29. Ibid., Aug. 4, 1866.
30. Manuscript letter. (New York Public Library, 42nd Street.)
31. Manuscript letter, Jan. 29, 1868. (New York Historical Society.)

32. Manuscript letters, March 4, 1857, Sept. 27 (year undated). (Mrs. H. C. Ingersoll Papers, Library of Congress.)
33. *National Anti-Slavery Standard,* Feb. 23, 1867.
34. Martyn, p. 356.
35. *National Anti-Slavery Standard,* April 27, 1867.
36. Manuscript letters. (Sumner Collection, Harvard College Library.)
37. Manuscript letter, July, 1867. (Giddings-Julian Papers, Library of Congress.)
38. Manuscript letter, Dec. 13, 1875. (James G. Blaine Papers, Library of Congress.)
39. Austin, *Wendell Phillips,* pp. 243–245.

CHAPTER FORTY-SEVEN
"Impeach the Rebel!"

1. Beale, pp. 370–371.
2. Ibid., p. 371.
3. Ibid., pp. 372–373.
4. Robert W. Winston, *Andrew Johnson* (New York, 1928), p. 343.
5. Ibid., pp. 344–345.
6. Oberholtzer, *A History of the United States,* I, 172.
7. Ibid., I, 172.
8. Winston, p. 345.
9. Oberholtzer, I, 402.
10. Claude G. Bowers, pp. 137–138.
11. Beale, p. 370.
12. Petroleum V. Nasby (David R. Locke) *Andy's Trip to the West* (New York, 1866) cover and p. 13.
13. Winston, p. 367.
14. McPherson, pp. 134–136.
15. Oberholtzer, I, 411.
16. *National Anti-Slavery Standard,* Nov. 17, 1866.
17. Beale, p. 403.
18. Claude G. Bowers, p. 158; Holzman, p. 171.
19. *National Anti-Slavery Standard,* Feb. 29, 1868.
20. Richard N. Current, *Old Thad Stevens* (Madison, Wisc., 1942), pp. 303, 304, 306.
21. Winston, p. 450.
22. Ibid., p. 453.
23. Ibid., p. 451; Holzman, p. 170.
24. Winston, pp. 451–453.
25. Ibid., p. 453.
26. Oberholtzer, II, 132–133.
27. Ibid., II, 133.
28. *National Anti-Slavery Standard,* May 23, 1868.

CHAPTER FORTY-EIGHT

"To Your Tents, O Israel"

1. *National Anti-Slavery Standard,* Dec. 28, 1867.
2. Ibid., Aug. 11, 1866.
3. Ibid., Aug. 11, 1866.
4. Ibid., March 27, May 30, June 20, 1868.
5. Ibid., Aug. 29, Sept. 26, Nov. 7, 1868.
6. Ibid., Nov. 14, 1868.
7. Carrie Chapman Catt and Nettie Rogers Shuler, *Woman Suffrage and Politics* (New York, 1923), p. 50.
8. *National Anti-Slavery Standard,* June 6, 1868.
9. Ibid., Aug. 21, 1869.
10. Ibid., July 3, 1869.
11. Ibid., July 3, 1869.
12. Mrs. Rheta Louise (Childe) Dorr, *Susan B. Anthony* (New York, 1928), p. 183.
13. Catt and Shuler, p. 73.
14. *National Anti-Slavery Standard,* May 29, 1869.
15. Ibid., May 29, 1869.
16. Ibid., May 29, 1869.
17. Ibid., May 29, 1869.
18. Ibid., June 12, 1869.
19. Ibid., Aug. 7, 1869.
20. Ibid., Oct. 23, 1869.
21. Martyn, p. 369.
22. Manuscript letter, quoted in Martyn, pp. 370–371.
23. Quoted in the *National Anti-Slavery Standard,* April 16, 1870.
24. See Note 19 in Appendix.
25. *National Anti-Slavery Standard,* April 16, 1870.

CHAPTER FORTY-NINE

The Citadel of State Street

1. George W. Curtis, *Wendell Phillips* (New York, 1884), p. 31.
1ᵃ David Donald, pp. 30, 36; Mandel, pp. 61–62, 82, 95, and passim.
2. Swift, p. 360; W. P. and F. J. Garrison, IV, 249.
3. See manuscript letter to R. D. Webb, Jan. 13, 1848 (Boston Public Library), and pamphlets and notes on labor found in his library after his death. (Martyn, pp. 379–380.) According to Korngold, Phillips's interest in labor should be dated later. (Korngold, pp. 366–367.)
4. Stearns, *Sketches from Concord and Appledore,* p. 217.
5. Phillips, *Speeches, Lectures, and Letters,* Second Series, p. 139; see also *Remarks at the Mass Meeting of Workingmen in Faneuil Hall, Nov. 2, 1865* (Boston, 1865.)
6. Phillips, *Speeches, Lectures, and Letters,* Second Series, p. 139.

7. Phillips, *Remarks at the Mass Meeting of Workingmen in Faneuil Hall*, pp. 7–9.

8. Ibid., pp. 13, 14, 19, 20.

9. Terence Powderly, *Thirty Years of Labor* (Columbus, Ohio, 1890), pp. 72–73.

10. *American Annual Cyclopedia, 1870* (New York, 1871), X, 473, 474.

11. Ibid., X, 474; Nathan Fine, *Labor and Farmer Parties in the United States* (New York, 1928), p. 29.

12. *National Standard*, Oct. 29, 1870.

13. Ibid., Oct. 29, 1870.

14. Jonathan Grossman, pp. 155–157.

15. *National Standard*, Nov. 5, 1870.

16. Ibid., Nov. 5, 1870.

17. Ibid., Nov. 5, 1870.

18. Ibid., Nov. 5, 1870.

19. Ibid., Nov. 5, 1870.

20. Ibid., Nov. 12, 1870.

21. Stearns, *Sketches from Concord and Appledore*, pp. 180–181.

22. *National Standard*, Nov. 12, 1870.

23. *American Annual Cyclopedia, 1870*, X, 477.

CHAPTER FIFTY

The Battle of Labor

1. Benjamin F. Butler, *Butler's Book* (Boston, 1892), pp. 414–425, Holzman, pp. 84–88.

2. *Life and Public Services of Major General Butler* (Phila., 1864), p. 84.

3. *Hansard's Parliamentary Debates* (London, 1862), June 13, 1862, Third Series, CLXVII, 611–618.

4. *Punch or the London Charivari*, July 5, 1862, XLIII, 9.

5. Howard P. Johnson, "New Orleans under General Butler," *The Louisiana Historical Quarterly*, April, 1941, XXIV, No. 2, pp. 531–532. Johnson adds: "It is true his rule at New Orleans was unnecessarily severe. . . . On the other hand New Orleans as a whole was a tough city and it gave Butler strong provocation for rough handling. . . . And the people themselves from beginning to end were, like General Butler himself, angry and rude. . . . Condemnation of his harshness is mainly condemnation of that generally vindictive spirit which seems to follow upon the heels of war. . . . Butler must appear less the monster that a subject people thought him than an embodiment . . . of the immemorial ways of the victor with the vanquished." (p. 532.)

6. Benjamin F. Butler, Letter to Edward L. Pierce, Aug. 15, 1861, *Private and Official Correspondence of General Benjamin F. Butler during the Period of the Civil War* (Privately Issued, 1917), I, 216.

7. *Commonwealth History of Massachusetts*, IV, 68; Holzman, pp. 13–14.

8. Wyman, p. 145.

9. John Russell Young, *Around the World with General Grant* (New York, 1879), II, 304.

10. James H. Wilson, *The Life of Charles A. Dana* (New York and London, 1907), pp. 483–484.

11. Butler, *Butler's Book*, p. 416.

12. Ibid., pp. 860, 871, 812.

13. Ibid., p. 104.

14. Benj. F. Butler, *Argument before the Tewksbury Investigation Committee,* July 15, 1883, p. 42.

15. Wyman, pp. 24–25.

16. Phillips, *The People Coming to Power* (Boston, 1871), p. 3.

17. Ibid., p. 3.

18. Ibid., p. 8.

19. Ibid., pp. 9–10.

20. Ibid., pp. 11–12.

21. Ibid., pp. 12–14.

22. Ibid., pp. 17, 21–22.

23. Ibid., p. 23.

24. *National Standard*, Nov. 4, 1871.

25. Ibid., Oct. 21, 1871. See also "The Foundation of the Labor Movement," *Speeches, Lectures, and Letters*, Second Series, pp. 152–154.

26. *American Annual Cyclopedia, 1871*, xi, 494; Fine, p. 30.

27. *American Annual Cyclopedia, 1871*, xi, 494–495.

28. *National Standard*, May 20, 1871.

29. Ibid., May 27, 1871.

30. Ibid., July 8, 1871.

31. Ibid., Oct. 21, 1871.

32. Ibid., Dec. 2, 1871.

33. Korngold, pp. 367, 369. "The system which he hoped would supplant Capitalism bears some resemblance to that advocated by Peter Kropotkin, who wished to form local cooperative and productive groups where 'loving treatment, moral influence, and liberty' would prevail." (Ibid., p. 370.)

34. Hofstadter, pp. 159–160.

35. Phillips, "The Foundation of the Labor Movement," op. cit., Second Series, pp. 158–159. See also Martyn, pp. 389–392.

36. "The Foundation of the Labor Movement," op. cit., p. 163.

37. Ibid., p. 167.

38. New York *Daily Tribune*, Dec. 7, 1871.

39. Ibid., Dec. 7, 1871.

40. Ibid., Dec. 7, 1871.

41. Phillips, "The Labor Question," *Speeches, Lectures, and Letters*, Second Series, pp. 172–175.

42. Ibid., pp. 169–170. See also Note 20 in Appendix.

CHAPTER FIFTY-ONE

Sumner's Humiliation—"Old White Hat"—Enlightening Jonathan

1. William E. Woodward, Meet General Grant (New York, 1928), p. 446.
2. William C. Church, Ulysses S. Grant (New York, 1897), p. 375.
3. Louis A. Coolidge, Ulysses S. Grant (Boston, 1917), pp. 326–327.
4. Allan Nevins, Hamilton Fish (New York, 1936), pp. 373–374.
5. Ibid., pp. 372–373.
6. Oliver Wendell Holmes, Ralph Waldo Emerson and John Lothrop Motley (Boston and New York, 1892), p. 447.
7. Storey, p. 421.
8. Edward L. Pierce, Memoir and Letters of Charles Sumner 4 vols. (Boston, 1893), IV, 552. Whittier launched a movement to rescind the offensive resolution. (Ibid., IV, 561–562.)
9. Martyn, pp. 424–425.
10. Ibid., pp. 425–427. Louis Ruchames ("Charles Sumner and American Historiography," Journal of Negro History, April, 1953), XXXVIII, No. 2) has ably charted the rise and fall in the barometer of Sumner's reputation: from George Haynes's evaluation, "No American of Sumner's day had a wider or more distinguished circle of personal friends. . . . No other American of his time had so wide and eminent an acquaintance abroad," Emerson's "I never knew so white a soul," and Schouler's ". . . to the sickly moral atmosphere of our Potomac capital he was like the advent of a north wind. . . . His sense of moral rectitude was sublime" to David Donald's "the arrogant Massachusetts solon" whose Crime against Kansas speech "reeked of the sewer" and George F. Milton's indictment of Sumner as an "eerie evil genius who sat in Daniel Webster's seat in the Senate spinning tenuous spider-webs of far fetched theory about Negro equality. . . . In his own opinion Charles Sumner was almost a demigod."

The change came, as Ruchames points out, with a change in the historical attitude towards the Abolitionists and Reconstruction. The Abolitionists were now wild-eyed fanatics, breeders of hatred and Civil War. William A. Dunning, making the first great overture of appeasement towards the South, fired the first gun against Sumner's reputation.

Yet as Prof. David Donald frankly admits in a recent book (Lincoln Reconsidered), when Sumner was not posturing from a pedestal, he could relax and become, as Mrs. Lincoln found, "the most agreeable and delightful of men." Mary Lincoln found the handsome Senator one of the most congenial men in Washington. Sumner and Mrs. Lincoln wrote each other notes in French; they went for carriage drives; they lent each other books and she sent him bouquets from the White House conservatory. The President too found that the Senator had qualities of personal charm. Mary Lincoln declared that her husband and the Senator ("the Abolitionist fanatic") used to talk and "laugh together like two schoolboys."

11. Manuscript letter on Sumner Resolutions to J. B. Smith, Esq. (Massachusetts Historical Society.)
12. Gamaliel Bradford, "Charles Sumner," Yale Review (April–July, 1916), V, 552.

13. Pierce, IV, 591.

14. See manuscript letter to Sumner, April 11, 1872. (Sumner Collection, Harvard College Library.) Note 21 in Appendix.

15. Cincinnati Correspondent, New York *World*, May 4, 1872; Wittke, *Refugees of Revolution*, pp. 250–253.

16. Oberholtzer, III, 27–28; Henry L. Stoddard, *Horace Greeley* (New York, 1946), p. 312.

17. Stoddard, *Greeley*, pp. 304, 313, 315.

18. Letter to John Sherman, July 16, 1872, *The Sherman Letters*, p. 337.

19. *The Nation*, July 4, 1872, XV, 1.

20. Constance Rourke, *Trumpets of Jubilee* (New York, 1927), p. 330.

21. Don C. Seitz, *Horace Greeley* (Indianapolis, 1926), p. 229.

22. Rourke, p. 348.

23. Oberholtzer, III, 54.

24. Claude G. Bowers, p. 391.

25. New York *Daily Tribune*, Jan. 7, 1868. See also issues of May 1, 1861 and Dec. 10, 1867; *Harper's Weekly*, July 6, 1872, p. 523; Chauncey M. Depew, *My Memories of Eighty Years* (New York, 1924), p. 93.

26. Oberholtzer, III, 55–56.

27. *Harper's Weekly*, 1872, xvi, passim.

28. Ibid., May 25, 1872, p. 416; July 13, 1872, pp. 548, 560; July 20, 1872, p. 573; Aug. 31, 1872, p. 665; Sept. 7, 1872, p. 692; Sept. 14, 1872, p. 713; Sept. 21, 1872, p. 732.

29. Conkling, p. 435, quoted in *DAB*, VII, 499.

30. *The Nation*, issues of Aug. 29, Sept. 12, Sept. 26, Oct. 10, Oct. 31, 1872; Seitz, pp. 385–386.

31. Seitz, pp. 385–386.

32. Ibid., p. 386.

33. W. P. and F. J. Garrison, IV, 260.

34. Martyn, pp. 400–402.

35. Gamaliel Bradford, "Horace Greeley," *The American Mercury* (April, 1924), I, No. 4, p. 390; Rourke, p. 355.

36. Oberholtzer, III, 65–66.

37. John T. Campbell, *The Great Problem of the Age: An Address on Labor Reform* (Phila. and Lancaster, Pa., 1872), back page cover.

38. Fine, pp. 31–32.

39. Herbert Paul, *Life of Froude* (New York, 1905), p. 202. See also reports on Froude and his lectures in the New York *Tribune*, Oct. 17, 19, 22, 24, 26, 1872. The Editor remarked prophetically: "The mission of Froude is to be no holiday progress. . . . It was not without reason that he said at the banquet on Tuesday night, quoting the misgiving of Falstaff, 'Would it were evening, and all were well!'" (Oct. 17, 1872.) A report of the lectures is also given in "Thumping English Lies," *Froude's Slanders on Ireland and Irishmen*, with preface and notes by Colonel James F. McGee (New York, 1872). The last must be read with a considerable degree of caution.

40. Paul, p. 205.

41. Ibid., p. 207.

42. Ibid., pp. 208–209.

43. Ibid., p. 211.

44. Ibid., p. 214.

45. Rev. Thomas N. Burke, *English Misrule in Ireland* (New York, 1877) "There is little doubt that Mr. Froude has met his match in combativeness and daring." (New York *Tribune*, Oct. 21, 1872.) For Burke's lectures as reported in the newspapers, see New York *Tribune*, Nov. 15, 20, 22, 27, 1872.

46. Martyn, pp. 404–405. See Phillips's comments on Froude in the course of his lecture on "Daniel O'Connell," New York *Herald Tribune*, Dec. 10, 1872.

CHAPTER FIFTY-TWO

The Louisiana Episode

1. George F. Hoar, *Autobiography of Seventy Years* (New York, 1903), 2 vols., I, 208.

2. See inflammatory report in the New York *World*, Jan. 5, 1875; Coolidge, p. 470.

3. Ibid., p. 471.

4. Jesse H. Jones, *His Last Battle, Wendell Phillips in Faneuil Hall on the Louisiana Difficulties* (Boston, 1897), p. 12.

5. Ibid., pp. 13–15.

6. Ibid., p. 27.

7. Ibid., pp. 30–31.

CHAPTER FIFTY-THREE

The Money Question—Daniel O'Connell—Old South Church

1. Martyn, p. 412.

2. *Sketches and Reminiscences of the Radical Club,* ed. by Mrs. John T. Sargent (Boston, 1880), p. 165.

3. Boston *Daily Globe*, Oct. 12, 1875.

4. Ibid., Oct. 12, 1875.

5. Phillips, *Who Shall Rule Us? Money or the People?* (Boston, 1878), pp. 5, 6, 8.

6. *Sketches and Reminiscences of the Radical Club,* p. 163.

7. Phillips, "Daniel O'Connell," *Speeches, Lectures, and Letters,* Second Series, pp. 389–390, 392, 394, 396–397, 406–407, 409.

8. *American Annual Cyclopedia, 1875,* XV, 479.

9. John R. Commons, et al, *History of Labor in the United States* (New York, 1918–1935), II, 87–88.

10. Foster Rhea Dulles, *Labor in America* (New York, 1949), p. 107.

11. Boston *Daily Globe*, Oct. 7, 1875.

12. Ibid., Nov. 1, 1875.

13. *American Annual Cyclopedia, 1875,* XV, 480.

14. Manuscript letters to Mrs. Helen Garrison, Spring and Dec., 1875. (Boston Public Library.)

15. Phillips, "The Old South Meeting House," *Speeches, Lectures, and Letters,* Second Series, pp. 237–238.

16. Phillips, *Who Shall Rule Us? Money or the People?,* pp. 3–5.

17. Thomas A. Bland, *Life of Benjamin F. Butler* (Boston, 1879), p. 192.

18. Ibid., p. 191.

19. Phillips, *Who Shall Rule Us? Money or the People?* p. 7.

20. See Note 22 in Appendix.

21. W. P. and F. J. Garrison, IV, 305; Oliver Johnson, p. 401.

22. W. P. and F. J. Garrison, IV, 305–307.

23. Phillips, "William Lloyd Garrison," *Speeches, Lectures, and Letters,* Second Series, p. 472.

CHAPTER FIFTY-FOUR

The Champion of Orthodoxy

1. *Sketches and Reminiscences of the Radical Club,* pp. 76–77.
2. Ibid., pp. 147–148.
3. Ibid., pp. 178–179.
4. Ibid., p. 296.
5. Ibid., pp. 163–164.
6. Ibid., p. 165.

CHAPTER FIFTY-FIVE

Lecturing

1. Martyn, p. 441.

Travel:	Street Life in Europe
Science:	The Lost Arts
Current Events:	The Times or The Lesson of the Hour
Reform:	Temperance, Labor, Woman, The Indians, or, in earlier days, Anti-Slavery
Political Economy:	Finance
Political Philosophy:	Agitation (his favorite college commencement address
Law:	Law and Lawyers, Courts and Jails
Foreign Affairs:	The Irish Question
Biography:	Toussaint, O'Connell, Sir Harry Vane, Sumner
Religion:	Christianity a Battle, Not a Dream

2. Ibid., pp. 511–512.

3. Manuscript letter, Oct. 7, 1857. (Cornell University Library.) But the New York *Tribune* of Dec. 13, 1872, remarks, for example: "Notwithstanding the cold weather, the hall (Steinway Hall) was well filled."

4. Manuscript letters to Sumner, Oct. 19, 1841; Jan. 24, 1869; March 7, 1853. (Harvard College Library.)

5. Manuscript letter, Aug. 24, 1852(?) (Boston Public Library.)

6. Martyn, p. 442. This and the following in a budget of manuscript letters that were in the possession of Martyn.

7. Ibid., pp. 442–443.

8. Ibid., p. 444.

9. Ibid., p. 526.

10. Ibid., pp. 528–529.

11. Ibid., p. 529. Martyn does not say whether Phillips told him these anecdotes personally or the orator's friends passed them on to him. He follows the tale of the Chinese philosopher with a letter addressed from Phillips to him, starting, "My Dear Friend."

12. Ibid., p. 527.

13. Anecdote related to Russell (Charles E. Russell, *The Story of Wendell Phillips*, Chicago, 1914), pp. 128–130.

14. Manuscript letter to Rev. Samuel May, Feb. 9, 1862. (New York Public Library, 42nd Street.)

15. Manuscript, 1875. (Harvard College Library.)

16. Manuscript dated Jan. 1864. (New York Historical Society.) See Note 23 in Appendix.

17. Exercises at the Dedication of the Statue of Wendell Phillips (Boston, 1916), p. 24.

CHAPTER FIFTY-SIX

Timid Scholarship

1. Phillips, "The Scholar in a Republic," *Speeches, Lectures, and Letters.* Second Series, pp. 341, 344, 349.

2. Ibid., p. 356.

3. Ibid., p. 356.

4. Ibid., pp. 358–359.

5. Ibid., p. 361.

6. Vernon L. Parrington, *Main Currents in American Thought* (New York, 1930), III, 146.

7. Sears, p. 313.

8. Martyn, p. 465.

9. Powell, pp. 95–96.

10. *Recollections of Dr. James Freeman Clarke,* quoted in Austin, *Phillips,* pp. 344–345. Prof. Hofstadter says of the Phi Beta Kappa oration: "The agitator who had given no quarter, expected none, and perhaps sensed the scholarship of the future would treat him in the same spirit as had the scholarship of his time." (op. cit., p. 161.)

11. Manuscript letter to Mrs. E. F. Crosby, quoted in Martyn, p. 469.

12. *Exercises at the Dedication of the Statue of Wendell Phillips* (Boston, 1882), p. 137.

CHAPTER FIFTY-SEVEN

Last Days

1. Stearns, *Sketches from Concord and Appledore,* p. 192.
2. Martyn, p. 510. It seems Martyn examined Phillips's memorandum book.
3. Manuscript letter to Wardwell, Aug. 7, 1878. (New York Public Library, 135th Street Branch.) See note 24 in Appendix.
4. Wyman, p. 28.
5. Martyn, p. 419.
6. Wyman, p. 30.
7. Thomas W. Higginson, *Wendell Phillips* (Boston, 1884), p. 14.
8. See Note 25, in Appendix.
9. Manuscript letter, May 14, 1883. (Dall Collection, Massachusetts Historical Society.)
10. Martyn, pp. 471–472.
11. George W. Woodberry, *Wendell Phillips, The Faith of an American* (Woodberry Society, New York, 1920), p. 303.
12. Sallie Holley, p. 147.
13. Manuscript. (A. A. Lawrence Collection, Massachusetts Historical Society.)
14. Martyn, pp. 472–473.
15. Ibid., p. 473.
16. "Harriet Martineau," *Speeches, Lectures, and Letters,* Second Series, p. 473.
17. Martyn, p. 480.
18. Ibid., p. 481.
19. Wyman, p. 30. Ann died April 24, 1886. (*Memorial Sketch of Ann Phillips,* p. 4, Martyn gives a wrong date.
20. *Memorials of Wendell Phillips.* Book of newspaper clippings. (Boston Public Library.)
21. Austin, *Wendell Phillips,* p. 366.
22. See Note 26 in Appendix.
23. Charles E. Russell, *The Story of Wendell Phillips,* p. 183. Charles A. Madison (*Critics and Crusaders,* New York, 1947) remarks of Phillips: he achieved his eminent place in American history not by virtue of his profound intellect or original genius, but by a combination of noble zeal and prime eloquence. He was not an innovator of a moral movement as Garrison was. But he was supremely the fighter for social justice. "To the very end and with undiminished vigor, he persisted undauntedly in his advocacy of the principles of freedom and justice and in laying the foundation for the rights of the mass of Americans which have made the United States the chief democracy in the world. . . . In his time the foremost defender of our democratic rights." (pp. 73, 79.)

Henrietta Buckmaster (Henkle) (*Let My People Go,* New York and London, 1941) vividly sums up Phillips contribution: "He was a creature of tingling nerves and uncanny prescience. The gentleman, the barrister, the dandy with the golden voice was the only revolutionist among them, the only one who saw the shape of the future in terms of a new life, unrelated to the old." (p. 319.)
24. George W. Curtis, *Wendell Phillips,* pp. 4–5.

NOTES

1.

The family of John and Sally Walley Phillips:
1. Thomas Walley m. Anna Dunn.
    Children: John, Samuel.
2. Sarah Hurd m. Francis Jenks, Jr., who died in 1837; she married in 1840 Professor Alonzo Gray of Brooklyn, N. Y.
    Children: Mary Elwell Jenks (b. 1824) m. Rev. R. S. Storrs of Brooklyn, N. Y.; John Phillips Jenks (1826-1828); Francis Jenks (b. 1828); Grenville Tudor Jenks (b. 1830); Ames Jenks; Alice Elizabeth Gray.
3. Samuel (1801-1817)
4. Margaret (b. 1802) m. Dr. Edward Reynolds of Boston.
    Children: John Phillips Reynolds (b. 1825); Adeline Margaret Reynolds (b. 1827); Miriam Phillips Reynolds (b. 1829); Anne Foster Reynolds (b. 1831); Margaret Elizabeth Reynolds (b. 1833); Adeline Ellen Reynolds (b. 1835); Augusta Theresa Reynolds (b. 1837).
5. Miriam m. Rev. George W. Blagden.
    Children: Anna Blagden (b. 1832); John Phillips Blagden (b. 1833); George Blagden (b. 1835); Edward R. Blagden (b. 1837); Thomas Blagden (b. 1839); Samuel Phillips Blagden (b. 1841); Sally Phillips Blagden (b. 1843); Miriam Phillips Blagden (b. 1845, d. 1849).
6. John Charles (1807-1878 m. Harriet Welch
    Children: Margaret Welch (b. 1835); John Charles Welch (b. 1838); Emily Susan Welch (b. 1842); Harriet Welch (b. 1845, died young); Miriam Welch (b. 1849); Anna Dunn (b. 1850); Caroline Crowninshield (b. 1852).

7. George William (1810-1880) m. Emily Blagden, sister of George W. Blagden. She died in 1842 and he married her sister, Mary Ann Blagden. She died in 1848 leaving no children.

   Children: Emily Blagden (b. 1842) m. Chas. A. Welch.

8. Wendell (1811-1884) m. Ann Terry Greene.

9. Grenville Tudor (1816-1863).

   (Albert M. Phillips, *Phillips Genealogies*.)

2.

Later a rift occurred. Phillips in 1846 attacked as infamous Justice Story's decision in the Prigg case "for giving a master what the terms of the Constitution did not give him, the right without legal process to seize and carry away his slave," and for declaring all state laws which required him to prove his property, unconstitutional and void. Said Phillips: "No oath of office, no obligations to the constitution of the United States can excuse an outrage on justice and humanity. The magistrate does not cease to be a man and neither the man nor the magistrate can shield his wrong acts from censure by alleging that he thought them right. The course of a Judge, no matter how pure his private character, no matter how high his fame as a jurist, who helps a master to regain his slave shall, whether he is living or dead, be branded as infamous so far as my voice and pen can affect it."

(*Liberator*, XVI:37, Sept. 11, 1846.)

3.

A national society was needed to concentrate the agitation of the whole country. Towards the end of 1833, a convention was held in Adelphi Hall, Philadelphia, and the American Anti-Slavery Society organized. Garrison at first played a quiet part in the proceedings, but was soon deputed to draft a "Declaration of Principles." This he did between ten at night and eight in the morning in the home of a colored woman delegate. When the committee found him, he was just ending his task, the shutters closed and the lamp burning. There was little to erase or amend, but the members decided to omit his attack on the Colonization Society. Garrison writhed somewhat before submitting. "Brethren," he finally remarked, "it is your report, not mine."

The Declaration of Sentiments was signed by sixty-three delegates who received copies of it printed on silk. It was the Magna Charta of the Anti-Slavery movement.

"We maintain that no man has a right to enslave or imbrute his brother—to hold or acknowledge him, for one moment, as a piece of merchandise—to keep back his hire by fraud—or to brutalize his mind by denying him the means of intellectual, social, and moral improvement.

The right to enjoy liberty is inalienable. To invade it is to usurp the prerogative of Jehovah. Every man has a right to his own body—to the products of his own labor—to the protection of law—and to the common advantages of society. It is piracy to buy or steal a native African, to subject him to servitude. Surely the sin is as great to enslave an American as an African.

Therefore, we believe and affirm—that there is no difference in principle between the African slave trade and American slavery:

That every American citizen who retains a human being in involuntary bondage as his property is, according to Scripture (Exodus XXI:16) a man stealer:

That the slaves ought instantly to be set free and brought under the protection of law.

That if they had lived from the time of Pharaoh down to the present period, and had been entailed through successive generations, their right to be free could never have been alienated, but their claims would have constantly risen in solemnity.

That all those laws which are now in force admitting the right of slavery, are, therefore, before God, utterly null and void; being an audacious usurpation of the Divine prerogative, a daring infringement on the law of nature, a base overthrow of the very foundations of the social compact, a complete extinction of all the relations, endearments, and obligations of mankind, and a presumptuous transgression of all the holy commandments; and that therefore they ought instantly to be abrogated.

We maintain that no compensation should be given to the planters emancipating their slaves:

Because it would be a surrender of the great fundamental principle that man cannot hold property in man:

Because slavery is a crime, and therefore is not an article to be sold.

Because the holders of slaves are not the just proprietors of what they claim; freeing the slave is not depriving them of property, but restoring it to its rightful owner; it is not wronging the master, but righting the slave—restoring him to himself:

Because immediate and general emancipation would only destroy nominal, not real property; it would not amputate a limb or break a bone of the slaves, but, by infusing motives into their breasts, would make them doubly valuable to the masters as free laborers: and

Because, if compensation is to be given at all, it should be given to the outraged and guiltless slaves, and not to those who have plundered and abused them.

We regard as delusive, cruel, and dangerous any scheme of expatriation which pretends to aid, either directly or indirectly, in the emancipation of the slaves, or to be a substitute for the immediate and total abolition of slavery.

We also maintain that there are, at the present time, the highest obligations resting upon the people of the free states to remove slavery by moral and political action, as prescribed in the Constitution of the United States . . .

These are our views and principles—these our designs and measures. . . . With entire confidence in the overruling justice of God, we plant ourselves upon the Declaration of our Independence and the truths of Divine Revelation, as upon the Everlasting Rock.

We shall organize Anti-Slavery Societies, if possible, in every city, town, and village in our land.

We shall send forth agents to lift up the voice of remonstrance, of warning, of entreaty, and of rebuke.

We shall circulate, unsparingly and extensively, anti-slavery tracts and periodicals.

We shall enlist the pulpit and the press in the cause of the suffering and the dumb.

We shall aim at the purification of the churches from all participation in the guilt of slavery.

We shall encourage the labor of freemen rather than that of slaves by giving a preference to their productions, and

We shall spare no exertion nor means to bring the whole nation to speedy repentance.

Our trust for victory is solely in God. We may personally be defeated, but our principles never! Truth, Justice, Reason, Humanity, must and will gloriously triumph. Already a host is coming up to the help of the Lord against the mighty and the prospect before us is full of encouragement.

Submitting this Declaration to the candid examination of the people of this country and of the friends of liberty throughout the world, we hereby affix our signatures to it, pledging ourselves, that, under the guidance and by the help of Almighty God, we will do all that in us lies, consistently with this Declaration of our principles, to overthrow the most execrable system of slavery that has ever been witnessed upon earth; to deliver our land from its deadliest curse; to wipe out the foulest stain that rests upon our national escutcheon; and to secure to the colored population of the United States all the rights and privileges which belong to them as men and as Americans—come what may to our persons, our interests or our reputations—whether we live to witness the triumph of Liberty, Justice, and Humanity, or perish untimely as martyrs in this great benevolent and holy cause.

Done at Philadelphia, the 6th day of December, A.D. 1833.

4.

"Song of the Abolitionist" by Garrison to the Air of Auld Lang Syne:

I

I am an Abolitionist!
    I glory in the name,
Though now by Slavery's minions hissed
    And covered o'er with shame:
It is a spell of light and power—

The watchword of the free:—
Who spurns it in the trial-hour,
A craven soul is he!

II

I am an Abolitionist!
Then urge me not to pause;
For joyfully do I enlist
In Freedom's sacred cause:
A nobler strife the world ne'er saw,
Th'enslaved to disenthral;
I am a soldier for the war,
Whatever may befall! . . .

IV

I am an Abolitionist!
No threats shall awe my soul,
No perils cause me to desist,
No bribes my acts control;
A freeman will I live and die.
In sunshine and in shade,
And raise my voice for Liberty,
Of nought on earth afraid.

V

I am an Abolitionist!
The tyrant's hate and dread—
The friend of all who are oppressed—
A price is on my head!
My country is the wide, wide world,
My countrymen mankind:
Down to the dust be Slavery hurled:
All servile chains unbind!

(*Liberty Bell*, 1842, pp. 64-66.)

5.
The first call for a World Convention sent out by the Executive Committee of the British and Foreign Anti-Slavery Society invited "friends of the slave in every nation and every clime." When the Committee learned that Boston Abolitionists

had appointed women as delegates, they sent out a second call which specified the delegates as "gentlemen." (*Letters of Theodore D. Weld, Angelina Grimké Weld, and Sarah Grimké.*)

6.

According to Professor Barnes, the American Anti-Slavery Society was slowly starving to death. Its New York executives were bankrupt and helpless, the State societies refused to pay their pledges, and the Society's treasury was bare. The Executive Committee resolved that so long as the State societies maintained their ban, "there is no alternative before us but that of bankruptcy." The delegates appointed a committee (Birney, Lewis Tappan, and Gibbons, a Garrison man) with power to decide the fate of the Society and adjourned. They prepared for a final liquidation of the Society.

It must be noted, however, that immediately after Lewis Tappan's exodus from the American Anti-Slavery Society, he organized the American and Foreign Anti-Slavery Society. The matter of dissolution, then, seems to have been an attempt to disrupt the Society rather than see it succumb to the "noxious" influence of Garrison.

7.

Letter of J. G. Whittier to Henry Wilson, November 18, 1850: "Can a Free Soil Man be chosen? This granted, we can then take the man who will best advance [?] the cause we have at heart." Among others to do honor to the party of freedom Whittier suggested Wendell Phillips.

(Manuscript letter, New York Public Library, 42nd Street.)

8.

Washington in the fifties was not an inspiring spectacle. It was a small straggling, overgrown, ill-kept city. The streets were full of grass and dirt. Cows even pastured in some of the principal ones. Houses were cheerless looking. Pennsylvania Avenue was paved with dust or mud according to the weather that prevailed. On a windy day, immense clouds of dust swept over the street, making it hard for pedestrians to see the way. On rainy days the avenue was a bank of thick black mud.

When one entered the strangers' gallery in the Senate, which was supported by iron pillars running round the circular part of the chamber, the following notice posted on the door met the visitor's eyes: "Gentlemen will be pleased not to place their feet on the board in front of the gallery, as the dirt from them falls upon the Senators' heads."

Four grates beneath the mantel shelves in the corridor, back of the Vice President's desk, and two Franklin stoves near the main entrance heated the Senate chamber. In front of the crackling fires, standing with their backs to the blaze and their coat tails spread, could be seen many renowned statesmen whiling away their spare moments spinning yarns, exchanging confidences, and poking fun at one another. They wore woolen shawls, heavy and warm, of sombre hue, principally gray or brown; the Senate was wrapped head and all in these big shawls. Many of the older men to keep warm made frequent pilgrimages to the open grates and were far more interested in the state of the fires than in any of the Union.

The Senators did their own writing, for they had no secretaries then. Upon each desk was a small box of sand for blotting. A number of Senators were fond of snuff. Two snuff boxes were on the Vice President's desk. Some of the pages carried snuff for emergency. Seward and Foote could not speak well without it.

(See Christian F. Eckloff, *Memories of a Senate Page, 1855–1859;* Edward Ingle, *Southern Sidelights;* William A. Butler, *A Retrospect of Forty Years.*)

9.

"Chauncey Depew, when over ninety, declared Phillips to have been the greatest of American orators and added that he himself had heard all the leading speakers from Clay and Webster through the administration of Wilson and was therefore competent to pronounce his judgment. . . ."

It was written of Phillips when he died that he did not have the "action" of Demosthenes, or the intense passion of Choate, or use the massive perorations of Webster, or have the impressive dignity of Everett: "Different from all these, Mr. Phillips's eloquence was that of Mr. Phillips . . . the most charming orator in America, if not in the world."

(Oswald G. Villard, "Wendell Phillips after Fifty Years," *American Mercury,* XXXIV (Jan. 1935), No. 133, 93–99.

10.

Subscription for Kansas Settlers, 1855:

Dr. Cabot	240
Cunningham Bros.	100
J. M. Forbes	300
Wendell Phillips	100
I. Bertram	100
G. Howland Shaw	100
Sam A. Eliot	100
Theo. Lyman	100
Henry Lee	50
Crowell	25
Gerrit Smith	250
W. R. Lawrence	100
Calvin Hall	50
L. B. Russell	25
E. R. Hoar	25
Sam'l Hoar	50
	1715
A. A. Lawrence	955
	$2670

(A. A. Lawrence manuscript, Massachusetts Historical Society.)

11.

To Higginson, June 14, 1854: "That you did not tell me and thus give me a chance to help you, instead of making a fool of myself in Faneuil Hall I will never forgive you—but I'll say nothing about it till we are both in jail—then we can discuss it at our leisure."

(Manuscript letter, Boston Public Library.)

12.

A prominent conservative of the Republican party was John Murray Forbes. He worked hard for the Union, yet he described his own position as follows: "The fact is, I am not good enough to be an Abolitionist, which demands a certain spirit of martyrdom, or at least self sacrifice and devotion to abstract principle which I am not yet up to. I am essentially a conservative, have rather a prejudice against philanthropy, and have been anti-slavery more because Slavery is anti-Republican, anti-peace, anti-material progress, anti-civilization than upon the higher and purer ground that it is wicked and unjust to the slave. I have no special love for the African any more than for the low-class Irish, but don't want to see either imposed upon. You cannot steal one man's labor or any part of it by law without threatening to steal, when you get strong enough, every man's labor and property and life. Hence to be anti-slavery is to be conservative." (Ware, *op. cit.*, p. 107.)

13.

Phillips objected to the fair and liberal resolutions on marriage and divorce at the 10th National Woman's Rights Convention, May 10, 1860. He said: "This convention is no Marriage Convention—if it were, the subject would be in order, but this Convention, if I understood it, assembles to discuss the laws that rest unequally upon women, not those that rest equally upon men and women. We have nothing to do with a question which affects both sexes equally." (*History of Woman Suffrage*, I, 732–733.)

Again to Caroline H. Dall, 1860: "I'm at sea on these points, have no advice to give—only know I shall not act on platform where marriage is held part of the Woman Rights question."

(Manuscript letter, Dall Collection, Mass. Historical Society.)

14.

"'Did you ever,' says Rabelais, "see a dog with a marrowbone in his mouth—the beast of all others, according to Plato, the most philosophical? If you have seen him, you might have remarked, with what devotion and circumspection he wards and watches it; with what care he keeps it; how fervently he holds it; how prudently he gobbles it; with what affection he breaks it; and with what diligence he sucks it.

"Anti-slavery is Mr. Phillips's bone, and no man can venture to indulge in a little philanthropy without provoking from that gentleman a sub-acidulous snarl. He dotes only on those who disagree with him, and all his converts immediately become the objects, not, perhaps, of his jealousy, but certainly of his suspicion. He loves his enemies because it is so delightful to pummel them, and he dilates with pleasure over some fresh and uncommon wickedness, just as a surgeon admires a large ulcer better than a cheek which health has incarnadined. . . .

"Mr. Phillips is a close communion reformer. You must take the wine out of his cup, or you shall not have a drop. You must receive the bread from his plate, or you shall not swallow a scrap. . . . A bigot of liberality, a sectarian anti-sectarian, a sour philanthropist, is not a pleasing object. Mr. Phillips should remember that hostility to human bondage cannot be monopolized by seven men in Cornhill, Boston, and that a presidential election is of more consequence in the world's turmoil than six anti-slavery bazaars.

"He lacks largeness of views to that deplorable extent that he cannot conceive of a tempest outside of a teapot. A little convention in a little village passing a little series of little resolutions, and just a little disturbed by the lewd and base, is to Mr. Phillips the most august of all possible human gatherings. . . . It is his misfortune, as it is that of the handful who consort with him, that they look at large events through the large end of the telescope, while, when little affairs are to be scrutinized, there is no microscope powerful enough to satisfy their desire for magnificence. . . .

"Everything must be done in the routine of a clique. You must subscribe to the *Liberator*, you must be mobbed twice a year—once in New York and once in Boston. You must think as Mr. Garrison thinks, and you must not think as anybody else thinks. If you are found faithful in these things, you are esteemed faithful in all. . . ."

(Horace Greeley's "Holier Than Thou," in the *New York Tribune* of December, 1860, reprinted in the *Liberator,* XXXI:I, January 4, 1861.)

15.

Phillips wrote an indignant letter to A. A. Lawrence holding him responsible for the action of the mob in breaking up the meeting. Said Phillips: Lawrence had refused to lift a finger, or utter a word of protest, or dissuade them at a moment when one word from a person in his position would have had such momentous weight. And he denounced the action of the mob as "bloody outrages on the friendless and unoffending."

(Manuscript letter, A. A. Lawrence Collection, Mass. Historical Society.)

16.

This was Phillips's tribute to Karl Heinzen: "It was men who had learned of him that, during that sad, dark winter of 1860 and 1861, when Boston was full of violence and almost conquered by the mob, passed that never to be forgotten vote, 'that they would protect Free Speech and Free Speakers.' Members of your Halle carried out that resolve, and four men by four, relieved every hour, guarded the houses of prominent Abolitionists, week after week, all night long."

(Manuscript, *Wendell Phillips Scrapbook*, Boston Public Library.)

17.

"If Mr. Lincoln," said the New York *Herald*, "had nothing better to offer upon this fearful crisis than the foolish consolations of his speech at Columbus, let him say nothing at all."

(Quoted in Barton, *Abraham Lincoln*, II, 16.)

18.

When Phillips felt that an alliance offensive and defensive had been made between the Supreme Court and the President, he advocated the abolition of the Court. "The nation must be saved," said he, "no matter what or how venerable the foe whose existence goes down before that necessity."

A Throttle the Court Bill, requiring two thirds of the justices to concur before they could render a decision, was passed by the House on January 13, 1868, but found its grave in a committee of the Senate.

(Oberholtzer, *A History of the United States Since the Civil War*.)

19.

With the official Proclamation of the Fifteenth Amendment, the *Standard* omitted from its title *National Anti-Slavery* and was issued as an independent journal of reform and literature. It contained eight pages (*Harper's Weekly* size). The prospectus announced: "The *Standard* will be radical in doctrine and independent of party. It will plead for abolition of Caste, and urge for the Negro Land, Education, and Protection. It will advocate for Indians and Chinese civil and political equality, secure equal rights for women, recognize the Labor question as closely allied in many respects to that of Slavery, and advocate a reduction of the hours of labor, a more equitable division of profits, and seek to extend the movement for Cooperation in all branches of Industry. It will seek to obtain justice for the oppressed everywhere, to strengthen the cause of Temperance, of Education, of Prison Reform, and to promote practical, unsectarian religion, and all that makes for peace and a true civilization."

(Issues of March 5 and July 30, 1870.)

Aaron M. Powell continued as editor, but Phillips was a regular contributor and the guiding spirit.

20.

Phillips once said to Joseph Arch that the first real achievement which the working men of Boston had obtained was the opening of the library on Sundays and that Mayor Pierce deserved credit for not vetoing the measure as his predecessors had done.

(Speech of William Murray delivered in Paine Hall, Boston, Sept. 18, 1894. Boston Public Library.)

Phillips must have been interested in the establishment of an Industrial Bank for Working Men, for in a letter, dated June 14, 1874, after thanking James G. Blaine for his telegram and intervention in his behalf, he added: ". . . for tho' I have no pecuniary interest in it, the Bank interests me as a valuable auxiliary for thrifty working men."

(James G. Blaine Papers, Library of Congress.)

21.

To Sumner, Phillips wrote, April 11, 1872: "I don't know how much, if any, you have to do with this Cincinnati Convention. But not knowing whom else to say it to, let me say to you that if it is reckoning on any sympathy or support from the Labor Movement—it will get *none* for C. F. Adams or Trumbull or G. Brown. I should myself and I judge most others of that ilk would support Grant in preference to either of those three!"

(Manuscript letter, Sumner Collection, Harvard College Library.)

22.

The charge of hypocrisy deliberately made by Fish against Sumner was not justified in the sense in which Sumner took it to his bosom. The added charge that Sumner had made an inefficient Chairman of the Foreign Relations Committee was "both petty and needless, and Fish should never have made it."

(Allan Nevins, *Hamilton Fish*. See pages 452–453, 455, 457, 464–465.)

23.

Another favorite was:

Count that day lost
Whose low descending sun
Sees at thy hand
No worthy action done.

These lines John Brown taught to each of his children.

(Manuscript, April, 1862, Boston Public Library.)

24.

Phillips's finances must have been in a precarious state. In a letter dated August 25, 1873, he writes: "Sell at once for the most we can get. Get 8000 if you can. . . . We must go to auction if no other way serves." In another letter, undated, to Davenport, he urges him to accept any offer to continue the mortgage three or four years.

(Manuscript letters, Harvard College Library.)

25.

A tablet was erected on the site of Phillips's Essex Street house:

HERE

WENDELL PHILLIPS resided during forty years,
Devoted by him to efforts to secure
The abolition of African slavery in this country.
The charms of home, the enjoyment of wealth and learning,
Even the kindly recognition of his fellow citizens,
Were by him accounted as naught compared with duty.
He lived to see justice triumphant, freedom universal,
And to receive the tardy praises of his former opponents.
The blessings of the poor, the friendless, and the oppressed
enriched him.
In Boston
He was born 29 November, 1811, and died 2 February, 1884.
This tablet was erected in 1894, by order of the City
Council of Boston.

(*Wendell Phillips Centenary*, 1811-1911, National Association for the Advancement of Colored People.)

26.

Phillips had planned to be buried in the beautiful suburb of Milton where he and his wife often passed their summers. Here he had purchased a lot, and here on the death of Ann the following year both were borne and finally interred. In referring to this, Theodore D. Weld said to Carlos Martyn: "Wendell did not care to lie amid the beat of hurrying feet, but wished to be out where the birds sing and the flowers bloom."

(Martyn, *op. cit.*, p. 487, footnote.)

ACKNOWLEDGMENTS

The author acknowledges with thanks permission to quote from material published by the following:

American Historical Association (Gilbert H. Barnes, *The Anti-Slavery Impulse (1830-1844)*, 1933).

Columbia University Press (Edith E. Ware, *Political Opinion in Massachusetts during Civil War and Reconstruction*, 1916).

Harcourt, Brace & Co. (Howard K. Beale, *The Critical Year*, 1930; William E. Du Bois, *Black Reconstruction*, 1935).

Henry Holt & Co. (Robert W. Winston, *Andrew Johnson*, 1928).

Houghton Mifflin Co. (Ralph W. Emerson, *The Journals of Ralph Waldo Emerson*, 10 vols., 1912; Henry G. Pearson, *The Life of John A. Andrew*, 2 vols., 1904; John G. Whittier, *The Complete Poetical Works of John Greenleaf Whittier*, 1904).

International Publishers Co. (Philip S. Foner, *The Life and Writings of Frederick Douglass*, 2 vols., 1950).

Alfred A. Knopf, Inc. (David Donald, *Lincoln Reconsidered*, 1956; Francis B. Simkins, *The South, Old and New*, 1947).

Little, Brown & Co. (Daniel Webster, *The Writings and Speeches of Daniel Webster*, National Edition, 1903).

MacRae Smith Co. (Ellis P. Oberholtzer, *Abraham Lincoln*, 1904).

New England Quarterly (Pieter Geyl, "The American Civil War and the Problem of Inevitability," June, 1951, XXIV, No. 2, 147-168).

Chas. Scribner's Sons (Allan Nevins, *The Emergence of Lincoln*, 2 vols., 1950).

The author also acknowledges with thanks permission to include as chapters several articles which appeared in the following periodicals—many of these articles have been revised or greatly enlarged:

Negro History Bulletin: "Five Bleeding Wounds,"—June, 1947; "Stealers of Men,"—April, 1948; "Animated Conversation,"—February, 1950; "On Freedom's Southern Line,"—May, 1948; "Barbarism at the Capitol,"—March, 1948; "Nine Old Men," February, 1948.

New England Quarterly: "The Armory of God," March, 1945; "Sons of Otis and Hancock," June, 1946.

Phylon: "Whipmaster and Scouts," First Quarter, 1947; "Philosopher of Agitation," Third Quarter, 1945.

BIBLIOGRAPHY

I. MANUSCRIPTS

The author has examined manuscript collections of letters and anti-slavery material in the following libraries:

Public Library of the City of Boston (Anti-Slavery Collection including the Garrison Papers; Chapman Collection; Folsom Collection; Weston Papers; and Letters listed under Wendell Phillips.)

Library of Congress (James G. Blaine Papers; S. P. Chase Papers; Giddings-Julian Papers. Add. 4; Mrs. H. C. Ingersoll Papers; Theodore D. Weld Papers; and manuscripts listed as Personal.)

Harvard College Library (J. R. Lowell Collection; Sumner Collection.)

Howard University (Moorland Foundation.)

Massachusetts Historical Society (Dall Papers; A. A. Lawrence Papers; Norcross Papers; Washburn Papers; and letters listed under Wendell Phillips.)

New York Historical Society (Manuscript letters listed under the names of Wendell Phillips and prominent persons of the period; also manuscripts listed under Anti-Slavery.)

New York Public Library (Main Division at 42nd Street and Branch at 135th Street; manuscripts listed under names of prominent persons of the period.)

Yale University Library (Manuscript letters listed under Wendell Phillips.)

Cornell University Library (Photostats of manuscript letters written by Wendell Phillips and kept in a file chiefly relating to anti-slavery matters. Photostats sent by Professor Otto Kinkeldey, Librarian of Cornell University Library.)

II. Newspapers, Periodicals, Encyclopedias, Etc.
Not Listed in Bibliography (Part III)

American Annual Cyclopaedia. 1870, 1871, 1875. New York, D. Appleton, 1871, 1872, 1876.

Boston Newspapers:
  Bay State Democrat
  Columbian Centinel
  Commercial Gazette
  Daily Advertiser
  Daily Globe
  Independent Messenger
  New England Galaxy
  Recorder
  Weekly Messenger
Congressional Globe. Edited by Blair and Rives (23rd to 30th Congress) and John C. Rives (31st to 38th Congress, 1st Session.) Washington, D. C., printed at the Globe Office for the Editors.
Dictionary of American Biography.
Emancipator, ed. by Rev. Joshua Leavitt, Oct. 12, 1837.
Harper's Weekly. New York, 1872.
Johnson's New Universal Cyclopaedia. Edited by Frederick A. P. Barnard and Arnold Guyot. 4 vols., 8 parts. New York, Johnson, 1881.
Liberator. Edited by William Lloyd Garrison and Isaac Knapp. Boston, 1831-1865.
Liberty Bell. By the Friends of Freedom. Boston, American Anti-Slavery Society, 1839-1858.
Nation. Vol. XV. New York, 1872.
National Anti-Slavery Standard, 1840-1870. New Series, National Standard, 1870-1871. New York, American Anti-Slavery Society.
New England Historical and Genealogical Register.
New York Newspapers:
  Daily News
  Daily Times
  Daily Tribune
  Express
  Evening Post
  Herald
  Independent
  Sun
  Times
  World

North American Review, New York, 1888.
Punch, or the London Charivari.
The Southern Literary Messenger, 1854.

III. BOOKS, ARTICLES, SPEECHES.

The following works have been examined in preparation for this biography:

ABDY, EDWARD STRUTT. Journal of a Residence and Tour in the United States. 3 vols. London, J. Murray, 1835.

ADAMS, ALICE DANA. The Neglected Period of Anti-Slavery in America (1808-31). Boston and London, Ginn, 1908.

ADAMS, CHARLES FRANCIS. Richard Henry Dana. 2 vols. Boston, Houghton, Mifflin, 1891.

ADAMS, HENRY. The Education of Henry Adams. Boston and New York, Houghton, Mifflin Co., 1918.

ADAMS, JAMES TRUSLOW. The Adams Family. New York, Literary Guild, 1930.

ADAMS, JAMES TRUSLOW. The March of Democracy. 2 vols. New York, Scribners, 1932-1933.

ADAMS, JOHN QUINCY. The Diary of John Quincy Adams. Edited by Allan Nevins. New York, Longsman, Green, 1929.

ADDISON, DANIEL DULANY. The Clergy in American Life and Letters. London, Macmillan, 1900.

ALBJERG, MARGUERITE HALL. "The New York Press and Andrew Johnson," *The South Atlantic Quarterly* (Durham, N. C., 1927). XXVI, 404-416.

ALCOTT, AMOS BRONSON. Sonnets and Canzonets. Boston, Roberts, 1882.

ALCOTT, LOUISA M. Her Life, Letters, and Journals. Boston, 1889.

American Anti-Slavery Society. Annual Reports. New York, 1834-1861, Nos. 1-7, 22-28.

American History Told by Contemporaries. 5 vols. Edited by Albert Bushnell Hart. Vols III and IV. New York, Macmillan, 1901-1902.

ANDREWS, ETHAN ALLEN. Slavery and the Domestic Slave Trade. Boston, Light and Stearns, 1836.

APPLETON, THOMAS GOLD. A Sheaf of Papers. Boston, Roberts Bros., 1875.

APTHEKER, HERBERT. American Negro Slave Revolts. New York, Columbia University, 1943.

APTHEKER, HERBERT. Essays in the History of the American Negro. New York, International, 1945.

APTHEKER, HERBERT. "Negro Casualties in the Civil War," *Journal of Negro History* (Jan. 1947), XXXII, No. 1, 10-80.

APTHEKER, HERBERT. "The Negroes in the Union Navy," *Journal of Negro History* (April, 1947), XXXII, No. 2, 169-200.

ARMSTRONG, RICHARD ACLAND. Latter Day Teachers. London, C. K. Paul, 1881.

ARMSTRONG, WILLIAM CLINTON. The Lundy Family and Their Descendants. New Brunswick, New Jersey, Heidingsfeld, 1902.

ARNOLD, ISAAC NEWTON. Abraham Lincoln. Chicago, Jansen, McClurg, 1885.

AUSTIN, GEORGE LOWELL. The History of Massachusetts. Boston, B. B. Russell, 1876.

AUSTIN, GEORGE LOWELL. Wendell Phillips. Boston, Lee and Shepard, 1888.

AVEY, ELIJAH. The Capture and Execution of John Brown. Elgin, Ill., Brethren Pub. House, 1906.

BALLOU, ADIN. A Discourse on the Subject of American Slavery. Boston, I. Knapp, 1837.

BANCROFT, FREDERIC. The Life of William H. Seward. 2 vols. New York and London, Harper, 1900.

BANCROFT, FREDERIC. Slave-trading in the Old South. Baltimore, Md., Furst, 1931.

BARBER, EDWARD W. "The Story of Emancipation," *Michigan Pioneer and Historical Society Collections.* XXIX (1901), 575-608.

BARBER, SAMUEL. Boston Common. Boston, Christopher Pub. House, 1916.

BARNES, GILBERT HOBBS. The Anti-Slavery Impulse (1830-1844). New York and London, Appleton-Century, 1933.

BARNES, GILBERT HOBBS. Letters of Theodore D. Weld, Angelina Grimké Weld, and Sarah Grimké. Edited by Gilbert Hobbs Barnes and Dwight L. Dumond. 2 vols. New York, Appleton-Century, 1934.

BARROWS, JOHN HENRY. Henry Ward Beecher, the Shakespeare of the Pulpit. American Reformers. Edited by Carlos Martyn. New York, Funk and Wagnalls, 1893.

BARRY, JOHN S. *A Historical Sketch of the Town of Hanover.* Boston, 1853.

BARTLETT, RUHL JACOB. John C. Fremont and the Republican Party. The Ohio State University Studies. Columbus, Ohio, 1930. No. 13.

BARTON, WILLIAM ELEAZAR. The Life of Abraham Lincoln. 2 vols. Indianapolis, Bobbs, Merrill, 1925.

BARTON, WILLIAM ELEAZAR. President Lincoln. 2 vols. Indianapolis, Bobbs, Merrill, 1933.

BASSETT, JOHN SPENSER. The Southern Plantation Overseer. Smith College Fiftieth Anniversary Publications. Vol. V. Northampton, Mass., Printed for Smith College, 1925.

BATCHELDER, SAMUEL FRANCIS. Bits of Harvard History. Cambridge, Harvard University Press, 1924.

BAUER, RAYMOND A. and BAUER, ALICE H. "Day to Day Resistance to Slavery," *Journal of Negro History* (Oct. 1942), XXVII, No. 4, 388-419.

BEALE, HOWARD KENNEDY. The Critical Year. New York, Harcourt Brace, 1930.

BEARD, CHARLES AUSTIN and BEARD, MARY RITTER. The Rise of American Civilization. 2 vols. New York, Macmillan, 1931.

BEARSE, AUSTIN. Reminiscences of Fugitive Slave Law Days. Boston, W. Richardson, 1880.

BEECHER, LYMAN. Autobiography, Correspondence, Etc. Edited by Charles Beecher. 2 vols. New York, Harper, 1865.

BEECHER, HENRY WARD. Wendell Phillips. New York, Fords, Howard, and Hulbert, 1884. pp. 409-425.

BENTON, THOMAS H. Thirty Years' View. 2 vols. New York, Appleton, 1886.

BESTON, HENRY. *See* Sheahan, Henry Beston.

BEVERIDGE, ALBERT JEREMIAH. Abraham Lincoln, 1809-1858. 2 vols. Boston, Houghton, Mifflin, 1928.

BILL, ALFRED H. Rehearsal for Conflict. New York, Knopf, 1947.

BIMBA, ANTHONY. The History of the American Working Class. New York, International Publishers, 1927.

BIRNEY, CATHERINE H. Sarah and Angelina Grimké. Boston, Lee and Shepard, 1885.

BIRNEY, JAMES G. Letters of James Gillespie Birney, 1831-1857, 2 vols., ed. by Dwight L. Dumond, New York and London, D. Appleton, Century, 1938.

BIRNEY, WILLIAM. James G. Birney and His Times. New York, Appleton, 1890.

BIRRELL, AUGUSTINE. Miscellanies. London, E. Stock, 1902.

BLACKMAR, FRANK WILSON. The Life of Charles Robinson. Topeka, Kansas, Crane, 1902.

BLAINE, JAMES GILLESPIE. Twenty Years of Congress. 2 vols. Norwich, Conn., Bill Pub. Co., 1884-1886.

BLAND, THOMAS AUGUSTUS. Life of Benjamin F. Butler. Boston, Lee and Shepard, 1879.

BOBBÉ, MRS. DOROTHIE [DE BEAR]. Fanny Kemble. New York, Minton, Balch, 1931.

BOLTON, SARAH KNOWLES. Famous Leaders Among Men. New York, Crowell, 1894.

BOND, HENRY. Genealogies of the Families and Descendants of the Early Settlers of Watertown, Massachusetts. Vol. II. Boston, Little, Brown and Co., 1855.

BOROME, JOS. A. "Some Additional Light on Frederick Douglass," Journal of Negro History, (April, 1953), XXXVIII, No. 2, 216-224.

The Boston Mob of "Gentlemen of Property and Standing." Proceedings of the Anti-Slavery Meeting Held in Stacy Hall, Boston, on the Twentieth Anniversary of the Mob. Boston, Wallcut, 1855.

—————. Boston Slave Riot and Trial of Anthony Burns. Boston, Fetridge, 1854.

BOTKIN, B. A. Ed. Lay My Burden Down. Chicago, University of Chicago, 1945.

BOWDITCH, VINCENT YARDLEY. The Life and Correspondence of Henry Ingersoll Bowditch. 2 vols. Boston and New York, Houghton, Mifflin, 1902.

BOWDITCH, WILLIAM INGERSOLL. Slavery and the Constitution. Boston, Wallcutt, 1849.

BOWERS, CLAUDE G. [ERNADE]. The Tragic Era. New York, Literary Guild, 1929.

BOWERS, RENZO DEE. The Inaugural Addresses of the Presidents. St. Louis, Mo., Thomas Law Book Co., 1929.

BRADFORD, GAMALIEL. "Charles Sumner," Yale Review, V (April-July, 1916), 541-556.

BRADFORD, GAMALIEL. Damaged Souls. Boston and New York, Houghton, Mifflin, 1923.

BRADFORD, GAMALIEL. "Horace Greeley," *The American Mercury.* I (April, 1924), No. 4, 385-393.

BRAWLEY, BENJAMIN GRIFFITH. A Social History of the American Negro. New York, Macmillan, 1921.

BREMER, FREDERIKA. The Homes of the New World. Translated by Mary Howitt. 2 vols. New York, Harper, 1853.

BROOKE, SAMUEL. Slavery and the Slaveholders' Religion. Cincinnati, Ohio, Published by the Author, 1846.

BROOKS, VAN WYCK. The Life of Emerson. New York, Literary Guild, 1932.

BROWN, MARY HOSMER. Memoirs of Concord. Boston, Four Seas Co., 1926.

BROWN, ROLLO WALTER. Lonely Americans. New York, Coward-McCann, 1929.

BROWN, WILLIAM B. Religious Organizations and Slavery. Oberlin, Ohio, Fitch, 1850.

BROWN, WILLIAM GARROTT. The Lower South in American History. New York, Macmillan, 1902.

BROWNLOW, W. G. and PRYNE, ABRAM. *Ought American Slavery to be Perpetuated, A Debate.* Phila., 1858.

BROWNE, WILLIAM HAND and JOHNSON, RICHARD MALCOM. Life of Alexander H. Stephens. Phila., Lippincott, 1878.

BRYCE, JAMES BRYCE, VISCOUNT. The American Commonwealth. 2 vols. New York, Macmillan, 1901.

BUCKINGHAM, J. S. *The Slave States of America,* 2 vols. London, 1842.

BUCKMASTER, HENRIETTA. (pseud.), see Henkle, Henrietta.

BUELL, WALTER. Joshua R. Giddings. Cleveland, Ohio, Williams, 1882.

BURKE, REV. THOMAS N. English Misrule in Ireland. New York, Lynch, Cole, and Meehan, 1877.

BUTLER, BENJAMIN F. Argument before the Tewksbury Investigation Committee, July 15, 1883. Printed by the Democratic Central Committee.

BUTLER, BENJAMIN F. Autobiography and Personal Reminiscences of Major General Benjamin F. Butler. Boston, Thayer, 1892.

BUTLER, BENJAMIN F. Private and Official Correspondence during the Civil War. 5 vols. Privately issued. Norwood, Mass., Plimpton Press, 1917.

BUTLER, FREDERICK. Memoirs of the Marquis Lafayette. Wethersfield, Conn., Deming and Francis, 1825.

BUTLER, WILLIAM ALLEN. A Retrospect of Forty Years. New York, Scribners, 1911.

CABLE, GEORGE W. Strange True Stories of Louisiana. New York, 1901.

CAIRNES, JOHN ELLIOTT. The Slave Power. London, Macmillan, 1863.

CALHOUN, JOHN CALDWELL. Works. Edited by Richard K. Crallé. 6 vols. New York, Appleton, 1857.

Campaign of 1848. Free Songs for the People. Boston, March, 1848.

CAMPBELL, JOHN T. The Great Problem of the Age. Phila., Pa., Labor Tribune, 1872.

CARLTON, FRANK TRACY. Organized Labor in American History. New York, Appleton, 1920.

CARMAN, HARRY JAMES and SAMUEL McKEE, JR. A History of the United States. 1 vol. New York, Heath, 1931.

CARNATHAN, W. J. "The Proposal to Reopen the African Slave Trade in the South, 1854-1860," *South Atlantic Quarterly* (Durham, N. C., 1926), XXV, No. 4, 410-429.

CARPENTER, STEPHEN D. Logic of History. Madison, Wisconsin, S. D. Carpenter, 1864.

CASH, W. J. The Mind of the South, New York, Knopf, 1941.

CATT, CARRIE CHAPMAN, and SHULER, NETTIE ROGERS. Woman Suffrage and Politics. New York, Scribners, 1923.

CHACE, ELIZABETH BUFFUM. Anti-Slavery Reminiscences. Central Falls, Rhode Island, Freeman, 1891.

CHACE, ELIZABETH BUFFUM and LOVELL, LUCY BUFFUM. Two Quaker Sisters. New York, Liveright, 1937.

CHADSEY, CHARLES ERNEST. The Struggle Between President Johnson and Congress over Reconstruction. Studies in History, Economics, and Public Law, Columbia University, New York, 1896-1898. VIII, no. 1.

CHADWICK, FRENCH ENSOR. Causes of the Civil War. The American Nation, A History. Vol. XIX. New York, Harper, 1906.

CHADWICK, JOHN WHITE. Theodore Parker. Boston, Houghton, Mifflin, 1900.

CHADWICK, JOHN WHITE. William Ellery Channing. Boston, Houghton, Mifflin, 1903.

CHAMBERLAIN, ALLEN. "Old Passages of Boston's Underground Railroad," *Magazine of History* (Tarrytown, N. Y., 1926). Extra no. 124, XXXI, no. 4, 31-43.

CHAMBERS, WILLIAM. Things as they Are in America. Phila., Pa., Lippincott, Grambo, 1854.

CHAMBERS, WILLIAM. American Slavery and Colour. London, Dix and Edwards, 1857.

CHANNING, EDWARD. A History of the United States. 6 vols. New York, Macmillan, 1921-1926. Vols. V and VI.

CHANNING, WILLIAM ELLERY. Slavery. Boston, Munroe, 1836.

CHANNING, WILLIAM ELLERY. Emancipation. Boston, Peabody, 1840.

CHANNING, WILLIAM ELLERY. A Letter to the Hon. Henry Clay on the Annexation of Texas to the United States. Boston, Munroe, 1837.

CHAPMAN, JOHN J. William Lloyd Garrison. Boston, Atlantic Monthly Press, 1921.

CHILD, LYDIA MARIA. The Evils of Slavery and the Cure of Slavery. Newburyport, Whipple, 1839.

CHILD, LYDIA MARIA. Letters. Collected by Harriet W. Sewall. Boston, Houghton, Mifflin, 1883.

CHILD, LYDIA MARIA. The Patriarchal Institution. New York, American Anti-Slavery Society, 1860.

CHURCH, ELLA RODMAN. "Lafayette's Last Visit to America," *Magazine of American History* (May, 1881). VI, no. 5, 321-329.

CHURCH, WILLIAM CONANT. Ulysses S. Grant. New York, De Fau, 1897.

CLARK, BENNETT CHAMP. John Quincy Adams. Boston, Little, Brown, 1932.

CLARK, GEORGE FABER. History of the Temperance Reform in Massachusetts. Boston, Clarke and Carruth, 1888.

CLARKE, FRANCIS. "Froude," *The London Mercury* (August, 1930). XXII, No. 130, 314-323.

CLARKE, JAMES FREEMAN. Anti-Slavery Days. New York, Lovell, 1883.

CLAY, HENRY. Speech of the Hon. Henry Clay Delivered in the Senate, Feb. 5 and 6, 1850. New York, Stringer and Townsend, 1850.

COBBE, FRANCES POWER. [Ed.] The Collected Works of Theodore Parker. Vol. V. London, Trübner, 1863.

COCHRAN, WILLIAM COX. The Western Reserve and the Fugitive Slave Law. Collections of the Western Reserve Historical Society. (Cleveland, Ohio, 1920). Publication 101.

COCKRUM, COL. WILLIAM MONROE. History of the Underground Railroad. Oakland City, Indiana, Cockrum Printing Co., 1915.

COFFIN, CHARLES CARLETON. Abraham Lincoln. New York, Harper, 1893.

COFFIN, LEVI. Reminiscences. Cincinnati, Ohio, Western Tract Society, 1876.

COIT, MARGARET L. John C. Calhoun. Boston, Houghton, Mifflin, 1950.

COLEMAN, McALISTER. Pioneers of Freedom. New York, Vanguard, 1929.

COLEMAN, MRS. GEORGE P. (Mary Haldane Begg). Virginia Silhouettes. Richmond, Va., Dietz Printing Co., 1934.

A Collection of Valuable Documents. Boston, Isaac Knapp, 1836.

COLLINS, WINFIELD HAZLITT. The Domestic Slave Trade of the Southern States. New York, Broadway Publishing Co., 1904.

COLVIN, DAVID LEIGH. Prohibition in the United States. New York, Doran, 1926.

COMMAGER, HENRY STEELE. Theodore Parker, Yankee Crusader. Boston, Little, Brown, 1936.

COMMONS, JOHN ROGERS and ANDREWS, JOHN B.; HOAGLAND, H. E.; MITTELMAN, E. B.; SAPOSS, DAVID J.; SUMNER, HELEN L.; PERLMAN, SELIG. History of Labour in the United States. 4 vols. New York, Macmillan, 1918-1935.

CONWAY, MONCURE DANIEL. Autobiography. 2 vols. London, Cassell, 1914.

COOKE, FRANCIS E. Story of Theodore Parker. Boston, Cupples, Upham, 1883.

COOLIDGE, LOUIS ARTHUR. Ulysses S. Grant. Boston, Houghton, Mifflin, 1917.

Correspondence between the Hon. F. H. Elmore and James G. Birney. New York, American Anti-Slavery Society, 1838.

CORWIN, EDWARD S. "The Dred Scott Decision in the Light of Contemporary Legal Opinion," American Historical Review, 1911, XVII, No. 1, 52-59.

COULTER, E. MERTON. The South during Reconstruction. Baton Rouge, Louisiana State University, 1947.

CRALLÉ, RICHARD K. Editor. Works of John C. Calhoun. 6 vols. New York, Appleton, 1857.

CRAVEN, AVERY. The Repressible Conflict, 1830-61. Baton Rouge, Louisiana State University, 1939.

CRAVEN, AVERY. The Coming of the Civil War. New York, Scribner's, 1942.

CURRENT, RICHARD N. Old Thad Stevens. Madison, Wisconsin, The University of Wisconsin, 1942.

CURRENT, RICHARD N. "John C. Calhoun, Philosopher of Reaction," Antioch Review (June, 1943), III, No. 2, 223-234.

CURTIS, GEORGE TICKNOR. Daniel Webster, 2 vols. New York, Appleton, 1870.

CURTIS, GEORGE WILLIAM. Wendell Phillips. New York, Harper, 1884.

CUTTING, ELIZABETH BROWN. Jefferson Davis, Political Soldier. New York, Dodd, Mead, 1930.

DANVERS HISTORICAL SOCIETY. Old Anti-Slavery Days. Danvers, Mass., Danvers Mirror Print., 1893.

DARLING, ARTHUR BURR. Political Changes in Massachusetts. Yale Historical Publications, XV. New Haven, Yale University Press, 1925.

DAUNT, WILLIAM JOSEPH O'NEILL. Personal Recollections of Daniel O'Connell. 2 vols. London, Chapman and Hall, 1848.

DAVIS, GRANVILLE. "Douglas and the Chicago Mob," American Historical Review (April, 1949), LIV, No. 3, 553-556.

DAVIS, JEFFERSON. Constitutionalist. His Letters, Papers and Speeches. Edited by Dunbar Rowland Jackson. 10 vols. Mississippi Department of Archives, 1923.

Days and Ways in Old Boston. Edited by William Sidney Rossiter. Boston, Stearns, 1915.

DEPEW, CHAUNCEY M. My Memories of Eighty Years. New York, Scribners, 1924.

DE WITT, D. M. "Vice President Johnson," Southern Historical Associations Publications (Washington, D. C., 1905). VIII, 437-442; IX, 1-23, 71-86, 151-159, 213-225.

DEXTER, LEWIS A. "The Legend of William Lloyd Garrison," Reprinted from The Social Studies (Feb. 1939). XXX, No. 2.

DICKEY, DALLAS C. Seargent S. Prentiss, Whig Orator of the Old South. Baton Rouge, Louisiana State University, 1945.

DICKINSON, REV. C. E. "The Come-Outer Movement," Ohio Church Historical Society (Oberlin, 1898). IX, 57-67.

Dodd, William Edward. Days of the Cotton Kingdom. Chronicles of America Series (New Haven, Yale University Press, 1919).

Dodd, William Edward. Expansion and Conflict. Riverside History of the United States, Boston, Houghton, Mifflin, 1915.

Donald, David. Lincoln Reconsidered. New York, Knopf, 1956.

Dorr, Mrs. Rheta Louise (Childe). Susan B. Anthony. New York, Stokes, 1928.

Douglass, Frederick. Life and Times. Boston, De Wolfe, Fiske, 1895.

Drake, Samuel Adams. Old Landmarks and Historic Passages of Boston. Boston, Little, Brown, 1900.

Drake, Thomas E. Quakers and Slavery in America. New Haven, Yale University, 1950.

Drewry, William Sidney. Slave Insurrections in Virginia, 1830-1865. Washington, D. C., Neale, 1900.

Du Bois, William Edward Burghardt. Black Reconstruction. New York, Harcourt, Brace, 1935.

Dudley, Harold M. "The Election of 1864," Mississippi Valley Historical Review (June, 1931-March, 1932). XVIII, 500-518.

Duffield, W. B. "Daniel O'Connell," Cornhill Magazine (London, 1899). New Series. VI (Jan.-June, 1899), 29-38.

Dulles, Foster Rhea. Labor in America. New York, Crowell, 1949.

Dumond, Dwight L. Antislavery Origins of the Civil War in the United States. Ann Arbor, University of Michigan, 1939.

Dunham, Chester F. The Attitude of the Northern Clergy towards the South, 1860-65, Toledo, Ohio, Gray, 1942.

Dunning, William Archibald. Reconstruction, Political and Economic. The American Nation, A History. New York, Harper, 1907.

Dyer, Brainerd. Zachary Taylor. Baton Rouge, Louisiana State University, 1946.

Eaton, Clement. Freedom of Thought in the Old South. Durham, N. C., Duke University, 1940.

Eaton, Clement. A History of the Old South. New York, Macmillan, 1949.

Eckenrode, Hamilton James. Jefferson Davis. New York, Macmillan, 1923.

ECKLOFF, CHRISTIAN FREDERICK. Memories of a Senate Page, 1855-1859. Edited by P. G. Melbourne. New York, Broadway Publishing Company, 1909.

EDDY, GEORGE SHERWOOD and PAGE, KIRBY. Makers of Freedom. New York, Doran, 1926.

"Elijah P. Lovejoy as an Anti-Catholic," *Records of the American Catholic Historical Society of Philadelphia* (Sept. 1951), LXII, No. 3, 172-180.

EMERSON, RALPH WALDO. The Complete Works of Ralph Waldo Emerson. 12 vols. Centenary Edition. Boston and New York, Houghton, Mifflin, 1932.

EMERSON, RALPH WALDO. The Journals of Ralph Waldo Emerson. 10 vols. Edited by Edward Waldo Emerson and Waldo Emerson Forbes. Boston and New York, Houghton, Mifflin, 1912.

EMERSON, RALPH WALDO. The Letters of Ralph Waldo Emerson. 6 vols. Edited by Ralph L. Rusk. New York, Columbia University Press, 1939.

Exercises at the Dedication of the Statue of Wendell Phillips. Boston Printing Department, 1916.

FAIRCHILD, JAMES HARRIS. "The Underground Railroad," *Western Reserve Historical Society* (Cleveland, Ohio). IV, Tract No. 87, 89-121.

The Farmer of Chappaqua Songster. New York, De Witt, 1872.

FESSENDEN, FRANCES. Life and Public Services of William Pitt Fessenden. 2 vols. Boston and New York, 1907.

FILLER, LOUIS. "Parker Pillsbury, An Anti-Slavery Apostle," *New England Quarterly* (Sept. 1946), XIX, No. 3, 315-337.

FINE, NATHAN. Labor and Farmer Parties in the United States. New York, Rand School of Social Science, 1928.

FISH, ANDREW. "The Reputation of James A. Froude," *Pacific Historical Review* (Glendale, California, 1932). I (June, 1932), No. 2, 179-192.

FISHER, GEORGE P. "Webster and Calhoun in the Compromise Debate of 1850," *Scribner's Magazine*. Vol. XXXVII. (Jan.-June, 1905), 578-586.

FISHER, SYDNEY GEORGE. The True Daniel Webster. Phila., Lippincott, 1911.

FITE, EMERSON D. The Presidential Campaign of 1860. New York, Macmillan, 1911.

FLEMING, WALTER LYNWOOD. The Sequel of Appomattox. Chronicles of America Series (New Haven, Yale University Press, 1919). Vol. XV.

FLOWER, FRANK A. History of the Republican Party. Springfield, Ill., 1884.

FONER, PHILIP S. Business and Slavery. Chapel Hill, N. C., University of North Carolina, 1941.

FONER, PHILIP S. The Life and Writings of Frederick Douglass. 2 vols. New York, International, 1950.

FORBES, JOHN MURRAY. Letters and Recollections of John Murray Forbes. Edited by Sarah Forbes Hughes. 2 vols. Boston and New York, Houghton, Mifflin, 1899.

FOSTER, HERBERT DARLING. Collected Papers. Hanover, N. H. Privately printed, 1929.

FLOWER, FRANK A. History of the Republican Party. Springfield, Ill., Union, 1884.

FOWLER, WILLIAM CHAUNCEY. The Sectional Controversy, New York, Scribner, 1862.

FOX, EARLY LEE. The American Colonization Society, 1817-1840. Johns Hopkins University Studies in Historical and Political Science (Baltimore, Md., The Johns Hopkins Press, 1919). Series XXXVII, No. 3.

FRANKLIN, JOHN H. From Slavery to Freedom, New York, Knopf, 1947.

FREEMAN, DOUGLAS SOUTHALL. R. E. Lee. 4 vols. New York, Scribners, 1934-35.

——————. A Fresh Catalogue of Southern Outrages Upon Northern Citizens. Anti-Slavery Tracts. New Series, No. 14. New York, American Anti-Slavery Society, 1860.

FROTHINGHAM, OCTAVIUS BROOKS. Theodore Parker. Boston, Osgood, 1874.

FROTHINGHAM, OCTAVIUS BROOKS. Gerrit Smith. New York, 1878.

FROTHINGHAM, PAUL REVERE. Edward Everett. Boston, Houghton, Mifflin, 1925.

FUESS, CLAUDE MOORE. Rufus Choate. New York, Minton, Balch, 1928.

FUESS, CLAUDE MOORE. Daniel Webster. 2 vols. New York, Little, Brown, 1930.

FUESS, CLAUDE MOORE. "Daniel Webster and the Abolitionists," *Massachusetts Historical Society Proceedings* (Boston, 1932). LXIV, 28-42.

GARDINER, JOHN HAYS. Harvard. American College and University Series. New York, Oxford University Press, 1914.

GARNER, JAMES W. *Reconstruction in Mississippi.* New York, Macmillan, 1901.

GARRATT, G. T. Lord Brougham. London, Macmillan, 1935.

GARRISON, WENDELL PHILLIPS, and GARRISON, FRANCIS JACKSON. William Lloyd Garrison. 4 vols. Boston and New York, Houghton, Mifflin, 1894.

GARRISON, WILLIAM LLOYD. The New Reign of Terror. Anti-Slavery Tracts. New Series, No. 4. New York, American Anti-Slavery Society, 1860.

GERRY, MARGARITA S. "The Real Andrew Johnson," *Century Magazine* (New York, 1927-1928). CXV, New Series, XCIII, 54-64, 218-230.

GEYL, PIETER. "The American Civil War and the Problem of Inevitability," *New England Quarterly* (June, 1951), XXIV, No. 2, 147-168.

GIDDINGS, JOSHUA REED. History of the Rebellion. New York, Follett Foster, 1864.

GOING, CHARLES BUXTON. David Wilmot. New York, Appleton, 1924.

GOODELL, WILLIAM. Come-Outerism. Boston, 1845.

GOODELL, WILLIAM. *Slavery and Anti-Slavery.* New York, The Author, 1853.

GOULD, ELIZABETH PORTER. Ezekiel Cheever. Boston, Palmer, 1904.

GRAY, WOOD. The Hidden Civil War. The Story of the Copperheads, New York, Viking, 1942.

Great Britain. Parliament. Hansard's Parliamentary Debates. 3rd Series. 1862. Vol. CLXVII. London, 1862.

GREELEY, HORACE. The American Conflict. 2 vols. Hartford, Conn., Case, 1864-1867. Vol. I.

GREENOUGH, CHARLES P. "The Rendition of Thomas Sims," *Massachusetts Historical Society Proceedings* (Boston, 1923). LV (1921-1922), 340-345.

GRIFFIN, SOLOMON BULKLEY. People and Politics. Boston, Little, Brown, 1923.

GRIMKÉ, ANGELINA EMILY. Appeal to the Christian Women of the South. The Anti-Slavery Examiner, No. 2. New York, 1836.

GRIMKÉ, ARCHIBALD H. William Lloyd Garrison. American Reformers. Edited by Carlos Martyn. New York, Funk and Wagnalls, 1891.

GROSSMAN, JONATHAN. William Sylvis, Pioneer of American Labor, New York, Columbia University, 1945.

HAGAN, H. H. "Wendell Phillips," The Sewanee Review (New York, 1913), XXI, 324-340.

HALE, EDWARD EVERETT. A New England Boyhood and Other Bits of Autobiography. Boston, Little, Brown, 1920.

[HALE, JAMES W.] Old Boston Town. By an 1801-er. New York, Nesbitt, [1883?]

HALL, CLIFTON RUMERY. Andrew Johnson, Military Governor of Tennessee. Princeton, N. J., Princeton University Press, 1916.

HAMILTON, HOLMAN. Zachary Taylor. Indianapolis, Bobbs-Merrill, 1941.

HAMILTON, J. G. DE ROULHAC. "Lincoln's Election and Slavery," American Historical Review (July, 1932). XXXVII, No. 4, 700-711.

HAMILTON, PETER JOSEPH. The Reconstruction Period. History of North America. Edited by F. N. Thorpe. Vol. XVI. Phila., Barrie, 1905.

HARRIS, N. DWIGHT. The History of Negro Servitude in Illinois, Chicago, McClurg, 1904.

HART, ALBERT BUSHNELL [EDITOR]. American History Told by Contemporaries. 5 vols. New York, Macmillan, 1901-1902. Vols. III and IV.

HART, ALBERT BUSHNELL [EDITOR]. Commonwealth History of Massachusetts. 5 vols. New York, The States History Co., 1927-1930.

HART, ALBERT BUSHNELL. Salmon P. Chase. American Statesmen. Boston and New York, Houghton, Mifflin, 1899.

HART, ALBERT BUSHNELL. Slavery and Abolition. The American Nation, a History. New York, Harper, 1906. Vol. XVI.

Harvard University Law School. Catalogue of the Officers and Students of the Law School of Harvard University, 1817-1887. Cambridge, Sever, 1888.

HAWORTH, PAUL LELAND. Reconstruction and Union. New York, Holt, 1912.

HAWORTH, PAUL LELAND. The United States in Our Own Times. New York, Scribners, 1920.

HAYNES, FREDERICK EMORY. Third Party Movements Since the Civil War. Iowa City, Iowa, The State Historical Society of Iowa, 1916.

HAYNES, GEORGE HENRY. Charles Sumner. American Crisis Biographies. Phila., Jacobs, 1909.

HAYWARD, EDWARD FARWELL. Lyman Beecher. Boston, The Pilgrim Press, 1904.

HEADLEY, PHINEAS CAMP. The Life of Louis Kossuth. Auburn, Derby and Miller, 1852.

HELM, T. C. "Wendell Phillips and the Abolition Movement," *The Reformed Church Review* (Phila., 1916) XX, Fourth Series, 196-226.

HELPER, HINTON ROWAN. The Impending Crisis. New York, Burdick, 1860.

HENKLE, HENRIETTA (Buckmaster, pseud.), Let My People Go, New York and London, Harper, 1941.

HERBERT, HILARY ABNER. The Abolition Crusade and its Consequences. New York, Scribners, 1912.

HERNDON, WILLIAM HENRY and WEIK, JESSE W. Life of Lincoln. New York, Boni, 1930.

HERRIOT, FRANK IRVING. "Memories of the Chicago Convention of 1860," *Annals of Iowa* (Des Moines, 1915-1921). XII, (1920), Third Series, 446-466.

HIBBEN, PAXTON. Henry Ward Beecher. New York, Doran, 1927.

HIGGINSON, THOMAS WENTWORTH. Travellers and Outlaws. Boston, Lee and Shepard, 1889.

HIGGINSON, THOMAS WENTWORTH. Wendell Phillips. Reprinted from the *Nation*. Boston, Lee and Shepard, 1884.

HILL, JAMES D. "Some Economic Aspects of Slavery, 1850-1860," *South Atlantic Quarterly* (Durham, N. C., 1927). XXVI, 161-177.

HILLARD, GEORGE STILLMAN. Memoir of Joseph Story. Boston, Wilson, 1868.

HILLIS, NEWELL DWIGHT. The Battle of Principles. New York, Revell, 1912.

History of Woman Suffrage. Edited by Elizabeth Cady Stanton, Susan Brownell Anthony, and Matilda Joslyn Gage. 3 vols. Rochester, S. B. Anthony, 1881-1889.

HITTELL, THEODORE H. History of California. 4 vols. San Francisco, Pacific and Occidental, 1885.

HOAR, GEORGE FRISBIE. Autobiography of Seventy Years. 2 vols. New York, Scribners, 1903.

HODDER, FRANK H. "The Genesis of the Kansas Nebraska Act," *Proceedings of the State Historical Society for Wisconsin, 1912.* (Madison, Wisconsin, 1913), pp. 69-86.

HODDER, FRANK H. "Some Phases of the Dred Scott Case," *Mississippi Valley Historical Review.* XVI (June, 1929-March, 1930), 3-22.

HOFSTADTER, RICHARD. "Ulrich B. Phillips and the Plantation Legend," *Journal of Negro History* (April, 1944), XXIX, No. 2, 109-124.

HOFSTADTER, RICHARD. The American Political Tradition and the Men Who Made It. New York, Alfred Knopf, 1948.

HOLLEY, SALLIE. A Life for Liberty. Edited by John White Chadwick. New York, Putnam, 1899.

HOLLIS, CHRISTOPHER. The American Heresy. London, Sheed and Ward, 1927.

HOLMES, OLIVER WENDELL. Ralph Waldo Emerson and John Lothrop Motley. Boston and New York, Houghton, Mifflin, 1892.

HOLMES, OLIVER WENDELL. The Autocrat of the Breakfast Table. Boston and New York, Houghton, Mifflin, 1891.

HOLZMAN, ROBERT S. Stormy Ben Butler. New York, Macmillan, 1954.

HOPKINS, VINCENT C. Dred Scott's Case. New York, Fordham, 1951.

HOSMER, JAMES KENDALL. The Appeal to Arms. The American Nation, A History. Vol. XX. New York, Harper, 1907.

HOWARD, BENJAMIN C. Reports of Cases Argued and Adjudged in the Supreme Court of the United States. December Term, 1856. Washington, D. C., Morrison, 1859.

HOWARD, JOSEPH. Life of Henry Ward Beecher. Phila., Hubbard Bros., 1887.

HOWE, DANIEL WAIT. Political History of Secession. New York, Putnam, 1914.

HOWE, MARK ANTHONY DE WOLFE. Boston. New York, Macmillan, 1907.

HOWE, MARK ANTHONY DE WOLFE. Boston Common. Boston, Houghton, Mifflin, 1921.

HOWE, SAMUEL GRIDLEY. Letters and Journals. Edited by Laura E. Richards, 2 vols. Boston, Estes, 1909-1910.

Hubbell, George Allen. Horace Mann. Phila., Fell, 1910.

Huberman, Leo. We the People. New York and London, Harper, 1932.

Hughes, Sarah Forbes. [EDITOR]. Letters and Recollections of John Murray Forbes. 2 vols. Boston and New York, Houghton, Mifflin, 1899.

Hull, Ernest R. That Arch-Liar Froude. Bombay, India, Examiner Press, 1919.

Hume, John F. The Abolitionists. New York, Putnam, 1905.

Hunt, Gaillard. John C. Calhoun. American Crisis Biographies. Phila., Jacobs, 1907.

Hunt, Gilbert J. The Tour of General Lafayette. New York, The Compiler, 1825.

Ingle, Edward. Southern Sidelights. New York, Crowell, 1896.

Jacobs, Harriet. Incidents in the Life of a Slave Girl. Edited by Lydia Maria Child. Boston, Published for the Author, 1861.

James, H. F. Abolitionism Unveiled. New York, Paterson, 1850.

Jay, William. An Inquiry into the Character and Tendency of the American Colonization and American Anti-Slavery Societies. New York, Leavitt, Lord, 1835.

Jay, William. Letters Respecting the American Board of Commissioners for Foreign Missions and the American Tract Society. New York, Bates, 1853.

Jay, William. Miscellaneous Writings on Slavery. Boston, Jewett, 1853.

Johnson, Allen. Stephen A. Douglas. New York, Macmillan, 1908.

Johnson, Howard Palmer. "New Orleans Under General Butler," Louisiana Historical Quarterly (April, 1941), XXIV, No. 2, 435-536.

Johnson, Oliver. William Lloyd Garrison and His Times. Boston, Houghton, Mifflin, 1881.

Johnston, Richard Malcom and Brown, William Hand. Life of Alexander H. Stephens. Phila., Lippincott, 1878.

Jones, Jesse H. His Last Battle, Wendell Phillips in Faneuil Hall on the Louisiana Difficulties. Boston, Wendell Phillips Memorial Association, 1897.

Jones, Wilbur D. "The British Conservatives and the American War," American Historical Review (April, 1953), LVIII, No. 3, 527-543.

JULIAN, GEORGE WASHINGTON. Political Recollections, 1840-1872. Chicago, Jansen, McClurg, 1884.

KASSEL, CHARLES. "Theodore Parker, A Study from the Life of Edwin Miller Wheelock," *The Open Court* (Chicago, 1923). XXXVII, 741-750.

KEMBLE, FRANCES ANN. Records of a Girlhood. 3 vols. London, Bentley, 1878.

KENNEDY, N. J. D. "Rufus Choate," The *Juridical Review* (Edinburgh, 1899-1900). XI-XII, 113-136.

KENNEDY, WILLIAM SLOANE. John G. Whittier. American Reformers. Edited by Carlos Martyn. New York, Funk and Wagnalls, 1892.

KIMBALL, JOHN CALVIN. Connecticut's Canterbury Tale, Its Heroine Prudence Crandall. Hartford, Conn., Plimpton, 1888.

KLINE, SHERMAN J. "The Old Man Eloquent," *Americana* (Somerville, N.J., Jan.-Dec., 1927). XXI, 479-497.

KNIGHT, LANDON. The Real Jefferson Davis. Battle Creek, Mich., The Pilgrim Magazine Co., 1904.

KORNGOLD, RALPH. Two Friends of Man. New York, Little, Brown and Co., 1950.

KOSSUTH, LAJOS. Kossuth in New England. Boston, Jewett, 1852.

KROUT, JOHN ALLEN. The Origins of Prohibition. New York, Knopf, 1925.

KRUM, JOHN M. "Death of Elijah P. Lovejoy, A Voice from the Past," *Journal of the Illinois State Historical Society* (Springfield, Ill.) IV (Jan. 1912), No. 4, 499-503.

LANDON, FRED. "Canada's Part in Freeing the Slave," Reprinted from the *Ontario Historical Society Papers and Records* (Toronto, 1919). Vol. XVII.

LANDON, FRED. "Benjamin Lundy, Abolitionist," *The Dalhousie Review* (Halifax, N. S., 1927). VII, 189-197.

LAWRENCE, GEORGE A. "Benjamin Lundy, Pioneer of Freedom," *Journal of the Illinois State Historical Society* (July, 1913). VI, No. 2, 175-205.

The Legion of Liberty and Force of Truth, New York, American Anti-Slavery Society, 1842.

Letters on American Slavery. Boston, American Anti-Slavery Society, 1860.

LEVASSEUR, A. Lafayette in America. Translated by John D. Godman. Phila., Carey and Lea, 1829.

Lewis, Lloyd. Myths after Lincoln. New York, Harcourt, Brace, 1929.

——————. Life and Public Services of Major General Butler. Phila., Peterson, 1864.

Lincoln, Abraham. The Writings of Abraham Lincoln. Edited by Arthur B. Lapsley. 8 vols. New York, Putnam, 1906. Vol. V.

Lincoln, Abraham. Complete Works. Edited by John G. Nicolay and John Hay. 2 vols. New York, Century, 1922.

Linn, William Alexander. Horace Greeley. Appleton's Historic Lives Series. New York, Appleton, 1903.

Lloyd, Arthur Y. The Slavery Controversy, 1831-1860. Chapel Hill, N. C., University of North Carolina, 1939.

Locke, David Ross. [Petroleum V. Nasby]. Andy's Trip to the West. New York, American News Co., 1866.

Locke, Mary Stoughton. Anti-Slavery in America, 1619-1808. Radcliffe College Monographs. No. 11. Boston, Ginn, 1901.

Lofton, Williston H. "Abolition and Labor," Journal of Negro History (July, 1948), XXXIII, No. 3, 249-283.

Longfellow, Samuel. Life of Henry Wadsworth Longfellow. 2 vols., Boston, 1886.

Loring, James Spear. The Hundred Boston Orators. Boston, Jewett, 1853.

Lovejoy, Joseph Cammet and Lovejoy, Owen. Memoir of the Reverend Elijah P. Lovejoy. New York, Taylor, 1838.

Lovell, Lucy Buffum and Chase, Elizabeth Buffum. Two Quaker Sisters. New York, Liveright, 1937.

Lovett, James D' Wolf. Old Boston Boys and the Games They Played. Boston, Privately Printed at the Riverside Press, 1906.

Lowell, James Russell. The Complete Poetical Works of James Russell Lowell. Cambridge Edition. Boston and New York, Houghton, Mifflin, 1896.

Lowell, James Russell. The Complete Writings of James Russell Lowell. 16 vols. Elmwood Edition. Boston and New York, Houghton, Mifflin, 1904.

Lundy, Benjamin. The Life, Travels, Opinions of Benjamin Lundy. Phila., Parrish, 1847.

Luthin, Reinhard H. Some Demagogues in American History American Historical Review (Oct. 1951), LVII, No. 1, 21-46.

McCall, Samuel W. Thaddeus Stevens. American Statesmen. Boston and New York, Houghton, Mifflin, 1899.

Macartney, Clarence E. Lincoln and His Cabinet. New York, Scribners, 1931.

MacDonagh, Michael. Daniel O'Connell and the Story of Catholic Emancipation. Dublin, Talbot Press, 1929.

MacDonald, William. Three Centuries of American Democracy. New York, Henry Holt, 1923.

Macy, Jesse. Anti-Slavery Crusade. Chronicles of America Series. New Haven, Yale University Press, 1919. XIII, Part 2.

Madison, Charles A. Critics and Crusaders. New York, Holt, 1947.

Maguire, John Francis. Father Mathew. New York, Sadlier, 1864.

Mandell, Bernard. Labor: Free and Slave. Workingmen and the Anti-Slavery Movement in the United States, New York, Associated Authors, 1955.

Martin, Asa Earl. Pioneer Anti-Slavery Press. *Mississippi Valley Historical Review.* II (March, 1916), No. 4, 509-528.

Martineau, Harriet. The Martyr Age. New York, Benedict, 1839.

Martyn, Carlos. Wendell Phillips, the Agitator. American Reformers. Edited by Carlos Martyn. New York, Funk and Wagnalls, 1890.

Massachusetts Anti-Slavery Society. Annual Reports. Boston, 1835-1856. Vols. IV-XXIV.

Massachusetts. House of Representatives. Report of the Joint Standing Committee on Federal Relations of the House of Representatives, March 22, 1855.

Massachusetts. House of Representatives. Report on the Joint Standing Committee on Federal Relations of the House of Representatives, April 4, 1855.

Massachusetts. Statutes. Acts and Resolves Passed by the Legislature of Massachusetts.

Massingham, Harold John. The Friend of Shelley. London, Cobden-Sanderson, 1930.

Masters, Edgar Lee. Lincoln the Man. New York, Dodd, Mead, 1931.

Mathew, Frank J. Father Mathew. London, Cassell, 1890.

Matlack, Lucius C. The History of American Slavery and Methodism. New York, 1849.

MAY, SAMUEL JOSEPH. The Fugitive Slave Law and Its Victims. Anti-Slavery Tracts. New Series, No. 15. New York, American Anti-Slavery Society, 1861.

MAY, SAMUEL JOSEPH. Some Recollections of Our Anti-Slavery Conflict. Boston, Fields, Osgood, 1869.

McCLURE, ALEXANDER KELLEY. Abraham Lincoln and Men of War Times. Phila., Times Publishing Co., 1892.

McCORMAC, EUGENE IRVING. James K. Polk. Berkeley, Calif., University of California Press. 1922.

McCRAY, FLORINE THAYER. The Life and Work of the Author of Uncle Tom's Cabin. New York, Funk and Wagnalls, 1889.

McCULLOCH, HUGH. Men and Measures. New York, Scribner's, 1888.

McDOUGALL, (MRS.) MARION G. Fugitive Slaves. Radcliffe College Monographs. No. 3. Boston, Ginn, 1891.

McELROY, ROBERT McNUTT. The Winning of the Far West. New York, Putnam, 1914.

McKEE, SAMUEL, JR. and CARMAN, HARRY JAMES. A History of the United States. 1 vol. New York, Heath, 1931.

McMASTER, JOHN BACH. A History of the People of the United States. New York, Appleton, 1885-1913. Vols. VII and VIII.

McMASTER, JOHN BACH. A History of the People of the United States during Lincoln's Administration. New York, Appleton, 1927.

McPHERSON, EDWARD. Political History of the United States during the Period of Reconstruction. Washington, D. C., Chapman, 1880.

MEAD, EDWIN DOAK. Emerson and Theodore Parker. Boston, American Unitarian Association, 1910.

MEAD, REV. ELWELL O. "The Underground Railroad in Ohio," *Ohio Church History Society* (Oberlin, 1899). X, 31-52.

MEADE, ROBERT D. Judah P. Benjamin, New York, Oxford, 1943.

MEIGS, WILLIAM MONTGOMERY. The Life of John C. Calhoun. New York, Neale, 1917.

Memorial of Wendell Phillips from the City of Boston. Boston, Rockwell and Churchill, 1884.

Memorials of Wendell Phillips. Book of Clippings. Boston Public Library.

—————. Memorial Sketch of Ann Phillips. Boston, Printed for Private Circulation, 1886.

MERRIAM, GEORGE SPRING. The Life and Times of Samuel Bowles. 2 vols. New York, Century, 1885.

MERRIAM, GEORGE SPRING. The Negro and the Nation. New York, Henry Holt, 1906.

MILLER, HENRY HORNBECK. Phillips Genealogy and Family History. Chicago, Privately Published, 1897.

MILTON, GEORGE FORT. The Age of Hate. New York, Coward-McCann, 1930.

MILTON, GEORGE FORT. The Eve of Conflict. Boston and New York, Houghton, Mifflin, 1934.

MINNERGERODE, MEADE and WANDELL, SAMUEL HENRY. Aaron Burr. 2 vols. New York, Putnam, 1927. Vol. II.

MOORE, ALBERT BURTON. The Presidential Campaign of 1860. New York, 1911.

MOORE, ALBERT BURTON. Southern Contemporary Opinion of Abraham Lincoln to July, 1861. Chicago, Mimeographed Dissertation, 1915.

MOORE, THOMAS. The Poetical Works of Thomas Moore. London, Oxford University Press, 1910.

MORDELL, ALBERT. Quaker Militant, John Greenleaf Whittier. Boston and New York, Houghton, Mifflin, 1933.

MORGAN, GEORGE. The True Lafayette. Phila., Lippincott, 1919.

MORISON, SAMUEL ELIOT. The Oxford History of the United States. 2 vols. London, Oxford University Press, 1928.

MORISON, SAMUEL ELIOT. Three Centuries of Harvard, 1636-1936. Cambridge, Harvard University Press, 1936.

MORSE, JOHN TORREY. Thomas Jefferson. Boston, Houghton, Mifflin, 1898.

MORSE, JOHN TORREY. John Quincy Adams. American Statesmen Series. Boston, Houghton, Mifflin, 1883.

MOTLEY, JOHN LOTHROP. Correspondence of John Lothrop Motley. Edited by George W. Curtis. 2 vols. New York, Harper, 1889.

MYERS, JOSEPH SIMMONS. The Genius of Horace Greeley. Journalism Series No. 6. Columbus, the Ohio State University Press, 1929.

MYERS, WILLIAM STARR. A Study in Personality, General George Brinton McClellan. New York, Appleton-Century, 1934.

MYRDAL, GUNNAR. An American Dilemma, The Negro Problem and Modern Democracy. 2 vols., New York, Harper, 1944.

NASBY, PETROLEUM V. See Locke, David Ross.

NEVINS, ALLAN. Fremont, The West's Greatest Adventurer. 2 vols. New York, Harper, 1928.

NEVINS, ALLAN. Hamilton Fish. New York, Dodd, Mead, 1936.

NEVINS, ALLAN. Ordeal of the Union. 2 vols., New York, Scribner's, 1947.

NEVINS, ALLAN. The Emergence of Lincoln. 2 vols., New York, Scribner's, 1950.

New England Anti-Slavery Society. Annual Reports. Boston, 1833-1835. Vols. I-III.

NICHOLS, ROY FRANKLIN. Franklin Pierce. Phila., University of Pennsylvania Press, 1931.

NICHOLS, ROY F. The Disruption of American Democracy. New York, Macmillan, 1948.

NICHOLS, DR. THOMAS LOW. Forty Years of American Life. London, Maxwell, 1864.

NICOLAY, JOHN GEORGE. A Short Life of Abraham Lincoln. New York, Century, 1906.

NYE, RUSSEL B. Fettered Freedom, Civil Liberties and the Slavery Controversy, 1830-60. East Lansing, Michigan State College, 1949.

OBERHOLTZER, ELLIS PAXON. Abraham Lincoln. American Crisis Biographies. Phila., Jacobs, 1904.

OBERHOLTZER, ELLIS PAXON. A History of the United States Since the Civil War. 5 vols. New York, Macmillan, 1917-1937.

OLIVER, JOHN W. "Louis Kossuth's Appeal to the Middle West," Mississippi Valley Historical Review (Cedar Rapids, Iowa, 1928). XIV, No. 4, 481-495.

OLMSTED, FREDERICK LAW. The Cotton Kingdom. 2 vols. New York, Mason, 1862.

OLMSTED, FREDERICK LAW. A Journey in the Back Country. 2 vols. New York, Putnam, 1907.

OLMSTED, FREDERICK LAW. A Journey in the Seaboard Slave States. 2 vols. New York, Putnam, 1904.

OLMSTED, FREDERICK LAW. A Journey Through Texas. New York, Dix, Edwards, 1857.

ORCUTT, WILLIAM DANA. "Ben Butler and the Stolen Spoons," North American Review (Jan.-June, 1918). CCVII, 66-80.

PALFREY, JOHN G. A Sermon After the Interment of the Late John Phillips. Boston, Munro and Francis, 1823.

Papers Relating to the Garrison Mob. Edited by Theodore Lyman. Cambridge, Mass., Welch, Bigelow, 1870.

PARKER, AMOS ANDREW. Recollections of General Lafayette on His Visit to the United States. Keene, N. H., Sentinel Printing Co., 1879.

PARKER, THEODORE. The Boston Kidnapping: a Discourse to Commemorate the Rendition of Thomas Sims. Boston, Crosby, Nichols, 1852.

PARKER, THEODORE. The Collected Works of Theodore Parker. Edited by Frances Power Cobbe. Vol. V. London, Trübner, 1863.

PARKER, THEODORE. The New Crime Against Humanity. Boston, Mussey, 1854.

PARKER, THEODORE. A Discourse Occasioned by the Death of Daniel Webster. Boston, Mussey, 1853.

PARKER, THEODORE. William Ellery Channing, The American Scholar. Edited with notes by G. W. Cooke. Boston, American Unitarian Association, 1907.

PARKER, WILLIAM. "The Freedman's Story," Atlantic Monthly, XVII, 276-295, March, 1866.

PARRINGTON, VERNON LOUIS. The Beginning of Critical Realism in America. Main Currents in American Thought. Vol. III. New York, Harcourt, Brace, 1930.

PARTON, JAMES. General Butler in New Orleans. New York, Mason, 1864.

PARTON, JAMES. Life of Thomas Jefferson. [Boston, 1874.]

PATRICK, REMBERT W. Jefferson Davis and His Cabinet. Baton Rouge, Louisiana State University, 1944.

PAUL, HERBERT WOODFIELD. Life of Froude. New York, Scribners, 1905.

PAULDING, JAMES KIRKE. Slavery in the United States. New York, Harper, 1836.

PAYNE, EDWARD F. Dickens Days in Boston. Boston, Houghton, Mifflin, 1927.

PEARSON, HENRY GREENLEAF. The Life of John A. Andrew. 2 vols. Boston, Houghton, Mifflin, 1904.

PHILLIPS, ALBERT MERRITT. Phillips Genealogies. Auburn, Mass., Hamilton, 1885.

PHILLIPS, ULRICH BONNELL. American Negro Slavery. New York, Appleton, 1918.

PHILLIPS, ULRICH BONNELL. The Economic Cost of Slaveholding in the Cotton Belt. Boston, Ginn, 1905.

PHILLIPS, ULRICH BONNELL. Life and Labor in the Old South. Boston, Little, Brown, 1929.

PHILLIPS, WENDELL. Argument against Repeal of the Personal Liberty Law. Boston, Wallcut, 1861.

PHILLIPS, WENDELL. Can Abolitionists Vote or Take Office under the Constitution? New York, American Anti-Slavery Society, 1845.

PHILLIPS, WENDELL. The Constitution, A Pro-Slavery Compact. New York, American Anti-Slavery Society, 1856.

PHILLIPS, WENDELL. "The Immediate Issue," The Equality of All Men Before the Law. Boston, Rand and Avery, 1865.

PHILLIPS, WENDELL. The People Coming to Power. Boston, Lee and Shepard, 1871.

PHILLIPS, WENDELL. Remarks at the Mass Meeting of Workingmen in Faneuil Hall, November 2, 1865. Boston, Voice Printing and Publishing Co., 1865.

PHILLIPS, WENDELL. Review of Lysander Spooner's Essays on the Unconstitutionality of Slavery. Boston, Andrews and Prentiss, 1847.

PHILLIPS, WENDELL. Review of Webster's Speech on Slavery. Boston, American Anti-Slavery Society, 1850.

PHILLIPS, WENDELL. Speeches, Lectures, and Letters. 2 vols. Boston, Lee and Shepard, 1894.

PHILLIPS, WENDELL. Vindication of the Course Pursued by the American Abolitionists. London, Tweedie, 1853.

PHILLIPS, WENDELL. Who Shall Rule Us? Money or the People? Boston, Rand, 1878.

PHILLIPS, WENDELL. Wendell Phillips Centenary, 1811-1911. National Association for the Advancement of Colored People. New York, no date.

PICKARD, SAMUEL THOMAS. Life and Letters of John G. Whittier. 2 vols. Boston, Houghton, Mifflin, 1894.

PICKETT, WILLIAM PASSMORE. The Negro Problem, Abraham Lincoln's Solution. New York, Putnam, 1909.

PIER, ARTHUR STANWOOD. The Story of Harvard. Boston, Houghton, Mifflin, 1913.

PIERCE, EDWARD L. Memoir and Letters of Charles Sumner. 4 vols. Boston, Roberts, 1893.

PILLSBURY, ALBERT ENOCH. Daniel Webster, the Orator. Brooklyn, New York, 1903.

Poems of American History. Collected and Edited by Burton E. Stevenson. Revised Edition. Boston, Houghton, Mifflin, 1922.

POLLARD, EDWARD A. The Life of Jefferson Davis. Atlanta, Ga., 1869.

POMEROY, MARCUS MILLS. The Life and Public Services of Benjamin F. Butler. New York, 1868.

PONSONBY, ARTHUR AUGUSTUS WILLIAM HARRY PONSONBY, BARON, and PONSONBY, DOROTHEA (P). Rebels and Reformers. London, Allen and Unwin, 1917.

PORTER, KATHERINE H. The Development of the American Lyceum. Chicago, Typewritten Dissertation, University of Chicago, 1914.

POSEY, WALTER BROWNLOW. "Influence of Slavery Upon the Methodist Church in the Early South and Southwest," Mississippi Valley Historical Review (Cedar Rapids, Iowa). XVII, 530-542.

POWDERLY, TERENCE VINCENT. Thirty Years of Labor. Columbus, Ohio, Rankin and O'Neal, 1890.

POWELL, AARON MACY. Personal Reminiscences. New York, Powell, 1899.

PRESTON, EMMETT D. "The Fugitive Slave Acts in Ohio," Journal of Negro History (Oct. 1943), XXVIII, No. 4, 422-477.

Proceedings of the First Three Republican National Conventions of 1856, 1860, 1864, Minneapolis, Minn., 1895.

The Pro-Slavery Argument. Phila., Lippincott, Grambo, 1853.

QUARLES, BENJAMIN. "Sources of Abolitionist Income," Mississippi Valley Historical Review (June, 1945), XXXII, No. 1, 63-76.

QUARLES, BENJAMIN. Frederick Douglass, Wash. D. C., Associated, 1948.

QUINCY, JOSIAH. Figures of the Past. Boston, Little, Brown, 1926.

QUINCY, JOSIAH. A Municipal History of Boston. Boston, Little and Brown, 1852.

QUINCY, JOSIAH P. "Memoir of Edmund Quincy," Proceedings of the Massachusetts Historical Society (Boston, 1905). Second Series (1903-1904), XVIII, 401-416.

RANDALL, HENRY STEPHENS. Thomas Jefferson. 3 vols. New York, Derby and Jackson, 1858. Vol. III.

RANDALL, JAMES GARFIELD. Constitutional Problems under Lincoln. New York, Appleton, 1926.

RANDALL, JAMES GARFIELD. Lincoln the Liberal Statesman. New York, Dodd, Mead, 1947.

RAY, P. ORMAN. "The Genesis of the Kansas Nebraska Act," *Annual Report of the American Historical Association* (Washington, D. C., 1916). I (1914), 259-280.

REDPATH, JAMES. The Roving Editor. New York, Burdick, 1859.

Report of the Proceedings Connected with the Great Union Meeting Held at the Academy of Music in the City of New York, December 19, 1859. New York, Davies and Roberts, 1859.

RHODES, JAMES FORD. History of the United States. 7 vols. New York, Macmillan, 1902-1907.

RICE, ALLEN THORNDIKE. Reminiscences of Abraham Lincoln by Distinguished Men of His Time. New York, North American Publishing Co., 1886.

RICE, MADELEINE H. American Catholic Opinion in the Slavery Controversy. New York, Columbia University, 1944.

RICHARDS, LAURA ELIZABETH (HOWE). Samuel Gridley Howe. New York, Appleton-Century, 1935.

RICHARDSON, JAMES DANIEL. Messages and Papers of the Presidents. 10 vols. Washington, D. C., Government Printing Office, 1896-1899.

ROBERTS, OCTAVIA. With Lafayette in America. Boston and New York, Houghton, Mifflin, 1919.

ROBINSON, HARRIET JANE. Massachusetts in the Woman Suffrage Movement. Boston, Roberts, 1881.

ROBINSON, WILLIAM M., JR. Justice in Grey. Cambridge, Harvard University, 1941.

ROGERS, NATHANIEL PEABODY. Collection from Newspaper Writings. Concord, N. H., French, 1847.

ROSS, ALEXANDER MILTON. Recollections and Experiences of an Abolitionist. Toronto, Roswell and Hutchinson, 1875.

ROSSITER, WILLIAM SIDNEY [EDITOR]. Days and Ways in old Boston. Boston, Stearns, 1915.

ROURKE, CONSTANCE M. Trumpets of Jubilee. New York, Harcourt, Brace, 1927.

RUCHAMES, LOUIS. "Charles Sumner and American Historiography," *Journal of Negro History* (April, 1953), XXXVIII, No. 2, 139-160.

RUSK, RALPH L. [EDITOR]. The Letters of Ralph Waldo Emerson. 6 vols. New York, Columbia University Press, 1939.

RUSSELL, CHARLES EDWARD. The Story of Wendell Phillips. Chicago, Kerr and Co., Cooperative, 1914.

SANBORN, FRANKLIN BENJAMIN. A. Bronson Alcott. 2 vols. Boston, Roberts, 1893.

SANBORN, FRANKLIN BENJAMIN. The Life and Letters of John Brown. Boston, Roberts, 1891.

SANBORN, FRANKLIN BENJAMIN. Recollections of Seventy Years. 2 vols., Boston, 1909.

SANBORN, FRANKLIN BENJAMIN. Dr. Samuel G. Howe. New York, Funk and Wagnalls, 1891.

SATTLER, JOHN WILLIAM. *Wendell Phillips: Speaker and Agitator* (Unpublished Doctoral Dissertation), Evanston, Ill., 1943.

SAVAGE, JAMES. A Genealogical Dictionary of the First Settlers of New England. Boston, Little, Brown, 1861.

SCHAFF, MORRIS. Jefferson Davis. Boston, Luce, 1922.

SCHEIPS, PAUL J. Lincoln and the Chiriqui Colonization, *Journal of Negro History* (Oct. 1952), XXXVII, No. 4, 418-453.

SCHLESINGER, ARTHUR M. The American as Reformer, Cambridge, Harvard University, 1950.

SCHMIDT, LOUIS BERNARD. "Wheat and Cotton During the Civil War," *Iowa Journal of History and Politics* (Iowa City, Iowa). XVI (1918), 400-439.

SCHOULER, JAMES. History of the United States of America. 6 vols. Washington, D. C., Morrison, 1880-1899. Vols. IV-VI.

SCHURZ, CARL. Henry Clay. 2 vols. Boston, Houghton, Mifflin, 1899.

SCHURZ, CARL. *Condition of the South*, 39th Congress, 1st Session. Senate Executive Document, No. 2, Washington, D. C.

SCUDDER, HORACE ELISHA. James Russell Lowell. 2 vols. Boston and New York, Houghton, Mifflin, 1901.

SEARS, LORENZO. Wendell Phillips. New York, Doubleday, Page, 1909.

SEDGWICK, HENRY DWIGHT. Lafayette. Indianapolis. Bobbs-Merrill, 1928.

SEITZ, DON CARLOS. Horace Greeley. Indianapolis. Bobbs-Merrill, 1926.

SEITZ, DON CARLOS. Lincoln the Politician. New York, Coward-McCann, 1931.

SELDES, GILBERT VIVIAN. The Stammering Century. New York, John Day, 1928.

Selection of Anti-Slavery Hymns. Boston, Garrison and Knapp, 1834.

SEVERANCE, FRANK HAYWARD. Old Trails on the Niagara Frontier. Buffalo, Matthews-Northrup, 1899.

SEWARD, FREDERICK WILLIAM. Reminiscences of a Wartime Statesman and Diplomat. New York, Putnam, 1916.

SHEEHAN, HENRY BESTON (HENRY BESTON). The Book of Vagabonds. New York, Doran, 1925.

SHEPPERSON, GEORGE. "Frederick Douglass and Scotland," Journal of Negro History (July, 1953), XXXVIII, No. 3, 307-321.

SHOTWELL, WALTER GASTON. Life of Charles Sumner. New York, Crowell, 1910.

SHULER, NETTIE ROGERS and CATT, CARRIE CHAPMAN. Woman Suffrage and Politics. New York, Scribners, 1923.

SIEBERT, WILBUR HENRY. The Underground Railroad. New York, Macmillan, 1918.

SIMKINS, FRANCIS B. The South Old and New. New York, Knopf, 1947.

SIMMS, HENRY H. A Decade of Sectional Controversy, 1851-1861. Chapel Hill, N. C., University of North Carolina, 1942.

SIMONS, ALGIE MARTIN. Social Forces in American History. New York, Macmillan, 1914.

Sketches and Reminiscences of the Radical Club. Edited by Mrs. John T. Sargent. Boston, Osgood, 1880.

SKINNER, HENRIETTA DANA. An Echo from Parnassus. New York, Sears, 1928.

SMALL, E. W. and SMALL, MIRIAM R. "Prudence Crandall," New England Quarterly (Dec. 1944), XVII, No. 4, 506-529.

SMALLEY, GEORGE WASHBURN. Anglo-American Memories. First Series. London, Duckworth, 1911.

SMEDLEY, ROBERT C. History of the Underground Railroad. Lancaster, Pa., Office of the Journal, 1883.

SMITH, DONALD EUGENE and WERTENBAKER, THOMAS JEFFERSON. The United States of America. New York, Scribners, 1931.

SMITH, ELBERT B. "Thomas Hart Benton: Southern Realist," American Historical Review (July, 1953), LVIII, No. 4, 795-807.

SMITH, GOLDWIN. The Moral Crusader, William Lloyd Garrison. New York, Funk and Wagnalls, 1892.

SMITH, THEODORE CLARKE. The Liberty and Free Soil Parties. Harvard Historical Studies. Vol. VI. New York, Longmans, Green, 1897.

SMITH, THEODORE CLARKE. Parties and Slavery. The American Nation, A History. Vol. XVIII. New York, Harper, 1906.

SNIDER, DENTON JAQUES. The American Ten Years War, 1855-1865. St. Louis, Mo., Sigma Publishing Co., 1906.

SNODGRASS, JOSEPH EVANS. "Benjamin Lundy," *Northern Weekly* (New York, 1868). II (March, 1868), No. 5, 501-520.

SNOW, CALEB HOPKINS. History of Boston. Boston, Bowen, 1825.

Social and Economic Forces in American History. The American Nation, A History. New York, Harper, 1913.

Southern Literary Messenger (Richmond, Va.). Vols. XXXIV-XXXV, July-August, 1862.

STAFFORD, WENDELL PHILLIPS. Wendell Phillips. New York. National Association for the Advancement of Colored People, 1911.

STAMPP, KENNETH M. "The Fate of the Southern Anti-Slavery Sentiment," *Journal of Negro History* (Jan. 1943), XXVIII, No. 1, 10-22.

STAMPP, KENNETH M. And the War Came. Baton Rouge, Louisiana State University, 1950.

STAMPP, KENNETH M. "The Historian and Southern Negro Slavery," *American Historical Review* (April, 1952), LVII, No. 3, 613-624.

STEARNS, FRANK PRESTON. Cambridge Sketches. Phila., Lippincott, 1905.

STEARNS, FRANK PRESTON. Sketches from Concord and Appledore. New York, Putnam, 1895.

STEARNS, FRANK PRESTON. True Republicanism. Phila., Lippincott, 1904.

STEPHENSON, NATHANIEL WRIGHT. Abraham Lincoln and the Union in the War of Secession. Chronicles of America Series. New Haven. Yale University Press, 1919. XIV. Part I.

STEPHENSON, NATHANIEL WRIGHT. The Day of the Confederacy. Chronicles of America Series. New Haven, Yale University Press, 1919. XV. Part I.

STEPHENSON, NATHANIEL WRIGHT. Lincoln. Indianapolis, Bobbs-Merrill, 1922.

STEVENS, CHARLES EMERY. Anthony Burns. Boston, Jewett, 1856.

STILL, WILLIAM. The Underground Railroad. Phila., Porter and Coates, 1872.

STODDARD, HENRY L. Horace Greeley. New York, Putnam, 1946.

STOREY, MOORFIELD. Charles Sumner. American Statesmen. Boston and New York, 1900.

STORY, JOSEPH. Life and Letters of Joseph Story. 2 vols. Edited by William W. Story. Boston, Little and Brown, 1851.

STOWE, CHARLES E. and STOWE, LYMAN BEECHER. Harriet Beecher Stowe. Boston, Houghton, Mifflin, 1911.

STOWE, HARRIET BEECHER. The Key to Uncle Tom's Cabin. Boston, Houghton, Mifflin, 1929.

STOWE, HARRIET BEECHER. Uncle Tom's Cabin. Boston, Houghton, Mifflin, 1929.

STOWE, LYMAN BEECHER. Saints, Sinners and Beechers. Indianapolis, Bobbs-Merrill, 1934.

STOWE, LYMAN BEECHER, and STOWE, CHARLES E. Harriet Beecher Stowe. Boston, Houghton, Mifflin, 1911.

STRINGFELLOW, BENJAMIN F. Negro Slavery No Evil, Boston, 1855.

STROUD, GEORGE M. A Sketch of the Laws Relating to Slavery. Phila., 1827.

STRUNSKY, ROSE. Abraham Lincoln. New York, Macmillan, 1914.

STRUNSKY, ROSE. "The Truth About Lincoln and the Negro," The New Review. II (May, 1914), No. 5, 258-269.

Studies in Southern History and Politics. New York, Columbia University Press, 1914.

SUMNER, CHARLES. His Complete Works. Statesman Edition. 20 vols. Boston, Lee and Shepard, 1910. Vol. V.

SUMNER, CHARLES. Recent Speeches and Addresses. Boston, 1857.

SUMNER, CHARLES. The Scholar, the Jurist, the Artist, the Philanthropist. Boston, Ticknor, 1846.

SUNDERLAND, LA ROY. Anti-Slavery Manual. New York, Piercy and Rud, 1837.

SWEET, WILLIAM WARREN. The Methodist Episcopal Church and the Civil War. Cincinnati, Ohio, Methodist Book Concern Press, 1912.

SWIFT, LINDSAY. William Lloyd Garrison. American Crisis Biographies. Phila., Jacobs, 1911.

SWINT, HENRY LEE. The Northern Teacher in the South, 1862-1870. Nashville, Tenn., Vanderbilt University, 1941.

SWISHER, CARL BRENT. Roger B. Taney. New York, Macmillan, 1935.

SWISSHELM, MRS. JANE GREY. Half a Century. Chicago, Jansen, McClurg, 1880.

SYDNOR, CHARLES S. The Development of Southern Sectionalism 1819-48. Baton Rouge, Louisiana State University, 1948.

TANNER, HENRY. The Martyrdom of Lovejoy. Chicago, Fergus Printing Co., 1861.

TAPPAN, LEWIS. A Sidelight on Anglo-American Relations, 1839-1858. Edited by Annie H. Abel and Frank J. Klingberg. Lancaster, Pa., The Association for the Study of Negro Life and History, 1927.

TATE, ALLEN. Jefferson Davis. New York, Minton, Balch, 1929.

TEN BROEK, JACOBUS. The Anti-Slavery Origins of the Fourteenth Amendment. Berkeley and Los Angeles, University of California, 1951.

THAYER, ELI. A History of the Kansas Crusade. New York, Harper, 1889.

THAYER, WILLIAM ROSCOE. Historical Sketch of Harvard University. Cambridge, Mass., The Author, 1890.

THOMAS, BENJAMIN P. Theodore Weld, Crusader for Freedom. New Brunswick, N. J., Rutgers University, 1950.

THOMPSON, CHARLES WILLIS. The Fiery Epoch, 1830-1877. Indianapolis, Bobbs-Merrill, 1931.

THOMPSON, GEORGE. Prison Life and Reflections. Hartford, 1853.

THOMPSON, MORTIMER. Great Auction Sale of Slaves at Savannah, Ga., March 2 and 3, 1859. Reported for the Tribune. New York, American Anti-Slavery Society, 1859.

————————. "Thumping English Lies," Froude's Slanders on Ireland and Irishmen. With preface and notes by Col. James E. McGee. New York, McGee, 1872.

TODD, CHARLES BURR. The Story of the City of New York, New York, Putnam, 1895.

THOREAU, HENRY DAVID. The Writings of Henry David Thoreau. 11 vols. Boston and New York, Houghton, Mifflin, 1893.

TREXLER, HARRISON A. Slavery in Missouri, 1804-1865. Baltimore, Johns Hopkins, 1914.

TRUMAN, MAJ. GEN. BENJ. C. "Anecdotes of Andrew Johnson," The Century Magazine, (1913), LXXXV, 435-440.

TUCKERMAN, BAYARD. Life of General Lafayette. 2 vols. New York, Dodd, Mead, 1889. Vol. II.

TURNER, EDWARD RAYMOND. "The Underground Railroad in Pennsylvania," Pennsylvania Magazine of History and Biography Phila., 1912). XXXVI, 309-318.

TURNER, LORENZO DOW. Anti-Slavery Sentiment in American Literature prior to 1865. Washington, D. C., The Association for the Study of Negro Life and History, 1929.

TURPIN, EDNA. Cotton. New York, American Book Co., 1924.

TYLER, ALICE FELT. Freedom's Ferment. Minneapolis, University of Minnesota, 1944.

United States. Bureau of Census. Seventh and Eighth Census, 1850 and 1860. Washington, Government Printing Office, 1853, 1864.

United States. Bureau of Census. Statistical View of the United States, Being a Compendium of the Seventh Census, 1850. By J. D. B. De Bow, Superintendent of the Census. Washington, D. C., Nicholson, 1854.

United States. Supreme Court. Reports of Cases Argued and Adjudged in the Supreme Court of the United States. December Term, 1856. By Benjamin C. Howard. Washington, D. C., Morrison, 1859.

USHER, ROLAND GREENE. The Rise of the American People. New York, Century, 1904.

VILLARD, FANNY GARRISON. William Lloyd Garrison on Non Resistance. New York, The Nation Press Printing Co., 1924.

VILLARD, OSWALD GARRISON. John Brown. Boston and New York, Houghton, Mifflin, 1911.

VILLARD, OSWALD GARRISON. "Wendell Phillips After Fifty Years," American Mercury. XXXIV (January, 1935), No. 133, 93-99.

VON HOLST, HERMANN EDWARD. John C. Calhoun. Boston, Houghton, Mifflin, 1911.

Walks and Talks About Historic Boston. Edited by Albert William Mann. Boston, Mann Pub. Co., 1917.

WANDELL, SAMUEL HENRY and MINNERGERODE, MEADE. Aaron Burr. 2 vols. New York, Putnam, 1927. Vol. II.

WARE, EDITH ELLEN. Political Opinion in Massachusetts during Civil War and Reconstruction. Studies in History, Economics, and Public Law. Vol. LXXIV, No. 2. New York, Columbia University Press, 1916.

WARREN, CHARLES. History of the Harvard Law School. 3 vols. New York, Lewis Publishing Company, 1908.

WARREN, CHARLES. The Supreme Court in United States History. 3 vols. Boston, Little, Brown, 1922. Vols. II and III.

WARREN, RAYMOND. The Prairie President. Chicago, Reilly and Lee, 1930.

WARREN, ROBERT PENN. John Brown, The Making of a Martyr. New York, Payson and Clarke, 1929.

WATSON, THOMAS EDWARD. The Life and Times of Thomas Jefferson. New York, Appleton, 1903.

WEBSTER, DANIEL. The Writings and Speeches of Daniel Webster. National Edition. 18 vols. Edited by Fletcher Webster. Boston and New York, Little, Brown, Taylor, 1903.

WEISS, JOHN. Life and Correspondence of Theodore Parker. 2 vols. New York, Appleton, 1864.

WELD, CHARLES RICHARD. A Vacation Tour in the United States and Canada. London, Longman, Brown, Green, and Longmans, 1855.

WELD, THEODORE DWIGHT. American Slavery As It Is. New York, American Anti-Slavery Society, 1839.

WELD, THEODORE DWIGHT. Letters of Theodore D. Weld, Angelina Grimké Weld, and Sarah Grimké. Edited by Gilbert Hobbs Barnes and Dwight L. Dumond. 2 vols. New York, Appleton-Century, 1934.

WERTENBAKER, THOMAS JEFFERSON and SMITH, DONALD EUGENE. The United States of America. New York, Scribners, 1931.

WEST, WILLIS MASON. History of the American Nation. New York, Ronald Press, 1929.

WESTERMANN, WILLIAM L. "Between Slavery and Freedom," American Historical Review (Jan. 1945), L, No. 2, 213-227.

[WESTON, A. W.] Report of the 20th National Anti-Slavery Bazaar. Boston, Yerrington, 1854.

WHITE, HORACE. The Life of Lyman Trumbull. Boston, Houghton, Mifflin, 1913.

WHITE, STEWART EDWARD. The Forty-Niners. Chronicles of America Series. Vol. XVI. New Haven, Conn., Yale University Press, 1918.

WHITLOCK, BRAND. LaFayette. 2 vols. New York, Appleton, 1929. Vol. II.

WHITTIER, JOHN GREENLEAF. The Complete Poetical Works of John Greenleaf Whittier. Household Edition. Boston and New York, Houghton, Mifflin, 1904.

WILBUR, HENRY WATSON. Lincoln's Attitude Towards Slavery and Emancipation. Phila., Jenkins, 1914.

WILLIAMS, GEORGE WASHINGTON. A History of the Negro Troops in the War of the Rebellion. New York, Harper, 1888.

WILLEY, AUSTIN. The History of the Anti-Slavery Cause in State and Union. Portland, Me., Brown, Thurston, and Hoyt, Fogg and Donham, 1886.

WILLIS, DR. FREDERICK LLEWELLYN HOVEY. Alcott Memoirs. Boston, Badger, 1915.

WILSON, HENRY. History of the Rise and Fall of the Slave Power in America. 3 vols. Boston, Osgood, 1874-1877.

WILSON, HILL PEEBLES. John Brown, Soldier of Fortune. Boston, Cornhill Co., 1918.

WILSON, JAMES HARRISON. The Life of Charles A. Dana. New York and London, Harper, 1907.

WILSON, JANET. "The Early Anti-Slavery Propaganda," More Books, The Bulletin of the Boston Public Library (Nov. 1944), XIX, 393-405.

WILSON, RUFUS ROCKWELL. New York Old and New. 2 vols. Phila., Lippincott, 1902.

WINSOR, JUSTIN [EDITOR]. Memorial History of Boston. 4 vols. Boston, Osgood, 1880-1881. Vols. III and IV.

WINSTON, ROBERT WATSON. Andrew Johnson. New York, Henry Holt, 1928.

WISE, JOHN SERGEANT. The End of an Era. Boston, Houghton, Mifflin, 1899.

WITHROW, W. H. "The Underground Railway," Proceedings and Transactions of the Royal Society of Canada. VIII (1902), Second Series, 49-77.

WITTKE, CARL. Against the Current, The Life of Karl Heinzen (1809-80), Chicago, University of Chicago, 1945.

WITTKE, CARL. Refugees of Revolution, The German Forty-Eighters in America, Phila., University of Pennsylvania, 1952.

WOLF, HAZEL C. On Freedom's Altar, Madison, Wisconsin, University of Wisconsin, 1952.

WOODBERRY, GEORGE EDWARD. Wendell Phillips, the Faith of an American. Heart of Man and Other Papers. New York, Harcourt, Brace, and Howe, 1920.

WOODLEY, THOMAS FREDERICK. Thaddeus Stevens. Harrisburgh, Pa., Telegraph Press, 1934.

WOODWARD, WILLIAM E. Meet General Grant. New York, Literary Guild, 1928.

WYMAN, LILLIE BUFFUM CHACE. American Chivalry. Boston, Clarke, 1913.

YOUNG, JOHN RUSSELL. Around the World with General Grant. 2 vols. New York, American News Co., 1879.

INDEX